Preface

This third edition of *European Union Politics* builds on the success of the previous two editions, published in 2003 and 2007. Now with a new co-editor, Nieves Pérez-Solórzano Borragán, the book has retained and updated many of the existing chapters, whilst bringing in a number of new contributors and co-authors. We are very pleased to include a chapter on Environmental Policy for the first time, as well as a chapter that discusses EU policy making.

As seems always to be the case in EU politics, much has changed over the past three years, and this caused some consternation among the editorial team. How should we deal with the fact that when the chapters were drafted the Lisbon Treaty remained in limbo, as we awaited the results of the Irish Referendum of 2 October 2009; and what would the results of European Parliamentary elections of June 2009 be? How might we acknowledge the impact of the post-2008 financial and economic crisis, when the recession that followed was still under way? And by the time you read this, will more countries have joined the European Union, over and above the 2009 membership of 27? We have tried as much as possible to embrace this uncertainty, whilst not being a hostage to it, leaving open the possibility of a range of different European futures.

This edited book remains true to its earlier ambition, which was to offer students of EU politics an introductory text that would be both accessible and challenging, written by authors who are experts in their field. It was designed with undergraduates in mind, particularly those coming to the topic of the EU for the first time; but we know that it has also proven a useful basic text for more advanced students. As in previous editions, we have sought to make the book an appealing prospect for students who might otherwise be deterred from further study of the European Union.

The large number of chapters in this volume (26 in this edition) should not be taken to imply that the book is comprehensive; but rather that it provides a solid overview of a range of topics, falling loosely under the rubric of EU politics. Other textbooks focus more specifically on history, theories, institutions, policies. This book aims to give a taste of all these areas of EU study. It should be stressed that for the majority of students the chapters in this book will be the starting point for their work on the EU. It would be disappointing if this were the only book they read on the subject.

Finally, a debt of gratitude goes to Ruth Anderson at OUP for her efficient handling of the early stages of the project. Later in the project she was replaced by Claire Brewer, who has been engaged and helpful as we worked towards the submission of the rather hefty typescript. Jo Hardern kept us in line at the end of the project as Production Editor. Thanks are also owed to the contributors, without whom this book really would not have been possible.

Mat Hope provided excellent research assistance, support that was funded by the Department of Politics at the University of Bristol through its Graduate Research Assistant/PhD scholarship scheme. Hannah Parrot did a professional job in compiling the index. We would also like to thank Rachel Minto for taking on the task of rebuilding the *European Union Politics* online resources pages. Rachel has provided readers of this book (both students and teachers) with an excellent supplementary resource. We very much hope that you will take advantage of it.

MC and NPSB
Oct. 2009

Contents

Detailed Contents

List of Figures

List of Boxes

CASE STUDIES

OTHER BOXES

List of Tables

About the Contributors

Ian Barnes is Jean Monnet Professor of European Economic Integration in the Lincoln Business School, University of Lincoln, UK.

Pamela Barnes is Principal Lecturer and Jean Monnet Chair in European Political Integration in the Lincoln Law School, University of Lincoln, UK.

David Benson is Lecturer in Environmental Management at the University of East Anglia, Norwich, UK.

Tanja A. Börzel is Chair of European Integration, Jean Monnet Chair and Director of the Centre for European Integration at the Otto-Suhr-Institute for Political Science, Free University of Berlin, Germany.

Marco Brunazzo is Assistant Professor of Political Science in the Department of Sociology and Social Research at the University of Trento, Italy.

Dimitris N. Chryssochoou is Associate Professor of European Integration in the Department of International and European Studies at Panteion University, Athens, Greece.

Clive H. Church is Emeritus Professor in the Department of Politics and International Relations, University of Kent, UK, and visiting Professor at the University of Sussex.

Michelle Cini is Professor of European Politics in the Department of Politics at the University of Bristol, UK.

Robert Dover is Senior Lecturer in International Relations in the Department of Politics, International Relations and European Studies, at Loughborough University, UK.

Ralf Drachenberg is a PhD candidate in the School of Social Sciences, Brunel University, Uxbridge, UK.

Michelle Egan is Associate Professor in the School of International Service at the American University, Washington DC, USA.

Morten Egeberg is Professor of Public Policy and Administration in the Department of Political Science and at ARENA, University of Oslo, Norway.

Rainer Eising is Chair of Comparative Government and Political Science in the Faculty of Social Science, Ruhr University, Bochum, Germany.

Gerda Falkner is Director of the Institute for European Integration Research at the Austrian Academy of Sciences, and Professor at the Department of Government, University of Vienna, Austria.

Eve Fouilleux is a CNRS researcher at CIRAD and CEPEL, University of Montpellier, France.

Andrew Jordan is Professor in Environmental Politics in the School of Environmental Sciences, University of East Anglia, Norwich, UK.

Ilias Kapsis is a former graduate student in the Law Department at the University of Bristol, UK.

Sonja Lehringer is a researcher in the Faculty of Social Science, Ruhr University, Bochum, Germany.

Jeffrey Lewis is Associate Professor in the Department of Political Science at Cleveland State University, USA.

Lauren M. McLaren is Associate Professor in the School of Politics and International Relations, University of Nottingham, UK.

Diana Panke is Lecturer in European Studies at University College, Dublin, Ireland.

Nieves Pérez-Solórzano Borragán is Senior Lecturer in Politics, Department of Politics, University of Bristol, UK.

David Phinnemore is Senior Lecturer in European Integration and Jean Monnet Chair in European Political Science in the School of Politics, International Studies and Philosophy, Queen's University, Belfast, Northern Ireland.

Ben Rosamond is Professor of Politics and International Studies in the Department of Politics and International Relations at the University of Warwick, UK.

Roger Scully is Professor of International Politics in the Department of International Politics, University of Wales, Aberystwyth, UK.

Michael Smith is Jean Monnet Professor of European Politics in the Department of Politics, International Relations and European Studies, Loughborough University, UK.

Carsten Strøby Jensen is Director of the Sociology Institute at Copenhagen University, Denmark.

Emek M. Uçarer is Associate Professor of International Relations in the Department of International Relations at Bucknell University, Lewisberg, PA, USA.

Derek W. Urwin was Professor of Politics and International Relations at the University of Aberdeen, UK. He is now retired.

Amy Verdun is Professor, Jean Monnet Chair in European Integration and Director of the European Studies Program in the Department of Political Science at the University of Victoria, Canada.

Alex Warleigh-Lack is Professor of Politics and International Relations in the School of Social Sciences, Brunel University, Uxbridge, UK.

Abbreviations

ACP	African, Caribbean, Pacific Countries
AER	Assembly of European Regions
AFSJ	Area of Freedom Security and Justice
AG	Advocate-General
AMCHAM	American Chamber of Commerce
AoA	Agreement on Agriculture
APEC	Asia Pacific Economic Co-operation
ARNE	Antiracist Network for Equality in Europe
ASEAN	Association of Southeast Asian Nations
BEUC	European Consumers' Bureau
BLEU	Belgium Luxembourg Economic Union
BSE	Bovine Spongiform Encephalopathy (Mad Cow Disease)
BTO	Brussels Treaty Organization
BUAV	British Union for the Abolition of Vivisection
CALRE	Conference of European Regional Legislative Parliaments
CAP	Common Agricultural Policy
CARDS	Community Assistance for Reconstruction, Development and Stability in the Balkans
CCP	Common Commercial Policy
CCTV	Closed-circuit television
CdT	Translation Centre for the Bodies of the European Union
CDU	Christian Democratic Union (Germany)
CEAS	Common European Asylum System
CEB	Council of Europe Development Bank
CEDEC	European Federation of Local Public Energy Distribution Companies
CEDEFOP	European Centre for the Development of Vocational Training
CEE	Central and Eastern Europe
CEEC	Countries of Central and Eastern Europe
CEEP	Centre Européen des Entreprises Publics (European Association for Public Sector Firms)
CEFIC	European Chemical Association
CEMR	Council for European Municipalities and Regions
CEN	European Committee for Standardization
CENELEC	European Committee for Electro-technical Standardization
CEPOL	European Police College
CFCA	Common Fisheries Control Agency
CFR	Charter of Fundamental Rights
CIREA	Centre for Information, Discussion and Exchange on Asylum
CIREFI	Centre for Information, Discussion and Exchange on the Crossing of Frontiers and Immigration
CIVAM	Network of French Alternative Farmers
CFI	Court of First Instance
CFSP	Common Foreign and Security Policy
CGS	Council General Secretariat
CLRA	Congress of Local and Regional Authorities
CM	Common Market or Community Method
CMO	Common Market Organization
CNJA	Centre National des Jeunes Agriculteurs (French young farmers' association)

CO_2	Carbon Dioxide	ECHA	European Chemicals Agency
CoA	Court of Auditors	ECHO	EC Humanitarian Office
CoE	Council of Europe	ECHR	European Convention on Human
CONNECCS	the European Commission's		Rights
	database on consultation and civil	ECJ	European Court of Justice
	society	ECSC	European Coal and Steel
COPA	Comité des Organisations		Community
	Professionelles Agricoles de la	ECOFIN	Council of Economics and Finance
	Communauté (European farmers		Ministers
	association)	ECOSOC	see EESC
COPS	see PSC	ECU	European Currency Unit
CoR	Committee of the Regions	EDA	European Defence Agency
COREPER	Committee of Permanent	EDC	European Defence Community
(or Coreper)	Representatives	EdF	Électricité de France
CPMR	Conference of Peripheral Maritime	EEA	European Environment Agency or
	Regions		European Economic Area
CPVO	Community Plant Variety Office	EEB	European Environment Bureau
CSG	Council Secretariat General	EES	European Employment Strategy
CSU	Christian Social Union (Germany)	EDU	European Drug Unit
CT	Constitutional Treaty	EEA	European Economic Area
CU	Customs Union	EEB	European Environmental Bureau
DG	Directorate-General	EEC	European Economic Community
E&T	Education and Training	EESC	European Economic and Social
EACEA	Education, Audiovisual and Culture		Committee
	Executive Agency	EFSA	European Food Safety Authority
EACI	Executive Agency for	EFTA	European Free Trade Association
	Competitiveness and Innovation	EIA	Environmental Impact Assessment
EAEC	European Atomic Energy	EIB	European Investment Bank
	Community	EiOP	European Integration Online Papers
EAGGF	European Agricultural Guidance	EJA	European Justice Area
	and Guarantee Fund	EMCDDA	European Monitoring Centre for
EAHC	Executive Agency for Health and		Drugs and Drug Addiction
	Consumers	EMEA	European Medicines Agency
EAP	Environmental Action Plan	EMU	Economic and Monetary Union (or
EASA	European Aviation Safety Agency		European Monetary Union)
EBRD	European Bank for Reconstruction	EMS	European Monetary System
	and Development	EMSA	European Maritime Safety Authority
EC	European Community or European	ENDS	Environmental Data Services Ltd
	Communities	ENISA	European Network and Information
ECA	European Court of Auditors		Security Agency
ECB	European Central Bank	ENP	European Neighbourhood Policy
ECDC	European Centre for Disease	ENPI	European Neighbourhood
	Prevention and Control		Partnership Instruments

EONIA	European Overnight Index Average	EURO-C	ETUC's consumer organization
EP	European Parliament	EURO-COOP	European Consumer Co-operatives
EPC	European Political Co-operation (or		Association
	European Political Community)	EURODAC	European Fingerprinting System
EPI	European Policy Integration	EUROFOUND	European Foundation for the
EPP	European People's Party		Improvement of Living and
ERA	European Railway Agency		Working Conditions
ERC	European Research Council	EUROJUST	European Union's Judicial
	Executive Agency		Cooperation Unit
ERDF	European Regional Development	EUROPOL	European Police Office
	Fund	EUSA	European Union Studies Association
ERPA	European Research Papers Archive	EUSC	European Union Satellite Centre
ESC	Economic and Social Committee	EWL	European Women's Lobby
ESCB	European System of Central Banks	FDP	Free Democratic Party (Germany)
ERDF	European Regional Development	FEU	Full Economic Union
	Fund	FNSEA	Fédération Nationale des Syndicats
ERM	Exchange Rate Mechanism		D'Exploitant Agricoles (French
ERRF	European Rapid Reaction Force		agricultural association)
ERT	European Round Table (of	FPU	Full Political Union
	Industrialists)	FRA	European Fundamental Rights
ESC	Economic and Social Committee		Agency
ESCB	European System of Central Banks	FRONTEX	European Agency for the
ESDP	European Security and Defence		Management of Operational
	Policy		Cooperation at the External
ESF	European Social Fund		Borders
ETF	European Training Foundation	FRY	Former Republic of Yugoslavia
ETS	Emissions Trading Scheme	FTA	Free Trade Area
ETSI	European Telecommunications	FYROM	Federal Yugoslav Republic of
	Standards Institute		Macedonia
ETSO	European Association of	GAC	General Affairs Council
	Transmission Systems Operators	GAERC	General Affairs and External
ETUC	European Trade Union Congress		Relations Council
EU	European Union	GATT	General Agreement on Tariffs and
EU3	UK, France and Germany		Trade
EUMC	European Union Military	GDP	Gross Domestic Product
	Committee or European Monitoring	GDR	German Democratic Republic
	Centre on Racism and Xenophobia	GEODE	Groupement Européen de Sociétés
EUMS	European Union Military Staff		et Organismes de Distribution
EU-OSHA	European Agency for Safety and		d'Énergie
	Health at Work	GMO	Genetically Modified Organism
EUR	Euros	GNI	Gross National Income
EURATOM	See EAEC	GNP	Gross National Product
EURELECTRIC	Union of the Electricity Industry	GNSS	Global Navigation Satellite System

GSA	European GNSS Supervisory Authority	MI5	Military Intelligence 5 (British Secret Service)
GWOT	Global War on Terror	MKD	Macedonian Denar
G8	Group of Eight Most Industrialized Countries	MLG	Multi-level Governance
		MOD	Ministry of Defence
HLWG	High-Level Working Group on Asylum and Immigration	MP	Member of Parliament
		MTR	Mid-term Review (CAP)
ICTY	International Criminal Tribunal of former Yugoslavia	NAFTA	North Atlantic Free Trade Agreement
IFIEC	International Federation of Industrial Energy Consumers)	NATO	North Atlantic Treaty Organization
		NEPI	New Environmental Policy Instruments
IGC	Intergovernmental Conference	NGO	Non-Governmental Organization
IMF	International Monetary Fund	NMG	New Modes of Governance
IMP	Integrated Mediterranean Programmes	NUTS	Nomenclature of Units for Territorial Statistics
IPA	Instrument for Pre-Accession Assistance	NY	New York
IPE	International Political Economy	OCA	Optimum Currency Area
IR	International Relations	OECD	Organization for Economic Co-operation and Development
ISAF	International Security Assistance Force	OEEC	Organization for European Economic Co-operation
ISPA	Instrument for Structural Policies for Pre-accession	OHIM	Office for the Harmonization of the Single Market (Trade Marks and Designs)
ISS	European Union Institute for Security Studies		
JAC	Jeunesse Agricole Chrétienne	OJ	Official Journal (of the European Union)
JASPER	Joint Assistance in Supporting Projects in Europena Regions	OMC	Open Method of Coordination
JEREMIE	Joint European Resources for Micro and Medium Enterprises	OSCE	Organization for Security and Cooperation in Europe
JESSICA	Joint European Support for Sustainable Investment in City Areas	PDB	Preliminary Draft Budget
		PES	Party of European Socialists
		PESC	Politique Etrangère et de la Sécurité Commune
JHA	Justice and Home Affairs		
JNA	Joint National Army (of Serbia)	PHARE	Poland and Hungary Aid for Economic Reconstruction
LI	Liberal Intergovernmentalism		
LMU	Latin Monetary Union	PJCCM	Policy and Judicial Co-operation in Criminal Matters
MC	Monetary Committee		
MEP	Member of the European Parliament	PLO	Palestine Liberation Organization
		PM	Prime Minister
MEQR	Measures having equivalent effect	PNV	El Partido Nacionalist Vasco (Basque Nationalist Party)
MFA	Minister of Foreign Affairs		
MGQ	Maximum Guaranteed Quantities	PPP	Purchasing Power Parity

PSC	Political and Security Committee (also COPS)	TEN-TEA	Trans-European Transport Network Executive Agency
OSCE	Organization for Security and Co-operation in Europe	TEU	Treaty on European Union
QMV	Qualified Majority Voting	TFEU	Treaty on the Functioning of the European Union
REA	Research Executive Agency	UEAPME	European Association of Craft, Small and Medium Sized Enterprises
REGLEG	Conference of European Regions with Legislative Powers		
RELEX	External Relations	UK	United Kingdom
SAA	Stability and Association Agreement	UN	United Nations
		UNFCCC	United National Framework Convention on Climate Change
SAPARD	Special Accession Programme for Agriculture and Rural Development	UNICE	European Confederation of National Employers' Associations
SCA	Special Committee on Agriculture		
SEA	Single European Act	UNHCR	Office of the United Nations High Commissioner for Refugees
SEM	Single European Market		
SFP	Single Farm Payment	UNMIK	United Nations Mission in Kosovo
SGP	Stability and Growth Pact	UNIPEDE	International Union of Producers and Distributors of Electrical Energy
SIS	Schengen Information System		
SLIM	Simpler Legislation for the Internal Market		
		UNSC	United Nations Security Council
SM	Single Market	US	United States
SME	Small and Medium-sized Enterprises	USA	United States of America
		USSR	Union of Soviet Socialist Republics (the Soviet Union)
SSC	Scientific Steering Committee		
TA	Treaty of Amsterdam	VAT	Value Added Tax
TACIS	Programme for Technical Assistance to the Independent States of the Former Soviet Union and Mongolia	VIS	Visa Information System
		VOC	Volatile Organic Compounds
		WEU	Western European Union
TCN	Third Country National	WTO	World Trade Organization
TEC	Treaty on the European Community	WWF	World Wildlife Fund for Nature
		YES	Young Workers' Exchange Scheme

Guided Tour of Learning Features

This book is enriched with a range of learning tools to help you navigate the text and reinforce your knowledge of the European Union. This guided tour shows you how to get the most out of your textbook package.

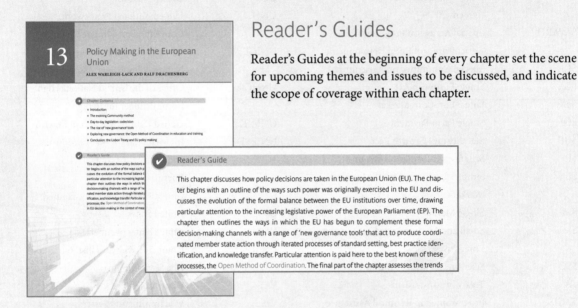

Reader's Guides

Reader's Guides at the beginning of every chapter set the scene for upcoming themes and issues to be discussed, and indicate the scope of coverage within each chapter.

13 Policy Making in the European Union
ALEX WARLEIGH-LACK AND RALF DRACHENBERG

Chapter Contents
- Introduction
- The evolving Community method
- Day-to-day legislation: codecision
- The rise of 'new governance' tools
- Exploring new governance: the Open Method of Coordination in education and training
- Conclusion: the Lisbon Treaty and EU policy making

Reader's Guide

This chapter discusses how policy decisions are taken in the European Union (EU). The chapter begins with an outline of the ways such power was originally exercised in the EU and discusses the evolution of the formal balance between the EU institutions over time, drawing particular attention to the increasing legislative power of the European Parliament (EP). The chapter then outlines the ways in which the EU has begun to complement these formal decision-making channels with a range of 'new governance tools' that act to produce coordinated member state action through iterated processes of standard setting, best practice identification, and knowledge transfer. Particular attention is paid here to the best known of these processes, the Open Method of Coordination. The final part of the chapter assesses the trends

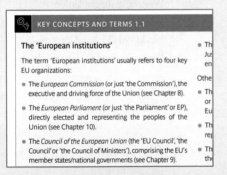

Boxes

Throughout the book, boxes provide you with extra information on particular topics that complement your understanding of the main chapter text.

KEY CONCEPTS AND TERMS 1.1

The 'European institutions'

The term 'European institutions' usually refers to four key EU organizations:

- The *European Commission* (or just 'the Commission'), the executive and driving force of the Union (see Chapter 8).
- The *European Parliament* (or just 'the Parliament' or EP), directly elected and representing the peoples of the Union (see Chapter 10).
- The *Council of the European Union* (the 'EU Council', 'the Council' or 'the Council of Ministers'), comprising the EU's member states/national governments (see Chapter 9).

The early days of the policy

The objectives of the CAP, which came into force from 1962, were laid down in the Treaty of Rome in 1957 (Article 39) and subsequently at the Stresa Conference in July 1958. Three general principles underpinned the policy: market unity; Community preference; and financial solidarity. The initial move in establishing a European agricultural market (applying the so-called market unity principle) was

Glossary Terms

Key terms appear in blue in the text and are defined in a glossary at the end of the book to aid you in exam revision.

ately
the

ther
the
ould
will
ents
ngly
ope
EU

KEY POINTS

• Ratification of the Treaty of Lisbon continued despite the 'no' vote in Ireland, with the Irish government committing itself to holding a second referendum before 31 October 2009.

• Although a blow to the prospects of the Treaty of Lisbon, the Irish 'no' will not bring an end to the EU, but will strengthen the resolve of opponents to contest its development.

Key Points

Each main chapter section ends with a set of key points that summarize the most important arguments.

? **QUESTIONS**

1. Why did it prove difficult to establish a momentum for the end of World War II?

2. How important was the development of international Ev as a necessary condition for European integration?

3. What lessons for the future could be adduced from the s

4. To what extent does the failure of the European Defence areas of policy that are not amenable to integration?

Questions

A set of carefully devised questions has been provided to help you assess your understanding of core themes, and may also be used as the basis of seminar discussion or coursework.

GUIDE TO FURTHER READING

■ Baun, M. J. *An Imperfect Union: The Maastricht Treaty* (Boulder Co: Westview, 1996). An introductory account o early development.

■ Church, C. and Phinnemore, D. *The Penguin Guide to the Amsterdam, Nice and Beyond* (London: Penguin, 2002). EU, and which reproduces the provisions of the Treaties in

■ Galloway, D. *The Treaty of Nice and Beyond* (Sheffield:

Further Reading

Reading lists have been provided as a guide to finding out more about the issues raised within each chapter and to help you locate the key academic literature in the field.

 WEBLINKS

• http://ec.europa.eu./ The Commission's web portal guid relations, and development policies.

• http://www.wto.org/ The website of the World Trade Orga tary on current trade issues and trade disputes, as well as larg negotiations.

• http://www.oecd.org/ The website of the Organisation which includes analysis of EU trade and economic policies.

Important Websites

At the end of every chapter you will find an annotated summary of useful websites on the European Union which will be instrumental in further research.

Guided Tour of the Online Resource Centre

www.oxfordtextbooks.co.uk/orc/cini3e/

The Online Resource Centre that accompanies this book provides students and instructors with ready-to-use teaching and learning materials. These resources are free of charge and designed to maximize the learning experience.

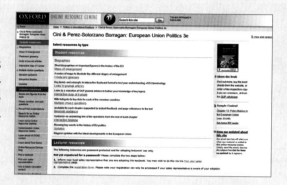

FOR STUDENTS

Interactive Timeline

An interactive timeline provides summaries of the key events in the history of European Union politics as you click on each date.

Biographies

Jean Monnet

Jean Monnet (1888-1979) is credited as one of the founding fathers of the European stages of post-Second World War European integration, undoubtedly influencing t War. Monnet was consulted by the French Foreign Minister Robert Schuman as to Europe. As both a businessman and a bureaucrat, Monnet proved to be an ideal integration.

Short biographies offer interesting background information on important figures in the history of the EU.

Maps

A series of maps have been provided to show you the different stages of EU enlargement and outline vital social and political facts about each member state.

Multiple Choice Questions

Question 1

Which treaty made the first moves towards a common market?

- ⊙ a) Treaty of Rome (1957)
- ○ b) SEA (1986)
- ○ c) TEU (1992)
- ○ d) Nice Treaty (2001)

A bank of self-marking multiple-choice questions has been provided for each chapter of the text to reinforce your understanding and to act as an aid to revision.

Flashcard Glossary

A series of interactive flashcards containing key terms and concepts allow you to test your understanding of the terminology of the European Union.

Revision Tips

A list of key points to consider in answering the end of chapter questions will help you to check your revision is on track.

Updates

Regular updates will be posted to keep you informed of the latest developments in the European Union.

Links to OUP Journal Articles

Links to relevant OUP journal articles allow students and lecturers to explore and research European Union politics in even greater detail.

FOR INSTRUCTORS

PowerPoint® Presentations

These complement each chapter of the book and are a useful resource for preparing lectures and handouts.

Essay, Seminar, and Quiz Questions

Essay, seminar, and quiz questions are provided for each chapter to offer a variety of methods for reinforcing the key themes.

Boxes and Figures from the Text

All boxes and figures from the text have been provided in high resolution format for downloading into presentation software or for use in assignments and exam material

1

Introduction

MICHELLE CINI AND NIEVES PÉREZ-SOLÓRZANO BORRAGÁN

 Chapter Contents

- Why a European Union?
- What is the EU?
- Who can join?
- Who pays?
- How is European policy made?
- The EU and its citizens
- The organization of the book

 Reader's Guide

This chapter provides a very brief introduction to European Union (EU) politics. Its aim is to help direct students who are completely new to the study of the EU by providing some initial building blocks which, it is hoped, will provide useful background for the chapters that follow. The chapter makes brief comments on what the EU is, why it was set up, who can join, who pays, how policy is made, and what role European citizens can play. The chapter ends by explaining how the book is organized.

Why a European Union?

The European integration process was initiated in the 1950s largely as a consequence of the negative experiences of the founding member states during and in the immediate aftermath of the Second World War. Maintaining peace was a primary objective at the time. Even though the idea of some kind of formalized system of European cooperation had been around for centuries, the form that the post-1945 Communities (and later Union) would take was—while drawing on familiar models of government—rather novel.

From the standpoint of the twenty-first century it is perhaps easy to forget how potent the anti-war rationale for European integration must have been in the 1940s and 1950s. In practice, however, this went hand-in-hand with the recognition that for (Western) Europe to get back on its feet economically, after the devastation of the war years, cooperation with neighbouring states was essential. Fundamental to this objective was Germany, considered the engine of the wider European economy. One might imagine how controversial such an idea would have been at the time. Surely, encouraging the reconstruction of Germany would pose a threat to the security of Western Europe? And wasn't this a case of short-term economic objectives trumping long-term geopolitical ones? Ultimately, however, these two ostensibly contradictory objectives of 'peace' and 'economic reconstruction' began to be viewed as mutually reinforcing. European integration—or rather the prospect of it—was the instrument that allowed this change of perspective to occur.

The EU has changed dramatically since the early days of the Community, and some argue that the original objectives of the 1950s are no longer relevant. Certainly, the prospect of war between West European member states of the European Union seems extremely slim now, demonstrating, one might argue, the success of the integration project. Yet at a general level, the concerns of the early post-millennium decades are not so much altered, though we might articulate these concerns using a different language.

Any explanation of why the EU exists must rest on the concept of 'security'. Yet since the early 1990s, this concept has undergone a metamorphosis. Whereas the 'old' definition of security implied *military* security—closely related to the notion of *defence*—the more contemporary variant is much more wide-ranging. For example, it encompasses notions of environmental hazard, migration flows, financial crisis, and demographic change. These new conceptualizations of security help to explain the increasing scope of the EU's competences since the 1980s. Two contextual 'events' have been crucial: the end of the Cold War in 1989; and the terrorist attacks on the World Trade Center in New York and the Pentagon in Washington DC on 11 September 2001 (now usually referred to as 9/11). While the former ended the bipolarity of the post-1945 period, the latter redefined security threats as internal as well as external, as more multi-dimensional and fluid, and as less predictable. Add to this a growing awareness of the threats posed to future generations from climate change, and to current populations from environmental pollution; extreme instability in financial markets; and, in the period following 2008, challenges—practical and intellectual—to the dominant neo-liberal, capitalist paradigm advanced, albeit in different ways, by the world's developed states; and it seems in retrospect that the period after 1989 has marked a transition phase during which a new world order was beginning to emerge.

The EU is as much a product of this new world order as it is an actor seeking to manage change, or an arena in which other actors attempt to perform a similar function. Thus there is no claim here that the EU alone can address these issues. It is but one response, one that is highly institutionalized, that facilitates agreement through procedural mechanisms such as qualified majority voting and norms of consensus (even if on the surface it may not always seem to be the case), all overseen by a goal-orientated, politically involved bureaucracy, a directly elected co-legislature, and an (at times) activist judicial system.

The EU is not just about security, however, no matter how broadly we define the concept. It also concerns welfare. Welfare, in this context, is linked to the concept of the 'welfare state'. In a welfare state, the state takes responsibility for the well-being and social condition of its citizens (rather than leaving them to fend for themselves). In its original form, the welfare state was a European construct, so it should come as no surprise to find that the EU has had ambitions in this direction. But while there is some element of redistribution of funds and central (EU-level) intervention involved in many European policies, when compared to the functions performed by its member states, the EU—in the sense of the European level of governance—performs a rather minimal welfare role. While some argue that this is right and proper, others would like to see the EU developing its activities further in this direction. Whether it should or not is a fundamental political question.

What is the EU?

The European Union is a family of liberal-democratic countries, acting collectively through an institutionalized system of decision making. When joining the EU, members sign up not only to the body of EU treaties, legislation, and norms (the so-called *acquis communautaire*), but also to a set of shared common values, based on democracy, human rights, and principles of social justice. Even so, members, and indeed the European institutions, are keen to stress the diversity of the Union—most obviously in cultural and linguistic terms. By 2007 the EU comprised 27 member states, and over 497 million people.

Since its establishment in the 1950s, commentators have argued over the kind of body the European Community (now Union) is (for an explanation of the distinction between EU and EC see Box 1.1). While there is a growing consensus that the EU now sits somewhere between a traditional international organization and a state, the question of whether it resembles one of these 'models' more than the other remains contested. Although it might seem fair to claim that the European Union is unique, or a hybrid body, even this point can be contentious where it prevents researchers from comparing the EU to national systems of government and international organizations.

KEY CONCEPTS AND TERMS 1.1

The 'European institutions'

The term 'European institutions' usually refers to four key EU organizations:

- The *European Commission* (or just 'the Commission'), the executive and driving force of the Union (see Chapter 8).

- The *European Parliament* (or just 'the Parliament' or EP), directly elected and representing the peoples of the Union (see Chapter 10).

- The *Council of the European Union* (the 'EU Council', 'the Council' or 'the Council of Ministers'), comprising the EU's member states/national governments (see Chapter 9).

- The *Court of Justice* (often called 'the European Court of Justice', 'the European Court' or the ECJ), the body that ensures compliance with European law (see Chapter 11).

Other EU bodies include:

- The *Court of Auditors* ('the European Court of Auditors' or ECA), which ensures the lawful management of the European budget.

- The *European Economic and Social Committee* (EESC), representing the opinions of organized civil society.

- The *Committee of the Regions* (CoR), which represents the opinions of the regions and local authorities.

- The *European Ombudsman*, which deals with complaints of maladministration against the European institutions.

- The *European Central Bank* (ECB), which takes responsibility for monetary policy and for foreign exchange.

- The *European Investment Bank* (EIB), which finances public and private long-term investment.

- The *European Data Protection Supervisor*, which safeguards the privacy of people's personal data.

- The *Office for Official Publications of the European Communities*, which publishes information about the EU.

- The *European Personnel Selection Office*, which recruits staff for the EU institutions and other bodies.

- The *European Administrative School*, which provides training in specific areas for members of EU staff.

Specialized agencies include:

- *Community agencies,* which fulfil specific technical, scientific or managerial tasks within the first pillar. These include:

  o Community Fisheries Control Agency (CFCA)

  o Community Plant Variety Office (CPVO)

  o European Agency for Safety and Health at Work (EU-OSHA)

  o European Agency for the Management of Operational Cooperation at the External Borders (FRONTEX)

  o European Aviation Safety Agency (EASA)

  o European Centre for Disease Prevention and Control (ECDC)

  o European Centre for the Development of Vocational Training (Cedefop)

  o European Chemicals Agency (ECHA)

  o European Environment Agency (EEA)

  o European Food Safety Authority (EFSA)

  o European Foundation for the Improvement of Living and Working Conditions (EUROFOUND)

  o European Fundamental Rights Agency (FRA); previously EUMC

  o European GNSS Supervisory Authority (GSA)

  o European Institute for Gender Equality (under preparation)

  o European Maritime Safety Agency (EMSA)

  o European Medicines Agency (EMEA)

  o European Monitoring Centre for Drugs and Drug Addiction (EMCDDA)

  o European Network and Information Security Agency (ENISA)

  o European Railway Agency (ERA)

  o European Training Foundation (ETF)

  o Office for Harmonisation in the Internal Market (Trade Marks and Designs) (OHIM)

  o Translation Centre for the Bodies of the European Union (CdT)

- *Common Foreign and Security Policy agencies*, which fulfil specific technical, scientific or managerial tasks within the second pillar. These include:

  o European Defence Agency (EDA)

  o European Union Institute for Security Studies (ISS)

  o European Union Satellite Centre (EUSC)

- *Police and judicial cooperation in criminal matters agencies*, which support member states' cooperation in criminal matters (third pillar). These include:

  o European Police College (CEPOL)

  o European Police Office (EUROPOL)

  o The European Union's Judicial Cooperation Unit (EUROJUST)

- *Executive agencies* which fulfil tasks relating to the management of one or more Community programmes. These include:

  o Education, Audiovisual and Culture Executive Agency (EACEA)

  o European Research Council Executive Agency (ERC)

  o Executive Agency for Competitiveness and Innovation (EACI)

  o Executive Agency for Health and Consumers (EAHC)

  o Research Executive Agency (REA)

  o Trans-European Transport Network Executive Agency (TEN-TEA)

- *EURATOM agencies and bodies*, which support the aims of the European Atomic Energy Community Treaty (EURATOM). These include:

  o EURATOM Supply Agency

  o Fusion for Energy

Source: http://europa.eu/agencies/index_en.htm.

The common institutions of the EU, that is, the Commission, Parliament, Council and Courts, along with many other bodies (see Box 1.1) are perhaps the most visible attribute of the European Union. These institutions are highly interdependent; and together they form a nexus for joint decision making in a now extremely wide range of policy areas. While many argue that the EU Council (comprising the EU's governments and support staff) still predominates as the primary legislator, the

importance of the European Parliament has grown substantially since the 1980s, so that it is now generally considered as a co-legislature. Ultimately, however, the member states remain in a privileged position within the EU, as it is they (or rather their governments) who can change the general institutional framework of the Union through treaty reform; or even—potentially—withdraw from the Union, though it seems highly unlikely that any state would take such a dramatic step.

 CHRONOLOGY 1.2

The Treaties

The Treaty of Paris, which set up the European Coal and Steel Community (ECSC), was signed on 18 April 1951. It came into force in 1952.

The Treaty of Rome, which set up the European Economic Community (EEC) and European Atomic Energy Community (EAEC or EURATOM), was signed on 25 March 1957. It came into force on 1 January 1958.

Since the 1950s there have been several revisions to these treaties. Note that these are not new (from-scratch) treaties; each revises earlier versions, beginning with the Treaty of Rome. The most important of these came after the mid-1980s.

● The *Single European Act* (SEA, or just 'Single Act') was signed in 1986. It came into force in July 1987.

● The *Maastricht Treaty* (creating a Treaty on European Union, or TEU) was signed February 1992. It came into force in November 1993.

● The *Amsterdam Treaty* (which revised the TEU) was signed in 1997. It came into force in 1999.

● The *Nice Treaty* (which revised the Amsterdam version of the TEU) was signed in 2000. It came into force in February 2001.

The Constitutional Treaty was signed in October 2004. After the negative outcome of the ratification referendums in France and the Netherlands in 2005, the Treaty could not enter into force (see Chapters 4 and 24).

The Lisbon Treaty (which revised the Nice version of the TEU) was signed in 2007. In 2008 the citizens of Ireland voted against the Treaty in a referendum. As a consequence, it was impossible for this Treaty to enter into force at the start of 2009.

Who can join?

From the very beginning of the project, the European Community (EC) was open to new members. The criteria for joining were rather vague, however. States had to be European, of course, but there was no real definition of what European actually meant. There was also an assumption that member states had to be democratic, but again, this was ill-defined,

and was not included in any treaty. This changed when in 1993 the Copenhagen European Council agreed that countries wishing to join the Union had to meet political and economic criteria; in other words, they must have working market economies and liberal democracies, and be able to take on board the Community *acquis communautaire* (the existing body of EU treaties, legislation, and norms). These conditions of membership became known as the Copenhagen Criteria and they have served ever since as the template for assessing a country's readiness to join the EU.

Although there had been enlargements in the 1970s (with the UK, Ireland, and Denmark joining in 1973) and the 1980s (with Greece joining in 1981 and Spain and Portugal in 1986), the end of the Cold War brought a very different phase in the history of the expansion of the EU. Without the Soviet threat and after a history of more than 30 years of successful cooperation with the EU under the aegis of EFTA (European Free Trade Area), Sweden,

Finland, and Austria became members in 1995. After gaining independence the former communist states saw in the EU the anchor supporting their political and economic transitions and the gateway ensuring their return to Europe. Yet accession would only be completed over a decade later as both the European Union and the new member states had first to adapt to the challenges of a larger and more diverse Union. It was not until May 2004 that the Czech Republic, Estonia, Hungary, Poland, Latvia, Lithuania, Slovakia, and Slovenia joined, along with two small island states, Cyprus and Malta. Bulgaria and Romania joined in 2007, while Croatia and Turkey were negotiating accession in 2009 and the

Figure 1.1 Map of Europe

Former Yugoslav Republic of Macedonia (FYROM) is expected to do so soon after. Other countries in the Western Balkans, such as Montenegro and Albania, have applied for EU membership but most of the former Yugoslav states are not so far advanced in their adaptation to the membership criteria. Further afield, Moldova, Ukraine, and Iceland are interested in closer ties with the EU.

The EU's enlargement experience to date is a successful one. The prospect of membership pushes reforms in the potential candidates and is a guarantee for stability in the entire region. Similarly, each successive enlargement has been accompanied by internal reforms that have, in most cases, strengthened the integration progress. However, the prospect of an EU of 30 or more is controversial in some member states, so it is likely that the question 'Who joins?' will become intrinsically linked to the EU's ability to communicate enlargement effectively to its citizens.

Who pays?

The European Union has its own budget, referred to either as the EU—or perhaps more accurately as the Community—Budget. Unlike national governments, the Union does not have the capacity to tax European citizens in a direct way, which begs the question: from where does this money come? In fact, the Community Budget has more than one source: it comprises 75 per cent of receipts from customs duties and sugar levies contributions at the EU's borders, VAT-based contributions (of 0.5 per cent), and national contributions provided by the member states, amounting to 1.25 per cent of Gross National Product (GNP). The EU budget is, however, relatively small. In 2008, it amounted to 129.1 billion, which is, for example, 15 per cent less than the British government's expenditure on the National Health Service. To avoid the annual wrangling over the budget, it was decided in the 1980s that the general framework of the budget would be decided on a multi-annual basis. Agreement on this framework, which is known as the 'Financial Perspective' is always controversial. This is not surprising, as the negotiations establish the amount to be paid by each individual member state, the overall levels of funding, as well as ceilings for particular policy areas such as agriculture or regional policy. After months of argument, the 2007–13 Financial Perspective was finally agreed in December 2005, including, for the first time, the new member states from Central and Eastern Europe. Some countries

negotiating, such as Germany and the Netherlands, were adamant that they would not sanction an increase in the overall budget. This left little room for manoeuvre. The new post-2004 member states were keen to ensure that they benefited from enhanced rights to regional aid, something those countries who had benefited in the past, namely Spain, Portugal, and Greece, were reluctant to concede. In the end, as is often the case, governments were really only concerned about the bottom line: whether their net contributions were stable, that is, whether what they paid into the budget was roughly in line with what they received from it. Although for the French this meant ring-fencing the Common Agricultural Policy (see Chapter 21), for the British it meant a staunch defence of their rebate, an extra payment made to compensate them for paying into the Budget a much higher proportion than they received.

The EU's budgetary process is a complex one. It involves the Commission, the EU Council, and the European Parliament. Negotiations may last several months if not years (the negotiations for the 2007 budget started in 2005) and it is always highly technical. The budgetary process provides an excellent illustration of the necessity of inter-institutional cooperation amongst Commission, Parliament and Council. While the European Parliament and Council act as the 'Budgetary Authority' for the budget, each has the final say over around half of the budget (the Council has the final say over agricultural spending—called 'compulsory expenditure; the Parliament has the final say over non-compulsory expenditure, the rest of the budget). It is the European Commission, however, that does the first draft of the budget (the Preliminary Draft Budget or PDB). So when it comes to the budget year-on-year (rather than the multi-annual Financial Perspective), it is not just the member states who have to agree amongst themselves; it is also necessary—for most policies—to get the parliamentarians on board. Although there is a technical dimension to it, the process is highly political. It is not surprising that disputes often leap out of the meeting rooms and corridors of the Brussels institutions and into the newspapers.

How is European policy made?

It is not easy to summarize the European policy process in just a few paragraphs. One reason for this is that there is no *one* way of making European policy. For example, the EU is divided into three pillars (see Figure 3.1). While the second and third pillars (which deal respectively with foreign and security policy, and policy and judicial cooperation in criminal matters) are largely intergovernmental, and use a decision-making process that is based largely on government-to-government cooperation, there is much more of a supranational quality to first pillar (EC pillar) decision making, which accounts for all other European policy areas. Moreover, variation across policy areas is now an important theme within the study of European Union politics. There are several decision-making procedures in operation, though the most common now is the codecision procedure (see Chapter 13). Focusing more on policy types rather than formal procedures, Helen Wallace has sought to group similar types together, identifying five 'modes' of European decision making: the classical Community method; the EU regulatory mode; the EU distributional mode; the policy coordination mode; and intensive transgovernmentalism (Wallace 2005).

In some of the earliest textbooks on the EC, the adage that 'the Commission proposes, the Council disposes' was often repeated. As a general statement of how policy making operates today, this presents an inaccurate picture. In the first (or EC pillar), it is certainly still true that the Commission proposes legislation (see Chapter 8), though this is not a helpful summary of the Commission's role in pillars 2 and 3. Indeed, in pillar 1, the Commission possesses the exclusive right of initiative: in other words, only the Commission can draft legislation. But as we shall see below, the Council increasingly plays the role of initiator in today's European legislative process.

In the EC pillar, it is fair to say that policy now emerges as a result of the interaction of a number of actors and institutions. First amongst these is what is sometimes referred to as the 'institutional triangle' of the European Commission, European Parliament, and the Council of the European Union (the EU Council). However, many other European, national and subnational bodies, including interest groups, also play an important role in the making of European policy (see Chapters 12 and 18). The functions, responsibilities, and obligations of these actors and institutions depend on the particular rules that apply to the policy under consideration. While there are rather different rules that apply to budgetary decisions and to the agreement of international agreements, and indeed for Economic and Monetary Union, much of the work of the EC pillar involves a process of regulation.

Legislative procedures

The *codecision procedure* is the main decision-making procedure for the European Community (the first pillar of the European Union). It is based on the principle of parity: that is, that no European decision can be taken without the agreement of both the EU Council and the European Parliament (see Figure 13.1).

The *consultation procedure* was the original EC decision-making procedure, as outlined in the Treaty of Rome. Consultation allows the European Parliament to give its opinion on Commission proposals before the Council takes a decision. Once the Parliament's opinion is made known, the Commission can amend its proposal if it sees fit, before the Council examines it. The Council can then adopt the proposal or amend it. If it wishes to reject the proposal, it must do so unanimously. Under the majority of procedures within the EC pillar, qualified majority voting now applies to votes taken in the EU Council. The use of unanimity is reserved for particularly sensitive political or constitutional issues. It is also in general use (with a few minor exceptions) in Pillars 2 and 3.

The *assent procedure* was introduced in the Single European Act. When this procedure is used, the Council has to get the agreement (or 'assent') of the European Parliament before policy decisions are taken. Under this procedure the Parliament can say 'yes' or 'no' to a proposal, but does not have any right to propose amendments to it. Assent is only used in a relatively small number of policy areas, for example EU enlargement and international agreements.

The *cooperation procedure* was introduced in the Single European Act, and was extended by the Maastricht Treaty. However, at Amsterdam, governments agreed to privilege the codecision procedure and cut back on areas where cooperation was used. It is now only used for economic and monetary union decisions.

Various legislative procedures govern the way that policy is made (see Box 1.3). The most common of these now is the codecision procedure. Codecision gives both the Parliament and the Council, as co-legislators, two successive readings of legislative proposals drafted by the Commission (see Chapter 13).

The procedure used is determined by the so-called legal basis underpinning the policy, which involves reference to a specific treaty provision. This provision also determines whether governments voting in the EU Council need to take their decisions on the basis of unanimity or a qualified majority vote (QMV). The legal basis is decided by the Commission, though the Commission's decision must be based on objective criteria so that it can be challenged through the courts if need be. Where there are grey areas, the choice of legal basis (and hence, legislative procedure) can be extremely contentious. This is because different procedures allow different configurations of actors and institutions a say in the policy process. This is particularly important in determining the relative importance of the Council, Parliament and Commission in the European policy process.

The 2000 Lisbon Strategy agreed by the member states, with the aim of making the EU the most competitive economy in the world, incorporated a new policy-making instrument, the so-called open method of coordination (OMC). Unlike the legislative procedures described above, the OMC provides a framework for member states to work towards policy convergence in areas of national competence such as employment, social protection, social inclusion, education, and youth and training, through sharing common objectives, policy instruments, best practice, and peer pressure to achieve policy convergence. The Commission, the Parliament, and the Court of Justice have a limited or no role in the process. The incorporation of new policy instruments is a clear example of the dynamism of EU governance (see Chapter 13).

The EU and its citizens

In the preamble to the Treaty of Rome, the member states stated their determination to lay the foundations for 'an ever closer union among the peoples of Europe'. As the chapters in this book will show, the process of European integration has deeply affected the lives of all Europeans—from everyday things such as the labelling on packets of crisps and the colour of their passports, to more complex and perhaps non-tangible changes such as the rights bestowed to them by virtue of being citizens of a member state. The Maastricht Treaty established a new citizenship of the Union (conceived of as a supplement to, not a substitute for, national citizenship), which conferred on every European citizen the right to move and reside freely in the Union; the right to vote for and stand as a candidate at municipal and European Parliament elections in whichever member state the EU citizen might reside; the right to petition to the EP and the European Ombudsman, and the right to diplomatic and consular protection. Such rights were further extended at Amsterdam, incorporating an anti-discrimination clause and member states' commitment to raise the quality of and guarantee free access to education. The Charter of Fundamental Rights (although without binding legal effect yet, as the Lisbon Treaty is pending ratification) summarizes the common values of the member states and brings together a set of common civil, political, economic and social rights (see Chapters 3 and 4).

However, almost since its inception the EU has struggled to communicate the rationale of integration to the citizens of Europe and to generate some sense of identification with the European project. European citizens tend to conceive of the EU as a remote entity suffering from a permanent democratic deficit. In other words, the EU's decision-making mechanisms are considered complex and opaque; it lacks a parliamentary chamber that holds the decisions of government to account; it is run by a set of political elites who have failed to consult citizens on the direction and objectives of the integration process; and more often than not it is portrayed by the media and national political leaders as the source of unpopular political decisions (see Chapter 23). This set of feelings translates into low voter turnout to European Parliament elections. Indeed, a record low was reached in 2004, when only 45.6 per cent of the EU electorate voted. Similarly, according to a Eurobarometer survey published in May 2008, only 49 per cent of European citizens feel some kind of attachment to the EU, compared with 91 per cent who feel primarily attached to their own countries. Unsurprisingly, a closer look at these data displays the variation that exists across member states, with 65 per cent of Belgian and 63 per cent of Polish citizens professing an attachment to the EU, but only 27 per cent of citizens in Finland or the United Kingdom feeling the same way.

While this detachment seemed less obvious and perhaps less significant in the early years of the integration process, the so-called 'permissive consensus' ended at Maastricht in 1992, with the negative outcome of the Danish referendum and the almost French 'non'. For the first time, the citizens of Europe contested the move towards further integration. Ever since, contestation has become the norm rather than the exception each time the direction of European integration has been put to the vote, as the ratification of the Nice Treaty, the Constitutional Treaty, and the Lisbon Treaty have shown. Hence, despite attempts to give more powers to the European Parliament, the introduction of the principle of subsidiarity to give more voice to localities and regions, the commitment to a permanent dialogue with civil society, plans for citizens' initiatives, and a communication policy aimed at 'listening better, explaining better and going local', European integration is still a politicized issue that generates negative mobilization of public opinion with regard to EU policies and institutions (see Chapter 24). 'We are not forming coalitions of states, we are uniting men,' said Jean Monnet. Yet European citizens have different interests, culture, language, and history. Any attempt to forge an ever closer union among the peoples of Europe needs to account for such a variety of goals, perceptions, and expectations.

The organization of the book

The book is organized into five parts. Part One covers the historical evolution of the European Community from 1945 to early 2009. Readers should note that at the time of writing, the 2009 European Parliament elections have not yet been held; and there remains considerable uncertainty over the ratification of the Lisbon Treaty. Chapter 2 focuses on the origins and early years of the European integration process. Chapter 3 covers the period from the Single European Act to the Nice Treaty; and Chapter 4 reviews the period from the Constitutional Treaty's failed ratification to the Lisbon Treaty.

Part Two covers the theoretical and conceptual approaches that have sought to explain European integration and EU politics. Chapter 5 reviews the fortunes of neo-functionalism; while Chapter 6 summarizes the key elements of the intergovernmental approaches to European integration. Chapter 7 has a wide remit, focusing on the new (or newer) theories of European integration and EU politics, including work on multi-level governance and new institutionalism.

Part Three deals with the European institutions: the Commission (Chapter 8); the EU Council (Chapter 9); the European Parliament (Chapter 10) and the European Courts (Chapter 11). It also includes a chapter on interest intermediation (Chapter 12).

Part Four covers a sample of European policies, which, though not aiming to be in any way comprehensive, demonstrates the various ways in which such policies have evolved, and—though to a lesser extent—how they operate. It starts in Chapter 13 with an overview of the EU policy process. Thereafter, Chapter 14 tackles external economic policy; Chapter 15, foreign, security, and defence policy; and Chapter 16, the single market. Chapter 17 discusses social policy; Chapter 18, regional policy; and Chapter 19, justice and home affairs. Chapters 20 and 21 deal, respectively, with Economic and Monetary Union (EMU) and the Common Agricultural Policy (CAP). Finally, Chapter 22 examines the EU's environment policy.

The final part of the book, Part Five, comprises four chapters, each of which deals with specific issues related to the politics of the European Union. The first, Chapter 23, discusses democracy and the democratic deficit; the second, Chapter 24, focuses on public opinion; and the third, Chapter 25 discusses Europeanization; and, finally, Chapter 26, enlargement.

PART ONE

The Historical Context

2

The European Community: From 1945 to 1985

DEREK W. URWIN

Chapter Contents

- Introduction
- The opening moves
- The Community idea
- Rome and the stalling of ambition
- The emergence of summits
- Conclusion

Reader's Guide

This chapter reviews the principal developments in the process of European integration from the end of World War II through to the mid 1980s. While ideas and arguments in favour of European unity have a much longer history, the war and its aftermath contributed to providing a greater urgency and different context to the issue. In the mid 1980s the European Community took a series of decisions that launched it firmly on a trajectory towards intensive political, economic, and monetary integration. Between these two points in time, neither the support for integration nor the institutional and structural forms it took were preordained or without opposition. The rate and direction of integration depended upon a shifting constellation of forces: the nature of interactions between federalist ideas and their supporters, national governments and their assessments of national self-interest, and the broader international environment. Within these parameters, the chapter looks at the emergence of international organizations in Western Europe in the 1940s, the establishment of the Community idea from the Schuman Plan through to the Treaty of Rome, and the factors that contributed towards the seemingly erratic progress towards ever closer union made by the European Community after 1958.

Introduction

The institutional structure and operation of the European Union (EU) can trace a direct line of descent back to the establishment of the European Coal and Steel Community (ECSC). Indeed, while the intervening decades may have witnessed extensive embellishment and refinement, the broad outline and principle remain those of 1951. However, the idea and dream of a politically integrated Europe possess a much longer pedigree. Across the centuries, numerous intellectuals and political leaders have argued for and have attempted to bring order and unity to the fragmented political mosaic of the European continent. As part of this long-standing dream, an increased intellectual agitation for unity in Europe emerged in the nineteenth century, but almost exclusively among people who were, at best, at the fringes of political decision making. Their arguments and blueprints held little appeal or relevance for political leaders. However, there did emerge a more widespread recognition that some form of economic cooperation might well contain some potential political advantages for states. Those schemes that did become operative, however, were either short-lived or, like the Zollverein established among German states, highly region specific and protectionist in their external mien.

The post-World War I peace process, by its emphasis upon national self-determination, made the continental political mosaic even more complex, so leading to a greater urgency for, and difficulty surrounding any process of, cooperation. After 1918, the hopes that had been invested in the League of Nations as a world body dedicated to a cooperative peace quickly foundered in a highly charged atmosphere of economic uncertainty and historic political antipathies. The Low Countries and the Nordic states explored possibilities of economic cooperation, but with no significant outcome. A few politicians, most notably perhaps Aristide Briand, the French Foreign Minister, did raise the idea of political integration. But in concrete terms this did not advance beyond the 1930 Briand Memorandum, a generalized proposal advocating a kind of intergovernmental union with its own institutional infrastructures within the League of Nations. Outside political circles, a plethora of associations expounded schemes for cooperation and integration, but failed to achieve any positive results. By the 1930s economic depression and crisis, and the rise of fascism, had led countries to look to their own defences; the outbreak of war in 1939 simply confirmed the absence of any radical change to the European world of states. The history of European integration, therefore, as it is conventionally understood today, essentially begins in 1945. The chapter that follows charts that history, focusing on the period between 1945 and 1985.

The opening moves

World War II was a catalyst for a renewed interest in European unity. It contributed to arguments that nationalism and nationalist rivalries, by culminating in war, had discredited and bankrupted the independent state as the foundation of political organization and international order, and that a replacement for the state had to be found in a comprehensive continental community. These ideas were most forcefully expressed in the political vision of the Italian federalist, Altiero Spinelli, who produced a blueprint for a United States of Europe as the overriding priority for the post-war peace. His arguments found strong favour among the various national Resistance movements. However, the new European administrations seemed to give European unity a low priority, concentrating more upon issues of national economic reconstruction. But for several reasons the siren voices of federalism were heard by, and swayed, a larger audience than had been the case in the interwar period, so enabling the possibility and dream of union to survive as an item on the European political agenda (see Box 2.1).

One important factor was the increasingly glacial international political climate. This division of Europe between East and West after 1945, and the subsequent Cold War between the world's two superpowers, the USA and the USSR, fuelled alarm in Western Europe about its own fragile defences in the light of what it feared were the territorial ambitions of the USSR. This led to a deep involvement of the USA in European affairs in the late 1940s. The consequent ideological bipolarization in turn helped propel Western Europe towards defining itself as an entity with common interests. This changing mood was assisted by a general concern over the parlous state of the national economies, a concern which helped generate a widespread belief that economic recovery would require both external assistance from the USA and collaboration on development and trade across the West European states. It was widely assumed across Western Europe that the lead in any moves towards closer collaboration, because of its wartime role, would be taken by the UK, and that, with Germany prostrate and militarily occupied, a British-French alliance would lie at the core of European organization. However, the initial moves

---

BOX 2.1

Issues and debates in the early years of European integration

Why European integration began, and the reasons why the subsequent plot developed the way it did have been the subject of intense debate. There has been a tendency, especially among those strongly committed to a federal Europe, to see development moving, if not smoothly, then nevertheless inexorably along a single plane towards a predetermined goal. Yet the history of integration since the formation of the ECSC in 1951 has not been like that. The rate of integrative progress has been far from consistent, and all arguments and pressures for further advances have had to contend with equally powerful countervailing forces pulling in the opposite direction. Nor was there anything preordained about the structural route taken in 1950, or that future developments would revolve largely around a Franco-German axis. There might, both then and later, have been broad agreement about the desirability and principle of a united Europe; but there has rarely been consensus on anything else. As Robert Schuman, the French Foreign Minister, commented in May 1950 when he unveiled his plan for a pooling of coal and steel resources, 'Europe will not be made all at once, or according to a single plan.'

In reality, the story of integration is complex, with numerous subplots, varying strategies, and different ambitions. As advocated by the federalists, the role of ideas and beliefs has always been central to the progress of integration. Even so, there has been tension within the federalist camp as to the most appropriate strategy to adopt. Simplifying the complex strands of thought somewhat, there have been two competing strategic schools. On the one hand, there are those who have followed the arguments of people like Altiero Spinelli who, in the Ventotene Manifesto of 1940 and his subsequent writings and actions, urged a once-and-for-all 'big bang' solution, an instantaneous and all-embracing transformation into a federal European state. On the other side was a more cautious and pragmatic strategy, encapsulated by the inputs of people like Jean Monnet and Robert Schuman, which envisaged a slower process of steady accretion through a series of limited actions and innovations. But while central and necessary, the force of ideas by itself has not been sufficient. The impact and rate of advance of the federalist impulse has been modified by the input and role of national governments—by their policies and by the degree to which integrative proposals have been seen as fitting with, or at the very least not seeming to threaten, what regimes perceive to be the national interests of their own states. The way in which processes of integration have developed over the past half-century, therefore, is the product of a complex interaction of centripetal and centrifugal pressures, of ideas, principles, and *realpolitik* scepticism. And all of this intricate dance has occurred within a broader and ever shifting international political and economic environment that itself has affected, sometimes positively and sometimes negatively, the degree of enthusiasm for, commitment to, and rate of progress of integration.

<table>
<tr><td colspan="3">**CHRONOLOGY 2.2**</td></tr>
</table>

Key dates in European integration, 1947–57

1947	March	Announcement of Truman Doctrine by the USA
		Signature of Treaty of Dunkirk by the UK and France
	June	Declaration of Marshall Plan by the USA
1948	January	Start of Benelux Customs Union
	March	Signature of Treaty of Brussels by the UK, France, and Benelux
	April	Establishment of Organization for European Economic Co-operation (OEEC) by 16 European states, the USA, and Canada
	May	The federalist Congress of Europe meets at The Hague
1949	April	Signature of the Atlantic Pact and formation of the North Atlantic Treaty Organization (NATO) by 12 states
	May	Treaty of Westminster establishes the Council of Europe
1950	May	Schuman Plan proposes a pooling of coal and steel resources by France, the Federal Republic of Germany, and any other state wishing to join them
	October	Proposal for a European Defence Community (EDC)
1951	April	Treaty of Paris establishes the European Coal and Steel Community (ECSC)
1952	May	Signature of EDC Treaty
	July	ECSC comes into operation
1953	March	Draft Treaty of a European Political Community (EPC)
1954	August	French Parliament rejects EDC. The EDC and EPC plans collapse
	October	Treaty of Brussels is modified to establish West European Union (WEU)
1955	June	Foreign Ministers of the ECSC states meet in Messina, Italy, to consider 'further European integration'
1957	March	Signature of Treaty of Rome establishes the European Economic Community (EEC) and the European Atomic Energy Community (EURATOM)

---

towards enhanced collaboration by governments were limited in scope, an exception being the wartime decision by the governments in exile of the Low Countries to establish a Benelux customs union. While governments were more typically interested primarily in security arrangements, they did little more than consider mutual aid treaties of the traditional variety. The only formal agreements to emerge were the 1947 Treaty of Dunkirk between the UK and France, and its 1948 extension in the fifty-year Treaty of Brussels (formally the Treaty of Economic, Social and Cultural Collaboration and Collective Self-Defence), which incorporated the Low Countries as signatories, and which was later to serve as the basis of the Western European Union (WEU). While these treaties listed economic and cultural cooperation as objectives, they were first and foremost mutual security pacts with promises of reciprocal assistance, specifically to guard against possible future German aggression. While other countries and federalists alike looked to the UK to take a lead, the British attitude towards anything more than cooperation between independent states was consistently negative, at best deeply sceptical, and at worst totally hostile.

By 1948 the Cold War was in full swing. Heightened alarm over events in Central and Eastern Europe helped to consolidate the final marriage between Western Europe and the USA, with the formation of the North Atlantic Treaty Organization (NATO) in 1949. NATO was the conclusion of a programme of American support first outlined in the Truman Doctrine of March 1947, which pledged American assistance for 'free peoples who are resisting subjugation'. It provided a protective shield behind which Western Europe was free to consider and develop its political and economic options without necessarily having to devote time and scarce resources to military defence. Equally, the USA, itself a federation, saw nothing inherently problematic about closer integration in Western Europe; indeed, also partly because of its own strategic interests, the USA lent its weight after 1947 to proposals for more intensive collaboration. The American commitment was strongly welcomed by the two leading states, the UK and France. But although they were expected to form the vanguard of the European future, neither saw this as leading to radical reconstruction. French European policy was dominated by the need to keep Germany weak and to control its future, a concern met by the military occupation of the country after 1945. The UK was suspicious of anything beyond close collaboration that might diminish its own sovereignty and freedom to act independently.

It was against this backdrop that the protagonists of a federal Europe nevertheless began to receive endorsement from a growing number of senior politicians from several countries. Soon, the dominant issue became not whether there should be integration, but rather what form it should take. Governments and political parties took positions on the question of whether this should only be intensive intergovernmental collaboration embedded in formalized treaties and arrangements, or something deeper that would embrace an element of supranationalism and the diminution of national sovereignty. This was the core of the debate at the Congress of Europe in 1948, which led to the establishment of the Council of Europe in 1949 (see Box 2.3).

Political developments were paralleled by activity on the economic front through the introduction of the European Recovery Programme, or Marshall Plan. The essence of the Plan was an American offer

---

CASE STUDY 2.3

The establishment of the Council of Europe

The Congress of Europe, a gathering of over 700 delegates or representatives of pro-integration or federalist organizations from 16 countries, along with observers from Canada and the USA, was held at The Hague (in the Netherlands) in May 1948. The Congress was too unwieldy to achieve any practical outcome, not least because it did not speak for governments. But in calling for a European federation or union, with its own institutions, a charter of human rights linked to a European court, a common market, and monetary union, it helped place integration more firmly and visibly on the agenda. It stimulated a process of discussion and debate that culminated in May 1949 in the establishment by ten states of the intergovernmental Council of Europe, the first post-1945 political organization on the continent. The Council, however, represented a victory for those, especially the UK, who wished only cooperation, not integration: decisions would require the consent of all its members, and hence it could not enforce any view or policy upon reluctant member states. Federalists accepted the final outcome of the Council only reluctantly, viewing it as a start that would not preclude a search for something better. By contrast, for others it epitomized the totality of what was desirable or necessary. In seeking to accommodate two very contrasting positions, the product was very much a dead end. More importantly, however, the Council of Europe represented a watershed. It convinced the protagonists of a united Europe that they would have to narrow their horizons even further. It brought the curtain down on the willingness to compromise in order to keep reluctant states and governments on board. It was, therefore, the point at which the post-war belief that the UK should and would take the lead in radical political reorganization came to an end.

of economic aid to Europe. The aid, however, was contingent upon the administration of the relief programme being collective, in order to maximize its benefits. The USA further insisted that the European participants in the programme had to decide themselves how aid was to be distributed across the countries involved. These were the basic tasks of the Organization for European Economic Cooperation (OEEC), established in April 1948. The OEEC was primarily concerned with macro-economic cooperation and coordination. Like the Council of Europe, it was intergovernmental in nature, only able to operate with the full consent of all its members. Both organizations, however, had to have some permanent institutions to enable them to perform their allotted functions satisfactorily. While limited in scope and bound very much by the principle of voluntary cooperation, both nevertheless reflected a growing realization in Western Europe of the interdependency of states, and that these states, especially against the backdrop of the Cold War, would prosper or fail together. And both contributed significantly to a learning curve among the participants about how one should go about collaborating. Yet it remained the case that both

organizations, in terms of the degree of integration and limitations on national sovereignty, operated on the basis of the lowest common denominator of intergovernmental cooperation. While this clearly met the needs of some states and governments, it was a situation that could not satisfy those who believed in the imperative of union (see Hogan 1987).

KEY POINTS

- World War II contributed to a new interest in European unity.

- The first post-1945 governments were more concerned with economic issues than with European integration.

- Federalists and supporters of integration expected the UK, because of its wartime role, to take the lead in reorganizing Europe.

- The Cold War heightened West European fears of insecurity and led to a massive American political and economic involvement in Europe.

- European international organizations established in the late 1940s were all intergovernmental in nature.

The Community idea

If union were to become a political objective, a different path had to be sought, and federalists had to acknowledge that such a path would prove acceptable to only some countries. The radical redirection of effort was provided by the then French Foreign Minister, Robert Schuman, who in May 1950 cut through the tangled debate to propose a pooling of coal and steel resources. The Schuman Plan was the blueprint for the European Coal and Steel Community (ECSC), formally established in April 1951 as Western Europe's first organization to involve the yielding of a degree of state sovereignty to a supranational authority (Diebold 1959).

That such a scheme could be proposed, drafted, and turned into reality was the outcome of a combination of shifting circumstances. It had an immediately identifiable and concrete goal, making it more attractive to senior politicians than an instantaneous federal transformation, no matter how strongly they might favour intensive integration. The drafter of the plan had been Jean Monnet, whose experiences as the supremo of national economic planning in France after 1945 had confirmed his long-held view that economic development and prosperity could best be achieved at a European rather than a national level, and that therefore the route to political integration was a long road that inevitably lay through economics. Equally importantly, Monnet had also consistently argued that peace and stability in Europe could only be achieved through a *rapprochement* between the historical rivals, France and Germany; for Monnet the two states had to form the core of any integrative venture. These were views to which Schuman also strongly subscribed. He was able to persuade his governmental colleagues in Paris of their virtues in part because of further changes in the international environment.

Relations between East and West had reached a nadir in 1948. One consequence was the decision by the USA, backed by the UK and a reluctant France, to form a German state out of the western military zones of occupation in the country. This decision and the establishment of an independent Federal Republic of Germany in 1949 destroyed at a stroke the foundation of France's post-1945 European policy. In addition, the compensatory decision to establish an International Ruhr Authority in April 1949 to supervise coal and steel production in West Germany's dominant industrial region failed to satisfy anyone. In 1950, with the Ruhr Authority increasingly ineffectual and on the point of being abandoned, Monnet's ideas offered France a way out of the dilemma, by indicating a strategy by which the new West Germany could be subject to external influence while it was still politically weak. Schuman's proposal proved equally attractive to the West German leader, Konrad Adenauer, who saw it as a potentially valuable element of his policy of tying the Federal Republic firmly to Western Europe politically, economically, and militarily. Submerging the country in European ventures, he hoped, would further reassure his neighbours that West Germany had abandoned the aggressive nationalism of the past. It is not insignificant that Schuman's announcement was for a structure enabling the pooling of French and West German coal and steel resources, which other countries were welcome to join if they wished. He further made it clear that a new structure would be created even if no other state wished to join: 'if necessary, we shall go ahead with only two [countries]'. Be that as it may, the Schuman Plan was

overtly about more than just coal and steel: Schuman emphasized that it would set down 'common bases for economic development as a first step in the federation of Europe'.

Hence, the formation of the European Coal and Steel Community (ECSC) was the product of a combination of integrationist impulses and ideas, national self-interest, and international circumstances. Hailed by Jean Monnet as 'the first expression of the Europe that is being born', the ECSC set in motion a groundswell that some 40 years later was to result in the European Union. While an invitation to join the new body was extended to all West European states, and especially the UK, only four other countries—Belgium, Italy, Luxembourg, and the Netherlands—felt able to accept the supranational principle of the ECSC. The institutional structure adopted by the ECSC—which included a supreme judicial authority—was to serve as a model for all future developments. The most innovative (and in the future a highly contentious) feature was the divided executive and decision-making structure: a High Authority vested with significant power to represent and uphold the supranational principle, and a Council of Ministers to represent and protect the interests of the governments of the member states (Poidevin and Spierenberg 1994).

However, if the ECSC were to be the first step towards deeper union, more had to be done. Monnet himself saw the ECSC as the opening phase of a process of sectoral integration, where the ultimate goal of political union would be the long-term culmination of an accretion of integrative efforts, of trust and experience, in a sector-by-sector linkage of specific economic areas and activities that ultimately would result in a common economic market (see Chapter 6). Discussions began more or less immediately on what—for example, transport or agriculture—would and should follow on from coal and steel as the next instances of sectoral economic integration.

The ECSC survived as a separate entity until 1967 when the merged European Communities (EC) was created. Its record of economic success, however, was rather mixed. Even though Jean Monnet had been appointed head of the High Authority, the latter failed to bring national coal and steel policies and practices fully under its control, and it had little or no control over or effect on other economic sectors. By themselves, these issues might in time have forced a re-evaluation of the strategy of sectoral integration. In the event, the direction taken by the latter was altogether surprising. The determining factor was a further transformation in the international climate, which had once again changed for the worse as armed conflict broke out in Korea during the ECSC negotiations. Concerned that the Asian war might be a prelude to war in Europe, the USA called for a strengthening of NATO, while simultaneously stressing that because of its global role and commitments, America itself could not provide the necessary additional resources. When the European members of NATO argued that their economies were too weak to bear substantial additional defence costs, the USA proposed a West German military contribution to NATO.

Only a few years after the overthrow of Nazism, the idea of a German army alarmed its neighbours. In France, the possibility of West German rearmament threatened once again to undermine the core of its European policy. Yet, prompted by Jean Monnet, who saw sectoral integration as a solution to the dilemma, the French government proposed a European Defence Community (EDC), modelled upon the ECSC, which would establish a Western European army that would include military units from all the member states, including West Germany.

However, the exercise failed when the French National Assembly refused to take a decision to ratify the Treaty in 1954 (see Box 2.4).

The consequences for integration of the EDC debacle seemed to be severe. It proved to be the high-water mark of the sectoral approach to integration. Only the ECSC survived the damage to the integration cause, and there were fears that it too would collapse. A somewhat disillusioned Jean Monnet announced his intention not to seek reappointment as President of the ECSC High Authority, in order to pursue the goal of integration as a private citizen. However, there remained across Western Europe a substantial degree of institutional cooperation built up over the previous decade: NATO, OEEC, the Council of Europe, and, of course, the ECSC. Within these networks there had survived in the little Europe of the ECSC Six a strong commitment to further integration. At a meeting of their foreign ministers at Messina in Sicily in June 1955, the six members of the ECSC took a decisive step forward. Taking as their core text the 1952 Dutch proposal for the abolition of quotas and tariffs within, and the introduction of a common external tariff for, the Community area, the foreign ministers agreed to launch 'a fresh advance towards the building of Europe'. This set in motion progress towards plans for a customs union and, ultimately, a common market, plans that culminated in March 1957 with the Treaty of Rome and the formation of the European Economic Community (EEC). Again, however, only the six members of the ECSC were willing to commit themselves to the leap of faith demanded by the Rome Treaty.

KEY POINTS

- The Schuman Plan offered a way in which France and the Federal Republic of Germany could become reconciled with each other, and a path towards integration that went beyond intergovernmental cooperation.

- The European Coal and Steel Community (ECSC) was the first step in an anticipated process of sectoral economic integration. It brought together six states that delegated some aspects of their sovereignty to a supranational authority.

- Hostility to, and the ultimate rejection by France of plans for a European Defence Community (EDC) led to its abandonment. The failure of the EDC contributed towards a discrediting of the sectoral strategy and threatened to destroy the whole process of integration.

- In 1955 the ECSC states launched a rescue operation and committed themselves to further integration, signing the Treaty of Rome two years later.

CASE STUDY 2.4

The European Defence Community

Under plans for a European Defence Community (EDC), German units would be part of a European army, all falling under an integrated European, and not an independent West German, command. The other member states would have only a proportion of their armed forces within the EDC framework. The EDC proposal was immediately seen by federalists and others as a significant second step towards integration. However, the question of the desirability or necessity of some form of political control over and direction of an EDC soon led to arguments for a European Political Community (EPC), something that would short-circuit sectoral integration by an immediate advance towards creating a comprehensive federation. The Dutch Foreign Minister, Johan Willem Beyen, took the argument one step further in 1952, suggesting a parallel drive to economic unity. Arguing that sectoral integration by itself was insufficient for economic development and unity, Beyen proposed that the EDC/EPC nexus be extended to embrace the construction of a customs union and common market (see Chapter 16).

Only the ECSC countries were willing to explore these possible new ventures. The UK declined a specific invitation to join the EDC, but because it wished NATO to be strengthened, it indicated support for a European army that would include a West German military contribution. The EPC idea remained at the draft stage, and Beyen's ideas were largely put on hold because it was clear, not least in the minds of supporters of further integration, that any advance down that road was dependent upon the success or failure of ratification of the EDC by the national parliaments of the proposed members. Ironically, the stumbling block was France, where the idea of a rearmed Germany, even within

the EDC, remained deeply perturbing. France had originally wanted, and perhaps had expected, the UK to be part of the new organization as an extra guarantee against any possible resurgence of German militarism, the well known British hostility to anything that smacked of supranationalism notwithstanding. In a sense, the French proposal for an EDC had been, for many of its politicians, a delaying tactic, perhaps even an idea so outrageous in its audacity that it would become mired in years of debate and argument. The extent to which the notion was embraced both within the ECSC states and beyond, and the speed at which the subsequent talks progressed, placed successive French governments, all short lived, weak, and concerned more with mere survival than innovation, in a quandary. Confronted by strong political and popular opposition, all were unable or unwilling to make the effort to secure a parliamentary majority for EDC ratification (Aron and Lerner 1957).

After almost four years of stalemate, France rejected the EDC in 1954 on a technicality (the vote was not on whether the treaty should be approved, but whether the parliament wished to discuss the treaty). With it fell the hopes for an EPC. The vote did not remove the issue of West German rearmament from the agenda. In a frantic search to salvage something from the wreckage, agreement was secured on a British proposal to revamp the 1948 Treaty of Brussels, bringing into it all the projected members of the EDC. A new body, the Western European Union (WEU), was established, linking together the UK and the ECSC states in a defence arrangement within which West German rearmament would occur. In reality, WEU remained more or less moribund until the 1980s, and a rearmed West Germany entered NATO as a full and equal member. The outcome, therefore, was the one result that France had hoped to avoid by its advocacy of an EDC.

Rome and the stalling of ambition

Because the new organization was to range over an extremely wide area of activity, the provisions of the Treaty of Rome were necessarily complex. Its preamble may have been less prescriptive than that of its ECSC predecessor, yet, in referring to the determination 'to lay the foundations of an ever closer union among the peoples of Europe', its implications were far reaching. More specifically, the Treaty

enjoined its signatories, among other things, to establish a common market, defined as the free movement of goods, persons, services and capital, to approximate national economic policies, and to develop common policies, most specifically in agriculture. Although the objectives of the Treaty were expressed in economic terms, as the preamble implied, a political purpose lay behind them. In

CHRONOLOGY 2.5

Key dates in European integration 1958 – 85

1958	January	Establishment of the EEC and EURATOM
1959	January	First tariff cuts made by the EEC
1961	July	Fouchet Plan for a 'union of states' proposed
1961	July – August	The UK, Denmark, and Ireland apply for EEC membership
1962	January	EEC develops basic regulations for a Common Agricultural Policy (CAP)
	May	Norway applies for EEC membership
1963	January	President de Gaulle vetoes British membership; signature of Franco-West German Treaty of Friendship and Reconciliation
1965	April	Treaty merging the executives of the three Communities signed in Brussels
	June	France walks out of the Council of Ministers and begins a boycott of EEC institutions
1966	January	The Luxembourg Compromise ends the French boycott
1967	July	The three Communities merged to form the European Community
	November	President de Gaulle vetoes British membership for the second time
1968	July	The EC establishes a customs union and agrees on a Common Agricultural Policy
1969	December	The Hague summit agrees to consider EC enlargement and supports greater policy cooperation and economic and monetary union
1970	October	Werner Report on economic and monetary union; Davignon Report on foreign policy cooperation leads to establishment of European Political Cooperation (EPC)
1972	March	The currency 'snake' established, limiting margins of fluctuation between participating currencies
1973	January	Accession of the UK, Denmark, and Ireland
1974	December	Paris summit agrees to establish the European Council and accepts the principle of direct elections to the European Parliament
1976	January	Tindemans Report published, recommending reform of the EC institutions
1979	March	Establishment of the European Monetary System (EMS)
	June	First direct elections to the EP
1983	June	Signature of Solemn Declaration on European Union by the heads of state and government
1984	February	EP approves the Draft Treaty Regarding European Union
	June	Fontainebleau summit of the European Council agrees to take action on a number of outstanding issues hindering progress on integration
1985	March	European Council agrees to the establishment of a single market by the end of 1992
	June	European Council agrees on a reform of the Treaty of Rome

aiming to create something more than a common market, the Treaty emphasized the principle that the problems of one member state would be the problems of all.

The institutional structure was modelled on that of the ECSC, with the quasi-executive and supranational European Commission intended to be the motor force of integration; its authority was counterbalanced by the Council of Ministers representing the member states. Facing these executive bodies was a much weaker assembly with little in the way of significant decision-making powers. The Assembly, which quickly adopted for itself the title of European Parliament (EP), was soon engaged in a perpetual struggle to enlarge its own authority, including a demand for implementation of the Treaty provision on direct elections. The final major EEC institution was the European Court of Justice, which rapidly, not least by its ruling that EEC law took precedence over national law, asserted itself as a major bonding force. The new EEC shared its assembly and court with the ECSC and the less significant European Atomic Energy Community (EURATOM), also set up in 1957 by a second Treaty of Rome to promote collaboration on the development of nuclear energy for peaceful economic purposes. The three Communities retained separate executive structures until 1967, when they were merged to form the European Communities (EC).

The Treaty of Rome set a target for its objectives. Within specified time limits the implementation and completion of a customs union, and then a common market, were to be achieved through a three-stage process. The auguries were initially bright. Under the leadership of a proactive Commission, early progress towards the goals of Rome was satisfactory. By 1961 EEC internal tariff barriers had been substantially reduced and quota restrictions on industrial products largely eliminated. Towards the end of the decade the EEC could proudly claim that the customs union had been implemented ahead of schedule. Internal EEC trade flourished, rates of economic growth were impressive, and work had begun on establishing a common agricultural policy. These positive advances raised hopes among those committed to the establishment of a political union that that goal might also be expedited. Indeed, Walter Hallstein, the forceful West German statesman and economist who served as President of the Commission from 1958 to 1967, could inform journalists that perhaps he should be regarded as a kind of Western European prime minister. The optimism, however, proved to be premature. Broadly speaking, the transformation of the EEC into a common market was scheduled to be spread over a period of 12 to 15 years. By the early 1970s, however, the EEC was seemingly no nearer that goal than it had been a decade earlier. A series of circumstances had led to its derailment.

The issues that the EEC was obliged to confront in the 1960s were issues that have remained central ever since. In simple terms, they related to the deepening and widening of the Community: the extent to which, and the rate at which, more intensive integration should be pursued, and how these aspects of integration should relate to the enlargement of the EEC. The specific context in which these issues emerged in the 1960s had a focal point in the French President, Charles de Gaulle. While he was generally supportive of the EEC as a means of retaining French influence in Western Europe, forging in particular a close relationship with Konrad Adenauer and the German economic giant across the Rhine in 1963, de Gaulle was suspicious of anything that might affect that influence and undermine French sovereignty. In 1961 he had tried to push the EEC down a somewhat different route, floating the idea of a 'Union of States' that would entail the incorporation of the EEC into a new intergovernmental organization for the coordination of foreign and defence policy. His proposal was given detailed institutional flesh in the subsequent Fouchet Plan. But the idea received at best little support outside West Germany, and was rejected in 1962 after a series of acrimonious meetings. While the smaller EEC members were concerned about being presented with some kind of Franco-German fait accompli, the episode merely added extra substance to de Gaulle's long-standing suspicions that the EEC, or anything like it, might well act as a brake on his ambitions for France.

Two further episodes heightened the mood of crisis. First, the immediate economic success of the EEC as a trading bloc after 1958 had persuaded other Western European states that had previously rejected involvement, to revise their opinion and seek membership. The most important candidate was the United Kingdom, which applied for membership in 1961. In 1963, and again in 1967, de Gaulle, against the wishes of his five partners, vetoed the British application on the grounds that the country, because of its Commonwealth links and close relationship with the USA, was not sufficiently committed either politically or economically to Europe or to EEC objectives. Although not subject to a veto, the other applicant states declined to proceed without the UK. Second, according to the schedule set by the Treaty of Rome, the EEC was expected to take some decisive decisions in 1966, including a move to an extension of qualified majority voting (QMV) in the Council of Ministers. At the same time the EEC was faced with approving financial arrangements for the Common Agricultural Policy (CAP) and a Commission proposal for enhancing supranational authority by giving more powers to itself and the EP. The latter proposal clearly involved a diminution of national sovereignty, as would any extension of qualified majority voting which would reduce the number of areas where unanimity across the member states was necessary. Instead, for many decisions a two-thirds majority would suffice, with the result that a state could be outvoted but not block the decision by exercising a veto. While the Treaty of Rome had envisaged a steady diminution of the right of a member state to exercise a veto, de Gaulle was not prepared to accept the increased risk of France being outvoted in key decisions. In 1965 he provoked a crisis by withdrawing all French participation in Council of Ministers business except for that dealing with low-level and routine technicalities. The EEC almost ground to a halt. The crisis was resolved only by the Luxembourg Compromise of 1966 (see Box 2.6).

Overall, the results of de Gaulle's actions seemed to indicate that political integration, as advocated

CASE STUDY 2.6

The Luxembourg Compromise

The Luxembourg Compromise (or Luxembourg Agreement) is the name often given to the agreement among the then six member states of the European Community, concluding the 'empty chair crisis' of 1965. The agreement stated that in cases of the vital national interest of one of the member states the Council would aim to find a consensus solution, thus creating a de facto veto right.

The Compromise had practical effects for both the Council and the Commission. In the case of the Council, member states were more willing to accept an extension of majority voting, knowing that in the final instance they could invoke the Luxembourg Compromise and veto unwanted legislation. In the case of the Commission, it meant that this institution had to make more of an effort to ensure that its proposals would not impact upon the vital interests of any member state. In so doing, it made the Commission much more cautious in its policy proposals. These effects were felt despite the fact that the Luxembourg Compromise was never recognized by the European Court of Justice as legally binding.

by federalists, was off the agenda, and that the future development of the EC would be more as an intergovernmental grouping of independent states. This shift of emphasis and mood seemed to be symbolized by the 1967 resignation of Hallstein as Commission President. To some extent, the early rapid progress after 1958 had been possible not only because of favourable internal and external economic conditions, but also because, apart from the furore over the Fouchet Plan, national leaders had remained relatively uninvolved in EEC business, being content to allow the Commission to push things forward. If, however, future progress was to be governed by the Luxembourg Compromise, a more positive national governmental input would be required. But even that might be insufficient as long as Charles de Gaulle remained in power. Hence, any way forward had to await the French President's retirement in 1969.

The emergence of summits

In 1969, at a summit meeting in The Hague in the Netherlands intended to discuss the options open to the EC, the six heads of government attempted to restore some momentum to the stalled organization. The Hague summit opened the way for the enlargement of the EC, especially for the British. It agreed to extend the budgetary competence of the European Parliament, and argued for more common policy. It also called for a move towards Economic and Monetary Union (EMU), initially through an exchange rate system for the EC, as an important step towards the ultimate goal of political union (see Chapter 20). In practice, the Hague meeting inaugurated summitry as a new style of EC decision making, recognizing that integration could only develop further if it was able to reconcile itself with national concerns. Summitry, that is, the use of European summits to set the political agenda of the Community, was to be formalized and placed on a regular footing with the establishment of the European Council in 1974 as a meeting place for the leaders of national governments (see Chapter 9).

Achievement of the objectives declaimed at The Hague was only partially successful. The first enlargement of the EC duly occurred in 1973 with the accession of the UK, Denmark, and Ireland (Nicholson and East 1987). The other candidate for membership in the 1960s, Norway, had already withdrawn from the final negotiations as a result of a referendum in 1972 which, against government advice, had rejected EC membership. Equally, the

EC began to be able to assert a more positive and united presence in international affairs. Represented by the Commission, it spoke with one voice in international trade negotiations, and after the 1970 Davignon Report on policy cooperation, the member states, through European Political Cooperation (EPC), developed an impressive and on balance quite successful structure and pattern of collaboration on and coordination of foreign policy (see Chapter 15). After the mid 1970s, two structural funds, the European Regional Development Fund (ERDF) and the European Social Fund (ESF), began to play an important role in providing aid for economic and employment restructuring. The CAP had also come fully on stream in 1972, though in its final form it developed as a protectionist device that shielded European farmers from the full impact of market forces and from the necessity of taking markets and demand into account when planning production (see Chapter 21).

However, while the balance sheet around the end of the 1970s did feature many positive aspects, there was also a debit side. The achievements gained could not disguise the fact that on the broader front of the ambitions of the Treaty of Rome, the EC still seemed to be marking time. A common market seemed to be as far away as ever, with the prospect of political union even more remote. The major integrative impetus propounded at the Hague summit had been Economic and Monetary Union. The leaders had set up a committee under the Luxembourg premier, Pierre Werner, to put some flesh on the proposal. The Werner Report of 1970 outlined a three-stage process for the full implementation of EMU by 1980 (see Chapter 20).

The decade, however, had not progressed very far before this rekindling of ambition was thwarted. In 1972 the EC did attempt to establish a European zone of stability by imposing limits on how far EC currencies would be permitted to float against each other (the so-called 'snake'), but this barely got off the ground. Undermined not least by the quadrupling of oil prices in 1973—the consequence of war in the Middle East—the 'snake' structure was already dead when it was abandoned in 1976. In addition, the EC experienced both rapidly growing unemployment and inflation in the 1970s. The consequent political and electoral pressures forced governments to turn more to national issues and national defence. Some stabilization was eventually achieved after 1979 with the relaunch—sponsored by the European Council—of a monetary policy. The European Monetary System (EMS) did, through an Exchange Rate Mechanism (ERM), have currency stabilization as an objective. However, by itself the EMS could not achieve monetary union. It was a more modest design and could only be a first step on the road back to EMU. In the 1980s the EMS was deemed, perhaps because of its modesty, to have had some success in curbing currency fluctuations, inflation and unemployment, thereby contributing to the return of EMU to the central EC agenda in 1989 (see Chapter 20).

On the broader integrative front, the initiative had passed firmly to the European Council. Its formation in 1974 confirmed the central role that had to be adopted by the heads of government in determining the future path of the EC. More specifically, it brought to an apogee the Franco-German axis that lay at the core of the EC and which had been, two decades earlier, an essential sub-theme for people like Monnet and Schuman. Formalized in a Treaty of Friendship and Reconciliation in 1963, the relationship and its significance for the EC was to become far more overt in the 1970s. While the two states might not always be able to impose their will upon their partners, their active consent was vital

for any progress to be made. Although the leaders of the two states, Valéry Giscard d'Estaing and Helmut Schmidt, accepted the need to utilize and develop the EC as an instrument of pragmatic integration, both tended to evaluate ideas in terms of national interest and were seemingly reluctant to pursue an advanced federalist route. That Franco-German drive had to await the leadership of François Mitterrand and Helmut Kohl, who came into power in 1981 and 1982 respectively (Simonian 1985). With the Commission seemingly downgraded and kept on a short leash, the real achievements that were gained could not conceal the fact that the EC was not progressing, or at least was doing so only minimally, towards the aims of the Treaty of Rome.

Nevertheless, the EC, and the European Council in particular, continued to pay lip service to the ideal of full economic and political union. From its commissioning of the 1976 Tindemans Report, which recommended strengthening the EC institutions and the adoption of more common policies, through to its 1983 Solemn Declaration on European Union, the European Council sponsored studies on how to advance the cause of union or rhetorically reasserted its faith in the ultimate goal. In 1974, the Council of Ministers had eventually agreed to implement the Rome requirement that the European Parliament should be elected directly by the national electorates. The first direct elections were held in 1979. They gave the EP a sense of greater legitimacy, a feeling that it now had a mandate to review existing structures and to urge the EC to progress to a more cohesive and genuine union. With its moves coordinated by the veteran federalist, Altiero Spinelli, who had been elected to the Parliament, the EP produced a Draft Treaty Establishing the European Union. While the European Council took no immediate action on the EP proposals, the Treaty nevertheless provided a working basis for and contributed towards the developments that within a decade led to the establishment of the European Union (EU).

At the end of the day, however, initiative and commitment had to come from the European Council. For this to happen, it needed to take on board a growing number of issues that it had earlier sought to shelve or avoid: the EC's budget and how national contributions to it were determined; the burgeoning costs, problems, and distorting consequences of the Common Agricultural Policy (CAP); the need to consider and develop further common policies; future enlargements; and a more detailed and positive response to how the EC should fit into a rapidly changing international world. Indeed, adapting to the international environment seemed to increase in urgency in the 1980s. European leaders began to worry that in a new economic era of high technology, which required massive investment, Western Europe was already lagging far behind the market leaders of the USA and Japan, Increasingly, the argument was heard that European survival and competitiveness in this brave new world could be achieved only through cooperation and a common front.

Moreover, the EC states had become alarmed in the late 1970s by an increasingly bellicose Soviet foreign policy that they feared might destabilize the West European status quo. After 1980 they became equally alarmed at the aggressive American response, fearing that they might be dragged into conflict by an American policy over which they had no influence. After 1985 and the arrival of Mikhail Gorbachev as leader of the USSR, the two superpowers began to talk to each other about means of reducing tension and accommodating each other's interests. Almost predictably, the EC states began to express concerns that the two superpowers might reach an agreement that would not take their interests into account.

This international background provided, as it often had done in previous decades, a necessary stimulus for more visible activity on the domestic West European front. Partly by choice and partly by necessity, European Council sessions turned to internal matters. At the core of this new activity was President Mitterrand of France. After the failure of his initial attempts to reflate the French economy after 1981, Mitterrand concluded that recuperation could more readily be achieved by means of European integration, especially when working in close harness with West Germany. With the encouragement of Mitterrand and others, there emerged, in short, a new sense of direction and purpose. In 1984 the Fontainebleau summit meeting of the European Council reached agreement on tackling a backlog of issues that had hitherto stalled the integration progress. With these agreements behind them, members of the European Council were able to take a series of decisions intended to advance the cause of union. They agreed to the establishment of a single internal market by the end of 1992 and to a major revision of the Treaty of Rome. In so doing, they pushed the EC decisively towards a more intense economic integration, the Treaty on European Union, and the establishment of the EU (see Chapter 3).

KEY POINTS

- The Hague summit of 1969 opened the way for the admission of new members to the EC and agreed to seek new initiatives in policy cooperation, especially economic and monetary union.

- The practice of summitry was institutionalized by the establishment of the European Council in 1974.

- In 1984 the European Council reached agreement on several important outstanding issues. This permitted it the following year to consider future developments. It committed the EC to a single internal market and a major overhaul of the Treaty of Rome. These initiatives were helped by concerns that Western Europe's international status, both political and economic, had declined.

Conclusion

The story of the events that led to the Treaty of Rome, and then to its reform in the 1980s, does not portray an inevitable and steady progression towards European union. Behind the rhetoric of inexorable progress towards the goal of 'an ever closer union', there lies a rather more complex reality. Thus, it might be more appropriate to liken the story of integration to a roller-coaster ride, where the uphill and downhill gradients that determined the speed of the ride were the product of a multitude of factors.

The history of the formative decades of European integration was the product of an array of complex interactions. The world of ideas and the agitation of committed federalists had to contend with and were counterbalanced by the roles played by national leaders and governments, and their assessment of how developments and proposals might impinge upon national self-interest. No matter how intricate the consequent dance, the steps and routines were influenced by and contained within parameters set by the broader flows of the international political and economic environment. And at the heart of this complex product lay the health of the relationship between France and West Germany. When all, or perhaps only most, of these factors were in positive conjunction with each other, progress could be rapid, significant, and impressive. When they were not, the process of integration was more likely merely to mark time.

? QUESTIONS

1. Why did it prove difficult to establish a momentum for integration in the years immediately following the end of World War II?

2. How important was the development of international European organizations between 1945 and 1950 as a necessary condition for European integration?

3. What lessons for the future could be adduced from the strategy of sectoral integration in the 1950s?

4. To what extent does the failure of the European Defence Community (EDC) suggest that there are some areas of policy that are not amenable to integration?

5. How important were the crises of the 1960s in shaping the future development of the European Community?

6. How important was the establishment of the European Council as a mechanism for promoting further integration in the European Community?

7. To what extent was a collaboration between France and the Federal Republic of Germany necessary for a process of integration to begin?

8. To what extent has the international political and economic environment stimulated or hindered processes of integration?

GUIDE TO FURTHER READING

■ Arter, D. *The Politics of European Integration in the Twentieth Century* (Aldershot: Dartmouth, 1993). A broad historical survey that also considers developments in Eastern Europe.

■ Burgess, M. *Federalism and European Union: The Building of Europe*, 1945–2000 (London: Routledge, 2000). A detailed revisionist history of the development of integration that highlights the central role of federalist ideas and influences.

■ Duignan, P. and Gann, L. H. *The United States and the New Europe* 1945–1993 (Oxford: Blackwell, 1994). A general survey that examines European developments from an American strategic and policy perspective.

■ Stirk, P. M. and Willis, D. (eds) *Shaping Postwar Europe* (London: Pinter, 1991). A collection of useful chapters surveying the various arguments and different kinds of integration sought from 1945 up to the formation of the European Community.

■ Urwin, D. W. *The Community of Europe* (London: Longman, 1995). A broad introductory survey of the post-1945 history of European cooperation and integration.

 WEBLINKS

● www.let.leidenuniv.nl/history/rtg/res1/   Leiden University's History Department has an interesting site on the history of European integration.

● http://europa.eu.int/abc/history/index-en.htm   The EU's own website includes a good chronology of events in the history of the European integration process.

● www.iue.it/LIB/SISSCO/UL/hist-eur-integration/Index.html   The European University Institute in Florence has a European integration history project that includes some helpful links.

● www.lib.berkeley.edu/GSSI/eu.html   The University of California at Berkeley runs this general EU gateway, which includes links to historical documents and research papers on the history of the EC.

 Visit the Online Resource Centre that accompanies this book for lots of interesting additional material. http://www.oxfordtextbooks.co.uk/orc/Cini_Borragan3e/

3

The European Union: Establishment and Development

DAVID PHINNEMORE

 Chapter Contents

- Introduction
- The European Union as a European union
- Reviewing the Union: 1996 IGC and the Treaty of Amsterdam
- Preparing for enlargement: the 2000 IGC, the Treaty of Nice, and the 'Future of Europe' debate
- Conclusion

Reader's Guide

The focus of this chapter is the emergence and development of the European Union (EU). Key issues include the significance for the idea of union of the Single European Act (SEA) (1986), the Treaty on European Union (TEU) (1992), and the pillar structure of the EU. The chapter also examines the origins and impact on the EU of the Treaty of Amsterdam (1997) and the Treaty of Nice (2000), presenting their key reforms and assessing the extent to which they contribute to the idea of the EU as a union. The chapter also introduces the 'Future of Europe' debate launched in 2001, which led to the adoption of the Treaty establishing a Constitution for Europe (2004) and subsequently the Treaty of Lisbon (2007).

Introduction

To what extent is the European Union a union? This may seem an odd question to ask, but an examination of what the EU was when it was formally established on 1 November 1993 and how it has since evolved, at least in terms of its formal structures, suggests that it remains less than its name implies. Indeed, whereas 'union' might conjure up ideas of coherence and uniformity, the EU today continues to be characterized as much by variation in its structure and exceptions for certain of its member states. Hence, voices are often heard calling for change. It is in part the desire to ensure that the EU behaves and acts as a union that has been behind the various reform attempts—successful or otherwise—that have dominated the EU's agenda ever since its creation. Indeed, since the TEU was agreed in December 1991, two major sets of treaty amendments have been introduced in addition to various other adjustments resulting from three enlargements (see Chapter 26). Each has sought to reform the EU (see Box 3.1). So too have the Constitutional Treaty (CT) and the Treaty of Lisbon (see Chapter 4).

This chapter discusses the structure of the EU and how this has been affected by certain key developments over the last 15 years. The chapter examines not only the origins of the EU, but also the background to and content of the Treaty of Amsterdam (1997) and the Treaty of Nice (2000). In between discussing how these have changed the EU and impacted on the idea of union, consideration is given to the significance of the launch of Economic and Monetary Union (EMU), a process which simultaneously promoted closer union and differentiated integration within the EU, thus suggesting that member states may integrate in different ways or at different speeds (see Chapter 20). A similar argument can be made of cooperation in the Schengen area (see Chapter 19). The chapter concludes by introducing the issues that the EU and its member states sought to address as part of the 'Future of Europe' debate that eventually led to the

drafting of the CT (see Chapter 4). Before then, however, the EU as a union and the TEU need to be considered.

CHRONOLOGY 3.1

Key events 1986–2004

1986	Single European Act signed (17 and 28 February)
1987	Single European Act enters into force (1 July)
1991	Maastricht European Council agrees Treaty on European Union (9–10 December)
1992	Treaty on European Union signed (7 February)
1993	European Union established (1 November)
1995	EU enlarges to 15 member states (1 January)
1996	1996 IGC launched (29 March)
1997	Amsterdam European Council agrees Treaty of Amsterdam (16–17 June) Agenda 2000 published (15 July) Treaty of Amsterdam signed (2 October)
1999	Stage III of EMU launched (1 January) Treaty of Amsterdam enters into force (1 May)
2000	2000 IGC launched (14 February) Nice European Council agrees Treaty of Nice (7–11 December)
2001	Treaty of Nice signed (26 February) Laeken European Council adopts Declaration on the Future of the Union (14–15 December)
2002	Introduction of the euro (1 January) Launch of the European Convention (28 March)
2003	Treaty of Nice enters into force (1 February)

The European Union as a European union

The idea of creating a European union has long been a goal of states committed to European integration. This was made clear in the 1950s when the six original members of the European Economic Community (EEC) expressed their determination in the first recital of the preamble to the Treaty of Rome 'to lay the foundations of an ever closer union among the peoples' (see Box 3.2). They reaffirmed this in 1972 when they expressed their intention to convert 'their entire relationship into a European Union before the end of the decade'. In joining them in the European Communities (EC), new members from 1973 (Denmark, Ireland, and the United Kingdom), 1981 (Greece), and 1986 (Portugal and Spain) also signed up to this goal. And reaffirmation of the commitment was central to the Solemn Declaration on European Union proclaimed at the Stuttgart European Council in June 1983 and, in part, inspired the Single European Act of 1986. This, as its preamble noted, was adopted in response to the member states' desire to 'transform' their relations into 'a European Union', to 'implement' this new entity and invest it 'with the necessary means of action'.

KEY CONCEPTS AND TERMS 3.2

European Union and European 'union'

Note the use of the word 'union' in these two treaty clauses.

DETERMINED to lay the foundations of an ever closer union among the peoples of Europe

Preamble, Treaty of Rome (1957)

By this Treaty, the HIGH CONTRACTING PARTIES establish among themselves a EUROPEAN UNION, hereinafter called 'the Union'

Article 1, Treaty on European Union (1992)

The Single European Act

The SEA brought about some significant reforms to the Treaty of Rome. In terms of policies, it introduced a range of formally new competences (environment, research and development, economic and social cohesion); established a deadline for the completion of the internal market and facilitated the adoption of harmonized legislation to achieve this; committed the member states to cooperate on the convergence of economic and monetary policy; and expanded social policy competences to include health and safety in the workplace and dialogue between management and labour. As regards the institutions, it expanded the decision-making role of the European Parliament (EP) through the introduction of the cooperation procedure to cover mainly internal market issues and the assent procedure governing association agreements and accession. It also extended the use of qualified majority voting (QMV) in the Council; allowed the Council to confer implementation powers on the Commission; and established a Court of First Instance to assist the European Court of Justice in its work. In addition, it gave formal recognition to the European Council and European Political Cooperation (EPC), the latter being the forerunner of the Common Foreign and Security Policy (CFSP). The fact that neither the European Council nor EPC were technically part of the EC was reflective of member states' differences on how much supranational integration they were willing to pursue (see Chapter 15). For some, there was a clear preference for intergovernmental cooperation. Evidently, the desire for a European union was not universal.

The establishment of the EU was not, however, far off. Despite being a very brief document and one that failed in many respects to meet the aspirations of integrationists, the SEA and the launch of the initiative to complete the internal market by the end of

From Intergovernmental Conference (IGC) to Treaty

The European Union and the European Community were both established by constitutive treaties concluded between their founding member states. If the current member states wish to reform the EU or the EC they need to amend the constitutive treaties. This is formally done via an Intergovernmental Conference (IGC) in which the member states negotiate amendments. Agreed amendments are then brought together in an amending treaty that all member states must sign and ratify. Ratification normally involves each member state's parliament approving the treaty by vote. In some member states, for either procedural or political reasons, treaties are also put to a referendum.

The Treaty on European Union

The impact of the Treaty on European Union (TEU) on the process of achieving 'ever closer union' was considerable. Most significantly it formally established the EU. In addition it promoted European integration in a whole variety of ways whether through the promotion of cooperation in the two new intergovernmental pillars on foreign and security policy and justice and home affairs or through the expansion of EC activities. Indeed, thanks to the TEU, the EC was given new competences in the fields of education, culture, public health, consumer protection, trans-European networks, industry, and development cooperation. Citizenship of the EU was also established. And, of course, the TEU set out the timetable for EMU by 1999. As for existing competences, some were expanded, notably in the areas of social policy, the environment, and economic and social cohesion, although in an attempt to assuage concerns of over-centralization of power, the principle of subsidiarity was introduced. Moreover, the TEU saw the establishment of new institutions and bodies including the European Central Bank, the Committee of the Regions, and the Ombudsman. As for existing institutions, the powers of the EP were increased—not least through the introduction of the new codecision procedure—greater use of qualified majority voting in the Council was agreed, the Court of Auditors was upgraded to an institution, and the European Court of Justice gained the power to fine member states.

1992 ushered in a period of renewed dynamism for the EC during the second half of the 1980s. At the time, calls for further steps towards European union were being made by senior European leaders such as the French President, François Mitterrand, and the German Chancellor, Helmut Kohl, as well as by the Commission President, Jacques Delors. All this plus the collapse of communist regimes in Central and Eastern Europe in 1989, the end of the Cold War, and the prospect of German unification led in 1990 to the launch of two Intergovernmental Conferences (IGCs) (see Box 3.3), one on EMU and a second on political union. Out of these emerged the Treaty on European Union (TEU).

The Treaty on European Union

Agreed at Maastricht in December 1991 and entering into force on 1 November 1993, the TEU—often referred to as the 'Maastricht Treaty'—was designed to expand the scope of European integration, reform the EC's institutions and decision-making procedures, and bring about EMU (see Box 3.4). Moreover, the goal of ever closer union was to be furthered by bringing together the EEC—now renamed the

European Community—the European Coal and Steel Community (ECSC), and the European Atomic Energy Community (EURATOM or EAEC) as part of an entirely new entity, to be called the 'European Union'. This was to be more than simply the existing supranational Communities. Established in 1993, it comprised not just their supranational activities but also intergovernmental cooperation in foreign and security policy matters and justice and home affairs.

This mix of supranational integration and intergovernmental cooperation meant that the new EU fell short of what might normally be considered a union: a political and legal entity with a coherent and uniform structure. Indeed, in an early assessment of the EU, Curtin (1993) referred to its constitutional structure as a 'Europe of bits and pieces'. Depending, for example, on the policy area, the roles of the relevant institutions involved in decision making differ. In the early years of the EC, there was essentially one approach, the so-called Community method—the use of supranational institutions and decision-making procedures to develop, adopt, and police policy. This would no longer be the case.

That the EU lacked and continues to lack uniformity in terms of its structures and policy-making procedures was and remains evident from the terminology widely used to describe it. For many, whether they are practitioners, academics, or others, the EU is structurally akin to a Greek temple consisting of three pillars. The first comprises the original Communities (the EC, EURATOM/EAEC and, prior to mid-2002, the ECSC—see Box 3.5), while the second and third consist of essentially intergovernmental cooperation in the areas of the Common Foreign and Security Policy (CFSP) and, originally, justice and home affairs (JHA) (see Figure 3.1 and Chapter 1). Changes in the relationship between the pillars since 1993 have meant that the boundaries between them have become blurred. Indeed, if the Treaty of Lisbon (2007) were to enter into force, the pillars would formally disappear (see Chapter 4).

To supporters of supranational integration, the establishment of the EU in 1993 on the basis of three

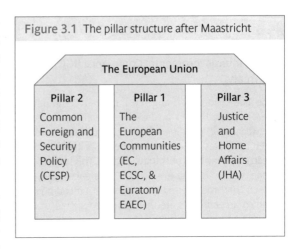

Figure 3.1 The pillar structure after Maastricht

pillars represented a clear setback. This was because the intergovernmental pillars threatened to undermine the supremacy of the Community method. For others, adopting a mix of supranational and intergovernmental pillars merely formalized existing practice. Even prior to the TEU, the member states were pursuing intergovernmental cooperation outside the framework of the EC. The most obvious examples were EPC and Schengen activities relating to the removal of border controls (see Chapter 19). These had been taking place since the early 1970s and mid 1980s respectively. All the same, the mix of supranationalism and intergovernmentalism, particularly given that the Community institutions, with the exception of the Council, were at best marginal players in pillars 2 and 3, meant that the EU, when established, was less of a union than many had either hoped or feared.

The idea of the new EU as a union was also undermined by other features of the TEU. First, plans for EMU—the most important new area of EC activity—were set to create a three-tier EU with the member states divided between those that would become full participants, those that would fail to get in (that is, fail to meet the convergence criteria), and those—the United Kingdom and Denmark—that either had availed or could avail themselves of opt-outs. Semi-permanent differentiation between member states in a major policy area would characterize the new EU.

CASE STUDY 3.5

The European Communities: from three to two

Originally there were three European Communities: the European Coal and Steel Community (ECSC), the European Economic Community (EEC), and the European Atomic Energy Community (EAEC), the EEC being formally renamed the European Community in 1993 thanks to the TEU (though it was often used informally as shorthand for the EEC before that date). Since then, the ECSC has been disbanded, its founding treaty having expired after 50 years, as envisaged, in July 2002.

Second, it was agreed that closer integration in the area of social policy would only be pursued by eleven of the then twelve member states. Resolute opposition to increased EU competences meant that new legislation resulting from the so-called 'Social Chapter' would not apply to the United Kingdom. Third, Denmark was later granted a de facto opt-out from involvement in the elaboration and implementation of foreign policy decisions and actions having defence implications. All this created the image of a partially fragmented EU.

That the TEU's provisions did not all apply to the same extent to all member states was significant, as such differentiation had never been enshrined in the EU's treaty base before. This is not to say that differentiation between member states had never existed. But it had been temporary, with new member states given strict time limits for fulfilling the requirements and obligations of membership. Hence, there were fears that the Maastricht opt-outs would set a precedent leading, at worst, to an à la carte EU, with member states picking and choosing the areas in

which they were willing to pursue closer integration. Such fears were initially assuaged when, at the time of the 1995 enlargement, the EU refused to consider any permanent exemptions or opt-outs from the existing *acquis communautaire* for the new member states. Austria, Finland, and Sweden had to and indeed did accept all the obligations of membership, including those concerning social policy, EMU and the CFSP, the latter being significant because each of the three countries was still notionally neutral.

KEY POINTS

- Despite 'ever closer union' being a long-established goal of the EC member states, the EU was not created until 1993.

- The EU lacks a uniform structure, consisting as it does of one supranational and two intergovernmental pillars.

- The TEU introduced opt-outs from certain policy areas for some member states.

Reviewing the Union: 1996 IGC and the Treaty of Amsterdam

That the EU, when it was created, was less than its title implied was recognized not only by those studying the EU but also those working in its institutions and representing its member states. Even those who drafted the TEU acknowledged that what they were creating was not the final product, but part of an ongoing process. In the TEU's very first article, the member states proclaimed that the establishment of the EU 'marks *a new stage* in the process of creating an ever closer union among the peoples of Europe' (emphasis added). They then proceeded to facilitate the process by scheduling an IGC for 1996 at which the TEU would be revised in line with its objectives. Among these was (and indeed remains) the idea of 'ever closer union'.

The 1996 IGC

Views on the purpose of the 1996 IGC differed. For the less integrationist member states, notably the United Kingdom, it would provide an opportunity to review and fine-tune the functioning of the EU and its structures. It was too soon to consider anything radical. For others, a more substantial overhaul was not ruled out. The IGC would provide an opportunity to push ahead with the goal of creating 'ever closer union', something that the EP was particularly keen to see, as its draft constitution of February 1994 demonstrated. Ever closer union, it was argued, was necessary if the EU wished to rectify the shortcomings of the structures created at

Maastricht and prepare itself, having enlarged in 1995 to 15 member states, to admit the large number of mainly Central and Eastern European (CEE) applicants (see Chapter 26). Enlargement was now on the agenda; the European Council at Copenhagen in June 1993 had committed the EU to admit CEE countries once they met the accession criteria. Moreover, several member states were growing increasingly impatient with the reluctance of the less integrationist member states to countenance closer integration. And there was also the need to bring the EU closer to its citizens. Popular reaction to the TEU had shown that more needed to be done to convince people of the value of union. Not only had the Danish people initially rejected the TEU in June 1992, but also the French people had only narrowly approved it three months later.

The shortcomings of the EU's structures were highlighted in reports produced by the Council, Commission, and EP in 1995. They all agreed that the pillar structure was not functioning well and that the intergovernmental nature of decision making in pillar 3 was a significant constraint on the development of cooperation in JHA areas. As for pillar 2, its inherent weaknesses had been highlighted by the EU's ineffective foreign policy response to the disintegration of Yugoslavia. Such shortcomings needed to be addressed, particularly given that enlargement was now firmly on the EU's agenda. Preparations would have to be made, notably where the size and composition of the institutions were concerned. In addition, there was the matter of QMV. Its extension to replace unanimity would be necessary if the EU was going to survive enlargement and avoid decision-making paralysis. Also needed within an enlarged EU, at least in the eyes of supporters of closer integration, were mechanisms that would allow those member states keen on closer integration to proceed without the need for unanimous agreement of the others. There was consequently much discussion of ideas concerning a 'core Europe', variable geometry, and a multispeed EU. It was against this background that preparations for reforming the EU took place. These began in earnest in 1995 with the formation of a

'Reflection Group'. Its report suggested three key aims for the 1996 IGC: bringing the EU closer to its citizens; improving its functioning in preparation for enlargement; and providing it with greater external capacity. In doing so, the report also promoted the idea of 'flexibility' mechanisms that would facilitate 'closer cooperation' among groups of willing member states.

The IGC was launched in March 1996, with the early stages of the negotiations confirming expectations that any agreement on reform would not be easily reached. Progress under the Irish presidency did, however, lead to a draft treaty being produced for the Dublin European Council in December 1996. This left many issues unresolved. And with a general election due in the United Kingdom in May 1997, it was clear that finalizing agreement on many of these would have to wait until after that had taken place. Certainly the Labour victory did make the job of drawing the IGC to a close easier for the Dutch presidency. However, differences between other member states now came into the open. Added to this, attention was being distracted away from the unresolved issues on the IGC's agenda by a new French government intent on seeing the EU commit itself to greater action on economic growth and employment.

The Treaty of Amsterdam

What eventually emerged was the Treaty of Amsterdam, which was signed on 2 October 1997. It attracted far less popular attention than the TEU had. This does not mean that it was an insignificant treaty. It certainly caught the attention of lawyers and practitioners, renumbering as it did all but four articles in the Treaty of Rome and TEU. Moreover, in terms of substantive changes to the EU, it added the establishment of 'an area of freedom, security and justice' to the EU's objectives and shifted much of JHA activity from pillar 3 into pillar 1—in what is often referred to as communitarization. In doing so, the thrust of cooperation in pillar 3 was refocused on police and judicial cooperation in criminal

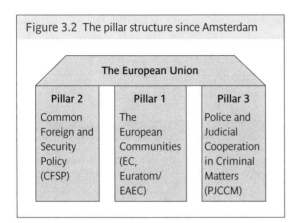

Figure 3.2 The pillar structure since Amsterdam

matters, and the pillar renamed accordingly (see Figure 3.1). At the same time, provision was made for Schengen cooperation to be incorporated into the EU. These developments meant greater coherence in EU activity. Yet the changes were also accompanied by increased differentiation. The United Kingdom, Ireland, and Denmark gained various opt-outs from both the new 'area of freedom, security and justice' and Schengen cooperation (see Chapter 19)

There was also the potential for further differentiation with the introduction of mechanisms for 'closer cooperation'. Under these, member states that wished to could use the EC framework to pursue enhanced cooperation among themselves. This was provided that the mechanisms were only used as a last resort, that a majority of member states would be participating and that the cooperation would be open to all other member states. Moreover, closer cooperation could not detract from either the principles of the EU and the *acquis* or from the rights of member states. Nor could it be pursued for CFSP matters. Such restrictions, as well as the de facto veto which each member state had over closer cooperation, meant that the provisions would be difficult to use. In fact, the first formal proposal to use the provisions on closer cooperation was not until 2008. All the same, the possibility of increasing differentiation within the EU was being established.

Where the Treaty of Amsterdam lessened differentiation within the EU was in its repeal of the UK opt-out from social policy. There was a bolstering of

the EC's social policy competences too (see Chapter 17). Moreover, an employment policy chapter was introduced, in part as an attempt to assuage popular concerns that the EU did not have its citizens' interests at heart. The need to make the EU more citizen-friendly was also behind other new emphases, notably the enhanced EC competences concerning consumer and environmental protection, a new emphasis on transparency and subsidiarity, and a reassertion that EU citizenship does not undermine national citizenship.

In terms of addressing the shortcomings of pillar 2, the IGC resisted calls for a communitarization of the CFSP, preferring to maintain existing intergovernmental arrangements. Reforms were, however, introduced in an attempt to improve the consistency of EU action by involving the European Council more, creating the post of High Representative, establishing a policy planning and early warning unit, seeking to develop long-term strategies, clarifying the nature of the different instruments available, defining more precisely the EU's concept of security (the so-called 'Petersberg tasks' of humanitarian and rescue tasks, peacekeeping and crisis management, including peacemaking), and allowing for 'constructive abstention' so that member states abstaining would not block CFSP initiatives (see Chapter 15). The desire to deepen integration further was asserted in the renewed commitment to a common defence policy and a common defence.

Finally, the Treaty of Amsterdam was supposed to prepare the EU institutionally for enlargement. Here it failed. Rather than agreeing reforms, it simply deferred to a later date the resolution of key questions, such as the size of the Commission, the redistribution of votes in the Council, and the nature of majority voting. Unanimity was replaced by QMV in some 19 instances, but even here, thanks to German insistence, progress was far less than anticipated or desired by many member states. This was underlined in a declaration issued by Belgium, France and Italy to the effect that further reform should be a precondition for the signing of the first accession treaties with applicant countries. The

Treaty of Amsterdam did not fail totally to introduce institutional reform. The size of the EP was capped at 700 members, and use of the assent and codecision procedures was extended, thus enhancing the legislative role of the EP. The EP's hand in the appointment of the Commission was also increased, as was its right to set its own rules for its elected members (see Chapter 10).

KEY POINTS

- Early experiences of the EU raised concerns about the functioning of the pillar structure.

- The desire not to be held back by more recalcitrant member states led to mechanisms for closer cooperation between interested and willing member states.

- Despite the acknowledged need to introduce institutional reforms in preparation for enlargement, the Treaty of Amsterdam failed to prepare the EU sufficiently to admit more than a handful of new members.

Preparing for enlargement: the 2000 IGC, the Treaty of Nice, and the 'Future of Europe' debate

With momentum in the late 1990s building towards enlargement to include the ten CEE countries as well as Cyprus and potentially Malta, the need to introduce institutional reform remained on the EU's agenda. Without such reform it was feared that policy making could grind to a halt. Moreover, there were concerns that enlargement could challenge the whole idea of union. Admitting ten CEE countries, most of which had been undergoing processes of wholesale transformation from command to fully functioning market economies was something that the EU had never done before. How to accommodate and integrate the new members became a major question. At the same time, the EU had to ensure that its *acquis* and the notion of union would be neither impaired nor undermined by enlargement, and that its institutions could continue to function as decision-making and decision-shaping bodies. Moreover, confronted with the prospect of what amounted to almost a doubling of its membership, the EU was faced with the challenge of ensuring that

the commitment towards 'ever closer union' would be maintained.

Enlargement moves centre-stage

Preparing the EU institutionally for enlargement had been a key objective of the 1996 IGC. However, the resulting Treaty of Amsterdam failed to deliver, as noted above. Instead it was decided to postpone reform. A Protocol therefore envisaged that at the time of the next enlargement, the Commission would consist of one national per member state provided that by then the weighting of votes within the Council had been modified either via a reweighting or through the adoption of a dual majority system of voting (see Chapter 9). The idea behind the reweighting was to compensate the larger member states for giving up 'their' second Commissioner. The Protocol also provided for an IGC to carry out a 'comprehensive review of … the composition and functioning of the institutions' at least one year before the membership of the EU exceeds twenty member states.

In reality the provisions of the Protocol were mainly ignored. For even before the Treaty of Amsterdam entered into force on 1 May 1999, the European Council in 1998 had identified institutional reform as an issue of primary concern for the EU. Then, in June 1999, it agreed to hold an IGC in 2000 to address the key institutional questions left unresolved at Amsterdam. The issues—the size and composition of the Commission, the weighting of votes in the Council, and the possible extension of QMV in the Council—became known as the 'Amsterdam leftovers'.

What pushed the European Council into calling an IGC for 2000 were changes in the EU's handling of the enlargement process. In July 1997, a matter of weeks after the Amsterdam European Council, the Commission had published Agenda 2000, its blueprint for enlargement. Following its recommendations, the Luxembourg European Council in December 1997 agreed to launch an inclusive accession process with all applicant states (excluding Turkey), but to open accession negotiations proper with only six of the applicants. It was felt at the time that six new members could be squeezed into the EU without necessarily holding an IGC. Within 18 months, however, attitudes towards enlargement were changing and, in the aftermath of the 1999 Kosovo conflict, the decision was taken to open accession negotiations with six more applicants and recognize all applicants including Turkey as 'candidate countries'. Opening up the possibility of large-scale enlargement made the need to address the Amsterdam leftovers more urgent. Hence an IGC was called.

The 2000 IGC

The 2000 IGC opened in February 2000 with only a limited agenda. This reflected the preferences of most member states for an IGC focused on the Amsterdam leftovers. Others, including the Commission and the EP, favoured a broader agenda. In a Commission-inspired Wise Men's Report published in October 1999, strong support was voiced for a reorganization of the treaties and the integration of the Western European Union (WEU) into the EU as a step towards a common defence policy. A Commission report in January 2000 also reminded the member states that it was incumbent on them to ensure that the IGC reformed the EU in such a way that it would remain flexible enough 'to allow continued progress towards our goal of European integration. What the Conference decides will set the framework for the political Europe of tomorrow'. The EU, it warned, 'will be profoundly changed by enlargement, but must not be weakened by it'. As for the EP, it came out strongly in favour of a wider agenda dismissing the 'excessively narrow agenda' adopted by the Helsinki European Council in December 1999 as one that 'might well jeopardize the process of integration'.

Such calls were initially overlooked by the IGC, although 'closer cooperation' was added to its agenda by the Feira European Council in June 2000. By this time, however, certain member states were beginning to think more openly about the future of the EU. Hence, negotiations were soon taking place against a backdrop of speeches from the German Foreign Minister, Joschka Fischer, advocating in a personal capacity 'a European Federation' (see Box 3.6) and the French President, Jacques Chirac, championing proposals for a European constitution. Other proposals on the future shape of the EU from, among others, the UK Prime Minister, Tony Blair, and his Spanish counterpart, José María Aznar, soon followed.

Many of the proposals were too ambitious for the IGC, where progress was already proving to be slow not least due to major differences on how best to deal with the Amsterdam leftovers. This was evident from the harsh words exchanged at the Biarritz European Council in October 2000. And the situation was not helped by the heavy-handed manner in which France, now holding the Council presidency, was managing the IGC. Accusations abounded that

From Confederacy to Federation: thoughts on the finality of European integration

Excerpts from speech by Joschka Fischer at the Humboldt University in Berlin, 12 May 2000:

'Quo vadis Europa?' is the question posed once again by the history of our continent. And for many reasons the answer Europeans will have to give, if they want to do well by themselves and their children, can only be this: onwards to the completion of European integration. A step backwards, even just standstill or contentment with what has been achieved, would demand a fatal price of all EU member states and of all those who want to become members; it would demand a fatal price above all of our people ...

The task ahead of us will be anything but easy and will require all our strength; in the coming decade we will have to enlarge the EU to the east and south-east, and this will in the end mean a doubling in the number of members. And at the same time, if we are to be able to meet this historic challenge and integrate the new member states without substantially denting the EU's capacity for action, we must put into place the last brick in the building of European integration, namely political integration ...

Permit me therefore to remove my Foreign Minister's hat altogether in order to suggest a few ideas both on the nature of this so-called finality of Europe and on how we can approach and eventually achieve this goal ...

Enlargement will render imperative a fundamental reform of the European institutions. Just what would a European Council with 30 heads of state and government be like? Thirty presidencies? How long will Council meetings actually last? Days, maybe even weeks? How, with the system of institutions that exists today, are 30 states supposed to balance interests, take decisions and then actually act? How can one prevent the EU from becoming utterly intransparent, compromises from becoming stranger and more incomprehensible, and the citizens' acceptance of the EU from eventually hitting rock bottom?

Question upon question, but there is a very simple answer: the transition from a union of states to full parliamentarization as a European Federation, something Robert Schuman demanded 50 years ago. And that means nothing less than a European Parliament and a European government which really do exercise legislative and executive power within the Federation. This Federation will have to be based on a constituent treaty.

I am well aware of the procedural and substantive problems that will have to be resolved before this goal can be attained. For me, however, it is entirely clear that Europe will only be able to play its due role in global economic and political competition if we move forward courageously. The problems of the twenty-first century cannot be solved with the fears and formulae of the nineteenth and twentieth centuries ...

Source: www.ena.lu.

---

the French were abusing their position as chair by promoting what was essentially a French agenda rather than seeking to broker compromises between the member states. At no point were the accusations louder than at the Nice European Council which, after more than four days, eventually agreed a treaty. Once tidied up, the Treaty of Nice was signed on 26 February 2001.

The Treaty of Nice

What the member states agreed at Nice attracted much criticism. Although it was rightly heralded as paving the way for enlargement, for many it produced suboptimal solutions to the institutional challenges raised by the prospect of an enlarged membership. All the same, the Treaty of Nice did equip the EU better to accept new members and avoid decision-making and institutional paralysis. For example, QMV was extended to nearly 40 more treaty provisions, albeit in many instances ones concerned with the nomination of officials rather than policy making, although some ten policy areas did see increased use of QMV. Reaching a decision using QMV did not, though, become any easier. Despite a reweighting of votes—each member state saw its number of votes increase, with the larger member states enjoying roughly a trebling and the smaller member states roughly a doubling—the proportion of votes required to obtain a qualified majority remained at almost the same level as before and was actually set to increase. Moreover, a new hurdle was introduced: any decision could, at the behest of any member state, be required to have the support of member states representing 62 per cent of the EU's total population.

The Treaty of Nice also provided for a staged reduction in the size of the Commission. From 2005, each member state would have one commissioner. Then, once the EU admitted its 27th member, the next Commission would comprise a number of members less than the total number of member states. There was, however, a proviso: an equitable rotation system would have to be agreed. Staying with the institutions, the cap on the size of the EP was revised upward to 732 and maximum sizes were agreed for the Committee of the Regions and the European Economic and Social Committee (see Chapter 18). Reforms were also introduced to the competences and organization of the European Court of Justice and the Court of First Instance (see Chapter 11).

The imminence of enlargement to fairly young democracies in Central and Eastern Europe, coupled with an awareness of existing institutional difficulties, also accounted for an enhanced stress on democracy and rights. Hence a 'yellow card' procedure was introduced for member states deemed to be at risk of breaching the principles on which the EU is founded. Thanks to the Treaty of Amsterdam, it had already been agreed that the voting and other rights of such member states could be suspended. Moreover, the Treaty of Nice revised the mechanisms for closer cooperation—now referred to as 'enhanced cooperation'. These become notionally easier to use mainly because the number of member states needed to start a project and the opportunities to block such were reduced. Enhanced cooperation could also now be used for non-military aspects of the CFSP. All this opened up the possibility of the EU becoming a less uniform entity.

At the same time, however, the Treaty of Nice arguably gave the EU a greater sense of coherence. In the area of CFSP, and following the development

of the European Rapid Reaction Force (see Chapter 15), it made the EU rather than the WEU responsible for implementing the defence-related aspects of policy. It also increased the focus on Brussels as the de facto capital of the EU. With enlargement, all European Council meetings would be held in Brussels.

Yet although the Treaty of Nice paved the way for a more 'European' EU by introducing the institutional reforms necessary for enlargement, it did little in terms of furthering the goal of 'ever closer union'. Integration-minded MEPs were quick to express their concerns, voicing particular criticism at the perceived drift towards intergovernmentalism and the consequent weakening of the Community method (Leinen and Méndez de Vigo, 2001). The new Treaty did, however, set in motion a process that drew on the speeches made by Fischer, Chirac, and others in 2000 and after to promote a debate on the future of the EU. To some, the Commission especially, this would provide an opportunity to create a stronger, more integrated EU with a less fragmented structure. Others, however, envisaged greater flexibility, a clear delimitation of competences and a weakening of commitments to 'ever closer union'.

Beyond Nice: the 'Future of Europe' debate

The initial terms of reference for the debate were outlined in a declaration adopted by the 2000 IGC in which the member states called for 'a deeper and wider debate about the future of the European Union'. This would focus, inter alia, on four issues: how to establish and monitor a more precise delimitation of powers between the EU and its member states; the status of the Charter of Fundamental Rights proclaimed at the Nice European Council; a simplification of the Treaties with a view to making them clearer and better understood; and the role of national parliaments in the European architecture. In addition, ways of improving and monitoring the democratic legitimacy and transparency of the EU

CASE STUDY 3.7

Laeken Declaration on the future of the European Union, December 2001 (excerpts)

[T]he Union stands at a crossroads, a defining moment in its existence. The unification of Europe is near. The Union is about to expand to bring in more than ten new Member States ... At long last, Europe is on its way to becoming one big family, without bloodshed, a real transformation clearly calling for a different approach from 50 years ago, when six countries first took the lead ...

The European Union needs to become more democratic, more transparent and more efficient. It has to resolve three basic challenges: how to bring citizens, and primarily the young, closer to the European design and the European institutions, how to organize politics and the European political area in an enlarged Union and how to develop the Union as a stabilizing factor and a model in the new multipolar world ...

Citizens often hold expectations of the European Union that are not always fulfilled ... Thus the important thing is to clarify, simplify and adjust the division of competences between the Union and the Member States in the light of the new challenges facing the Union ...

A first series of questions that needs to be put concerns how the division of competence can be made more transparent. Can we thus make a clearer distinction between three types of competence: the exclusive competence of the Union, the competence of the Member States and the shared competence of the Union and the Member States? At what level is competence exercised in the most efficient way? How is the principle of subsidiarity to be applied here? And should we not make it clear that any powers not assigned by the Treaties to the Union fall within the exclusive sphere of competence of the Member States? And what would be the consequences of this?

The next series of questions should aim, within this new framework and while respecting the *'acquis communautaire'*, to determine whether there needs to be any reorganization of competence. How can citizens' expectations be taken as a guide here? What missions would this produce for the Union? And, vice versa, what tasks could better be left to the Member States? What amendments should be made to the Treaty on the various policies? How, for example, should a more coherent common foreign policy and defence policy be developed? Should the Petersberg Tasks be updated? Do we want to adopt a more integrated approach to police and criminal law cooperation? How can economic policy coordination be stepped up? How can we intensify coopera-

tion in the field of social inclusion, the environment, health and food safety? But then, should not the day-to-day administration and implementation of the Union's policy be left more emphatically to the Member States and, where their constitutions so provide, to the regions? Should they not be provided with guarantees that their spheres of competence will not be affected?

Lastly, there is the question of how to ensure that a redefined division of competence does not lead to a creeping expansion of the competence of the Union or to encroachment upon the exclusive areas of competence of the Member States and, where there is provision for this, regions. How are we to ensure at the same time that the European dynamic does not come to a halt? In the future as well the Union must continue to be able to react to fresh challenges and developments and must be able to explore new policy areas. Should Articles 95 and 308 of the Treaty be reviewed for this purpose in the light of the *'acquis jurisprudentiel'*? ...

Who does what is not the only important question; the nature of the Union's action and what instruments it should use are equally important. Successive amendments to the Treaty have on each occasion resulted in a proliferation of instruments, and directives have gradually evolved towards more and more detailed legislation. The key question is therefore whether the Union's various instruments should not be better defined and whether their number should not be reduced.

In other words, should a distinction be introduced between legislative and executive measures? Should the number of legislative instruments be reduced: directly applicable rules, framework legislation and non-enforceable instruments (opinions, recommendations, open coordination)? Is it or is it not desirable to have more frequent recourse to framework legislation, which affords the Member States more room for manoeuvre in achieving policy objectives? For which areas of competence are open coordination and mutual recognition the most appropriate instruments? Is the principle of proportionality to remain the point of departure? ...

[H]ow can we increase the democratic legitimacy and transparency of the present institutions ...?

How can the authority and efficiency of the European Commission be enhanced? How should the President of the Commission be appointed: by the European Council, by the European Parliament, or should he be directly elected by the citizens? Should the role of the European Parliament be strengthened? Should we extend the right of codecision or not? Should the way in which we elect the members of the European Parliament be reviewed?

Should a European electoral constituency be created, or should constituencies continue to be determined nationally? Can the two systems be combined? Should the role of the Council be strengthened? Should the Council act in the same manner in its legislative and its executive capacities? With a view to greater transparency, should the meetings of the Council, at least in its legislative capacity, be public? Should citizens have more access to Council documents? How, finally, should the balance and reciprocal control between the institutions be ensured?

A second question, which also relates to democratic legitimacy, involves the role of national parliaments. Should they be represented in a new institution, alongside the Council and the European Parliament? Should they have a role in areas of European action in which the European Parliament has no competence? Should they focus on the division of competence between Union and Member States, for example through preliminary checking of compliance with the principle of subsidiarity?

[A] third question concerns how we can improve the efficiency of decision making and the workings of the institutions in a Union of some 30 Member States. How could the Union set its objectives and priorities more effectively and ensure better implementation? Is there a need for more decisions by a qualified majority? How is the codecision procedure between the Council and the European Parliament to be simplified and speeded up? What of the six-monthly rotation of the Presidency of the Union? What

is the future role of the European Parliament? What of the future role and structure of the various Council formations? How should the coherence of European foreign policy be enhanced? How is synergy between the High Representative and the competent Commissioner to be reinforced? Should the external representation of the Union in international fora be extended further? ...

[A further question] concerns simplifying the existing Treaties without changing their content. Should the distinction between the Union and the Communities be reviewed? What of the division into three pillars?

Questions then arise as to the possible reorganization of the Treaties. Should a distinction be made between a basic treaty and the other treaty provisions? Should this distinction involve separating the texts? Could this lead to a distinction between the amendment and ratification procedures for the basic treaty and for the other treaty provisions? ...

The question ultimately arises as to whether this simplification and reorganization might not lead in the long run to the adoption of a constitutional text in the Union. What might the basic features of such a constitution be? The values which the Union cherishes, the fundamental rights and obligations of its citizens, the relationship between Member States in the Union?

Source: European Council, 'Laeken Declaration on the Future of Europe', 15 December 2001 (via www.ena.lu).

---

and its institutions would be sought. The aim was to bring them closer to the citizens. A further IGC and treaty would follow.

The agenda for the 'Future of Europe' debate appeared quite limited. However, by the time the debate was formally launched by the Laeken European Council in December 2001, the reference to 'inter alia' had been seized on and a whole raft of often wide-ranging questions had been tabled for discussion. In all, the resulting 'Laeken Declaration' contained more than 50 questions. These dealt with matters ranging from the democratic legitimacy of the EU to the future of the pillar structure and cooperation in the area of social exclusion (see Box 3.7). Also, it had been agreed that the debate would not feed directly into an IGC. Instead a Convention comprising representatives of member state governments, members of national parliaments, MEPs, and

Commission representatives as well as governmental representatives and MPs from the 13 candidate countries would be established to explore how the questions raised in the Laeken Declaration could be answered. Only after the Convention had completed its work would the IGC meet (see Chapter 4).

For supporters of integration disappointed by the Treaty of Amsterdam and the Treaty of Nice, this 'Future of Europe' debate was welcomed as providing a further opportunity to promote the idea of 'ever closer union'. Developments they had in mind included the adoption of a European constitution, something that the EP in particular had long been championing and the French and German governments had publicly endorsed. The EP was also keen to see the communitarization of a strengthened foreign policy and remaining third-pillar matters, formal recognition of the EU's legal personality, election of the Commission president, simplification of decision-making procedures, and an extension of its own powers (Leinen and Méndez de Vigo 2001). Many of these ideas were shared by the Commission, which also proposed removing existing opt-outs (European Commission 2002c). They would also be fed, along with a range of other ideas from various sources, into the work of the Convention. The challenge it faced would be to come up with acceptable answers. Whether these would result in a further step along the road to 'ever closer union' and whether they would be accepted by national governments and electorates remained to be seen.

KEY POINTS

● Changes in the approach the EU was adopting towards enlargement in 1999 gave greater urgency to the need to address the Amsterdam leftovers and agree institutional reform.

● The Treaty of Nice may have paved the way for enlargement, but to many it provided suboptimal solutions to the institutional challenges posed by a significantly larger EU.

● While criticized for potentially weakening the EU, the Treaty of Nice initiated a process designed to respond to calls for a European Federation and a European Constitution.

Conclusion

In the history of the EU and its predecessors there has rarely been a point when ideas for increased integration have not been aired. This has been particularly true of the period from the mid 1980s during which treaty reform and IGCs have become almost permanent items on the agenda of the EU. As a result, the EU that was established in 1993 has evolved in a variety of ways. The member states have agreed to expand the range of policies in which the EU has a competence to act; they have adjusted the decision-making powers of the institutions; and they have embarked on some major integration projects, notably EMU and the adoption of the euro in 2002, and enlargement that has brought the membership to 27.

Consequently, the EU has assumed during its first ten years—and still retains in 2009—many of the characteristics of a union. For some it resembles or is becoming a **superstate**. Yet for many, particularly supporters of political union, it has always been a much looser and more fluid organization than its name suggests. Its pillar structure embodies a complex mix of intergovernmental cooperation and supranational integration that brings together in various combinations a range of supranational institutions and the member states to further a variety of policy agendas. Adding to the complexity are the various opt-outs that Denmark, Ireland, and the United Kingdom have

in certain policy areas, notably regarding certain JHA matters and in particular Schengen, as well as the differentiated integration created by EMU and emergence of the eurozone. Moreover, successive rounds of treaty reform have sought to facilitate a more multi-speed EU through the introduction and refinement of mechanisms for enhanced cooperation. All this raises questions about how uniform the EU is and will be.

What the various rounds of treaty reform also reveal, however, is that the EU has taken on more responsibilities and is at least aware of the challenges raised by its complex structure and procedures, particularly in the light of enlargement. This is not to say that its member states have warmed to the challenges, introduced appropriate reforms, streamlined the EU, or decided what its finalité politique should be. There has been and there still remains considerable difference of opinion. This was evident in the negotiation of the Constitutional Treaty (2004), its rejection, and the adoption of the replacement Treaty of Lisbon (2007). As the next chapter shows, several of the envisaged reforms could make the EU more like the union that its name implies. On balance, however, they would do little to transform the EU. It has been since its establishment in 1993, and remains, a complex, indeed messy, mix of supranationalism, intergovernmentalism and differentiated forms of integration.

QUESTIONS

1. Is it appropriate to describe the EU in terms of 'pillars'?

2. What is meant by 'ever closer union'?

3. Do opt-outs and mechanisms for enhanced cooperation undermine the EU as a union?

4. What impact did the Treaty of Amsterdam have on the pillar structure of the EU?

5. Why did the 1996 IGC fail to adopt the institutional reforms necessary to prepare the EU for enlargement?

6. Did the Treaty of Nice prepare the EU adequately for enlargement?

7. Why was the agenda for the 'Future of Europe' debate expanded between Nice and Laeken?

8. To what extent is the EU structurally a complex mix of supranationalism, intergovernmentalism and differentiated forms of integration?

 GUIDE TO FURTHER READING

■ Baun, M. J. *An Imperfect Union: The Maastricht Treaty and the New Politics of European Integration* (Boulder Co: Westview, 1996). An introductory account of the establishment of the EU in 1993 and its early development.

■ Church, C. and Phinnemore, D. *The Penguin Guide to the European Treaties: From Rome to Maastricht, Amsterdam, Nice and Beyond* (London: Penguin, 2002). A comprehensive guide to the treaty base of the EU which reproduces the provisions of the Treaties in their current form.

■ Galloway, D. *The Treaty of Nice and Beyond* (Sheffield: Sheffield Academic Press, 2001). A detailed analysis of key reforms introduced by the Treaty of Nice.

■ Lynch, P., Neuwahl, N., and Rees, W. (eds) *Reforming the European Union from Maastricht to Amsterdam* (London: Longman, 2000). A volume assessing developments in the EU during the 1990s, paying particular attention to the reforms introduced by the Treaty of Amsterdam.

■ Monar, J. and Wessels, W. (eds) *The European Union after the Treaty of Amsterdam* (London: Continuum, 2001). An informative collection of studies explaining the significance for the EU of the institutional and policy reforms introduced by the Treaty of Amsterdam.

 WEBLINKS

● http://europa.eu/abc/treaties/index_en.htm   The EU's treaties.

● http://ec.europa.eu/archives/igc2000/index_en.htm   Archives of the 2000 IGC.

● http://www.ena.lu/   On-line archive on the development of the EU.

 Visit the Online Resource Centre that accompanies this book for lots of interesting additional material. http://www.oxfordtextbooks.co.uk/orc/Cini_Borragan3e/

4 From the Constitutional Treaty to the Treaty of Lisbon

CLIVE CHURCH AND DAVID PHINNEMORE

Chapter Contents

- Introduction
- The European Convention, the 2004 IGC, and the Constitutional Treaty
- The 'no' votes: crisis and reflection
- 'Negotiating' the Treaty of Lisbon
- The main elements of the Treaty of Lisbon
- An appraisal
- Ratification
- The significance of the Treaty of Lisbon and the ratification experience
- Where next for the EU and its treaties?
- Conclusion

Reader's Guide

This chapter explores the origins and evolution of the Treaty of Lisbon. The origins lie both in the Constitutional Treaty (CT) of 2004 and in the French and Dutch referendum defeats of May and June 2005, which led to a period of so-called reflection. Then, mainly under the German Council Presidency, there was an emphatic drive to resolve underlying political disagreements amongst the EU's member states and produce not a constitution but an orthodox amending treaty to carry forward the basic reforms of the Constitutional Treaty. This process succeeded in getting a deal by October 2007 with a text acceptable to all member states, embedding most of the changes negotiated in 2002–4 into consolidated treaties that were somewhat more comprehensible than the existing texts. However, while parliamentary ratification went successfully, a referendum in Ireland saw a defeat for the Treaty in June 2008. In part this symbolized a rejection of some elements of the Treaty but it also owed much to a deeper unease about the EU, which an active opposition was able to exploit. Hence the Union again found itself in crisis.

Introduction

Given the political difficulties the process of treaty amendment has caused, it is perhaps surprising that the EU has pursued it so doggedly over the last few years, especially after the two resounding 'no' votes in 2005. Opponents put this down to an unholy lust for power on the part of a basically anti-democratic European elite seeking to replace national and popular sovereignty by a centralized, and probably neo-liberal, superstate. The truth is less dramatic. Many European decision makers believe the enlarging Union needs substantial institutional reform if it is to develop effectively. This must take precedence over the opposition of those who query the EU project because their countries have held a referendum, but who offer no better alternative text. And the opposition overlooks the fact that the reforms have been more democratically devised and directed than in previous treaty reforms. In other words, it is not a Manichean war between good and evil, but a normal political conflict over the governance and direction of the Union.

In any case, the EU set out in the early years of the new century to try and get better institutional arrangements than those provided by the much criticized Treaty of Nice. This grew out of an awareness of the latter's weaknesses, the existing proliferation of treaties, pressures from the German Länder for a clarification of their rights vis-à-vis the EU, and elite desires for making the Union more democratic and effective through a process of constitutionalization. After a sketchy debate the Laeken Declaration was adopted in December 2001 (see Chapter 3) and a representative Convention launched to consider a large number of questions about the future of the Union. The Convention met in Brussels from February 2002 until July 2003 and produced a 'Draft Treaty Establishing a Constitution for Europe'. This was then revised by an intergovernmental conference (IGC) and signed in Rome in October 2004. Ratification proceeded smoothly at first, with a positive referendum in Spain. However, in May and June 2005, referendums in France and the Netherlands rejected the Constitutional Treaty.

Many observers thought that the CT was dead, but during a so-called 'period of reflection' other states continued to ratify it. Although little serious reflection took place, eventually the German Council Presidency led a push for a new deal, seeking to agree with the other member states a detailed mandate for a new IGC which would preserve many of the innovations of the CT but within an orthodox treaty that would have nothing of the 'constitutional' about it. This was achieved by a rapid, secretive, and technical IGC. The new Treaty, embodying the points laid down in the mandate, was signed in Lisbon in December 2007. The thought behind this strategy was that it was the constitutional element that had alarmed people; removing this would therefore permit easy parliamentary ratification.

To begin with, this was the case. However, on 12 June 2008 the Irish rejected the treaty, just as they initially had refused the Treaty of Nice. The reasons for this were partly related to the text itself but also to specific Irish issues and an underlying popular angst. The rejection nevertheless threw the Union into a new crisis. This time there was no reflection period, the ball being quickly and firmly left in the Irish court. By the end of the year, with all except three other states having completed ratification, the Irish government, having secured various clarifications and concessions, notably general agreement on all member states having a Commissioner, committed itself to hold a second referendum, just as with Nice.

This chapter therefore looks initially at the background of the CT and, in particular, the reasons for the 'no' votes. It then goes on to trace the emergence of the Treaty of Lisbon and to explain and assess its main points. Next it describes the ratification process, giving special attention to the reasons for the Irish rejection. Finally it asks what the significance of the new treaty and the ratification process is, and what this might mean for the future of the Union. It also suggests that, even if Lisbon is finally ratified, arguments about reform are likely to continue.

The European Convention, the 2004 IGC, and the Constitutional Treaty

The origins of the Constitutional Treaty are manifold, but its rise owes much to the 'Future of Europe' debate set in motion by the Nice European Council in 2000 and furthered by the Laeken Declaration adopted a year later (see Box 4.1 and Chapter 3). Although the 'debate' attracted little popular input and few governments tried to promote discussion, there was sufficient political support to move towards a further round of treaty reform. This time, in recognition of the need to engage citizens more in the process, the question of how to reform the EU would not be left simply to an IGC. Instead, and drawing on the approach for the Charter of Fundamental Rights in 1999–2000, a 'Convention on the Future of Europe' was established to debate options and make proposals. This 'European Convention' comprised representatives of national governments, members of the European Parliament (EP) and of national parliaments as well as representatives from the Commission and the 13 candidate countries, along with observers from other EU institutions and bodies. It was chaired by a Praesidium led by former French President and MEP, Valéry Giscard d'Estaing.

Although there were doubts about the potential of the Convention, it proved itself an active, and up to a point an open, forum. It responded positively to Giscard's observation at the inaugural plenary that the best option was to produce a single text rather than a set of possibilities. Through a mixture of plenary sessions, working groups, study circles and praesidium meetings it began to move towards a European constitution. In the spirit of openness and transparency, all its papers were posted on the web and its plenary sessions were open to the public. Yet the Convention failed to attract much media or popular attention. It remained anonymous and restricted to an essentially self-selecting EU elite, skilfully steered by Giscard.

The Convention was only just able to meet its deadline and present its draft to the European Council in June 2003. Although a minority of Eurosceptics sketched an alternative vision, the vast majority of *conventionnels* accepted it, which made it hard to ignore. This was acknowledged by EU leaders at the Thessaloniki European Council, which declared that the draft was a 'good basis' for further negotiations. They also allowed for a further period of textual polishing. IGC negotiations began surprisingly soon afterwards, in September 2003. However, no member state was willing to adopt the draft without amendment, several having serious reservations about some of its contents. In particular, Spain and Poland objected to a proposed new double majority voting system in the Council. Others had doubts about provisions on the Commission, the proposed Union Minister for Foreign Affairs, the reformed Presidency, the respective powers of the EP and the Council; the extension of qualified majority voting (QMV) and the revision processes envisaged. Given this and poor preparation and chairing by the Italian Presidency, it proved impossible to get agreement at the European Council in December.

The sense of crisis then whipped up by the media and opposition politicians had a partly beneficial effect, since it focused minds on the outstanding issues. It also led to a cooling-off period that allowed the incoming Irish Presidency some time to consider how various problems with the draft could be resolved. Its task was made easier by a change of government in Spain in March 2004 and the adoption by the Polish government of a more accommodating position on the double majority issue. Negotiations resumed and, within little more than a month, agreement was reached. The European Council in Brussels in June 2004 duly adopted the Treaty establishing a Constitution for Europe. The text—90 per cent of which had come from the Convention draft, despite

CHRONOLOGY 4.1

From Nice to Lisbon

2001	26 February	Treaty of Nice signed
	7 March	'Future of Europe' debate launched
	15 December	Laeken Declaration
2002	28 February	Inaugural plenary session of the European Convention
2003	20 June	Parts I and II of the *Draft Treaty establishing a Constitution for Europe* presented to the Thessaloniki European Council
	18 July	Complete *Draft Treaty* presented to the President of the European Council
	29 September	IGC opens
2004	18 June	European Council agrees a *Treaty establishing a Constitution for Europe*
	29 October	*Treaty establishing a Constitution for Europe* signed
2005	29 May	French electorate reject the *Constitutional Treaty* in a referendum
	1 June	Dutch electorate reject the *Constitutional Treaty* in a referendum
	16–17 June	European Council announces a 'pause' in ratification
2006	15–16 June	European Council agrees extension to the 'period of reflection'
	14–15 December	European Council
2007	1 January	Germany assumes Presidency of the Council
	25 March	Berlin Declaration adopted on 50th anniversary of the signing of the *Treaties of Rome*
	21–22 June	European Council adopts IGC mandate for new '*Reform Treaty*'
	23 July	IGC opens
	18–19 October	Informal European Council adopts *Treaty of Lisbon*
	13 December	*Treaty of Lisbon* signed
2008	12 June	Irish electorate reject *Treaty of Lisbon* in a referendum
	11–12 December	European Council agrees concessions to Irish government in exchange for commitment to complete ratification before 1 November 2009
2009	1 January	Original scheduled date for the entry into force of the *Treaty of Lisbon*
	2 October	Second Irish referendum held

the IGC having made 80 amendments—was subsequently tidied up and authentic versions produced in each of the 21 official languages of the enlarged EU. The complete version of the Constitutional Treaty was then signed on 29 October 2004 at a ceremony in Rome, in the same building where representatives of the original six member states had signed the 1957 Treaty of Rome.

The document they approved was a lengthy one divided into four parts. These were supplemented by annexes, protocols, declarations and a final act (see Box 4.1). It was designed to replace all the existing treaties and become the single constitutional document of the Union. Yet, although it was all in one volume, for many of those who had hoped, or feared, that the Convention and IGC would produce

BOX 4.1

Structure of the Constitutional Treaty

Preamble

Part I

Part II: The Charter of Fundamental Rights

Part III: The Policies and Functioning of the European Union

Part IV: General and Final Provisions

Protocols (36)

Annexes (2)

Final Act

Declarations (50)

a short, succinct constitution, it was a disappointing text: 482 pages in length, complex and impenetrable, and doing little to promote transparency and accountability. This was despite a concise Part I, clear headings and a single numeration.

The document began with a preamble setting out the purpose of the EU. This was followed by a core Part I outlining the fundamentals of the EU. This included everything that one needs to know about what the EU does and how it does this, making it the most innovative and constitutional of the four parts. Part II contained the Charter of Fundamental Rights. The longest element was Part III, which contained detailed rules expanding on the provisions of Part I by bringing much of the existing Treaty on European Union (TEU) and Treaty establishing the European Community (TEC) into line with them. Part IV and the Final Act contained legal provisions common to international treaties, such as revision and ratification procedures. The protocols and declarations provided more detailed specifications and interpretations of what is found in the four parts.

In terms of content, not much was new. The vast bulk of the document came from the existing treaties, albeit slightly altered. The innovations, alongside the replacing of all the existing treaties, lay mainly in the overall structure of the Union, the style

of its operation, changes to the institutions, the addition of the Charter, and alterations to the revision process. Policy and powers changed rather less. The CT abolished the European Community and the pillars, replacing it with the single Union normally recognized by public opinion. This inherited the legal personality of the Community along with its symbols and the primacy of its law. However, the Union committed itself to respecting its member states, who were recognized as conferring powers on it. And member states were given the right to leave.

Its style also changed, with the simplification and unification of the way it made rules through the 'ordinary legislative procedure' involving joint decision making by the Council and the EP. And its rules were rechristened as laws and not directives and regulations. There was also a new focus on values and rights along with democratic improvements, including new powers for both the EP and national parliaments. The CT also envisaged citizens' initiatives. Accompanying all this was an extended use of QMV, although unanimity would still be required for a range of sensitive and constitutional issues, such as measures relating to tax harmonization, the accession of new members, and revisions of the Constitutional Treaty. A change to what constitutes a qualified majority was also planned, with a double majority consisting of 55 per cent of member states representing 65 per cent of the EU's population generally being necessary.

The new treaty also maintained most of the present institutions. However, it upgraded the European Council (giving it a permanent president), limited the size of both the EP and the Commission, formalized the use of team presidencies in the Council, and established a new post of Union Minister for Foreign Affairs. The holder was to be at the same time a member of the Commission and the Chair of the Foreign Affairs Council, while being assisted by an External Action Service. The constitutional nature of the document was intensified by the addition of the Charter of Fundamental Rights. This was made binding on the member states but only when they were applying EU law. And further guarantees were given to the UK that the Charter did not increase EU powers. Part IV also introduced a number of easier revision procedures, to avoid the Union being forced to call an IGC for all alterations to its treaties.

As to what the EU can do, the CT specified that its rationalizing changes did not mean any accretion of power. It also clarified the Union's policy competences. It explained what the EU's exclusive competences are—customs union, competition, monetary policy for the eurozone, common commercial policy—and identified those areas where competence is 'shared' with the member states. These include the internal market, social policy, the environment, and the area of freedom, security and justice. In other areas, the EU's role was restricted to supporting and coordinating complementary actions; that is, powers which are explicitly conferred by the member states and are not the EU's by right. Few new competences were conferred through the CT. A number of areas—tourism, civil protection, administrative cooperation, energy—were specifically mentioned for the first time in any detail, but each of these is an area where the EU has already been active.

Generally speaking, the CT simplified the structure, terminology and operation of the Union, as well as attempting to make it more comprehensible, democratic, and efficient. Unfortunately, people rarely came to terms with the simplification and restructuring it brought. The text was not easily available and was poorly publicized. And other issues got in the way. Indeed, while the Convention and the IGC succeeded in providing one document, they did not, as responses and ratification were to show, involve the people and increase the EU's legitimacy in the desired way.

KEY POINTS

- The European Convention attempted to be both more open and more innovative than previous IGCs.

- The IGC took two attempts to produce a slightly amended text.

- The CT attempted to be a single set of rules for a streamlined and more democratic EU.

The 'no' votes: crisis and reflection

With little popular and, in many cases, political understanding or appreciation of the Constitutional Treaty, ratification by all 25 member states was always going to be a challenge. This was recognized in a Declaration adopted by the IGC that envisaged the matter being referred to the European Council if, once four-fifths of member states had ratified, some were encountering 'difficulties'. Ratification at first proceeded relatively smoothly even if not in a uniform or coordinated manner, since some member states, as was their right, chose to have referendums along with parliamentary consideration. In the event, the Lithuanian parliament led the way, ratifying in November 2004. It was followed by Hungary and Slovenia before Spain held the first referendum in February 2005. The outcome was, as expected, positive, although low turnout and scant knowledge of the treaty meant the vote was

essentially an expression of support for EU membership. The same could also be said for several, if not most, of the subsequent positive votes in national parliaments. It was not true, however, of the French referendum on 29 May when 53.3 per cent of voters—mainly rural, low income and public-sector based—rejected the CT. It was equally not true of the Dutch referendum three days later, which saw an even larger majority (61.07 per cent) say 'nee'. Both defeats attracted a high turnout. The far from overwhelming endorsement in the Luxembourg referendum in July did little to create a sense that the CT was a text that commanded popular support, even if by then the Cypriot, Latvian, and Maltese parliaments had also voted in favour. Not surprisingly, the UK government, after some hesitation, postponed its planned referendum, as did the Irish and Danes.

It was clear that the CT itself was only one element of the problem. This was partly because the text was problematic and partly because, as a complicated compromise document, it was hard for supporters of integration to sell, especially as some of them judged that it fell short of their aspirations. The issues it addressed were also poorly appreciated, thus making room for other concerns, few of which originated in the treaty. So, while a significant proportion of those who voted 'nee' in the Netherlands did so for reasons associated with the CT, detailed studies of the French referendum made little reference to the text. French worries were essentially national and social concerns, seeing the EU as becoming too liberal. Paradoxically, the portions of the treaty that seem to have motivated this were in Part III and came straight from the existing treaties. This was possibly—as with the TEU in Denmark in 1992—the result of people coming to realize what had been agreed in the past and of the provision of texts of the treaties rarely, if ever, being read before.

Therefore it has been widely, and rightly, assumed that popular rejection of the CT was part of a broader malaise that has at its roots a general dissatisfaction with national governments and, especially, a basic alienation from the EU. The former had much to do with domestic political frustration over government strategy, unemployment, threats from globalization, and social welfare difficulties.

However, some 'European' issues—albeit unconnected to the Constitutional Treaty—such as the 'Bolkestein' directive on services, Turkey's potential membership, and the orientations of the Barroso Commission—did feature. Beyond this, the increasing pace of treaty reform and the unsettling implications of enlargement seemed to have intensified the underlying malaise. Yet little had been done to address it, with efforts to communicate 'Europe' being generally half-hearted and for the most part failing abysmally. This had both allowed the gap to widen and questioned the commitment of political elites to making the process of European integration inclusive. Nevertheless, ratification continued well after the two 'no' votes, so that 18 states had actually ratified the Treaty on 21–22 June 2007. All the same, the CT was effectively dead and the EU found itself faced with a constitutional crisis.

KEY POINTS

- The CT could only have entered into force if it had been ratified by all member states.

- 'No' votes in the French and Dutch referendums reflected a range of concerns, not all of which were connected with the CT, together with a failure of governments to engage the people in debates about European integration.

'Negotiating' the Treaty of Lisbon

EU leaders were at a loss as what to do to extricate the Union from its latest crisis. For sure there was little leadership. The UK government deliberately sought to avoid discussion of the subject during its Council Presidency in late 2005. There were no formal statements of what the French and Dutch wanted in place of the rejected CT. Despite bright ideas from academics and others about how to get the EU out of its current bind, and the Commission's work on Plan D to improve its communication

efforts, the political resolve to find a solution to the 'no' votes was lacking.

In 2006 the Austrian Council Presidency talked bravely of resuscitation but was unable to overcome national disagreements. Equally the EP tried to stimulate debate. However, the issue soon began to slip down the public agenda even though Belgium and Estonia completed ratification. The best the Commission could come up with was the idea of a Declaration for the 50th Anniversary of the Treaty of Rome. Yet many in Germany, including Chancellor Angela Merkel, made it clear that they supported the revival of the Treaty at the right time. Others, however, felt otherwise, the veteran Luxembourg Prime Minister Jean-Claude Juncker observing that Europe had lost its bearings. Not surprisingly the reflection period was, in June 2006, extended for a further year.

During the autumn of 2006, with the Finnish Council Presidency doing its best to ensure that the reflection process did not die completely, new ideas did emerge from Nicholas Sarkozy, Andrew Duff, and Margot Wallström, and others. Enquiries were carried out into the cost of not having a constitution and a Committee of Wise Men was set up under Giuliano Amato. And the Spaniards and Luxembourgers were beginning to rally ratifiers under the umbrella of the 'Friends of the Constitutional Treaty'. More significantly, the Finns began passing on findings from their consultations to the Germans who would shortly be assuming the Council Presidency. Indeed, the German Presidency would play a huge part in actually reviving the substance of the CT. Merkel was a believer in the Treaty. She felt it absolutely necessary for the EU, especially as there was no realistic alternative. Pressure had been brought on the Austrian Presidency to agree that the Germans should be charged with real action. Then, in October 2006 Merkel declared that it would be the German Presidency's intention to produce a road map for action by June 2007. Her underlying assumption seems to have been that the real problems lay with the member states and that these had to be settled confidentially. If this was done, then referendums could be avoided and parliamentary ratification achieved. The process would therefore be very tightly controlled with discussions being limited to a very small group of nationally-appointed 'sherpas' and followed by a short 'technical' IGC.

Not everybody shared Merkel's enthusiasm. The UK government was very cautious overall and the Poles and Czechs wished that the question of what to do would simply go away. However, a Berlin Declaration designed to reassure people about the EU's ambitions and achievements was adopted in March, providing an opportunity for the Germans to begin discussions on how to proceed. A questionnaire on issues to be addressed was soon being circulated and in May there were contacts with various European leaders. The election of Nicholas Sarkozy to the French Presidency added political weight to Merkel's plans. By 14 June, when a list of outstanding issues was circulated, much progress had been achieved. Less than a week later an unprecedentedly detailed mandate for an IGC was produced. The first half outlined the amendments to be made and the second half specified more precisely where, and how, they were to be inserted in the two basic treaties. This was then approved, along with a decision to launch an IGC, by the European Council on 21 June 2007 after last-minute concessions, notably to the UK and Poland.

The incoming Portuguese Council Presidency made completing the negotiations on a new amending treaty its overriding objective. The IGC commenced work on 23 July and continued over the summer. Foreign ministers, assisted by MEPs, considered progress at Viano de Castelo on 7–8 September and a final draft was achieved on 2 October. Various loose ends were sorted, notably offering further concessions to Bulgaria, Poland, and especially Italy, which threatened to veto a deal over its allocation of EP seats. An informal European Council in Lisbon on 18–19 October brought the negotiations to a close. Following legal refinements to the text, a replacement to the Constitutional Treaty was signed in Lisbon on 13 December.

KEY POINTS

- The reflection period failed to produce any clear answer to the ongoing crisis.

- The German Presidency followed a tightly controlled strategy to secure member state agreement on an IGC mandate to transfer much of the CT into a conventional amending treaty.

- Under the Portuguese Presidency a technical IGC produced the Treaty of Lisbon.

The main elements of the Treaty of Lisbon

The Treaty of Lisbon is, in one sense, a simple document with only seven articles (see Box 4.2). However, the first two are extremely long, as they contain a whole series of amendments to the existing treaties. Article 1, dealing with the TEU, contains 61 instructions on amending the treaty, while the second, amending the renamed TEC—now the Treaty on the Functioning of the EU (TFEU)—contains eight horizontal changes and 286 amendments. The remaining articles make it clear that the Treaty of Lisbon has unlimited effect, that accompanying Protocols are also valid, and that the TEU and TFEU will be renumbered. In addition to the Treaty text proper there are 13 legally binding Protocols, an Annex, a Final Act, and 65 numbered Declarations. Five of the Protocols—covering the role of national parliaments, subsidiarity, and proportionality, the Eurogroup, permanent structured cooperation, and the EU's planned accession to the European Convention on Human Rights—were originally part of the CT. The remaining eight are new, including some dealing with the continuing significance of competition, the application of the Charter in the UK and Poland, or interpreting shared competences, values, and public services. There are also various transitional institutional arrangements. The final two Protocols repeal or adapt existing Protocols to reflect changes brought about by the new Treaty. As a result, assuming it is ratified and comes into effect, the Treaty of Lisbon itself will actually disappear from view, leaving behind considerably changed versions of the TEU and TFEU, which will be the basis for EU governance. Thankfully, consolidated versions of these, including the new numbering, have been made available.

The reworking and reshaping of the TEU has resulted in a treaty that provides a fairly succinct outline of the purpose and structure of the EU, notably in terms of aims, objectives, principles, and institutions (see Box 4.3). It also includes a good deal of detail on enhanced cooperation and, especially, on external action. The TEU may now

---

BOX 4.2

Structure of the Treaty of Lisbon

Article 1	Amendments to the *Treaty on European Union*
Article 2	Amendments to the *Treaty on the Functioning of the European Union* (formerly the *Treaty establishing the European Communities*)
Article 3	Duration
Article 4	On amendments to existing protocols and the Treaty establishing the European Atomic Energy Community
Article 5	Renumbering
Article 6	Ratification
Article 7	Languages
Protocols	(13)
Annex	(1)
Final Act	
Declarations	(65)

BOX 4.3

Structure of the Consolidated Treaty on European Union (TEU)

Preamble	
Title I	Common Provisions
Title II	Provisions on Democratic Principles
Title III	Provisions on the Institutions
Title IV	Provisions on Enhanced Cooperation
Title V	General Provisions on the Union's External Action and Specific Provisions on the Common Foreign and Security Policy
Title VI	Final Provisions

have a more constitutional feel about it, since it deals with major facets of the Union, but it has exactly the same legal status as the TFEU and cannot be used to override it. The TFEU is much longer, with seven Parts and 358 articles and many Declarations (see Box 4.4). It now starts with a set of common provisions and rules on citizenship which are followed by the longest section: Part III, which

deals with policies. External relations, institutional and budgetary provisions make up the bulk of the rest. The order is perhaps slightly more logical than in the past.

Together, the TEU and TFEU make up a simplified and somewhat more efficient Union. Firstly, in structural terms, the key change is that Lisbon brings matters into line with common practice. Hence the

---

BOX 4.4

Structure of the Consolidated Treaty on the functioning of the European Union (TFEU)

Preamble	
Part One	Principles
Title I	Categories and Areas of Union Competence
Title II	Provisions having General Application
Part Two	Non-Discrimination and Citizenship of the Union
Part Three	Union Policies and Internal Actions
Title I	The Internal Market
Title II	Free Movement of Goods
Title III	Agriculture and Fisheries
Title IV	Free Movement of Persons, Services and Capital
Title V	Area of Freedom, Security and Justice
Title VI	Transport
Title VII	Common Rules on Competition, Taxation and Approximation of Laws
Title VIII	Economic and Monetary Policy
Title IX	Employment
Title X	Social Policy
Title XI	The European Social Fund
Title XII	Education, Vocational Training, Youth and Sport
Title XIII	Culture
Title XIV	Public Health
Title XV	Consumer Protection
Title XVI	Trans-European Networks
Title XVII	Industry
Title XVIII	Economic, Social and Territorial Cohesion
Title XIX	Research and Technological Development and Space
Title XX	Environment
Title XXI	Energy
Title XXII	Tourism
Title XXIII	Civil Protection
Title XXIV	Administrative Cooperation
Part Four	Association of the Overseas Countries and Territories
Part Five	External Action by the Union
Title I	General Provisions on the Union's External Action
Title II	Common Commercial Policy
Title III	Cooperation with Third Countries and Humanitarian Aid
Title IV	Restrictive Measures
Title V	International Agreements
Title VI	The Union's Relations with International Organizations and Third Countries and Union Delegations
Title VII	Solidarity Clause
Part Six	Institutional and Financial Provisions
Title I	Provisions governing the Institutions
Title II	Financial Provisions
Title III	Enhanced Cooperation
Part Seven	General and Financial Provisions

Community disappears and the Union becomes the sole structure of integration. And the latter inherits all the powers of the Community, including legal personality, institutions, and policy mix. Apart from the Common Foreign and Security Policy (CFSP) everything will function according to the basic Community method. Equally there are still many opt-outs from parts of the system, while the facilities for enhanced cooperation have been increased.

Secondly, despite the talk of a superstate, the Treaty of Lisbon makes it abundantly clear that the EU is a body based on powers conferred by the member states, enshrined in the treaties and subject to subsidiarity and proportionality. And member states have rights of action, consultation, recognition, support, and, now, secession. The EU can also give up competences, although it has yet to do so, and legal harmonization is subject to clear limits. Equally the institutions can operate only within defined boundaries. The EU's powers are categorized as exclusive, shared, or supportive, which makes it clear that they are not all-embracing or self-generated.

Thirdly, EU policies are not greatly expanded. Energy, tourism and civil protection are written more clearly into the TFEU, while space, humanitarian aid, sport, and administrative operation are added for the first time. In energy there is now specific reference to combating climate change and providing for energy solidarity. The main change is the way that rules on justice and home affairs matters are brought into the mainstream. If Lisbon is ratified they will be governed by normal Union procedures and not subject to special, more intergovernmental, procedures. This is a significant development.

Fourthly, in terms of decision making, the Treaty of Lisbon makes codecision the basic legislative process. The procedure is extended to some 50 new areas. Inside the Council, QMV is extended to some 60 new instances. And QMV is due to be based not on the current complicated formula but on a double majority of the member states (55 per cent) and the populations they represent (65 per cent). In doing so, the proportional weight of larger member states like the UK increases. Member states have also retained unanimity or emergency brakes in areas

like tax harmonization, the CFSP, criminal matters, and social security. And, to satisfy the Poles, old-style QMV can be invoked until 2017, after which a form of the Ioannina Compromise will apply.

Fifthly, there are significant changes in institutional arrangements. The EP receives extra powers, notably over the budget and treaty changes. It will also have a virtual veto on the appointment of the President of the Commission. The European Council also emerges strengthened and formalized as an 'institution', now meeting every three months, and given a new role in external relations and overall strategy. This points to the continuing influence of member states. Special arrangements for the Eurogroup are also provided. The Commission gains an expanded role in the area of freedom, security, and justice, thanks to the communitarization of the remaining pillar 3 activities, and in foreign affairs. Thus the High Representative of the Union for Foreign Affairs and Security Policy will be a Vice-President of the Commission, as well as chairing the Foreign Affairs Council. The High Representative will be assisted by an External Action Service drawing on existing Commission and national diplomatic services. The General Affairs Council will continue to be chaired by the rotating Council Presidency. In 2014 the size of the Commission is also due to be reduced to the equivalent of two-thirds of the member states, though the latter can change this by a unanimous decision. The Courts' jurisdiction has been extended, albeit not to diplomacy and police matters. Other institutions are largely unchanged.

A sixth facet is a new emphasis on values and rights. The former are expanded and given more prominence while the latter are given a dual boost. Applicant states will also be required to respect them as a condition of membership. Hence the Charter of Fundamental Rights is given legal status, subject to safeguards for national jurisdictions insisted on by the UK. Additionally, the Union can now sign up to the wider, independent, European Convention on Human Rights.

Lastly, Lisbon tries to make the Union more democratic. Thus democracy now has a separate Title in the TEU. This includes the provision for a citizens' initiative. National parliaments also gain new rights to query proposed EU legislation on subsidiarity grounds, though these are not as extensive as some wished.

It is also worth noting briefly what from the CT will not make its way via Lisbon into the revised treaties. The constitutional language and references have gone, along with the treaty-based mention of the Union's symbols. Acts of the Union are no longer to be called laws. Equally, the term Union Minister for Foreign Affairs will no longer be used. This is not as insignificant a change as some critics claim.

KEY POINTS

- The Treaty of Lisbon is not designed to have a lasting existence of its own, since its function is to amend the two treaties—the TEU and TEC—on which the Union is based.

- The TEU and TEC are extensively altered and modernized, and, in the case of the latter, renamed to become the TFEU.

- Together, the TEU and TFEU create one structure, the Union, with characteristics fairly close to those of the past.

An appraisal

The first question to be asked is whether the Treaty of Lisbon improves on the much criticized CT. It is certainly much more obviously a treaty since, as well as leaving out constitutional language and symbols, it no longer proposes to abolish all the other treaties and takes typical amending treaty form. Hence any claims that it is still 'a constitution' must rest on the contents or the style. At worst it is constitutionalization without a constitution. At the same time it connects the reforms slightly more closely with the EU's past arrangements than the CT did. However, it can hardly be regarded as simpler to understand and read than its predecessor. The aftermath of the constitutional crisis meant that Lisbon had to be an amending treaty, which translates into long lists of proposed changes that are not easy to follow. Critics claim that this was a deliberate attempt to make the Treaty unreadable, but this falls down in the face of the demands of legal continuity and the fact that the existing treaties are all like this, and that consolidated versions of the treaties were made available earlier than ever before.

Perhaps the more important question is whether the Treaty succeeds in its intention of increasing the democratic legitimacy and the efficiency of the Union. On the first point, many would claim that the Irish rejection shows that it fails. However, this is a somewhat self-interested view of democracy, ignoring the clear democratic improvements in Lisbon giving more powers to parliaments, both national and European, introducing the citizen's initiative and signing up to the ECHR and the EU's own Charter. The more precise delimitation of the powers of the Union and the insistence that these are conferred on the Union by its member states underlines the role of national democracy in the EU. This is reinforced by the elevation of the European Council's role, equal status among member states and their right to secede from the Union. The expansion of ECJ jurisdiction can also be seen as reinforcing the legal and democratic nature of the Union, even if critics see this as an example of creeping competence. Conversely, some believe that the changes in the CFSP downgrade the Commission to the benefit of the member states. As to efficiency, the slimming down of the Commission, the introduction of a European

Council President, the linking of the High Representative with membership of the Commission, the use of simpler voting procedures, and the extension of codecision are likely to make the Union more efficient. However, whether such changes, which are often contested, will wholly transform things is very doubtful. At best the improvements will be incremental. And the reinforcement of national governmental and parliamentary powers could well militate against faster and less contentious decision making.

Thus Lisbon introduces a wide-ranging series of changes, the actual importance of which cannot yet be estimated. Merkel and others certainly intended the Treaty to shake things up, hence the insistence that it is implemented almost irrespective of what Ireland ultimately decides. They may succeed. However, the new Union will remain remarkably like the old one. The most recent round of treaty change will not turn the EU world upside down.

KEY POINTS

● The Treaty of Lisbon is much more obviously and deliberately a treaty than the CT, hence it remains complex and difficult to read.

● The Lisbon Treaty seeks to make the EU more democratic and efficient but this has not always been appreciated.

● Despite the range of changes introduced, its effects are not likely to be revolutionary.

Ratification

Whether the reforms contained in the Lisbon Treaty come into force clearly depends formally on whether it is ratified (see Table 4.1). In an initial phase of ratification the prospects looked good, with a majority of member states completing the process relatively easily via parliamentary endorsements. This was interrupted by the Irish rejection, although ratification did not grind to a halt. It continued into late 2008, by which time very few ratifications remained outstanding. That ratification proceeded from the outset so quickly and seemingly problem free was in no small part due to the nature of the Treaty of Lisbon. As a reworked version of the CT, minus its constitutional and other symbolic trappings, the Treaty was deemed to be sufficiently far removed from its predecessor for member states previously committed to ratification via referendum to obviate the need for popular endorsement. Confirmation that there were no transfers of sovereignty to warrant a popular vote came from official sources in Denmark and Netherlands. This was welcomed by the Treaty's supporters across the EU, as were the UK and Portuguese governments' insistence that they would resist calls for a referendum. Hungary won the race to be first to ratify on 17 December (see Table 4.2). Malta and Slovenia quickly followed suit, with the Romanian, French, and European parliaments approving in February 2008. The ratification process also got under way in the UK. A second wave of approvals came in March and April, beginning with Bulgaria and followed by Slovakia, Austria, Portugal, and Denmark. Germany and Belgium also made progress. By the end of May Germany had successfully completed parliamentary approval, as had Luxembourg. Three more emphatic ratifications then followed on 11 June, the day before the Irish referendum, in Estonia, Finland, and Greece.

Much to the annoyance and frustration of Eurosceptic groups and other opponents of the Treaty, only Ireland found itself obliged to hold a referendum. The result was, however, very much to their liking. On a turnout of 53.1 per cent, a clear majority of 53.2 per cent voted against ratification (see Table 4.3). The arguments against Lisbon varied. To begin with, there was the general lack of knowledge and understanding of the text and its significance. It was

Table 4.1 Ratification of the Lisbon Treaty

As of 1 March 2009		Date	Yes	No	Abstain	Absent	Total	Referendum
Austria	Nationalrat	09.04.08	151	28	4	0	183	
	Bundesrat	24.04.08	58	4	2	0	64	
Belgium	Chambre	10.04.08	116	18	7	9	150	
	Sénat	07.03.08	48	8	1	14	71	
	Regional	*by 07.08*	*N/A*	*N/A*	*N/A*	*N/A*	*N/A*	
Bulgaria	Grand N Ass	21.03.08	193	16	0	31	240	
Cyprus	House of Reps	03.07.08	31	17	1	7	56	
Czech Republic	Chamber	18.02.09	125	61	11	3	200	
	Senate	06.05.09	54	20	5	2	81	
Denmark	Folketing	24.04.08	90	25	0	64	179	
Estonia	Riigikogu	11.06.08	91	1	0	8	100	
EU	EP	20.02.08	525	115	29	116	785	
Finland	Eduskunta	11.06.08	151	27	1	21	200	
France	Ch Deputés	06.02.08	336	52	22	167	577	
	Senat	10.02.08	265	42	13	1	321	
	Congrès (Jt)	14.02.08	560	181	N/A	N/A	908	
Germany	Bundestag	24.04.08	569	23	2	7	601	
	Bundesrat	23.05.08	66	0	3	0	69	
Greece	Voulis	11.06.08	268	17	15	0	300	
Hungary	Az Orsàg Hàza	17.12.07	325	5	14	42	386	
Ireland	Dail	02.04.08	*No vote taken*				166	*
	Senead	07.05.08	*No vote taken*				60	
Italy	Camera	31.07.08	551	0	0	0	630	
	Senato	23.07.08	286	0	N/A	40	326	
Latvia	Saeima	08.05.08	70	3	1	26	100	
Lithuania	Seimas	08.05.08	83	5	23	30	141	
Luxembourg	Chamber of D	29.05.08	47	1	3	9	60	
Malta	House of Reps	29.01.08	65	0	0	0	65	
Netherlands	Tweede Kamer	05.06.08	111	39	0	0	150	
	Ertse Kamer	08.07.08	60	0	0	15	75	
Poland	Sejm	01.04.08	384	56	12	8	460	
	Senate	02.04.08	74	17	6	0	97	
Portugal	Ass of Republic	23.04.08	208	21	0	1	230	
Romania	Chamber	04.02.08	387	1	1	80	332	
	Senate	04.02.08	*Counted with Chamber*				137	
Slovakia	Narodna Rada	10.04.08	103	5	1	41	150	
Slovenia	Drzavni zbor	29.01.08	74	6	0	10	90	

Table 4.1 Ratification of the Lisbon Treaty *(continued)*

As of 1 March 2009		Date	Yes	No	Abstain	Absent	Total	Referendum
	Drzavni svet		*Not Involved*				40	
Spain	Congreso	26.06.08	322	6	2	20	350	
	Senado	14.07.08	232	6	2	17	257	
Sweden	Riksdag	20.11.08	243	39	13	54	349	
United Kingdom	Commons	11.03.08	346	206	0	94	646	
	Lords	18.06.08	*No vote taken*				670	

* Ireland was the only country holding a referendum to ratify the Lisbon Treaty. It rejected the Lisbon Treaty on 13 June 2008. Ireland has agreed to rerun the referendum in October 2009.

Table 4.2 The Irish 'no' to Lisbon

	Total	%
No	752,451	46.6
Yes	862,415	53.4
Spoilt	6,171	0.4
Turnout	1,621,037	53.1

also a large factor in encouraging voters to abstain. This linked to the impression that the text was ultra complex and had little meaning for ordinary people who, in any case, were not really interested in coming to terms with it. In other words, many Irish voters returned to the 'Don't know, vote No' stance of 2000. However, there were a number of points at which specific elements of the Treaty did surface, notably the regular loss of an Irish commissioner, the timing of which was misunderstood; the perceived threat to neutrality, which was seen in some quarters as not merely being done away with but replaced by obligatory conscription in a European army; and the threat to the Irish ban on abortion, which was coupled with talk of enforced recognition of same-sex marriages. Governmental inability to counter such arguments when levelled by a highly organized and effective opposition also played a part in the rejection.

Although the Irish rejection was a bitter blow to Lisbon's supporters, it did not bring the process of ratification to an end. Various non-ratifiers made a point of pushing ahead. Notable among these was the UK government, which completed parliamentary ratification the following week. Final parliamentary votes came in the Netherlands, Cyprus, Spain, and Italy in July. Finland deposited its 'instruments of ratification' with the Italian government in early autumn and the Swedish parliament approved the Treaty in late November. This left only three countries, apart from Ireland, still to complete ratification: Germany and Poland, where the respective Presidents had yet to sign off the ratification bill; and the Czech Republic, where, following a positive ruling by the Constitutional Court and with the threat of the President refusing to sign, MPs decided to postpone their vote until early 2009.

KEY POINTS

- Parliamentary ratification proceeded without undue difficulty into summer 2008.

- The main causes of the 'no' vote in Ireland were a lack of knowledge and understanding of the Treaty of Lisbon, together with specific national concerns.

- The 'no' vote did not 'kill off' the Treaty, and ratification continued.

Table 4.3 The Irish 'no': reasons for rejection

	%	Hard No	SoftNo
Any mention of information, knowledge, understanding	45	38	65
Lack of information, knowledge, understanding, treaty too complex	42	37	57
Not sure of opinion, so voted no	3	1	10
Any mention of issues attributed to Lisbon	26	30	14
Treaty of Lisbon a bad deal, bad for Ireland	8	9	5
Loss/diminution of Irish neutrality	5	6	3
Loss of Irish Commissioner	4	4	2
Any mention of attitudes to referendum process	20	22	14
Didn't have confidence in government	6	6	6
Don't like being told how to vote	4	5	2
Not convinced by 'yes' arguments	3	3	1
Loss of power/independence/identity	16	19	6
Loss of power/domination by large countries	13	15	5
Loss of/threat to Irish independence	3	4	1
Any mention of aspects of European integration	6	7	3

Sources: Milward Brown MS, Post-Lisbon Treaty Referendum Research Findings, Dublin, September 2008 (http://www.reformtreaty.ie/eutreaty/DFAFinalreport.pdf).

The significance of the Treaty of Lisbon and the ratification experience

The Treaty of Lisbon was a second attempt to realize reforms that many European leaders think necessary to make the EU fit for the world into which it is moving, but in a format more acceptable to European opinion. Critics suggest that the determination to press on with reforms apparently rejected in 2005 is a piece of arrogance that is either mindless or a deliberate attempt to foist a superstate on the nations and peoples of Europe. There may be an element of this, but it is more a pragmatic matter of ensuring that the EU changes in line with its expanding membership and the demands of the world in which it has to operate. The fact that the idea was endorsed by those who actually have to work the system deserves to be remembered.

The fact that Lisbon substantively repeats the CT is a starting point and not something that need be concealed. Pretending that this was not so was a peculiarly British idiocy reflecting the sulphurous nature of UK anti-Europeanism. It was also an argument that placed too much stress both on understanding the difference between a constitution and a treaty and on the importance attributed by opponents to the constitutional status of the CT. Stripping off the constitutional element was seen as the way to defuse the opposition experienced in 2005 and since. But this was to overlook the fact that opposition to the CT was based on a whole range of often contradictory stances and beliefs, many of them related more to the EU in general and the way western European society has been developing than to the document's terms. More important are the depth and organization of opposition to treaty reform mobilized by the events of 2005. While this is often marginal, come referendums it is likely to express itself. Hence the ratification crisis is again seen as symbolizing an underlying alienation from the Union which is decreasingly being accepted as a wholly good thing. The crisis is also revelatory of the failure of governments to give real attention to dealing with the opposition, a failure most egregiously demonstrated in the one country where there was least room for it: Ireland.

So, is there a crisis of legitimacy? It is quite clear that there is a major problem in the old member states of Western Europe whose populations are now much less inclined to identify with the EU than they used to. This is because of their economic unease, their lack of confidence in the future, and their feeling that their interests are not being taken into account by 'Brussels'. Yet much of the opposition to Lisbon, as with the CT, came from people who described themselves as good Europeans. Their objections were not to integration as such but to the EU's style and strategy over the last 15 years. Lisbon served as a symbolic surrogate for such doubts. While the Irish vote was certainly a hammer blow for EU elites, it would be wrong to think that it was a death warrant for Lisbon. As in 2005, it actually opened a tense period of crisis, thanks in part to the way it revived anti and Eurosceptic forces across Europe, which appear set to do well in the 2009 EP elections, and the way this conflicted with member state governments' commitments to the reforms it

contained. The Irish rejection also forced the Danes to postpone a referendum on ending their opt-outs. European markets and the EU's standing in the world were also affected. It certainly forced the EU to give more attention to institutional questions at the expense of the policy issues which both friends and foes alike believe should be its main concern. However, talk of the demise of the EU remains much exaggerated. While there is clearly vocal and active opposition, this needs something special like a referendum to make an impact. Once the crisis is over, apathy and lack of interest are likely to reassert themselves. Moreover, the Union has continued to function fairly normally and has not lost confidence, even though some would see this as arrogance.

Interestingly, the Irish 'no' vote seemed much less of a protest against enlargement and immigration than the votes of 2005. Enlargement was hardly discussed, Turkey not at all. Immigration was a somewhat disguised issue. Equally, the assault on the text was much less motivated by left-wing critiques of the EU's economic stance despite the gathering economic gloom. In other words the 'no' vote symbolized other kinds of political concerns (see Chapter 24). While the Anglo-Saxon world has tended to see the 'no' as a justifiable protest against an undemocratic Union, there was another view. For some supporters of integration there were two problems: there was a democratic problem created by a minority of 0.2 per cent of the EU population, with no right to claim to speak for all the peoples of Europe, blocking the wishes of the majority; secondly the 'no' vote itself was brought about by people who did not agree on what they wanted in its place and in some cases had based their decision on bare-faced lies. Hence the Irish had to accept the logic of and responsibility for their rejection.

KEY POINTS

- Abandoning the language of 'constitution' in the Treaty of Lisbon failed to pacify opposition.

- Governments had a case but failed to engage with a well-organized opposition.

- Hence the Irish 'no' opened a new period of crisis over EU reform.

Where next for the EU and its treaties?

How the crisis spawned by the Irish 'no' will play out is unclear. The fact that 23 countries had completed ratification by December 2008 encouraged the EU leaders to leave it to Dublin to come up with a solution. A general assumption was that if all other member states ratified, it would increase the pressure on Ireland and oblige voters to consider the possible threat to Irish membership when they voted again. It would also make it clear that the Treaty was neither dead nor up for revision. However, there could be some concessions. Hence the European Council in December 2008 agreed that, assuming Lisbon entered into force, the size of the Commission would not be reduced, allowing Ireland to retain 'its' Commissioner. Moreover, provided the Irish government committed itself to completing ratification before 1 November 2009, three legal guarantees, acknowledging popular Irish concerns, would be given, namely: Lisbon does not alter EU competences on taxation; nothing in the Treaty affects Irish neutrality; and the Irish Constitution's provisions on the right to life, education and the family would not be affected by Lisbon, its provisions on justice and home affairs, or the Charter of Fundamental Rights. These guarantees would be included in the treaty governing Croatia's accession to the EU. Note was also taken of the 'high importance' the EU attaches to workers' rights and various public services. This was enough for the Irish government. Indeed, satisfied with what was on offer, the Taoiseach, Brian Cowen, immediately confirmed that he was 'prepared to go back to the Irish people' in 2009.

If this second vote says 'yes', and presuming other difficulties in Poland, Germany, and especially the Czech Republic are overcome, the Treaty should enter into force before the end of 2009. This will not stop critics and other discontented opponents of Lisbon, who by then may well be more strongly represented in the EP. This was certainly the hope of Libertas and its leader Declan Ganley who, as EU leaders were meeting to agree the concessions to be made to Ireland, was launching a pan-European anti-Lisbon campaign for the 2009 EP elections. However, divisions within Libertas and among other opponents may prove a problem. So the Union will struggle on. And the conflict between the political class and the populist defenders of the peoples' rights will probably remain latent. This is unlikely to affect enlargement to either Croatia or Iceland despite the threats of Sarkozy and Merkel. However, a second rejection could call enlargement beyond EU (28–29) into question, partly in order to 'punish' opponents and partly to justify the belief that without Lisbon enlargement is impossible. The lost opportunities contained in Lisbon are also likely to be stressed in dealings with Russia and in seeking to confront other challenges such as climate change and the financial crisis. If there were a second Irish 'no', this would certainly sap the enthusiasm for reform. Many zealots might, however, ask whether it was worth carrying on the fight for a deal that is, in any case, flawed. A second 'no' may well also mean an end to grand treaty-making experiments, with much more modest sectoral changes being essayed in future. Suggestions that Ireland will be more or less excluded, either by being forced to withdraw or by being left behind by the use of enhanced cooperation provisions, seem unlikely to come about. They ignore the support that Ireland could attract and the virtual impracticality of many of the bright ideas.

KEY POINTS

- Ratification of the Treaty of Lisbon continued despite the 'no' vote in Ireland, with the Irish government committing itself to holding a second referendum before 31 October 2009.

- Although a blow to the prospects of the Treaty of Lisbon, the Irish 'no' will not bring an end to the EU, but will strengthen the resolve of opponents to contest its development.

- The impact on Ireland's position within the EU in the light of non-ratification remains uncertain.

Conclusion

Despite all the talk of the CT and the Treaty of Lisbon creating a superstate, what comes out of all this is the fact that the EU is a body dependent on its member states and defined by its treaties. There is no underlying 'Europe' to fall back on as there is a Denmark, a Netherlands, or a Slovakia. It is because of this dependence on the treaties that amendments to them are so sensitive and controversial. They raise the question of what the EU is, what it should be and where it might go. Given this, the likelihood is that the existing treaties will occasionally need to be revised so that they are kept up to date. Many states do this fairly regularly with their constitutions. There is often a pragmatic need for change as well as idealists pushing for more integration. And opponents of Lisbon argue for change too, in some cases even for clearer, shorter, more constitution-like documents. So pressure for reform will not go wholly away even if Lisbon is ultimately defeated.

The problem with Lisbon was that EU leaders bet heavily that dropping the constitutional element and going for a mainly parliamentary ratification would head off the kind of opposition that emerged in 2005.

To an extent the bet paid off, but because Ireland at least believed it should have a referendum, ratification was never going to be a dead cert. And it rather looks as though the Irish government behaved like most others and made little attempt to devise a convincing case and campaign strategy. This allowed an opposition to mobilize and to good effect, even if some of the more persuasive arguments deployed presented Lisbon and the EU decidedly inaccurately.

This all points, and certainly not for the first time, to the need for the EU's institutions and, more importantly, its member states to engage citizens in meaningful and informed debate on what the EU is, can and should be. It needs to be recognized that the EU is far from static; it remains a work-in-progress and therefore subject to and often in need of revision. Moreover, as the formal abandonment of the CT showed, non-ratification of a treaty neither reduces the need for change nor precludes either the EU's development or further attempts to reform it. As such, whatever its fate, the Treaty of Lisbon is unlikely to be the last chapter in the history of EU treaty reform.

? QUESTIONS

1. Why did the EU embark on a process of institutional reform?
2. Why was the Constitutional Treaty rejected in France and the Netherlands?
3. Why did the member states decide to continue with the reform process after 2005?
4. What kind of a document is the Treaty of Lisbon?
5. How does the Treaty of Lisbon compare with the Constitutional Treaty?
6. Why was the Treaty of Lisbon rejected in Ireland?
7. Why does it matter that the Treaty of Lisbon was rejected in Ireland?
8. What enabled the Irish government to commit to a second referendum in 2009?

GUIDE TO FURTHER READING

- Amato, G., Ziller, J. et al *The European Constitution: Cases and Materials in EU and Member States' Law* (Cheltenham: Elgar, 2007). A series of useful essays touching on ratification, referendums, and innovations.

■ Church, C. H. and Phinnemore, D. *Understanding the European Constitution: An Introduction to the EU Constitutional Treaty* (London: Routledge, 2006). An accessible discussion of the origins, key themes, and content of the Constitutional Treaty, and which reprints Part I of the Treaty.

■ Eriksen, E. O., Fossum, J. E., and Menéndez, A. J. (eds) *Developing a Constitution for Europe* (London: Routledge, 2005). An academic study of the rationale for a European Constitution and the process that led to the adoption of the Constitutional Treaty.

■ Gros-Verheyde, N. (coordinator) (2007) 'Treaty of Lisbon: Here is What Changes', *Europolitique*, 3407, 7 November (available at www.europainfo.at/dokumente/Europolitics_3407_special_treaty). A detailed, journalistic summary of what is included in the Treaty of Lisbon and how it was negotiated.

■ Sutton, M. (2007) 'The IGC 2007: The European Union Comes of Age?', *European Public Law*, 14/1: 55 – 68. An enthusiastic appraisal of the Lisbon Treaty.

 WEBLINKS

● http://european-convention.eu.int   European Convention website.

● http://europa.eu.int/scadplus/cig2004/   Archives of the 2003 IGC.

● http://www.consilium.europa.eu/showPage.asp?id=1297&lang=en&mode=g   The—sketchy—official site of the 2007 IGC.

● http://europa.eu/lisbon_treaty/index_en.htm   The EU's own Lisbon website.

● http://www.lisbon-treaty.org/wcm/index.php   A source of documentation on the Lisbon Treaty with a news-ticker.

 Visit the Online Resource Centre that accompanies this book for lots of interesting additional material. http://www.oxfordtextbooks.co.uk/orc/Cini_Borragan3e/

PART TWO
Theories and Conceptual Approaches

5

Neo-functionalism

CARSTEN STRØBY JENSEN

Chapter Contents

- Introduction
- What is neo-functionalism?
- A brief history of neo-functionalism
- Supranationalism and spillover
- Critiques of neo-functionalism
- The revival of neo-functionalism
- Conclusion

Reader's Guide

This chapter reviews a theoretical position, neo-functionalism, which was developed in the mid 1950s by scholars based in the United States. The fundamental argument of the theory is that states are not the only important actors on the international scene. As a consequence, neo-functionalists focus their attention on the role of supranational institutions and non-state actors, such as interest groups and political parties who, they argue, are the real driving force behind regional integration efforts. The chapter that follows provides an introduction to the main features of neo-functionalist theory, and to its historical development since the 1950s. It focuses, more specifically, on three theses advanced by neo-functionalists: the spillover thesis; the elite socialization thesis; and the supranational interest group thesis. The chapter also considers the main critiques of the theory to explain why it went out of fashion in the 1970s. The final section scrutinizes the revival of interest in neo-functionalism beginning in the late 1980s and 1990s, as well as providing some examples of how today's neo-functionalists differ from those of the 1950s.

Introduction

Neo-functionalism is often the first theory of European integration studied by students of the European Union. This is largely for historical reasons, as neo-functionalism was the first attempt at theorizing the new form of regional cooperation that emerged at the end of the Second World War. Although few researchers of European integration would now accept all neo-functionalist arguments, the theory remains important because its concepts and assumptions became part of the so-called Monnet Method of European integration. Indeed, at times it has been difficult to separate the theory of integration from the reality of the EC/EU. This has been something of a curse for neo-functionalism, as it has meant that its success as a theory became inextricably tied to the success of the European integration project. But it does mean that it is possible to chart the history of the EC/EU through the lens of neo-functionalism, as we shall see below.

The chapter begins by asking: 'What is neo-functionalism?' The purpose of this first section is to outline the general characteristics of the theory. The second section then summarizes the rise and fall from grace of neo-functionalism between the 1950s and the 1970s. The third section examines three theses that form the core of neo-functionalist thinking. These are: (a) the spillover thesis; (b) the elite socialization thesis; and (c) the supranational interest group thesis. These three arguments help to expose neo-functionalist beliefs about the dynamics of the European integration process. The fourth section reviews the main criticisms of the neo-functionalist school, while the final section turns to more recent adaptations of neo-functionalist ideas, accounting for the renewal of interest in this approach to the study of regional integration at the beginning of the 1990s and in the 2000s. The chapter concludes that neo-functionalism remains part of the mainstream theorizing of EU developments, even though there have been some major changes in the way neo-functionalism is used today compared with its original application in the 1950s.

What is neo-functionalism?

The story of neo-functionalism began in 1958 with the publication by Ernst B. Haas (1924–2003) of *The Uniting of Europe: Political, Social and Economic Forces 1950–1957* (Haas 1958). In this seminal book, Haas explained how six West European countries came to initiate a new form of supranational cooperation after the Second World War. Originally, Haas's main aim in formulating a theoretical account of the European Coal and Steel Community (ECSC) was to provide a scientific and objective explanation of regional cooperation, a grand theory that would explain similar processes elsewhere in the world (in Latin America, for example). However, neo-functionalism soon became very closely associated with the EC case and, moreover, with a particular path of European integration. However, some argued that despite its scientific language, neo-functionalism was imbued from the outset with pro-integration assumptions that were not made explicit in the theory.

Three characteristics of neo-functionalist theory help to address the question of what is neo-functionalism. First, neo-functionalism's core concept is that of spillover. This is covered in more detail later in the chapter. It is important to note at this point, however, that neo-functionalism was mainly concerned with the process of integration (and had little to say about end goals, that is, about how an integrated Europe would look). As a consequence, the theory sought to explain the dynamics of change to which states were subject when they cooperated. Haas's theory, then, was based on the assumption that cooperation in one policy area would create pressures in a neighbouring policy area, placing it on the political agenda, and ultimately leading to further integration. Thus, spillover refers to a situation where cooperation in one field necessitates cooperation in another (Hooghe and Marks 2007). This might suggest that the process is automatic, that is, beyond the control of political leaders. However, when we look at the various forms of spillover identified by Haas, we will see how this 'automatic' process might be guided or manipulated by actors and institutions whose motives are unequivocally political.

A second, albeit related, point which helps to explain neo-functionalism concerns the role of societal groups in the process of integration. Haas argued that interest groups and political parties would be key actors in driving integration forward. While governments might be reluctant to engage in integration, groups would see it as in their interest to push for further integration. This is because groups would see

integration as a way of resolving problems they faced. Although groups would invariably have different problems and, indeed, different ideological positions, they would, according to neo-functionalists, all see regional integration as a means to their desired ends. Thus, one might see integration as a process driven by the self-interest of groups, rather than by any ideological vision of a united Europe or shared sense of identity.

Finally, neo-functionalism is often characterized as a rather elitist approach to European integration. Although it sees a role for groups in the integration process, integration tends to be driven by functional and technocratic needs. Though not apolitical, it sees little role for democratic and accountable governance at the level of the region. Rather, the 'benign elitism' of neo-functionalists tends to assume the tacit support of the European peoples—a 'permissive consensus'—upon which experts and executives rely when pushing for further European integration (see Box 5.1).

 KEY CONCEPTS AND TERMS 5.1

Features of neo-functionalism

- Neo-functionalism is a theory of regional integration that seeks to explain the process of (European) integration. It is a theory that focuses on the supranational institutions of the EU.

- The theory was particularly influential in the 1950s and 1960s.

- Its main focus is on the 'factors' that drive integration: interest group activity at the European and national levels; political party activity; the role of governments and supranational institutions.

- The driving force of integration is the self-interest of groups and institutions. They may well have different goals in mind, but the actions they choose, in order to achieve those goals, drive forward the integration process.

- European integration is mostly seen as an elite-driven process—driven by national and international political and economic elites.

- The concept of spillover is the key concept within neo-functionalism.

A brief history of neo-functionalism

Neo-functionalism is very much connected to the case of European integration. Indeed, most neo-functionalist writers have focused their attention on Europe (Lindberg 1963; Lindberg and Scheingold 1970, 1971). This was not their original intention,

however. Rather, an early objective was to formulate a general or grand theory of international relations, based on observations of regional integration processes. Political and economic cooperation in Latin America was one of the cases investigated to that end (Haas and Schmitter 1964; Mattli 2005). It was in Europe, however, that political and economic integration was best developed and most suited to theoretical and empirical study. Therefore Europe and European integration became the major focus of neo-functionalists during the 1960s and 1970s.

With the benefit of hindsight the success of neo-functionalism is understandable, as it seemed that the theory explained well the reality of the European integration process at that time. Until the 1970s, neo-functionalism had wide support in academic circles, though after that it lost much of its appeal. Indeed, it almost disappeared as a theoretical and empirical position in the study of European integration. One reason for this was that neo-functionalism lacked a theoretically solid base for its observations. Another reason was that the kind of incremental political integration that neo-functionalism predicted did not take place. From the mid 1970s, political cooperation seemed less compelling, and researchers became more interested in other kinds of theories, especially those that stressed the importance of the nation state. Even Haas was among those who recognized the limitations of neo-functionalism. On this point he wrote that 'the prognoses often do not match the diagnostic sophistication, and patients die when they should recover, while others recover even though all the vital signs look bad' (Haas 1975: 5).

After the early 1990s neo-functionalism underwent a sort of revival. The new dynamism of the EC/EU, a consequence of the single market programme (see Chapter 16), made theories focusing on processes of political integration relevant once again (Tranholm-Mikkelsen 1991). And even traditional critics of neo-functionalism, such as Paul Taylor, accepted the need to examine this approach more closely. On this point, Taylor (1993: 77) wrote that 'The student of the European Community . . . needs to return to the writings of . . . the neo-functionalists—whose writings for many years have been unfashionable. They provide the essential context of theory in which to place the practice of diplomacy and even the speeches of Prime Ministers so that they might be better understood.'

Since this revival of interest in neo-functionalism, a number of scholars have sought to adapt the theory to their own research agendas—whether on the European integration process writ large, on specific policy areas, or on the role of the supranational institutions. Correspondingly there were, following Haas's death in 2003, a number of attempts to evaluate and re-evaluate the importance of the neo-functionalist contribution to our understanding of the development of the European Union (for example, in a special issue of the *Journal of European Public Policy* in 2005). These new approaches and evaluations will be reviewed towards the end of this chapter.

KEY POINTS

- Neo-functionalism was fashionable amongst elites and academics until the 1970s.

- From the 1970s, other theoretical and conceptual approaches seemed to fit the reality of European integration much better than neo-functionalism, and the theory became obsolete.

- In the 1990s, with the revival of the integration process, there came also a renewed interest in neo-functionalism. This led to a wave of further research, which used certain elements of the neo-functionalists' conceptual toolkit. During the mid 2000s there have been further attempts to develop the theoretical framework of traditional neo-functionalism.

Supranationalism and spillover

The key question asked by neo-functionalists is whether and how economic integration leads to political integration; and if it does so, what kind of political unity will result? In this respect neo-functionalism differs from other traditional approaches to international relations theory. More realist IR positions have stressed the power games that occur between states. Among neo-functionalists it was believed that economic integration would strengthen all the states involved, and that this would lead to further political integration. The fundamental idea was that international relations should not be seen as a zero-sum game, and that everybody wins when countries become involved in processes of economic and political integration.

Another important aspect of neo-functionalist theory is related to the development of supranational institutions and organizations. Supranational institutions are likely to have their own political agendas. Over time, neo-functionalists predict, the supranational agenda will tend to triumph over interests formulated by member states. As an example one might look at how the European Parliament (EP) operates. Members of the European Parliament (MEPs) are directly elected within the member states. One would therefore expect it to be an institution influenced very much by national interests. In the Parliament, however, MEPs are not divided into groups relating to their national origin. They are organized along party political and ideological lines (see Chapter 11). In other words, Social Democrats from Germany work together with Labour members from the UK, and Liberals from Spain work with Liberals from Denmark. According to neo-functionalist theory, MEPs will tend to become more European in their outlook as a consequence of these working practices, though this may be disputed empirically. This is often referred to as 'elite socialization'. The fact that MEPs work together across borders makes it difficult for them to focus solely on national interests. This also makes the EP a natural ally for the European Commission in its discussions with the EU Council, even if the institutions do not always agree on matters of policy.

Political integration is therefore a key concept for neo-functionalists, though it is possible to identify a number of different understandings of political integration in their writings. Lindberg (1971: 59), for example, stressed that political integration involves governments doing together what they used to do individually. It is about setting up supranational and collective decision-making processes.

By contrast, Haas saw political integration in terms of shifts in attitudes and loyalties among political actors. In 1958 he famously wrote:

> Political integration is the process whereby political actors in several distinct national settings are persuaded to shift their loyalties, expectations and political activities toward a new center, whose institutions possess or demand jurisdiction over the pre-existing national states. The end result of a process of political integration is a new political community, superimposed over the pre-existing ones.

(Haas 1958: 16).

Neo-functionalist writers developed at least three different arguments about the dynamics of the integration processes: (a) the spillover thesis; (b) the elite socialization thesis; and (c) the thesis on supranational interest groups. The following subsections set out the content of these theses and the following section presents critiques of these arguments.

Spillover

Spillover is neo-functionalism's best-known concept, one that has been widely used both by social scientists and by practitioners. According to Lindberg (1963: 10), the concept of spillover refers to a process where political cooperation conducted with a specific goal in mind leads to the formulation of new goals in order to assure the achievement of the original goal. What this means is that political cooperation, once initiated, is extended over time in a way that was not necessarily intended at the outset.

In order to fulfil certain goals, states cooperate on a specific issue. For example, the original aim may be the free movement of workers across EU borders. But it may soon become obvious that different national rules concerning certification prevent workers from gaining employment in other EU states. For example, nurses educated in one member state may not be allowed to work in another because of differences in national educational systems. As a consequence, new political goals in the field of education policy may be formulated so as to overcome this obstacle to the free movement of labour. This process of generating new political goals is the very essence of the neo-functionalist concept of spillover.

> Spillover refers ... to the process whereby members of an integration scheme—agreed on some collective goals for a variety of motives but unequally satisfied with their attainment of these goals—attempt to resolve their dissatisfaction by resorting to collaboration in another, related sector (expanding the scope of mutual commitment) or by intensifying their commitment to the original sector (increasing the level of mutual commitment), or both.

(Schmitter 1969: 162).

A distinction is often drawn between different types of spillover. Functional (or technical), political, and cultivated spillover constitute three different kinds of spillover process (Nye 1971; Tranholm-Mikkelsen 1991; Rosamond 2005; Moravcsik 2005; Niemann 2006; see also Box 5.2).

An example of functional spillover—where one step towards cooperation functionally leads to another—can be seen in the case of the Single Market (see Chapter 16). The Single Market was functionally related to common rules governing the working environment. This meant that some of the trade barriers to be removed under the Single Market Programme took the form of national regulations on health and safety, as the existence of different health and safety standards across the Community prevented free movement. The functional consequence of establishing a Single Market was, then, that the member states ended up accepting the regulation of certain aspects of the working environment at European level, even though this had not been their original objective (Jensen 2000).

Political spillover occurs in situations characterized by a more deliberated political process, where national political elites or interest groups argue that supranational cooperation is needed in order to solve specific problems. National interest groups focus more on European than on national solutions and tend to shift their loyalty toward the supranational level. Interest groups understand that their chances of success increase when they support European rather than national solutions.

KEY CONCEPTS AND TERMS 5.2

Types of spillover

- Functional spillover takes place when cooperation in one sector/issue area 'functionally' creates pressures for cooperation in another related area.

- Political spillover refers to situations characterized as a more deliberate political process, as when actors (national or supranational, political, or private) find it more useful to argue for European rather than for national solutions.

- Cultivated spillover refers to situations where supranational actors such as the European Commission push the process of integration forward during the intergovernmental negotiation process. The Commission acts not only as mediator but also as political entrepreneur during these negotiations.

This type of spillover is closely related to a thesis which argues that European integration promotes shifts of loyalty among civil servants and other elite actors.

Cultivated spillover refers to situations where supranational actors—the European Commission in particular—push the process of political integration forward when they mediate between the member states (Tranholm-Mikkelsen 1991; Niemann 2006). For example, the Commission may only take heed of arguments that point toward further political integration ('more' Europe) during the negotiation process, while ignoring or rejecting arguments that are primarily based on national interests.

Supranational institutions may use special interests as a means of driving forward the integration process. These special interests may be promoted through so-called 'package deals', where steps are taken to treat apparently discrete issues as a single (composite) item, enabling all (or the majority of) actors to safeguard their interests (Lindberg and Scheingold 1970: 116). For example, if one member state has an interest in a certain policy area, such as preventing cuts in agricultural spending, while another has interests in industrial policy, these member states may agree, formally or informally, to support each other in negotiations. As a result the two policy areas can be easily linked within the bargaining process, particularly where an an entrepreneurial actor such as the Commission takes the initiative.

Thus spillover processes may be seen partly as the result of unintended consequences. Member states might deliberately accept political integration and the delegation of authority to supranational institutions on a particular issue. However, as a result of that decision, they may suddenly find themselves in a position where there is a need for even more delegation. As a result, Lindberg and Scheingold are right to stress that political integration need not be the declared end goal for member states engaging in this process. The latter have their own respective goals, which are likely to have more to do with policy issues than with integration. As Lindberg and Scheingold write: 'We do not assume that actors will be primarily or even at all interested in increasing the scope and capacities of the system per se. Some will be, but by and large most are concerned with achieving concrete economic and welfare goals and will view integration only as a means to these ends' (Lindberg and Scheingold 1970: 117). In this sense the establishment of supranational institutions such as the EU may be seen as the result of unintended conse-

quences of actions among the actors involved in decision making.

Elite socialization

The second aspect of neo-functionalist theory concerns the development of supranational loyalties by participants such as officials and politicians in the decision-making process. The thesis here is that, over time, people involved on a regular basis in the supranational policy process will tend to develop European loyalties and preferences (Pentland 1973). For example, Commission officials are expected to hold a European perspective on problem solving so that their loyalty may no longer be to any one national polity, but rather to the supranational level of governance.

We can well imagine how participants engaged in an intensive ongoing decision-making process, which may extend over several years and bring them into frequent and close personal contact, and which engages them in a joint problem-solving and policy-generating exercise, might develop a special orientation to that process and to those interactions, especially if they are rewarding. They may come to value the system and their role within it, either for itself or for the concrete rewards and benefits it has produced, or that it promises (Lindberg and Scheingold 1970: 119).

Thus neo-functionalists predicted that the European integration process would lead to the establishment of elite groups loyal to the supranational institutions and holding pan-European norms and ideas. This elite would try to convince national elites of the advantages of supranational cooperation. At the same time neo-functionalists also predicted that international negotiations would become less politicized and more technocratic. The institutionalization of the interactions between national actors, and the continued negotiations between different member states, would make it more and more difficult for states to adhere to their political arguments and retain their credibility (Haas 1958: 291). As a result, it was expected that the agenda would tend to shift towards more technical problems upon which it was possible to forge agreement.

 CASE STUDY 5.3

Functional spillover: from Single Market to Economic and Monetary Union

The establishment of the Single Market increased the possibilities for companies in Europe to trade across borders. This generally implied a growth in trade among the countries in the European Community. However, the increased level of transnational trade in the European Community made companies and countries more exposed to fluctuations in national currencies, which demonstrated the functional advantages inherent in a common European currency. From that perspective Economic and Monetary Union can be seen as a consequence of a functional logic connecting growth in trade across borders in the EU with the functional need for a common currency so as to reduce risks related to expanding trade.

The formation of supranational interest groups

According to neo-functionalist theory, civil servants are not the only groups that develop a supranational orientation. Organized interest groups are also expected to become more European, as corporations and business groups formulate their own interests with an eye to the supranational institutions (see Chapter 13). As economic and political integration in a given region develops, interest groups will try to match this development through a process of reorganization, to form their own supranational organizations. For example, national industrial and employers' organizations established a common European organization, BUSINESSEUROPE (formerly UNICE), in 1958, at much the same time as the European Community was established. In so doing, their intention was to influence future Community policy. Early neo-functionalists also saw a similar role for political parties.

Furthermore, neo-functionalists believed that interest groups would put pressure on governments to force them to speed up the integration process. These groups were expected to develop their own supranational interest in political and economic integration, which would ally them to supranational institutions, such as the European Commission. Thus, 'in the process of reformulating expectations and demands, the interest groups in question approach one another supranationally while their erstwhile ties with national friends undergo deterioration' (Haas 1958: 313).

Before we examine criticisms of the neo-functionalist approach, it is important to stress the following point: neo-functionalism is often compared to or is seen as connected with federalism. Federalists argue that the EU should establish strong federal institutions leading in the end to the creation of a federation with some similarities to the USA. Sometimes neo-functionalism is seen as a theoretical approach that supports a federalist agenda. Neo-functionalists, like federalists, talk about processes of political integration, and about the advantages of this process (see Box 5.4). However neo-functionalists like Haas (1971: 20–1) stressed that neo-functionalism and federalism are very different in several respects. The most important of these is that federalism is a political position, while neo-functionalism is both theoretical and scientific. Federalists are interested in how things ought to be (taking a normative stance), while neo-functionalists analyse the processes of integration and disintegration from a scientific point of view. However, critics of neo-functionalism would most likely dispute the claim that neo-functionalism is devoid of a political agenda.

BOX 5.4

Neo-functionalist expectations about the European institutions

Neo-functionalists have formulated theories that they have used to predict the behaviour of the European institutions.

- The European Commission is expected to act as a 'political entrepreneur' as well as a mediator. The Commission will, according to neo-functionalist theory, try to push for greater cooperation between the member states in a direction that leads to more and more supranational decision making.

- The European Court is expected not only to rule on the basis of legal arguments, but also to favour political integration. In this way, the Court will seek to expand the logic of Community law to new areas.

- The European Parliament is expected to be a supranationally oriented institution and to be the natural ally of the European Commission. Although MEPs are elected by the nationals of their home country, they are divided politically and ideologically in their daily work. Neo-functionalists expect MEPs to develop loyalties towards the EU and the 'European idea', so that they would often (though not always) defend European interests against national interests.

- The EU Council is expected to be the institution where national interests are defended. However, neo-functionalists would also expect member states to be influenced by the logic of spillover, which would lead them to argue for greater economic and political integration, despite their national interests. The member states are also expected to be influenced by the fact that they are involved in ongoing negotiations in a supranational context. This makes it difficult for a member state to resist proposals that lead to further political integration.

Critiques of neo-functionalism

We now review briefly the main criticisms of neo-functionalism made by observers such as Haas (1975, 1976), Moravcsik (1993, 1998, 2005), Taylor (1990, 1993), Keohane and Nye (1975), Keohane and Hoffman (1991) and Schmitter (2005).

Neo-functionalism has been criticized on both empirical and theoretical grounds. At an empirical level the criticism focuses on the absence (or slow pace) of political integration in Western Europe during the 1970s and early 1980s. Neo-functionalism had predicted a pattern of development characterized by a gradual intensification of political integration, a development that by the 1970s had clearly not taken place. The French boycott of the European institutions in the mid 1960s had led to a more cautious phase in the evolution of the Community, and recognition of the importance of political leaders as constraints on the process of integration. Indeed, with the European Community having suffered numerous crises, it could even be argued that the integration process had reversed. Moravcsik writes that:

> Despite the richness of its insights, neo-functionalism is today widely regarded as having offered an unsatisfactory account of European integration … The most widely-cited reason is empirical: neo-functionalism appears to mispredict both the trajectory and the process of EC evolution. Insofar as neo-functionalism advances a clear precondition about the trajectory in the EC over time, it was that the technocratic imperative would lead to a 'gradual', 'automatic' and 'incremental' progression toward deeper integration and greater supranational influence.

(Moravcsik 1993: 476).

Haas even talked about the possibility that there might be a disintegrative equivalent to spillover, which might be labelled 'spillback'!

However, alongside these empirical critiques lie theoretical objections which cover a broader spectrum. Here we shall focus on three main types of criticism. The first set of objections was aimed at the theses advanced by neo-functionalists. An example of this is Taylor's challenges to the elite socialization thesis, and to the idea that supranational loyalties would emerge in institutions such as the Commission. Taylor (1990) pointed out that, rather than integration making officials more European, it was the interests of the member states in having 'national' civil servants in the Commission that increased as political integration intensified. Member states became increasingly aware of the need to ensure that they reached 'their' quota of European civil servants (Taylor 1990: 180) and that their interests were represented. Moreover, it was surmised that European civil servants would become more nationally orientated when vital political issues were on the agenda (see also Hooghe 2002).

Correspondingly, Risse (2005) has argued that if the neo-functionalists were right, farmers and women should be among the most EU-supportive citizens in Europe, which is definitely not the case:

> Haas seemed to have assumed … that those who profit most from European integration are also more likely to shift their loyalties toward Europe than others. If this were true, two groups should be more supportive of European integration than they actually are. First, farmers are arguably the

one professional group who profit most from the EU ... Yet, there is no indication that farmers identify with EU to any considerable degree. Their satisfaction with the EU's perform-ance appears also to be rather low. Second, we would expect women to be in general more supportive of European inte-gration than men, given that it was EU that pushed gender equality, particularly equal treatment and equal pay in the workplace ... But there is a gender gap in support for the EU, with men being in general more supportive of integration than women.

(Risse 2005: 297).

The second set of objections was based on criticism of the theories formulated by Haas himself. By the late 1960s Haas had accepted that the prediction that regional organizations such as the EU would develop incrementally, propelled forward by vari-ous dynamics such as spillover, failed to encapsulate the reality of European cooperation (Haas 1975, 1976). He recommended a different approach to regional integration, based on theories of interde-pendence which were being developed in the mid 1970s by Keohane and Nye (1975, 1976) amongst others. This approach argues that institutions such as the EC/EU should be analysed against the back-ground of the growth in international interdepend-ence, rather than as regional political organizations (Haas 1976: 208). Referring to European integra-tion, Haas wrote that 'What once appeared to be a distinctive "supranational" style now looks more like a huge regional bureaucratic appendage to an intergovernmental conference in permanent ses-sion' (Haas 1975: 6). In so arguing, Haas himself abandoned the theory he had been so instrumental in developing.

Haas had argued that one of the factors reducing the level of predictability or inevitability of integra-tion was the replacement of traditional forms of functional policy links (that is, functional spillover) by what he referred to as 'deliberated linkage'. In essence, what Haas was saying was that political forms of spillover were replacing the original func-tional logic. This meant that over time the political linkage of package deals became more and more central and more and more complex, increasing the

uncertainty surrounding the integration process both for the researcher and for the participant (Haas, 1976: 209). Haas emphasized another, and possibly more important, deficiency: that the theory of regional integration had focused too narrowly on the region as an isolated entity, ignoring the impact of external factors.

In the third group of objections to the theory, it was argued that neo-functionalism had placed undue emphasis on the supranational component in regional integration. Critics suggested that greater importance should be attached to the nation state, and that regional forms of cooperation should be analysed as intergovernmental organizations. This line of attack was adopted by Moravcsik (1993, 1998, 2005) amongst others, under the rubric of lib-eral intergovernmentalism (see Chapter 7):

Whereas neo-functionalism stresses the autonomy of supranational officials, liberal intergovernmentalism stresses the autonomy of national leaders.

(Moravcsik 1993: 491).

This can be read as a claim that the nation state remains the core element in an understanding of international relations, including interpretations of the development of cooperation within the EU framework. If we accept this thesis, it obviously imposes limits on opportunities for political inte-gration. The assumption appears to be that political integration is based exclusively on the aggregate interests of the single nation state and on its deter-mination to survive. Nation states are thus prepared to cede formal competence to supranational institu-tions only if by so doing they ensure, or possibly regain, control of specific areas of policy.

Finally, there is also a different type of criticism, which relates to what we might call the elitist nature of neo-functionalism. This criticism attacks the prescriptive implications of the approach rather than the theory itself and so is of a different order to the critiques already outlined. The argument here is that neo-functionalism is not merely a sci-entific and objective theory of regional integration, but has also become an essential part of a model of

European integration. It is this model, which some call the 'Monnet Method' or the 'Community Method', that is subject to the criticism that it does not involve European citizens in this momentous process of change, and that it is therefore undemocratic. Neo-functionalism sees integration primarily as a process of functional or technocratic change, with experts largely running the show. As pointed out by Risse: '… Haas was not that much concerned about mass public opinion and the loyalties of the ordinary citizens, as he regarded European integration as an elite affair' (Risse 2005: 297). This has led to accusations that neo-functionalist integration implies 'integration by stealth'. Not only is this not an appropriate model for European integration in the early twenty-first century, it is also no longer an accurate depiction of the process itself, though as we shall see in Chapter 22 on the democratic deficit, not everyone would agree that things have changed very much from the early days of the Community.

Neo-functionalism first and foremost focused on political and administrative elites and on the processes that developed the cooperation between national elites. The assumption was that if the elites started to cooperate then the populations would follow their line of policy. The experience related to different national referendums about EU treaties points to the fact that the unilateral focusing on political elites is a major weakness in neo-functionalist theory. Although the political and administrative elites at the national and European level, for

example, agreed upon the new constitution or the Lisbon Treaty, this did not mean that the voters followed the elites. In this respect one could say that neo-functionalism as a theoretical tradition has a blind spot in the lack of understanding of the need for the EU to establish legitimacy among the peoples of Europe.

As the above suggests, the original neo-functionalist project has been subjected—from many different angles—to critical reappraisal at both the theoretical and empirical levels. Yet this did not mean that neo-functionalism died as a theoretical project. As we shall see in the next section, neo-functionalist theory experienced a sort of renaissance at the beginning of the 1990s and in the 2000s, as neo-functionalist concepts such as 'spillover' were revisited so as to explain contemporary developments in European integration.

KEY POINTS

- Neo-functionalism is criticized on both empirical and theoretical grounds.

- On empirical grounds it was argued that neo-functionalism no longer fitted with the reality of the EC in the 1970s.

- On theoretical grounds, critics denied the existence of elite socialization, stressed the importance of the international dimension of integration, and sought to reposition the nation state at the heart of the study of the European integration process.

The revival of neo-functionalism

After years of obsolescence, there was a revival in interest in neo-functionalism at the beginning of the 1990s. There are a number of reasons for the theory's renewed popularity. The first has to do with general developments in the European Community. The Single European Act and the creation of the Single

Market (see Chapter 16) marked a new phase of economic and political cooperation in Western Europe in the mid 1980s. And the processes of integration associated with these developments seemed very much in line with the sort of spillover predicted by neo-functionalist theory (Tranholm-Mikkelsen 1991).

However, this renewed interest in neo-function-alism involved much more than just a step back to the 1960s. Rather than simply adopting the traditional or classical model, many of those who sought to reuse neo-functionalist theory accepted it as a partial theory, that is, as a theory which would explain some but not all of the European integration process. This contrasts with the earlier ambition of the neo-functionalists—to create a grand theory of European integration.

An important contribution to this new approach was made by Stone Sweet and Sandholtz (1998; see also Stone Sweet and Brunell 1998 and Stone Sweet 2004). Although these authors are not neo-functionalists in any traditional sense, they do claim that their theoretical considerations have 'important affinities with neo-functionalism' (Stone Sweet and Sandholtz 1998: 5). They argue that the traditional distinction made in the theoretical literature on European integration—that it is either supranational or intergovernmental— is no longer sufficient. While both tendencies are represented in the real world of European politics, they appear differently in different policy areas within the Union, so that some are characterized by intergovernmentalism, others by supranationalism (Stone Sweet and Sandholtz 1998: 9). However, Stone Sweet and Sandholtz do not use the spillover concept when they seek to explain processes of political integration and the formation of supranational institutions. Instead they develop what they call a 'transaction-based' theory of integration. This draws attention to the increasing levels of transactions (such as in the field of trade, communications, and travel) across EU borders, which in turn increase demands for European-level regulation (Stone Sweet and Sandholtz 1998: 11). In time, these demands generate a process of institutionalization leading to the establishment of what the authors call 'supranational governance'.

One of the supranational institutions analysed using this approach was the European Court of Justice (Stone Sweet and Caporaso 1998; Stone Sweet 2004; see also Chapter 12). Stone Sweet and Caporaso observe how the Court interprets the Treaty expansively within its rulings. In doing so, they confirm their theses about the autonomy of the EU's supranational institutions and about supranational governance, and their theoretical relation to neo-functionalism. And elsewhere, Stone Sweet and Brunell explain the extent to which their analysis is similar to that formulated by Haas:

> Our results provide broad support for some of the core claims of 'neo-functionalist' theory, first developed by Ernst Haas ... Haas ... tried to show that market expansion and political development could be connected to one another through positive feedback loops that would push steadily for more of both. We formalized these insights as hypotheses, gathered data on the processes commonly associated with European integration, and tested our hypotheses in different ways. The evidence support Haas's basic intuitions.

(Stone Sweet and Brunell 2004: 52).

Others have also used the European Court to provide evidence of the existence of neo-functionalist dynamics in the EC. Burley and Mattli (1993) argue that the European Court has been a very important institution in the building of a supranational community as it has played an active role in the creation of Community authority in legal matters. They stress that the founding member states of the Community had no intention of giving the Court supremacy over national legal systems. However, the European Court was able to develop its doctrine over the course of the 1960s and 1970s. According to Burley and Mattli, the Court has also been able to advance political integration by using technical and apolitical arguments in the legal arena, a process which is close to the type of integration mechanisms proposed by neo-functionalist theory.

Along similar lines, references to neo-functionalist theory have increased dramatically since the beginning of the 1990s. And in policy areas such as defence (Guay 1996), social policy (Jensen 2000), and telecommunications (Sandholtz 1998), attitudes among European civil servants (Hooghe, 2001), competition policy (McGowan 2007), and transnational liberties (Newman 2008), authors have discussed neo-functionalism as a possible frame for explaining specific forms of integration. During the 2000s there have also been some important attempts at further developing the original neo-functionalist framework. Arne Niemann (2006), for example, argues that the process of integration should not be seen as an automatic process, but rather as a process that can occur under certain conditions.

Integration is no longer viewed as an automatic and exclusively dynamic process, but rather occurs under certain conditions and is better characterized as a dialectic process, i.e. the product of both dynamics and countervailing forces. In addition, instead of a grand theory, the revisited approach is understood as a wide-ranging, but partial, theory (Niemann 2006: 4–5).

Niemann's work focuses particularly on the traditional elite perspective in neo-functionalist theory:

66 ...[W]hile elites are still attributed a primary role for decision outcomes, the wider publics are assumed to impact on the evolution of the European integration process, too. 99

(Niemann 2006: 5).

Niemann similarly discusses the original neo-functionalist concepts of spillover and argues for the relevance of a new form of spillover: 'social spillover' (Niemann 2006: 37ff). Through this concept Niemann tries to combine the traditional spillover concept with the socialization thesis discussed above, arguing that this new concept of social spillover can capture processes that lead to a low level of European integration:

66 In contrast to early neo-functionalism, which assumed constant learning and socialization, the revisited framework departs from the presumption and is concerned with delimiting the scope of social spillover. 99

(Niemann 2006: 42)

Conclusion

Since the first writings of Haas in the 1950s, theories of regional integration, or neo-functionalism as it is more popularly called, have had their ups and downs. As a means of explaining cooperation between states in the 1960s, neo-functionalism became very popular. The new types of cooperation that developed after the Second World War, especially in Europe, demanded new research perspectives. Neo-functionalism was able to describe and explain these developments in a way that was novel and of its time. In the period after the war, the fashion was for grand theorizing, the construction of scientific theories that would explain the 'big picture'. Nowadays, theorists (and particularly those working on the EU) are content to devote their energies to the generation of less ambitious, middle-range theories (see Chapter 7) that explain only part of the process.

Focusing on the supranational aspects of the new international organizations, neo-functionalism explained cooperation using concepts like spillover

and loyalty transfer. States were expected to cooperate on economic matters in order to realize the economic advantages that come with increased levels of trade. This would lead to demands for political coordination across state borders, and in some cases to the establishment of supranational institutions. Cooperation in one policy area would involve cooperation in new areas, thereby initiating an incremental process of political integration. Over time, the supranational institutions would become more and more independent and able to formulate their own agendas, forcing the national states to delegate further competences to the supranational level.

Yet by the mid 1970s neo-functionalism was no longer a credible position to hold. Even traditional proponents of the theory, like Haas, argued that it could not fully explain European developments in regional cooperation. Indeed, he accepted that the European Community did not develop in the way that neo-functionalists had predicted. States remained key actors and it became hard to distinguish supranational institutions from more traditional international organizations.

Supranationalism did experience a revival in the beginning of the 1990s, however. The establishment of the Single Market and the creation of the EU at Maastricht opened the door to new interest in supranational developments and institutions. The EU suddenly began to look much more like the kind of institution that Haas and others predicted would emerge as a result of regional economic and political integration. But although there was some interest in neo-functionalism at this time, most of the 'new' neo-functionalists felt free to pick and choose from those elements of the theory that best suited their research agendas. Finally, despite the renaissance of the theory in the 1980s and 1990s, neo-functionalism is still rarely considered as at the forefront cutting edge of research on European integration and EU politics. It seems that the mainstream now belongs more to variants of intergovernmentalism and other newer competing theories of the EU (see Chapters 6 and 7), even if there have been some recent attempts to develop the original neo-functionalist theoretical framework in new directions (for example, Niemann 2006).

? QUESTIONS

1. What do neo-functionalists mean by political integration?

2. How helpful is the spillover concept in explaining the development of European integration since the 1950s?

3. How can private interest groups influence the processes of political integration?

4. How convincing is Moravcsik's critique of neo-functionalism?

5. According to neo-functionalist theory, what role do the supranational institutions play in the European integration process?

6. What evidence is there that 'loyalty-transfer' among the civil servants in the supranational institutions actually occurs?

7. Does the conduct of the European Court support the neo-functionalist thesis?

8. Why is it very difficult for neo-functionalism to analyse and explain (a) the rejection of the constitution by the French and Dutch voters at the referendum in 2005 or (b) the rejection of the Lisbon Treaty by the Irish voters in 2008?

GUIDE TO FURTHER READING

■ *Journal of European Public Policy*, 'The Disparity of European Integration: Revisiting Neo-functionalism in Honour of Ernst Haas', Vol. 12, No. 2, 2005. A special issue of this journal with contributions from Phillip C. Schmitter, Andrew Moravcsik, Ben Rosamond, Thomas Risse, and others. This is the latest up-to-date evaluation of neo-functionalism and its contribution to the study of European integration.

■ Moravcsik, A. *The Choice for Europe: Social Purpose and State Power from Messina to Maastricht* (London: UCL Press, 1998). The seminal text on liberal intergovernmentalism by its key proponent. It includes a very useful critique of neo-functionalism.

■ Niemann, A. *Explaining Decisions in The European Union* (Cambridge: Cambridge University Press, 2006). Niemann uses neo-functionalism to explain decision-making processes in the European Union. One of the most interesting recent attempts to use and develop neo-functionalism.

■ Sandholtz, W., and Stone Sweet, A. (eds) *European Integration and Supranational Governance* (Oxford: Oxford University Press, 1998). An edited volume which develops the notion of supranational governance, drawing on aspects of neo-functionalist theory.

■ Tranholm-Mikkelsen, J. 'Neo-functionalism: Obstinate or Obsolete? A Reappraisal in the Light of the New Dynamism of the EC', *Millennium: Journal of International Studies,* vol. 20, no. 1, 1991, pp. 1 – 22. The key reference for examining the application of neo-functionalism to the post-1985 period.

WEBLINKS

● http://globetrotter.berkeley.edu/people/Haas/haas-com0.htm   An interview with Ernst Haas a few years before his death.

Visit the Online Resource Centre that accompanies this book for lots of interesting additional material. http://www.oxfordtextbooks.co.uk/orc/Cini_Borragan3e/

6

Intergovernmentalism

MICHELLE CINI

 Chapter Contents

- Introduction
- What is intergovernmentalism?
- Hoffmann and his critics
- Beyond classical intergovernmentalism
- Liberal intergovernmentalism and its critics
- Conclusion: the future of intergovernmentalism

 Reader's Guide

This chapter provides an overview of intergovernmentalist integration theory, focusing particularly on the works of Stanley Hoffmann and Andrew Moravcsik. It first introduces the basic premises and assumptions of intergovernmentalism, identifying its realist underpinnings and the state-centrism which provides the core of the approach, before examining in more detail the specific characteristics of Hoffmann's work. The subsequent section also examines some of the ways in which intergovernmentalist thinking has contributed to different conceptualizations of European integration. The topics covered in this section are confederalism; the domestic politics approach; and institutional analyses that emphasize the 'locked-in' nature of nation states within the integration process. Last, but certainly not least, the chapter provides a brief review of Moravcsik's liberal intergovernmentalism, which since the mid 1990s has become the main focal point for intergovernmentalist research.

Introduction

From the mid 1960s to the present day, intergovernmentalism—in one shape or another—has provided students of the European Community/Union with a conceptual account of the European integration process. For decades, students of European integration learnt about the two competing approaches which explained (and in some cases predicted) the course of European integration: neofunctionalism (covered in Chapter 5) and intergovernmentalism. Although this dichotomy was supplemented by a new division, in response to the 'governance turn' (see Chapter 7), intergovernmentalism, or rather, contemporary variants of intergovernmentalism, continues to dominate much of the academic discourse on European integration. It is in this sense that one might see it still as the dominant paradigm for explaining European integration at the start of the twenty-first century, even if some researchers into EU politics might contest this claim.

This chapter provides a general introduction to the arguments and critiques of intergovernmentalist theory. It does so by focusing on the works of Stanley Hoffmann (whose early writings date from the 1960s), and Andrew Moravcsik (who began to make an impact on the field in the early 1990s). It also unpacks some of the premises and assumptions underpinning intergovernmentalist thinking. The chapter begins by addressing the question: 'What is intergovernmentalism?' This section outlines the general characteristics of the approach. The section that follows introduces Hoffmann's early ideas; this section also addresses the main criticisms of his particular brand of intergovernmentalism. Hoffmann's groundbreaking insights into the phenomenon of European integration, together with critiques of his work, led to new developments in European integration theory from the 1970s onwards. Although these might not always be termed 'intergovernmentalist' in any narrow sense of the word, they are premised upon a 'state-centrism' which owes much to Hoffmann's work. Important examples of these 'variants' of intergovernmentalism are dealt with in the remainder of the chapter. The first highlights the confederal characteristics of the European Union (EU). The second draws attention to the importance of domestic politics; while the third groups together a more institutionalist kind of research that shows how states, still central actors, become 'locked into' the European integration process. The final section—and perhaps the most crucial—looks at the work of Andrew Moravcsik and more specifically at his 'liberal intergovernmentalist' (LI) theory of European integration. Although this is an extremely rich and influential theory, LI has been widely criticized. Some of these criticisms are addressed towards the end of the chapter.

What is intergovernmentalism?

Intergovernmentalism provides a conceptual explanation of the European integration process. In this account, intergovernmentalism is characterized by its state-centrism. In other words, intergovernmentalism privileges the role of (national) states within European integration. It sees integration as a zero-sum game in which the winner takes all, claims that it is limited to policy areas that do not touch on fundamental issues of national sovereignty, and argues that 'European integration is driven by the interests and actions of nation states' (Hix 1999: 15).

Intergovernmentalism is drawn, whether explicitly or implicitly, from classical theories of international relations, and, most notably, from realist or neorealist analyses of inter-state bargaining. Realism

Intergovernmentalism as theory and method

In this chapter, intergovernmentalism is defined as a theory of European integration. What this implies is that intergovernmentalism is an approach that explains what European integration (or European cooperation) is. Intergovernmentalism may also serve as a model of European integration. This is something rather different. This sort of intergovernmentalism is prescriptive in the sense that it is likely to *advocate* reducing the role of the supranational institutions (European Commission, European Parliament, and the Courts) in favour of a greater role for the European Council and EU Council, representing national governments. It might also imply a reinstatement of unanimous voting in the Council and the repatriation of European policies to the national level.

incorporates the claim that international politics concerns the interaction of self-interested states in an anarchic environment, where there is no global authority capable of securing order (Morganthau 1985). From this perspective, states are rational, unitary actors that define their interests based on an evaluation of their position in the system of states (Rosamond 2000: 131). State interest is, therefore, primarily about survival, with other concerns, such as economic growth, of secondary importance. Thus the theory 'is centred on the view that nation states are the key actors in international affairs and the key political relations between states are channelled primarily via national governments' (Nugent 1999: 509).

Neo-realism (Waltz 1979), like realism, sees states as self-regarding actors co-existing in an anarchical system. However, it also understands that there is some potential for order, on the basis of international cooperation (see Axelrod 1984; Keohane 1988) if only as a rational means to state survival. According to neo-realists, regimes are arenas for the negotiation of zero-sum agreements, with the outcomes of those negotiations shaped by the distribution of state power within the regime. Yet, despite the promise of international cooperation, neo-realism

also makes the assumption that states have their own distinctive problems and concerns, and that they face very different internal ircumstances. This means that their policy preferences (or interests) will often fail to converge. As a consequence, any attempt to build a community *beyond the state* will be fraught with difficulties, and may even intensify the sense of difference felt across state borders. Neo-realists accept that international institutions of all kinds are established to reduce the level of anarchy within the states system, and see the European Union as just another of these institutions, albeit within a highly institutionalized setting. While neo-realists have not been particularly interested in any explicit way in European integration (yet see de Grieco 1995, 1996), their influence on intergovernmentalism is clear (Rosamond 2000: 132). It should be stressed however, that intergovernmentalism and (neo-)realism are not synonymous (Church 1996: 25).

Intergovernmentalism is not just associated with EU politics. It also refers to a type of decision making that occurs within all international organizations. International organizations are intergovernmental bodies, in that they serve as arenas in which states meet to discuss common issues, to share ideas and to negotiate agreements. They are usually based on international treaties, and membership is voluntary. They tend not to have powers of taxation, and rely therefore on member-state contributions for their operation. Generally, they do not have independent powers, and usually find it difficult to enforce decisions where individual members are recalcitrant (McCormick 2002: 4). While some international organizations stray from this model, intergovernmentalists apply this kind of framework to their understanding of the European Union, albeit with some modification.

According to intergovernmentalists, there are costs and benefits attached to involvement in European integration. (Note, however, that intergovernmentalists may prefer to talk of European *cooperation*, rather than of integration). Participation in cooperation of this kind will rest on a weighing up of the pros and cons of membership and on the extent to which European integration improves the efficiency of bargains struck among its member states. The main aim in engaging in this qualitative cost–benefit analysis is to protect their national interests.

Cooperation within the EU, then, is essentially conservative and pragmatic. It rests on the premise that common solutions are often needed to resolve common problems. To put it another way, cooperation has nothing to do with ideology or idealism, but is founded on the rational conduct of governments as they seek to deal with the policy issues that confront them in the modern world. For intergovernmentalists, European integration is normal or even 'mundane' (O'Neill 1996: 57) behaviour on the part of state actors. There is nothing particularly special about it, other than it has taken a highly institutionalized form since the 1950s. As international cooperation always occurs simultaneously on a variety of levels and taking many different forms, cooperation within the EU is deemed to be only one example of a more general phenomenon. This is why intergovernmentalists are reluctant to admit that there is a European integration *process*, as such. Rather, they see cooperation occurring in fits and starts, and not as a trend heading inexorably in one direction towards some sort of European political community or federal state.

Thus, as an institutionalized form of inter-state cooperation, European integration facilitated the survival of the West European state in the bi-polar context of the post-1945 period (see Box 6.2). It is perhaps not surprising to find, therefore, that in the early 1990s some intergovernmentalists supported the view that European integration would probably not survive the end of the Cold War (Mearsheimer 1990). Yet even if this prediction has proved inaccurate, there is no disputing that the nation state has survived (O'Neill 1996: 54).

At the heart of the intergovernmental thesis lies a particular conception of the sovereignty of national states. Sovereignty remains a very emotive word, particularly when used in the context of European Union politics. It has various meanings, holding associations with 'notions of power, authority, independence, and the exercise of will' (Nugent 1999: 502). One useful definition states that sovereignty

---

 CASE STUDY 6.2

The European rescue of the nation state

In his book *The European Rescue of the Nation State* (1992), the economic historian Alan Milward analysed European integration in the 1940s and 1950s. He argued that the European integration process in the post-1945 period 'saved' rather than undermined the nation state. Governments at this time had a number of difficult problems to resolve, arising out of increasing interdependence and increased disaffection from social actors. The successful delivery of policy programmes was a matter of survival for the states of Western Europe (Rosamond 2000: 138). European integration became a means to this end. As Rosamond (2000: 139) notes, 'The idea of integration as a progressive transfer of power away from the state managed by emerging supranational elites is given little credence by this hypothesis.' Rather, the key actors are governmental elites.

However, read in a particular way, Milward's work can be seen as challenging the standard polarization of intergovernmentalism and supranationalism. Integration does not necessarily entail the drift toward supranational statehood, and states can be seen as controlling agents with an interest in the promotion of degrees of integration (Rosamond 2000: 139).

---

implies 'the legal capacity of national decision makers to take decisions without being subject to external restraints' (Nugent 1999: 502); another claims that sovereignty is 'the right to hold and exercise authority' (McCormick 2002: 10). However, many use the word sovereignty as little more than a synonym for 'independence', and this is particularly the case in public discourse (for example, when journalists or politicians discuss sovereignty).

According to intergovernmentalism, not only are the member states deemed to be the most important actors by far, they also manage to involve themselves in European integration without ceding sovereignty. This implies that states remain very much in control of the process. Accordingly, European cooperation implies at most a *pooling* or *sharing* of sovereignty, as opposed to a *transfer* of sovereignty from the national to the supranational level (Keohane and Hoffmann 1990: 277).

Intergovernmental cooperation might also involve a delegation of sovereignty. Intergovernmentalists accept that European integration can indeed involve a transfer of functions from the state executive, and, to a lesser extent, from the parliaments of the member states, to the European institutions—to the Commission and the Court of Justice in particular. The argument is that national governments find it in their interest to hand over certain (regulatory) functions in order to make cooperation work more effectively (that is, to make the commitments they have entered into more credible). This emphasis on delegation colours how intergovernmentalists understand the role of the EU's institutions. Rather than assuming that these institutions are capable of playing an independent or autonomous role within the European integration process, intergovernmentalists tend to stress that the so-called supranational actors, the Commission in particular, are little more than the servants of the member states. While these institu-

tions may be permitted a more important role in less controversial areas of policy, the functions they perform in more sensitive policy domains is severely curtailed. The European institutions that really matter, then, are the EU Council (of national ministers) and the European Council (of heads of state and government), while the role of the other European institutions is considered much more peripheral.

> **KEY POINTS**
>
> - Intergovernmentalism has been influenced by realist and neo-realist assumptions that privilege the role of the state and national interest in explaining European integration (or cooperation).
>
> - Intergovernmentalists believe that sovereignty rests with the EU's member states, although it may be in states' interests to share/pool sovereignty and to delegate it to European-level institutions.

Hoffmann and his critics

Intergovernmentalism, as a theory of European integration, emerged in the mid 1960s, from a critique of neo-functionalist theory (see Chapter 5) and as a reaction to federalist assumptions that the European Community (EC) would eventually transform itself into a fully-fledged state. By the end of the 1960s it had become the dominant paradigm used to explain European integration, replacing the earlier neo-functionalist orthodoxy and reflecting more accurately, it seemed, the practice of European integration by that time. After the then French President General Charles de Gaulle's 'boycott' of the European institutions in mid 1965, his so-called 'empty chair policy', and the signing of the accord which came to be known as the Luxembourg Compromise in early 1966 (see Chapter 2), a tide turned in the history of European integration. The persistence of the national veto post 1966, instability in the international political economy, and institutional changes which privileged the Council of

Ministers (now the EU Council) and institutionalized the European Council as key decision makers within the Community (O'Neill 1996: 57–9), all pointed to the limits of supranationalism and to the continued primacy of state actors in European politics. That the Commission began to play a more cautious role post 1966 than it had done in the early years of the EC was also an important factor supporting the intergovernmental thesis.

It was Stanley Hoffmann who laid the foundations of the intergovernmentalist approach to European integration. Most of the state-centric variants of integration theory of the 1970s and afterwards drew on his work. Hoffmann's intergovernmentalism began by rejecting neo-functionalist theory, claiming that in concentrating on the *process* of European integration, neo-functionalists had forgotten the *context* within which it was taking place (Rosamond 2000: 76). More specifically, Hoffmann rejected neo-functionalist claims that

European integration was driven by a sort of snowball effect known as spillover (see Chapter 5), arguing that this was more an 'act of faith' than a proven fact. He stressed that international politics remained characterized by a perpetual conflict over interests (O'Neill 1996: 61).

According to Hoffmann, there was nothing inevitable about the path of European integration (Cram 1999: 60) and neither was there evidence of any political will to create a federal state in Europe (O'Neill 1996: 63). If anything, the federalist rhetoric did little more than highlight the enduring qualities of the nation state, in that it sought to replicate it on a European scale. As for neo-functionalism, not only did it ignore the global context within which European integration was occurring, he argued, it also missed the importance of cultural differences that were continuing to influence how states perceived their interests. Thus Hoffmann contrasted the idea of 'the logic of integration' against his own preferred 'logic of diversity', hammering home the point by stating that European integration involved a dialectic of fragmentation and unity (Hoffmann 1966). This diversity was a consequence of the unique context of internal domestic politics, and of global factors (that is, the situation of the state in the international system), both of which contributed to inexorable centrifugal forces placing limits on European integration (Rosamond 2000: 76).

Hoffmann's intergovernmentalism offered a 'systematic contextualization' (Rosamond 2000: 75) of the events of the mid 1960s, drawing on empirical studies of French presidential politics under President Charles de Gaulle. In this sense it was much more than just an application of realist theory to the European Community case. Indeed, Hoffmann's view was that in the post-1945 period, nation states were dealing with regional issues in very different ways than had earlier been the case. While he accepted that traditional, exclusive notions of sovereignty were now obsolete, and that there was a blurring of the boundaries between the national state and international organizations (Hoffmann 1966: 908), this did not mean that nation states and national governments had lost their significance. National sovereignty and the nation state were being tamed and altered, he argued, but the latter was not being superseded (Hoffmann 1966: 910–11); and while the national dimension may well have seemed less important in the immediate post-1945 period than it had in earlier times, it had not taken long for states to reassert themselves (Hoffmann 1995: 867–9). Indeed, national states had proven themselves extremely resilient actors in international politics (O'Neill 1996: 60). 'The nation-state is still here, and the new Jerusalem has been postponed because the nations in Western Europe have not been able to stop time and to fragment space' (Hoffmann 1966: 863). Thus, from the title of one of his best-known articles, he claimed the nation state to be 'obstinate' not 'obsolete' (Hoffmann 1966). Despite the fact that societal changes posed real challenges for the nation state, state governments remained powerful for two reasons: first, because they held legal sovereignty over their own territory; and second, because they possessed political legitimacy, as they were democratically elected (George and Bache 2001: 13).

Although he recognized the successes of European cooperation, its distinctive characteristics, and the possibility that it may produce more than zero-sum outcomes (Hoffmann 1995: 4), Hoffmann argued that the events of the 1960s highlighted the *differences* between member states as much as pointing to *common interests*. This was an important argument, since 'preference convergence' was deemed a prerequisite for European integration. Thus where states met with uncertainty, and as supranational institutions began to develop agendas of their own, national governments would respond by going their own way.

Hoffmann's starting point was the political rather than the technocratic (Rosamond 2000: 78). Crucial in this account was the distinction that he made between high and low politics. Whereas high politics (the political sphere) was said to touch on national sovereignty and issues of national identity, low politics (the economic sphere) tended to be more technocratic and much less controversial. According to Hoffmann, there were clear boundaries between more dramatic economic integration possible in areas of low politics, and the 'impermeable' and very 'political' domain of high politics (O'Neill 1996: 61), where integration would not occur. While functional spillover might occur in the former, there could be no assumption that states would allow it to be transferred to the latter.

Although Hoffmann's analysis was based very generally upon realist assumptions, he differed from realists in his approach to the concept of the state. Indeed we might say that:

> Hoffmann's intergovernmental position was more sophisticated than that of realists ... and his political awareness was also greater than that of the neo-functionalist writers who tended to adopt a rather simplified pluralist view of political processes.

(George and Bache 2001: 13).

To Hoffmann states were more than just 'black boxes'; they represented communities of identity and belonging:

> [T]hey are constructs in which ideas and ideals, precedents and political experiences and domestic forces and rulers all play a role.

(Hoffmann 1995: 5).

Hoffmann was particularly critical of the earlier theorists of European integration who had adopted a simplistic and unrealistic view of how governments defined their interests. He argued that these interests were not reducible to power and place alone (Hoffmann 1995: 5), but were calculated on the basis of various historical, cultural, and indeed political concerns.

However, Hoffmann's intergovernmentalism has been subject to a number of critiques. Many of these involved a rejection of his rigid demarcation between high and low politics (O'Neill 1996: 65). Even in the 1970s, there were claims that the existence of European Political Cooperation (EPC), the forerunner to today's European foreign policy (see Chapter 15), and an area of 'high politics', seemed to disprove this particular aspect of his theory. Similarly, recent events, most notably the establishment of the

single currency and the common foreign and security policy, point in that direction as well. Indeed, since the 1960s, Hoffmann has softened his line on this issue, accepting that there are limits to the usefulness of the traditional distinction between low and high politics.

Hoffmann was also criticized for playing down the constraints imposed on states as a consequence of their increasing 'interdependence' (O'Neill 1996: 65; see Box 6.3). Moreover, it was argued that he failed to take into consideration the novelty and the complexity of the European integration project. The EC, it was claimed, was about more than just the creation of a regional regime, and bargains struck at European level could not simply be reduced to a set of national interests (Rosamond 2000: 79).

 KEY CONCEPTS AND TERMS 6.3

Interdependence and intergovernmentalism

Interdependence theory emerged in the 1970s, its key proponents being Robert Keohane and Joseph Nye (1975). Its main influence on intergovernmentalism was to set it in a broader context than had earlier been the case. It was argued that 'Many of the factors that have influenced ... [the] development [of the EC] have applied to it alone, but many have not' (Nugent 1999: 511). In other words, in many instances what we might consider to be the effects of European integration are really the effects of a much wider phenomenon. Changes to the international political economy—international modernization in particular—have led to greater and greater levels of interdependence, and these have changed the way in which states and other non-state actors relate to each other in the international sphere (Nugent 1999: 511).

While interdependence theory cannot really be considered a discrete theory of European integration, it does add to our understanding of the background conditions that facilitate or constrain the integration process, and helps to make the point that the EC might not be quite as unique as some (such as the neo-functionalists) have claimed. While it highlights the fact that states may not always be able to act unconstrained within the international system, it is best viewed as a response to a rather specific weakness in intergovernmentalism, rectified by an increasing emphasis on the global dimension.

While Hoffmann's intergovernmentalism was not a theory in any systematic sense (Church 1996: 26), but was, rather, part of an approach which dealt with the wider phenomenon of regional cooperation, it was extremely influential in shaping the way scholars of European integration thought about the (then) European Community. As such it set the agenda for future research undertaken in the field of integration theory from the 1970s onwards. Thus, accepting the limits of Hoffmann's approach as it was constructed in the 1960s did not mean opting for a supranational theory of integration. Rather, it allowed the door to be opened to new variants of intergovernmentalism, some of which are dealt with in the section that follows.

KEY POINTS

- Stanley Hoffmann was the key proponent of intergovernmentalism in the mid 1960s. His work on French, European, and international politics led him to critique the work of the neo-functionalists.

- Hoffmann distinguished between high and low politics, arguing that while functional integration might be possible in less controversial areas (the economic sphere), states would resist any incursion into areas of high politics (the political sphere).

- Critics have questioned Hoffmann's use of the high/low politics distinction, based on empirical evidence (such as recent moves towards foreign policy integration) and for not taking into consideration the novelty and the complexity of the European integration project. However, his approach has been extremely influential.

Beyond classical intergovernmentalism

This section presents some examples of how Hoffmann's intergovernmentalism has been supplemented and adapted since the 1960s. While setting aside for the moment the most important example of this adaptation (liberal intergovernmentalism), which is dealt with later in the chapter, this section first deals with confederalism; second, with the 'domestic politics approach' to European integration; and finally with a number of analyses that have sought to explain how states become locked into the European integration process.

Confederalism

As a model or framework for European integration, the idea of confederation (Forsyth 1981) seems closely allied to intergovernmentalism. A confederation may be viewed as a particular type of intergovernmental arrangement, in which national sovereignty remains intact despite the establishment of a common institutional framework (O'Neill 1996: 71). O'Neill calls it the antithesis of federalism, a concert of sovereign states. Wallace stresses that there must be no assumption that confederation will lead ultimately to unity. Rather, it implies that the 'Community is stuck, between sovereignty and integration' (W. Wallace 1982: 65).

Confederal approaches draw attention to the institutionalized nature of the European integration process, recognizing (in contrast to intergovernmentalism) its distinctiveness. Along similar lines, Paul Taylor (1975) has argued that confederation (or confederalism) is a helpful supplement to intergovernmentalism, allowing us to move beyond its inherent constraints, while retaining its state-centric core. In this respect, Wallace points to the importance of supranational/international law in differentiating confederalism from intergovernmentalism. Taylor puts it rather differently. He suggests that '[t]he salient feature of confederal Europe is that the scope of integration is extensive ... but the level of integration is low' (Taylor 1975: 343). Moreover '[t]he Europe of this Confederal phase of integration is ... decentralized but highly interdependent, potentially autarchic but in practice united by intense practices of consultation' (Taylor 1975: 343). It is also characterized, he claims, by the defensive posture of national governments against the further extension of the powers of supranational actors, by an interpenetration of European politics into the domestic sphere, and by an oscillation between advanced proposals for integration and retreats into national independence. Much of this argument is state-centric, with Taylor arguing that the nation state is likely to be strengthened through confederation. As such it adds to intergovernmentalist understandings of European integration by characterizing the framework within which cooperation and integration take place.

The domestic politics approach

In the 1970s and 1980s, an approach that focused on domestic politics and policy making became fashionable in the field of European integration studies. Although not a theory of European integration per se, the approach was critical of intergovernmentalism's failure to capture the transnational nature of the EC policy process (Church 1996: 26) and sought, as a consequence, to focus attention on the impact of domestic politics on EC policy making (Bulmer 1983). In this we can identify the origins of what today would be called the 'Europeanization' literature (see Chapter 25). We might also see this approach as one that links Hoffmann's intergovernmentalism to later state-centric research projects—and particularly to liberal intergovernmentalism (Rosamond 2000: 76).

The idea behind the domestic politics approach was that it was said to be impossible to understand the European Community without taking domestic politics into consideration (Bulmer 1983). Thus Bulmer sought to identify the domestic determinants of preference formation (Rosamond 2000: 80). One way of doing this was to undertake in-depth case studies of the European policy process, which allowed researchers to establish variations in patterns of policy making, emphasizing the linkages between the national and supranational dimensions of European politics. Bulmer was particularly interested in two dimensions of domestic politics: policy-making structures and attitudes towards the EC (Bulmer 1983).

There are a number of elements involved in this approach, which when taken together provide a framework for analysing the behaviour of member states. First, the national polity was considered the basic unit of the EC/EU. Second, each national polity was acknowledged to be different in terms of its unique socio-economic characteristics; and it was these differences that shaped national interests. Third, European policy was deemed to be only one facet of national political activity. Fourth, the national polity lay at the juncture of national and European politics. And finally, an important lens through which one might understand these elements was that of the 'policy style' concept (Bulmer 1983: 360).

The importance of the domestic politics approach is that it demonstrated how intergovernmentalists had failed to look in any coherent way *within* the member states when analysing the European integration process (Bulmer 1983). Although it was stated earlier in this chapter that intergovernmentalism is closely related to (neo-)realism in international relations, newer variants of intergovernmentalism have also been greatly influenced by neo-liberal ideas. Neo-liberalism, as an approach to the study of international relations, is concerned with the *formation* of state preferences (Rosamond 2000: 135) or 'national interests'. Whereas neo-realism is focused exclusively on politics between nations, neo-liberalism draws attention to the content of the 'black box' of domestic politics and tries to address from where national interests originate. It therefore places the national polity, rather than just national executives, or governments, at the heart of the European integration project. Although the influence of neo-liberal ideas in the domestic politics approach may not be explicit or direct, the concerns are very much the same. This is a point that will be picked up again when we come to look at the work of Andrew Moravcsik.

The 'locking-in' of states

As a more recent example of how intergovernmentalism has evolved, a number of analyses explain how states have become *locked into* the European integration process. These draw heavily on a particularly German approach to the study of federalism, in which 'interlocking politics' (*Politikverflectung*), characterizes interactions between different levels of government (Risse-Kappen 1996: 60–1). While these approaches rest on state-centric premises, they move quite far beyond classical intergovernmentalism and show how European integration is about much more than inter-state bargains. In the process, they emphasize the importance of institutional factors (see Chapter 7) and show how intergovernmentalist ideas may provide a starting point from which new arguments about and analyses of the European integration process develop.

Wolfgang Wessels (1997) has advanced an argument about European integration that rests soundly on state-centric premises in that it sees national interests as the primary driving force of integration. It also, however, links 'integration processes to the evolution of the state' (Wessels 1997: 274–5). He called this his 'fusion thesis'. In this approach, Wessels argues that after 1945, West European states became increasingly responsible for the welfare of their citizens, enhancing their legitimacy as a consequence. But for the welfare state to persist, national economies needed to be strong. In order to maintain economic growth to this end, states recognized the need to open up their markets, which led governments to rely more and more on the joint management of shared policy problems. This is what Wessels means when he talks of the 'fusion' of the West European states (1997: 273)—in essence a 'merger of public resources located at several state levels whereby steering instruments are increasingly used in concert' (Wessels 1997: 274). This amounts to much more than a pooling of sovereignties. As states have become more interdependent, they have

lost the ability to act autonomously, blurring the lines of accountability and responsibility that connect citizens to the state. He claims that it is increasingly difficult to reverse these trends without drastic action being taken.

Also grounded in state-centrism, Fritz Scharpf (1988) drew an analogy between German federalism and the European Community. He did this to explain how European integration has become almost irreversible because of the intense institutionalization to which it has been subject. Like Wessels, Scharpf focuses on how EC decision making offered states the ability to solve problems jointly. He argues, however, that the outcomes of these decisions are likely to be suboptimal, in that they do not emerge from any assessment of the best available solutions, but are reached through a process of bargaining which inevitably leads to compromises being struck. In other words, as national interests determine policy positions, creative (and rational) problem solving is not possible (Scharpf 1988: 255). As such, no member state is likely to be entirely satisfied by what the process of integration has to offer. This is something that will contribute over time to the slowing down of European integration. Yet the institutionalization of the decision-making process means that retreating from integration is not an option. As such, states are trapped in a Community from which they cannot escape, in a paradox characterized by Scharpf as 'frustration without disintegration and resilience without progress' (Scharpf 1988: 256), which he labels a 'joint decision trap'.

More recently, historical institutionalists have sought to explain how states become locked into the European integration process through a process of path dependence. The argument, advocated by Paul Pierson (1998) amongst others, is that the more states integrate, the more future options become constrained (see Chapter 7). While this does not imply an inevitability about the 'process' of integration, it does mean that the only way of escaping from further integration is by provoking a dramatic break with past practice, a so-called 'critical juncture'.

KEY POINTS

- Confederalism complements intergovernmentalism, by acknowledging the institutionalized character of the European Community.

- The domestic politics approach claimed that it is impossible to study European integration without looking at policy making within the member states.

- Wessels's fusion thesis, Scharpf's joint decision trap and Pierson's path dependence explain how states have, over time, become locked into the European integration process.

Liberal intergovernmentalism and its critics

In 1988, Robert Putnam published an influential article in which he explored the dynamics of domestic and international politics using the metaphor of 'two-level games' (Putnam 1988). To explain this concept we need to understand that 'two-level games' are played by states. The first game deals with how states define their policy preferences (or national interest) at home within the domestic environment. The second game is played on the international stage and involves the striking of inter-state bargains.

Putnam's core point is that national executives play games in two arenas more or less simultaneously. At the domestic level, power-seeking/enhancing office holders aim to build coalitions of support among domestic groups. At the international level, the same actors seek to bargain in ways that enhance their positions domestically by meeting the demands of key domestic constituents (Rosamond 2000: 136).

Putnam's main aim was that of providing a framework for analysing the myriad entanglements involved in domestic–international interactions (Putnam 1988: 433). This image of the two-level game is helpful in that it provides a starting point for understanding Moravcsik's influential theory of liberal intergovernmentalism (LI).

Moravcsik's Liberal Intergovernmentalism

Since the early 1990s, Andrew Moravcsik's theory of liberal intergovernmentalism has become one of—if not the—most important account of the European integration process. It has become a touchstone against which all integration theory is now judged, 'a model of parsimony and clarity' (Risse-Kappen 1996: 63), even for those who do not agree with its assumptions, its methods, or its conclusions. Drawing on and developing earlier intergovernmentalist insights, it offers a theoretical approach that is much more rigorous than its antecedents (George and Bache 2001: 13), incorporating within it both realist and neo-liberal elements (Rosamond 2000: 136), and dealing explicitly with the interface between domestic and international politics. It was 'initially presented as a framework for synthesizing theories into a coherent account of large EU decisions taken under unanimity, though it can be applied to other types of decisions as well' (Dinan 2000: 280).

The European Union is identified as a successful intergovernmental regime designed to manage economic interdependence through negotiated policy coordination. The theory is based on assumptions drawn from the 'rational actor model', in that it assumes that states behave rationally, 'which means that the actions of states are assumed to be based on utilizing what are judged to be the most appropriate means of achieving their goals' (Nugent 1999: 509). In true intergovernmentalist fashion, LI emphasizes the importance of the *preferences* and *power* of states. While national politicians embody state interests that reflect domestic policy preferences, all decisions made by the EU are ultimately the result of bargaining amongst states. Agreements are (usually) reached on a lowest-common-denominator basis, with clear limits placed on the transfer of sovereignty to supranational agents. Thus, according to Moravcsik, '[t]he broad lines of European integration since 1955 reflect three factors: patterns of commercial advantage, the relative bargaining power of important governments, and the incentives to enhance the credibility of inter-state commitment' (Moravcsik 1998: 3). When economic or commercial concerns converge, integration takes place.

There are two separate dimensions to LI: the supply side and the demand side. The argument is that both the *demand* for cooperation, which derives from the national polity, and the *supply* of integration,

arising out of inter-state negotiations, are important in understanding European integration outcomes. To explain the link between the demand and supply sides, the theory is divided into three steps, each of which is explained by a different set of factors (and drawing on different theories): economic interest; relative power; and credible commitments (Moravcsik 1998: 4).

First, drawing on liberal theories of *national preference formation*, and applying a domestic politics approach, Moravcsik shows how 'state goals can be shaped by domestic pressures and interactions which in turn are often conditioned by the constraints and opportunities that derive from economic interdependence' (Nugent 1999: 509). Thus he identifies underlying societal factors that provoke an international demand for cooperation. National political institutions are subject to myriad pressures from nationally based interests, provoking a process of preference formation. State preferences are formed, and these feed into inter-state negotiations, as groups compete with each other for the attention of government elites. To put it another way, policy preferences at national level are constrained by the interests of dominant, usually economic, groups within society. Resting on a very

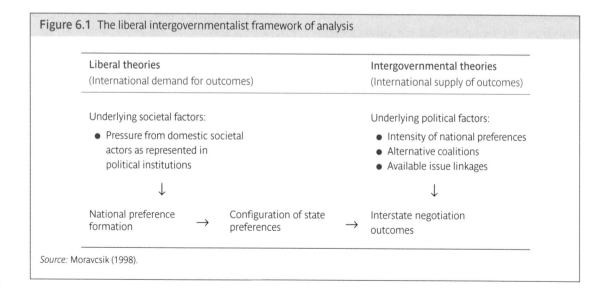

Figure 6.1 The liberal intergovernmentalist framework of analysis

Liberal theories (International demand for outcomes)	Intergovernmental theories (International supply of outcomes)
Underlying societal factors: • Pressure from domestic societal actors as represented in political institutions	Underlying political factors: • Intensity of national preferences • Alternative coalitions • Available issue linkages
↓	↓
National preference formation → Configuration of state preferences	→ Interstate negotiation outcomes

Source: Moravcsik (1998).

pluralistic understanding of state–society relations, national governments end up representing these interests in international forums. Thus Moravcsik sees national interests as derived from the domestic politics of the member states and not the 'sovereign state's perception of its relative position in the states system' (Rosamond 2000: 137), that is, from geo-political concerns. As Moravcsik has claimed: 'the vital interest behind General de Gaulle's opposition to British membership in the EC ... was not the pursuit of French *grandeur* but the price of French wheat (Moravcsik 1998: 7).

The second and supply-side strand of LI is based on *intergovernmentalist theories of inter-state relations*, with European integration supplied by inter-governmental bargains (such as treaty reforms) (Moravcsik 1998: 7). This part of LI 'draws on general theories of bargaining and negotiation to argue that relative power among states is shaped above all by asymmetrical interdependence, which dictates the relative value of agreement to different governments' (Moravcsik 1998: 7). Thus, this second element in the theory emphasizes the centrality of strategic bargaining among states and the importance of governmental elites in shaping inter-state relations. At this point, states are considered as unitary actors, and supranational institutions are deemed to have a very limited impact on outcomes. In other words, the theory focuses mainly on the European and EU Councils. This generally involves a two-stage process of negotiation. First governments must resolve the policy problems that confront them, taking decisions to that effect; and only second do they try to reach agreement on institutional mechanisms that would allow them to implement those decisions. The process by which states engage in inter-state bargaining is important. Various strategies and techniques, such as 'coalitional alternatives to agreement', the linking of issues and threats of exclusion and inclusion, shape outcomes. A bargaining space (a sort of window of opportunity) is formed out of the amalgamation of national interests, with the final agreement determining the distribution of gains and losses. This points to the restrictive range of possible integration outcomes. Yet Moravcsik accepts that inter-state bargains can lead on occasion to positive-sum outcomes (Hix 1999: 15). As a consequence, governments will bargain hard to gain the upper hand. Not surprisingly, the power of individual states is very important in determining whose interests matter. And as such Moravcsik focuses his attention largely on the preferences of the largest EU states: UK, France, and Germany. In stressing the point that integration *benefits* states, that states face few constraints in the Council, and that inter-state negotiations enhance their domestic autonomy, the issues of why governments engage in European integration when it might otherwise seem like an irrational thing to do is addressed by this part of the theory (Rosamond 2000: 138).

The third element within LI is that of *institutional delegation*. The argument here is that international (European) institutions are set up to improve the efficiency of inter-state bargaining. 'To secure the substantive bargains they had made ... governments delegated and pooled sovereignty in international institutions for the express purpose of committing one another to cooperate' (Moravcsik 1998: 3–4). Thus, the European institutions create linkages and compromises across issues, where decisions have been made under conditions of uncertainty, and where non-compliance would be a temptation. In other words, institutional delegation reflects the desire for 'credible commitments'.

In this respect Moravcsik's work has been influenced by the liberal institutionalism of Robert Keohane (1989). Keohane views institutions as ways of facilitating positive-sum bargaining ('upgrading the common interest') among states, but claims that there is no evidence that supranational institutions bias the outcomes of decisions away from the longer-term self-interest of the member states (Rosamond 2000: 143). In line with this sort of thinking, according to Moravcsik, 'The entrepreneurship of supranational officials ... tends to be futile and redundant, even sometimes counterproductive (Moravcsik 1998: 8).

CASE STUDY 6.4

Moravcsik's five case studies

In his book *The Choice for Europe*, Andrew Moravcsik applies his theory of liberal intergovernmentalism to five cases in the history of the European integration process.

The five cases are:

1. The negotiation of the Treaty of Rome (1955–8)

2. The consolidation of the common market and the Common Agricultural Policy (CAP) (1958–69)

3. Monetary Cooperation and the setting up of the European Monetary System (EMS) (1969–83)

4. The negotiation of the Single European Act (SEA) (1984–8)

5. The negotiation of the Treaty on European Union (TEU) (1988–91).

In each case, Moravcsik—drawing on secondary historical and some documentary sources—argues that what was important in driving elite support for European integration was national economic interest. This line of argument was contrary to conventional wisdom usually put forward by historians at the time that geopolitical factors were what mattered most in explaining European integration. Moravcsik makes the case that geopolitics, such as France's pursuit of a policy of *grandeur*, though not irrelevant, were merely a secondary consideration as national governments established their bargaining positions on history-making decisions.

Together, these three elements result in integration outcomes (treaty change, for example). Applying the theory to actual cases in the history of European integration, Moravcsik came to the following conclusions. First, he concluded that the major choices made in favour of European integration were a reflection of the preferences of national governments and not of supranational organizations. Second, he stressed that these national preferences reflected a balance of domestic economic interests, rather than any political bias of politicians or national strategic security concerns. Finally, he stressed that the outcomes of the negotiations reflected the relative bargaining power of the states,

and that the delegation of decision-making authority to supranational institutions reflected the wishes of governments to ensure that commitments made were adhered to (George and Bache 2001: 14). In short, Moravcsik is arguing that: 'European integration can best be explained as a series of rational choices made by national leaders' (Moravcsik 1998: 18).

Critiques of Liberal Intergovernmentalism

Although Moravcsik's theory of liberal intergovernmentalism (LI) has been subject to criticism, there is no doubt that it remains an extremely useful way to organize data and to construct empirical studies. At the same time, it presents a serious challenge for competing models that seek to explain the European integration process (Rosamond 2000: 145). This is largely because liberal intergovernmentalism has been said to offer an 'almost uncompromising framework' (Nugent 1999: 510), which can be hard, if not impossible, to reconcile with alternative interpretations of European integration and EU politics.

Perhaps the most often repeated criticism of LI is that it simply does not fit the facts. This tends to be argued on the basis of empirical analyses and specific case studies of EU politics. This is, however, part of a related criticism, which is that Moravcsik's work has too narrow a focus to be called a theory of European integration, as it is 'too selective with his empirical references when seeking to demonstrate the validity of ... [the] framework in the EU context' (Nugent 1999: 510). In other words, thus far liberal intergovernmentalism has been applied only to those cases that will (almost inevitably) result in proving that the theory is correct. It has been claimed by Scharpf (1999: 165), for example, that applying the theory to cases of *intergovernmental negotiation*, where economic integration is the main concern and where decisions were taken on the basis of unanimous voting in the Council, will invariably lead to the conclusions that Moravcsik reaches. 'Given this focus for his attention, it is hardly surprising that Moravcsik comes to the view that the EC is primarily motivated by the aggregation and conciliation of national interests' (Wincott 1995: 602). However, in 'harder' cases, where international negotiations are not the primary form of decision taking, and where majority voting applies, LI may not produce such clear-cut results.

The critique is often set out in the following way: that Moravcsik's theory may well apply for the majority of 'history-making' decisions (Peterson 1995) which deal with the future of European integration: that is, high profile policy steps of major constitutional significance, which often involve treaty change and occur through inter-state negotiations (Wincott 1995: 602). However, LI is much less able to explain the way in which the EU works in matters of day-to-day politics.

The second criticism that is often made of Moravcsik's work is that his conception of the state is a rather narrow one. Liberal intergovernmentalism pays little attention to the way in which the 'state' may be broken down into its component parts. Critics argue that in order to understand fully how governmental positions (or preferences) are determined (Nugent 1999: 510), a more subtle analysis of domestic politics is required. Indeed, as George and Bache (2001: 14) claim: '... in some ways it [LI] was less sophisticated in its account of domestic politics than was that suggested by Hoffmann'. In Moravcsik's pluralist or liberal view, the primary determinant of government preferences is the balance between *economic* interests (George and Bache 2001: 14). But in practice, there is a huge range of diverse influences that are likely to impinge on national preference formation. Risse-Kappen (1996: 63) points, for example, to the potential importance of the impact of domestic structures. On this basis, Moravcsik's account is too simplistic when it focuses solely on economic and (to a lesser extent) geo-political concerns (Wincott 1995: 600–1). Moreover, it is argued that the two-level game metaphor does not depict the reality of EU politics today—and that the EU is now much more of a multi-level than a two-level polity (see Chapter 7).

Third, and highly important as a critique of liberal intergovernmentalism, is that the theory understates the constraints faced by key policy makers. The case of the single market programme is often used to back up this argument. There are, however, a number of dimensions to this general critique. First, it is frequently argued that Moravcsik plays down to too great an extent the role of supranational actors within the European integration process. In other words, he does not provide a full enough account of the supply side of his model when focusing solely on inter-state negotiations. As the roles of the European Commission and the European Court of Justice (ECJ) are deemed relatively unimportant, if not entirely irrelevant in terms of policy outcomes, their interests and strategies do not figure particularly strongly in Moravcsik's work. This assumption about the supranational institutions' potential influence over integration outcomes (even at times in history-making decisions) has been contested by many academics.

Moravcsik's portrayal of the Commission as exercising a role of little more than a facilitator in respect of significant decision making has attracted particular criticism, with numerous empirically based studies claiming to show that the Commission does exercise an independent and influential decision making role, be it as *animateur*, a policy entrepreneur, or a motor force (Nugent 1999: 510–11).

Cram (1994), for example, has provided empirical evidence of how the Commission has been able to influence policy outcomes, by means of its policy entrepreneurship. Wincott (1994) and Burley and Mattli (1993) have highlighted the ECJ's impact on European integration through its innovative legal rulings in cases such as those pertaining to human rights (see also Chapter 11). Pollack's analysis (1997a) has shown how, despite the fact that supranational institutions tend to operate within the boundaries set by member state preferences, they are able to exploit the differences between these preferences in order to promote their own independent agendas. As Rosamond (2000: 143) points out, this adds an institutional dimension to intergovernmentalism, whilst retaining many of its core characteristics.

A similar point also applies to non-state 'transnational' actors, such as European firms and European interest groups. Cowles (1995) has demonstrated, for example, the importance of business groups in the 1980s in influencing the single market project (see also Chapter 16). While she accepts that these groups were not the sole cause of the '1992' programme:

> [I]ntergovernmental theory cannot explain the activities of the key non-state actors in the 1992 process. The single market programme was not merely the result of conventional statecraft. Nor were Member States' actions predicated solely on the basis of domestically defined interest group activity, as suggested by a recent version of intergovernmentalism [LI] ... Indeed, the story of the ERT [European Round Table of Industrialists] points to the fact that non-state actors—and in particular, multinational enterprises—also play two-level games in EC policy making

(Cowles 1995: 521–2).

This point is not just about which actors and institutions matter in the process of European decision making. It also reflects Moravcsik's emphasis on the more formal aspects of that process, at the expense of the informal, 'behind-the-scenes' dimension. If informal politics matter in shaping policy outcomes, this may mean that actors who appear on the surface to be responsible for decision taking may not really be in control of the process. As Wincott has stated—again of the single market case—'... the basic, innovative policy techniques required for the internal market programme had been fashioned in the daily work of the supranational institutions long before the Member States considered these issues' (1995: 606). As such, the substance of inter-state negotiations had already been framed well before intergovernmental conferences and European summits met to take their formal decisions (see also Box 6.5, which argues some similar points from the perspective of a number of different cases).

Finally, Wincott has criticized LI for not being a theory, at least in his understanding of the term. He makes this claim, as he believes that a rigorous theory ought to spell out the conditions under which it might be refuted or disproved. Wincott argues that

 CASE STUDY 6.5

The Maastricht Treaty and the UK's bargaining position: a critique of liberal intergovernmentalism

In an interesting article published in 1998, Anthony Forster sought to test the liberal intergovernmentalist (LI) thesis in three policy cases, each of which relates to the UK's role in the negotiation of the Maastricht Treaty (Forster 1998). The three dossiers covered in the article were (a) social policy; (b) foreign and security policy; and (c) increasing the powers of the European Parliament. The article, which is grounded in the empirical study of the three cases, casts doubt on LI's explanation of national preference formation. It also questions the extent to which governments always act as purposive and instrumental actors; whilst challenging the LI conception of bargaining.

Moreover, in a critical final paragraph, Forster states that:

... this article can only conclude by expressing serious doubts about LI's ambitious claim to provide a parsimonious predictive and explanatory theory. From a methodological perspective, the theoretical approach is simply too complex, often requiring unknowable or nonexistent information, to provide a 'toolkit' for explaining and predicting the actions of governments (Anderson 1995). Above all, however, LI's empirical foundations are weak. In particular its inadequate conceptualization of the state raises very large question marks over the value of an approach consciously 'derived independently of the matter being studied', rather than based on empirical evidence (Moravcsik 1993: 477). In the final analysis, LI is thus perhaps best regarded less as a theory of intergovernmental bargaining, than as pre-theory or analytical framework. It provides some very useful insights but, as empirical testing proves, it must be supplemented by other models in order to explain fully how and why a government chooses among various outcomes. Similarly, other models are needed to explain the determinants of politicians' choices among competing alternatives. The irony is that, like neo-functionalism, LI's aspiration to generality ultimately renders it 'oddly apolitical' (Moravcsik 1993: 477).

Source: Forster (1998).

LI does not do this, but engages in an act of closure on certain types of argument about European integration. As such, he claims that LI should be considered an 'approach' rather than a theory—one which brings together three existing theories (preference formation, intergovernmental bargaining, and institutional delegation) to provide a 'pre-theory' or 'analytical framework' (Forster 1998: 365) that can be applied to the European integration process. Not surprisingly, these points, along with all the others mentioned above, are vehemently rejected by Moravcsik.

KEY POINTS

- Liberal intergovernmentalism provides a tripartite explanation of integrative outcomes: as national preference formation; inter-state bargaining; and institutional delegation.

- The theory supplements a rich account of bargaining inside the Council, with a concern for how national interests (or preferences) are formed. Moravcsik argues that it is mainly powerful domestic economic interests that determine national interest.

- Moravcsik is criticized for focusing only on 'history-making decisions' (treaty change in particular) and for ignoring day-to-day politics and the multi-level character of the European Union.

Conclusion: The future of intergovernmentalism

This chapter has reviewed the general approach to European integration known as 'intergovernmentalism'. Associated in its classical form with the work of Stanley Hoffmann, the chapter has shown how intergovernmentalist premises (and more specifically, state-centrism) have provided the foundations for a range of theories and models that have sought to specify the structure of the EC, the nature of decision making, and the 'locking-in' of states within the European integration process. Andrew Moravcsik's work now provides the core of the intergovernmentalist thesis, one that allies intergovernmentalism to neo-liberalism.

But what future might we imagine for intergovernmentalism? While it continues to provide inspiration for scholars of European integration, new developments within the study of the European Union have tested the resilience of intergovernmentalist arguments. Yet intergovernmentalism has been flexible enough to adapt to new conditions and new theories that appear to resonate with today's European integration process, whether in the form of Moravcsik's 'liberal' variant of the theory, or in Schimmelfennig's account of liberal intergovernmentalism as a partial explanation of the enlargement case (2004) (see Box 6.5). As we shall see in the next chapter, there are many who contest the (liberal) intergovernmentalist account of European integration. But for anyone wishing to study the EU, it makes an important contribution to our understanding of what European integration is or might be.

QUESTIONS

1.   How plausible are intergovernmentalist accounts of European integration?

2.   Why do you think Andrew Moravcsik's theory of liberal intergovernmentalism has been so influential?

3.   What are the main critiques of liberal intergovernmentalism?

4.   How useful a model for explaining the EU is confederalism?

5.   What are the main elements of Stanley Hoffmann's intergovernmentalism?

6.   How central is the nation state within the process of European integration?

7.   In what sense and to what extent is European integration a 'mundane' affair?

8.   How might Moravcsik respond to recent critiques of his liberal intergovernmentalism?

 GUIDE TO FURTHER READING

■ Hoffmann, S. *The European Sisyphus. Essays on Europe 1964–1994* (Oxford: Westview Press, 1995). An excellent collection of Stanley Hoffmann's work, showing how his ideas have changed (or not) over the years. Includes seminal articles published in the 1960s which set the scene for future intergovernmentalist writings.

■ Moravcsik, A. *The Choice for Europe. Social Purpose and State Power from Messina to Maastricht* (London: UCL Press, 1998). The seminal liberal intergovernmentalist book. Chapter 1 'Theorizing European Integration' covers both a critique of neo-functionalism and sets out the characteristics of LI in some detail.

■ O'Neill, M. *The Politics of European Integration. A Reader* (London: Routledge, 1996), Chapter 4. Ostensibly a 'reader', but also includes a useful chapter on state-centric approaches to European integration.

■ Rosamond, B. *Theories of European Integration* (Basingstoke: Macmillan, 2000), Chapter 6. The most recent, overarching text on European integration theory, with numerous references to intergovernmentalism, and a specific chapter devoted to 'Intergovernmental Europe'.

■ Schimmelfennig, F. 'Liberal Intergovernmentalism' in A. Wiener and T. Diez (eds) *European Integration Theory* (Oxford: Oxford University Press, 2004). An interesting chapter on liberal intergovernmentalism, which uses enlargement as a case study for how LI and social constructivism (see Chapter 7) might enter into a dialogue.

 WEBLINKS

● http://eiop.or.at/erpa/   European Research Papers Archive. A collection of online working papers relating to EU studies, where much innovative theoretical work is showcased for the first time.

● www.princeton.edu/~amoravcs   Andrew Moravcsik's home page. Includes access to published and forthcoming papers.

 Visit the Online Resource Centre that accompanies this book for lots of interesting additional material. http://www.oxfordtextbooks.co.uk/orc/Cini_Borragan3e/

7 New Theories of European Integration

BEN ROSAMOND

Chapter Contents

- Introduction
- The limits of the classical debate
- Institutionalism and the EU
- Theories of policy making and the EU
- Multi-level governance
- Social constructivist approaches to the EU
- International relations and international political economy revisited
- Conclusion

Reader's Guide

This chapter deals with recent theoretical work on the European Union. It concentrates upon approaches which, in various ways, seek to depart from the established theoretical positions established by neo-functionalism (see Chapter 5) and intergovernmentalism (see Chapter 6). This chapter commences with a discussion of how 'newer' approaches identify the limitations of the 'classical' debate. Much of this discussion hinges on how analysts characterize the EU. For many the EU is best conceived of as a political system, which suggests that the theoretical tools of conventional political science and policy analysis might have greater explanatory power than approaches from the discipline of International Relations (IR). To explore the plausibility of this proposition, this chapter discusses in turn the contribution to EU studies of new institutionalist political science (see new institutionalism), approaches from policy analysis, the idea of multi-level governance, and constructivism. The chapter also explores how IR theories might be brought back into EU studies. The purpose of the chapter, aside from introducing the contemporary theoretical repertoire in EU studies, is to show how the EU raises significant questions about the nature of authority, statehood, and the organization of the international system in the contemporary period.

Introduction

Much of the academic work on the European Union remains under the spell of the classical debate between neo-functionalism and intergovernmentalism (see Chapters 5 and 6). There is a rationale for continuing to explore the opposition between these two schools. Thinking in this way forces us to address key issues of continuity versus change in European politics. Does the growth of the EU imply the transcendence of the European nation-state system? If so, does this bring to the fore a new group of activist supranational institutions and confirm the rise to prominence of powerful non-state actors?

Alternatively, are the member states the key actors in this process and are the EU's key dynamics intergovernmental? These rival academic discourses have their equivalents in the policy world. The strategy of the founding fathers of integration (such as Jean Monnet and Robert Schuman) has often been thought of as 'neo-functionalist', while politicians still tend to use a vocabulary that is underwritten by statist and intergovernmentalist assumptions.

However, recent years have witnessed concerted attempts to 'think otherwise' about the EU. This chapter deals with these new theoretical approaches. It is worth pausing for thought to consider what 'new' might mean in this context. The term implies, after all, that some theories are old or perhaps redundant. In particular, many academics who offer new theoretical prospectuses tend to begin with the proposition that the classical terms of debate—as represented by the rivalry between neo-functionalism and intergovernmentalism—fail to capture adequately what is going on in the contemporary European Union. This chapter is attentive to this premise and begins with a deeper discussion of its soundness as a proposition for theoretical departure.

This discussion alerts us to the importance of thinking carefully about theoretical work. Theory is not simply a self-indulgent exercise. Nor can it be side-stepped by any serious student of the EU.

Rather, being conscious about the theoretical propositions chosen by authors is vital, because alternative readings of the EU and European integration follow from alternative theoretical premises. That said, writers rarely (these days at least) attempt to construct 'grand theories' of integration. Instead, since the 1970s, they have tended to build theories to aid understanding and explanation of elements of (a) the integration process and (b) EU governance. Even the direct descendants of neo-functionalism and intergovernmentalism have limited ambitions. For example, Sandholtz and Stone Sweet's theory (1998) of supranational governance explicitly 'brackets' (that is, sets aside) the origins of the EU, because the theory has no way of explaining this. Moreover, Moravcsik (2001) has emphasized that his liberal intergovernmentalism is not intended to be a comprehensive theory of European integration, but rather a theory of intergovernmental bargaining only.

These caveats still do not bypass the objection that the old neo-functionalist–intergovernmentalist debate fails to capture highly significant attributes of the present EU. The principal objection, explored in the first substantive section of this chapter, is that 'old' theories are rooted in an outdated conception of what the EU is. However, we need to be aware that the study of the EU is not something that simply ebbs and flows with the real-world development of European integration and the evolution of the European Union. It is also—and perhaps more predominantly—bound up with the developments in social scientific fashion. Many scholars think about this in terms of theoretical 'progress'—that is, as social science in general and political science in particular 'improve' their techniques, so we can expect objects of study such as the European Union to be treated more rigorously than hitherto. The alleged consequence is that theoretical advancement delivers more robust and reliable results, thereby advancing our empirical knowledge of the EU.

KEY CONCEPTS AND TERMS 7.1

Institutions and the new institutionalism

For most students of politics, 'institution' brings to mind phenomena such as the legislative, executive, and judicial branches of government—what we might think of as ongoing or embedded sets of formalities, often underwritten or codified by constitutional prescription. Early political science dealt with the study of this sort of institution. Scholars explored how such bodies operated, how they interacted and how they supplied sets of rules that helped to account for the ways in which political systems operated. Often such studies concluded that institutional patterns reflected the character of a country's politics. This 'old' institutionalism was criticized—especially by behaviouralists—for an over-emphasis on the formal, codified aspects of politics at the expense of looking at the nitty-gritty of politics: the interaction of groups in pursuit of their interest and the basis, form, and consequences of individual and collec-

tive political behaviour. However, classical institutional studies did bequeath a concern with the impact of rules upon the behaviour of actors and thus upon political outcomes more generally. 'New' institutionalism proceeds from the axiom that 'institutions matter' as shapers of and influences upon actor behaviour (rather than as mere expressions of political culture). This is combined with a broader definition of 'institution' to embrace not only formal rules, but also forms of ongoing social interaction that form the 'compliance procedures and standard operating practices' in the political economy, to borrow Peter Hall's well established definition (Hall 1986: 19). Thus, from the new institutionalist vantage point, we may be talking about anything from written constitutional rules through to norms or even collectively-recognized symbols when we speak of institutions. With this in mind, it is hardly surprising that the EU has become a favoured venue for the practice of new institutionalist political science.

The limits of the classical debate

As the previous two chapters have indicated, the legacies of neo-functionalism and intergovernmentalism remain intact in much current writing about integration and the EU. Moreover, even when analysts of the EU attempt to offer an alternative point of theoretical departure, they invariably set their coordinates with reference to the established neo-functionalist and intergovernmentalist positions. There is always a danger that the histories and trajectories of neo-functionalism and intergovernmentalism can end up being caricatured in such accounts. It is not the job of this chapter to offer a revisionist reading of the classical theoretical literature; suffice to say that the early texts of integration theory repay careful reading by present-day students. This is not just because of the obviously useful legacies of ideas such as 'spillover'. It is also true to say that the ways in which these 'old' theories are criticized is open to contest. Indeed, the idea that there is a convenient and rigid division between 'new' and 'old' theories is open to

considerable critical scrutiny (see Haas 2001, 2004; Rosamond 2005).

The 'old' debate has been criticized on at least three interrelated counts: its alleged inability to capture the reality of integration and the EU; its supposed entrapment in the disciplinary wilderness of International Relations and its so-called 'scientific' limitations.

On the first of these, neo-functionalists—in particular—were heavily criticized for the lack of correspondence between their theory of integration and the unfolding reality of European integration. The assertion of intergovernmental politics from the mid 1960s, the obstinacy of nationalist sentiment within the member states, and the peculiarity and non-replicability of the European experience all provided serious body blows to neo-functionalist discourse by the mid 1970s (see Chapter 5). Similarly, intergovernmentalism is open to the charge that it offers only a partial representation of both integration and EU governance. The focus on politics between member-state executives and the claim that substantive change in European integration is traceable only to intergovernmental bargains stands at variance with a lot of the empirical evidence gathered by those at the coal face of EU studies (see Chapter 6). However, while much of what goes on within the EU—in terms of day-to-day legislative and regulatory activity—is bound up with the actions of 'non-state actors', this does not mean that neo-functionalism is necessarily best placed to make a comeback.

To take an example, one of the big debates to emerge in the literature of the late 1980s and early 1990s concerned the origins of the single market programme as codified in the Single European Act (SEA) (1987) (see also chapters 3 and 16). Intergovernmentalists homed in on the SEA as an obvious case of treaty reform initiated by an intergovernmental bargain. It was argued that change became possible because of the convergent interests of the three most powerful member states (France, Germany, and the UK). Moreover, these national preferences emerged out of processes of domestic political exchange in all three countries (Moravcsik 1991). Against this it was claimed that the SEA represented the formal consolidation of practices that had emerged in recent years. This in turn reflected acts of institutional creativity by the Commission, the jurisprudence of the Court of Justice and processes of institutional interaction (Wincott 1995). At the same time, neo-functionalists found some evidence of spillover as initiatives to create the single market prompted calls for incursions into the realms of social policy and monetary union (Tranholm-Mikkelsen 1991). But while the evidence for this spillover was impressive, it was also true that there was a lot more going on in the Communities besides progression to the single market and beyond. In any case, other (newer) theoretical perspectives had developed strong explanations of how and why the single market and subsequent progress to monetary union came about.

The next criticism of 'old' theories builds on the allegation that they emerge from the disciplinary homeland of International Relations. From this vantage point, IR is claimed to be a discipline preoccupied

with two core themes: questions of war and peace, and relations between *states*. European integration was originally of interest to IR scholars because European states seemed to be embarking on a project that sought to undermine and eliminate the recurrent causes of war on the continent. This led IR-derived theories into two ways of thinking. Neo-functionalists became concerned with the progressive mechanics of the integration process, while intergovernmentalists developed an interest in the ways in which diplomacy between national governments either survived or became institutionalized in the context of European integration.

This in turn sparks two types of complaint. The first is that the EU is about a lot more than the 'integration question'. Simon Hix (1994, 2005) makes the point that the question of whether there should be more or less *integration* does not motivate the behaviour of most of the actors involved in the business of the EU. Rather, he argues, these are individuals and groups pursuing their interests within a complex political system. As analysts of the EU, we are in fact confronted with the evergreen political science question of 'who gets what, when, how?' to use Harold Lasswell's classic formulation (Lasswell 1950). If we think that the 'integration question' is all that the EU is about, then we fall into the same trap as those politicians who conceptualize the EU in terms of the simple zero-sum opposition between 'nation state' and federal 'superstate'. This leads to the second type of complaint. This maintains that we need to break out of the 'state fixation' that characterizes so much of the routine academic and political discourse about the EU. For one thing, many—perhaps most—students of the EU would want to argue that the EU has evolved into a peculiar form of polity or political system that does not really fit into any established template for understanding the state. On the other hand, the EU is a system that delivers coherent and binding policy outputs. The allegation is that IR perspectives fail to deal with these criticisms.

The third criticism of the classical debate brings together a number of concerns about the type of theory involved. Neo-functionalism in particular has been criticized as a 'grand theory'—an attempt to develop a set of general 'laws' about the dynamics of regional integration across the world. Such attempts at overarching theory came under intense scrutiny in the early 1970s and it is no coincidence that this was the period in which neo-functionalism was abandoned by its foremost practitioners. In place of grand, universal theories, social scientists became more interested in developing 'middle-range theories'. As the name suggests, middle-range theories do not have totalizing ambitions; they seek to explain aspects of a phenomenon rather than its whole. As we will see below, most contemporary theoretical work is concerned with explaining aspects of the policy process and regulatory fabric of the EU. Theories *of* European *integration* are by and large obsolescent (though see Haas 2004).

Of course, this criticism often merges with the critique of International Relations to suggest that the problem with IR is that it continues to trade in the currency of grand theory. Another way of thinking about this problem is to identify 'old' theory as concentrating on the *form* that integration would take. For many contemporary scholars of the EU, this is simply an irrelevant question. What merits attention and explanation are the processes through which the EU delivers authoritative outputs, and not the 'big picture' question of what the EU is becoming.

It would be a mistake to think that these criticisms have been completely decisive and have ushered EU studies into a new theoretical age. Each is contested, and even where scholars agree that there is some substance in the above argument, many argue that the theoretical landscape is more nuanced and complex than many of the critics of classical theory suggest. Yet not all critiques would take the failures of neo-functionalism and intergovernmentalism to match 'reality' as a legitimate starting point. Theorists working in what is sometimes called the 'constitutive' tradition regard the relationship between theory and reality as intimate and problematic and would choose altogether different criteria for evaluating theories than their ability to correspond to and/or predict the 'real' world.

Moreover, the dismissal of International Relations as a parent discipline has been taken to task by those who suggest that what goes on within IR departments and journals bears little resemblance to the grand theorizing and state-fixated area of study depicted by the critics. In any case, it is a bold claim that overstates the extent to which the study of European integration was ever cordoned off as a sub-field of IR. The likes of Ernst Haas, Karl Deutsch, Leon Lindberg, and Philippe Schmitter studied the early communities as self-conscious (and often pioneering) exponents of the latest political science (Haas 2001, 2004; Ruggie et al 2005). Integration theory's most obvious connection to IR was its contribution to the emergence of International Political Economy (IPE), a sub-area that explicitly emphasizes the fuzziness of the boundaries between domestic politics and international relations (Katzenstein, Keohane and Krasner 1998). Others suggest that IR theories retain a valuable place in EU studies because they act as valuable tools for understanding the global environment within which the EU operates (Hurrell and Menon 1996; and Peterson and Bomberg 1999).

The third point—the type of theorizing involved in the 'old' debate—is less a criticism than an observation about how the study of a phenomenon (in our case the EU) is bound up with the ebbs and flows of social science, as much as it is related to the context supplied by that phenomenon.

Markus Jachtenfuchs (2001) draws a distinction between a classical phase of integration theory where the 'Euro-polity' was the dependent variable and the contemporary 'governance' phase in which the 'Euro-polity' becomes the independent variable. In the other words, the EU has shifted from being a phenomenon that analysts seek to explain to becoming a factor that contributes to the explanation of other phenomena. This amounts to moving from asking 'Why does integration occur?' to posing the question 'What effect does integration have?' While the evolution of the European Union may explain why the nature of EU studies (and the theoretical work that informs them) has shifted in this way, it is clearly not the only reason. It is important to remember that the preoccupations and fashions of political science also change over time. For example, the growth of policy analysis as a key component of EU studies reflects a more general explosion of policy analytic work. In particular this has concentrated upon less formal, 'softer' forms of governance, thereby exposing a dense array of informal institutional mechanisms and non-hierarchical policy methodologies within the EU system. Theoretical development (or, for some, progress) in a particular field is about assimilating the currently predominant conceptual toolkit and the preoccupations of social science. Some would say that this delivers progress in a field in the form of better explanations of the reality of the object of enquiry (in our case the EU) and more rigorous forms of social science. Others would argue that our knowledge of the social world is governed by prevailing conceptions of what counts as valid knowledge, thereby skewing the game in favour of some forms of theory over others.

> **KEY POINTS**
>
> ● Recent years have seen renewed interest in theorizing the EU. Most scholars accept that there has been a significant shift towards newer styles of theoretical work.
>
> ● Critics of the classical debate regard neo-functionalism and intergovernmentalism as theories that ask the wrong sorts of question about the EU.
>
> ● Discussion of the obsolescence of 'old' theories raises some interesting questions about the nature and purpose of theory.

Institutionalism and the EU

By the standards of regional integration schemes worldwide, the EU is heavily institutionalized. It possesses a distinctive set of supranational institutions as well as a number of intergovernmental bodies. The treaties define the roles of these various institutions as well as the ways in which they are supposed to interact.

Four points are worthy of note. First, the founders of the European Communities sought to capture their desired balance between national and supranational forces through careful institutional design. Most accept that the balance has altered over time, but the formal institutional structure of European integration has remained remarkably resilient for half a century. Second, close observers of the EU often note the growth of distinct cultures within the various institutions. It is not just that there is a particular modus operandi within the Commission, but that individual Directorates-General (DGs) of the Commission possess distinct institutional cultures (see Chapter 8). The same is true of different Councils (see Chapter 9). Third, scholarship has revealed the existence of various informalities within the formal institutional shape of the EU. This work suggests that much that is decisive within the policy process is the consequence of regularized practices that do not have formal status within the treaties. In spite of that, these established routines are frequently defined as institutions. Fourth, much recent scholarly effort has been directed at understanding the *multi-level* character of the EU's institutionalized polity. Thus EU institutions (whether formal or informal) are not simply constituted by the world of Brussels and Strasbourg, but by a dense network of institutions that extend into the fabric of domestic and local polities. So much of the corpus of EU studies involves the analysis of formal and informal institutions and the impact that institutionalized practices have upon policy outcomes. At the same time, as studies of the EU have multiplied in recent years, so the wider world of political science has become infused with the so-called 'new institutionalism' (Hall and Taylor 1996).

It would be a mistake to regard the new institutionalism as a single theoretical perspective. Institutionalists agree, more or less, that institutions matter.

Institutions contain the bias individual agents have built into their society over time, which in turn leads to important distributional consequences. They structure political actions and outcomes rather than simply mirroring social activity and rational competition among disaggregated units (Aspinwall and Schneider 2001: 2).

Importantly, institutionalists of different hues have alternative accounts of just *how much* institutions matter. Aspinwall and Schneider (2001) think about institutional political science as a spectrum. At one end of this spectrum sits an economistic-rationalist position that sees institutions as the consequence of long-run patterns of behaviour by self-seeking agents. Institutions in this account are both modifiers of the pursuit of self-interest and a medium through which actors may conduct their transactions with greater efficiency. At the opposite end of the spectrum is a sociological position where actors' interests are actually constructed through processes of institutional interaction. Hall and Taylor's landmark discussion (Hall and Taylor 1996) identifies three subspecies of institutionalism: rational choice, historical, and sociological. Each of these has a presence in EU studies (see Table 7.1).

Rational choice institutionalism is the most obvious way in which rational choice approaches to politics have infiltrated EU studies (Dowding 2000). This is a close relative—in terms of foundational theoretical premises—of Moravcsik's liberal intergovernmentalism. Rational choice theory—perhaps

the dominant (though much criticized) strand in contemporary American political science—is based on the idea that human beings are self-seeking and behave rationally and strategically. The goals of political actors are organized hierarchically. They form their preferences on the basis of their interests. Institutions are important because they act as intervening variables. This means that institutions do not alter preference functions, but will have an impact upon the ways in which actors pursue those preferences. Consequently, changes in the institutional rules of the game, such as the introduction of the codecision procedure (which gave the Council and the European Parliament co-legislative power in certain areas) or alterations to the voting rules within the Council (from unanimity to qualified majority) will induce actors to recalculate the ways in which they need to behave in order to realize their preferences.

By and large, rational choice institutionalists have been interested in how their theory develops propositions about the changing relative power of institutional actors in the policy process. Scholars of this persuasion assume that institutional actors seek policy outcomes that correspond as closely as possible to their preferences. This is why institutions are created in the first place (the so-called functionalist theory of institutional design). The construction of formal models, often deploying the type of reasoning found in formal economic analysis, allows for empirical research on specific cases to

Table 7.1 The 'new institutionalisms'

TYPE OF INSTITUTIONALISM	Rational choice institutionalism	Historical institutionalism	Sociological institutionalism
RESEARCH OBJECTIVE	The changing relative power of institutions	The long-term effects of institutions	The role of culture OR persuasion and communicative action

Source: Hall and Taylor (1996).

be mapped against formal decision. Thus EU studies have developed lively debate about matters such as the agenda-setting power of the various institutions. Another key component of the rationalist argument has been the application of 'principal-agent analysis' to EU politics. Here self-regarding actors ('principals') find that their preferences are best served by the delegation of certain authoritative tasks to common institutions ('agents'). In the EU case, this approach provides powerful explanations for member states' decisions to create and assign tasks to supranational institutions such as the Commission and the European Court of Justice (Pollack 2002).

For their proponents, rational choice perspectives offer rigorous foundations for the development and testing of falsifiable hypotheses around a series of core shared propositions. This improves knowledge in a progressive and cumulative way. Scholars work from a set of (admittedly stylized) assumptions to produce progressively better understandings of how the EU works. For their opponents, rational choice institutionalists miss the point. Their focus on formal rules leads them to ignore the various informal processes that grow up around the codified practices. It is these informalities that better explain policy outcomes. Moreover, rational choice accounts of actor preferences tend to leave these fixed rather than recognizing the ways in which processes of socialization can mould interests and identities.

Historical institutionalists are interested in how institutional choices have long-term effects. Institutions are designed for particular purposes in particular sets of circumstances. They are assigned tasks and in this process acquire interests and ongoing agendas. If institutions interact with one another in a decision-making process, then patterns that are constitutionally prescribed or evolve in the early lifetime of the institutions concerned may 'lock in' and also become ongoing. This 'lock in' means that a 'path-dependent' logic may set in. The ongoing nature of institutional interests (their continuing bureau-shaping agendas and their preference for self-preservation)

KEY CONCEPTS AND TERMS 7.2

Rational choice and the science of EU studies

Supporters of rational choice institutionalism believe that this approach to the EU is able to build knowledge in a systematic way. Scholars working under the auspices of rational choice subscribe to particular methods of theory building. This usually involves the development of models capable of generating hypotheses, which can then be subjected to confirmation or disconfirmation through exposure to hard empirical evidence. Such work relies on the deployment of (often quite stylized) assumptions and the use of game theory as a tool of analysis. The substantial work of Geoffrey Garrett and George Tsebelis (for example Tsebelis 1994; Garrett and Tsebelis 1996) yields the counter-intuitive claim that the codecision procedure has strengthened the Council at the expense of the Commission and the European Parliament. The analysis is sophisticated, but relies on the assumption that institutions' preferences are arranged along a continuum according to the amount of integration that they favour. For critics, this type of work may produce intriguing results, but it relies too much on unrealistic assumptions and describes games that bear no relation to the complex interactions that take place between EU institutions on a day-to-day basis. Another dimension to this debate is that rational choice institutionalists often advance the view that theirs is a more rigorous form of political science than that offered by either EU studies 'traditionalists' or those of a more constructivist persuasion.

means that institutions become robust and may well outlive their creators. This also means that institutions may have an impact that their creators could not have foreseen, not least because they survive to confront new circumstances and new challenges. But these new challenges are met through the prism provided by pre-existing institutions. Thus the range of possible action and policy choice is constrained. Policy entrepreneurs may attempt to redesign institutions to meet current needs, but they do so in the face of institutional agendas that are locked in and which are, therefore, potentially difficult to reform.

Like the other two variants of institutionalism, historical institutionalism is not exclusive to EU studies. But its applications are obvious. That said, scholars use this basic template in various ways. Paul Pierson's well-known discussion of path dependency (Pierson 1998) looks at the problem of unintended consequences. He argues that the immediate concerns of the architects of the European Communities (EC) led them, at a critical juncture, into acts of institutional design that ultimately helped to erode the capacity of national governments to control the governance of their economies. So while the intention of West European governments of the 1950s may have been to rescue the nation state (Milward 1999), Pierson's work suggests that the long-term consequence of their deliberations may have been to engineer precisely the obverse. The implications for research from this theoretical insight are quite interesting. It pushes students of the EU to think about policy pathways: how particular EU-level competences emerge over time as a result of specific decisions. We are asked to think about how rational acts at one point in time influence rational action in the future.

Less wedded to rational actor assumptions is other historical institutionalist work such as that of Kenneth Armstrong and Simon Bulmer (1998) in their extensive study of the single market. Armstrong and Bulmer are more interested in the way that institutions can become carriers of certain ideas, values, and norms over time. Once again we are directed towards thinking about how such normative and ideational 'matter' is loaded into institutions at their inception. But students of the EU are also invited to explore how institutional cultures (say of the Commission generally or of specific DGs) impact upon all stages of the policy process, influence action and policy choice, and (perhaps) assist in the conditioning of the interests of actors.

This last comment provides a link to sociological institutionalism, a strand of literature that is closely bound up with the constructivist 'turn' in international and European studies (see Risse 2004; Wiener 2006 for comprehensive overviews). This is discussed later in the chapter, so the exposition in this section will be relatively brief. It is important to note that sociological institutionalists tend to reject the other institutionalisms because of their inherent 'rationalism'. The

meaning of this term is again discussed below, but for now it is worth remembering that sociological institutionalists/constructivists operate with a quite distinct ontology (an underlying conception of the world). This boils down to a very particular take on the nature of actors' interests. While rational choice and (most) historical institutionalists see interests as exogenous (external) to interaction, so sociological institutionalists see them as endogenous (internal). In other words, interests are not pre-set but rather the product of interaction between actors.

This leads sociological institutionalists towards a concern with two broad issues: the 'culture' of institutions and the role of persuasion and communicative action within institutional settings (Börzel and Risse 2000). By 'culture' is meant the emergence of common frames of reference, norms governing behaviour and 'cognitive filters'. In this account, 'institutions do not simply affect the strategic calculations of individuals, as rational choice institutionalists contend, but also their most basic preferences and very identity' (Hall and Taylor 1996: 948). With this in mind, sociological institutionalist analysis of the EU looks at the ways in which ongoing patterns of interaction and 'normal' forms of behaviour emerge within institutional settings. As one writer puts it, 'institutions have theories about themselves' (Jachtenfuchs 1997: 47). Thus institutions contribute to actors' understandings of who they are, what their context is, and what might be the motivations of other actors. This sort of work aims to add substance to often heard claims such as the idea that different Directorates-General of the European Commission function in quite distinct ways. Another area in which the application of this sort of thinking seems appropriate is the investigation of whether formally intergovernmental processes such as those associated with the Common Foreign and Security Policy (CFSP) conform to established patterns of inter-state interaction, or whether they bring about new norms of exchange between the envoys of member states, thereby transforming long-established norms of inter-state politics.

The roles of communication, argument and persuasion are seen as particularly important in these contexts. This is likely to occur in settings where norms have been established, but these deliberative processes also contribute to the establishment of common understandings. Thus, sociological institutionalists often embark upon empirical quests for so-called 'norm entrepreneurs'—'well placed individual actors … [who] … can often turn their individual beliefs into broader, shared understandings' (Checkel 2001: 31). Sociological institutionalism is not simply interested in the EU level of analysis. A lot of work is being done on the interaction of national and European-level norms and in particular the ways in which 'European' norms filter into the existing political cultures of the member states.

> **KEY POINTS**
>
> - The EU has become a major venue for the application of 'new institutionalist' political science and for debates between its main strands.
>
> - Rational choice institutionalists are interested in how the relative power of actors shifts in accordance with changes in institutional rules.
>
> - Historical institutionalists focus on the long-term implications of institutional choices made at specific points in time.
>
> - Sociological institutionalists pay attention to the 'culture' of institutions and the ways in which patterns of communication and persuasion operate in institutional settings.

Theories of policy making and the EU

One of the major features of EU studies in recent years has been the growth of work that draws on theories of public policy making. This is barely surprising. The EU is a major source of authoritative policy outputs in Europe. Moreover, most observers agree that there has been a substantial 'drift' of policy-making competence from member states to the European level since the initiation of the Communities in the 1950s. Consequently, there is an obvious and increasing need to make sense of how policy is made in this context. This confirms the idea, discussed above, that the EU is about rather more than 'integration'. If we think of the EU as a policy system, then it follows that scholarship needs to explore the ways in which policy agendas are set, policies are formulated, decisions are made and legislation is implemented.

This also constitutes a move away from the idea that the key EU outputs are 'big' history-making decisions such as treaty revisions. Much of what the EU does is in the area of technical regulation and the finer points of economic governance. Others—such as those scholars associated with the multi-level governance school discussed below—note that different patterns of policy making occur in different areas of EU activity. Thus, the politics of agricultural regulation might be quite dissimilar to the politics of merger control. This suggests that detailed empirical scholarship is needed on a sector-by-sector basis if we are to properly comprehend the complexity of EU governance. However, this does not mean that theory is irrelevant or marginal to this enterprise. All political science—however empirical—is informed by theory.

The EU has always been a port of call for theoretical work constructed elsewhere in the social sciences, and the concern with the minutiae of policy making suggests an important role for theories of policy analysis. In their discussion of EU decision making, John Peterson and Elizabeth Bomberg (1999) suggest that different levels of action in the EU require different sorts of theory. They identify three levels of action: super-systemic, systemic and meso (sectoral). At each level, analysts are interested in different variables—respectively, changes in the wider environment of the EU, institutional change, and resource dependencies. Thus, each level requires different theoretical tools. IR theories work well at the super-systemic level, while new institutionalist theories suit the systemic level of analysis.

At the sectoral level, where regulatory complexity prevails and where 'stakeholders' in the policy process exchange information and resources, Peterson and Bomberg recommend the deployment of policy network analysis (see also Peterson 2004). The concept of policy networks provides a way of thinking about complex decision-making situations characterized by ongoing relations between multiple 'stakeholding' actors. They are situations where ideology is largely secondary and expertise is at a premium. This is not to say that politics is absent. On the contrary, policy network analysis deals with the politics of influence and mutual dependency in situations where power is dispersed. The actors involved in policy networks have, by definition, an interest in policy outcomes. In national contexts— where the policy network approach was first developed—emphasis was placed upon the relationships between government departments, pressure groups, and various agencies and organizations. The main insight of such work was that networks often involved the ongoing exchange of resources between their component members. The impact of such work is that it guides us away from thinking about policy making in terms of rule-bound interactions between (constitutionally defined) institutions that are organized hierarchically. It emphasizes the need to understand the specific relations of mutual dependency that obtain in different sectors.

Opinion is divided as to whether policy network analysis has a place in the study of the EU. Kassim (1994), for example, criticizes policy network approaches for neglecting the interaction of institutions that is so central to a proper understanding of the EU policy process. Peterson, on the other hand, points to the regulatory, uneven, fluid, and multi-actor character of the EU policy game as ample justification for the application of the policy network template to the EU. Also, as Richardson (2001) reminds us, the concept of policy networks (as opposed to the rather more rigid idea of 'policy communities') is fluid and adaptable, and thus well-suited to the fact that EU policy making is segmented complex, and populated by multiple stakeholders.

The take-up of this approach by students of the EU begs the interesting question of whether the tools used to study national governance and policy making can be applied straightforwardly to the European level. This takes us back to some of the fundamental issues discussed at the beginning of this chapter. But policy network analysis is not alone in making this assumption.

Another good example emerges from the work of Giandomenico Majone (1994, 2005) who has been a central figure in the development of the idea of the 'regulatory state'. The regulatory state literature offers a view of how the management of advanced capitalist economies has shifted in recent times in the face of challenges posed by changes in the global economy. In Majone's terms, the EU has many of the key features of a regulatory state, the paradigm example of which is the United States. Regulatory states are distinct from positive interventionist states. Whereas the latter involve government intervention to engineer the redistribution of resources (usually through the mechanism of the welfare state), so the former busy themselves only with the rectification of market failure. Much of what the EU does is bound up with the regulation of the single market. It lacks the welfare function associated most with the post-war (west) European state. The EU's relatively modest resources are best targeted at regulatory forms of policy making. But Majone's point is that regulation is a form of governance that is becoming widespread across the western world. It is not a development unique to the EU. However, the EU can be thought of as a set of regulatory institutions created by the member states to solve problems of market imperfection. In this respect Majone's analysis shares a lot with principal-agent analysis (discussed above).

Not everyone would agree that the EU is solely a regulatory state, but the model of negative market integration/regulation is increasingly seen as one important dimension of the way in which governance in Europe is delivered, even if after 2008 the model has been increasingly challenged in the context of financial crisis. The regulatory mode of governance proceeds from quite distinct logics when compared to the classic 'Community method'. It is worth noting that much of the earlier theoretical work in EU studies was concerned with exploring the dynamics of the Community method. The growth of regulation within the EU policy process has therefore forced a corresponding recalibration of theory. One thing that would appear to unite political scientists working on the EU with, on the one hand, scholars of international political economy and, on the other, analysts of national and subnational policy making is an interest in *governance*. This is usually defined in terms of the range of actions and institutions that supply order. What we conventionally understand as *government* is one way in which order is delivered, but the literature on governance suggests that the traditional methods of public regulation, intervention, and legislation are being displaced and that authority is becoming dispersed amongst a variety of actors. The state retains a key role in governance, but its role is being reformulated and, arguably,

residualized. The EU is thought of as a very interesting and pertinent laboratory for the exploration of these trends, a point taken up by the literature on multi-level governance.

KEY POINTS

- The status of the EU as a polity that is responsible for the delivery of coherent and meaningful policy outputs challenges us to think about it in terms other than the classical theoretical discourse of integration.

- With this in mind, many have sought to treat the EU as a policy system. This requires the application of the tools of policy analysis. Many of these approaches, such as policy network analysis, originally emerged in the study of national political systems.

- A slightly different take on this question is to think about the EU in terms of trends that are shaping the ways in which governance is delivered in modern complex societies.

Multi-level governance

Much of the work introduced in the previous section builds on the claim that policy making within both nation states and the EU is a complex affair that cannot be captured by static models of the decision-making process focusing on formal legislative institutions. Analysts who adopt the theoretical language of policy networks and the regulatory state force us to question whether there is any meaningful distinction between policy making at different levels of governance. Perhaps the crucial changes are taking place in terms of policy-making styles rather than policy-making levels. We can take this a little further to say that the character of governance in Europe has changed significantly over the past 50 years. If we adopt this position, then we might suggest that the boundaries between national policy making and European policy making have been blurred to the point of insignificance. The EU policy process is not something that simply happens at the

European level. It penetrates into national political and legal systems in complex ways. So while there has been an undoubted 'drift' of authority in various policy areas to the European level, we need to move away from the image of there being two distinct domains of politics in Europe—the national and the supranational/European level. This claim represents a direct challenge to theories such as Moravscik's liberal intergovernmentalism (LI) (see Chapter 6).

The term 'multi-level governance' (MLG) has become commonplace in EU studies in recent years and the term is usually used to capture the peculiar qualities of the EU's political system. As with most of the literature discussed in this chapter, the growth of MLG language in EU studies is an echo of work within several fields including IR, local government and policy analysis. The two leading proponents of the idea define MLG as 'the dispersion of authoritative decision making across multiple territorial levels' (Hooghe and Marks 2001: xi). Rather than thinking about the extent to which Europe has become 'integrated', it is helpful to explore how loci of authority have shifted over the past half-century. Hooghe and Marks find that authority has become more dispersed since the late 1950s. So while there has been a drift of authority from the national to the European level, there has also been a general devolution of decision-making competence in most west European countries. At the same time, however, national governments remain important sites of authority.

So we have a picture of the EU policy process comprising several tiers of authority (the European, the national, and the subnational). But the idea of MLG goes beyond this. It also emphasizes fluidity between these tiers, so that policy actors may move between different levels of action. Moreover, dispersion of authority is uneven across policy areas.

At present MLG remains more of an organizing metaphor than a theory. It is within this metaphor that particular approaches—such as policy network analysis—can sit comfortably. But it does rest on some fundamental theoretical preconceptions that differentiate it squarely from LI. We have already noted the departure from the conceptions of political space offered by two-level game theorists. It is also worth saying that MLG proceeds from a more pluralistic and organizational conception of the state than the likes of LI. This means that analysts beginning with an MLG frame of reference dispute quite fundamentally the intergovernmentalist account of what the EU is. The MLG version of the EU is a 'set of overarching, multi-level policy networks [where] ... [t]he structure of political control is variable, not constant across policy space' (Marks et al 1996: 41). In many ways MLG represents an attempt to capture the complexity of the EU, but it also represents a clear denial of the idea that there can be a single all-encompassing theory of the EU.

KEY POINTS

- The literature on multi-level governance (MLG) encourages us to think about the EU as a political system across multiple levels.

- MLG is premised on the idea that authority has gradually moved away from national governments over the past half-century and has become dispersed among a variety of private and public agents.

Social constructivist approaches to the EU

Constructivism has been the big news in International Relations theory over the past few years. The work of constructivist scholars like Alexander Wendt (1999) has come to pose a serious challenge to the established schools of IR theory. Until recently, the main debate in mainstream IR was between forms of realism and liberalism. While realists offer a state-centric view of the world that emphasizes the primacy of self-help and power, liberals contemplate the ways in which international cooperation, commerce, and institutionalization are able to temper tendencies towards war in the international system. Constructivists note that both of these approaches are *rationalist*, that this, that they operate with a view of the world (an ontology) that sees interests as materially given. They also adhere to a positivistic conception of how knowledge should be gathered. This involves a commitment to 'scientific' method, the neutrality of facts, and the existence of observable realities (S. Smith 2001: 227). While such sentiments characterize much social science, they are not shared universally. Ranged against rationalism is a range of reflectivist and interpretivist approaches—such as postmodernism, and critical theory—that begin from wholly different premises.

The appeal of constructivism—or at least the type of constructivism that has entered the IR mainstream in the last decade—is that it claims to offer a middle way between rationalism and reflectivism. Constructivists such as Wendt see interests as socially constructed rather than pre-given, which means that regularities in the international system are the consequence of collective (or 'intersubjective') meanings. Constructivists are interested in how collective understandings emerge and how institutions constitute the interests and identities of actors. However, some authors believe that constructivism can and should share the rationalist commitment to developing knowledge through clear research programmes, refutable hypotheses, and the specification of causal mechanisms that produce regularities. Many—though certainly not all—IR constructivists aspire to this ambition.

The editors of the first collection of constructivist essays on the EU accept that the various authors occupy different positions along the continuum between rationalism and reflectivism (Christiansen, Jørgensen, and Wiener 2001). Moreover, the commitment to 'break bread' with rationalist theories such as liberal intergovernmentalism varies from author to author. That said, constructivists argue that they are best placed to study integration as a *process*. While intergovernmentalists recommend that the EU be studied as an instance of inter-state bargaining and comparativists think about the EU as a political system, constructivists purport to investigate the character of the move from a bargaining regime to a polity (Christiansen, Jørgensen, and Wiener 2001: 11). Thus if we think about European integration as a process bound up with change, then it makes sense to draw on a metatheoretical position that treats reality as contested and problematic. This means that constructivist-inspired work should focus on 'social ontologies and social institutions, directing research at the origin and reconstruction of identities, the impact of rules and norms, the role of language and political discourse' (Christiansen, Jørgensen, and Wiener 2001: 12).

More concretely, as Risse (2004) notes, constructivists are predisposed to think about how human agents interact in ways that produce structures (be they norms, institutions, shared cultural understandings, or discourses) that simultaneously shape and influence social interaction and the possibilities for action that follow. Constructivists endeavour to understand the constitution of interests and (thus) identities. Moreover, they are interested in the ways in which institutions act as arenas for communication, deliberation, argumentation, persuasion, and socialization. Constructivists also touch base with discourse analysts (Wæver 2004) to emphasize the power resident in the capacity to create meaning and so frame policy choices in often non-negotiable ways.

Perhaps the best way to unravel constructivism in EU studies is to mention a few examples of what constructivists actually work on. Many are interested in how European identities emerge. So the idea of a 'European economy' a 'European security community', or 'European citizenship' should not be read as a consequence of actors' interests changing rationally in response to external material changes such as the onset of globalization or the end of the Cold War. Rather, constructivists insist that we need to investigate the ways in which these identities are constructed through the use of language, the deployment of ideas, and the establishment of norms. We also need to pay attention to the ways in which these norms and ideas are communicated and to the processes of learning and socialization that take place among actors. 'Norms' are particularly important in the constructivist vocabulary. These are defined as 'collective expectations for the proper behaviour of actors with a given identity' (Katzenstein 1996: 5). It is through the internalization of norms that actors acquire their identities and establish what their interests are. This is what constructivists mean when they talk about the 'constitutive effects' of norms.

The constructivist research agenda in EU studies (which has much in common with that of sociological institutionalism outlined earlier in this chapter) also pays attention to the ways in which European-level norms, ideas and discourses penetrate into the various national polities that make up the EU (Börzel 2002).

International relations and international political economy revisited

In recent years attempts have been made to 'bring IR back in' to the study of the European Union. Two in particular stand out: (a) the possibility that the EU can be studied as an instance of the so-called 'new regionalism' that has emerged in recent years across the world as (perhaps) a response to globalization, and (b) the growing significance of the EU as an actor on the world stage.

The EU and the 'new' regionalism

Regional integration—especially in the form of free-trade areas and customs unions—is not a new phenomenon. However, the period since the mid 1980s has been characterized by the growth of many regional economic blocs in the global political economy. Among the most conspicuous are the North American Free Trade Agreement (NAFTA), Asia Pacific Economic Co-operation (APEC), and Mercosur in South America. Not surprisingly, these cases of 'regionalism' have generated considerable scholarly interest and analysts have been keen to explore the possibility that their more or less simultaneous emergence has something to do with exposure to common stimuli.

The most obvious explanation for the revival of regional integration is the development of **globalization**. Globalization is a deeply contentious topic, but is usually thought of as a combination of things like heightened capital mobility, intensified cross border transactions, the multinationalization of production, and the spread of neo-liberal economic policy norms—in short, the growth of market authority at the expense of formal political authority. This debate is very complex, but one line of argument is that regionalism (as represented by NAFTA, Mercosur, and so on) is the primary way in which states have responded to globalization. The move to regionalism suggests that states have seen fit to pool resources in order to recapture some of the authority that globalization has taken away—a type of collective insurance against globalization.

Debate exists over the extent to which states actually and effectively lead the creation of regional integration schemes. This is where a distinction between regionalism and regionalization is important in the literature. While regionalism describes state-led projects of institution building among groups of countries, regionalization is a term used to capture the emergence of a de facto regional economy, propelled by the cross-border activities of economic actors, particularly firms. The question here is whether the formal institutions of regional integration are created to deal with and regulate this emergent transnational economic space, or whether the growth of cross border activity is stimulated by the decisions of governments. These are empirical questions at one level, but the two positions in this particular debate emerge from two different theoretical accounts of the world—one largely state-centric and one not.

There is also a debate in international economics about the impact of regional agreements on the global economy. All of the instances mentioned above are actual or aspirant free-trade areas. The question is whether the creation of regional free-trade zones creates or diverts trade on a global scale. Put another way, it asks whether we are heading for a regionalized world (of competing regional blocs) or a globalized world. Again, such matters can be measured empirically, but theoretical intervention is needed if we are to fully understand the meaning of a term like 'globalization'. Notice also how much of the foregoing implies a particular type of relationship between globalization and statehood and, it should be said, between structure and agency. Alternative accounts place differential emphasis upon the structural qualities of globalization—its ability to set imperatives and shape the behaviour of actors.

The theoretical relevance of the questions raised in the preceding paragraphs becomes especially apparent when we think about their application to the EU. Thinking theoretically, as James Rosenau and Mary Durfee (1995) point out, involves asking the 'of what is this an instance?' question. The 'new regionalism' literature forces us to ask whether the EU is a comparable case with, say, NAFTA. If the answer is yes, then the study of comparative regional *integration* is brought back in with the EU as one of the primary cases.

Of course, the EU is at best a deviant case of regionalism. Its longevity rules out any claim that the EU was *created* as a response to global economic upheavals in the late 1970s and early 1980s. Moreover, compared with other cases of regionalism the EU is considerably more institutionalized and much more deeply integrated. To use the EU as a benchmark case against which other regional projects should be measured is clearly a fallacy. Yet at the same time the acceleration of economic integration through the single market programme and progress towards monetary union has coincided with the growth of regional projects elsewhere.

The problem is not a new one for theoreticians of European integration. In many ways, the problem defined the project of the first generation of integration theorists. For neo-functionalists, comparison was a 'must' because only then might a generalizable theory of regional integration emerge from the case study supplied by the European Communities. Integration theorists and their critics have long grappled with the so-called $n = 1$ problem, that is, the uncomfortable possibility that the European Union may be nothing other than an instance of itself.

There are two suggestions as to how the field of EU studies might be reunited with the study of comparative regional integration without the EU becoming the paradigm case. The first follows Warleigh's (2006) argument that EU studies offer a rich and fertile range of ideas for scholars interested in questions of governance beyond the nation state, the interplay between domestic politics and collective institutions, and the possibilities for post-national democracy and legitimacy. The second suggested strategy involves the rediscovery of some of the neglected themes of classical integration theory, particularly neo-functionalism, where there was an overt emphasis on the study of the requisite material and cognitive background conditions for the formation and consolidation of regional projects.

The EU as an actor

The external policy of the EU is discussed at length elsewhere in this book (see Chapters 14 and 15). The task here is to concentrate on what this might mean for the ways in which we might conceptualize and theorize the EU's role in the global political economy.

The question that first emerges is whether we can conceptualize the EU as an *actor*. That is to say, is the EU a discernible entity with its own capacity to act on the basis of its own interests? To be sure, the EU possesses certain formal roles in world politics and in the management of the global economy. It speaks with a common voice in international trade negotiations and has the makings of an embryonic foreign and security policy (M. Smith 2001). On the other hand it consists of 27 member states, all of which

CASE STUDY 7.3

The EU and statehood

Much of the routine political discourse surrounding European integration bothers itself with the question of whether the EU is becoming a 'federal superstate', which, by definition, is supplanting the powers of its constituent member states. While such debates will seem simplistic to close students of the EU, they open up interesting avenues for theorists. Without doubt, the EU lacks some of the classical indices of 'statehood' as it has come to be understood (not least in Europe) over the past three and a half centuries. For example, the EU lacks fixed territorial boundaries and does not possess monopolistic control over the legitimate means of violence. It does not engage in extensive programmes of redistribution, yet it does exercise meaningful and emphatic authority over the governance of its constituent economies, and by extension over the lives of hundreds of millions of Europeans. Moreover, the presumption of many current theorists is that the EU is sufficiently similar to national political systems to allow the deployment of the tools of normal political science and policy analysis. But statehood also has external dimensions. Thus world politics has developed into a game played between states with the notion of 'sovereignty' as the ultimate rule. Much contemporary International Relations literature debates the extent to which processes such as globalization have begun to transform this system. Yet the language of statehood, international politics, sovereignty, and diplomacy remains central to world politics. We might argue that the condition for admission to the world polity remains the achievement of statehood. So the question becomes whether the EU is being constituted and shaped by the existing world system or whether it is contributing to a radical reshaping of world politics.

operate as actors within the current international system (note how the very phrase 'inter-national system' connotes an order founded on the interaction of authoritative national states).

That the EU is not a state (at least in the conventional modern sense of the term) is not really in dispute. But is it becoming one? If this is the case, then we might want to argue that the EU is an embryonic state writ large, formed through the gradual merger of its component member states. This might then allow us to slot the EU—as a constituent unit of the international system—into long-established theories of IR, such as realism. This would construe the EU as an entity seeking to advance its own interests and, particularly, to render itself secure from external threat.

However, we might be reluctant to arrive at this conclusion. The EU might appear to be a unique entity, lacking those decisive authoritative attributes normally associated with modern (supposedly sovereign) nation states. If we think about the image of the EU that is described by the literature on multi-level governance (discussed earlier in this chapter) and then project outwards, then students of integration are confronted with something that seems to fit very badly with conventional theories of IR (Ruggie 1998: 173–4). Indeed, rather than trying to fit the EU into IR theory, perhaps IR theorists need to look carefully at their established theoretical toolkits if they are to properly comprehend the EU. Theories such as neo-realism and neo-liberal institutionalism (which dominate theoretical discourse in IR, especially in the United States) are built around the idea of states as the dominant units of analysis in the world system. The EU might be a freak occurrence, specific to the peculiarities of Europe, but the ways in which the boundaries between domestic and international politics have become blurred along with the styles of governance that have evolved may well have a much wider application.

One rider to this is that the EU's external action takes place, whether in terms of foreign policy or commercial (trade) policy, in conditions that still respond to the rules of state-centred inter-national politics. Thus, for the EU to acquire legitimacy and recognition as a valid actor in the system, we might hypothesize that it has to conform to the rules of that system. This in turn would create pressures for the EU to become state-like. Therefore, the paradox is that while the EU may appear to transcend the international system, it is still in meaningful ways constituted (as constructivists would put it) by the norms of that very system.

Conclusion

The revival of interest in theory in EU studies has occurred within the context of some serious thinking about the role of theory in political science. Some of the 'new' theories discussed in this chapter have emerged from a concern to render theoretical work more rigorously 'scientific'. Other newer approaches have emerged from positions that explicitly challenge the rationalist mainstream in social science. Others theorists still—notably certain constructivists—try to occupy a middle position between rationalism and reflectivism. These debates have begun to intrude into EU studies and have been played out more extensively in the broader International Relations literature.

Theoretical reflection and debate simply bring out into the open assumptions that reside in any empirical discussion of the EU. Alternative theories have different accounts of social reality and sometimes lead to quite different strategies for acquiring valid knowledge about that world. This translates eventually into a set of disagreements about matters fundamental to this book: what sort of entity is the EU and how should it be studied?

Much of the 'new' theoretical work introduced above represents a self-conscious departure from thinking about the EU in terms of 'integration'. Its status as a supplier of authoritative policy outputs suggests that the toolkit of political science and policy analysis might be useful. At the same time, however, the fact that the EU is not a state as conventionally understood poses all sorts of challenges to those seeking to understand not only European integration but also the nature of world order in the early twenty-first century. The EU may offer a clear indication of what a 'denationalized' world order might look like. It sits between nation states and the international system and arguably transforms both through its very existence.

The facts that the EU is multidimensional, that integration is uneven, and that EU governance is composed of multiple, coexisting policy modes all force us to think carefully about how the nature of authority is changing. The trick—as employers of the 'multi-level governance' metaphor remind us—is to think about the EU as part and parcel of this changing pattern of governance. To treat the EU as a political system 'above' national political systems ignores the complex interpenetration of the domestic and the supranational in contemporary Europe. The task of theories—whether drawn from the formal disciplinary domains of 'International Relations' or 'political science'—is to offer ways of organizing our thoughts about what is going on in this context. We might continue to be confused about the complexity of the EU, but the present vibrant theoretical culture in EU studies at least gives us a chance of being confused in a reasonably sophisticated way.

QUESTIONS

1. Is it fair to say that Comparative Politics provides a better disciplinary homeland for EU studies than International Relations?

2. Can there be a single institutionalist research agenda in EU studies?

3. How helpful is the idea of 'multi-level governance' for organizing the way we think about the EU?

4. How might one study the EU from a policy networks perspective?

5. What added value do social constructivists bring to the study of the EU?

6. How might we go about theorizing the EU's role in the world?

7. To what extent is it possible to compare the EU with other instances of 'regionalism' in the global political economy?

8. Why is it important to theorize European integration and the European Union?

 GUIDE TO FURTHER READING

■ Christiansen, T., Jørgensen, K. E., and Wiener, A. (eds) *The Social Construction of Europe* (London: Sage, 2001). A collection of constructivist-inspired readings of aspects of European integration. Contains critical responses and a notable new essay by Ernst Haas, the founder of neo-functionalism.

■ Cini, M. and Bourne, A. K. (eds) *Palgrave Advances in European Union Studies* (Basingstoke: Palgrave Macmillan, 2006). A collection on the state of the art in EU studies with numerous theoretical insights.

■ Jørgenson, K. E., Pollack, M. A., and Rosamond, B. (eds) *Handbook of European Union Politics* (London: Sage, 2007). A wide-ranging survey of the EU literature that includes a helpful section on EU theories—including the new theories addressed in this chapter.

■ Rosamond, B. *Theories of European Integration* (Basingstoke: Palgrave, 2000). A critical discussion of past and present theories of integration.

■ Wiener, A. and Diez, T. (eds) *European Integration Theory* 2nd edn (Oxford: Oxford University Press, 2009). Practitioners of a wide variety of theoretical perspectives discuss and apply their approaches to the EU.

 WEBLINK

● http://eiop.or.at/erpa/ European Research Papers Archive. A collection of online working papers relating to EU studies, where much innovative theoretical work is showcased for the first time.

 Visit the Online Resource Centre that accompanies this book for lots of interesting additional material. http://www.oxfordtextbooks.co.uk/orc/Cini_Borragan3e/

PART THREE

Institutions and Actors

8

The European Commission

MORTEN EGEBERG

Chapter Contents

Reader's Guide

This chapter provides a general introduction to the European Commission. It argues that it is more productive to compare the Commission to national executives or to a government than to a secretariat of a traditional international organization. It begins with a summary of the Commission's functions within the EU's policy process. It then considers the question of Commission influence and autonomy, before moving on to look at the structure and demography of the organization, that is, at the role of the President of the Commission and the Commissioners, at the Commissioners' personal staffs, at the Commission administration, and at committees and administrative networks that link the Commission to national administrations and interest groups. The chapter concludes by emphasizing that the Commission is moving away from its intergovernmentalist roots towards becoming much more of a European(ized) institution than it was at its inception.

Introduction

To many observers, the Commission is a unique institution. It is much more than an international secretariat but not quite a government, though it has many governmental characteristics, as we shall see. The Commission encompasses elements of both intergovernmentalism (a national dimension) and supranationalism (a European dimension). It is the opposing pull of these two elements that forms the focal point of this chapter. By exploring the national and supranational features of the Commission's organization, the chapter reopens the question: what sort of institution is the European Commission?

The Commission dates back to the High Authority of the European Coal and Steel Community. It represented a considerable institutional innovation, and it still is if we compare the institutional arrangement of the EU with international organizations around the world. What constitutes its most innovative aspect is the fact that for the first time in the history of international organizations a separate executive body, with its own political leadership, had been set up *outside* the ministers' council. The concept of an Assembly, later the European Parliament, was already known from the United Nations, NATO, and the Council of Europe. An international court of justice had been in place in The Hague since the early twentieth century. An independent executive, on the other hand, was something quite new.

The chapter begins with a brief review of the Commission's main functions, which revolve around its role in the EU policy process. These involve the Commission in agenda setting, and more specifically in the drafting of legislation, in the implementation of policies (albeit at arm's length) and the management of programmes, and in the formulation and negotiation of certain aspects of the EU's external relations. Moreover, the Commission also has a role to play in mediating between the Parliament and Council and amongst national government and non-state actors involved in European policy making, and in presenting its own, or a European, perspective on issues and events. The second section focuses on the question of Commission influence and autonomy, viewing this matter through the lens of integration theorists (see Chapters 5–7). In the sections that follow, attention turns to organizational features and their behavioural consequences, with the focus first on the Commission President and College of Commissioners; second, on the Commissioners' cabinets (their personal staffs); third, on the Commission Administration; and finally on the role of committees and external administrative networks. In perusing these sections, however, readers should be aware that the Commission has recently undergone a major organizational reform, which has in recent years altered some of the Commission's structure and processes. However, the conclusions to the chapter are likely to hold true all the same—that the Commission is becoming a more European institution than it ever was in the past.

The functions of the Commission

The European Commission is, like governments, composed of a political executive wing (the Commissioners and their staffs) and an administrative wing (the 'services'). It has a wide range of functions within the EU system—policy initiation, the monitoring of policy implementation, the management of European programmes, an important external relations role, and other functions which involve it as a mediator amongst the 27 member states and between the EU Council and the European Parliament (EP), as well as asserting its own European identity. The Commission is clearly involved in the EU's policy process from start to finish. In much the same way as are national executives, the Commission is responsible for the initiation and formulation of policies, usually in the form of legislative, budgetary, or programme proposals. To put it bluntly, the Commission drafts the legislation. It is in this sense that in the majority of policy areas—that is, in those policies falling under the first or EC pillar of the EU, such as the Single Market (see Chapter 16)—the Commission performs an exclusive agenda-setting role. Other actors, such as the European Council (the heads of state/government), the EP, national officials, and interest groups, may also take initiatives and advance policy proposals. But it is generally up to the Commission to decide whether these ideas will be picked up and subsequently passed on to the legislature in the form of a formal legislative proposal, even if in practice these sorts of policy initiative quite often originate from outside the Commission. By contrast, under the two more intergovernmental pillars—the Common Foreign and Security Policy (CFSP) or second pillar, or the third pillar covering Police and Judicial Cooperation in Criminal Matters (formerly within Justice and Home Affairs)—the Commission does not have an exclusive agenda-setting role, although it may still be active in developing policy programmes. However, executive tasks of the Justice and Home Affairs area have gradually been transferred to the Commission. Under the EU's Foreign and Security Policy, the Secretary-General of the Council has also been appointed as the High Representative for the Union's CFSP (see Chapter 15). The strengthening of the Council's General Secretariat in this respect presents a direct challenge to the Commission's executive role, and illustrates the considerable tension between intergovernmentalism and supranationalism in this particular policy arena.

Also very much in line with the functions performed by national executives, the Commission has an important role to play in the implementation of European policies. What this means in an EU context is that the Commission is responsible for the *monitoring* of implementation within the EU's member states. In much the same way as occurs in Germany, the execution or putting into effect of policy remains largely the responsibility of the state (in this context meaning the regional or *Land*) governments. However, before implementation can occur at the national or subnational level it may be necessary for secondary (or administrative) legislation to be agreed. This is because laws made by the Council, usually together with the EP, tend to take the form of broad policy guidelines or frameworks rather than detailed steering instruments. Thus it is up to the Commission, in close cooperation with the member states, to detail and fill in EP/Council legislation by agreeing more specific rules, often in the form of *Commission* directives or regulations, in what is called delegated legislation. Only in very few policy areas, such as competition policy, is the Commission responsible for implementation in the sense of handling individual cases.

Finally, the Commission's external representation role has become increasingly important, particularly since the early 1990s. Just like national governments, the Commission staffs and runs delegations (in effect, EU embassies) around the world. There are no fewer than 130 offices in non-member countries. Also under the rubric of external representation the Commission acts as the main negotiator for the Union in trade and cooperation negotiations and within international bodies such as the World Trade Organization (WTO) (see Chapter 14).

The Commission also performs other less tangible and more diffuse functions within the EU. Important amongst these is its role as a mediator amongst the EU's member states, and between the EP and the Council. Thus, the Commission does its best, once it has produced a proposal, to ensure that agreement is reached within the Union's legislative bodies. After having agreed a policy proposal internally (see below for more on the internal functioning of the Commission), the officials who drafted the proposal may attend meetings of the relevant EP committee and plenary sessions (see Chapter 10), the relevant Council working party, the Council Committee of Permanent Representatives (COREPER), and the relevant Council ministerial meeting (see Chapter 9) in order to defend their line, and, if necessary, to mediate between conflicting parties. The Commission also presents policy documents to heads of state/government at European Council (summit) meetings and at Intergovernmental Conferences (IGCs). The Commission not only helps in the process of achieving a final agreement but also has its own institutional position to advance, one that may involve the presentation of a more European picture of events than emerges from national quarters (or even the EP).

Commission influence

It is all very well to state that the Commission is involved at almost all stages of the EU policy process (at least in pillar 1/EC affairs), but to what extent does the Commission have any real influence? In studies of the European Commission, there is a great deal of dispute over whether Commission initiatives make a significant difference or not to EU outcomes.

On the one hand, intergovernmentalists believe national governments are the real driving forces in the European project. In the *liberal* intergovernmentalist version of this theoretical stance (see Chapter 6), it is accepted that the Commission has an important role to play in pillar 1 policies (such as the internal market, agricultural policy, and regional policy). However, they claim that the authority it exercises as an agenda setter and overseer of implementation at the national level is merely a derived and delegated authority (Moravcsik 1998). According to this view, the Commission may facilitate intergovernmental cooperation, but it has no real power basis of its own, as the Commission's powers are decided upon and framed by the member states within treaty negotiations.

Intergovernmentalist thinking on the role of the Commission is countered by those whose approach might be labelled as 'supranationalist' or 'institutionalist'. Most of these institutionalists would argue

that there is ample evidence that the Commission has displayed strong leadership and on a number of occasions has even had a profound effect on the outcomes of 'history-shaping' and frame-setting IGCs, and European Council meetings. For example, Armstrong and Bulmer (1998) assign a highly significant role to the Commission (and indeed to other EU institutions) in the process that led to the creation of the Single Market. The Single Market Programme is one of the important frameworks within which the Commission operates under the first (EC) pillar. Institutionalists argue that treaty-based frameworks, which are the main focus of intergovernmentalists, are quite often vague and ambiguous constructions that need to be translated into practical politics through day-to-day policy making. And when it comes to this sort of crucial follow-up work the Commission is one of the key actors.

Another, but related, scholarly dispute questions the extent to which the Commission is able significantly to affect decisions even within its own organizational boundaries. Not surprisingly perhaps, to many intergovernmentalists the Commission appears very much as an arena permeated by national interests. From this perspective, Commissioners, their personal staffs (*cabinets*), as well as officials in the Commission's departments (services), are primarily pursuing the interests of their respective nation states. By contrast, institutionalists tend to emphasize that the Commission, like other institutions, furnishes individual actors with particular interests and beliefs, and that it may even be able to resocialize participants so that they gradually come to assume supranational identities.

KEY POINTS

● Intergovernmentalists see the Commission as relatively insignificant.

● By contrast, institutionalists (supranationalists) view the Commission as having an independent impact on policy outcomes.

The President and the Commissioners

The European Commission has both a political and an administrative dimension. While there is no doubt that the actions of the administrative branch also have political significance, there is still a useful distinction to be made between the Commission's political leaders—the 'College of Commissioners'—and the officials who sit in the Commission's services (or departments).

The 'College' consists of 27 Commissioners, including the President of the Commission. Within the Commission's internal decision-making process contentious issues that have not been resolved at the lower echelons of the Commission are lifted to this highest political level in the last instance. The College strives to achieve consensus through arguing and bargaining. If this does not result in a consensus, voting may take place, although this seems to be relatively rare. When it does happen, all Commissioners, including the President, carry the same weight—one vote each—and an absolute majority is necessary for a final decision to be reached. Since the College operates on the basis of the principle of collegiality—in other words, since all Commissioners are collectively responsible for all decisions taken—it would be reasonable to assume that a relatively large proportion of all decisions is referred to the College. However, due to the present size of the College, more issues seem to be dealt with through direct interaction between the President and the particularly affected Commissioner(s). Thus, one asks whether 'presidentialization' is taking place, meaning that the President changes from

being a 'primus inter pares' to becoming a 'primus super pares' (Kurpas et al 2008). It is now accepted that the work of the College is subject to the President's political leadership (see below). And like a national prime minister, the President also has at his disposal a permanent secretariat, the Secretariat-General (or General Secretariat as it is sometimes called), which has been strengthened over the last years.

Commissioners have policy responsibilities (portfolios), which normally involve oversight of one Commission department. These departments are known as Directorates-General or simply as DGs. As DGs tend to be organized sectorally (according to purpose) or functionally (according to process), one might expect this to provide a particular source of conflict amongst Commissioners. This expectation is explained in Box 8.1.

Although Commissioners are supposed not to take instruction from outside the Commission, and do not represent national governments in any formal sense, they are, nevertheless, nominated by them. Previously, larger countries had two Commissioners each, while the other member states had to make do with one each. From 2004 on, all governments nominate only one Commissioner each. A major concern has been to avoid the College becoming too large, since this could threaten its decision-making capacity. With too many Commissioners one also faces difficulties finding meaningful portfolios of a reasonable size. For example, in 2007, the new Commissioner from Romania

Politics in the Commission

How politics within the Commission is a reflection of the sectoral and functional specialization of the Commission's organizational structure

The weekly Brussels newspaper, *European Voice* (31 May–6 June 2001) reported that the then Transport Commissioner Loyola de Palacio was set for a clash with the Environment Commissioner Margot Wallström over the future direction of EU transport policy. 'Officials from Wallström's services have only just begun studying de Palacio's White Paper on transport after it was released for consultation between Union executive departments. But already they say there are "things missing" from the 120-page document that are likely to prompt criticism from Wallström.' The newspaper reported that Wallström was likely to intervene with some concerns raised by environmental interest groups over the policy proposal, which seeks to freeze road traffic at its current 44 per cent share of all transport, but makes no attempt to reduce its overall growth. 'Green groups say the White Paper fails to live up to the Amsterdam Treaty obligation to bring environmental objectives into all policy areas. ... Environmentalists insist the proposal will make it harder for the EU to comply with its Kyoto obligations to reduce greenhouse gas emissions.'

became Commissioner for multilingualism, not a particularly broad or meaningful policy responsibility. Before appointing Commissioners, however, the national governments must first agree on a candidate for the Commission Presidency. This is necessary if the new President is to be given an opportunity to influence the composition of the College. Over time the President's role in selecting his colleagues has grown. In the revisions to the Treaty, agreed at Amsterdam in 1997, the President is able, for the first time, to reject candidates nominated by member governments. The President also has the final say in how portfolios are allocated and even has the right to reshuffle the team during the Commission's five-year term of office by redistributing dossiers (portfolios).

National governments have increasingly seen their role in the make-up of the College of Commissioners diminish. By contrast, the European Parliament has gradually gained more of a stake in the process in a number of different ways, indicating that the EU has taken some steps in the direction of a parliamentary system. First, from the very start, the EP has been able to dismiss the entire College by taking a vote of no confidence. Second, the term of office of the Commissioners has been extended from four to five years, so as to bring it into close alignment with the term of the EP. This means that the appointment of a new College takes place after the EP elections, to allow MEPs to have a say on the matter. Not only is the EP consulted on the choice of President, but it also has the right to approve their appointment. In fact, the outcome of the 2004 European elections was probably decisive for the choice of a candidate close to the European Peoples' Party (EPP), since this party formed the largest group in the EP. Moreover, the

Growing party-politicization of the Commission?

The weekly Brussels newspaper *European Voice* (27 January–2 February 2005) reported that socialist members of the European Parliament were challenging the Commission's five-year work plan over what they saw as a lack of concern for social rights and the environment. The Commission President had told the Parliament that his team's main objective was to stimulate economic growth. Paul Nyrup Rasmussen, President of the European Socialist Party, criticized the Commission's plan for being old-fashioned. But Hans-Gert Pöttering, leader of the centre-right European Peoples' Party described the Commission's programme as realistic and ambitious: 'Anyone who neglects the nurturing of European competitiveness will be responsible for the fact that in the future we will have no European social model to preserve.' (p. 6)

EPP had a say as regards the person nominated as Commission President. Former Prime Minister of Portugal, José-Manuel Barroso, had been a Vice-President of the EPP and was this party's candidate. Steps have also been taken to render the Commission more directly accountable to the Parliament, as illustrated by the fact that the EP committees now scrutinize nominated Commissioners and the political programme of the Commission (see Box 8.2).

What kind of College demography (composition) does this inspire? First, it means that the political leadership of the Commission always has a fixed mix of nationals. Second, it tends to bring people into the College who have the same political party background as the national government nominating them. Over time, nominations to Commission posts have included people with impressive political experience, and it is now quite usual to see prominent national ministers in the list of nominees. Such a recruitment pattern obviously furnishes the College with political capital, though probably not in a strict party-political sense. A coherent party platform for the College is almost unthinkable under the current appointment procedure. Instead, Commissioners' nationality is likely to be a more crucial background factor to take into account in explaining their conduct (Wonka 2008). This is so since national governments, lobbyists, and the like tend to contact 'their' Commissioner as a first port of call, when they want to obtain information or have a say at the very highest level of the Commission. And Commissioners may also become involved in social networks with their compatriots—for example, in gatherings at their respective Permanent Representations (their national embassies to the EU) in Brussels.

It should not be concluded from this, however, that Commissioners act primarily as agents of the national government that nominated them. In fact, a Commissioner's portfolio, or DG affiliation, is also quite important in order to explain their behaviour with regard to a particular decision. Like national ministers, Commissioners see multiple and often conflicting role expectations imposed upon them: at one and the same time they are supposed to feel some allegiance, albeit informal, to the geographical area from which they originate, to champion Commission interests, to advance their own portfolio, and to assume a party-political role (Egeberg 2006a). Balancing these diverse pressures is not always an easy task.

KEY POINTS

- The European Commission is composed of a political leadership in the form of the College of Commissioners.

- Commissioners are nominated by national governments, but they are expected to act independently and seem to do so to a considerable extent.

- Steps in the direction of a parliamentary system have been taken.

- The Commission President has gained more powers since the 1980s, so that the current President is no longer simply 'first among equals'.

Commissioners' cabinets

Like many national ministers in Europe, Commissioners have their own political secretariat or private office. The Commissioner's 'cabinet' (note that the French pronunciation is often used), as it is called, is organizationally separate from the administrative services of the Commission. It is composed of people trusted by the Commissioner in question, and who may be hired and fired at the Commissioner's discretion. Consequently, their tenure can last only as long as their Commissioner's. A cabinet consists of about six to seven advisers, plus a number of clerical staff. Their role is to help push Commissioners' ideas down to the services, on the one hand, and on the other, to edit and filter policy proposals coming up from the DGs before they are referred to the Commissioner and the College. As an integral part of this 'editorial work' a Commissioner's cabinet frequently interacts with other cabinets in order to register disagreements and pre-empt objections that might be raised at the level of the College. Due to the principle of collegiality, in essence a form of mutual responsibility, each of the 27 cabinets covers all Commission portfolios. Thus, a Commissioner's cabinet is vital as a source of information about issues beyond their own remit. Ahead of the weekly meeting of the College, the *chefs de cabinet* (cabinet heads) convene to ensure that the Commission acts as coherently and cohesively as possible. These inter-cabinet gatherings are chaired by the Secretary-General, the administration's top official.

In addition to the role played by cabinets in coordinating, both vertically and horizontally, the flow of information within the Commission, they also have important functions at the interface between the Commission and the outside world. Cabinets are crucial points of access for governments, lobbyists, and other actors and institutions keen to influence the Commission (see Chapter 12). Their role is to assist Commissioners in this respect, with cabinet members responsible, amongst other things, for writing Commissioners' speeches, standing in for them, and representing them at conferences and meetings. Cabinets have also acted as a kind of liaison office between the Commissioners and 'their' respective governments, particularly via 'their' Permanent Representations. Thus, they are able to inform the national governments about forthcoming Commission proposals that might become politically interesting from a national point of view, whilst at the same time acting as a conduit for information about national positions on policy initiatives under consideration in the Commission.

Cabinets have often been portrayed as national enclaves. This description was appropriate given that (in the past) the nationality of cabinet personnel almost directly reflected the nationality of the lead Commissioner. Since the Prodi Commission,

however, at least three different nationalities should be represented in each cabinet, and the head or the deputy head of the cabinet should be of a different nationality from that of the Commissioner. In 2004, at the start of the Barroso Commission, the formal requirements were clearly over-fulfilled: 96 per cent of the cabinets contained more nationalities than formally prescribed and 57 per cent of the personnel were non-compatriots of their respective Commissioners (Egeberg and Heskestad 2008). Moreover, at least half of cabinet members should be recruited from within the Commission services. This may also have interesting implications for the role of nationality in the cabinets since those coming from the Commission administration may have weaker ties to any particular national constituency. Those who have come to the cabinets from outside the Commission have for the most part served in national administrations, but some have also come from other kinds of organizations, for example from the political party to which the Commissioner belongs.

Before the Prodi Commission's reforms of the cabinet system in 1999, one would probably have concluded that the structure as well as the demography of these bodies would tend to foster kinds of intergovernmental patterns of behaviour within the Commission. However, the structure and demography of the cabinets have changed. Thus, multinational staffing and an increased emphasis on internal recruitment seem to fit better with institutionalist explanations. As a consequence of these reforms, it would seem very likely that the role of cabinets as the interface between national governments and the Commission will be profoundly redefined.

KEY POINTS

- Each Commissioner is supported by a personal staff, known as a 'cabinet'.

- The cabinet, traditionally a 'national enclave' within the Commission, has become significantly more multinational in recent years.

The Commission services

As is the case in national executives, the political leadership of the Commission is served by an administrative staff. In the Commission this administration is often referred to as the Commission 'services' (see Box 8.3). Key components of the Commission's administration are the Directorates-General that are roughly equivalent to the administrative components of national government departments, and which now cover almost all possible policy fields. The basic principles of organizational specialization are also quite similar to those of national ministries. While DG Agriculture and DG Justice, Freedom and Security reflect a sectoral organization, DG Budget and DG Personnel and Administration are organized around the functions they perform. Precisely because they are functionally orientated, DG Budget and DG Personnel and Administration are also said to be the Commission's horizontal services, that is, the administrative units that are assigned coordination tasks or that deal with issues cutting across sectoral departments. The Secretariat-General is the most important of these horizontal services. As the permanent office of the Commission President it plays an important role in shaping a coherent policy profile for the Commission as a whole, and also has a crucial part to play in managing relationships between the Commission and other key institutions inside and outside the Union. The role of Secretary-General, the head of the secretariat, very much parallels that of a permanent secretary within national prime ministers' offices so that they may be identified as the first among equals of the administrative heads. Examples of other horizontal services are the Press and Communication Service, the Statistical Office (Eurostat), the Translation Service, and the Legal Service. The Legal Service provides much of the Commission's legal expertise, though lawyers are also found in large numbers in other parts of the Commission. Thus, the Legal Service primarily serves as an expert body which other departments consult. It makes sure that

legislative proposals drafted within the DGs comply with the technical and linguistic standards that are deemed appropriate for EU legislation, thereby pre-empting future challenges to European legislation in the European or domestic Courts (see Chapter 11).

Headed by a Director-General, DGs usually consists of several Directorates, with each of these headed by a Director. Each Directorate is further split into Units. Obviously, some tasks and new policy initiatives do not fit well into this strictly specialized hierarchical structure. To meet such needs, special task forces or interdepartmental working groups are created. Sometimes these temporary or ad hoc bodies become institutionalized and end up as new DGs or departments. The DGs usually have a total permanent and full-time staff of about 300–700 each, but their size varies considerably. The Commission employs approximately 24,000 officials. In addition there are about 6,000 people on temporary contracts. The most prestigious posts belong to the so-called AD category, which consists of around 12,500 officials mainly engaged in policy making and policy management. When the scholarly literature deals with 'Commission officials' it is referring to staff in this category (rather than those performing executive, clerical and manual tasks).

In addition to staff paid by the Commission, the services also include approximately 1,000 AD-category officials seconded from member governments. These seconded officials, or 'detached national experts', have their salaries paid by their national employer. In the early days of the High Authority of the European Coal and Steel Community, the forerunner of the Commission (see Chapter 2), most officials were appointed on temporary contracts or seconded from the member states. Over time this has changed. As we have seen, an overwhelming majority of the posts are now permanent, while temporary jobs might be used for hiring personnel who might provide additional expertise on particular policy issues that are under consideration in the services.

BOX 8.3

The Commission services

General services

European Anti-Fraud Office

Eurostat

Press and Communication

Publications Office

Secretariat-General

Policies

Agriculture and Rural Development

Competition

Economic and Financial Affairs

Education and Culture

Employment, Social Affairs and Equal Opportunities

Energy and Transport

Enterprise and Industry

Environment

Executive Agencies

Maritime Affairs and Fisheries

Health and Consumers

Information Society and Media

Internal Market and Services

Joint Research Centre

Justice, Freedom and Security

Regional Policy

Research

Taxation and Customs Union

External relations

Development

Enlargement

EuropeAid Cooperation Office

External Relations

Humanitarian Aid Office

Trade

Internal services

Budget

Bureau of European Policy Advisers

European Commission Data Protection Officer

Informatics

Infrastructures and Logistics

Internal Audit Service

Interpretation

Legal Service

Office for Administration and Payment of Individual Entitlements

Personnel and Administration

Translation

Recruitment of new AD-category candidates for a career in the Commission services is based largely on the meritocratic principle. What this means is that appointments should be made on what a person has achieved in their educational and professional career so far, rather than on any other criteria, such as a candidate's social or geographical background, their gender, or the extent to which an applicant has 'good contacts'. This principle is inherently linked to understanding of what a modern and well-functioning bureaucracy should look like

if it is to avoid nepotism, favouritism, and corruption. Thus, in accordance with this principle, those who want to embark on a Commission career are normally required to hold a university degree. Subsequently, they have to pass a competitive exam called the *concours*. The *concours* is modelled on the French standard entry route into the higher civil service, which means in practice that all applicants have to pass written as well as oral tests. These tests are arranged in the member states on a regular basis and may involve thousands of applicants. However, no more than 150–700 reach what is called the 'reserve list', and even these lucky few are still not guaranteed a job; rather they have to wait for a vacancy and hope that they will be contacted about it.

A loose quota system (in the form of 'targets') regulates more or less the intake of new recruits on a geographical basis. As a result, those hired should be drawn proportionately from all member states, so that larger countries provide more candidates than smaller ones. In a way this sort of quota arrangement is at odds with the meritocratic principle outlined above; however, the huge number of qualified applicants should nevertheless provide for a highly professional staff. This system does ensure that the Commission—or rather, the AD category—is not over-populated by staff from only a few of the EU's member states (see Box 8.4).

Once in post, seniority matters for promotion at the lower levels of the AD category. In addition to

an official's immediate superior, the staff unions also play a significant role in decisions about promotion at this level. For appointments as Head of Unit and above, achievements in earlier positions matter more than seniority as a criterion for promotion. The role of staff unions is also considerably reduced at these senior levels. Instead, nationality has traditionally reappeared as a crucial factor, and increasingly so, the more senior the level of the appointment. Obviously, the narrower the pyramid, the more complicated it has become to manage the national quota system in a fair manner, while at the same time paying heed to merit as the basic norm for promotion. In these cases, national governments are often keen to look after 'their share' of jobs, and it has conventionally been up to Commissioners and their cabinets to intervene if the 'balance' is deemed to be threatened. In addition to concerns about proportionality, a top official's immediate subordinate and superior should be of a different nationality. The argument goes that a multinational chain of command will prevent policy proposals from reflecting narrow national concerns.

It would seem that while the services should continue to maintain a broad geographical balance, nationality is, subsequent to Prodi Commission reforms, no longer allowed to be the determining factor in appointing a new person to a particular post. The aim was clearly to abolish the convention of attaching national flags to senior positions. New and strict procedures seem in fact to have effectively encapsulated processes in which top officials are appointed: senior Commission officials themselves seem to orchestrate such processes, and Commissioners, who take the final decision usually adhere to the shortlist of candidates presented to them (Egeberg 2006b). New member states may claim a reasonable share of posts at all levels of the hierarchy, and this has meant that highly experienced national officials have had to be brought into the senior ranks of the Commission administration. However, these officials also have to compete for vacant jobs and are subject to the same strict appointment procedures (see Box 8.5).

 CASE STUDY 8.4

Personnel policies

How personnel policies in the Commission are increasingly 'normalized', i.e. becoming more similar to such policies within national ministries

The weekly Brussels newspaper *European Voice* (21–27 February 2002) published a small notice that neatly illustrates how personnel management in the Commission has become more multifaceted than we might expect to find in international institutions. While balancing meritocracy and a proper national balance has been the dominant concern, gender equality has also become an issue in the Commission. In the notice, the European Ombudsman calls for urgent action over *ethnic* imbalance. He says the Commission does not take possible racism in recruitment seriously enough. 'When I look around the various institutions—the Commission, Parliament and Council—the only staff I see from ethnic groups are security guards and cleaners. Given that an estimated 30 million people of ethnic minority origin live in the EU, I wonder why so few appear to be in more senior posts.'

Commissioners' limited control over the appointment of top officials

The weekly *European Voice* newspaper (12–18 October 2006) reported that the Commissioner for enterprise, Gunther Verheugen, when launching a document that set out ways to reduce the burden of red tape on EU businesses, had criticized top officials in the Commission for obstructing his 'better regulation' proposal. He suggested that Commissioners should have more power to pick their directors-general to ensure they do their political masters' bidding. Verheugen's suggestions were rejected by the Personnel and Administration Commissioner Siim Kallas who argued that the whole point of Commission staff reforms had been to 'oppose political appointments based on criteria other than merit'(p. 2). But, according to *European Voice*, 'Verheugen's comments echoed recent criticism of the Commission by German Chancellor Angela Merkel who said in a speech in Berlin that Commissioners' lack of control over their directors-general was "unthinkable" for a German minister' (p. 2).

In accounting for the behaviour of Commission officials, how important is their national background? Given the enduring interest that national governments have shown towards recruitment and appointments, we are led to think that nationality matters very much indeed. However, the attention devoted to the issue does not necessarily correspond to the impact that national origins might have. There is no doubt that officials bring to the Commission administrative styles and general attitudes that can be linked to their country of origin. For example, officials stemming from federal states like Germany or Belgium seem to view the prospect of a federal Europe more favourably than do those from unitary states, probably because the former are already familiar with that kind of system (Hooghe 2001). However, the extent to which experience of national administration affects the Commission must depend on the career patterns of the officials involved. In the early years of the Commission, when many officials were on temporary contracts or secondments from their national

governments, more Commission officials were imbued with national styles and attitudes. Under the current staffing regime, though, relatively few officials have in fact had the opportunity to acquire much administrative experience back home. Thus, they are arriving at the Commission without much 'baggage' in this respect.

Although a considerable number of Commission officials are without administrative experience in their home country, they may still make interesting interlocutors for their compatriots. A common language and nationality facilitate interaction so that Commission officials become points of access for those keen to know what is going on in the Commission. Moreover, officials of the same nationality often socialize together in Brussels and this may be enough to sustain a sense of national belonging. However, there is virtually no evidence of a direct link between an official's nationality on the one hand and their decision behaviour in the Commission on the other hand, as organizational roles and decision-making procedures tend to diminish this sort of variation in conduct (Suvarierol 2008). In fact, the attachment of officials to their DGs seems far more important than their national background as an explanation for the preferences and choices they make in their daily work (Curtin and Egeberg 2008; Trondal et al 2008).

Certain organizational characteristics suggest that the behaviour of Commission officials is intergovernmentally driven in the sense that it reflects national interests and influence. These include the temporary contracts systems and, in the past, the national quotas. Strict quotas might have served to legitimate national identities and, consequently, national policy orientations, while seconded personnel may have an incentive to pursue the interests of their current employer back home—usually their national government. However, there are also a number of organizational features that suggest that the institutionalist perspective is more accurate. Examples include the fact that specialization in the Commission occurs according to sector or function rather than geography; that there is a clear majority of permanent posts; that recruitment is basically on merit; that the Commission comprises multinational units and chains of command; and that there are lifelong career patterns, which facilitate the resocialization of personnel. Over time these institutional factors have gained in importance: the proportion of officials on temporary contracts or secondments has been constantly declining; and recruitment on merit and internal promotion to senior levels in the Commission has gained ever increasing support, particularly from the European Courts, the staff unions, and, indeed, the College of Commissioners. However, the current practice of allowing new member states to have a share of the senior jobs in the Commission immediately after accession probably represents the most serious challenge to further development in this direction.

KEY POINTS

- The Commission's administrative services comprise sectoral and functional (horizontal) departments, called Directorates-General (DGs).

- Officials' actual decision behaviour is probably best explained by their DG affiliation.

- Officials within the services are recruited on a merit basis with a view to an appropriate geographical balance among member countries.

Connecting to national administrations: committees and networks

In order to assist the Commission in its preparatory work on new legislation and in other forms of policy making, approximately 1,200 expert committees have been established. The practical work on a policy initiative often starts in such a committee, which is usually composed of national officials and other experts. Committees of this sort are supposed to provide additional expertise on a particular subject and thus complement the work of the Commission's permanent staff. They may also serve as an arena for floating policy ideas and anticipating future reactions to them. Involving interest organizations that might ultimately be affected by a new proposal might make political support and legitimacy more likely. The Commission particularly welcomes European-level interest groups (see Chapter 12). In policy areas where these sorts of interest organizations have been lacking, the Commission has actively tried to encourage their formation. This is understandable, since it is far more convenient to communicate with one group representing a particular interest than with 27 or more, all representing different national, sectional interests. Encouraging the establishment of tran-

snational interest groups may serve other purposes as well, though. Like the Commission itself, interest-group systems structure themselves primarily along functional and sectoral lines, rather than territorially. Thus, the Commission may see transnational interest groups as future partners in an evolving EU polity.

Commission officials chair expert committees and advisory groups, calling officials from member governments to participate. The Commission covers their travel expenses, and they are expected to behave like independent experts and not as government representatives. In general, national officials participating in Commission committees assign considerably less weight to the role as government representative than those attending Union Council committee meetings (Egeberg, Schaefer, and Trondal 2003).

When committee work comes to an end, the policy proposal is processed in the administrative and political ranks of the Commission before it is submitted to the Council and the EP. When a final decision has been reached in the Council, the issue is again handed over to the Commission for implementation. As mentioned earlier, some Council directives may need to be supplemented by rules of a more technical nature. This kind of legislative work is delegated to the Commission in the same way as national legislatures may let governments hammer out specific regulations. In order to monitor the Commission's legislative activity, however, the Council has set up about 250 so-called comitology committees (also sometimes known as 'implementation committees'). The membership of these committees are formal representatives of national governments, though it is the Commission that calls and chairs the meetings, sets the agenda, submits the proposals requiring discussion, and writes the protocols. Some comitology committees are only entitled to advise the Commission (advisory committees). Others have competence to overrule the Commission's proposals under certain conditions (management committees and regulatory committees). In practice, however, the Commission usually gets its own way, though this is not to say that national representatives have no influence. It is, of course, also quite possible that the Commission deliberately chooses proposals that national governments are likely to endorse (see Christiansen and Larsson 2007).

When it comes to the implementation of EU policies at the national level, the Commission has to rely on member-state administrations, since the Commission does not itself possess agencies at this level. This may result in considerable variation in administrative practices across countries. However, there are signs that national regulatory authorities that often work at arm's length from ministries become kind of 'partners' of the Commission in implementation as well as in policy-preparation processes. Due to these authorities' 'semi-detached' status, they seem to be in a position in which they might be able to serve two masters simultaneously: both the national ministry *and* the Commission. Within a range of policy sectors (like competition, telecommunications, environment, or food safety) we observe transnational networks of national agencies in which the Commission constitutes the hub (Egeberg 2006b). Do we then see a multi-level genuine *Union* administration emerging?

KEY POINTS

- Expert committees have an important role to play in the preparatory work of the Commission.

- Comitology committees monitor the Commission when it is issuing delegated legislation.

- National officials behave less 'intergovernmentally' in Commission committees than in Council committees and comitology.

- Issue-specific networks are emerging among the Commission and semi-detached national agencies.

Conclusion

The Commission has often been portrayed as a hybrid and unique organization because of its mix of political and administrative functions. This is understandable if the Commission is compared with the secretariat of a traditional international organization, since such secretariats are not expected to have a political will of their own. However, the Commission is probably better compared to a national executive. Like governments, the Commission is headed by executive politicians who are responsible for various administrative services. In a fashion similar to national executives, the Commission is authorized to initiate and formulate policy proposals, and to monitor the implementation of policies. The Commission has not, however, achieved full control of all executive tasks at the EU level, sharing its executive function in some respects with the EU Council. Most importantly, perhaps, the Union's Common Foreign and Security Policy (CFSP) is largely the executive responsibility of a strengthened Council Secretariat.

This chapter has focused on how the various parts of the Commission are organized and staffed, and how these structural and demographic features might be related to the way decision makers actually behave. Are these features mainly conducive to intergovernmental ways of behaving, or do they instead evoke patterns of decision making that are more in line with what institutionalists would predict? At all levels—the College, the cabinets, the services, and the committees—there are components that are certainly more in line with intergovernmental decision processes than with other kinds of processes. However, those organizational components that work in the opposite direction are becoming more and more important. These components tend to focus attention along sectoral, functional, partisan or institutional cleavages, that is, on lines of conflict and cooperation that cut *across* national boundaries, and that evoke non-territorial feelings of belonging among Commissioners and their officials. If these trends persist, the Commission is set to become much more of a European institution than in the past, though one which will inevitably continue to exhibit a mix (albeit a different mix) of both intergovernmental and supranational characteristics.

? QUESTIONS

1. To what extent is the Commission comparable with national governments?

2. How influential is the Commission within the EU policy process?

3. How important is the national background of Commissioners in shaping their preferences and decisions?

4. What is the role of the Commissioners' cabinets?

5. How are the Commission services organized, and what are the possible implications for patterns of conflict within the Commission?

6. How might nationality affect decision making within the services?

7. What is comitology?

8. Which roles do national officials evoke in EU committees?

GUIDE TO FURTHER READING

■ Cini, M. *From Integration to Integrity. Administrative Ethics and Reform in the European Commission.* (Manchester: Manchester University Press, 2007). This book is the first to examine how the European Commission has addressed concerns about its ethical standards since 1999.

■ Dimitrakopoulos, D. G. (ed.) *The Changing European Commission* (Manchester: Manchester University Press, 2004). This book focuses in particular on the Prodi Commission: the College, the administrative reforms and relationships to member states and the Council.

■ Egeberg, M. (ed.) *Multilevel Union Administration: The Transformation of Executive Politics in Europe* (Basingstoke: Palgrave, 2006). This book deals with politics within the Commission as well as between the Commission and other institutions, in particular national administrations, from an organization theory perspective.

■ Nugent, N. *The European Commission* (Basingstoke: Palgrave, 2000). This is probably the most empirically rich and balanced textbook on the Commission.

■ Spence, D., with Edwards, G. (eds) *The European Commission* (London: John Harper Publishing, 2006). This anthology also covers most topics, and is particularly detailed and informative on the structure and personnel of the Commission.

 WEBLINKS

● http://ec.europa.eu   This is the official website of the European Commission. It has links to its work programme, documents, calendar, the Commissioners, the services, and the delegations.

● www.eurunion.org   The European Union in the United States. The website of the EU delegation of the European Commission, based in the USA.

● www.cec.org.uk   The European Commission Representation in the UK.

 Visit the Online Resource Centre that accompanies this book for lots of interesting additional material. http://www.oxfordtextbooks.co.uk/orc/Cini_Borragan3e/

9

The Council of the European Union

JEFFREY LEWIS

Chapter Contents

- Introduction
- The heart of EU decision making
- The Council and the European Council: not the same thing
- How does the Council work?
- The layers of Council decision making
- Institutional evolution over time, and current challenges
- Conclusion: national, supranational, or both?

Reader's Guide

This chapter examines the heart of decision making in the EU, the Council of the European Union (or EU Council). The Council is the EU institution that unabashedly represents national interests in the European integration process, and as such it is a site of intense negotiation, compromise building, and at times acrimonious disagreement amongst the member states. The Council is not a single body, however, but more a composite of national officials working at different levels of specialization and political seniority—think of it as a system of decision making. From the heads of state and government to the ministers, and all the way down the ladder to the expert level *fonctionnaires* (officials), the Council embeds governments of the EU into a complex collective decision-making system that deeply penetrates into the national capitals and domestic politics of the member states. The result, as this chapter explains, is the most advanced and intensive forum of international cooperation between sovereign nation states in the modern world. This chapter looks at the organization and functioning of the Council, at its component parts (the European Council, the EU Council, the Committee of Permanent Representatives—COREPER—working groups, and the Secretariat), and at how it has evolved as an institution over time.

Introduction

The focus of this chapter is the Council of the European Union, also known as the Council and the more antiquated (but still preferred by many) 'Council of Ministers'. The Council is the epicenter of EU decision making and plays a pivotal role in the making of European policy. Although ostensibly representing the interests of the EU's 27 member states, the Council is also a European institution; and though formally one of the EU's legislative bodies, it is also an important arena for inter-state diplomacy and negotiation.

To explore these seemingly paradoxical traits of the EU Council, this chapter begins by outlining the way in which the institution is structured. The first section also emphasizes the difference between the EU Council and the European Council (the latter comprising heads of state and government rather than just national ministers). In the second section,

the operation of the Council comes under scrutiny. Here the focus is on the presidency, which rotates from member state to member state, as well as on the relationship between the Council, the Commission, and the Parliament. In the third section, the layers of Council decision making are peeled away, and we focus, from the top down, on European Council summits, on Council meetings themselves, on the work of COREPER (involving senior national civil servants), and that of the more technical working groups. This section also considers the increasingly important role of the Council's own officials in the Council General Secretariat (CGS). Finally, the chapter turns to consider some of the challenges facing the Council: the institutional challenges, the democratic deficit, and the wider implications of enlargement.

The heart of EU decision making

The Council of the European Union is the institutional heart of decision making in the EU. It is the institution designed to represent the member states, and as the creation of sovereign nation states, it was unsurprisingly endowed with extensive legislative and executive functions. The central legislative function is that all EU proposals (originating from the Commission) must be approved by the Council before becoming EU law. Despite newer decision-making procedures granting the European Parliament a more coequal status (called codecision), the Council remains at the core of the EU's legislative process. The Council has a central executive function as well: to provide strategic leadership and steer the pace and direction of European integration.

Legally speaking, there is only one Council, but this is misleading since in reality there are numerous formations organized by policy specialization (see Box 9.1). Each Council formation manages a

specialized policy sector, and the participants authorized to adopt legislative acts are the national ministers from each of the member states who hold domestic responsibility for that sector. Hence, the 27 EU ministers of agriculture preside over the Agricultural and Fisheries Council (AGFISH), the environmental ministers over the Environment Council, and so on.

Historically, the 'senior' Council formation with general institutional responsibilities and charged with overall EU policy coordination has been the foreign affairs ministers, who meet as the General Affairs and External Relations Council (GAERC) (See Box 9.2).

Since the dawn of the euro, and, some argue, earlier, the finance and economics ministers have increased in stature through their work on the Economic and Financial Affairs Council, otherwise known as ECOFIN. A subset of ECOFIN, made up of those member states that subscribe to the euro,

---

BOX 9.1

Council formations

General Affairs and External Relations (GAERC)

Economic and Financial Affairs (ECOFIN)

Justice and Home Affairs (JHA)

Employment, Social Policy, Health and Consumer Affairs (EPSCO)

Competitiveness

Transport, Telecommunications, and Energy

Agriculture and Fisheries (AGFISH)

Environment

Education, Youth, Culture

Source: Council's website.

 CASE STUDY 9.2

Renovating the General Affairs Council

Following widespread agreement in the latter half of the 1990s that the Council's premier ministerial body—the General Affairs Council—was impossibly over-tasked and increasingly dysfunctional, the European Council decided at the 2002 Seville meeting to split the GAC's work into two tracks:

- General Affairs

- External Relations.

Since 2002, the GAC has been reforged as the GAERC, or General Affairs and External Relations—although the cast of characters remains largely the same.

The 'new' General Affairs portion is tasked with 'preparation for and follow-up to the European Council meetings, including the necessary coordination of all preparatory work, overall coordination of policies, institutional and administrative questions, horizontal dossiers which affect several of the European Union's policies and any dossier entrusted to it by the European Council, having regard to operating rules for the Economic and Monetary Union' (Article 2A, Rules of Procedure).

The External Relations (or Foreign Policy) portion is assigned 'the whole of the European Union's external action, namely common foreign and security policy,

European security and defence policy, foreign trade, development cooperation and humanitarian aid' (Article 2B, Rules of Procedure).

Technically, the two strands operate independently, with their own meetings and agendas, but in practice the GAERC tends to meet on the same day(s) back to back, with the foreign affairs ministers at both. One big difference, if the Lisbon Treaty ever enters into force, would be who runs each grouping: the new Foreign Policy chief would chair the External Relations portion and the member state holding the rotating Presidency would chair the General Affairs portion. Whether this new arrangement imparts greater coherence to the work of the foreign ministers and renews the leadership role of 'General Affairs' is an open question.

Perhaps to keep the 'Eurojargon' fresh or perhaps just another example of the opacity of the EU's inner workings, the Lisbon Treaty refers to the 'General Affairs Council' and the 'Foreign Affairs Council' (Articles 16.6 and 236). So perhaps some day the GAERC will be redubbed the GAFAC.

Sources: Presidency Conclusions, Seville European Council, 21–22 June 2002; Council Decision of 15 September 2006 adopting the Council's Rules of Procedure, OJ L 285/47, 16.10.2006; Consolidated Versions of the Treaty on European Union and the Treaty on the Functioning of the European Union, OJ C115, Volume 51, 9 May 2008.

---

meet additionally in a Council formation known as the Eurogroup. The newest Council additions include the interior/home affairs ministers, who meet in the Justice and Home Affairs Council, and the defence ministers, who meet in a 'jumbo' Council format with the foreign ministers to discuss European Security and Defence Policy (ESDP).

The policy segmentation of the Council's work into distinct, compartmentalized formations is a hallmark of how the EU works. Each formation has its own pace and legislative agenda, with some meeting monthly (GAERC, ECOFIN/Eurogroup, AGFISH) and some no more than twice per year (Education, Youth, Culture). Each Council also has its own organizational culture, often including a set of informal (unwritten) rules and distinctive working habits. For example, some, such as the GAERC, rely on highly restricted lunchtime sessions to discuss issues of particular importance or sensitivity. And the GAERC has institutionalized the right to meet on the day before all European Council summits, to conduct final preparatory negotiations and adopt a definitive agenda for the heads of state and government (see Box 9.2). Another informal rule is for the Eurogroup finance ministers to avoid substantive macroeconomic policy discussions that affect non-euro EU members without also holding those discussions in the ECOFIN Council—interpreted by many observers as a norm that safeguards against 'us versus them' attitudes between the euro and non-euro members. Taken together, 'the Council' is a multifaceted decision-making structure operating across a wide range of policy domains, with negotiations taking place concurrently. In one guise or another, the Council is almost continually in session.

The ministers are but the tip of the iceberg, however. If it were only a matter of the ministers meeting a few days per month, the EU would be an inchoate and chaotic decision-making system. The work of the Council involves a much larger contingent of national officials. First, there are the EU permanent representatives who staff the Committee of Permanent Representatives (COREPER). COREPER is responsible for preparing forthcoming Council meetings, and this often involves intensive discussions to pave the way for agreement by the ministers. The EU permanent representatives (two per member state: each appoints their own EU ambassador and a deputy) live in Brussels, meet weekly, and literally 'eat, drink, and breathe EU issues seven days a week' (Barber 1995). Each member state also maintains a Permanent Representation in Brussels run by the EU ambassador and deputy and staffed by policy specialists from different national ministries.

But that is still not all. The bulk of day-to-day Council activity takes place at the expert working group level. At any point in time, the Council is composed of approximately 200–250 working groups. Even assuming one national expert per group, that means that there will be between 5,400 and 6,750 national officials shuttling to and from the national capitals or posted to the Permanent Representations. Working group officials are tasked with examining proposals in the early stages of negotiation, and the groups serve as a clearing house in which less controversial and/or more technical issues are settled. The working groups also act as an early warning system for complications or political issues that need addressing at the level of COREPER or the ministers.

In total, the Council involves thousands of national officials meeting in dozens of working groups, COREPER, or ministerial settings each week to negotiate and decide on EU proposals. If one adds up all of the national civil servants and policy specialists involved, earlier estimates put the total number working on EU affairs at around 25,000 (Wessels and Rometsch 1996: 331). Taking into account a dozen newcomers since then, and the growth of policy activity in the foreign, security, military, and justice fields, this number today must be closer to 40,000+! At base, this figure neatly captures the classic neo-functionalist meaning of the term *l'engrenage* ('caught up in the gears') and what Ernst Haas insightfully forecast as the Council's 'concept of engagement' (Haas 1958, 522-23).

Of all the EU institutions, how the Council actually operates is perhaps the least documented. Part of this stems from inaccessibility, but more important is the Council's enigmatic appearance. It is the 'chameleon' of EU institutions (Wallace 2002) because it blurs intergovernmental and supranational organizational traits and behaviours. The standard, glossary image of the Council is one of a stronghold of individualistically orientated national actors who focus more or less exclusively on their own self-interests rather than on the welfare of others or the group as a whole. This interpretation of the Council also forms a basic theoretical foundation for intergovernmentalist approaches. But the Council is a more complex and variegated institutional construct. The Council, as an institution, equals more than the sum of its parts (the member states). National actors in the Council also act collectively, and many develop a shared sense of responsibility that the work of the Council should move forward and that the legislative output of the Council (even if in only one specialized policy area) should be a success. As a chamber of continuous negotiation across a wide range of issues, national actors often develop long-term relations of trust, mutual understanding, and obligations to try and help out colleagues with domestic political difficulties or requests for special consideration. Council participants can also develop collective interests in the process of joint decision making itself. This can become a kind of 'global, permanent interest' in addition to the specific national interest on a given subject or proposal. In short, the member states who participate in the system also become socialized into a collective decision-making system. As one leading scholar on the Council has summarized the enigma, 'The Council of the EU is both an institution with collective EU functions and the creature of member governments' (Wallace 2000: 16).

The Council and the European Council: not the same thing

No portrait of the Council would be complete without including the role of the European Council. The European Council is the pre-eminent political authority for the EU because it brings together the 27 heads of state and government (and the President of the European Commission). Overall strategic guidance for the EU is supplied by the European Council, and the Prime Ministers, Chancellors, and Presidents meeting in the high-profile summits have assumed extensive responsibility for such key subjects as institutional reform, the budget, enlargement, and foreign, security, and defence policy. Issues such as future national budgetary contributions, relative voting weights, or how to finance new foreign policy missions have proven too politically charged for the ministers to settle and they have relied on the European Council to break deadlocks, overcome interministerial discord (especially between finance and foreign affairs), and broker the big, interlocking package deals for which the history-making 'constitutional' turning points in the EU are famous. The European Council meets formally at least twice a year (June and December), and at least twice more as 'informal' gatherings organized around a specific topic or theme (such as the March 2008 summit on a renewed 'Strategy for Growth and Jobs'). The European Council can also convene on an emergency basis, such as the September 2008 'Extraordinary Meeting on the Situation in Georgia' following Russia's military actions in Abkhazia and South Ossetia. European Council summits attract intense public scrutiny, covered by some 1,200 journalists, and, increasingly, accompanied by large turnouts of protesters (ranging from farmers to anti-globalization groups) which have led to violent clashes with police (such as the 2001 Gothenburg summit in Sweden).

The European Council was created in the early 1970s, and by 1974 was informally institutionalized. Many EU scholars credit the European Council with holding the Union together during the nearly two decades of Eurosclerosis. For the first dozen years or so, the European Council was not a legally recognized part of the Community's institutional system, and was not acknowledged in the Treaties until the Single European Act (SEA) of 1986. Thus, the European Council was considered an extra legal institution of the EU, and although it receives mention in the 'common provisions' section of the TEU, it is still separate from the original European Community institutions, to defray the image of becoming too closely controlled by the member states and avoid upsetting the delicate institutional balance between intergovernmentalism and supranationalism. While the European Council rarely makes a decision on a specific proposal (though there is nothing legally preventing it from doing so), the summits supply the EU with critical navigation, and the usual output for a meeting is a 30+ page *communiqué* (known as the 'Presidency conclusions') which summarizes positions on issues and sets priorities for future EU policy making. The as yet unratified Lisbon Treaty contains a big innovation for the European Council's leadership (see Box 9.8 for a summary) by removing the grouping from the regular rotating Presidency (see below) and creating a new permanent President who would chair all summits and provide a single face for the Union externally.

> **KEY POINTS**
>
> - The Council was designed to represent the member states, and has both executive and legislative functions in the EU system of governance.
>
> - The work of the Council is compartmentalized into nine sectoral formations.
>
> - The Council involves a large number of national officials (40,000+) who meet at the ministerial, COREPER, and working-group levels as well as coordinating EU policy positions back home.
>
> - The European Council is a signal component of the Council, bringing the heads of state and government together in multi-annual summits to discuss the most pressing business and provide strategic guidance.
>
> - As an institution, the Council is enigmatic: it is both defender of the national interest and a collective system of decision making, blurring the theoretical distinctions between intergovernmentalism and supranationalism.

How does the Council work?

The most common way to portray the Council is as a hierarchy of levels. The European Council forms the top level, followed by the ministerial level (with the GAERC and ECOFIN as *primus inter pares*, or first amongst equals). Below them is the COREPER level, which serves as a process manager between the ministers and the working groups who form the base of the hierarchy. This portrayal is not wrong, but it is distorted. The reality is a more labyrinthine and nuanced decision-making system, with significant variation by issue area. In some policy areas and with issues that are of a highly technical nature, the specialists in the working group may forge substantive agreement on important issues. In other cases, the permanent representatives who meet in COREPER conduct the detailed negotiations over substance, perhaps because of their legal expertise in applying Treaty articles, or institutional memory in a specific policy area, or sometimes to 'keep the lid' on a controversial subject that risks becoming hamstrung by the ministers. It is also not uncommon,

particularly when a Presidency is not run efficiently (see below), for a ministerial meeting or even a European Council summit to have the detailed, technical minutiae of a proposal on its agenda for discussion. In organizational imagery, the actual operation of the Council is perhaps closer to a network relationship of interorganizational authority than a corporate hierarchy, which is the typical portrayal.

The role of the rotating Presidency

The Council Presidency rotates between member states every six months. The Presidency is responsible for planning, scheduling, and chairing meetings of the Council and European Council. The same goes for all meetings of COREPER and the working groups. The Presidency also represents the EU internationally by acting as a spokesperson in EU external affairs. The true genius of the rotating Presidency is that it acts as a great equalizer between big and small states, giving tiny Luxembourg the same chance to run things as, say, Germany, France, or Britain. The rotation is set to give variation between big and small, newer and older member states (see Box 9.3).

Holding the chair carries formidable logistical duties, as the Council's work is organized into a six-month calendar. Planning for the Presidency typically begins 18 months prior to the start date. The Czechs, who held the Presidency in the first half of 2009, began planning for their 1 January 2009 start date back in the summer of 2006. They also increased staff at their Brussels Permanent Representation by approximately 100 people to handle the Presidency workload (in comparison, the Czech delegation totalled 58 in 2005). Despite the workload, the Presidency is highly coveted by member states as a chance to run things, since that member state not only organizes meetings but has a close involvement in setting the agenda—what issues are covered and in what order—and in finding solutions: brokering deals, suggesting compromises, drafting conclu-

sions. A newer innovation is the institutionalization of greater coordination between Presidencies into an 18-month work programme organized by a 'Presidency trio'. The idea behind the 18-month programme is to enhance continuity and formalize greater coordination in the Council's work. The 'trio's' programme is scrutinized, debated as necessary, and approved by the GAERC (Article 2.4, Rules of Procedure). The first 'trio' (2007–8) consisted of Germany, Portugal, and Slovenia; the second 'trio' (2008–9) was France, the Czech Republic, and Sweden (see Box 9.3 on the sequencing).

The EU Presidency involves much quiet diplomacy, behind the scenes and often in bilateral conversations at the margins of meetings (known as 'confessionals') in order to make progress on new proposals as well as to deal with the inevitable unexpected developments and crises as they arise. Running the Presidency is a real art form, and involves subtle diplomatic skills such as knowing in what order to call on member states during discussions to ensure the best chances of success (or failure), when to call for coffee breaks, and how to time the right moment for suggesting a 'Presidency

---

BOX 9.3

Council Presidency rotations 2009–20

Czech Republic	January–June 2009	Latvia	January–June 2015
Sweden	July–December 2009	Luxembourg	July–December 2015
Spain	January–June 2010	Netherlands	January–June 2016
Belgium	July–December 2010	Slovakia	July–December 2016
Hungary	January–June 2011	Malta	January–June 2017
Poland	July–December 2011	United Kingdom	July–December 2017
Denmark	January–June 2012	Estonia	January–June 2018
Cyprus	July–December 2012	Bulgaria	July–December 2018
Ireland	January–June 2013	Austria	January–June 2019
Lithuania	July–December 2013	Romania	July–December 2019
Greece	January–June 2014	Finland	January–June 2020
Italy	July–December 2014		

Source: Council Decision, 5002/07, 1 January 2007.

compromise'. The Presidency can be an important source of leadership in the EU, and member states see their turn at the helm as a chance to leave their imprint on the integration process.

The Presidency is a great example of the Council's enigmatic identity, since the country holding the position must simultaneously work to advance collective European solutions and be on the lookout for a particular set of national interests. This can be a delicate balancing act, especially in policy areas where there are highly mobilized domestic constituencies and costly economic issues at stake. Member states that handle this balancing act with a deft touch can accumulate a great deal of political capital and respect. The Finnish Presidency of 1999 helped earn that country a reputation for being very communitarian and skilful at compromise building despite being relative newcomers to the EU game. Likewise, it is possible to be seen as using the Presidency to pursue a narrower national agenda or to push through new policies without widespread support, as the French found out during their rotation in 2000 when smaller states accused the Presidency of trying to force through new voting weights which advantaged the big states.

Relations with other EU institutions

From the earliest days of the Union, interactions between the Council and Commission have constituted the main pulse and dynamic of European integration. But as the two institutions were created with a certain degree of inbuilt tension, with the Council representing individual member states and the Commission representing the 'European' interest, relations have at times been quite strained. The worst crisis in the history of the Union, the empty chair crisis of 1965, was prompted when French President de Gaulle felt the Commission had overstepped its authority in seeking to obtain its own sources of revenue (see Chapter 2). During other periods, relations between the Council and the Commission have been smoother, such as the period

in the late 1980s when the bulk of legislation to create the Single Market was adopted in a steady stream by the Council. More recently, signs of strain have shown up again in areas of foreign policy, between the External Affairs Commissioner and the Council's Secretary-General and High Representative of CFSP, over who should represent the EU internationally. The Lisbon Treaty attempts to resolve this problem with a very hybrid institutional solution. Should the Lisbon Treaty enter into force, the EU will have a Foreign Policy chief who would at the same time be a central Council actor *and* a Vice-President of the Commission in charge of the external relations portfolio (see Box 9.8).

In contrast to the Commission, relations with the European Parliament for most of the Union's history were very much at arm's length and mostly one sided. Prior to the Maastricht Treaty, the Council merely had to consult the EP before adopting legislation, and proposed EP amendments were not binding (see Chapter 10). This all changed when the codecision procedure was introduced to selected issue areas, the essential feature of this procedure being that the EP is a coequal legislator with the Council, since it is now much more difficult for the Council to ignore or overrule EP amendments. Since the 1990s, with each new Treaty (Maastricht, Amsterdam, Nice), codecision has been introduced or extended to more issue areas. The Lisbon Treaty has gone even further, codifying codecision as the EU's 'ordinary legislative procedure' rather than something exceptional or allowed under certain circumstances (Article 289). Under codecision rules, where the Council disagrees with EP amendments there is a procedure known as 'conciliation' where the two sides meet to reach compromise on a final text. Conciliation meetings, and compromise-seeking negotiations to stave off conciliation with an 'early' (first or second reading) agreement have dramatically intensified Council–EP relations since the mid 1990s. Working relations between the Council and EP have improved to the point where the number of codecision files that are concluded by compromise (during the first or second reading) without the need for lengthy conciliation negotiations has steadily increased. Today, 85 per cent of all codecision agreements are reached without the need for conciliation. The growth of codecision represents a new dynamic of inter-institutional networking in the EU and shows how the legislative process has evolved to become more like that of other bicameral federal political systems (Lewis 2005a).

KEY POINTS

- The Council has a clear hierarchical structure from the heads of state and government down to the experts in the working groups, but in practice the lines of authority and decision making are more akin to a complex network relationship.

- Leadership of the Council is supplied by a rotating Presidency which alternates every six months and is coordinated by the 18-month work programme of the 'Presidency trio'.

- The Council Presidency is both a huge job of planning and chairing meetings and a huge reward for all member states to have an equal chance at running things.

- Relations with the Commission are an integral part of the EU's federal-like system of overlapping powers, and the Commission's right of initiative gives them the '28th' seat at the table.

- Relations with the European Parliament have become more intense as the codecision procedure has grown and the EP is treated more like a colegislator.

The layers of Council decision making

Despite the aforementioned relevance of the network metaphor, the following section looks at the Council hierarchically, moving from the European Council to the Council of the EU, then to COREPER and the Council's working groups. The section also considers the growing range of functions performed by the Council's own bureaucracy, the General Secretariat.

European Council summitry

Since the 1970s, the European Council has been at the heart of the major 'history-making' moments of European integration. This includes the creation of the European Monetary System in the late 1970s, the resolution of major budgetary disputes in the early 1980s, launching new intergovernmental conferences that would lead to new Treaty agreements (SEA, TEU, Amsterdam, Nice), and so on. As the grouping that brings together the heads of government and state (in the case of France and Finland), no other EU body can match the political authority of the European Council. As a result, the summit conclusions greatly enhance the legitimation of daily decision making at the ministerial, COREPER, and working group levels. For instance, following the European Council's special meeting in October 1999 in Tampere, Finland to discuss the creation of a 'common area of freedom, security, and justice', the policy area of Justice and Home Affairs experienced a great burst of activism, including a new influx of Commission proposals and the adoption of several new directives by the JHA Council in areas covering immigration, asylum policy, and cross-border crime (see Chapter 19).

The Ministers' Council(s)

In terms of formal decision-making authority, the ministers are the national representatives empowered to vote and commit member states to new EU legislation (Article 16.2). As we shall see, a lot of informal decision making takes place in COREPER and the working groups, but the distinction between formal (juridical) and informal (de facto) decision-making authority is important to understand, since the ministers are the elected officials who are accountable to their domestic constituencies for the policies adopted in Brussels.

Three Council formations have more work and meet more frequently than the others: GAERC, ECOFIN/Eurogroup, and AGFISH. These three meet each month, usually for one or two days. The workload is particularly intense during certain periods, such as at the end of a Presidency when there is a final push to complete a legislative calendar.

The types of legislative acts adopted by the ministers vary by policy area. In traditional 'Community pillar' (first pillar) affairs, legislation is typically in the form of directives, regulations, or decisions. For Justice and Home Affairs (third pillar) and Common Foreign and Security Policy (CFSP) (second pillar), most legislative acts are made in the form of a joint action or a common position.

There are also rules for voting. Voting rules divide into two main categories: unanimity and qualified majority voting (QMV), though some procedural issues are passed by a simple majority vote. The key to how the Council reaches decisions is to understand the different dynamics between unanimity and QMV. Under the unanimity decision rule, any member state can block a proposal with a 'no' vote. If a delegation wants to signal disagreement with some aspect of a proposal, but not block adoption by the others, they can abstain. Abstentions do not count as 'no' votes. Since the 1986 Single European Act, many areas of policy are no longer subject to unanimity, though key areas which still are include CFSP, JHA, taxation, and institutional reform.

QMV now applies to most areas under the first ('Community') pillar and its reintroduction with

---

BOX 9.4

The qualified majority voting system

The post-Nice QMV is based on a 'triple majority' system. This will change if the Lisbon Treaty comes in to force. First, there must be a majority of votes in favour (currently 255 votes out of 345), based on the following member state weightings:

	Weighted votes
Germany, France, Italy, United Kingdom	29
Spain, Poland	27
Romania	14
Netherlands	13
Belgium, Czech Republic, Greece, Hungary, Portugal	12
Austria, Sweden, Bulgaria	10
Denmark, Ireland, Lithuania, Slovakia, Finland	7
Cyprus, Estonia, Latvia, Luxembourg, Slovenia	4
Malta	3
EU 27 total	345

Second, two-thirds of all member states must vote in favour (at least 18 in an EU 27). Third, the qualified majority should represent at least 62 per cent of the EU's total population (for 2009 that equals 308,445,700 out of a total EU 27 population of 497,493,100).

Sources: Treaty of Nice (2001/C 80/82); Council Decision 16079/08, 1 December 2008, Amending the Council's Rules of Procedure.

---

the SEA was considered a crucial precondition for establishing a Single Market by the 1992 deadline. Under QMV rules, each member state has a 'weighted' vote based crudely on population size. In anticipation of Eastern enlargement, the voting weights were reconfigured at the Treaty of Nice, creating a controversial reweighting and a complicated 'triple-majority' system of adopting legislation (see Box 9.4). The French, for example, insisted on keeping a parity weighting with Germany despite having 23 million or so fewer national citizens. Spain and

Poland also came out disproportionately ahead in the weightings, while Belgium actually gave up some relative voting power.

However, one of the most substantively important changes for the Council contained in the Lisbon Treaty is a revision of QMV to begin—should the Treaty be ratified—after 1 November 2014 (see Box 9.8), which simplifies the procedure by dropping weighted votes entirely and revising the thresholds for population and member state majorities. Thus the anticipated 'new' system for QMV in 2014 will still be based on a 'supermajoritarian' decision-making rule, but on a 'double majority' calculation that is arguably easier to understand and fairer to all. Those in favour of the new QMV system successfully argued that the current weightings distort voting power to the disadvantage of some (notably Germany) and to the advantage of others (notably France, Poland).

But even where QMV applies, voting is a relatively uncommon occurrence. Rarely is there ever a show of hands; typically, the Presidency summarizes discussion and announces that a sufficient majority has been reached, or asks if anyone remains opposed, and, if not, notes the matter is closed. Voting is also unpopular in the EU because there is a highly ingrained culture of consensus, and it is simply considered inappropriate to 'push for a vote' where there are one or more delegations with remaining objections or difficulties. As a result, actual voting

and the use of votes to signal protest are fairly rare. We can see this empirically by the low incidence of contested votes (that is, voting 'no' or 'abstaining') (see Table 9.1).

Using data from 2004–6 as a reference, we can see that contested votes occur in fewer than 15 per cent of all legislative acts and barely 10 per cent of all Council actions. This affirms the deep-seated 'consensus-seeking' assumption in everyday Council negotiations. But the potential recourse to the vote (the so-called 'shadow of the vote') is a powerful reminder to delegations to avoid becoming isolated by simply saying 'no' and being unwilling to compromise. For this reason, Council participants claim that the fastest way to reach consensus is with the QMV decision rule.

A feature common to all formations of the Council is how the agenda is structured. The agenda has two parts: Part A contains issues that need no further discussion and are approved in a single block by the ministers at the beginning of each meeting. This can be quite a long list of 20–30 items, known as 'A points', and not necessarily in the ministers' areas of expertise. Part B is the portion of the agenda which does require discussion by the ministers. These issues, known as 'B points', are the focus of the ministers' discussions.

The meetings themselves take place in Brussels (except during April, June, and October, when they are held in Luxembourg as part of an agreement

Table 9.1 Contestation and consensus in Council negotiations, May 2004–December 2006

	Legislative Acts	Other Acts	Total
Uncontested (1215)	85.8% (357)	91.1% (858)	89.5%
Negative Votes	8.9% (37)	6.2% (58)	7.0% (95)
Abstentions	5.3% (22)	2.8% (26)	3.5% (48)
Total (1358)	100% (416)	100% (942)	100%

Note: absolute number of acts in parentheses

Source: Mattila, 2008: p. 27, Table 2.1.

from the 1960s over how to divide where the European institutions would be located). The official residence of the Council is the Justus Lipsius building, inaugurated in 1995 and named after the sixteenth-century philosopher. The meetings take place in large rooms equipped with rectangular tables and surrounded by interpreters' booths to provide simultaneous translation into the official EU languages. The meetings are far from intimate; typically, each delegation (and the Commission) will have three seats at the table (minister, permanent representative, assistant) and up to another half dozen who are waiting in the margins for a specific agenda point to be discussed. Normally, there are more than 100 people in the room at any one point, with lots of bilateral conversations, note passing, and strategizing going on at the same time as the individual who has the floor and is speaking.

COREPER

COREPER is the preparatory body of the Council, making it one of the most intense sites of negotiation in the EU. Whereas the ministers meet monthly at best, COREPER meets weekly. Officially, COREPER is charged with 'preparing the work of the Council', which reveals remarkably little about how important the committee has become in making the Council run smoothly. Whereas any particular ministerial Council will be focused on a particular sectoral issue or set of policies, the members of COREPER negotiate across the entire gamut of EU affairs and thus hold the unique responsibility for maintaining the performance of the Council as a whole. In short, COREPER acts as a process manager in the Council system between the ministers and the experts in the working groups. As an institution, COREPER has a unique vantage point because it is vertically placed between the experts and the ministers and horizontally situated with cross-sectoral and inter-pillar policy responsibilities.

Because of the heavy workload in preparing upcoming Councils, since 1962 COREPER has split into two groups: I and II (see Box 9.5). COREPER I

BOX 9.5

Division of labour between COREPER I and II

COREPER II

General Affairs and External Relations Council

Justice and Home Affairs

Multiannual budget negotiations

Structural and cohesion funds

Institutional and horizontal questions

Development and association agreements

Accession

IGC personal representatives (varies by member state and IGC)

COREPER I

Single European Market (Internal Market, Competitiveness)

Conciliation in areas of codecision

Environment

Employment, Social Policy, Health and Consumer Affairs

Transport, Telecommunications, and Energy

Fisheries

Agriculture (veterinary and plant-health questions)

Education, Youth, and Culture

---

is made up of the deputy permanent representatives, responsible for preparing the so-called 'technical' Councils (Competitiveness, Environment, Transport, and so on). The ambassadors (who hold the title of 'EU permanent representative') preside over COREPER II and primarily work to prepare the monthly GAERC meetings as well as issues with horizontal, institutional, or financial implications. COREPER I and II are functionally independent bodies (responsible for different formations of the Council), though the EU ambassadors in COREPER II have a more senior status with the national capitals. The permanent representatives live in Brussels and hold their positions for several years; some stay for a decade or longer, often outliving their political masters (ministers, prime ministers) and providing crucial continuity in the representation of national interests. The selection of an EU ambassador and deputy is considered a top appointment by member states, and some argue this may be the single most important posting that a member state will make.

The most critical feature of COREPER is nowhere discernible in the Treaties, namely the intensity of the negotiations that take place to prepare the ministers' meetings. Aside from the weekly meetings, COREPER also holds restricted lunch sessions (not even the translators are allowed in the room) to sort out the most sensitive and tricky problems. The permanent representatives also sit beside the minister at Council meetings, and attend European Council summits. But putting a finger on the precise value added by COREPER is tricky, since the permanent representatives have no formal decision-making authority. It is clear, however, that COREPER is an important de facto decision-making body, seen by the steady stream of 'A points' which are sent to the ministers for formal adoption. Over the years, COREPER has functioned under a fairly heavy cloak of confidentiality and insulation from domestic politics and domestic constituent pressures. This insulation enables a level of frankness in COREPER discussions essential to reaching compromise across so many different subject areas.

Because of the intensity of negotiations and the long periods of tenure, COREPER officials often develop close personal relations with one another, based on mutual trust and a willingness to try and help each other. In this kind of normative environment and under the pressures to keep the Council moving forward, the permanent representatives are always on the lookout for ways to reach compromise. At times, the search for collective solutions can border on collusion, and the permanent representatives will at times 'go out on a limb' to sell the results of an agreement back home to the relevant authorities. The permanent representatives also exemplify the enigmatic identity of the Council—in order to succeed, they must at the same time represent a national set of interests and share a responsibility for finding collective solutions. COREPER

illustrates how the Council is more than just defending national interests; it is also a collective decision-making process embedded in social relations and informal norms of mutual responsiveness, empathy, and self-restraint.

Working groups

The expert group is the workhorse of the Council. Currently numbering over 200, the working group level is a vast network of national officials who specialize in specific areas (such as food safety, the Middle East, olive oil, and financial services) and form the initial starting point for negotiations on any new proposal or issue. The working group is also used in the later stages of negotiation to contemplate specific points of disagreement, and can serve as a convenient way to place a proposal in 'cold storage' until the political climate is more favorable for an agreement. Some working groups are permanent, while others are ad hoc and disappear after tackling a specific question or issue. The working groups are staffed with officials travelling from the capitals or from the Brussels-based Permanent Representations, depending on the issue area involved. The purpose of the working group is to presolve as much technical and fine detail as possible, while leaving areas where there is disagreement or the need for political consideration to the permanent representatives or the ministers who have neither the time, nor, in many cases, the substantive knowledge to hold such finely grained discussions.

It is easy to assume the working group level is well catalogued, orderly, and coherent, but the reality is much the opposite. The working group level suffers from bureaucratic sprawl in the Council system, and because it covers such a wide range of issues and policy sectors, it is on the whole very difficult to monitor. For example, in 2008, over 50 groups were linked to the GAERC alone (18 covering horizontal questions (such as enlargement and legislative codification) and 36 dealing with external relations (such as Africa, sanctions, terrorism, and the Middle East peace process).

The working group 'expert', though a vital part of the Council's performance, is not always appreciated at other levels of the Council. The permanent representatives meeting in COREPER, for example, can view their own national experts with some disdain for what one described as their 'bloody single-mindedness' over technical merits without an appreciation of political realities or the broader picture. Likewise, an expert will sometimes feel undermined when a permanent representative or a minister concedes a point that they spent five months defending as absolutely essential at the working group level.

Council General Secretariat

The Council employs a bureaucracy of approximately 3,300 officials known as the Council General Secretariat (CGS). Jobs are carefully allotted to all 27 member states, with the majority being linguistic and clerical positions. For instance, the CGS legal service numbers 201 employees, of whom 83 are linguistic experts. In 2007 the CGS had 1,226 staff devoted to translation and document production. The top jobs are the 'A grade' (policy-making) positions, which number about 300 in total. At the very top are the highly prestigious Secretary-General and Deputy Secretary-General positions, which are only filled after an agreement is made by the heads of state and government. The CGS is the administrative backbone and institutional memory of the Council. Organizationally, the CGS is divided into the Private Offices of the Secretary-General and the Deputy Secretary-General, a Legal Service, a Press Office, and eight Directorates-General for different policy areas (see Box 9.6).

The CGS is officially charged with keeping a record of all meetings, including note taking (and producing the minutes of the meeting), and translating all documents into the EU's 23 official languages. The CGS is also an important asset and ally of the Presidency, providing logistical assistance, offering advice, and helping to find constructive solutions (the famous 'Presidency compromise'). Over the years, the CGS has earned the reputation of being a dedicated, highly professional team. The commitment of the CGS personnel to the Council's work has also earned them the reputation of being 'honest brokers' and helping the presidency find solutions acceptable to all (see Box 9.7).

Perhaps the key factor in the ascendance of the CGS in EU politics is the office of the Council Secretary-General. In the history of the EU, the position has only changed hands five times. There is no official rule about how long a Secretary-General serves, but the long tenure of the position gives the Council an important element of continuity and leadership. Under Niels Ersbøll, the

---

BOX 9.6

Organization of the Council General Secretariat

Office of the Secretary-General and High Representative of CFSP

Office of the Deputy Secretary-General

Private Office (Top advisors to the Secretary-General and the Deputy Secretary-General)

Legal Service

Directorate-General A: Personnel and Administration

Directorate-General B: Agriculture and Fisheries

Directorate-General C: Internal Market, Competitiveness, Industry, Research, Energy, Transport, Information Society

Directorate-General E: External Economic Relations, Common Foreign and Security Policy

Directorate-General F: Press, Communication, Protocol

Directorate-General G: Economic and Social Affairs

Directorate-General H: Justice and Home Affairs

Directorate-General I: Protection of the Environment, Consumers, Health, Foodstuffs, Education, Youth, Culture, Audiovisual

Source: Council's website.

The Council General Secretariat as an honest broker

The CGS has earned a reputation for finding creative EU solutions to deadlocked negotiations and helping to defuse potential political crises. In particular, the CGS legal staff, which is well versed in the intricacies of the Treaties, is a team of committed Europeanists and an important source of supranational entrepreneurship in the EU. As of 2009 the long-standing head of the Council's Legal Service was Director-General Jean-Claude Piris. He is legendary for his ability to innovate legal solutions to seemingly intractable problems. The most famous is his work on devising a Danish 'opt-out' to the Maastricht provisions on joining the Single Currency and foreign policy cooperation with defence implications (following Denmark's 'no' vote). The opt-outs were a creative way to make the TEU palatable to Danish voters yet avoided renegotiating the entire Treaty. Although some point out that the Danish opt-outs also had

the unintended consequence of creating a precedent for other member states to use in the future when they disagreed with new EU policies, creating new momentum for an à la carte EU (pick and choose).

The CGS has also become such a skilful advisor to the rotating Presidency that some member states ask the CGS for help with domestic coordination meetings on EU policy. For instance, during the 1998 Austrian Presidency, members of the GCS were asked to travel to Vienna and brief the cabinet ministers on the state of the Agenda 2000 negotiations, which covered reform of EU spending policies and the 2000–6 budget. As one advisor in the Secretary-General's office recalls, the trip to Vienna was designed so that the CGS would 'orchestrate an internal coordination meeting' among the Austrian ministries to help produce a set of presidency conclusions (interview, Brussels, May 2000). This example nicely illustrates how the CGS is entrusted as an honest broker.

---

long-serving Secretary-General (1980–94) from Denmark, the CGS was transformed from relative obscurity to a central position in Council negotiations, albeit a behind-the-scenes role that is not often credited in public (Hayes-Renshaw and Wallace 1997: 108-109). The position of Secretary-General was granted new authority following the decision by the heads of state and government at the 1999 Cologne European Council to upgrade

the office to include the title of High Representative of Common Foreign and Security Policy (unofficially dubbed 'Mr CFSP') and to appoint the then Secretary-General of NATO, Javier Solana, to the position (see Box 9.7 for more). The Deputy Secretary-General is now entrusted with the task of overseeing the day-to-day operations of the Council, and participates in the weekly COREPER II meetings.

KEY POINTS

- European Council meetings (summits) are the source of most 'history-making' decisions in the history of European integration.

- The European Council is under great demand to provide leadership and overall guidance in setting the pace and direction of the integration process.

- The ministerial Councils are divided by policy. Three (the GAERC, ECOFIN/Eurogroup, AGFISH) stand out for the level of work and frequency of meetings.

- COREPER is the official preparatory body for the Council, which gives the EU ambassadors and deputies the pri-

mary responsibility of prenegotiating and discussing the agendas of every upcoming Council session.

- The working groups are the biggest single dimension of the Council's work, involving thousands of national experts and handling the technical and fine-grained detail of specific proposals.

- The Council has a permanent secretariat, the CGS, which helps facilitate meetings, takes notes, translates documents, and serves as an advisor to the presidency.

Institutional evolution over time, and current challenges

Of all the accolades that one can find written about the Council's ability to forge compromise among sovereign states with divergent interests, few claim that the Council is an efficient decision-making system. It takes about 18 months on average for a new proposal to work its way through the stages of negotiation in the Council and with the EP, though there are some cases that take much longer. A few notorious examples include the directive on lawnmower noise (84/538/EEC), negotiated over a dozen years to harmonize the maximum decibel level mowers can make, or the chocolate directive (2000/36/EC), which took 26 years to reach agreement on a common definition for 'chocolate products'!

The ministers' meetings in particular show signs of strain. Never known for their punctuality and often the brunt of jokes for their lack of preparedness, the ministers do not always hold highly productive meetings. One former British minister, Alan Clark (1993: 139), recalls his fondness for Council meetings in his memoirs : 'The ministers arrive on the scene at the last minute, hot, tired, ill or drunk (sometimes all of these together), read out their piece and depart.' This has become more problematic as the competences of the EU have evolved and agendas have grown more extensive, even overloaded. For example, GAERC agendas grew from an average of 8.4 items per meeting in 1990 to 36.2 in 2000 (Gomez and Peterson 2001: 7-8). One implication is that as agendas continue to swell, the actual discussions over substance are taking place at the level of COREPER, seen by the growth of 'A points', which are merely rubber-stamped by the ministers. In 1995, the proportion of items on the GAERC agenda that were passed without debate was 34 per cent of the total agenda; in 2000, that figure had increased to 54 per cent (Gomez and Peterson 2001: 9). Another implication of this overload is that overall coordination is increasingly left to the European Council. In light of these dysfunctions and in antic-

ipation of adding new members from the east, the Lisbon Treaty has devised a number of important institutional revisions for the Council (see Box 9.8). Whether the Lisbon Treaty is eventually adopted remains to be seen, but few Council participants believe the current system can continue for much longer without fundamental reform.

If internally the Council shows signs of strain and overload, the external problem of credibility with EU citizens is of equal concern. Since the 1990s, the issue of the 'democratic deficit' has been at the top of the EU's agenda. But the inner workings of the Council have so far avoided scrutiny. Reducing the democratic deficit has centred on reforming the EU's decision-making procedures, increasing involvement by the European Parliament, and introducing the subsidiarity principle to keep decisional authority as close to the citizen as possible. But addressing the democratic deficit inside the Council remains controversial. Every member government pays lip service to the need for the Union to be more transparent, more accessible, and more connected to EU citizens, but there is less agreement among them on how best to accomplish this task in Council deliberations. One innovation was to hold 'public debates' by broadcasting select Council meetings on television and the internet, but this has the perverse effect of stifling real dialogue, since the ministers simply began reading from set speeches. Instead of increasing the transparency of the Council's work, public debates merely promote the reading of 'successive monologues' (Galloway 1999). The Council's Rules of Procedure have become more detailed on requirements for deliberations 'open to the public' (via TV and the internet). Specifically, this is to include open sessions on the adoption of codecision acts, the 'first deliberation on important new legislative proposals' that do not involve codecision, and, within the GAERC, an open 'public policy debate' on the 18-month Presidency 'trio' programme (Article 8, Rules of Procedure).

BOX 9.8

Lisbon Treaty reforms and the Council

Should the Lisbon Treaty be ratified, the Council will change in the following ways:

New qualified majority voting system (Article 16): Possibly the single most contentious item debated during the Lisbon IGC was how to reform the system of qualified majority voting. The new design is a double majority system that scraps the controversial voting weights reset during the Nice Treaty in anticipation of future enlargements. The new system would take effect from 1 November 2014 and would be based on two threshold requirements:

- at least 55 per cent of the member states (that is, at least 15 in an EU27)

- representing at least 65 per cent of the total EU population.

An additional clause requires at least four member states to form a 'blocking minority'. This provides safeguards against hypothetical big-state coalitions that could be used to block legislation (any three of the big four—Germany, France, Britain, Italy—represent more than 35 per cent of the EU's population).

European Council President (Article 15): Part effort to improve coherence and part effort to leverage Europe's ability to speak with a single voice, the idea of a senior statesperson to represent the Union and Chair the summits of the heads of state and government was an institutional innovation widely hailed in national capitals. The European Council appoints the President by qualified majority for a term of 2.5 years (renewable once). The Council President cannot wear a 'double hat'—they must not simultaneously hold a national office (Article 15.5). The European Council President is expected to:

- chair meetings of the European Council and drive forward its work

- ensure the preparation and continuity of the work of the European Council

- endeavour to facilitate cohesion and consensus

- issue a report to the EP after each summit.

Upgraded Foreign Policy Chief (Article 18): Upgrading the 'Mr CFSP' post was an early consensus of the Constitutional Convention. While some members, such as the British, could not ultimately swallow the proposed title change—to EU Foreign Minister—the agreed title 'High Representative of the Union for Foreign Affairs and Security Policy' still carries with it a substantial enhancement of institutional clout. It is the area where, practically speaking, the EU gains the most visible international legal personality. Lauded as Europe's answer to Henry Kissinger's famous quip back in 1973, 'I wouldn't know who to call if I wanted to talk to Europe,' the political significance is to enhance the policy-making coherence of CFSP and ESDP.

For scholars of the EU, the new post is intriguing because it explicitly blurs the institutional boundaries between the Council and Commission in ways previously unheard of. To avoid organizational chaos in EU external relations, the new foreign policy 'supremo' is not only a top Council actor, but a Vice-President of the Commission in charge of the sizable external relations budget. Duties would include:

- chairing the External Relations portion of the GAERC

- attending European Council meetings

- serving as a Vice-President of the Commission and running the External Relations DG

- representing the EU externally and conducting high-level diplomacy.

Enhanced Cooperation (Article 20): Seen by many as the formalization and legitimation of an à la carte (pick and choose) Europe. This was packaged as a way to 'further the objectives of the Union, protect its interests and reinforce its integration process' but a more cynical way of putting it is that vanguard or core members can no longer be held back in policy areas by the most reluctant integrationists. Enhanced cooperation is, however, considered 'a last resort' when 'cooperation cannot be attained … by the Union as a whole'. Outsiders may still participate in deliberations but they have no voting rights. Adopted acts would only bind participating member states and do not become part of the EU *acquis*.

Source: Consolidated versions of the Treaty on European Union and the Treaty on the Functioning of the European Union, OJ C115, Volume 51, 9 May 2008.

CASE STUDY 9.9

How Turkey might imbalance the 'big state' club of voting power in the Council

The eventual membership of Turkey is one of the EU's most politicized issues. In the press, the issue is often presented as whether Turkey is part of 'Europe', touching on the identity politics of Islam and Christianity stretching back over the centuries. Academics tend to focus more on the high hurdles Turkey faces in meeting the *acquis communautaire* or passing the constitutionally required referendum on the subject in France. Less attention is paid to how radically Turkey could shake up the delicate balancing of national power within the Council. The problem, in a nutshell, is this: overnight Turkey would become the first or second most powerful vote on the Council, leapfrogging the French, the British, the Italians, the Spanish, the Polish, and eventually overtaking the Germans. By current demographic projections, Turkey would be the most populous state in a future hypothetical EU sometime around 2015 and hence the most powerful vote on the Council. Thus it is likely that behind the more vocal worries of smaller members such as Austria and Greece lie deep reservations by many of the founding and big-state members who are concerned about the institutional and decision-making implications of 'absorbing' such a large and heterogeneous newcomer.

Population/ Projections (millions)	Year			
	2005	2008	2015	2025
Turkey	72.7	75.8	82.5	90.5
Germany	82.4	82.4	82.0	80.6
France	62.9	64.1	66.3	68.5
United Kingdom	60.4	60.9	62.2	63.8
Italy	58.1	58.1	57.7	56.2
Spain	40.3	40.5	40.5	39.6
Poland	38.6	38.5	38.3	37.4

Source: Summary demographic data, US Census Bureau, International Database, 2008.

While the EU doggedly remains hard to predict, there are two areas that show signs of posing future challenges with potentially unsettling implications. The first issue is enlargement (see Chapter 26). Can the Council continue to operate the same in an EU of 27+ member states? Some believe that the Council will become such an unwieldy and heterogeneous body that it will become little more than a 'talking shop' of ministers. An EU of 27 places strain on the Council's decision-making structures—originally built for six members—and will likely slow down the pace and output of new legislation even further. Enlargement is also likely to increase the workload on COREPER and the expert groups, which will hold greater responsibilities for discussing substantive issues and finding agreements at their levels. Finally, how easily the Council's decision-making system can consolidate its new members will depend on how quickly and extensively they become socialized to the EU's normative environment. If for example, the new members are slow to absorb the established norms of compromise and accommodation, the Council may develop a more rigid 'veto culture' or even divide into different voting blocks along geographic or GDP lines. Of particular concern is the future admission of Turkey, which could alter the balance of national voting power in the Council in dramatic and unpredictable ways (see Box 9.9).

The second issue is differentiation and variable geometry. How will the Council change as the EU becomes more polycentric and differentiated? 'Enhanced' forms of cooperation, which were for the first time incorporated into the Treaties with Nice, pose certain risks in altering the very finely tuned mechanisms of exchange and consensus-seeking which has become a reflexive habit among Council participants. While many view differentiation as a method of promoting diversity and preventing the blockage of integration by reluctant or recalcitrant members, others see differentiation as setting a dangerous precedent for different 'classes' of membership which challenge the principle of equality.

Conclusion: national, supranational, or both?

The Council is the main decision-making body of the EU. It is the premier EU institution for representing national interests and power. But it is also a collective system of governance that locks member states into permanent negotiations with one another. National officials who participate in this system have developed their own 'rules of the game' which include a culture of behaving consensually through compromise and mutual accommodation. Thus, strictly speaking, the Council is both an institution that represents national interests and a body at the supranational level that makes collective decisions. When examined closely, researchers often find evidence that the Council blurs the traditional distinctions between the national and European levels, between intergovernmentalism and supranationalism. As a leading study of the Council concludes, national officials who participate in this system face a 'continuous tension between the home affiliation and the pull of the collective forum' (Hayes-Renshaw and Wallace 1997: 279). It is this feature more than any other that really distinguishes the Council of the European Union from other international institutions and forums of inter-state cooperation.

Whether the Council can continue to operate as it did for the first 50 years remains open to debate. There are signs of strain on decision makers, as agendas continue to balloon and the lines of coordination

and coherence between Councils atrophy. Enlargement of the EU to 27+ members risks stretching the system to the point of paralysis. Even at 15, following the 'Nordic round' of enlargement in 1995, many Brussels insiders characterized the Council as operating 'over capacity'. In pragmatic terms, the decision-making system originally made for six cannot function the same at nearly 30; Council participants claim that such a large table is now needed for meetings that many rely on small-screen televisions strategically placed in front of each delegation, to see the face of the person talking.

There are also serious questions of democratic accountability which remain unanswered, as Council deliberations continue to be obscure and mysterious to EU citizens. Reshuffling the formations of the ministers' meetings or splitting the work of 'general affairs' into an internal institutional and external foreign policy format is no substantive remedy. Council reform faces sharp trade-offs between greater transparency that is ineffective (public debates leading to set speeches) and more effective decision making that takes place behind closed doors and out of the public spotlight (lunches, restricted sessions).

Finally, the new focus on differentiated integration could have perverse effects on Council decision making as some member states may find themselves excluded from certain discussions altogether, as we already see in areas of eurozone policy making (see Chapter 20). This would have the unprecedented effect of creating different tiers or classes of membership. On the other hand, the EU has shown a remarkable capacity over the years to cope with crises and innovate new governance solutions. The current halfway-house status of the Lisbon Treaty is only the most recent illustration of this. The issue of 'institutional reform' is thus likely to be unresolved for some time, and, in a governance system this advanced, may even be an endemic feature of the EU's agenda.

? QUESTIONS

1. In what manner does the Council perform both legislative and executive functions in the European Union?

2. What kind of institution is the Council? Is it intergovernmental or supranational?

3. Do big states outweigh smaller states in power resources and influence in the Council? If so, how? If not, why not?

4. How do the member states coordinate the representation of national interests in Council negotiations?

5. What role does the rotating Presidency play in EU governance?

6. How does the Council General Secretariat act as a 'neutral umpire' and facilitator of meetings? How might this detract from the influence of the Commission?

7. How have Council–EP relations changed since the 1990s?

8. How and why have European Council summits increased in importance over time?

GUIDE TO FURTHER READING

- de Bassompierre, *G. Changing the Guard in Brussels: An Insider's View of the EC Presidency* (New York: Praeger, 1988). A candid, highly readable account of the role of the rotating Presidency.

- Hayes-Renshaw, F. and Wallace, H. *The Council of Ministers*, 2nd edn (New York: St. Martin's Press, 2006). The definitive study of the Council as a decision-making institution, newly updated to reflect changes since the mid 1990s.

- Naurin, D. and Wallace, H. (eds) *Unveiling the Council of the European Union: Games Governments Play in Brussels* (London and New York: Palgrave Macmillan, 2008). An edited volume that presents new data and contrasts different approaches to theorizing Council decision making.

- Tallberg, J. *Leadership and Negotiation in the European Union* (Cambridge: Cambridge University Press, 2006). A systematic account of how the rotating Presidency matters, informed by a sophisticated model in the 'new institutionalism' tradition.

- Westlake, M. and Galloway, D. *The Council of the European Union*, 3rd edn (London: Cartermill, 2004). A comprehensive study, including a useful comparison of the working methods of different formations of the Council.

WEBLINKS

- http://consilium.europa.eu   The Council's official homepage. The website includes links to specific policies and brief summaries for each Council formation's main purpose. Some links offer considerable insight, such as the Council's own 'Codecision Guide' for national delegations (http://www.consilium.europa.eu/cms3_fo/showPage.asp?id=447&lang=EN&mode=g). Under the 'Press' heading, one can find the calendar of upcoming meetings as well as the agendas and a photo archive. Access to Council documents online (including the minutes to Council meetings since 1999) has improved considerably over the last decade. To locate recent Council acts there are several ways to proceed, including a 'simple search' using keywords in the Public Register; or by date, through the 'monthly summary of Council acts'.

- http://www.consilium.europa.eu/cms3_fo/showPage.asp?id=695&lang=en&mode=g   The listing of the websites of current and former EU Presidencies. Here one can find basic news, information about a Presidency's legislative priorities, upcoming agendas, and the always important 'Presidency conclusions' of European Council summits.

- http://www.consilium.europa.eu/cms3_applications/applications/solana/index.asp?lang=EN&cmsid=246   The homepage of Javier Solana, unofficially known as 'Mr. CFSP'. The information available here is voluminous, including press releases and statements, speeches, articles, and a monthly calendar that lists his peripatetic schedule. Even more personable is his YouTube page found here: http://www.youtube.com/user/EUHRSolana.

Visit the Online Resource Centre that accompanies this book for lots of interesting additional material. http://www.oxfordtextbooks.co.uk/orc/Cini_Borragan3e/

10 The European Parliament

ROGER SCULLY

Chapter Contents

- Introduction
- The origins and development of the European Parliament
- The powers and influence of the European Parliament
- The internal politics of the European Parliament
- Elections, the people, and the European Parliament
- Conclusion

Reader's Guide

This chapter examines the European Parliament (EP), and its role within the institutional system of the European Union (EU). Unlike the bodies covered in the previous two chapters, the Commission and the EU Council, the EP has only fairly recently assumed prominence in the EU's governing structures. The first section of the chapter outlines the origins of the Parliament as an essentially marginal institution within the developing structures of European cooperation. The following section then reviews in detail the significant increases in powers experienced by the EP in recent times, and discusses how these have transformed the importance of the chamber. After that, the chapter goes on to examine the complex internal politics of the EP, namely its membership, organization, and working practices. Finally, the chapter considers the 'electoral connection'—in other words, the links between the EP and the European public. The general conclusion is that the European Parliament has been strikingly successful in gaining more powers, but far less successful in linking the EU to the peoples of Europe.

Introduction

Compared to many national and even subnational legislatures, the European Parliament enjoys a relatively low public profile. Scholars of the European Union, too, have not traditionally devoted substantial attention to the EP, judging it less important than other governing institutions of the Union. For much of its life, the EP could have justly been labelled a 'multi-lingual talking shop'. This is no longer the case. Since the mid 1980s, the EP has undergone probably more substantial changes than any other major EU body. And the cumulative effect of many of these changes has been to enhance greatly the importance of the Parliament within the Union's governing structures. This chapter examines the development of the EP, and its role within the EU's political system. As with parliamentary institutions in other systems, to understand the role of the European Parliament adequately we must consider three major topics. These are:

- The *legislative work* of the Parliament: its role in developing and shaping policies and laws.
- The *internal politics* of the Parliament: the organizational structures of the chamber, and the competition within it between different political parties and ideologies.
- The *representative role* of the Parliament: as a chamber comprised of elected representatives, its role as 'voice of the people' in linking the political system to the public.

As we shall see, while the EP has developed considerably as an institution, it still faces significant challenges with regard to the representation dimension. These challenges matter not just for the Parliament, but potentially for the EU as a whole. Before examining all this, however, it is necessary to give a brief overview of the origins and development of the EP.

The origins and development of the European Parliament

For much of its life, the European Parliament has been fairly marginal to the development of European integration and to the politics of the EU. To understand that, and to appreciate how much has changed since the mid-1980s, we must be aware of the EP's rather modest origins.

What is now the European Parliament began life as the Common Assembly of the nascent European Coal and Steel Community (ECSC) in 1952. This new assembly was not central to the plans of the 'founding fathers' of integration: 'In Jean Monnet's vision, it was, together with the European Court of Justice, an institution of control and scrutiny, not of decision making' (Neunreither 2000: 133). Thus the new chamber was given limited and specific responsibilities. It could discuss policies and scrutinize their execution. And it could, in principle, dismiss the High Authority, the forerunner to today's

European Commission (see Chapter 8) for gross mismanagement. But over new policies and laws it could only issue opinions to which other institutions were not compelled to respond. A further source of weakness was that the Assembly's membership was not directly elected by voters, but drawn from member states' national parliaments. This provided a direct link between the European Coal and Steel Community and national political systems, but it also ensured that the Common Assembly, as well as having restricted powers, could only ever be a part-time institution, as its members still had national parliamentary responsibilities to fulfil.

The assembly met originally in Strasbourg. Among the many reasons for this was the symbolism of a parliamentary chamber meeting to discuss European cooperation in a city that had long been disputed territory between France and Germany.

Support staff for the Assembly were originally based in Luxembourg, alongside the ECSC High Authority. As the EU has increasingly centred its operations in Brussels, the EP has come to conduct more of its business and base more staff in the EU capital. However, rather than locate all EP activities there, national governments have continued to insist (against the wishes of most MEPs) that the Parliament hold regular plenary sessions in Strasbourg, and maintain some staff in Luxembourg. This situation hampers the work of the EP, requires costly duplication of buildings and other facilities, and generates some understandable ridicule.

The original Common Assembly consisted of 78 nominated national parliamentarians from the then six ECSC member states. By the time of the 2009 elections, the European Parliament (as it had renamed itself in 1962) comprised 734 elected representatives from 27 states (see Box 10.1 for a description of how the composition of the EP has changed over time). The Rome Treaty in the late 1950s had called for the Chamber to become an elected institution. Yet the first European Parliament elections did not take place until 1979. A central reason for this delay was that governments and parties hostile to the development of stronger European-level institutions foresaw an elected European Parliament being in a powerful position to argue for greater powers. After all, the EP would be (indeed, it remains to this day) the only directly elected European institution, and it could use this democratic status to argue for enhanced powers. Such fears proved well founded, and whatever wider concerns remain regarding EP elections (see below), the

---

CHRONOLOGY 10.1

The growth of the EP

Year	No. of MEPs	No. of member states	Status of MEPs	Title of chamber
1952	78	6	Nominated	ECSC Common Assembly
1958	142	6	Nominated	EC Common Assembly
1973	198	9[a]	Nominated	European Parliament
1979	410	9	Elected	European Parliament
1981	434	10[b]	Elected	European Parliament
1986	518	12[c]	Elected	European Parliament
1994	567	12[d]	Elected	European Parliament
1995	626	15[e]	Elected	European Parliament
2005	732	25[f]	Elected	European Parliament
2007	785	27[g]	Elected	European Parliament
2009	734*	27	Elected	European Parliament

[a] Enlargement to Denmark, Ireland, and UK
[b] Enlargement to Greece
[c] Enlargement to Spain and Portugal
[d] German enlargement and seat redistribution
[e] Enlargement to Austria, Finland, and Sweden
[f] Enlargement to Cyprus, Czech Republic, Estonia, Hungary, Latvia, Lithuania, Malta, Poland, Slovakia, and Slovenia
[g] Enlargement to Bulgaria and Romania
* The number of MEPs was reduced in most member states in line with the provisions of the Nice Treaty.

elected Parliament has proven a strong advocate of both closer European integration generally and more powers for itself in particular (Corbett 1998; Rittberger 2005). By the mid 1990s, the EP was no longer a marginal institution, but a central, 'mainstream' part of the Union's governing system.

KEY POINTS

- The European Parliament originated as an unelected, part-time institution with limited powers.

- The EP's powers were originally restricted to supervision and scrutiny of other institutions, apart from the ability to remove the High Authority in exceptional circumstances.

- Over time, the chamber has changed its name to the European Parliament, grown substantially in size, and become an elected institution.

The powers and influence of the European Parliament

Since the 1970s, treaty amendments and institutional agreements have greatly enhanced the European Parliament's power. (Box 10.2 summarizes the major changes described below). The first major advance for the Parliament came in the realm of the Community budget. Two treaties in the 1970s granted the EP the right to propose modifications to planned 'compulsory' spending (mainly on agriculture), to insist on amendments to 'non-compulsory' spending, and the right (if supported by an absolute majority of all MEPs and two-thirds of those voting) to reject the budget outright. This power has been exercised twice, in 1979 and 1984. The Parliament's budgetary role was further enhanced from the late 1980s onwards by a series of 'Inter-Institutional Agreements' between the Council, Commission, and Parliament, which meant that Parliamentary approval was henceforth needed for increases in most areas of EU spending; these agreements ran parallel to multi-year budgetary deals that, by fixing for several years ahead broad spending priorities, allowed the Parliament to give greater attention to monitoring EU expenditure.

The Parliament has made more limited progress in terms of executive oversight, in part because the EU political system lacks a clear executive branch to oversee. Many executive functions, notably in foreign affairs, remain in the hands of national governments who yield only reluctantly, and to a limited extent, to scrutiny from the EP. Nonetheless, the Parliament can dismiss the Commission and would have used this power in March 1999, in response to evidence of Commission mismanagement, had they not been pre-empted by the Commission's resignation. The EP's powers over the Commission were enhanced by the Maastricht and Amsterdam Treaties, which first gave the chamber veto power over the new Commission nominated by national governments, and then separate vetoes over both the Commission President-designate and the entire team of Commissioners. In 2004, these powers gave the Parliament sufficient political leverage to require changes to the team under the new Commission President, José Manuel Barroso, before parliamentary approval could be obtained (see Box 10.3). In addition, day-to-day scrutiny of the Commission is increasingly pursued by EP committees.

The growth of the EP

Year	Event	Impact on EP powers
1970	Treaty changes on budget	Greater budgetary powers for EP
1975	Treaty changes on budget	More budgetary powers for EP; EP given considerable influence over non-CAP spending
1980	*Isoglucose* judgment of ECJ	Right of consultation for EP reinforced
1987	Entry into force of Single Act	Cooperation procedure introduced for some legislation, giving EP greater scope for delay, amendment and blocking laws; assent powers to EP on some matters
1993	Maastricht Treaty enters into force	Codecision procedure introduced for some legislation; EP given approval power over nominated Commission
1999	Amsterdam Treaty enters into force	Codecision procedure altered in EP's favour and extended in scope; EP given formal right to veto Commission President nominee
2003	Nice Treaty enters into force	Further extension of scope of codecision procedure

Appointing the Barroso Commission

The appointment of the European Commission in 2004 illustrated the powers that the EP now possesses in term of executive oversight, and also the willingness of MEPs to use these powers.

Mr Barroso, the centre-right Portuguese Prime Minister at the time, was nominated by national governments of the EU member states in June 2004, shortly after the 2004 EP elections. The following month, he appeared before the European Parliament to seek endorsement for his nomination. Although this was forthcoming, Barroso received opposition from a significant number of MEPs; the final vote (413 in favour, 251 against, with 44 abstentions) saw him winning significantly less than two-thirds support.

However, Mr Barroso's problems became more serious when he sought to win approval for the team of Commissioners to work under him as President. Several of the nominees (agreed between Mr Barroso and the respective national governments of each nominee) did not impress EP Committees when forced to undergo 'confirmation hearings' by those committees. Opposition was particularly strong to the Italian nominee, Rocco Buttiglione. Mr Buttiglione was the prospective Commissioner on Justice, Freedom and Security; but when appearing before the EP's Civil Liberties Committee he made disparaging comments regarding homosexuals and women that rendered him unacceptable to many MEPs, particularly on the left.

Mr Barroso, along with the Italian Prime Minister, initially refused to withdraw Mr Buttiglione from the list of Commission nominees. However, on the day that the approval vote was due to occur (27 October 2004), Mr Barroso was forced to postpone the vote when informed that he was likely to be defeated. A delay of some weeks occurred before agreement was reached on an alternative Italian commissioner (Franco Frattini), and the Commission team won a comfortable majority in the EP in November.

The greatest advances made by the EP, however, have been in the area of EU law making. Prior to the Single European Act (SEA), the EP's role here was very limited. EU laws (other than Commission legislation) were processed via consultation (see Chapter 13). Under this legislative procedure, the Parliament could offer opinions but could not force the Commission or Council to respond to them. Aside from using delaying tactics (such as postponing the formal presentation of its opinion), the EP had no mechanism by which to influence legislation.

Strong lobbying of national governments for greater parliamentary powers bore some fruit in the SEA. Consultation was retained for most laws. But for much legislation related to the Single Market initiative, the cooperation procedure was introduced. This allowed Parliament to propose amendments to draft legislation (which, if supported by the Commission, could be overturned only by a unanimous Council but accepted by a qualified majority of states), or to issue a veto on pieces of legislation that could only be overturned by a unanimous Council of Ministers. This was undoubtedly a significant advance for the EP. The SEA also gave the EP assent power (that is, a simple yes or no vote) over matters like association agreements and the accession of new member states to the Union. This means that any EU enlargement has to be agreed by the EP. Equally, any future enlargement of the EU could be stopped by a vote in the EP, even if it had been agreed by the governments of all 27 member states.

The Maastricht Treaty produced a further significant change; after Maastricht, around one-quarter of laws were processed under another new procedure, codecision. Codecision laws were designated as Joint Acts of the EP and the Council of Ministers (rather than the Council alone), and the Parliament was granted the ability to exercise an irrevocable veto over legislative proposals. Most observers saw this as a considerable step forward. As Duff has noted: 'Maastricht marks the point in the Community's development at which the Parliament became the first chamber of a real legislature ... The codecision procedure means that it has now come of age as a law-making body (Duff 1994:31). The way in which Maastricht originally shaped the codecision procedure did cause concern among many MEPs because it appeared to allow for the Council, at the end of the procedure, to reject a compromise with Parliament and impose a 'take it or leave it' choice on MEPs. This possibility led MEPs to revise their Rules of Procedure so as to make it as unlikely as possible that governments would try to back MEPs into a corner. The 1997 Amsterdam Treaty revised codecision slightly, in a manner somewhat beneficial to the Parliament, and also extended it to further areas of EU law. The 2001 Nice Treaty extended the scope of codecision even further, so the most important European legislation now falls under the procedure, with almost all the rest processed under consultation. Were the Lisbon Treaty ever to be enacted, codecision would become the standard procedure, applied almost universally.

It is clear that the EP has become a much more powerful institution than it used to be. But how does the contemporary EP compare to other parliaments, such as those in EU member states, in terms of power and influence? Such comparisons are difficult to make with great precision. But two things are fairly clear. The first is that even after the expansion of codecision, the EP's formal powers are still more limited than those of many national parliaments, most of which have formal approval power over all pieces of legislation. But the second, and possibly more important, point is that the EP actually *uses* its powers to a greater extent than do most national legislatures. Parliamentarians in most national chambers are bound by strong ties of party loyalty to support or oppose a government, and most governments have secure majorities that allow them effective control over parliaments. In the EP, with no clear government to either support or oppose, and with party loyalties also rather more diffuse, one sees a much greater willingness to exploit available powers to the full. Those who have attempted to evaluate the European Parliament's influence in comparative perspective thus tend to conclude that the EP actually ranks higher in this respect than many of its national counterparts (Scully 2000; Bergman and Raunio 2001).

The internal politics of the European Parliament

Life inside the European Parliament is complex. This complexity arises not only from the detailed and technical nature of the EU policies with which the Parliament spends much of its time dealing. Complexity is virtually inherent in the multinational, multilingual and multiparty political environment that the EP constitutes. This section of the chapter highlights some of the major features of politics within the Parliament.

MEPs in the 2009–14 Parliament will represent well over 100 separate national parties from the 27 member states. The Parliament thus encompasses a huge diversity of political viewpoints and previous political experiences. Although turnover at each election tends to be high (well over half of the members elected in June 2004 had not previously been MEPs), there are also many who have built long-term political careers at the European level. To an increasing extent, MEPs are professional politicians for whom being in the EP is a full-time job. Although some parties have been known to use the EP as a sort of 'political retirement home'—the current EP contains several former national prime ministers among its membership—most members work hard. The EP was once known for high levels of absenteeism amongst members compared to national parliaments; this is no longer the case. The EP also used to be known as a bastion of pro-integrationist opinion: in part because those less interested in the EU were more reluctant to stand as candidates for the EP. However, recent parliaments have included steadily growing numbers of Eurosceptic and anti-EU figures. The 2004 enlargement of the EU probably also contributed to changing the general ethos of the Parliament. A major survey of MEPs conducted by the European Parliament Research Group in 2006 found that those from the ten new member states were more right wing, and less supportive of closer European integration, than MEPs from the old 15 member states (Farrell et al 2006).

Individual national party delegations to the EP join together in multinational party groups, based broadly around political ideology. Being members of both national parties and European party groups, nationally elected yet working in a European institution, makes the task of the individual MEP as a representative potentially quite complicated. Most MEPs recognize the importance of balancing the interests of the several different constituencies that they represent. The party groups seek to bring together like-minded members from different states, yet they must always remain aware of differing national traditions and interests. Recent research has shown that in parliamentary votes the groups attain levels of intraparty unity that are, given the diversity of membership of the larger groups in particular, very high. Differences within the Parliament are structured far more frequently along party lines than national ones, and the voting unity of the party groups in the EP is much higher than that of the two parties in the US Congress (Hix et al 2006). Yet this unity must often be built on the basis of substantial 'give and take' between national delegations within the group, with agreement often following the lowest common denominator; even so, dissent from party group positions most often occurs when large numbers of MEPs from one or more national delegation refuse to support a group line (Hix 2002).

Although the party groups are ideologically based, intergroup relations in the Parliament have traditionally been based on cooperation rather than confrontation. The largest groups in the chamber have always been from the centre right (the European People's Party (EPP) group of Christian Democrats and some Conservatives) and the centre left (the Party of European Socialists (PES) group, renamed the Progressive Alliance of Socialists and Democrats (S & D) in 2009. For many years, these two blocs cooperated in sharing out most of the senior posts in the EP, as well as seeking consensus in most other matters before the Parliament. Recent years, however, have witnessed growing levels of voting division along left/right lines in the chamber, and some instances of public conflict between the major groups. A prime example has been the election of the Parliament's President. The two leading groups had long shared this job (which is held by each incumbent for two-and-a-half-years, half of a five-year EP term) between them and supported each other's candidates when the other group's 'turn' came around. In both July 1999 and January 2002, however, a PES candidate sought (unsuccessfully) the Presidency in opposition to candidates endorsed by the EPP. But in July 2004 and January 2007 the old EPP–PES duopoly was reasserted, with first Josep Borrell, a socialist, elected with EPP support, and two-and-a-half years later, a Christian Democrat, Hans-Gert Poettering, elected with socialist backing.

Party interests play an important part in the organization of business in the EP. The parliamentary hierarchy is headed by the Conference of Presidents, comprising the President of the EP, 14 Vice-Presidents and the leaders of the political groups. This body handles much of the scheduling of parliamentary business, and the allocation of things like committee chairships. The business of the Parliament itself is organized very tightly. The parliamentary timetable defines specific weeks as set aside for plenary sessions (usually one four-day session per month in Strasbourg, with a few additional 'mini-sessions' of two days in Brussels), other weeks being for committee work (usually two weeks in a month), with the balance of time reserved for 'party group weeks' and 'constituency weeks'. This hyperorganization of the parliamentary timetable extends also into the conduct of plenary sessions. Largely because of the need for extensive translation facilities, time for debates and individual contributions is planned very closely, literally almost down to the second.

The EP has a now well-established system of permanent committees (20 in the 2004–9 Parliament; see Box 10.4). These committees cover most areas of EU policy, and individual committees undertake both legislative work (scrutinizing draft legislation and drawing up amendments) and oversight activity (looking into the conduct of policy) in their area of responsibility. Some committees have also taken on a broader role: the Institutional Affairs Committee in previous parliaments (now the Constitutional Affairs Committee) sought to develop visionary proposals for deepening integration; the Women's Rights and Gender Equality Committee has often sought to broaden the degree to which gender-related considerations are incorporated into the EU; and the Foreign Affairs Committee has rarely felt itself restricted to discussing matters fitting directly within the Union's Foreign Security and Defence Policy. Many committees contain considerable expertise on their subject matter within their membership, and the committee system as a whole is widely regarded as the place where the bulk of the serious work of the Parliament is done. That work can sometimes be shaped by the influence of strong committee chairs. But, at least as often, committee work is led by the group coordinators appointed by the major party groups to each committee. And, on particular matters of policy, there is considerable scope for individual MEPs to have an impact, particularly if they are appointed *rapporteur*—the person delegated by a committee to prepare its report on a specific topic.

CASE STUDY 10.4

The Committees of the 2004–9 European Parliament

Committee Name

Foreign Affairs

Development

International Trade

Budgets

Budgetary Control

Economic and Monetary Affairs

Employment and Social Affairs

Environment, Public Health and Food Safety

Industry, Research and Energy

Internal Market and Consumer Protection

Transport and Tourism

Regional Development

Agriculture and Rural Development

Fisheries

Culture and Education

Legal Affairs

Civil Liberties, Justice and Home Affairs

Constitutional Affairs

Women's Rights and Gender Equality

Petitions

 CASE STUDY 10.5

The problems of multi-lingual parliamentary plenary sessions

The 27 member states of the EU produce, collectively, 23 main official languages for the Union (to say nothing of other minority languages like Catalan and Welsh). MEPs are permitted—indeed, expected—to make plenary speeches in their native language. But even with the provision of excellent translation facilities, the resulting 'Tower of Babel' effect can often hamper the cut and thrust of debate when the EP is in plenary session.

At a minimum, debate becomes more cumbersome. When speakers are using some of the less common languages (say Czech or Finnish) their words are translated into certain 'core' languages (usually English and French) before being re-translated into other tongues (like Italian and Latvian). Even when translation is entirely successful this can produce bizarre consequences; for example, a joke can potentially produce three waves of laughter!

Often the effect of translation is to lose subtleties of meaning, the passion of speeches, and even to produce total misunderstandings. The classic case occurred in the late 1990s. A French MEP was lamenting that discussion of an issue was not employing the common sense of the country people of Normandy, from where he hailed. Those hearing the English translation, however, were told that solving the problem in question needed Norman wisdom. To a large section of his audience—those familiar with the British comedian called Norman Wisdom—the serious point this MEP was seeking to make was thus entirely lost.

Plenary sessions include the great set-piece occasions of the EP's business. MEPs are frequently addressed by prime ministers and foreign ministers of member states, and sometimes of third countries. And on some occasions, as with the debates held over the nominations of new Commission Presidents, or that over the possible resignation of the Santer Commission in 1999, these can be genuinely dramatic events. Far more commonly, however, plenary sessions are tedious in the extreme: speeches tend to be more about putting certain views on the record than trying to persuade people, while Voting Time witnesses large numbers of votes, often on unrelated topics, being held one after the other. The problems of a multilingual institution also hamper plenary debates, making it often boring at best, confusing, and even farcical at worst (see Box 10.5).

Where does power ultimately lie in the EP? Compared to the executive-dominated parliaments of many countries in Europe, power in the EP is much more widely diffused. The lack of a controlling government party in the chamber, the importance of committees, and the multiparty and multinational nature of the institution all make the EP a highly complex and relatively 'de-centred' institution. This complexity, and the fact that some of the EP's major powers require the mobilization of 'super-majorities' (an absolute majority of all MEPs, not simply a majority of those participating in a particular vote) before they can be deployed, make compromise and coalition building a necessity and place a premium on subtle political skills. But this sort of environment also grants individual parliamentarians who possess such political skills greater scope to achieve substantive policy objectives in the EP than their national counterparts can achieve in most other parliamentary institutions.

KEY POINTS

- The membership of the EP comes from many different national political parties, is increasingly dominated by full-time MEPs, and now includes a significant number of Eurosceptics as well as integration enthusiasts.

- Party groups draw together individual national party delegations into broadly ideological collectives. The groups often have to compromise between different national viewpoints. The groups organize much of the work of the EP.

- Committees are where much of the detailed work of the EP is done. They provide opportunities for individual MEPs to make an impact on policy.

- EP plenary sessions are hampered by translation problems, and, with rare exceptions, tend to be dull and undramatic.

Elections, the people, and the European Parliament

Elected parliaments are a central, defining feature of democratic political systems. Their importance is more than simply symbolic. That institutions comprising the chosen representatives of the people be able to debate and give assent to major items of public policy, to voice public grievances, and to hold the executive to account, plays an important practical role in legitimating public authority. Put more simply, elected parliaments connect the people to the political system, and make legitimate the things done in the name of that political system. As the only elected institution in the EU, how well does the EP connect the people to the Union, and help legitimate the exercise of public authority at a European level?

EP elections are, in many respects, quite extraordinary exercises in democratic politics. In June 2009, many millions of people across 27 different countries voted (or at least were able to vote if they so wished) for a common legislative institution (Table 10.1 summarizes the number of MEPs elected in each country, and the method of election). This is an event that has no equivalent anywhere in the world, and to many people has had a powerful symbolism. But when one examines the elections more closely it becomes more difficult to sustain one's enthusiasm. EP elections are generally characterized by low turnouts, campaigns that fail to address seriously major issues facing the EU, and little popular interest or engagement.

Public participation in European elections is almost invariably at much lower levels than in national parliamentary elections. Moreover, as Figure 10.1 shows, average turnout levels across the Union have fallen in each of the last five elections, even as the

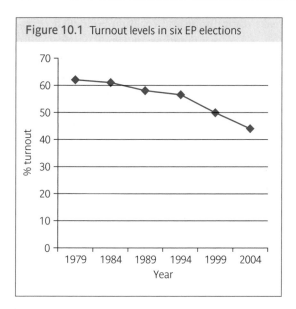

Figure 10.1 Turnout levels in six EP elections

EP has seen its powers grow considerably. Research on EP elections has suggested that one major reason for low (and declining) turnout is the widespread public perception that the elections are relatively unimportant. Such perceptions are in turn facilitated by the behaviour of political parties: in most member states, the major parties tend to focus their campaigns for EP elections on familiar national issues.

While the behaviour of parties is quite rational, in other words, emphasizing the themes most salient to voters, the outcome is election campaigns that do little to educate voters about the EU, or persuade them that there is much substantively at stake when they go to the polls. Rather, EP elections are treated by most parties and the vast majority of voters as second-order national elections, rather than contests where alternative visions of Europe might be offered, debated about, and decided upon by voters (Van der Eijk and Franklin 1996). Given that the elections are widely perceived as not mattering much, many voters take the opportunity to deliver a protest vote against government parties, who tend to do worse than opposition parties. But recent elections have also witnessed growing support for explicitly Eurosceptic or anti-EU parties, who now have significant representation in the EP (see Table 10.2).

Direct measures of public attitudes indicate very limited public awareness of the European Parliament. Although political elites now recognize the growing importance of the chamber, there is little or no evidence of this translating into public perceptions of a similar nature. The Eurobarometer survey of public opinion across the EU conducted in autumn 2008 (Eurobarometer No. 70) found only 53 per cent of citizens claiming to have recently heard anything about the EP. And 26 per cent of the sample correctly answered that the next set of elections to the Parliament was due to be held in 2009! The survey evidence does not suggest public hostility to the EP; but rather that the majority of the public neither know nor care enough to develop anything as active as hostility. Answers to survey questions about the Parliament by most citizens almost certainly embody a high degree of what public-opinion specialists term 'non-attitudes': in short, voters may be able to answer a question on the EP but such answers draw on little more than a general attitude towards the EU as a whole. Overall, it is difficult to dissent from the view that the Parliament suffers from a 'failure to even begin to penetrate the consciousness of so many of its electors' (Blondel et al 1998: 242).

Does this matter? Probably so, in two respects. It matters in an immediate sense for the EU as a whole. As stated earlier, elected parliaments are normally vital for the legitimation of the wider political system of which they are a part. Some in the EU have hoped that enhancing the powers of the elected institution might enhance the wider public legitimacy of European-level governance. Thus far, there is no sign that this strategy has worked or will work, as the public popularity of the EU has generally declined, even as the EP has grown more important (Farrell and Scully 2007; see also Chapter 24). In addition to this general implication for the EU, there is a specific implication for the EP itself. The Parliament has used its status as an elected body as an effective lever with which to attain its own empowerment. The EP's failure to build strong public support, either for itself or for the wider EU, may well lead in time to a fundamental questioning of the EP's role. As one sympathetic observer has suggested, 'it risks ... [an] insidious withering away of its basis of legitimacy because of voter disinterest' (Neunreither 2000: 135; see also Scully 2000).

Table 10.1 Representation in the 2009–14 European Parliament

Country	No. of MEPs	Population (millions)	Constituency type	People per constituency (average in millions)
Austria	17	8.1	National	8.1
Belgium	22	10.2	Regional	3.4
Bulgaria	17	7.7	National	7.7
Cyprus	6	0.8	National	0.8
Czech Rep.	22	10.3	National	10.3
Denmark	13	5.3	National	5.3
Estonia	6	1.4	National	1.4
Finland	13	5.1	National	5.1
France	72	60.4	Regional	7.6
Germany	99	82.0	National	82.0
Greece	22	10.5	National	10.5
Hungary	22	10.2	National	10.2
Ireland	12	3.7	Regional	0.9
Italy	72	57.6	National	57.6
Latvia	8	2.4	National	2.4
Lithuania	12	3.5	National	3.5
Luxembourg	6	0.4	National	0.4
Malta	5	0.4	National	0.4
Netherlands	25	15.8	National	15.8
Poland	50	38.6	Regional	3.0
Portugal	22	10.8	National	10.8
Romania	33	21.6	National	21.6
Slovakia	13	5.4	National	5.4
Slovenia	7	2.0	National	2.0
Spain	50	39.4	National	39.4
Sweden	18	8.9	National	8.9
UK	72	58.6	Regional	4.9

Table 10.2 The European Parliament in spring 2009

Party group	Political orientation	No. of MEPs (% of total)
European People's Party/European Democrats	Centre right (Christian Democrats and Conservatives	288 (36.7%)
Party of European Socialists	Centre left	200 (27.6%)
Alliance of Liberals and Democrats	Liberal	100 (12.7%)
Europe of Nations	Eurosceptic and generally right wing	44 (5.6%)
Greens/European Free Alliance	Environmentalist and some regionalists	43 (5.5%)
European United Left/Nordic Green Left	Left wing	41 (5.2%)
Independence/Democracy	Eurosceptic/anti-EU	22 (2.8%)
Non-attached	Various	30 (3.8%)

KEY POINTS

- As the elected institution, the EP ought to link the people and the EU, and thus build legitimacy for the Union.

- EP elections see low (and falling) turnout levels, and little debate about Europe featuring in the campaigns.

- Public knowledge of the EP is very limited, and this lack of public awareness and interest may bring the role of an elected EP into question.

Conclusion

The European Parliament is no longer a marginal part of the European Union's political system. It is a significant player in making EU policy, and it is thus important that students of the Union understand how the EP works. However, while the Parliament has been strikingly successful in accruing greater powers for itself, it has been far less effective in developing a profile with and support from the peoples of Europe. Addressing this task, rather than gaining powers, is surely now the major challenge facing the European Union's elected Parliament.

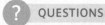

QUESTIONS

1. If the EP had been a powerful institution right from the beginning, how might the EU have developed differently?

2. Why did national governments increase the powers of the EP during the 1980s and 1990s?

3. Are there further powers that the EP ought to seek, in addition to those it now has?

4. Some people have suggested that the European Commission be elected from among the membership of the EP, rather than separate from the Parliament and nominated by national governments. How might this innovation alter the internal politics of the EP if it were ever implemented?

5. Are MEPs European politicians, national ones, both, or neither?

6. Do European Parliament elections serve any valuable purpose?

7. What practical steps could the EP take to build awareness and support of the institution among the European public?

8. Are European elections a waste of time?

GUIDE TO FURTHER READING

■ Van der Eijk, C. and Franklin, M. (eds) *Choosing Europe? The European Electorate and National Politics in the Face of Union* (Ann Arbor, MI: University of Michigan Press, 1996). The classic—though pessimistic—study of European Parliament elections and all their faults.

■ Hix, S., Noury, A. G., and Roland, G. (2006) *Democratic Politics in the European Parliament* (Cambridge: Cambridge University Press). An important study of the internal politics of the EP, drawing on an extensive data set of voting records in the chamber.

■ Jacobs, F., Corbett, R., and Shackleton, M. *The European Parliament*, 6th edn (London: John Harper, 2008). A superb introduction to the ins and outs of the EP, written by two long-time parliamentary officials and one MEP.

■ Rittberger, B. *Building Europe's Parliament: Democratic Representation Beyond the Nation State* (Oxford: Oxford University Press, 2005). By far the best scholarly study of the historical development of the EP.

■ Scully, R. *Becoming Europeans? Attitudes, Behaviour and Socialisation in the European Parliament* (Oxford: Oxford University Press, 2005). A study refuting widespread conjectures about MEPs 'going native' in Europe, and drawing some important implications from this finding for how we understand and study the EP.

WEBLINKS

● www.europarl.eu.int   The home page of the EP's own multilingual website, with considerable information on the members and activities of the Parliament, and links to official documents.

● www.lse.ac.uk/Depts/eprg   The home page of the European Parliament Research Group, a multinational team of researchers who study the EP. The page includes contact details of leading scholars, details of published work and ongoing research, a series of working papers, and data from major surveys of MEPs conducted in 2000 and 2006.

● www.elections2004.eu.int   This link contains detailed results for EP elections, analysed by party group and by member state.

Visit the Online Resource Centre that accompanies this book for lots of interesting additional material. http://www.oxfordtextbooks.co.uk/orc/Cini_Borragan3e/

11

The Courts of the European Union

ILIAS KAPSIS

Chapter Contents

- Introduction
- The history of the Court of Justice
- Composition, structure, and procedure
- Jurisdiction
- 'Judicial activism' and the member states
- Conclusion

Reader's Guide

This chapter examines the courts of the European Union (EU), which include the Court of Justice of the European Communities (ECJ), the Court of First Instance (CFI), and the European Civil Service Tribunal. It focuses on issues of structure and procedure, the extent of the Courts' jurisdiction, and their role in the promotion of European integration. The chapter also discusses the critique directed at the ECJ for the way it exercises its judicial powers, as this allegedly involves political considerations unacceptable for a judicial body. Lastly, the chapter takes into account recent developments in European integration, including the failure in 2005 of the Constitutional Treaty and the difficult ratification of the Lisbon Treaty.

Introduction

The judicial arm of the European Union comprises the Court of Justice of the European Communities (ECJ or 'the Court'), the Court of First Instance (CFI), and the judicial panels. These courts have the task of ensuring that Community law is interpreted and applied in the same way across the Union. In addition to these courts, there is a Court of Auditors whose function it is to control the revenues and expenditures of the Community. As the roles of the ECJ and the CFI are more important for EU citizens, this chapter will focus on these two Courts and on the judicial panels attached to the CFI. The chapter also focuses on the judicial activities (and their political ramifications) of the courts under the first pillar (the Community pillar), where the Courts have more power than in the second (Common Foreign and Security Policy) or the third pillar (Police and Judicial Cooperation in Criminal Matters).

The history of the Court of Justice

The Court of Justice was created in 1951 by the Treaty establishing the European Coal and Steel Community (ECSC). The Court's task was to ensure that 'in the interpretation and application of this Treaty … the law is observed'. The Court's powers were extended in 1958 by the Treaties of Rome establishing the European Economic Community (EEC) and the European Atomic Energy Community (EURATOM). It would subsequently serve all three Communities, thus emerging as a supranational court with compulsory jurisdiction over all areas falling within the scope of the three Treaties. The ECJ's decisions were binding on Community institutions, member states, and individuals. In 1986 the Single European Act (SEA) introduced significant amendments to the Treaties and provided for the establishment of the Court of First Instance (CFI) attached to the Court of Justice. This was intended to reduce the ECJ's workload and improve its efficiency. The CFI began its work in 1989. The SEA also excluded matters of foreign policy from the ECJ's jurisdiction.

The establishment of the European Union by the Maastricht Treaty in 1992 constituted an enormous step forward for European integration but, initially at least, it had little impact on the powers of the ECJ. In the EU's new three-pillar structure, only the first pillar remained within the jurisdiction of the ECJ. As the second and third pillars concerned sensitive policy areas touching upon core issues of national sovereignty, member states preferred to keep them intergovernmental, thus pre-empting any influence by the Court. Subsequently, the Treaty of Amsterdam gave new powers to the Court by transferring into the Community pillar certain policies previously belonging to the third pillar, such as external border control, asylum, and immigration. The Court's powers in the field of police and judicial cooperation in criminal matters were at the same time extended. However, the ECJ was to have no power to review the validity of operations carried out by national law-enforcement agencies or the exercise of the member states responsibilities in the field of maintaining law and order and safeguarding internal security.

The Treaty of Nice entered into force in 2003, introducing further significant amendments to the Court structure. The CFI is no longer attached to the ECJ but is now a Court in its own right. The Nice Treaty also provided for the establishment of specialized 'judicial panels' attached to the CFI. These were intended to reduce the workload of the CFI by relieving it of insignificant cases in specific areas. The first judicial panel, the Civil Service Tribunal, was established in 2004 to deal with litigation concerning EU staff, and performs de facto the work of an industrial relations tribunal for the EU institutions.

The Constitutional Treaty (CT) envisaged a significant increase in the powers of the ECJ as, had it been ratified, the CT would have given the Court full jurisdiction over the provisions of Treaty and would have increased its activity in a number of areas, including, with the incorporation of the Charter of Fundamental Rights (see Chapter 4), the issue of human rights. Even so, certain earlier restrictions to the Court's jurisdiction would have remained in place. The Court would have continued to lack jurisdiction on foreign policy matters (CFSP); and in the third pillar, the Court would still have had no power to review the validity of operations conducted by law enforcers or the acts of member states maintaining law and order and internal security. The exclusion of these elements remains in place in the Lisbon Treaty which was signed in December 2007. If ratified, the Lisbon Treaty would create a new 'Area of Freedom, Security and Justice' and the Court would therefore have general jurisdiction in this new area subject to the exceptions mentioned above. The Court would still be denied any jurisdiction on CFSP but would be able to exercise its authority in proceedings to make sure that the exercise of CFSP powers did not affect the competences of the Union and vice versa. Moreover, the Court would have jurisdiction to rule on the legality of decisions adopted by the Council under CFSP, which imposed restrictive measures on natural or legal persons.

This summary of the history of the ECJ demonstrates the increasing involvement of the Court in European affairs. This is a predicable development, as the deepening of European integration demands the existence of a judicial authority with sufficient constitutional powers to ensure the effective interpretation and application of EU law in the Community and in its member states. Given the diverse political and legal traditions in the different member states, the Court can—through its decisions—help to reconcile this diversity and in so doing secure compliance with European-level

agreements. However, the Court's ability to influence member states' policies has its limits, since ultimately member states are in position to curtail the Court's activities by amending the Treaties. Similarly, the power of the member states is well established in the second and third pillars of the EU, where the Court's jurisdiction, while increased, is still sorely restricted.

Over the years the Court has sought to exploit the general and often vague provisions of Treaties to expand its authority and the competences of the Community. One of the main techniques that the Court has used is the teleological (or purposive) interpretation of the Treaties, that is, 'the Court reading the text—and the gaps in the text—of the Treaty in such a way as to further what it determines to be the underlying and evolving aims of the Community enterprise as a whole' (Craig and De Búrca 2007: 274). Teleological interpretation offers flexibility, but by enabling the Court to be creative in its interpretation of the Treaties it compromises the consistency and predictability of its decisions. The frequent use of teleological interpretation when issuing rulings associated with political issues has raised concerns about the Court overstepping its judicial powers. Although the criticism is not unfounded, the Court's acts have been driven by necessity and have had the implicit acceptance of national governments who, at the end of the day, implemented the Court's decisions. These issues will be further addressed later in the chapter when examining the issue of judicial activism.

Lastly, strengthening of the role of the Court is an important factor in efforts to advance democracy within the EU. According to Carrubba (2003: 76), '[w]ithout an independent judiciary capable of ensuring that not even powerful political actors are above the law, an important democratic check is missing'. The Court has worked over the years to secure its independence and to protect the institutional balance within the EU, thus arguably advancing democracy in a Union whose democratic credentials are permanently subject to critique (see Chapter 23).

Composition, structure, and procedure

The ECJ is based in Luxembourg and is made up of 27 judges (one judge per member state) and eight Advocates-General (AGs). The judges hear cases and adopt decisions, whereas AGs deliver impartial and independent opinions—prior to the final decision-making stage—in open court. Their opinions are not binding on the judges but have a real impact on the final outcome of a case. The judges and AGs of the ECJ are appointed by the member states in accordance with their national traditions. These are usually individuals 'whose independence is beyond doubt and who possess the qualifications required for appointment to the highest judicial offices in their respective countries or who are juriconsults of recognised competence' (Article 223 TEU). The appointment of women as judges is very rare and for a long period there was none in the ECJ. The first female judge, Fidelma Macken, was appointed by Ireland in 1999.

Five of the Advocates-General are appointed by the five larger member states (Germany, France, Spain, Italy, and the United Kingdom) and three are appointed on a rotating basis by the remaining members. The Treaty of Lisbon provides that the number of AGs will increase to 11. Poland will nominate one of the new AGs, with Germany, France, Spain, Italy, and the United Kingdom retaining their prerogative. As before, the remaining five will be nominated on a rotating basis by the other member states. Finally, the Court also appoints a Registrar for six years who is responsible for procedural and administrative matters.

The appointment of judges must be 'by common accord of the governments of the member states'. The process is private, taking the form of a diplomatic meeting that may raise concerns about the possible political nature of the appointment. The Treaty of Lisbon provides for the establishment of a panel authorized to give opinions on the candidates' suitability. The judges are appointed for staggered terms of six years, which allows for a partial replacement of judges every three years. They are eligible for reappointment and there is no retirement age. The judges and AGs cannot be removed during their term in office and their duties end on their death or resignation. A judge or AG can be dismissed by the unanimous decision of the other judges and AGs if they no longer fulfil the requisite conditions or meet the obligations arising from the office. The judges elect a President by secret ballot for a renewable three-year term. The President directs the judicial and administrative activities of the Court and presides at sessions of the Grand Chamber. Following an election process similar to that of the judges, the AGs elect the so-called First Advocate-General for a one-year term.

The ECJ sits in chambers of three or five judges or in a Grand Chamber consisting of 13 judges. Grand Chambers are used in important cases or if a member state or a Community institution so requests. The Court sits as a full Court only in exceptional cases as laid down by the *Statute of the Court of Justice*. This would include proceedings concerned with the dismissal of a European Commissioner. The Chambers are presided over by their own respective President, who is elected by the same process used to elect the President of the Court as a whole.

The procedure before the ECJ has a written and an oral stage. The written stage is the more important, comprising the application to the Court, the submission of the documents supporting the application, the defences, the communication to the parties of relevant documents, and statements of case. In the oral stage, which takes place in open court, the judge assigned to the case presents to the Court a report containing a summary of the facts and the arguments of the parties. At that point, the legal representatives of the parties may make oral submissions to the Court. The oral stage also includes examination of any witnesses or experts, as well as the delivery of the opinion of the Advocate-General. The final decision is adopted by a majority where necessary but no mention of dissenting opinions is made in the judgment, with the latter signed by all judges and delivered in open court. This practice helps to maintain the anonymity and thereby the independence of the judges (Chalmers and Tomkins 2007: 123). The judgment is subsequently published with a summary in the EU's *Official Journal*, and a more detailed version appears in the official law report. The decisions of the ECJ are final. In other words, there is no appeal process.

The Court of First Instance consists of 'at least' one judge per member state and as such it currently has 27 judges. It began its work in 1989 and was initially attached to the ECJ. The Treaty of Nice gave the CFI an independent status and more cases were transferred to it, such as the right to decide on certain preliminary rulings. To date, the CFI has made a significant contribution to the development of administrative law, especially in the fields of competition and external trade law (Chalmers and Tomkins 2007: 125). Unlike the ECJ, its cases do not involve sensitive political and constitutional issues. This allows the CFI to focus more on purely legal issues and fact finding. The rules for the appointment of judges at the CFI and their terms of office are similar to those of the ECJ. It does not have AGs but, when necessary, one of its judges will be appointed to per-

form this task. The judges of the CFI elect a President for a renewable three-year term. They also appoint their own Registrar. Like the ECJ, the CFI usually sits in Chambers of three or five judges but it may also sit in a Grand Chamber of thirteen judges. In special cases the CFI may sit as a full court. The judgments of the CFI are subject to appeal to the ECJ on points of law: in other words, appeals can be made only on the legal argumentation and never on the assessment of the facts. The CFI delivers its judgments in open court following written and oral proceedings. There are no dissenting or concurring opinions.

Finally, the European Civil Service Tribunal was created in 2004 by the Treaty of Nice to reduce the workload of the CFI by relieving it of cases involving the EU's administration (including, for example, Commission officials). The Civil Service Tribunal consists of seven judges appointed by the Council for a renewable term of six years. A committee of seven people chosen from former members of the Court of Justice and the Court of First Instance and lawyers of recognized competence advises the EU Council on these appointments. The members of the tribunal have to be individuals 'whose independence is beyond doubt and who possess the ability required for appointment to judicial office' (Article 225a EC). The Tribunal elects its own President, whereas the number of judges sitting to hear cases varies. The procedure has a written and an oral stage; and its decisions can be appealed on points of law to the CFI.

KEY POINTS

- The ECJ is currently composed of 27 judges and eight Advocates-General whose duty is to perform the tasks assigned to the Court by the Treaties.

- The CFI was created to lessen the workload of the ECJ. It consists of 27 judges and unlike the ECJ it does not have permanent AGs.

- The European Civil Service Tribunal is attached to the CFI and consists of seven judges. It was created to relieve the CFI of its workload by handling disputes involving the civil servants of the Community.

Jurisdiction

The ECJ has often used its jurisdiction to adopt decisions that have a substantial political impact on the operation of the Community and on the Community's relationships with its member states. As far as judicial procedures are concerned, the distinction is often made between direct actions, which are brought directly to the Community Courts, and references for preliminary rulings, which reach the Community Courts via the intermediation of national courts.

Direct actions

Direct actions begin and end in the Community Courts. They can be brought by individuals, 'legal persons' (that is, companies, organizations), member states, or Community institutions. Actions brought by individuals and legal persons are handled by the CFI and on appeal by the ECJ. Actions brought by the member states and Community institutions are normally handled by the ECJ. However, since the Treaty of Nice the CFI has jurisdiction over certain direct actions brought by member states against the Community institutions, such as where a Community institution fails to act and thus infringes the EC Treaty (Article 232 EC).

There are three types of direct action: infringement proceedings; actions for judicial review (also known as annulment procedure); and actions for damages. The EC Treaty provides the Commission and member states with the power to bring infringement proceedings before the ECJ against member states failing to fulfil their Community obligations (Article 226–228 EC). Such a situation could arise, for example, if national law was inconsistent with Community law or if the latter was not implemented by member states in a timely or proper fashion. Therefore infringement proceedings aim at securing member-state compliance. These proceedings have an administrative stage and a judicial stage. The administrative stage involves the Commission and the member state that infringed Community law. Its aim is to resolve the matter through a process of negotiation. If the administrative stage fails, the Commission may bring the case to the Court, thereby initiating the judicial stage. If the ECJ confirms the alleged infringement, it will declare that the member state has failed to fulfil an obligation under the EC Treaty. The member state must comply with the decision and end the infringement; otherwise the Commission may bring a new action before the ECJ asking for the imposition of a penalty payment (Article 228). The latter may be a lump sum or periodic payment, or both. The provision

---

BOX 11.1

Infringement proceedings (Articles 226 – 228) initiated by the Commission against Greece

In 1991 the Commission initiated infringement proceedings against Greece, alleging the failure of the latter to comply with Community law on the disposal of toxic waste in Crete, where a rubbish tip was situated at the mouth of the river Kouroupitos. The tip operated in breach of Community law, which required that toxic and dangerous waste be disposed of without endangering human health and without harming the environment. The Greek government cited popular opposition to its plans to create new waste sites in the area for its failure to close the tip. The Court rejected the argument and in 1992 issued a judgment declaring that Greece was in breach of its Community obligations. Five years later, after the Greek government failed to comply with the 1992 judgment, the Commission once again brought the case to the ECJ. The ECJ, with its 2000 decision, imposed a payment of €20,000 for each day of delay in implementing the measures necessary to comply with the 1992 judgment. The new ruling proved more effective and along with pressure exercised on Greece by other Community institutions the closure of the tip was secured.

Source: Case C-387/97 *Commission v. Greece* [2000] ECR I-5047.

KEY CONCEPTS AND TERMS 11.2

Types of binding Community acts

Article 249 EC provides for three main types of binding act:

- Regulations have general application and are binding and directly applicable in all member states. Directly applicable means that they do not normally require member states to adopt measures for their implementation.

- Directives are addressed to all or some of the member states. Directives lay down specific binding objectives that have to be achieved by specific dates, and leave to the discretion of the member states the decision on how best to achieve these objectives.

- Decisions are addressed to individuals and are binding in their entirety.

for a penalty payment was added by the Maastricht Treaty as a means of making the proceedings more effective in ensuring member-state compliance with European law (see Box 11.1).

Judicial review of Community acts by the Courts is intended to ensure that the Community is subject to judicial scrutiny and control. Community Courts have jurisdiction to review the legality of acts of the Community institutions intended to produce legal effects. This scope of judicial review includes regulations, directives, and decisions (see Box 11.2), but also any other act that has binding force or which produces legal effects. If the action taken is successful, the Court will declare void the act concerned. The annulment of a Community act may occur due to a lack of competence if a Community institution adopts an act that it has no power to adopt under the EC Treaty. This may be due to the infringement of an essential procedural requirement such as where a Community institution fails to comply with a requirement to give reasons for its decision; it may be due to the infringement of the EC Treaty or of any rule of law relating to its application; or it may involve a misuse of powers, for example where a Community institution exercises its powers for an unauthorized purpose.

The institutions of the Community and the member states have the right to bring an action of

judicial review to the Court, but natural and legal persons—in other words, individuals and companies—are able to do so only if they pass a strict admissibility test, which denies access to most private applicants. The main reason given by the ECJ in *Unión de Pequeños Agricultores v. Council* (2002) for the denial of this right was that these applicants could use alternative judicial remedies available to them under Community law, including the use of national courts. A potentially more convincing reason may be that the Court's aim is to prevent a flood of individual cases that would hamper its work (Arnull 2006: 93). The Lisbon Treaty would amend the current admissibility test, giving more private applicants access to the Court.

In addition to the review of Community acts, the EC Treaty also provides a right to legal action in cases where a Community institution has *failed to act*, thereby infringing the Treaty (Article 232 EC). Lastly, Community law provides for compensation to be paid to individuals for damages suffered as a consequence of illegal activities by Community institutions (Article 288 EC).

References for preliminary rulings

Community law may arise in national courts where European legislation is directly applicable or where legislation has been applied by national agencies. In such cases national courts will have to apply Community law. They may also have to resolve conflicts between Community and national laws. The diverse legal and judicial traditions among member states, along with the lack of sufficient knowledge and experience of Community law among national judges, requires a mechanism that involves the ECJ, allowing it to offer authoritative interpretations of Community law and to coordinate action at the national level. Preliminary references provide such a mechanism. Without it, the coherence and application of Community law would be at risk since different national courts could give contradictory interpretations of Community law provisions. According to

Article 234 of the EC Treaty, national courts *may*—and where the decision to be adopted is final, not subject to further appeal, *must*—refer questions of Community law arising in the cases examined by them to the ECJ. The ECJ will then provide the required answers and the national courts will use this information when adopting their decision. It is up to the ECJ to *give the correct interpretation* of Community law and up to the national court *to apply* it to the particular case. The national court is not obliged to make a reference if the meaning of the Community provision is clear or if the Court has already ruled on the issue in a previous case. The relationship between national courts and the ECJ is cooperative and non-hierarchical. The reference to the ECJ does not take the form of an appeal but is aimed only at clarifying specific issues of interpretation and application of Community law. The ECJ's jurisdiction concerns the interpretation of the Treaty; the validity and interpretation of acts of the institutions of the Community and of the European Central Bank; and the interpretation of the statutes of bodies established by an act of the Council, where those statutes so provide. Note that the Lisbon Treaty would extend the preliminary rulings jurisdiction under the third pillar, awarding the ECJ general jurisdiction in the Area of Freedom, Security and Justice.

Preliminary rulings have played a central role in shaping the Community legal order and the relationship between the Community and its member states. Moreover, they have familiarized national courts with Community law. Some of the cases have had immense political significance. Indeed, some of the most important legal principles of Community law, such as supremacy, direct effect, and state liability, have been defined by the ECJ in response to preliminary references. In the *Van Gend en Loos* (1963) case, for example, the ECJ defined the principle of direct effect for the first time. The Court held that the Community constitutes a new legal order independent of member states and created by member states' voluntary agreement to surrender part of their sovereign rights. This new legal order not only imposed obligations but also conferred rights on individuals independently of the legislation of the member states. These rights had to be protected by national courts. Where a provision of Community

law is sufficiently clear, precise, and unconditional, it should be given direct effect, that is to say an individual can directly rely on it in a national court. As a result of *Van Gend en Loos*, individuals acquiring rights under Community law could ask national courts to protect these rights from breaches committed by, say, their own government. This implies a significant incursion of Community law into the domain of national sovereignty. Thus in individuals and in the national courts, the ECJ found two powerful allies in its efforts to force member states to comply with European law. While national governments might willingly ignore the ECJ's decisions where there are no effective sanctioning mechanisms against them, the Maastricht Treaty introduced the possibility of fines and penalty payments. Thus governments could not engage in this kind of behaviour any longer, especially since many of these kinds of cases reflected a popular demand for the effective protection of rights that had been given to individuals by the Community (see Box 11.3).

In *Costa v. ENEL* (1964), the Court defined the principle of supremacy for the first time. It established that Community law, irrespective of its nature (whether it is a Treaty provision or provision of a directive), could not be overridden by domestic law irrespective of the nature of national law (for example, a constitutional provision or a statutory provision). In other words, if there is a conflict between Community law and national law, Community law must prevail. Since then, in its famous *Francovich* (1991) ruling, the Court defined the principle of state liability. It declared that individuals can seek compensation for loss suffered as a result of member states' breach of Community law in national courts. Interestingly, the Court created this new remedy without relying on the text of the EC Treaty that allowed individuals to seek compensation only for losses suffered by illegal acts of the *Community* institutions (Article 288 EC). In *Francovich*, the Court held that a remedy against member states was 'inherent in the system of the Treaty' and that the effectiveness of Community law and the protection of individual rights would be weakened if individuals were unable to seek compensation against states breaching Community law (see Box 11.4).

CASE STUDY 11.3

The *Van Gend en Loos* case and the principle of direct effect

A Dutch tribunal submitted to the ECJ a question concerning the direct application of Article 12 (now 25) of the EEC (now EC) Treaty in the territory of a member state. Article 12 was addressed to member states and required the latter 'to refrain from introducing between themselves any new customs duties on imports or exports or any charges having equivalent effect and from increasing those which they already apply in the trade with each other'. The Van Gend en Loos company claimed that the Dutch custom authorities had raised the import duty for a quantity of chemicals it imported from Germany into the Netherlands, contrary to Article 12.

The case had great legal and political significance. If individuals were allowed to invoke, in national courts, provisions of EC law to protect their interests, this would be a significant incursion of the Community and the European Court into the realm of national sovereignty. The Belgian and Dutch governments intervened in the case and argued

that the ECJ had no jurisdiction, as issues relating to whether the EEC Treaty prevailed over Dutch legislation or other agreements entered into by the Netherlands and incorporated into Dutch national law should be decided exclusively by the national courts. The government in The Hague also argued that if there was a breach of Community law by a member state, the solution to the problem should come from the use of infringement proceedings. Through their arguments, the member states seemed to exclude the involvement of individuals in the efforts to ensure implementation of Community law in national territory.

The ECJ rejected these arguments and established that the Community constitutes a new legal order of international law for the benefit of which the member states have limited their sovereign rights, and the subjects of which comprise not only member states but also their nationals. The Court concludes from this a fundamental principle: that of the direct effect of Community law.

Source: Van Gend en Loos Case 26–62.

CASE STUDY 11.4

Francovich and Bonifaci v. Italy (1991) and state liability for breach of Community law

The applicants brought proceedings against Italy for failure to implement Directive 80/987, which provided employees with a minimum level of protection in the event of their employer's insolvency. The Directive established that the member states should give specific guarantees for payment of unpaid wage claims. The applicants, who were owed wages by their insolvent employers, sued the Italian government, claiming that the latter had to pay them either the sums payable under the Directive or compensation for the damages suffered due to the non-implementation of the Directive. The ECJ rejected the first argument but accepted the second, concerning the right to compensation. The Court stated the full effectiveness

of Community law would be impaired and the protection of rights which it grants would be weakened if individuals were unable to obtain compensation when their rights were infringed by a breach of Community law for which a member state was responsible. As a result, the principle of state liability for breaches of Community law is inherent in the Treaty. The Court found further support for its argument in Article 5 (now 10) EC, which provides that member states are required to take all appropriate measures to ensure fulfilment of their obligations under Community law, including the obligation to nullify the unlawful consequences of a breach of Community law.

Source: Francovich and Bonifaci v. Italy, C-6/90 and C-9/90.

The principles of direct effect, supremacy, and state liability demonstrate the great value of the preliminary rulings procedure for the development of the Court's jurisprudence and its influence on political processes in Europe. Moreover, they demonstrate

the Court's great success in exploiting the procedure to advance the goals and reach of Community law at the national level. It also transforms the EU's relationship with national courts from a horizontal to a de facto vertical form of cooperation, where the

Court, operating as a European Supreme Court, is able to impose its rulings on national courts. Finally, these cases illustrate the application of a teleological approach to the provisions of the Treaty, allowing the Court to adopt important legal doctrines and principles on the basis of a creative interpretation of the Treaty text. This has led to concerns about the Court overstepping its judicial powers and becoming too political. The chapter now addresses this issue.

KEY POINTS

- Direct actions begin and end in the Community Courts. They can be brought by individuals and 'legal persons', such as companies, member states, and Community institutions.

- There are three types of direct action: infringement proceedings, actions for judicial review, and actions for damages.

- Preliminary rulings provide national courts with the right to refer to the ECJ for guidance on issues of Community law arising in cases brought before them.

- Direct actions and references for preliminary ruling have played a crucial role in the establishment of the legal order of the Community and shaped the relationship between Community law and the member states.

'Judicial activism' and the member states

The ECJ's involvement in politically sensitive issues has not been limited to its relationship with the member states but has also concerned EU inter-institutional relations and the promotion of Community policies. The significance of the Court in shaping inter-institutional relations can be seen in a series of important decisions ('*Les Verts*' (1986), *Commitology* (1988), and *Chernobyl* (1990)), where the Court ruled that the acts of the European Parliament were subject to judicial review and that the latter should be given the right to stand as an applicant in the procedures, even though this was not explicitly provided for in the Treaty. These decisions led to the redrafting of the relevant Treaty provisions in the TEU and the Treaty of Nice, giving the EP first limited and then full standing rights in the Court in judicial review cases. These cases show that the Court has helped to strengthen the position of the European Parliament, the only institution directly elected by the people. On several occasions the Court has demonstrated its commitment to the promotion of democratic principles within the EU. By way of example, in *Commission v. Council* (1987), the Court made it clear that the Community institutions had, under the EC Treaty, the obligation to give reasons for their acts, which would then be checked by the Court.

With regard to the promotion of Community policies, the free movement of goods is an illustrative example. Article 28 EC prohibits 'quantitative restrictions on imports and all measures having equivalent effect'. Its aim is to prevent member states from restricting the trade of goods by placing quotas on the amount of imported goods or adopting measures having equivalent effect (MEQR) to quotas. The Court, in two seminal decisions, *Dassonville* (1974) and *Cassis de Dijon* (1978), adopted a very broad interpretation of MEQR, including in the prohibition of Article 28 not only national rules that directly discriminate against imports, but also rules which, without discriminating against imports, have a negative impact on the trade of goods within the Community. Such rules concern inter alia the shape, size, or weight of the product. The broad scope the Court has given to the meaning of MEQR has had a very positive impact on the establishment of a single market for goods in the Community by forcing member states to make policy adjustments by amending considerable parts of their domestic legislation (see Chapter 16).

More recently, in *Viking (2007)* and *Laval (2007)*, the ECJ recognized the workers' right to strike as a fundamental right within the EU but held that the exercise of this right might infringe employers' rights of freedom of movement and establishment under Articles 49 and 43 EC. Industrial action in such cases must be justified and proportionate. The decision has been characterized as 'disappointing', because the Court subordinated the right to strike to free movement, showing that its primary concern is the removal of barriers to intra-Community trade rather than the promotion of human rights (Davies 2008: 147). The impact of these decisions on national laws and policies is likely to be dramatic.

Occasionally, national courts express their disagreement with the ECJ's rulings but finally accept them, thus fostering integration and policy change (Obermaier 2008: 735). National governments seem to have followed a similar stance. While they have largely excluded the Court's jurisdiction from politically sensitive areas, such as security, defence, and foreign policy, they have cautiously accepted the expansion of the role of the Court in European affairs and its controversial rulings in other areas. They have even amended their national constitutions to safeguard the unhindered implementation of Community law (Hartley 2007: 238). There are various explanations for the governments' reaction. One may be that the ECJ's decisions serve the governments' own interests, while they have few reasons to fear the Court's activism, since they are always in a position to retaliate effectively. Governments may be able to amend the EU treaties and/or their national constitutions, or insert opt-outs that would deprive the Court of jurisdiction. Or they could merely fail to comply. Indeed, the numerous infringement proceedings and a new provision in the EC Treaty providing for financial penalties against violators indicate that state compliance is a real problem for the ECJ.

Regarding opt-outs, the UK and Ireland attached a Protocol to the Treaty of Amsterdam containing opt-outs that limit the impact on these countries of policies concerning visas, asylum, immigration, and other policies related to free movement of persons. Article 2 of the Protocol '... was evidently designed to protect the United Kingdom (and Ireland) even from judges as inventive as those of the Court of Justice' (Arnull 2008: 1193). However, in the complex and difficult political environment of the enlarged European Union, the Court with its strong commitment to the advancement of EU aims may be a useful tool in the effort to maintain stability and consistency and to advance European integration. Moreover, the Court's activism was stronger in periods when implementation of Community law by member states was facing problems (Craig and De Búrca 2007: 73), indicating that the Court may be able to offer solutions that advance common values when political processes fail.

KEY POINTS

- The Court's decisions have considerable political impact, not only on the relationships between the Community and member states, but also on both EU inter-institutional relations and the promotion of Community policies

- National courts and governments appear to support the ECJ's decisions despite occasional opposition. Member states can only restrict the Court's power through Treaty change or the agreement of opt-outs.

- The Court, with its strong commitment to European integration, could be a useful tool in advancing common values in periods when political processes fail.

Conclusion

The ECJ has '… no rival as the most effective supra-national judicial body in the history of the world' (Stone Sweet 2004: 1). The European Courts have greatly assisted in shaping and advancing an unprecedented project that has promoted political stability and economic prosperity in Europe after a long period of instability in the first half of the twentieth century. The twenty-first century has brought new challenges to the Courts of the Union. The Eastern enlargement that increased the number of member states from 15 to 27, the failed ratification of the Constitutional Treaty, and the still incomplete ratification of the Lisbon Treaty constitute new challenges not only for the Courts but also for the Union as a whole. One of the most pressing problems facing the Courts at present concerns their ever growing workload. The establishment of the CFI and the Civil Service Tribunal and the limited access of individuals to the Courts can help manage this workload. However, the recent enlargement of the Union is expected to complicate matters again. While additional judges from the new member states were appointed to the Courts, there are still a number of issues creating uncertainty. Rasmussen (2007: 1661),

for example, has questioned the efficiency of the new scheme, pointing to the diversity of cultures and the inexperience of the new judges on European matters. One might therefore ask the questions: will judicial activism be affected by enlargement?; and: how consistent will the decisions of the ECJ be in this new environment?

Moreover, the Court may find itself operating within 'an ideological crisis without precedent' (Rasmussen 2007: 1665) that has hit the Union following the failure of the Constitutional Treaty in popular referendums in France and the Netherlands and the difficulties that subsequently plagued the ratification of the Lisbon Treaty, rejected by Irish voters in a referendum in 2008. While it is still premature to assess the impact of these developments on the operations of the courts, it is clear that in recent years the ECJ has been more silent than in the past, and its level of activism has fallen. This may be a transitory condition. However, what is certain is that European integration will not advance without judicial support offering legitimacy and consistency to the European Union's still-expanding range of policies.

? QUESTIONS

1. What is the role of the Court in the process of European integration?

2. Why were the judicial panels established? What function does the European Civil Service Tribunal perform?

3. How does Community law ensure member state compliance with their Community obligations? What is the contribution of the Court?

4. Who can bring an action for judicial review and why does this matter?

5. To what extent and in what ways is the preliminary rulings procedure necessary?

6. What is the political significance of the ECJ's rulings in *Van Gend en Loos*, *Costa v. ENEL*, and *Francovich*?

7. Do you agree with the criticism of the Court's judicial activism?

8. What is the likely impact of the EU's eastward enlargement on the operation of the EU Courts?

GUIDE TO FURTHER READING

■ Arnull, A. *The European Union and its Court of Justice,* 2nd edn (Oxford: Oxford University Press, 2006). This volume records and analyses the contribution the Court has made to shaping the legal framework within which the Community operates.

■ Arnull, A. and Wincott, D. (eds) *Accountability and Legitimacy in the European Union* (Oxford: Oxford University Press, 2002). This contains an interdisciplinary collection of essays considering various aspects of accountability and legitimacy in the EU. Two of the essays examine the judicial architecture of the EU after Nice and the rule of law in the EU.

■ Craig, P. and De Búrca, G. *EU Law: Texts, Cases and Materials*, 4th edn (Oxford: Oxford University Press, 2007). This successful textbook offers an exhaustive analysis of the role of the Court and the relationship between EU and national courts.

■ Hartley, T. *The Foundations of European Community Law*, 4th edn (Oxford: Oxford University Press, 2007). This text offers a detailed analysis and assessment of the powers of the Court and the relationship between Community law and national law.

■ Horspool, M. and Humphreys, M. *European Union Law* (Oxford: Oxford University Press, 2008). The book provides an accurate account of the institutional structure of the European Union in an accessible manner.

 WEBLINKS

● http://www.curia.eu.int   The official website of the Community Courts.

● http://www.ena.lu   Online archive on the development of the EU that contains a section on the European Court of Justice.

● http://www.jeanmonnetprogram.org/index.html   This is the website of the Jean Monnet Centre for International and Regional Economic Law and Justice at the NYU School of Law. It contains, amongst other things, the Jean Monnet Working Papers, which feature the most current scholarship on EU Law.

● http://eur-lex.europa.eu/en/index.htm   EUR-Lex provides direct free access to European Union law, specifically the Official Journal of the European Union as well as the treaties, legislation, case law and legislative proposals.

 Visit the Online Resource Centre that accompanies this book for lots of interesting additional material. http://www.oxfordtextbooks.co.uk/orc/Cini_Borragan3e/

12 Interest Groups and the European Union

RAINER EISING AND SONJA LEHRINGER

Chapter Contents

- Introduction
- The EU institutions and interest groups
- EU democracy and civil society
- European interest groups
- The Europeanization of interests
- Conclusion

Reader's Guide

This chapter examines the role of interest groups in the European Union (EU) in the context of the broader system of interest intermediation that now exists at the European level. It also considers the way in which the EU as a political institution influences interest group structures and activities in both European and domestic political arenas. The chapter begins with a brief overview of the relationship between the EU institutions and interest groups and examines the steps taken thus far to regulate that relationship. It then looks at the structure of the system, focusing in particular on two salient aspects: the difference between national and EU organizations; and the difference between business and diffuse interests. Finally, the chapter addresses the Europeanization of interest intermediation (see also Chapter 25), to discuss how EU membership may have altered the structure and activities of domestic interest groups.

Introduction

The EU institutions do not make policy in a vacuum, and the links that they have with civil society take many different forms. Interest groups have a particularly important role to play in connecting European-level institutions with the citizens of the European Union, as well as in mediating between them. Frequently, they are expected to socialize their members into democratic politics, to give a voice to citizens between elections, to participate in constructing a general will out of the specific concerns of groups, and to serve as 'schools for democracy'. In recent years, the EU institutions have stressed civil society participation in EU policy making as a way of enhancing the democratic quality of the European Union (European Commission 2001, 2002a). Nonetheless, authors continue to look upon the contribution of interest groups to European democracy differently. Caporaso (1974) criticized European interest organizations for pursuing only very narrowly

defined interests and thereby undermining the legitimacy and accountability of the European institutions. In contrast, other authors have suggested that interest organizations offer European civil society the opportunity to participate in both EU policy making and institution building (Heinelt 1998).

Before evaluating these views on the role of interest groups, the following sections set out the broad terrain of EU interest intermediation. The first section highlights the institutional setting, while the second delineates the efforts that the EU institutions have made to regulate the access of interest groups and to incorporate civil society into EU policy making. The third section summarizes the structure of the EU interest group system, while the fourth discusses how the EU may have affected the structure and functions of domestic interest groups, through a process which is now referred to as Europeanization.

The EU institutions and interest groups

According to institutional theory (see Chapter 7), political institutions, such as the EU, have important effects on interest organizations (see Box 12.1). They not only form an **opportunity structure** within which interest groups can pursue their interests, but they also set up committees and bodies to consult regularly with groups (Mazey and Richardson 2002); delegate policy making and implementation powers to them (Falkner et al 2005); support a variety of interest groups by providing finance, organizational help and granting privileged access (Aspinwall and Greenwood 1998, Pollack 1997a, Smismans 2004, 2006b); and pursue their own policy preferences in alliances with groups that are supportive of their case (see Eising 2009). Four characteristics of the EU are particularly relevant in this context: first, the EU is a highly dynamic

system; second, the EU is a complex system that is horizontally and vertically differentiated; third, the EU is a system that favours consensus building; and finally, the EU is regarded as suffering from a democratic deficit (see Chapter 23).

Since the mid 1980s, the EC (and after 1993, the EU) has extended its competences far beyond market integration to include areas such as environmental policy, justice and home affairs, and foreign and security policy. This steady accretion of powers gives some indication of the dynamism that characterizes the European political agenda. This has had important consequences for interest groups. From a short-term perspective, the dynamic political agenda makes it difficult for interest organizations to forecast short-term political developments in the European Union. Therefore they are often uncertain

KEY CONCEPTS AND TERMS 12.1

Lobbies and interest groups

The literature on the European Union's interest groups rests largely on a body of research in the field of comparative politics. In this literature, interest groups have been labelled and defined in a variety of ways which, in turn, reflect specific approaches and normative assessments. Lobbies, pressure groups, non-governmental organizations (NGOs), social movement organizations and interest organizations are the most common terms used to characterize interest groups in this literature.

The term 'lobbyist' originated in the nineteenth century, when individuals waiting in the British parliamentary lobby exerted influence on members of legislatures to pass bills on behalf of unknown customers. Lobbying was then almost exclusively regarded as a commercial activity. Later, attempts by organizations to influence public bodies were also included in this narrow definition. Since the 1920s, the term 'pressure group' has increasingly been used in the political science literature as a term that is considered familiar and therefore needing little explanation. Its meaning comes close to that of a lobby group in that it centres on

the functions of these groups to influence—or put pressure on—parliament or the government. The term 'interest group' refers to the underlying rationale of these groups and has less negative connotations. Members join groups as they share common attitudes, or interests (Truman 1951: 34). 'Interest organizations' refers to interest groups that are highly formalized. This highlights the continuity of organizations as well as their ability to cope with complexity via differentiation. It also draws attention away from particular leaders and members within an organization, and towards the effects of the organizational form. The term 'non-governmental organization' (NGO) brings along a normative outlook and is often used by diffuse interests to avoid the 'interest group' label that is frequently associated with selfish inside lobbying. Beyers, Eising and Maloney (2008) propose three factors that define an actor as an interest group: organization (which excludes broad movements and waves of public opinion), political interests (also called political advocacy), and informality (no aspiration to public offices and no competition in elections, but the pursuit of goals through frequent informal interactions with politicians and bureaucrats).

about political options and stakes, particularly in the early phases of the policy process. This forces interest groups to devote considerable resources to monitoring EU developments. From a long-term perspective, the number of groups operating at the European level has steadily increased and so has the number of interests that are present in the European arena (see Table 12.1). The most active phases of group formation were the period between the foundation of the European Communities and the early 1960s, and the period between the formulation of the Single European Act and the enactment of the Maastricht Treaty. Many groups were created in direct response to or in anticipation of European institution building and regulation. In several cases the formation of European interest groups triggered responses from competing interests, which led to even more groups being established. As a result, the interest group landscape in the EU has become much more diverse over time. Initially, the interest group system consisted mostly of economic groups. However, groups representing diffuse interests, such

as environmental groups or development NGOs, have become more vocal since the 1970s and 1980s. And while only a limited number of national groups from the six founding members were initially present in the European arena, nowadays EU policies attract the attention of organizations from the 27 member states and beyond, such as multinational firms. With the Eastern enlargement, the interest in EU-level issues has widened considerably, making for greater internal heterogeneity.

The EU's second relevant characteristic with regard to interest groups is its pronounced horizontal and vertical differentiation. Horizontal differentiation implies that the importance of interest groups varies substantially across pillars, institutions, and policy areas. In the first pillar, for example, interest groups have relatively good access to the European institutions. This is much less the case in the EU's two other pillars. These second and third pillars operate more intergovernmentally, allowing national governments to prevent interest groups from gaining access to the EU policy process. For

Table 12.1 The evolution of European associations from 1950 to 2000

| Type of association | Number of associations per year | | | | | |
	1950	1960	1970	1980	1990	2000
Industry	17	92	141	180	219	278
Services	18	45	85	129	187	254
Diffuse interests	13	21	33	59	99	147
Agriculture	4	45	67	90	111	125
Professions	2	11	15	25	37	48
Regions	0	1	1	2	9	12
Various interests	6	6	9	12	15	18
Total	60	221	351	497	677	882

Note: The table combines several CONECCS categories to form more general ones. These reclassifications build on previous European Commission directories and on the missions of the interest groups in Brussels. The number of groups in 1950 is the aggregated number of European associations founded since 1843 and that still existed in 1950.

Source: CONECCS, May 2002.

most interest groups, then, the first pillar provides the greatest potential for access to the EU institutions, not least because it comprises the vast majority of the Union's regulatory and distributive policies. In the first pillar, the European Commission is the most important point of contact for interest groups at the European level. Its monopoly over policy initiation (see Chapter 8) grants the Commission a crucial role in agenda setting and policy formulation. And, as 'guardian of the treaties', it also plays an important role in monitoring member states' and non-state (or private) actors' compliance with Community law. However, interest groups will rarely approach the Commission as a collegiate body. Rather, they tend to maintain relations with one or several Commission Directorates-General (DGs) that are responsible for specific areas.

With its growing legislative competences, particularly since the introduction of the codecision procedure in the Maastricht Treaty, the relevance of the European Parliament (EP) for interest groups has increased. However, it is still considered to be less important than the Commission or the EU

Council, since its influence on EU policy making continues to vary according to the issue at hand and the decision-making procedure applied (see Chapter 10). Within the Parliament, the heads of the Standing Committees and the *rapporteurs* responsible for particular dossiers are the most important addressees for interest group demands. Since MEPs are elected by national voters, they are more amenable to national pressures than the Commission and also more open to protectionist demands than the Commission and the EU Council, as seen in the debate over the service liberalization. Parliamentarians are more responsive to 'weak' (or what are often called 'diffuse') interests, including those representing the environment, consumers or, large groups such as the unemployed and pensioners (Kohler-Koch 1997: 6–7; Pollack 1997a).

Owing to its pivotal position, the EU Council is a highly relevant contact for interest groups. However, the Council and its administrative machinery, the Committee of Permanent Representatives (COREPER) and the Council Working Groups (see Chapter 9), are rarely lobbied directly. Rather, domestic interest groups tend to address their concerns to individual members of national government departments. Although the Council's policy positions often evolve along national lines, in part as a consequence of the pressure by domestic interests, the European Council remains more removed from interest group pressure. Not only does it comprise the heads of state and government as well as the President of the European Commission, thus representing general interests to a greater degree, but formally it also needs to meet only once every six months, lessening its impact on the minutiae of day-to-day politics.

As the EU's judiciary, the European Court of Justice (ECJ) monitors compliance with and interpretation of EU law. European law takes precedence over national law and grants rights to individual citizens that national courts must uphold. Notably, the preliminary rulings procedure (see Chapter 11), which allows national courts to refer questions of European law to the ECJ, enables interest groups to challenge the compatibility of domestic and EU law. However, in practice, to take a case to the ECJ usually demands that a body of EU law already exists. Even when this is the case, the outcome of such action is uncertain, the financial costs are heavy, and the duration of the case is generally lengthy, which means that this avenue is not available to all citizens and interest groups and will be worthwhile only when the stakes are perceived to be especially high.

Finally, the European Economic and Social Committee (EESC) was set up to channel the opinions of organized interests into the European policy process. The EESC is a tripartite body composed of individual members who are nominated by the EU member states and who represent employers, workers, and other interests. It is generally considered to be of minor importance for the representation of interests within the EU. This is because direct contacts between the EU institutions and interest organizations are now much more important and frequent than this institutionalized forum for interest intermediation. Nonetheless, during the debate about the role of civil society in European democracy

(see below), the EESC sought to establish itself as an important voice of European civil society (see EESC 2004) and has consequently developed several proposals for strengthening its participation in EU policy formation and institution building (Smismans 2003).

Policy making in the EU is not confined to the European institutions, however. The European Union is vertically differentiated and increasingly regarded as a multi-level system (Marks and Hooghe 2001; see also Chapter 7), implying that many different public actors located at different territorial levels within the EU share political authority. Hence, multiple points of access are open to interest organizations (Pollack 1997a). Groups must take heed of political developments at both the European and national levels and need to be present at both levels (as well as in any relevant regional and local political arenas) if they hope to see their interests well represented and defended. They also need to ensure that their strategies are coordinated across each level. In reality only a minority of interest groups is able to pursue multi-level strategies in the sense of establishing routine contacts with political institutions at each level. This is because they are tied to their local, regional, national, or European memberships in one form or another, and must also make sure that they use their resources as efficiently as they can.

A third feature of the EU is its preference for consensus building. This is a consequence of the unpredictability of the EU policy agenda and the complexity of the EU's political system (see Katzenstein 1997; Kohler-Koch 1999). For member states, consensual decision making guarantees some protection against being outvoted in the EU Council when vital interests are at stake. Decision making by consensus, rather than on the basis of a majority, implies that EU institutions and the national governments need to take the opinions of all relevant interest groups into account to prevent groups opposed to the legislation from ultimately blocking the agreement. Hence national groups can no longer rely on the national veto in the EU Council.

The EU's fourth characteristic, its perceived legitimacy deficit, is discussed in more detail in the next section. These four characteristics—dynamics, complexity, reliance on consensus, and a perceived democratic deficit—affect the ways in which interest groups have sought to influence the European institutions as well as the ways in which these institutions incorporate interest groups into EU policy making.

KEY POINTS

- Political institutions, such as the EU, form a political opportunity structure that influences the formation and behaviour of interest groups.

- The EU's institutional setting (its dynamic political agenda; its complexity and multi-level character; and its reliance on consensus) shapes the interest group system and interest intermediation within the EU.

- There are multiple points of access to the EU policy process, including the Commission, the Parliament, the Council, and the Court, as well as national political institutions.

EU democracy and civil society

The fragile legitimacy of the European Union also has important consequences for the involvement of interest groups in EU policy making. Following the referendums on the Maastricht Treaty, the debate about the democratic deficit intensified in the 1990s. Interest groups have always been important to the EU institutions. The European Commission and the EESC in particular have emphasized the contribution interest organizations can make to input and output legitimacy. As the Commission puts it: 'By fulfilling its duty to consult, the Commission ensures that its proposals are technically viable, practically workable and based on a bottom-up approach. In other words, good consultation serves a dual purpose by helping to improve the quality of the policy outcome and at the same time enhancing the involvement of interested parties and the public at large' (2002a: 5). According to this reasoning, EU institutions draw on external sources of information in order to perform their policy functions effectively. Thus they rely on the expertise of interest groups to design public policy. At the same time, involving interest groups adds an element of functional representation to the imperfect dual legitimacy of the EU that is based on the representation of citizen interests through the EP and of territorial interests through the EU Council (see European Commission 1992b, 1999, 2001, 2002a). Interest groups' ability to define, aggregate, and articulate the interests of their members or their constituencies helps European institutions monitor social change and take on board new political concerns.

The contacts between EU institutions and interest groups range from a variety of informal ad hoc consultations to more formal institutionalized arrangements in EU committees. While these practices differ across EU institutions, there is a common trend to develop better defined frameworks to institutionalize consultations with interest groups.

The European Commission has traditionally preferred not to regulate these consultative practices but to apply existing administrative rules and to operate on the basis of self-regulatory principles. In 1992, the Commission proposed 'an open and structured dialogue' that aimed at making the access of interest groups more transparent (European Commission 1992b). In its 2001 White Paper on European Governance the Commission, in response to the perceived democratic deficit, made recommendations on how to enhance democracy in Europe and increase the legitimacy of the institutions. It launched a series of measures aimed at achieving input legitimacy by incorporating expert advice in EU policy making. Some of these measures include web-based registers of experts and expert committees, consultative and comitology committees, as well as a comprehensive code of practice for providers and users of expert advice (Greenwood 2007). In the same year, the Commission signed protocols with the EESC and the Committee of the regions to involve interest groups earlier in the policy-making process and thus enhance their function as intermediaries between the EU and civil society and the regions.

In the follow-up to the White Paper, the Commission adopted a set of general principles and minimum standards for consulting interest groups (European Commission 2002a: 15). These standards established its obligation to ensure clear and concise communications; to announce open public consultations on a single access point on the internet; to ensure an adequate coverage of the target groups; and to acknowledge the receipt of comments by reporting on the results of open public consultations on the internet (European Commission 2002a: 19–22). These principles and standards were expected to enhance the transparency and accountability of consultations and to ensure that all interested parties were being properly consulted. Regarding output legitimacy, the standards were aimed at enhancing the effectiveness and coherence of EU policies. According to critics, the standards are insufficient to streamline the consultation patterns of the Commission, given their non-binding character and the omission of other established modes of consultation. Moreover, building linkages with public interests has been deemed an unsuitable strategy to cope with the democratic deficit because EU-level interest groups are rather removed from domestic constituencies (Warleigh 2001).

At present, the Commission is leading the agenda on lobbying regulation at the EU level. In 2005 Commissioner Siim Kallas presented the European Transparency Initiative (ETI) as a reaction to the mistrust of European citizens towards lobbyism and EU institutions (see Box 12.2). According to the Estonian Commissioner, 'lobbyists can have a considerable influence on legislation, in particular on proposals of a technical nature' but 'their transparency is too deficient in comparison to the impact of their activities' (Kallas 2005: 6). As a consequence he sought to enhance financial accountability of EU funding, to strengthen the integrity and independence of the EU institutions, and to impose stricter controls on lobbying. In 2006, the Commission acted on that suggestion by publishing a Green Paper on the European Transparency Initiative, containing actions for a more structured framework for interest representation, for minimum consultation standards, and for the disclosure of beneficiaries of EU funds in order to be 'accountable to the taxpayer' (European Commission 2006). As in 1992, the Commission opted for voluntary registration and optional compliance with a code of conduct. After an open consultation with citizens and interest groups, the Commission launched a voluntary register for lobbyists seeking to influence policy making. The register distinguishes among three main categories of lobbyists: professional consultancies and law firms; corporate lobbyists and trade associations; and NGOs and think tanks. The requirements for inclusion in the register vary for all three, particularly regarding financial disclosure. Inclusion in the register requires acceptance of a 'Code of Conduct for Interest Representatives'. This contains specific rules that lobbyists need to follow in their relations with the EU executive (European Commission 2008). The only exception to this is where a Code of Conduct already exists, which contains identical or more stringent requirements. A plan is already in place to evaluate the register by 2009, with the option to make registration mandatory.

Due to its function and composition, the European Parliament has a different perspective on civil society participation from those of the Commission and the EESC. As elected representatives of the European citizens and subject to public

---

CHRONOLOGY 12.2

The European Transparency Initiative (ETI)

November 2005	Commissioner Kallas launches the European Transparency Initiative in a speech titled *The need for a European Transparency Initiative* (Kallas 2005: Nottingham/Speech/05/130)
May 2006	Publication of the European Commission's Green Paper—*European Transparency Initiative* (COM(2006) 194 final)
October 2006	Publication of the European Economic and Social Committee's *Opinion on the European Transparency Initiative Green Paper* (CESE 1373/2006)
February 2007	Publication of the Committee of the Regions's *Opinion on the European Transparency Initiative Green Paper* (2007/C 146/07)
March 2007	Publication of the European Commission's *Communication Follow-up to Green Paper—European Transparency Initiative* (COM(2007) 127 final)
May 2007	The European Parliament adopted a resolution titled *The development of the framework for the activities of*

interest representatives (lobbyists) in the European institutions (INI/2007/2115)

April 2008	Motion for a European Parliament resolution including a call for a mandatory register common to all three institutions (A6-0105/2008), adopted by the Parliament in May 2008
May 2008	Publication of the *European Commission's Communication European Transparency Initiative: A Framework for relations with interest representatives (Register—Code of Conduct)* (COM(2008) 323 final)
June 2008	The European Commission launched a voluntary lobbyists register (http://ec.europa.eu/transparency/regrin/)
December/2008 February 2009	An inter-institutional working group is formed to report on the feasibility of establishing a common lobbyists register.
Mid 2009	The European Commission reviews the success of the voluntary lobbyists register after its first year.

Source: https://webgate.ec.europa.eu/transparency/regrin/infos/officialdocuments.do?locale=en#en).

---

scrutiny, MEPs regard interest group influence as potentially problematic in two respects. First, as their response to the White Paper on European Governance shows, they maintained that 'the European and national parliaments' rather than civil society groups 'constitute the basis for a European system with democratic legitimacy'. They consider organized civil society as important but also as 'inevitably sectoral', so that it 'cannot be considered as having its own democratic legitimacy' (European Parliament 2001: points 8, 11a). In other words, the parliamentarians do not consider func-

tional representation by interest groups as an equivalent to citizen representation by parliament. Secondly, concerns about the lack of transparency involved in interest group influence and a desire to ensure the integrity of its members explain the EP's preference for a stricter lobbying regulation. In 1996, the EP established a register of interest groups. After registration and on acceptance of a code of conduct, interest representatives receive a pass that eases access to the EP and is valid for a year. Under the rules of parliamentary procedures, the MEPs and their assistants are also obliged to indicate their paid activities and the donations they receive, clarifying any relationship they might have with groups outside the Parliament. In 2008 and in the context of the ETI debate, the EP argued for a single mandatory register of lobbyists for all EU institutions following the United Nations model.

Beyond the institutional preferences described above, the EU's attempts at addressing legitimacy issues through civil society participation have been incorporated into the latest treaty revisions. Thus the 2004 Constitutional Treaty provided a preliminary effort at strengthening and institutionalizing civil society participation by including a new Title VI on 'The Democratic Life of the Union'. Under this title Article I-47 the principle of participatory democracy enshrined the EU's commitment to an open, transparent, and regular dialogue between institutions and representative associations and civil society; and to a citizens' initiative allowing citizens (no less than one million who are nationals of a significant number of member states) to submit to the Commission any appropriate proposal on matters where they consider that a legal act of the Union is required for the purpose of implementing the Treaty. While the principle as such has disappeared from the Lisbon Treaty, a Title II on 'Provision

on Democratic Principles' includes a new Article 11 stipulating the same commitment to an open, transparent and regular dialogue and to the citizens' initiative.

KEY POINTS

- In recent years, the EU institutions—notably the European Commission and the Economic and Social Committee—have come to stress the importance of civil society consultations for the legitimacy of EU policies, and have taken measures to institutionalize political participation.

- The EU institutions do not regulate interest group activity in any comprehensive way. The implications of the European Transparency Initiative are not yet obvious.

- Due to its different status in the EU political system, the European Parliament takes a different stance on interest group participation from those of the European Commission or the Economic and Social Committee.

- The Lisbon Treaty enshrines the commitment to an open, transparent, and regular dialogue and to the citizens' initiative

---

European interest groups

The number and variety of interest organizations operating at the EU level are vast. In fact, it is hard to quote an accurate number of interest groups. Estimates range from 1,300 (European Public affairs Directory 2005) and 2,600 (Kallas 2005:5) to 5,000 (Marks and McAdam 1999). The inconsistency of these data results from a number of factors, including complexities in identifying and classifying actors (Beyers et al 2008), differing data sources (Berkhout and Lowery 2008), as well as the lack of transparency in many of these figures. While different sources do not yield a common figure, they do at least provide some consistent indications of growth

over time, with the key growth period appearing to be the early 1990s (Greenwood 2007:12; see also Table 12.1).

There are various ways of classifying interest groups, for example according to type, number, or the homogeneity of their members, the kind of interests they represent, or whether they operate at a national or European level or both. In this chapter whether groups operate at the national or European level and the difference between business and non-business interests will be considered in greater detail because, as it will be explained below, these criteria have particularly important implications for the EU policy process.

EU and national groups

It is important to distinguish between national and EU interest groups (the latter are sometimes called 'Eurogroups'), because their organizations and constituencies differ and also because they pursue different strategies when representing their interests.

Typically, EU interest groups are composed of national associations rather than individuals. About two-thirds of EU interest organizations are in fact federations of national interest groups, while the remaining groups comprise either the direct membership of other organizations (such as firms), or a combination of these two elements (Aspinwall and Greenwood 1998). An example of the latter is the European Chemical Association (CEFIC), which brings together both national associations and individual firms. National groups tend for the most part to be composed of individual members. EU interest groups provide expertise and arguments that they then use to persuade the EU institutions of the merits of their cases. National associations tend to represent their interests to national members of the EU institutions as well as to their national administrations and governments, emphasizing the national character of their interests. Generally, EU associations have fewer functions than their national members and, as a consequence, their resources are much smaller. To different degrees they serve to create links among their memberships, to provide and distribute information on EU activities, to develop common positions and to promote the interests of their members (Lindberg 1963: 98). Compared to national associations, they concentrate on the representation of interests rather than on the provision of services to their members. Moreover, owing to the multinational composition of their membership and the heterogeneity of the national settings represented by these bodies, EU groups often have real difficulty in reaching agreement internally on important policy questions as well as in ensuring their members' compliance with agreements that were struck within the EU institutions (see Haas 1958).

Despite these differences, a fairly elaborate division of labour has evolved between the EU associations and their national counterparts. European interest groups are far more visible at the European Union level than are national associations (Eising 2004) and have increasingly become important intermediaries between their national members and the EU institutions. This holds particularly when the EU political agenda is set and when policies are being formulated by the EU institutions. On the other hand, national associations are more vocal than EU associations when EU policies are being transposed into domestic law or being implemented by the national public administration.

Business interests

At first glance, the EU interest group system looks broadly pluralist (see Streeck and Schmitter 1991). Both the large number of groups and their huge variety suggest that many interests are represented in the EU institutions. Usually no interest group enjoys a clear monopoly of representation in any one policy area. Of the EU groups present in the agricultural sector, for example, many reflect particular product specializations. Some of these compete and bargain not only with groups across policy areas, such as with environmental or consumer groups, but also with groups within the agricultural domain. Coalitions are generally fluid and depend on shared interests.

Business interest organizations clearly outnumber non-business interests: about 80 per cent of the EU organizations can be categorized as producers' professional or employers' interest organizations (see Table 12.1). One reason for this is the quick response from business interests to European integration. Business Europe (formerly UNICE, the Union of Industrial and Employers' Confederations of Europe), which is the primary European association of national producers' and employers' associations for private firms, was set up as early as 1958. The equivalent public sector association, the CEEP (Centre Européen des Entreprises Publics) followed soon after in 1961. Another body, EUROCHAMBRES, the federation of the chambers of commerce in the European Union, which represents SMEs, was also founded in 1958. Apart from these EU federations, there are a number of cross-sectoral associations that have a direct membership of firms. For example, the American Chamber of Commerce (AmCham) represents the European Council of American Chambers of Commerce and has a total of 10,000 European and American corporate members. The European Round Table of Industrialists is composed of 45 executives of leading European firms. The Round Table was particularly influential in pushing for acceptance of the Single Market Programme in the mid 1980s (Cowles 1997; see also Chapter 16).

Along with CEEP and Business Europe, the European Trade Union Confederation (ETUC) is the most important social partner in the EU. The term European social partner refers to those organizations at EU level that are engaged in the European social dialogue as provided for under Articles 138 and 139 EC. The social dialogue arose in the mid 1980s as part of the drive by Jacques Delors to build a social aspect into the Single European Market (SEA) of 1986. The SEA included Article 118b which urged the Commission to 'endeavour to develop the dialogue between management and labour at European level which could, if the two sides consider it desirable, lead to relations based on agreement'. In 1992, the Maastricht Treaty included a Social Agreement which provided the legal basis for this mechanism. The Amsterdam Treaty incorporated the social dialogue procedure in Articles 138 and 139. The competences of the social partners in the social field are defined extensively:

KEY POINTS

- Social partners are procedurally involved in the genesis of any Commission initiative in the social policy field.

- They may decide on how they wish to implement their agreements—'either in accordance with the procedures and practices specific to management and labour and the member states or, in matters covered by Article 137, at the joint request of the signatory parties, by a Council decision on a proposal from the Commission' (Article 139.2 EC).

- They may decide on autonomous agreements in all social policy fields—even those not falling under the competences of EU institutions as defined in Article 137 EC.

Consequently the social partners are allowed not only to provide technical information, to indicate the position of their members, or to suggest alternative courses of action, but they also have the right to formulate and/or implement the policies themselves.

The involvement of large firms in direct membership organizations (rather than in federations) can undermine the ability of business federations to aggregate interests along national lines and discipline their members' behaviour. The EU institutions may even prefer to cooperate with these kinds of organizations, as they are able to agree on common positions more easily than the EU federations. Indeed, large firms have become increasingly important in the interest group landscape, as is clear when we look at the restructuring of associations since the 1980s. Within Business Europe, for example, large firms were able to secure top positions in the standing committees, giving them a key role in the formulation of joint positions (Cowles 1997). Moreover, in several sectors, such as automobiles, chemicals, and biotechnology, large firms, by acting independently outside the framework of interest organizations or by forming direct membership organizations, seem to have acquired greater influence than either the national or the EU federations. Individual lobbying by large firms is commonplace nowadays, with these firms often having better access than the EU and national associations to both EU and domestic political institutions. This has led scholars to characterize EU interest intermediation as a form of 'elite pluralism' (Coen 1997, 1998; Cowles 2001).

Yet the extent to which the business community is able to pursue its interests effectively varies enormously across time and issues. Moreover, business is far from being a unitary actor. For example, within the Single Market Programme from the late 1980s, many economic sectors such as transport, electricity and gas, and telecommunications were liberalized despite strong resistance from incumbent firms. In the case of electricity liberalization, even Europe's largest utility, Electricité de France (EdF), had to accept the loss of its monopoly position on the French market, despite its best attempts to defend that position.

Yet it remains relevant to ask whether the strong presence of the business community is a result of the greater variety of interests needing representation, or whether it has more to do with firms being better able to form interest groups and pursue their interests than are the more diffuse, non-economic interest groups. Interest group theories have predominantly focused on the latter reason, raising important questions about the democratic implications of interest group activity.

Diffuse interests

In general, 'diffuse' interests, such as those pursued by religious, social, human rights, consumer, and environmental groups, are characterized by their broad scope and lack of clear membership. Aside from a small number of European federations, they also tend to lack a high degree of organization at the EU level. An important reason is that, with increasing group size and a lack of social control, potential members have strong incentives to free ride on the provision of collective goods. Due to ideological differences, differential linkages to national member organizations, overlapping responsibilities, and scarce EU funds, organizations of this kind sometimes end up competing with each other. When this happens it can limit their effectiveness as intermediary organizations for their domain. There are fewer diffuse interest organizations than business interest organizations in the European Union, even though the relative number of diffuse interests has increased in the past decade (Greenwood 2007). One reason for this is a relative lack of activity on the part of the EU institutions. In the early years of the European integration process, non-governmental organizations (NGOs) did not generally focus their activities on the European Community. Even well into the 1970s, welfare and social policy groups were conspicuously absent from Brussels (Harvey 1993: 189–90). Only intense regulatory activity has provoked the mobilization of diffuse interest groups at the EU level (see Box 12.3). For example, the foundation of the European Environmental Bureau (EEB) came about as a consequence of the EC's first environmental programme

in 1974. For the vast majority of non-business interests it was only in the 1980s that their numbers began to increase. In many cases, this came about as a response to new European programmes. For example, the growth of anti-poverty groups in the second half of the 1980s was a direct consequence of new EU programmes in this policy area (Harvey 1993: 190). By the mid 1990s, some 13 European environmental associations and networks were present at the EU level (Hey and Brendle 1994: 389), reflecting the new regulatory powers in this policy area. Today the EEB is the most comprehensive European environmental organization, bringing together more than 140 national associations. It has to share space with other environmental organizations and coalitions. It is part of the Green 10, a coordinated network of the ten leading environmental NGOs active at EU level. As with the EEB, the Green 10 are dominated by well equipped organizations like Greenpeace, the World Wide Fund for Nature, and Friends of the Earth.

The only exceptions to the process depicted above are the domestic consumer organizations. They formed the BEUC (Bureau Européen des Unions des Consommateurs), the European consumer association, in 1962 with the support of the European Commission, as a response to market integration (Young 1997: 157–8). BEUC brings together 41 member organizations from 30 countries.

Even though the degree of bias in the interest group system has been reduced as diffuse interest groups in the EU became more active in the 1990s, thus displaying the largest growth rate of all EU level groups, the extent of change has not equated that of some countries, such as the United States where citizen groups constitute much larger parts of the interest group population (Baumgartner and Leech 1998: 102-106).

The Commission and the Parliament have sought to improve the organizational capacities of diffuse interest groups by offering them financial support to enhance their standing in the policy process. These grants amount only to a small proportion of the EU budget. However, to the interest groups concerned, EU funding can be of major importance

The European Women's Lobby (EWL)

Founded in 1990, the European Women's Lobby (EWL) is the largest alliance of women's non-governmental organizations in the European Union, bringing together thousands of women's organizations throughout Europe. In 2008, the EWL comprised 28 national coordination departments in European Union countries and 19 European-wide member organizations. It claims to represent approximately 2,000 direct member organizations (see http://www.womenlobby.org/). The EWL works for the advancement of equality between women and men as well as the mainstreaming and monitoring of a feminist gender-equality perspective in all areas of EU policy. Between 1994 and 1997, the EWL worked for the inclusion of a new gender-equality clause into the Treaty of the European Union to overcome the absence of non-work-related issues in the EU's equal opportunity policies at that time (see Helfferich and Kolb 2001). By using a double strategy (at both the European and national levels), the lobby succeeded in having its demands taken up by governmental representatives and, in the end, included in the Treaty's amendments.

After the European Union decided to create a group of experts, the so-called 'Group of Wise Men', to advise member states on what issues should be taken up in the Amsterdam Treaty revision, the EWL assembled a 'Wise Women's Group' to work on a comprehensive position

paper. Several position papers and a survey were followed by a large campaign meant to raise consciousness in the member states and by Europe-wide petitions, which prompted the European Parliament to ask members of the EWL to present their position in a hearing. Thus the EWL was able to submit its own precise proposal for amendments. Important aspects of the EWL position were then integrated into the EP's position at the Intergovernmental Conference (IGC). The following innovations included in the Amsterdam Treaty are said to be at least partly the result of the campaign by the Europeans Women's Lobby:

- Article 3 of the Treaty incorporates the principle of gender mainstreaming to all policies of the EU.

- Women were added to the new article on anti-discrimination. Article 141 was extended to include equal pay for equal work. The right to and principle of equal treatment were enshrined in the Treaty.

Similar success stories about interest groups rarely appear. In this context it is important to bear in mind that several external factors enabled the EWL to have such an impact on public policy, namely the new mandate of the EU for social policy due to the northern enlargement and the legitimacy crisis of the EU after the signature of the Maastricht Treaty; the decision to revise the Treaty of the European Union in an IGC created a helpful policy window.

(see Pollack 1997a: 581). In 2000, the Commission estimated that its funding for diffuse interest groups was around €1 billion. However, there are no clear-cut criteria for the distribution of funding. Some EU budget lines grant interest groups mid-term financial security, while others provide financial means on a year-by-year basis, endangering the continuity of the organizations' work and even their survival; and funding is also made available within specific EU programmes. For example, in 2004, the European Environmental Bureau received 52 per cent of its financial resources from the Commission while 24 per cent came from other public authorities. Only 8 per cent of its resources were member contributions. The Social Platform, the leading umbrella citizen interest group, receives 90 per cent of its funding from the European Commission and

BEUC received about 50 per cent of its financial resources from the EU institutions in 2005.

Some members of diffuse interest groups fear that the support given by EU institutions is little more than a convenient way for the EU to give a human face to the Single Market. Moreover, there is a perceived risk that interest organizations might become too dependent on the EU institutions, thus influencing the organizations' political positions and activities. Financial support might allow the EU institutions to co-opt interest organizations, limiting their opposition to European initiatives. For these reasons, some associations, such as Greenpeace, do not accept EU funding. Yet there is 'no ready evidence of attempts by the Commission to steer networks towards, or for that matter away from, particular policy positions' (Harvey 1993: 191).

Nonetheless, little is known about the extent to which EU programmes draw the attention of these groups away from areas in which no such public funding is available. In sum, financial support enables 'weak' interest organizations to participate in decision making while simultaneously allowing the Commission to broaden its support base to improve its expertise on the divergent arguments of different groups, and to claim that the legitimacy of EU policies has increased.

KEY POINTS

- Interest groups in the European Union do not form a consistent unitary actor. For example, the differentiation between EU and national groups and between business and diffuse interests has important implications for the EU policy process.

- Business interest organizations outnumber non-business interests by approximately 4:1.

- The social partners have extensive rights, such as the right to formulate and/or implement European policies themselves.

- The Commission and the EP provide material and procedural support in order to enable 'weak' interest organizations to participate in decision making.

The Europeanization of interests

There is no doubt that the European integration process has provoked an increase in interest group activity at the European level. But the EU may also have important consequences for *national* interest groups. These may take a number of different forms.

First, the growing importance of EU policy may lead national interest groups to redefine their interests. In the short term, new opportunities and risks posed by EU policies may trigger a process of reassessment within domestic organizations. In the longer term, the presence of the European institutions and the importance of their policies may mean that national groups begin to look at issues from a European perspective rather than continuing to define problems in purely national terms (Katzenstein 1997).

Second, as a consequence of the European integration process, domestic interests will increasingly have to coordinate interest representation at a variety of different levels of governance. As the EU extends its remit, more and more issues of concern to interest groups are likely to involve the European institutions. To cope with these changes, domestic interest groups may feel the need to *adapt* to the new circumstances through various inter- and intra-organizational changes (see Lehmkuhl 2000; Grote and Lang 2003).

Third, the impact of the EU on domestic patterns of interest intermediation is as yet unclear. As one might expect, EU interest groups are much more involved than national groups in policy making at the EU level, while national groups dominate the domestic political arena. While large firms can easily afford to be present in both the domestic and the European arenas (see Coen 1997, 1998), this holds only for a minority of national interest organizations (Eising 2009). For example, despite the emergence of new European policies, the majority of German, British, and French trade associations continue to lobby domestic political institutions rather than the EU institutions when seeking to represent their interests (Eising 2007). Relations with domestic institutions need not necessarily weaken because of European integration. Rather, European integration may even contribute to a strengthening of existing ties (Benz 1998: 583) in cases, for example, where there is some uncertainty over new EU legislation that prompts national actors to exchange information or to reinforce domestic alliances. The degree of impact seems to be down to organizational, issue-specific, and systemic factors (see Box 12.4).

So, how does the EU affect the influence of interest organizations and state institutions? No agreement exists in the literature about whether European integration strengthens the influence of state institutions or that of interest organizations on public policy. On the one hand, three factors support the hypothesis that multi-level policy making strengthens state actors. First Andrew Moravcsik (1998) has emphasized that European integration strengthens national executives because these act as gatekeepers between the national and the European arenas and obtain more resources from European integration than other actors. It appears that European integration strengthens their capacity to set the domestic

political agenda, control policy information, legitimize political actions, and contain the ability of opposing actors to veto their political initiatives. Secondly, according to Edgar Grande (1994), domestic interest organizations may also lose ground due to what he calls the 'paradox of weakness'; in other words, the involvement of public actors in EU negotiations can enable them to actually gain autonomy vis-à-vis private actors as the reference to negotiation pressures in the EU may help them to turn down unwarranted interest group demands. Finally, the complexity of the EU multi-level system and the allocation of competences to a multitude of public actors are said to make it difficult for interest organizations to identify 'the' decisive locus of political authority in the EU (Grande 1994).

 CASE STUDY 12.4

The response of British and German chemical interest associations to European integration

Besides economic internationalization, European integration has transformed the environment for organized collective action in a fundamental way. Grote and Schneider (2006) have analysed the Europeanization of national associations in the chemicals sector in Germany and the United Kingdom since the 1970s. Their study is grounded in organizational ecology as a framework of analysis.

They identify four main areas that entail major challenges to business associations: economy, technology, society, and politics. Other than in sectors that display high technological and economic dynamics such as telecommunications, for the chemical industry politics appeared to be the main factor imposing the need for adaptation on business associations. In particular, Grote and Schneider delineate the increasing regulatory activities of the EU between 1980 and 1996. Notably, in February 2001, the Commission issued the White Paper on a 'Strategy for a future Policy on Chemicals' that prepared the so-called REACH regulation (Registration, Evaluation, Authorisation and Restriction of Chemicals) in which new and old chemical substances are to be subjected to a control procedure. In addition to the effects of EU regulation, some Europeanization effect was present in the emergence of new organizational forms, like European-level associations.

At the organizational level, political regulation was highly relevant for the associational responses to the EU. In that respect, the EU was seen as being more important than the national government, a significant change compared to the early 1980s. In the population of chemical industry associations, change was much less pronounced. In Germany, the corporatist structure and hierarchical ordering of interorganizational relations remained unchanged. In the UK, the structure of chemical associations remained much more fragmented, with a less hierarchical ordering of relations than was indicated in earlier studies. While German groups tended to retain their organizational format, the British pattern exhibited some variation of organizational format and the selection of new alliances. Regarding the linkages with other organizations, UK associations tended to leave the business of representation either to their counterparts at the EU level or to government departments. By contrast, German associations have grown accustomed to the EU and entertain good relations with all types of actors. More generally, political developments at the European level did not put 'uniform pressure on organized interests in different countries to undertake the same modifications, aimed at the same objectives, with the same pace of adaptation' (Grote and Schneider 2006:140), but allowed for cross-national variations. Their adaptation to the EU was embedded in specific institutional contexts and reflected specific evolutionary trajectories.

On the other hand, several authors doubt that European integration generally strengthens state actors vis-à-vis interest organizations. They highlight various aspects of the EU institutional setting or emphasize the cooperation of public and private actors in EU policy networks. Some authors argue that the EU multi-level system enhances the influence of interest organizations by increasing the number of potential access points (Pollack 1997a). Thus easy access to and the resource dependencies of the EU institutions may tip the balance in favour of private players. Other institutionalist arguments emphasize the legal opportunities of the EU system as EU law can enable interest organizations and

their constituencies to proceed against established domestic rules and practices.

Finally, studies drawing on the literature about policy networks or advocacy coalitions pose a conceptual challenge to the claim that private interests lose out to public institutions. They emphasize that European policies are predominantly made in constellations that consist of both private and public actors and that may stretch from the EU level into the member states. In sum, strong arguments exist for both the perspective that the EU strengthens the state and the point of view that the EU empowers private actors, leaving the evidence on this question inconclusive for now.

KEY POINTS

- The increase in European regulation may cause domestic interest groups to redefine or 'Europeanize' their interests.

- Interest groups may change in order to retain some control over public policy as it becomes more Europeanized.

- European integration can strengthen the ties between domestic institutions and interest groups.

- It is unclear whether European integration strengthens national governments at the expense of interest groups or vice versa.

Conclusion

European integration has left its mark on interest representation in Europe. A new multi-layered interest group system has emerged to reflect the multi-level institutional set-up of the EU. While the EU is characterized by numerous points of access for interests, potentially a source of confusion, it also—because of its preference for consensual decision making—grants interest groups an important say in the European policy process. Moreover, the EU institutions actively promote the formation of European-level groups, by providing funds for weaker, more diffuse interests and supporting those involved in implementing European policy. Over time, the perspective on interest groups has changed. While they are still considered to be important contributors to EU policy making, they are increasingly regarded as representatives of civil society in the EU.

Compared to national groups, those operating at the EU level tend to perform a narrower set of functions, acting as information brokers, representing the interests of their affiliates, and providing linkages to other interest organizations and to the EU institutions. Some even argue that interest groups have the potential to remedy the EU's democratic deficit (see Chapter 23), as they allow for greater political participation. However, this kind of argument has to recognize that there is a potential bias built into the system of EU interest representation. The system is highly asymmetric, with the large majority of all groups representing business interests, and only a minority more diffuse social interests. Lacking in organizational capacity, the latter are highly dependent on support from the European institutions. Moreover, interest groups offer a different sort of representation than do bodies such as national parliaments or subnational regional authorities. It is therefore questionable whether the institutionalization of civil society participation in which the European Commission and the Economic and Social Committee have engaged offers an appropriate remedy to the problems of democracy and accountability from which the European Union is currently suffering.

? QUESTIONS

1. How have the European institutions sought to institutionalize, regulate, and structure interest group activity?
2. In what way and to what extent does the EU support interest groups? Why does it do this?
3. In what way do interest organizations benefit the European Union?
4. How does the institutional setting of the EU impact upon interest intermediation?
5. How important is each European institution as an addressee of interest group demands?
5. What are the similarities and differences between national and EU groups?
6. Why are there more business than non-business interests present in the EU?
7. In what sense has there been a Europeanization of interest intermediation?

≋ GUIDE TO FURTHER READING

■ Balme, R. and Chabanet, D. (eds) *European Governance and Democracy. Power and Protest in the EU* (Lanham: Rowman & Littlefield, 2008). This study explores the interplay between collective action and democracy in the EU and its member states through a wealth of case studies (civil society interests, regional policy, unemployment and poverty, women's rights, migration policy, and environmental protection).

■ Beyers, J., Eising, R., and Maloney, W. (eds) *The Politics of Organised Interests in Europe: Lessons from EU Studies and Comparative Politics* (West European Politics 31:6, 2008). This volume examines the accomplishments of the present interest group literature and identifies potential avenues for future research.

■ Greenwood, J. *Interest Representation in the European Union,* 2nd edn (Basingstoke/New York: Palgrave Macmillan, 2007). This textbook provides a useful introduction to the role of interest groups in the European Union.

■ Mahoney, C. *Brussels versus the Beltway: Advocacy in the United States and the European Union* (Washington DC: Georgetown University Press, 2008). This comparative analysis explores what determines US and EU advocacy strategies and policy success. It analyses the importance of institutional structures, the types of issues, and the characteristics of the interest groups.

■ Smismans, S. (ed.) *Civil Society and Legitimate European Governance* (Cheltenham UK/Northampton USA: Edward Elgar, 2006). This edited volume presents a variety of theoretical perspectives and empirical analyses that centre on the role of civil society in EU democracy.

WEBLINKS

- www.euractiv.com   This internet newsletter, as well as being of general interest, provides a listing of EU-level interest organizations, structured according to categories of interest. The section on EU priorities and opinion provides useful dossiers about the governance reforms of the European Union. The section on public affairs provides more specific information on lobbying and non-governmental organizations. The website also provides useful links to the official EU documents on these issues and to position papers of private actors and member states.

- http://ec.europa.eu/transparency/index_en.htm   This website allocates all the information pertaining to the European Transparency Initiative.

- http://ec.europa.eu/civil_society/index_en.htm   This site provides information on the dialogue and consultations of the Commission with civil society.

- Individual interest organizations usually also have their own websites. Here are some examples:

  - www.businesseurope.eu/Content/Default.asp   Business Europe

  - www.beuc.org   The European Consumers Association

  - www.eeb.org   The European Environmental Bureau

  - www.etuc.org   The European Trade Union Confederation

  - www.socialplatform.org   The Platform of European social NGOs

  - www.green10.org   Group of leading environmental NGOs active at EU level

  - www.alter-eu.org/en   The Alliance for Lobbying Transparency and Ethics Regulation

 Visit the Online Resource Centre that accompanies this book for lots of interesting additional material. http://www.oxfordtextbooks.co.uk/orc/Cini_Borragan3e/

PART FOUR

Policies and Policy Making

13 Policy Making in the European Union

ALEX WARLEIGH-LACK AND RALF DRACHENBERG

Chapter Contents

- Introduction
- The evolving Community method
- Day-to-day legislation: codecision
- The rise of 'new governance' tools
- Exploring new governance: the Open Method of Coordination in education and training
- Conclusion: the Lisbon Treaty and EU policy making

Reader's Guide

This chapter discusses how policy decisions are taken in the European Union (EU). The chapter begins with an outline of the ways such power was originally exercised in the EU and discusses the evolution of the formal balance between the EU institutions over time, drawing particular attention to the increasing legislative power of the European Parliament (EP). The chapter then outlines the ways in which the EU has begun to complement these formal decision-making channels with a range of 'new governance tools' that act to produce coordinated member state action through iterated processes of standard setting, best practice identification, and knowledge transfer. Particular attention is paid here to the best known of these processes, the Open Method of Coordination. The final part of the chapter assesses the trends in EU decision making in the context of measures proposed in the Treaty of Lisbon.

Introduction

Decision making at the EU level is a complex affair. There are, for the time being, 27 different national governments which must be involved. The EU's supranational political institutions, the European Commission and the European Parliament, often play very important roles. In certain policy fields, such as monetary policy, particular specialized institutions have the principal parts; in the case of monetary policy, for instance, that institution is the European Central Bank (ECB). A wide range of non-state actors such as trade unions, interest groups, and non-governmental organizations (NGOs) will mobilize to try to shape policy decisions. And always in the background is the balancing act that decision makers in Brussels (and Strasbourg, Luxembourg, and Frankfurt) must manage between the various levels of the system that we know as the EU—the 'European' level, the national level, and the subnational level (local and/or regional governments).

In some areas of policy—for example, tax—the EU has either no or very few powers. In others, such as agriculture or competition, it has essentially replaced the individual member states as the locus of meaningful power. This balance of powers between the EU and its member states changes over time, and although some areas of policy remain rather resistant to Europeanization—again, tax is a good example—others have been progressively transplanted from national to EU levels over the lifetime of the Union. A case in point is environmental policy, in which the EU initially had no formal powers whatsoever, but in which it is now often seen as the leading actor in the world (see Chapter 22).

To complicate matters further, the EU makes its policy decisions in a variety of ways. These different configurations of the decision-making system or decision rules change the balance of power between the different levels in the system, and the different institutions at EU level, according to the issue at hand. These decision rules have changed signifi-

cantly over time, moving away from the orthodox Community method (Coombes 1970), to a variety of different mechanisms and revisions to the method itself. We return to this issue below.

John Peterson (1995) divides EU decision making into two basic types: those of 'history-making' proportions, and those of daily law-making. When it comes to the initial category of really major issues—such as setting out a strategy for the EU as a whole over a period of years, or agreeing changes to the treaties—member state governments have all meaningful power. Meeting at head of government or head of state level in the European Council, they make complex bargains and ensure that the package of proposals that results from such summits is acceptable to all of them, by means of the unanimity rule. Thus any member state can veto a proposal they find unacceptable, even as part of a bigger compromise package. Recent rounds of proposed treaty change have been prepared by Conventions: that is to say gatherings of representatives from the EU institutions, member states, and civil society which have drafted the text of proposed new treaties. These Conventions have been influential in shaping the content of recent treaties, but the power to decide upon what to do with Convention recommendations remains firmly with the member state governments, as their treatment of the Draft Constitution in 2003 made clear.

In daily decision making, the standard operating pattern in pillar 1 has in recent years become a sharing of formal legislative power between the member states (via the EU Council) and the EP, played out against a backdrop of furious network building. This process, known as codecision, has had a fundamental impact on the life and relevance of the EP in particular by increasing its legislative role from marginal to coequal of the Council (see Chapter 10 and Figure 13.1). However, this emerging standardization of the legislative process is not the whole story, for it is complemented by the increasing use of the so-called 'new' or 'soft' governance tools such as benchmarking or the Open Method of Coordination (OMC), in a way that arguably takes place outside the pillar structure altogether. These recently adopted governance tools give essentially no role to either the European Court of Justice (ECJ) or the EP, although they can involve a range of civil society actors, and produce EU decisions of a rather different kind: not legislation, but recommendations, advice on best practice, and guidelines. Explaining the impact of these new governance tools on EU decision making is one of the core objectives of this chapter.

Moreover, when the member states see benefits of cooperating at EU level in a new policy issue, but want to ensure this cooperation remains entirely under their control, or as near to that as is possible, they create new silos to contain this cooperation. An obvious example here is the creation of the so-called pillar structure in the Treaty on European Union, which gave the EU new competences in issues such as foreign policy, defence policy, and immigration, but kept those firmly away from the Commission and EP, as well as the ECJ, in separate 'pillars' of the EU, where a decision rule of intergovernmentalism operates, just as in the European Council (see Table 13.1).

There is evidence that the pillar structure is flexible. Policy issues can be shifted from one pillar to another, as member states become accustomed to cooperation in that issue or calculate that they would obtain better results if they moved away from intergovernmentalism. Several matters of immigration policy, for example, have travelled from their original location in pillar 3 to pillar 1, where the Commission and EP enjoy their full range of powers. Pillar 1 remains where the EU produces most of its legislation. On the other hand, where particular member states are reluctant to see the EU take action in a particular area of policy, they may decide to be flexible in a different way and to opt out rather than use their veto power. For example, the single currency is currently adopted by 16 member states, with the remainder either joining at some point in the future when they qualify for entry or, in the cases of the UK, Denmark, and Sweden, deciding to retain their national currencies.

The structure of this chapter is as follows. First, and briefly, we explore the evolution of the Community method. Next, we investigate the mechanics of EU policy making through a focus on the codecision process. The following section focuses on the recent trend towards 'soft policy', and is followed by a case study of how one of the 'new modes of governance', the OMC, has worked in a key area of its application, namely education and training policy. In our conclusions we evaluate the mixture of hard and soft forms of decision making in the EU and assess the impact on this balance of the Treaty of Lisbon, should it eventually be ratified.

Table 13.1 The three pillars of the EU (post-Nice)

Pillar	Title	Key Functions	Inter-Governmental?
I	European Community	Single market and 'flanking policies'	No
II	Common Foreign and Security Policy	Foreign and defence policies	Yes
III	Police and Judicial Cooperation in Criminal Matters	Cross-border crime; anti-terrorism policy	Yes

The evolving Community method

The original Community method was famously analysed by David Coombes (1970). He described a mode of integration that depended upon a two-way separation of political powers, with the Commission and Council of Ministers enjoying a near monopoly on decision making and agenda setting (in other words, getting issues onto the legislative agenda). The EP had extremely few powers. Interest groups were encouraged to lobby, but had no formal powers beyond the rather weak European Economic and Social Committee (EESC). The emphasis was clearly upon 'hard' legislation, and although progress was often very difficult to obtain, as witnessed by the empty chair crisis of the 1960s, and the so-called Eurosclerosis of the 1970s, the system was relatively simple. Unanimity in Council was the decision rule in all legislative decisions.

The process of adapting the Community method began in earnest in the mid 1980s, as part of the drive to complete the Single Market by adopting the Single European Act (SEA). In order to secure this important objective, the member states agreed to give up their veto powers in a specified range of issues, in a recognition that the goal of market integration was worth some sacrifice of national sovereignty (Sandholtz and Zysman 1989). This introduced qualified majority voting (QMV) to the EU, meaning that only a certain proportion of the member states need to accept a measure for it to obtain the support of the Council as a whole. QMV does not apply to every area of legislation; it is ruled out in pillars 2 and 3, and applies to most but not all issues included in pillar 1. Furthermore, the bar for a qualified majority is set quite high, at roughly 70 per cent of the weighted votes of the member states. Nonetheless, it is an historic departure from the normal practice of international organizations, and has contributed enormously to the success of EU decision making by making it possible to overcome resistance from a small number of member states where consensus cannot be obtained.

The SEA also paid attention to the EP, in order to address certain aspects of the democratic deficit (Warleigh 2003) but also to recognize that through its canny use of its internal rules and few formal powers, the EP was already becoming a more central player in decision making. The assent procedure was introduced in certain policy areas, and this gave the EP the ability to reject, but not to amend, certain proposals. Over time, for the same underlying reasons and also, perhaps, to drive a wedge between the Commission and the EP (Moravcsik 1999), the powers of the EP have grown (see Chapter 10).

Currently, the elaboration of the classic functions of government in the EU is rather fuzzy. There is clearly a separate judiciary, the Court of Justice of the European Communities, and the Court of First Instance (see Chapter 11), in conjunction with the national legal systems. But the executive and legislative functions of the EU are mixed responsibilities. The task of being the EU's executive, that is, holding responsibility for ensuring that EU policy is carried out properly, is chiefly performed by the Commission, with the ECJ also given powers to rule in cases of alleged non-compliance with EU policy by member states. However, the new modes of governance, such as benchmarking and best practice exchange, allow the member states to coordinate their policies without creating a new common European policy; under these forms of decision making it is arguable that the member states are also given an executive role since they are responsible for their own compliance with the measures they have agreed.

The legislative function of the EU in pillar 1 is a triangle between Council, Parliament, and Commission. Formally speaking, no legislative proposal can be made unless it comes from the Commission, which gives the latter significant power over the EU agenda, although both Council and EP have been known to make successful 'requests' for a proposal to the Commission.

Table 13.2 Types of formal decision in the EU

Type of Decision	Legally Binding?	On Whom?
Decision	Yes	The specific group or person involved, for example a particular member state or firm
Regulation	Yes	All member states, regarding both substance of the decision and the manner of implementation
Directive	Yes, but limited	All member states regarding substance, but with manner of implementation free.

Moreover, even under the codecision procedure, the Commission plays a key role in the early stages of the decision-making process, and is able to shape the positions adopted by the EP and the Council. At the other end of the process, formal decisions about the content of policy are left to the Council and EP, as under assent and codecision both institutions must agree the content of policy for it to reach the statute book.

The products of the EU formal decision-making process are of three kinds: *regulations, directives*, and *decisions*. These differ in the degree to which they are binding on the member states or the specific legal persons to whom they are applied (see Table 13.2).

Most EU policy is in the form of directives, which gives the member states the maximum leeway on issues of implementation. This is important to note because it allows the different national systems to find their own methods of achieving an agreed common goal. It also means, however, that the EU institutions have fewer powers to oversee implementation of policy than might otherwise be the case even under the 'hard' forms of legislation produced by the Community method. Moreover, in pillars 2 and 3, EU decision making depends almost entirely upon the collective will of the member states, with the EU functioning much more in keeping with the established modus operandi of an international organization (see Box 13.1).

 CASE STUDY 13.1

Decision making in pillars 2 and 3

In Pillars 2 and 3 the member states have kept the lion's share of decision-making power to themselves. In pillar 2, the European Council sets the overall agenda, with formal decisions made by the heads of state and government or, via the General Affairs Council, by national foreign ministers. In either case, unanimity is required. Much of the day-to-day work is delegated either to COREPER or to specialist committees, such as the Political and Security Committee, which comprise national representatives. These can be civilian or military officials, depending on the issue under discussion. The Commission is involved in the coordination and

planning of such committee meetings, alongside national officials, but does not have the right of initiative. The EP has no formal role.

In pillar 3, the member states remain dominant, but share more power with the Commission and EP than they do in pillar 2. Many decisions were switched from pillar 3 to pillar 1 by the Amsterdam Treaty, and thus made subject to codecision. Those areas which remain in pillar 3 are decided using the consultation process, giving a limited role to the EP, and the Council shares the right of initiative with the Commission. QMV, however, does not apply.

Day-to-day legislation: codecision

To understand codecision, it helps to remember that it is a *process*, and that what happens at one stage of the process has an impact on what happens at the next stage either by opening up new possibilities or by restricting the scope for action (see Figure 13.1). This is reflected in the idea of the 'policy chain', which is a metaphor for the interlocking stages of the decision-making process as the particular issue moves from conception to implementation amidst complex feedback loops and inter-linkages (Hudson and Lowe 2004). A typical codecision process for a new EU directive would take place roughly as follows.

Given the fuzzy separation of powers in EU decision making both horizontally (at EU level) and vertically (between the EU and national/subnational levels), it is unsurprising that the decision-making process is characterized by a scramble for influence. This process of *hustling* (Warleigh 2000) begins before the proposal is published, as actors with an interest in the subject of the proposed legislation attempt to shape its content right from the outset if they are aware it is in gestation. The Commission is also often open to input from member states and the EP, in order to avoid making proposals that would not get these other institutions' support. The Commission

Table 13.3 A typical codecision policy chain

Policy Stage	Activity
Proposal planning	Commission drafts proposal, after consultation with outside interest groups, MEPs and national governments.
Proposal issuing	Commission publishes proposal, normally after internal debate between different Directorates-General.
Scrutiny	Proposal is scrutinized by the national governments, EP, interest groups, and advisory committees (EESC, CoR).
Consensus formation	Member states attempt to reach a 'Common Position' in Council; EP generates a consensus in committee and then secures plenary support. Interest groups and advisory committees produce analysis papers and suggestions for amendments. Legislation may be finalized at this stage if Council and EP reach agreement.
Amendment	Council and EP return their respective amended drafts, which often reflect the desires of interest groups, to the Commission.
Reissue	Commission reissues a revised proposal.
Second scrutiny	Council and EP decide their respective positions on the revised draft.
Legislation	Council and EP agree text of new law, either immediately or after convening a 'conciliation committee' to resolve their differences.
Implementation	New directive becomes law in each member state. Its implementation is monitored by interest groups.
Adjudication (if necessary)	Implementation is found to be insufficient: interest group reports the member state in question to the Commission, which can prosecute the state in question at the ECJ.

Figure 13.1 The codecision procedure

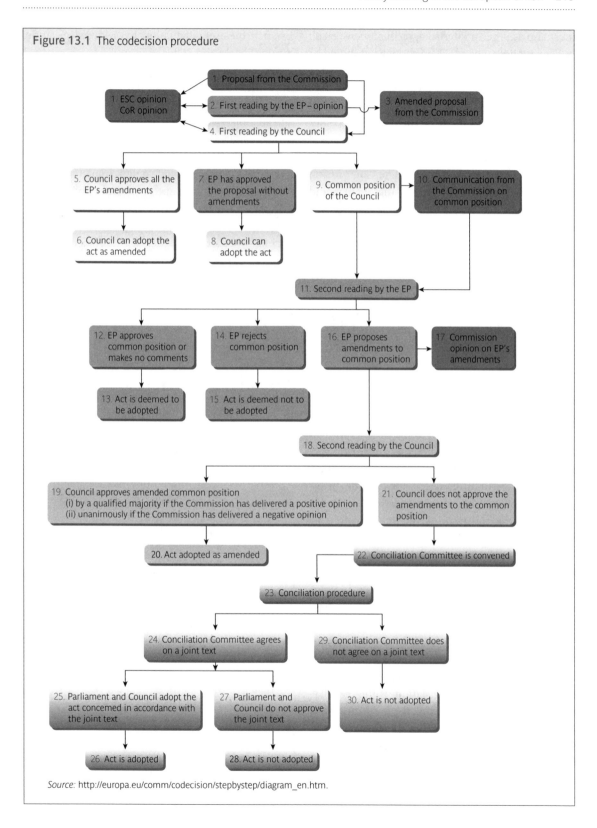

Source: http://europa.eu/comm/codecision/stepbystep/diagram_en.htm.

must also achieve an internal agreement between all its Directorates-General (DGs) about what should be included in the proposal, reconciling what can often be divergent intra-institutional preferences (see Chapter 8).

Once the proposal is public, the hustling becomes even more intensive. Further interest groups will become active, as at this stage it is easier to be aware of a proposal and its likely contents. The Commission may receive suggestions from the EESC and Committee of the Regions (CoR). The Council and EP will solidify their positions, and behind the scenes there is often regular contact between national ministers, COREPER and MEPs at this stage, in order to prepare the ground for a possible conciliation process, or even avoid it altogether by reaching early agreement (Garman and Hilditch 1998). Codecision requires a qualified majority in the Council and an absolute majority of MEPs to support the proposal. Thus it is logical for actors in both the Council and the EP to seek allies in each other's institutions as well as their own: a national minister opposed to the proposal, for example, may reinforce their effort to assemble a blocking minority in the Council with an attempt to help prevent the necessary majority crystallizing in the EP. Consequently, complex coalitions involving actors from EU institutions, national governments, and interest groups are formed.

The Commission receives amended versions of the proposal from both the EP and the Council. It then tries to revise the proposal to satisfy the other two institutions; if this process works, the legislation can be agreed. If the revision process does not work, the remaining points of dispute are clarified, and a conciliation committee may be convened. This committee involves equal numbers of representatives from EP and Council. Its task is to broker inter-institutional agreement on outstanding problems with the proposed legislation. If the conciliation committee is unsuccessful, the legislation falls. If it works out, the legislation is put to the vote in the EP and the Council; if the relevant majorities are to be found, the legislation is passed, and if not, it falls. The conciliation process has entrenched something of a culture of collaboration between the EP and

Council, meaning that failure to produce legislation is rare (Shackleton 2006).

Once the legislation is agreed, the member states implement it according to their own national systems and processes but with a care to ensure the agreed objective is met by each of them. Where implementation is not complete, member states can be prosecuted by the ECJ. That said, the Commission has no powers to inspect policy implementation, except in competition and agriculture policies, so it is in reality the task of citizens or interest groups to report problems to the Commission, which then decides whether the evidence is sufficient, or the political climate conducive, to such a challenge (Alter 2001). Such cases *do* occur, and the right of the Court to impose fines on member states for non-compliance with EU legislation was written into the Maastricht Treaty.

In sum, the codecision policy chain is complex, but suitable for producing workable policy. Despite its intricacy, it is able to involve a great array of actors, and it has proven to be capable of both evolving over time and extending its application to growing numbers of issue areas. We now turn to the OMC and ask whether this judgement also holds there.

KEY POINTS

- The Community method began as a two-way separation of powers at EU level, between the Commission and the Council, and with unanimous voting required in the Council.

- Over time, the Community method was adapted to introduce two very significant new components: qualified majority voting, and what has become a very powerful legislative role for the European Parliament.

- EU decision-making processes change over time and according to the policy area. An example is the use of the 'pillar structure', to keep certain areas of policy firmly under intergovernmental control.

- In day-to-day policy making in pillar 1, the key for success is the formulation of a successful policy network that can broker an alliance between the necessary range of institutions and non-state actors to secure the required majority in the Council and EP.

The rise of 'new governance' tools

In addition to the traditional Community method, the EU has recently included various so-called 'new modes of governance' (NMG) in its arsenal of policy-making instruments. The label 'new' might actually be considered misleading, because while a specific form of governance might be new to the European level, it may have existed for years at national or at international level, as in the OECD, for instance. It might be new in a given EU policy area, but not unprecedented in the EU system as a whole; a new mode of governance may be used in combination with other NMGs, or even with the Community method, in a particular issue area. How we study EU governance conceptually has implications for what we see and for what we consider to be 'new' here (Smismans 2006b).

Moreover, while NMGs can be understood to include any form of policy instrument which deviates from the classical Community method (Scott and Trubek 2002), others are rather similar to it, so it is right to argue that the distinction between new and old or hard and soft modes of governance is one of degree rather than of category (Laffan and Shaw 2006). Furthermore, these new modes of governance are not a homogeneous group, as they include a variety of policy-making instruments, such as framework directives, soft law, co-regulation, partnership models, voluntary agreements, and the social dialogue. While these policy-making instruments differ from each other, they all have certain common characteristics. New modes of governance are essentially voluntary and informal means of cooperation, which establish frameworks in which policy issues can be discussed and negotiated. As they are a form of 'soft law', they do not impose legally binding action or detailed obligations on the member states or national social partners, and they can be easily adapted to national circumstances. They promote flexibility and participation, which can lead to knowledge creation and perhaps to more effective policy, through deliberation (see Box 13.2). They are often applied in policy areas where the national situation differs substantially or where limited competences at EU level exist.

While applying new approaches to public administration and law is a wider international phenomenon (Scott and Trubek 2002; de Búrca 2003; Caporaso and Wittenbrink 2006), there are also some specific reasons for the European Union to utilize NMG. Generally, the use of NMG can be seen as a pragmatic accommodation of the emerging needs of the Union and a reaction to the rigidities of the Community method (Scott and Trubek 2002). More specifically, the application of NMG in the European Union can be traced to two parallel developments: the search for more legitimacy and the limited capacity of the Community method to add to the EU's stock of policy competences.

In order to gain support from European citizens for the European project, the EU sought ways of increasing its legitimacy, as demonstrated by the European Commission in its *White Paper on European Governance* (European Commission 2001). By increasing the participation of actors from

---

 KEY CONCEPTS AND TERMS 13.2

Characteristics of new modes of governance (NMG)

Participation: Having more and different actors participating in the policy-making process

Multi-level: Policy coordination involves actors from various levels of the political system

Subsidiarity: Policy design is decided at the lowest, most appropriate level

Deliberation: Policy learning and policy transferability are part of the policy-making process

Flexibility: The use of soft law ensures flexibility to adapt policy strategies quickly if needed

Knowledge creation: Some NMG use tools like benchmarking or peer review, which can lead to the creation of new knowledge

civil society in the policy-making processes as well as moving into policy areas that are regarded as being of direct concern to the citizen, the EU has been able to use NMG as a partial response to some of its legitimacy problems by increasing the range of actors who have a say in policy making (Eberlein and Kerwer 2002).

Moreover, by the 1990s, the EU had reached the point at which the integration process, in the wake of the advancing economic integration project, was approaching core areas of national sovereignty for the welfare state, such as employment and social policy. Many actors considered that further EU activity in these areas was necessary to balance the economic integration process, but member states nonetheless remained wary about yielding more sovereignty in these areas. Thus an alternative to the Community method was required so that the EU could play a role without threatening what is often highly-prized diversity in these issue areas at national level (Borrás and Jacobsson 2004). In this context the development and use of NMG can be seen as a compromise, as it retains member state responsibility for a policy area while giving the EU a coordinating and possibly policy-shaping role that member states could accept. The Commission, on the other hand, supported the use of new modes of governance because they offer the possibility to expand EU activities into further policy areas (Héritier 2002a).

Without doubt the best known new mode of governance is the Open Method of Coordination (OMC), created as a package by the 2000 European Council meeting in Lisbon on the basis of various existing instruments from previous processes like the European Employment Strategy (EES) (European Council 2000). The OMC is a voluntary and informal mode of intergovernmental cooperation, which does not impose policy solutions or proposals on the member states and which can easily be adapted to national circumstances. It is designed to be a method of benchmarking best practices in a decentralized approach in line with the principle of subsidiarity (European Council 2000). The OMC has now been introduced as a form of policy making in various policy areas. However, there is no uniform OMC process, because different policy areas apply the method according to their particular circumstances (see Box 13.3). There are several factors explaining the variation in OMC processes. These are: whether or not there is a (strong) treaty provision in the area of policy concerned; the role of the different institutions; the extent to which other actors can participate in the process; the existence of benchmarks, indicators and targets; and the possibility for sanctions (see Box 13.4).

In order to outline the specificities of an OMC process, the development and functioning of the

---

CASE STUDY 13.3

The ideal-type OMC as defined by the Lisbon strategy

The open method of coordination takes place in areas that fall within the competence of the member states, such as employment, social protection, social inclusion, education, youth and training. This method has several steps:

- fixing guidelines for the Union, combined with specific timetables for achieving the goals that they set in the short, medium and long terms

- establishing, where appropriate, quantitative and qualitative indicators and benchmarks against the best in the

world, tailored to the needs of different member states and sectors as a means of comparing best practice

- translating these European guidelines into national and regional policies by setting specific targets and adopting measures, taking into account national and regional differences

- periodic monitoring, evaluation and peer review organized as mutual learning processes.

Source: European Council (2000).

CASE STUDY 13.4

Five European benchmarks in education and training

By 2010

- The average rate of early school leavers should be no more than 10 per cent.

- The total number of graduates in maths, science, and technology should increase by at least 15 per cent, while the gender imbalance in these subjects should be reduced.

- 85 per cent of 22-year-olds should complete upper secondary education.

- The number of low-achieving 15-year-olds in reading, mathematics, and science should halve.

- The average participation of working adults population in lifelong learning should rise by at least 12.5 per cent.

Source: European Council (2003).

OMC in the education and training (E&T) policy area will be examined in more detail. Very often the OMC in employment is used as a case study, as it is the oldest OMC process, with a strong legal basis that existed even before the Lisbon Strategy was launched. However, we propose examining the potential of the OMC as a mode of governance in education and training policy because this is more illustrative of OMC in practice, as it is an a priori very lightly Europeanized policy area, with a very limited legal base for EU action and an almost negligible EU role prior to the Lisbon European Council.

Exploring new governance: the Open Method of Coordination in education and training

Education and training is an intriguing policy area, in which a combination of circumstances limits the choice of tools and forms of cooperation possible. First, there is a treaty base (Articles 149 and 150 EEC) that grants the EU only supporting competences, excluding legally binding Community initiatives. Second, the enormous diversity of national E&T systems makes any harmonization particularly difficult, even were there sufficient political will. Consequently, the work of the EU in the field of E&T was limited until the late 1990s to carrying out European Education programmes such as ERASMUS, and no real policy making took place. At the end of the 1990s the first attempts were made to improve cooperation in E&T, by adopting the 'Rolling Agenda', which ensures the Council pays ongoing attention to education and training issues,

especially regarding employment, the development of quality standards, and professional mobility; and establishing networks outside the EU framework, such as the Bologna Process in higher education. However, it was not until the European Council in Lisbon in 2000 that policy making really started. This European Council formulated two imperatives relevant to education and training: first, it set the goal for the EU 'to become the most competitive and dynamic knowledge-based economy in the world', thereby creating an important link between education and employment policies and making improvements in E&T a necessity for the EU's competitiveness. Second, the European Council required the EU to 'undertake a general reflection on the concrete future objectives of education systems'. This arguably amounts to the member states giving themselves permission to overstep the explicit Treaty base in order to realize their new objectives while avoiding binding legislation (Hingel 2001).

In general terms the OMC in E&T functions very similarly to the template created at Lisbon. The member states define common objectives and benchmarks, and work on them according to an agreed programme and timetable (see Box 13.3). Clusters and peer learning activities are carried out in order for participants to identify best practices and to learn from each other; and this is supported by continued checking and monitoring on the implementation, which happens through a reporting exercise. The work programme Education and Training 2010 holds all of these elements together by serving as the framework for the OMC in E&T.

Most of the learning about best practice occurs within the so-called clusters. These are expert groups which concentrate on specific aspects of the E&T policy area, organizing the peer learning activities and discussing current developments. Each of the clusters is made up of member state representatives, Commission experts, and, sometimes, social partners. The work of the clusters is coordinated in the Education and Training 2010 Coordination Group (ETCG), which organizes the planning and implementation of the clusters and peer learning activities and oversees the reporting exercise. Two main documents are published as part of the reporting exercise. The indicator and benchmark document is potentially more critical and perhaps negative, as it is purely Commission driven. The joint document, on the other hand, is based on national reports submitted by the member states, and their representatives are involved in the whole reporting process, both before and after collecting the data. It is this report which is the main 'naming and shaming' instrument used to encourage laggards to catch up.

The Commission and the Council are the main actors in the OMC in E&T. At first sight, the Council has by far the most significant role, since it has both the first word, deciding on the objectives, indicators and benchmarks, *and* the last word, adopting the reports and Council conclusions. However, the role of the Commission should not be overlooked, as the Commission is often the initiator, driver, and main agenda setter in the OMC process. The role of the EP in the OMC in E&T, on the other hand, is very limited, as it is only informed of decisions. While the involvement of non-state actors besides government representatives is officially promoted, the practical participation of social partners, regional governments, and civil society at large depends very much on the national traditions and political structures in the member states. For example, federal states usually involve their regions in the OMC processes more fully than more centrally organized member states.

Although it is difficult to quantify the impact of OMC measures in E&T policy, it is fair to say that the OMC in E&T has substantial consequences for policy making at both European and national levels, albeit with a significant degree of variation between the member states and with clear limits to the convergence of national policies and systems. Some member states already had policy in keeping with the emerging European consensus, and thus needed to change less; in some cases, member states have adopted the new EU standards as their own national equivalents; in other cases, member states have been somewhat cavalier in their approach to OMC. However, the OMC has shifted the context in which member states make policy on E&T issues, and has locked in a new link to *competitiveness* rather than social policy. Furthermore, national E&T policy making is increasingly regarded as having joint objectives in a European context, as participating in the OMC in E&T contributes to the transfer of concepts such as transparency, peer learning method, lifelong learning, learning outcomes, and permeability from the European to the national level. As an illustration, the European qualification framework led, in many member states, to the voluntary creation of national qualification frameworks. This is not always easy because member states might use the same concepts and terminology but have a different understanding of them: *competence* in English versus *Kompetenz* in German is a good example of this. However these transferred concepts often lead to new national policy discussions and approaches.

While using the OMC in the E&T policy area has not led to the transfer of any formal competences to the EU, it is also indisputable that the Commission has gained significant influence in this field. This can be seen, for example, in the variety of issues in which the EU is now involved, ranging from school and pre-school education to higher education and adult learning, and the increasing visibility and significance of the EU Commissioner for Education and Training vis-à-vis national ministers. Furthermore, there is now a substantial increase of policy output at European level in E&T as a direct consequence of this form of governance (European Commission 2008). Moreover, there has been a clear uploading of national issues and approaches via the OMC in this area, such as that by Belgium and France on 'equity' and teacher education.

In sum, while the OMC in E&T is a relatively young and 'weak' way of making policy decisions, it is a very successful one. EU cooperation and policy making in E&T have significantly increased over the last few years, and the Commission has gained an important role for itself. The OMC has led to more

political commitment by the member states towards cooperation in E&T at European level—a major change to the situation prior to the 2000 Lisbon European Council.

> **KEY POINTS**
>
> - The use of New Modes of Governance in the European Union is an attempt to respond to the legitimacy debate around the EU, and a recognition that a limit to integration had been reached with the Community method.
>
> - New Modes of Governance are not homogenous and some of them are not necessarily new inventions as such, having existed for years at national or international level.
>
> - The OMC instrument is used differently according to the specific conditions of the policy areas, and thus the OMC template provided by the Lisbon Strategy is not always followed entirely. Consequently there is not one OMC, but many.
>
> - The Commission has established for itself a significant role as initiator, driver, and agenda setter in the OMC in education and training.
>
> - European integration in the E&T policy area has increased significantly since using the OMC as a governance form.

Conclusion: the Lisbon Treaty and EU policy making

The EU makes policy decisions in a range of complex ways. New treaties are agreed by the member states only; the same goes for setting EU strategic directions, which are established by the European Council. Some policy areas, such as tax, remain almost entirely national competences. When the EU uses formal procedures to make 'day-to-day' decisions, the balance of power between the national and EU levels, and between the EU institutions, changes over time and according to policy area. The so-called pillar system is a good but limited example

of this variation, as even in pillar 1 there are significant differences in the distribution of power. For example, even today the EU has strong powers in competition policy, but the EP has at best a small role in this policy area, with power concentrated in the hands of the Commission in a way redolent of the original Community method. In environment policy, however, EU competence has grown from zero to impressive levels, and most policy decisions are made using both QMV in Council, and codecision, giving the EP a significant degree of power

Table 13.4 EU decision-making procedures by policy area: an indicative sample

Policy area	Formal EU power	Forms of governance/decision making	Treaty base	Noteworthy trends
Employment	Shared competence	a) OMC b) CM*	128 EC 129 EC	Strong use of both instruments
Social policy	Shared competence	a) OMC b) CM	144 EC 137 EC	The new social OMC is aimed at deepening EU social policy, but CM still main tool
Environmental policy	Shared competence	a) OMC b) CM	175 EC 175 EC	Shift to voluntary action and away from regulation
Cohesion policy	Supportive competence	CM	161–162 EC	Lisbon Treaty would introduce codecision and extend QMV
Education and Training policy	Supportive competence(weak)	a) OMC b) CM**	149–150 EC 149–150 EC	Increased EU activity due to OMC procedure
Macro-economic policy	Shared competence	OMC	99–100 EC	Broad Economic Policy Guidelines recommend aims; Lisbon Treaty would introduce codecision and extend QMV
Common agricultural policy	Shared competence	CM	37 EC	Lisbon Treaty would introduce codecision and extend QMV
Fiscal surveillance	Supportive competence	OMC	104 EC	Lisbon Treaty would introduce neither codecision nor QMV
Competition policy	Exclusive competence (very strong)	CM	83, 89 EC	Lisbon Treaty would extend use of QMV, but not introduce codecision
Immigration and Asylum policy	Shared competence	a) CM b) OMC	67 EC 61, 63 EC	Immigration now part of pillar 1, most action under CM

* Community method (CM)
** Harmonization of national laws is explicitly ruled out

where formal procedures are used, although there are also clear signs of a shift towards NMG in this policy area. This kind of variation is the result of bargains between the member states when they agree a change to the EU treaties or a new Treaty entirely. If the EU is complicated, this is because the member states prefer it that way. Moreover, when the EU uses new modes of governance to make policy decisions, this can also happen in a variety of ways. The OMC is the best known such method, but it is by no means the only one. Moreover, even in a single policy area the OMC can be applied in a variety of ways, for example in employment and social policy.

EU decision making will remain complex rather than uniform in the coming years. As indicated in Table 13.4, the Lisbon Treaty, if ratified, will alter the balance between the EU institutions in some policy areas, with a trend towards extending the use of QMV in Council, whilst also adding to the range of policies subject to codecision. This is likely to increase the role and influence of the EP, and standardize the formal balance of power between the Council, Commission, and EP, whilst also making it harder for national governments to use their veto. The introduction of a new method of calculating the threshold for a qualified majority—55 per cent of the member states, where this also represents 65 per cent of the total EU population—should also simplify formal legislation somewhat. The abolition of pillar 3, with the transfer of issues it encompasses to pillar 1, will also contribute to the standardization of the EU's formal legislative processes.

However, the simplification of QMV, its extension, and the increased use of codecision are not the whole story. It will still be necessary to hustle frantically in order to shape the content of EU legislation. Indeed, this process would even be extended if the new Treaty is ratified, since the latter also introduces a new role for national parliaments in EU decision making: it would enable an alliance between half the national parliaments and either the Council or the EP to block a new piece of EU legislation on the grounds of subsidiarity. Such a step may be welcome to boost the EU's legitimacy and to involve national parliamentarians' engagement with EU legislation, but it may well make the decision-making process more complex.

Intriguingly, as Table 13.4 demonstrates, new modes of governance are often deployed as a *complement* to the Community method as well as a *substitute* for it, and are often most effective when combined with it. The politics of EU decision making remains complex, however: although clearly new modes of governance can add to the range of policy issues in which the EU is active, they also, where used, return the EU to the institutional balance of the early days of the Community method with a role for the Commission, Council/member states, and interest groups, but almost none for the EP or the ECJ. Formal policy-making methods offer a very different balance of power, but it must nonetheless be acknowledged that where the member states so choose, they continue to be able to deepen the integration process while ensuring that the perceived cost to their sovereignty can be limited in creative ways. It is this that makes EU decision making so fascinating.

QUESTIONS

1. What was the original Community method, and why was it adapted?
2. What is the role of policy networks in EU decision making?
3. To what extent has codecision altered the balance of power between the EP, the Commission, and the EU Council?
4. To what extent has the 'pillar structure' of the EU been altered since it was set up by the Maastricht Treaty, and why?

5. Why was the use of new modes of governance considered necessary in EU politics?

6. How has the use of the OMC impacted on European integration in education and training policy?

7. Do new modes of governance represent a lasting paradigm shift in EU approaches to policy making?

8. To what extent, and in which ways, can non-state actors influence policy making in the European Union?

 GUIDE TO FURTHER READING

■ Héritier, A. 'New Modes of Governance in Europe: Policy Making Without Legislating?', in A. Héritier (ed.) *Common Goods: Reinventing European and International Governance* (Boulder, CO: Rowman and Littlefield, 2002), pp.185–206. An excellent analysis of whether new forms of governance are becoming the main form of decision making in the EU.

■ Peterson, J. and Bomberg, E. *Decision-making in the European Union* (Basingstoke: Palgrave, 2009). An indispensable book on EU decision making.

■ Phinnemore, D. and Warleigh-Lack, A. (eds) *Reflections on European Integration* (Basingstoke: Palgrave, 2009). An interesting collection of essays by leading academics and policy makers on the development of both the EU system and EU studies.

■ Radaelli, C. M. *The Open Method of Coordination: A New Governance Architecture for the European Union?* (Stockholm: Swedish Institute for European Policy Studies, SIEPS Report 2003/1). A very useful piece of research that provides an insight into the advantages and disadvantages of the OMC as a policy-making tool.

■ Scott, J. and Trubek, D. M. (2002) 'Mind the Gap: Law and New Approaches to Governance in the European Union', *European Law Journal*, 8/1: 1-18. A key reference when discussing the emergence of the 'new governance' concept, and comparing it with the Community method.

 WEBLINKS

● www.eu-newgov.org   The website of the Integrated Project on New Modes of Governance, coordinated by the Robert Schuman Centre for Advanced Studies at the European University Institute in Florence.

● http://eucenter.wisc.edu/OMC/   This is the OMC forum of the University of Wisconsin's European Center of Excellence, which makes recent forthcoming work on the OMC available to researchers, policy makers, and students.

● http://ec.europa.eu/education/index_en.htm   The European Commission's website on Education and Training policy, outlining the main activities of the European Union in this field.

 Visit the Online Resource Centre that accompanies this book for lots of interesting additional material. http://www.oxfordtextbooks.co.uk/orc/Cini_Borragan3e/

14 European Union External Relations

MICHAEL SMITH

Chapter Contents

- Introduction
- Institutions and policy making: the common commercial policy
- Institutions and policy making: development assistance policy and monetary policy
- The EU's external economic policy objectives
- Obstacles and opportunities: the EU as a power in the world economy
- Conclusion

Reader's Guide

This chapter focuses on the external economic relations of the EU—the longest-established area of EU international policy making and action. The chapter begins by examining institutions and policy making in the 'Community pillar', where the Commission plays a central role in initiating and conducting policy, and looks especially at the Common Commercial Policy. It goes on to look at two areas of 'mixed competence', where policy responsibility is shared between the EU institutions and national governments: development assistance policy and international monetary policy. The chapter then proceeds to explore the substance and impact of EU external economic policies, and to assess the role of the EU as a global 'economic power'. The conclusions draw attention to a number of tensions and contradictions in EU external economic policies.

Introduction

The European Union is unquestionably one of the largest concentrations of economic power in the global arena. As can be seen from Table 14.1, the Union possesses 'assets' in the form of economic resources, human resources, and territory that put it at least on a par with the United States, Japan, China, Russia, and other leading economic actors, and well ahead of several of them. Equally, in trade, investment, and other forms of international production and exchange, the EU can be seen as a potential economic 'superpower', not least because it constitutes the largest integrated market in the world. It is rich, it is stable, and it is skilled, and thus it inevitably occupies a prominent position in the handling of global economic issues. This fact of international economic life has only been underlined by the accession of the 12 new member states between 2004 and 2007 (see Chapter 26).

Basic to the conversion of this economic potential into economic power and influence, as in so many other areas of EU policy making, is the institutional context for the conduct of external economic policy. From the very outset in the 1950s, with the establishment of the customs union, the EEC had to develop a Common Commercial Policy to handle its relations with partners and rivals in the world economy. During the 1960s, the Community also initiated what was to become a wide-ranging and complex development assistance policy, primarily to manage relations with the ex-colonies of Community members. As early as the 1970s, there was a proposal also to establish a Monetary Union, with an external monetary policy, but this did not finally become established (and then only for some EU member states) until the twenty-first century. Each of these key areas of external economic policy presents the EU with distinct institutional problems, and with distinct opportunities for the exertion of international influence.

The purpose of this chapter is to explore these areas of external economic policy, to link them with the institutions and policy-making processes that they generate within the EU, and to explore the ways in which these create challenges and opportunities for the EU in the global arena. By doing this, the chapter will expose a number of areas in which there are tensions and contradictions within EU policies, as well as linkages between them; it will also enable us to evaluate EU policies towards major partners and rivals in the global arena and the extent to which the EU has been able to establish itself as a global 'economic power' by converting its potential into action.

Table 14.1 The European Union and its major rivals in the global political economy

	Population (m)	Area (million sq km)	GDP (€ bn)	Share of world trade %
China	1,321	9.6	2,226	Imports 8.0 Exports 11.7
India	1,130	3.3	718	Imports 2.2 Exports 1.4
Japan	128	0.4	3,139	Imports 5.5 Exports 6.4
Russia	142	17.1	851	Imports 2.2 Exports 3.3
USA	303	9.8	10,048	Imports 18.5 Exports 11.0
EU 27 (2005)	493	4.2	10,957	Imports 18.9 Exports 18.1

Source: http://ec.europa.eu/trade/en/ (all figures for 2007 except where noted).

Institutions and policy making: the common commercial policy

The core of the EU's external economic relations is the Common Commercial Policy (CCP). Established by the Treaty of Rome, but not fully implemented until the late 1960s, the CCP is the means by which the EU manages the complex range of partnerships, negotiations, agreements, and disputes that emerge through the operation of the customs union (on the customs union, see Chapter 16). As we shall see later, the definition of 'commercial policy' has broadened considerably since the initiation of the EEC, but it is important to understand the core principles and policy-making procedures of the CCP as the basis for understanding the whole of the Union's external economic policies.

As established in the Treaty of Rome, the CCP was based on Article 113 of the Treaty—since amended to become Article 133 of the consolidated treaties in the late 1990s. Article 133 sets out not only the principles on which the CCP is to be pursued, but also the policy-making processes through which it is to be implemented. In terms of principles, as set out in Box 14.1, the CCP embodies not only a set of aims for the external policies of the Union, but also a set of far broader aims in relation to the operation of the world trade system. This key tension is at the heart of the successes registered and the difficulties encountered by the CCP, since it sets up a series of contradictions: is the EC to achieve the aim of prosperity and stability for Europeans at the cost of international stability and development? Or is it to privilege the aim of global prosperity and development at the expense of the EU's citizens and their welfare? The reality, of course, is that there is a complex balancing process for EC policy makers as they utilize the instruments of the CCP.

What are those instruments? Essentially, they fall into two broad areas. The first deals with what might be called trade promotion: the activities that develop the EC's international activities and organize them around certain core practices. These instruments

fall partly within the control of the EC itself, but are also to be found in the broader global institutions and rules established in the world arena. Thus the EC has developed a complex range of trade and commercial agreements, covering almost every corner of the globe. Some of these are bilateral, with individual countries such as Russia; others are inter-regional, covering relations with groupings such as ASEAN (the Association of Southeast Asian

---

BOX 14.1

The Common commercial policy (extracts from European Community Treaty)

Article 131

By establishing a customs union between themselves, Member States aim to contribute, in the common interest, to the harmonious development of world trade, the progressive abolition of restrictions on international trade and the lowering of customs barriers ...

Article 133

1. The Common Commercial Policy shall be based on uniform principles, particularly in regard to changes in tariff rates, the conclusion of tariff and trade agreements, the achievement of uniformity in measures of liberalization, export policy and measures to protect trade such as those to be taken in the event of dumping or subsidies.

2. The Commission shall submit proposals to the Council for implementing the Common Commercial Policy.

3. Where agreements with one or more states or international organizations need to be negotiated, the Commission shall make recommendations to the Council, which shall authorize the Commission to open the necessary negotiations ... The Commission shall conduct these negotiations in consultation with a special committee appointed by the Council to assist the Commission in this task and within the framework of such directives as the Council may issue to it.

Nations); others still are multilateral, with the prime example being the World Trade Organization (WTO) In all of these areas of trade promotion, the EC aims to establish stable partnerships and relationships, often with a set of formal rules, which enable trade to develop and diversify.

A second set of CCP instruments are those of trade defence. Here the EC is concerned to counter perceived unfair trade practices by its key partners, such as the dumping of goods at unrealistically low prices on the EU market, the subsidization of goods, or the creation of barriers to EC exports. To support it in these areas, the Community has developed a battery of trade tools: anti-dumping and anti-subsidy measures, rules of origin, sanctions, and other punishments. But it does not exercise these powers in isolation; frequently the Community works through the WTO to counter what are seen as unfair practices, using the WTO dispute settlement procedures to defend itself at the global level. Trade and partnership agreements also include procedures for dealing with trade disputes, as a matter of routine, and sometimes linkages are made with other areas of external policy such as those on human rights and development assistance (see below).

The policy processes through which the CCP is implemented are those of the 'Community pillar', making use of the 'Community method'. This is why in this section we talk of the EC and not the EU (see Chapter 1 for further explanation of the distinction between the two). In practical terms, this means that the Commission has the power of initiative, not so much on legislation as on the initiation, conduct, and implementation of commercial policy agreements. In many cases, the Commission will propose 'negotiating directives' in which its negotiating mandate is set out; where this is the case, the Council has to approve the mandate as well as any changes in it, and the Commission is monitored by a special Council committee, the so-called '133 Committee' of member state representatives. In other areas, the Commission has delegated powers to apply regulations (for example on anti-dumping cases) subject to monitoring and approval by the Council. The Commission has developed a sophisticated appara-

tus for the conduct of trade negotiations and the conduct of 'commercial diplomacy' through its delegations and specialist missions such as that to the WTO in Geneva. It might be argued on this basis that in this area the EC has effectively displaced the national trade policies of the member states (in contrast to the position on foreign and security policy, where the member states remain supreme).

As time has passed, the Community has had to respond to the changing nature of world trade and exchange, and the CCP has been reshaped to reflect the key trends. In a number of instances, this has exposed the continuing tension between the national preferences of the member states and the 'European' perspective of the Commission, thus raising questions about the extent to which the EC has really undermined the independence of national commercial policies. A key issue here is that of competence: in the Treaty of Rome and for a long time afterwards, the CCP was assumed to be about trade in manufactured goods, but the changing global economy has given a much more prominent role to trade in services (for example, aviation services or financial services) and to related questions such as that of 'intellectual property' (the trade in ideas, such as those embodied in computer software). In order to cater for these changes, the scope of article 113 and then 133 has had to be expanded, and this has not always been a simple process, as member states have found reasons to resist the expansion of the Commission's role.

Another area of tension, which has existed from the earliest days of the Community, reflects the linkage (or the gap) between 'internal' EC policies and the Community's external relations. As internal integration reaches new areas, it is inevitably found that these have external policy consequences. Thus, in the early days of the Community, the Common Agricultural Policy (CAP) was recognized to be not only a policy about what went on within the Community, but also a policy about the regulation of food imports, and so it has remained ever since. More recently, the completion of the 'single European airline market' during the late 1990s raised questions about who was to negotiate with countries such as the USA about the regulation of international air routes. Only after a prolonged struggle was it agreed that the Community (and thus the Commission) could exercise this power. A large number of other 'internal' policy areas, such as competition policy, environmental policy, and industrial policy, are inevitably linked to the global economy, and this will continue to be an issue for the conduct of the CCP and related policies.

As a result of these trends and processes, the CCP has in a sense 'spread' to encompass new areas of external commercial policy, especially in the area of regulatory policy. The EU has become engaged with a very large number of international institutions in the conduct of these policies, and has developed a complex web of agreements with which to manage them. Not all of the EU's international economic policies fall into this framework, however, and we will now turn to look at two of the most important of these.

> **KEY POINTS**
>
> ● The Common Commercial Policy sets the framework for internal coordination of EU commercial policies, but also sets out principles for the EU's international activities; these two elements can conflict and set up tensions.
>
> ● The key instruments of EU external commercial policies can be seen as those of 'trade promotion' and 'trade defence'. They need to be balanced and can come into conflict.
>
> ● The key method of external commercial policy making is the 'Community method' based in pillar 1 of the EU and on Community competence, but there is still a residual role for member states, and a number of areas demonstrate 'mixed competence'.
>
> ● The changing nature of commercial policy on the global level creates tensions between the 'internal' development of the integration process and the 'external' demands of global institutions and trading partners or competitors.

Institutions and policy making: development assistance policy and monetary policy

From the very earliest days of the EEC, there has been pressure for the Community and now the Union to expand the scope of its international economic policies. Thus from the 1960s onwards there has been a continuing concern with development assistance policy, stimulated originally by the process of decolonization in the French empire, and since the 1970s there has been a realization that the process of monetary integration in Europe must be accompanied by some form of international monetary policy. In contrast to the trade and commercial policy area, though, these areas have never been subject to the full 'Community method' and thus to the leading role of the Commission. As a result, they demonstrate distinctive patterns of institutions and policy making.

Let us first look at Community policies on development assistance. Starting in the early 1960s, a series of increasingly ambitious agreements between the EEC, its member states, and a growing range of ex-colonies created a unique system for the multilateral management of development assistance issues. Box 14.2 summarizes the key phases in this process, especially the progression from the 'Yaoundé system' to the 'Lomé system' and then to the present 'Cotonou system' (each taking its name from the place in which the agreements were finalized). It can be seen from this summary that the successive conventions have set progressively larger ambitions for the scope of the activities they cover, and also that they have covered an increasing number of partners from less developed countries (as well as a growing EC and then EU). As a result, the 'Cotonou

CHRONOLOGY 14.2

Key stages in the evolution of the EU's relations with African, Caribbean, and Pacific (ACP) countries

1963: First Yaoundé Agreement (renewed 1969)

● Reciprocal preferential trade access between EEC member states and associated states (former colonies of member states)

● European Development Fund

● Joint Council of Ministers, Joint Parliamentary Assembly, and Committee of Ambassadors

1974: Lomé Convention (renewed 1979, 1984, 1990, 1995)

● Includes former British colonies; African, Caribbean, and Pacific Group established with Secretariat in Brussels

● ACP partners increase from 46 (1974) to 68 (1995)

● Non-reciprocal trade preferences

● Schemes to support ACP agricultural prices (STABEX, 1979) and mineral export prices (MINEX, 1984)

2000: Cotonou Agreement

● Twenty-year agreement (entered into force April 2003)

● ACP partners 78 (2006)

● Multilateral agreement to be supplemented by bilateral or minilateral Economic Partnership Agreements (EPAs) by December 2007

● Conditionality: aid payments linked to democratic government and human rights provisions

Source: European Commission (http://ec.europa.eu/development/en).

(ACP) countries. Processes were established to create and maintain a stable partnership, in which the ACP group would have its own collective voice, and to underpin the development of the poorest economies in the face of an unstable world economy. As time passed, however, there was criticism that the Lomé framework was increasingly irrelevant to the development of a global economy, and as a result the Cotonou system places a much greater emphasis on what might be called 'bottom up' processes of development, in which individual ACP countries or groups of them produced their own plans for sustainable development to be negotiated with the EU. The Cotonou system also contains markedly more in the way of what has come to be called 'conditionality'; in other words, provisions that make the granting of EU aid conditional on good governance, observance of human rights, and the introduction of market economics. As such, it parallels broader developments in the provision of aid on the global scale.

The EU's development assistance policies have thus had to respond to the changing nature of the global economy. Not only the Lomé and Cotonou frameworks have felt this pressure: over a wide range of other development assistance activities, the EC and then the EU have had to adjust, to take account of new linkages (for example between trade and development, environment and development, and so on), and to balance the needs of the developing countries against those of the EU and its member states. The most acute tensions come in the area of agricultural policy: the CAP does demonstrable damage to the economies of some of the poorest countries, by depressing commodity prices, preventing free access to the European market, and subsidizing EU exports. Here again, we can see that external economic policy is closely connected to internal policy processes, and it is not always a profitable linkage.

Central to the problems encountered by the EU's development assistance policies are two factors. The first is an 'internal' institutional problem: the mixture of policy competences between the EU and its member states. The second is an external factor: the ways in which development assistance policies have become increasingly politicized in the contemporary global

system' now covers well over half of all countries in the international system, including some of the very richest and a large number of the very poorest.

The initiation of the Lomé system in the 1970s was widely felt (especially by EC member states) to herald a revolution in development assistance policy by setting up an institutionalized partnership between the EEC and the African, Caribbean, and Pacific

Table 14.2 EU net bilateral and multilateral overseas development assistance (ODA), 2007

Country	Amount (US$ millions)
United Kingdom	12,034
France	10,312
Germany	10,257
Netherlands	5,329
Sweden	3,854
Spain	3,643
Italy	3,533
Denmark	2,173
Belgium	1,921
Austria	1,464
Finland	820
Ireland	984
Greece	407
Portugal	385
Poland	283
Luxembourg	269
Hungary	153
Czech Republic	149
Slovak Republic	51
Slovenia	42
Cyprus	19
Lithuania	18
Latvia	11
Estonia	10
Malta	8
Romania	3
Bulgaria	(no data)
EU 27 total (bilateral and multilateral)	68,099
USA	22,092
Japan	11,884

Source: EU Donor Atlas 2008; Volume 1 (European Commission/Organisation for Economic Cooperation and Development, January 2008) found at http://ec.europa.eu./development/index.en.cfmp.

arena. In terms of the EU's institutional make-up, development assistance policy is an area of 'mixed competence', in which policies proposed and implemented at the EU level coexist with national policies for international development. Thus, although the EU claims to be the world's largest donor of development aid, the majority of that figure consists of aid given by member states as part of their national programmes (see Table 14.2). The complex programmes that have evolved at the European level are also, unlike the Common Commercial Policy, the result of a complex division of powers between the European institutions and the national governments represented in the Council. As a result, the Commission and the Community cannot claim to speak for Europe in this area, although their policies and initiatives have had considerable influence on the ways in which development assistance is targeted and allocated. Agreements such as the Lomé and Cotonou conventions are mixed agreements, and the Council collectively and the member states individually have the power to ratify or not to ratify them.

In addition to the problems created by internal institutional factors, EU development assistance policies have to contend with the fact that issues of economic and social development have become intensely politicized within the global arena. This means that aid is not simply an economic matter; it has become linked to problems of human rights, of 'good governance', and of statehood in the less developed countries, and the EU has had to develop mechanisms to deal with this. There has been an increasing tendency to concentrate the EU's development assistance policies, especially through the EuropeAid development office, and to link them with the operation of agencies such as the European Community Humanitarian Office (ECHO). Since the end of the Cold War, there has also been a series of conflicts, for example in the former Yugoslavia and in Afghanistan, in which the EU has played a key role in coordinating reconstruction and post-conflict economic assistance. As a result, the EU's development assistance policies have moved away from their primary focus on the ACP countries, and a far wider range of recipients has been identified. Among these, post-Communist regimes and those involved in conflict form a key focus, as do the poorest countries, who are granted additional concessions in terms of free access to the European market for their goods.

Development assistance policy thus represents a long-established yet continually changing focus in the EU's external economic relations. Far less well established is the management of the international monetary relations that are an inevitable consequence of the adoption of the euro by sixteen of the EU's member states. It has long been the ambition of enthusiasts for European integration to see the establishment of a 'real' European currency that might rival the US dollar on the world stage. Although there was significant European monetary coordination during the 1980s and 1990s, it was only with the adoption of the euro in 2000 that this became a political and economic reality (and then only for a certain number of EU member states, now in a minority since the enlargement of 2004). The euro experienced a harsh baptism, declining against the dollar continually for two years or more, but then recovered during 2003–5 as the dollar itself came under pressure. Since then, it has maintained considerable strength not only against the dollar but also against European non-member currencies such as the British pound, especially after the onset of the global financial crisis in late 2008. This is not the place to discuss the internal workings of the euro, but it is important to note that the launching of the euro has created at least a partial alternative to the dollar; it has become part of the currency reserves of a wide variety of countries, and it has become a target for those concerned at their overwhelming reliance on the US currency.

The euro is managed through a complex institutional process in which the European Central Bank (ECB) plays a key role. Because it has not been adopted by all of the EU member states, it exists alongside the remaining national currencies such as the pound sterling, the Danish kroner, and the Polish zloty; whilst the governments of the non-euro countries are represented in a number of the bodies overseeing the euro and responsible for economic performance in the EU as a whole, there is differential membership, which gives rise to a number of

frictions and tensions. The result is a complex picture of overlapping institutions, and this has its implications for international monetary management. The euro is a common currency among a number of countries, but it is not managed by a single government: the ECB does not report to a European Finance Minister, and there is no EU system of taxation or macro-economic management. Yet the establishment of the euro has led to calls for adjustment of membership in international financial institutions such as the International Monetary Fund (IMF) to reflect the fact that 15 governments (as of late 2008) have merged their currencies into one. Not surprisingly, the United States has been prominent among those who note that 'euroland' should have only one voice in such bodies as the IMF or the World Bank, and that the persistence of the national representations is an anomaly.

KEY POINTS

- Development assistance and monetary policy are in their different ways two key areas of 'mixed competence' in EU external relations. Thus the EU has potentially important influence in both areas but has to contend with complex internal policy processes as well as international demands.

- Development assistance policy is an area with a long 'history' and one in which the EU can claim global leadership. But there are tensions between the EU's policy framework, global rules, and the needs of developing countries.

- Key problems in development assistance include those caused by the emergence of 'new issues' such as those concerning the environment or human rights, and the increasing 'politicization' of the area.

- European monetary policy has a shorter 'history', despite efforts from an early stage to move towards a common currency. It also lacks full coverage of the EU's member states. Nonetheless, the 'eurozone' has established a key role in international monetary management.

- As with development assistance, there is a potential—and often actual—tension between the internal demands for 'eurozone' monetary stability and coordination and the external challenge of a changing global economy. This is particularly clear in the context of global financial crisis.

The EU's external economic policy objectives

As noted above, the EU is nothing if not explicit about many of its external economic policy objectives. The tone is set by the provisions of article 133 of the Treaties, in which the Common Commercial Policy is established according to explicit principles, applying not only to the EEC and then to the EU but also to the broader management of international commercial relations. This has been backed up over the years by an extremely wide-ranging and sophisticated series of trade agreements with a wide range of partners, which go into great detail about the privileges and concessions to be given to specific partners. This can be seen as establishing an elaborate hierarchy or 'pyramid of privilege' in which the EU manages and adjusts its relations with individual partners (or groups of partners, as in the ACP case). From time to time, this set of arrangements raises questions about exactly how particular partners should be dealt with: for example, in the case of China, the EU has had to change its approach as the country has developed economically, and as it has increasingly become integrated into the global economy through membership of the WTO and other international bodies.

At the same time, the EU has to balance its external obligations against the internal needs of the member states and of European producers and consumers. We have already noted that the CAP provides extensive safeguards (often said to be discriminatory) for EU farmers, but this is often at the expense of consumers whose food bills are higher because of the protectionism built into the CAP. Likewise, during 2005–6, there was a major crisis in trade between the EU and China because of a surge of Chinese textile and clothing exports; this led to the imposition of quotas on Chinese products, but this in turn brought howls of anguish from EU retailers who had ordered products from China only to see them prevented from entering the European market (see Box 14.3). A large number of the disputes between the EU and the United States (who between them account for the majority of disputes brought before the WTO) have been exacerbated by the lobbying of producer groups both in the EU and the USA, which has created political problems around disputes that might in earlier times have been managed in a technocratic manner by officials and experts.

 CASE STUDY 14.3

The EU, China, and the 'Textile Wars' of 2005

During the early 2000s, the rapid growth of Chinese exports created a challenging situation for the EU (as it did for other major importers such as the USA). In particular, the phasing out of the Multi-Fibre Arrangement, an international agreement that allowed importers to impose quotas if they were threatened with a surge of cheap imports, led to a major increase in Chinese penetration of the European market for cheap textiles and clothing. The EU was faced with a dilemma: on the one hand, the remaining European textile producers, concentrated in 'southern' member states such as Italy, Portugal, and Greece, demanded protection; on the other hand, 'northern' member states with rapidly growing markets for cheap T-shirts and other products felt the heat from their consumer and retail lobbies. The European Commission was faced with an almost impossible choice—whether to live up to its international obligations and thus offend powerful internal groups, or to impose restrictions and thus potentially renege on its international commitments. The climax of the problem was reached in 2005, when frantic negotiations produced a set of compromise agreements based on voluntary restraints by China whilst shiploads of clothing products were trapped in European ports. The compromise agreements expired in 2007–8 without an immediate renewal of the crisis—perhaps because of the European economic slowdown and slackening of demand.

The net result of these cross-cutting tensions and pressures is a complicated picture in which the EU professes its commitment to the global management of trade issues but often acts as if it wishes to pursue its own interests in a unilateral manner. Some of the same sorts of tensions emerge in relation to development assistance, as has already been noted: the EU trumpets its commitment to international development and claims to be a pioneer of new types of development assistance policies, but there is always a balance to be struck between the broader international aims, those of the EU as a collective, and those of individual member states. This is institutionalized in the EU, thanks to the mixed nature of the institutional framework and the need to get agreement from the member states on major policy initiatives, and also reflects a number of powerful historical and cultural forces arising from the history of the European empires.

In international monetary policy, we have also noted the tensions between the requirements of internal management of the euro and the pressures of the global economy. The ECB has as almost its only major policy objective the achievement of monetary stability and the reduction of inflation, but this has been held responsible for some of the problems experienced by EU economies during the early 2000s, and thus for their inability to compete on a global level. Whatever the truth or the final conclusion of that argument, there is no doubt that the major economies of 'euroland' have often underperformed against their major global rivals, and that the need to bed down the eurozone system has contributed to this problem. It can also be argued that the primacy of monetary stability in the eurozone has made it more difficult for the eurozone countries and the ECB to respond rapidly to international financial crises such as those in the late 1990s, where unfavourable contrasts were drawn between the speed of movement of the US system and the lack of movement from Europe, or that of 2008 and after, where national measures predominated at some crucial stages.

The EU thus has to face up to a number of tensions emerging from its pursuit of external economic policies. These have become more significant as the EU (either as a whole or through major subgroups such as the eurozone countries) has expanded its role in the global economy, and as the linkages between economic, political, and security activities have become more pronounced. One way of stating these tensions is in terms of the competing demands of multilateralism, inter-regionalism, bilateralism, and unilateralism in EU external economic policies. Each of these patterns can be seen in current EU policies, and they have to be held in a complex and fluctuating balance by a set of collective institutions and individual member states with competing interests.

KEY POINTS

- The EU has a general aim of 'organizing' its external environment through commercial agreements, and of creating a 'pyramid' of partners in the global economy.

- The demands of external commitments can come into conflict with internal pressures from different interests within the EU.

- This is part of a general problem created by the need for responses to a changing global environment, but can express itself in concentrated disputes and crises for the EU.

- The EU also faces the need to balance between different types of relationships: multilateral, inter-regional, and bilateral. In addition, internal pressures can lead to unilateral behaviour by the Union.

Obstacles and opportunities: the EU as a power in the world economy

As noted earlier, the EU has enormous potential for influence and activity in the global economy, but it is equally clear from the argument here that it faces a number of important constraints on its capacity to turn potential into reality. We have already noted that a series of complex balances have to be struck in the making and implementation of EU external economic policies:

- Between the collective interests of the EU as a whole and those of individual member states or groups of member states.

- Between the claims and competences of specific institutions and the pressures generated by different sectors of external economic policy.

- Between the claims of different partners and rivals in the global arena, which demand different patterns of incentives and resources from the EU.

- Between the economic dimension of the EU's involvement in the global arena and the increasing levels of politicization that accompany international economic transactions.

- Between the competing claims of multilateralism, inter-regionalism, bilateralism, and unilateralism in the pursuit of EU policies, often within cross-cutting institutional frameworks with complex patterns of demands.

In some ways, of course, these are no more demanding than the problems confronting any national government in the globalizing world economy. All governments and international institutions are subject to at least some if not all of these dilemmas. In the case of the EU, though, they are compounded by the fact that the EU itself is founded on a series of institutional compromises and a process of continuous negotiation. This makes the competing claims more obvious and in some ways less manageable than they might be for a national government, no matter what its size or complexity.

Against this, the EU has considerable assets and opportunities in the global economy. We have already noted that the EU is the world's 'champion trader', with a key position in the exchange of goods, services and ideas, and its position as manager of the world's largest integrated market provides it with opportunities as well as with challenges. In recent years, the Community through the Commission has sought to exploit a number of these opportunities and to establish itself as a key player in the emerging global economy. Thus it has become increasingly active in leading global trade negotiations, with varying levels of success; it has taken a leading role in the handling of international environmental issues such as those dealt with by the Kyoto Protocol on global warming (see Box 14.4); it

---

BOX 14.4

The EU and the Kyoto Protocol

The EU has established what many would see as a global leadership role in the implementation of the Kyoto Protocol. This international agreement was reached in 1999 and sets targets for the reduction of greenhouse gas emissions. Whilst the EU has been prominent in supporting the Protocol, and has for example established its own internal 'emissions trading' scheme to help in achieving the targets it sets, other major 'emitters', most particularly the USA and China, have failed to ratify and thus to implement the Protocol. The EU spent a lot of time in the early 2000s building a coalition that could bring the protocol into force despite the absence of the USA (to enter into force, the Protocol had to be ratified by countries representing a set proportion of global emissions, and since the USA is by far the largest 'offender', its absence was a severe handicap). Eventually, with the crucial ratification by Russia, the Protocol entered into force in 2005. Whilst the USA is still not part of the Protocol, it has moved towards the EU's position, especially after the coming to office of Barack Obama in 2009, and seems likely to sign up to a successor Protocol to be implemented from 2012.

has pursued its claim to be a leader in the provision of international development assistance and increasingly of humanitarian aid and disaster relief; and it has begun to exercise material influence, albeit often indirectly and haltingly, on the conduct of international monetary policy.

This means that the EU has increasingly become acknowledged as a 'power' in the global economy. It has acquired the legal and institutional apparatus with which to pursue this ambition, and, as we have seen, that this legal and institutional framework gives it the capacity to carry out a number of important 'state functions' to preserve and enhance the prosperity of its citizens in a changing world economy. It has been able to establish itself as a key participant in global economic processes, both in formal institutional terms and in less formal terms of engagement in fundamental processes of trade, production, and exchange. In this, it has had to cope with challenges created by a number of other international economic 'powers' such as the USA, Japan, and (increasingly) China and India. It has created an impressive network of international economic partnerships, and has in many cases been able to link these with increasingly political conditions or requirements, for example through the use of economic sanctions. It has also taken an increasing role in global governance through its support for the regulation of international economic conditions through multilateral action.

It remains unclear in some respects what the EU as a global economic 'power' is for or against. As we have seen, this is a reflection of the complex institutional and other forces operating on its external economic policies, and the cross-cutting pressures to which its policy-making processes are subject. The result is a constant disparity between the EU's claims to global economic distinctiveness and the reality of its untidy policy-making processes. One thing that is clear, however, is that the enlarged EU of 27 members will continue to pursue an ambitious external economic policy and will continue to have a significant global economic impact.

> ### KEY POINTS
>
> - The EU faces a complex 'balancing act' in the global economy, as outlined in previous sections.
>
> - In this it is constrained by internal complexities and differences of interest.
>
> - But there are considerable opportunities for leadership, especially in 'new' areas such as environment and humanitarian support.
>
> - The EU is thus a key participant in 'global governance', and its role in this area is expanding.
>
> - Nonetheless, there are still uncertainties about the EU's overall aims and impact within the global arena, and these affect both the EU and its key partners.

Conclusion

This chapter has dealt with the core elements of the EU's external economic policies: institutions and policy making, aims and objectives, constraints and opportunities, and the impact of the EU's activities. It has done so by focusing especially on three areas of policy: external trade and commercial policy, development assistance policy, and monetary policy. Each of these areas of policy has its own characteristic 'history' in terms of the evolution of institutions, and in terms of the EU's international engagement. We have seen that the Common Commercial Policy was almost built into the foundations of the EEC because of the need to manage the customs union, whilst the development assistance policy responded to the need to deal with the ex-colonies of the EU's member states; and the EU's international monetary policy emerged directly from the internal integration process expressed in the establishment of the euro. In each of these cases the history matters, because it situates the external policy in a certain framework of institutional development, and also because it locates the policy in terms of the development of the global economy.

It is also clear that in each of the policy areas we have explored there is a complex and shifting array of pressures and demands, to which the EU has more or less successfully responded. The 'internal' pressures—from member state governments, from producer or consumer groups, and from competition between the institutions—intersect with the external pressures created by globalization, by competition from major established and emerging economies, and by the pursuit of the EU's sizeable ambitions in a changing world. In these areas, the EU has for a long time had to deal with real and pressing policy dilemmas, which are a natural product of its assumption of major 'state functions'.

Despite these contradictory pressures and the difficulties of constructing policy in a global economy, the EU can claim in its external economic relations to have gone some distance 'beyond the nation state'. This does not mean that the member states are redundant: far from it, they are a major source of policy pressures and challenges for the Union's institutions, and they are a key source of the legitimacy which has been acquired by those institutions in the context of global governance. But there are also the legitimacy that has been acquired by decades of steadily deepening involvement in the global economy and the acquisition of the knowledge and skills that go with it. These are what give the EU's external economic relations a distinctive significance and impact, and makes them a key subject for study.

QUESTIONS

1. What are the key sources of the EU's power in the global economy, and how have they changed in importance during the course of European integration?

2. What are the key features of the distribution of power between the EU institutions in issues of trade and commercial policy? Has the balance of power between the institutions changed, and if so, how and why?

3. How has the changing nature of world trade affected the EU's Common Commercial Policy?

4. What does it mean to say that development policy and monetary relations are areas of 'mixed competence' in the EU, and how does that affect processes of policy making?

5. Why is it appropriate to describe the EU's development policies in terms of a 'pyramid of privilege'?

6. What are the key differences between the Lomé and Cotonou systems of EU development policy?

7. Why has the EU not become a 'monetary superpower' since the establishment of the euro? What developments might enable it to become one?

8. What contribution does the EU make to the governance of the global economy? Does this contribution match its potential?

GUIDE TO FURTHER READING

- Eeckhout, P. *External Relations of the European Union: Legal and Constitutional Foundations* (Oxford: Oxford University Press, 2004). This is a detailed legal analysis, best used when you already know something about the legal and institutional frameworks.

- Hill, C. and Smith, M. (eds) *International Relations and the European Union* (Oxford: Oxford University Press, 2005). Chapters 4, 8, 11, 12, and 14 deal with various aspects of policy making and implementation in the EU's external economic relations.

■ Holland, M. *The European Union and the Third World* (Basingstoke: Palgrave/Macmillan, 2002). Still the best general treatment of the aid and development issue, including the negotiation of the Lomé and Cotonou Agreements.

■ McGuire, S. and Smith, M. *The European Union and the United States: Competition and Convergence in the Global Arena* (Basingstoke: Palgrave, 2008). Chapters 3–7 cover a number of dimensions of EU–US economic relations.

■ Verdun, A. (ed.) *The Euro: European Integration Theory and Economic and Monetary Union* (Lanham, MD: Rowman and Littlefield, 2002). Analysis of the political economy of the euro, including discussion of its international role.

WEBLINKS

● http://ec.europa.eu./   The Commission's web portal guides you to separate websites for trade, monetary relations, and development policies.

● http://www.wto.org/   The website of the World Trade Organization, which contains analysis and commentary on current trade issues and trade disputes, as well as large amounts of detailed information about trade negotiations.

● http://www.oecd.org/   The website of the Organisation for Economic Cooperation and Development, which includes analysis of EU trade and economic policies among a wide range of other studies.

● http://www.apcsec.org/   The website of the Secretariat for the African, Caribbean, and Pacific (ACP) states, who are the EU's partners in the Cotonou Convention.

● http://www.ecb.eu/   The website of the European Central Bank, and which includes studies on the international role and impact of the euro.

Visit the Online Resource Centre that accompanies this book for lots of interesting additional material. http://www.oxfordtextbooks.co.uk/orc/Cini_Borragan3e/

15

From CFSP to ESDP: the EU's Foreign, Security, and Defence Policies

ROBERT DOVER

Chapter Contents

- Introduction
- Some history: European Political Cooperation
- The changing context of European foreign policy
- Common Foreign and Security Policy
- European Security and Defence Policy
- The Lisbon Treaty and the institutional framework
- The global war on terror
- Conclusion

Reader's Guide

This chapter outlines the key historical, institutional, and thematic developments within the EU's foreign, security, and defence policies. It argues that the EU has been an awkward foreign and security policy actor, unable to formulate a cohesive identity or the credible capabilities with which to project itself on the world stage. This is because of the post-World War II pre-eminence of the North Atlantic Treaty Organization (NATO) as a security actor binding US political, economic and military capabilities into the Western European area, allowing European governments to free ride. Since 1991 and the end of the Cold War both the EU and NATO have been seeking to position themselves in the foreign and security policy spheres; the dawn of a new age of asymmetric military threats typified by terrorist attacks on mass transit systems focused the EU's security efforts on to 'homeland security' whilst a resurgent Russia has refocused Europe's attentions on its bellicose neighbour to the east. A lack of coordination and the unilateral actions of member governments are still the hallmarks of this policy sphere and look set to be so for the foreseeable future.

Introduction

Nearly two decades after the negotiators at the Maastricht Intergovernmental Conference (IGC) of 1992 confirmed that 'a common foreign and security policy is hereby established' (Article J, Treaty on European Union), the EU has not moved much closer towards a supranational foreign policy. As a Union of 27 countries and 499 million people, and with an economy now broadly comparable to that of the United States, the absence of a functioning EU foreign policy suggests that the EU remains a 'civilian superpower'. However, whilst the Maastricht, Amsterdam and Nice Treaties failed to reduce intergovernmentalism in foreign policy cooperation, member governments managed to create a highly bifurcated system in which the focus of the policy has switched to Brussels whilst national ownership of some aspects (wars of choice, relations with Russia, and intelligence) has been increased considerably. The move towards a 'Brusselsized' Common Foreign and Security Policy (CFSP) is a slow and piecemeal process that is now largely taking place outside treaty-making IGCs and which will never come to a fully federal conclusion (see Box 15.1).

BOX 15.1

Objectives of CFSP

The five key objectives of CFSP, as established in the Maastricht Treaty (Article 11), and reaffirmed in the Amsterdam and Lisbon Treaties are: to safeguard the common values, fundamental interests, independence, and integrity of the Union in conformity with the principle of the United Nations Charter; to strengthen the security of the Union; to preserve peace and strengthen international security, in accordance with the principles of the United Nations Charter (including those on external borders); to promote international cooperation; to develop and consolidate democracy and the rule of law, and respect for human rights and fundamental freedoms.

The Lisbon Treaty not only identified these core elements but also described how these objectives should be met:

● The principles behind CFSP and guidelines for implementation should be defined by the European Council.

● Common policies and actions should be established by the European Council to frame the way the EU deals with individual countries and regions. These should result in defining and pursuing common policies and actions, and a high degree of coordination.

● Consistency between different areas of external action and other EU policies shall be done by the Council and Commission, assisted by the High Representative.

The centralization of CFSP goes against many of the preferences held by member governments on foreign, security, and defence policy. European governments have sought to retain their sovereignty over these issues and have only allowed a federalist march towards a truly pan-European policy in certain areas, such as development (see Chapter 14), procurement, policing, and peacekeeping. These are areas that do not impinge on core national sovereignty, where there are no requirements to provide additional funding or capabilities, and in which there are pre-existing agreements. Expansions into 'federal' security and defence policies have occurred in a piecemeal fashion and on issues that are at the periphery of NATO's established remit. For example, the Amsterdam Treaty, which came into force in 1997, produced political mechanisms through which the EU could remain in regular contact with a large number of non-EU countries through troika meetings. These function to assist the government holding the EU's Presidency in discharging its responsibilities, and are made up of

CHRONOLOGY 15.2

CFSP

1947 Dunkirk Treaty—Anglo-French agreement on mutual defence should the other be attacked.

1948 Brussels Treaty Organisation (BTO) is formed to promote joint security between UK, France, Belgium, Netherlands, and Luxembourg.

1949 – North Atlantic Treaty Organisation (NATO) is founded by the USA, UK, France, Belgium, Netherlands, Denmark, Norway, Italy, and Luxembourg.

1954 – West Germany and Italy join the BTO and this enlarged BTO is renamed the Western European Union (WEU).

1962 – Failure of French attempt (Fouchet Plan) to develop closer political and military cooperation through an intergovernmental framework.

1970 – European Political Cooperation instituted; following the 'Luxembourg Report', members agree to cooperate more fully in the foreign policy sphere.

1986 – The Single European Act codifies the status of the EPC as part of the EC.

1992 – The Maastricht Treaty establishes that CFSP is the successor to EPC; includes the statement that CFSP would, in time, lead to a common defence policy and common defence.

1993 – The 'Eurocorps' is created: a small European army inaugurated by President Mitterrand (France) and Chancellor Kohl (Germany).

1996 – The Amsterdam Treaty is negotiated, reinforcing the Maastricht proposals in more specific terms and strengthening the position of the Commission in foreign and defence policy formation but without moving significantly from an intergovernmental framework.

1998 – December: Anglo-French summit at Saint Malo, Prime Minister Blair and President Chirac (France) agree to take positive and concrete steps to support the formulation of a common European defence initiative.

1999 – The Cologne Council puts capabilities at the heart of the ESDP—the capabilities catalogue is formulated but not met with the capabilities required for the EU to operate in this sphere.

2001 – The Nice Treaty provides for the development of an EU military capacity, the creation of permanent political and military structures, and the incorporation into the Union of the crisis-management functions of the WEU (entered into force 1 February 2003).

2002 – February: EU delegation begins work in Afghanistan to support post-conflict reconstruction.

– May: EU carries out first-ever practice crisis-management exercise under the ESDP banner.

– December: EU and NATO formalize the Berlin Plus arrangements that provide the EU with access to NATO assets.

2003 – January: EU ministers approve the first action under ESDP, sending assistance to FYROM.

– March 20: US and UK forces invade Iraq against the wishes of the French and German governments, who on 5 March say they will block a second UN Resolution.

– April: France, Belgium, Germany, and Luxembourg call for deeper cooperation on ESDP.

2004 – March: terrorists attack commuter trains entering Madrid.

– June: EU pledges €200m to support the reconstruction of Afghanistan.

2005 – May: German and French governments affirm that the Constitutional Treaty is an important milestone in the development of the EU's external identity.

– July 7: London public transport system is attacked by four bombers.

– September: EU decides by QMV to retain email and mobile phone communications for two years.

2006 – January: the EU 3 (UK, France, Germany) decide to end negotiations with Iran over its attempts to acquire advanced nuclear technologies.

– EU Border Assistance Mission to Rafah (Palestine) begins.

2007 – 1 January: EU Operations Centre opens in Brussels; additional Operation Centres become available in Paris, London, Potsdam, Rome, and Larrisa.

– June: EU Police Mission to Afghanistan begins, and is set to last three years.

– Ongoing disputes with Russia concerning energy security, ballistic missile defence systems, Russian intelligence activity in Europe, and alleged cyber warfare against Estonia.

– December: negotiations result in the Lisbon Treaty.

2008 – March: deployment of 3,000 troops into Chad and Central African Republic.

– August: Russia invades Georgia; French President Sarkozy (holding Presidency of the EU) leads the fractured European response.

– October: EU Monitoring Mission in Georgia (EUMM Georgia) begins.

representatives from the government holding the EU Presidency at the time, the next EU Presidency, the Secretariat of the Council, and the appropriate representative from the Commission. The aim of this policy was to give a global voice and diplomatic leverage to the EU similar to that of an autonomous government. However, with member governments vigorously pursuing independent foreign policies and some actively seeking to diminish the EU as a foreign policy actor, these efforts have been only moderately successful. International influence has been achieved, however, through the appointment of Special Representatives or Monitoring Missions in regions where there are or have been particularly acute crises. These have so far included the Great Lakes (Africa), the Middle East, the Former Yugoslav Republic of Macedonia (FYROM), Ethiopia, Afghanistan, the Central African Republic, and Georgia. These Special Representatives have given the EU a direct role in solving the problems in these areas and, in Bosnia, have proved a very high-profile and critically acclaimed symbol of the EU's external relations policy (Toal 2005).

The overarching aims of this chapter are to provide a guide to historical and institutional developments in EU foreign, security, and defence policy and to explain why these have occurred (see Box 15.2). The chapter will also analyse some of the main contemporary debates in CFSP and European Security and Defence Policy (ESDP), as well as those issues relevant to the medium- and long-term future of the policies.

Some history: European Political Cooperation

The EU has a very well established reputation as a 'civilian superpower', a reputation that is in part founded on the size and strength of its collective economy and the number of citizens who are able to call themselves 'European'. The first attempt at extending this economic responsibility to foreign affairs came with the establishment of the European Political Cooperation (EPC) framework. This was a product of the Luxembourg Report of 1970, later to be incorporated into the European Community (EC) by the 1987 Single European Act (SEA). Even within the 1987 regime, however, EPC was distinct from regular Community procedures. Bringing EPC within the Treaty from 1987 indicated a willingness in the Union to draw external relations away from the intergovernmental and Atlanticist stranglehold over the policy.

EPC was principally a means of coordinating meetings between foreign ministers. Until 1987 EPC did not have its own institutions and was managed by the troika, led by the country holding the EU Presidency. The problem with this set-up was that the Presidency (and troika) changed every six months, and as such there was limited scope for continuity and long-term planning. This hindered EU efforts to formulate common positions (Cameron 1999).

The pre- and post-1987 EPC regimes were quite similar in that the Commission and European Parliament remained subservient to the member states. However, after 1987 the role of the Commission became more extensive in economic negotiations, such as those concerning the General Agreement on Tariffs and Trade (GATT), as well as in areas where its competence over trade matters impinged on the external relations function of EPC.

EPC was often criticized for being weak and lacking in substance (Nuttall 1992; Allen 2002), but it did generate joint positions during the 1980s that gave some sense of a European view of the world. However, EPC's light-touch approach and its loose framing made it ill equipped to project a common European vision at the end of the Cold War and led to further accusations that it was purely reactive. Arguably, the absence of a common European response to the collapse of the Soviet Union was due to a lack of common foreign policy identity, that is, a sense of the EU as a unified political actor. It was also due to the governments' (and their intelligence agencies') disarray over the collapse—something they had all failed to predict despite the mounting evidence. As an intergovernmental organization, the EEC and then the EU was as politically cohesive as its members decided it should be, through their day-to-day and Treaty-based negotiations. Thus it is often problematic to identify an EU identity in this sphere, and somewhat simpler to highlight the preferences of individual member states.

> **KEY POINTS**
>
> - EPC was set up in the 1970s. It was reformed within the Single European Act in 1987.
>
> - Although EPC was able to secure opportunities for dialogue amongst the EC's members, it was frequently criticized for being purely reactive.
>
> - EPC was unable to forge a common response to the end of communism and the collapse of the Soviet Union in the late 1980s and early 1990s, though it can be argued that the expectations placed upon it were too great.

The changing context of European foreign policy

Despite the absence of an agreed European view about the end of the Cold War, the EU was well placed to play a leading role in the new economic world order. Organizations like NATO had, however, lost their raison d'être with the fall of communism. What NATO did bring was the potential engagement of the United States in Europe, something that the German and UK governments saw as being particularly important, and which the new Central and Eastern European members who had enjoyed the political and economic support of the USA have also seen as vital.

The collapse of the Soviet Union removed some significant barriers to the EU's eastern enlargement. It also allowed members of the European Free Trade Area (EFTA) (Sweden, Finland, Austria, Norway) to submit applications to join the EU, since the need, from a European perspective, for a 'buffer zone' between Russia and 'the West' was greatly reduced with cessation of Cold War hostilities. The debate between respective EU governments about whether to enlarge the Community immediately or whether to add first to the Community's competences was resolved with the very European compromise of extending competences (for example, developing Economic and Monetary Union (EMU), reforming the central administrative institutions of the EU, and codifying a foreign and security policy), whilst at the same time preparing for enlargement and the challenges of a post-Cold War Europe.

A more developed form of foreign policy cooperation was made possible by the end of the Cold
War as the events of this time created a necessary
policy space, whilst avoiding American and British
accusations that the Community was trying to
undermine NATO and US involvement in Europe.
Moreover, the new policy arrived at an opportune
time for EU–US relations; the US and particularly
President Bill Clinton, who took office in 1993, saw
an opportunity to reap a 'peace dividend' by limiting US involvement in mainland Europe. This
would only be possible, however, if EU member
governments were able to shoulder more of the
security burden in Europe.

Common Foreign and Security Policy

The sections that follow consider the evolution of a
new Common Foreign and Security Policy through
its various treaty incarnations at Maastricht and
Amsterdam.

The Maastricht Treaty

The European Council at Maastricht saw agreement
on a Common Foreign and Security Policy (CFSP),
which was to form the second pillar (pillar 2) of the
new European Union. Pillar 2 was to be intergovernmental, involving very little input from the
European Commission and European Parliament.
Moreover, the CFSP's decision-making framework
rests on member state unanimity in the Council,
giving each government the ability to veto any
policy initiative or operation. As a consequence, EU
foreign and security policy was to be a lowest common denominator process, with policy outputs that
were extremely conservative.

CFSP sought to assist EU governments in formulating common foreign policy positions. However,
as the CFSP was positioned outside the Community
decision-making structures, this was problematic.
This is because there are many economic issues
within pillar 1—the supranational European
Community pillar—that have an impact on the
EU's external relations (see Chapter 14). Similarly,
pillar 3 (Justice and Home Affairs), which deals with
issues such as immigration, asylum, terrorism, and
trafficking, uses decision-making procedures that
vary from those in CFSP and also has obvious external dimensions that make coordination difficult
(see Chapter 19). The coordination of European
external policy across the three pillars was to be
achieved by giving the Commission and the
Parliament some formal roles, which were later
expanded upon. The Treaty states that the Commission should be 'associated with all aspects of the
CFSP' and that it has an equal right of initiative on
external relations with member governments. In
pillar 1, by contrast, the Commission has sole right
of initiative. The European Parliament has to be
'kept informed' of policies and initiatives being
conducted under CFSP, whilst the European Court
of Justice has no role at all. These latter two institutions have been kept out of CFSP policy making to
ensure that the member states' pre-eminence in the
policy is maintained.

The enactment of the Treaty on European Union
(TEU) provided three identifiable sources of external
relations policy in the EU, binding the states and
supranational institutions together. First are the
member states, with their own foreign, defence, and
security policies pursued independently of CFSP.
Second is the coordinating CFSP framework, which
places a responsibility on member states to 'inform
and consult each other [on] matters of foreign and
security policy' with the aim of increasing the

BOX 15.3

Key instruments of CFSP

The Maastricht Treaty provided CFSP with the following key instruments:

- Common Positions: these require member states to adopt national policies that comply with a stated EU position on a particular issue. For example, the EU has a Common Position on Myanmar (Burma). This aims to bring pressure on the Burmese government to change its policies towards the opposition. The Common Position bans visas for senior members of the government, military, and security forces, freezes any assets held in the EU and suspends all high-level political visits from the EU.

- Joint Actions: these are operational actions agreed by the member states that fall under the flag of the EU and therefore CFSP. For example, Joint Action 2002/210/CFSP (11 March 2002) established the European Union Police Mission in Bosnia and Herzegovina (BiH), which was the first EU civilian crisis-management operation under CFSP/ESDP. It aimed to establish strong and sustainable policing arrangements by 2005. The EUPM was made up of around 500 seconded policemen and more than 300 international civilian and local staff. A similar Joint Action of 4 February 2008 was set up to help bolster Kosovo's legal framework and to promote the rule of law through active mentoring (Council Joint Action 2008/124/CFSP).

---

international leverage they can exert working together. The Council can establish a Common Position (see Box 15.3), as it has done in the case of the eradication of landmines, and then it falls to national governments to ensure that their policies are in line with these common positions. Thus, the EU has played a very strong role in supporting the international norm established by the 1997 Ottawa Treaty to ban the use of and eradicate stocks of anti-personnel landmines. The Union pledged in excess of 400 million euros between 1999 and 2005 to various projects that seek to end the use of mines and clean up mine-affected areas, whilst the European Parliament and Commission have also performed a monitoring role to ensure compliance with the terms of the Ottawa Treaty (European Commission 2005a). Following on from Common Positions, the EU can adopt a 'Joint Action', which requires a unanimous vote. Joint Actions allow the EU to go beyond merely consulting on issues (as had been the case under the EPC framework), obliging member states to conform to the positions they adopt. Third, the Commission, with its extensive responsibilities over trade policy and its large number of overseas representations, provides a third source of foreign policy stimuli in the EU (see Chapter 14).

The Maastricht Treaty also stated that the EU should work towards creating a common defence policy and eventually a common defence. This would later be used as the basis for developing a European Security and Defence Policy (see below). In the meantime, the Treaty established a review procedure for CFSP. This began with the setting up of a reflection group of civil servants in 1996, and culminated in an Intergovernmental Conference and the Amsterdam European Council in June 1997.

The British and French governments disagreed at Amsterdam as to how the policy should develop. The British felt that the Yugoslav experience confirmed that the EU was incapable of formulating a common foreign policy (see Box 15.4), whilst the French government argued that the Yugoslav experience demonstrated why a common policy was required (Howarth 2000). Very few could argue, however, with the proposition that CFSP had achieved remarkably little in its first few years. There seemed to be hardly any cooperative and collaborative work of substance on foreign policy amongst national governments. Moreover, common positions were weak, often reflecting disagreements and a lowest common denominator style of politics.

CASE STUDY 15.4

The EU and the Balkans

The Yugoslavian civil war was an enormous wake-up call for the EU as well as profound embarrassment. After Jacques Poos's rather optimistic statement that 'now is the hour of Europe', and the negotiations to codify CFSP, the EU's response to Yugoslavia 1991–5 highlighted the weaknesses within the EU's foreign and security policies. In unilaterally recognizing Slovenian independence in June 1991 the German government hastened the crisis; this in turn led to the recognition of independence of Croatia and Macedonia (June 1991 and September 1991 respectively) and political moves to establish a sovereign Bosnia following the Dayton Accords in 1995. These attempts to fracture the federation of Yugoslavia prompted a military response from the predominantly Serb Yugoslav National Army (JNA) under the civilian control of Slobodan Milosevic.

The EU's response to the genocide, displacement of populations, and imperial conquests has been widely condemned as inadequate (Bellamy 2002). The institutional historical memory of the First and Second World Wars and country allegiances to Croatia and Serbia partially guided EU governments in the early stages of the conflict. There was strong evidence that Croatian forces had been armed by Germany, whilst the French and British governments held historical allegiances with Serbia. This created problems early on in formulating a 'European' response. The need for unanimity in EU foreign policy meant that statements and policies that blamed one side or the other in the conflict were politically untenable. These allegiances were less

prominent after events such as the siege of Sarajevo in 1994 where a prevailing international norm of revulsion at the military action led to a more universal approach.

The United States played a very low-key role in the early stages of the civil war (1992–4), which further exposed the EU's inability to formulate a credible policy towards the conflict. Without being able to deploy a credible threat of military force, international agreements brokered with Milosevic were breached with impunity by the Serbs. It was only when the USA began to take an active role in brokering peace that the implied threat of the use of military force saw these agreements honoured.

Furthermore, the EU seemed obsessed with trying to deploy the levers of economic foreign policy to bring the conflict to a close. Economic sanctions and infrastructural aid were policies that EU governments could agree on. However, both the sanctions regime and the distribution of aid and infrastructural support were strongly criticized by practitioners and academics alike as ineffective; and yet economic foreign policy was a policy area where the EU was more confident and experienced (Keane 2004)., Since the fall of Milosevic, the EU has sought to pacify Serbia with the promise of EU entry if it tempers its nationalistic rhetoric and posturing, and has effectively offered Croatia membership in exchange for its assistance with the war crimes tribunals. The EU has also promoted stability in the Balkans through acting as a guarantor for Bosnian and Kosovan sovereignty. In these reconstruction and peace-building activities the EU has looked effective, in stark contrast to its attempts as a war-fighting power.

The Amsterdam Treaty

From the perspective of the British government, the Amsterdam Treaty was negotiated during a change of government, with the right-wing Eurosceptic Conservative Party replaced by the pro-EU social democratic Labour Party. Labour won their victory in May 1997, a matter of weeks before the Amsterdam Treaty was to be concluded. Whereas the Conservative government of John Major had been undermined by infighting over the 'European question', the 'New' Labour government of Tony Blair had been elected on a pro-European platform that

promised to change the way in which the European debate was conducted in Britain (Forster 2002b). However, the change of government in the UK came too late for the Amsterdam Treaty's CFSP revision. Efforts to give the EU a defence identity were very slight indeed. Of the changes that were introduced, 'constructive abstention' was notable. This provision enabled less than a third of member states to opt out of a Joint Action without vetoing it for the others. This was later replaced by the so-called Enhanced Cooperation provisions.

Two further significant measures were agreed by the Amsterdam European Council. The first was the creation of the High Representative for CFSP. The holder of this position was also to act as the Secretary-General of the EU Council. The second was the creation of the Policy Planning and Early Warning Unit, which resides in the Council Secretariat and has become known as the 'Policy Unit'. The unit was expanded in 2001, when the ESDP was established by the Treaty of Nice (see below), to incorporate officials from the newly created Military Staff (EUMS). These initiatives served to bring external relations closer to Brussels and away from the member states, with representatives of the Union performing more visible functions than in the past. Even so, the member states have still managed to guarantee the continuation of carefully protected intergovernmentalist working methods and, as a consequence, their pre-eminence over this policy field.

Finally, the Amsterdam Treaty also introduced, in Article 13.2, the notion of a 'common strategy'. This is decided unanimously by the European Council on the basis of a recommendation by the Council. One such strategy has been agreed (towards Russia). It is implemented by adopting Joint Actions and Common Positions that can be achieved through a qualified majority vote unless a member state argues that the measure runs contrary to its core national interest, in which case it can exercise a veto (Article 23.2).

European Security and Defence Policy

As already noted, the Maastricht Treaty did more than just set up the CFSP. It also looked forward to a point in the future when the EU would cooperate on matters of defence. However, it was not until 1998 that a window of opportunity opened that would allow steady convergence on defence to begin.

The Saint Malo Process

A process that began at the port of Saint Malo in France (December 1998) opened the way for a new phase in European foreign policy cooperation, one that involved defence issues and would contribute to a gradual militarization of the European Union. 'The Saint Malo Process' was led by the UK and French governments. For the newly elected Labour government in the UK the initiative aimed to bring defence cooperation into the heart of the European programme, and as such became a symbol of the UK government's pro-European leanings. It was also an initiative to prevent the French, Italian, and Spanish governments from forcing military and security policy onto the agenda in a way that disadvantaged British interests (Dover 2007).

But Saint Malo also has to be seen in a more general political context. The main 'European' issue of the day was the development of the single currency, which the UK government felt it could not support. As a consequence, Blair put out a call to his cabinet ministers to find policy areas in which the UK could further advance integration (Dover 2007). The Ministry of Defence (MoD) was the only Department to reply to this call, with a proposal for deepening European defence integration without undermining NATO's role. The MoD proposal resulted in the Pörtschach Declaration of October 1998, in which Blair stated his desire to see closer European cooperation on defence, and the Saint Malo Declaration of December 1998, which pledged Anglo-French cooperation on defence issues within a EU framework.

For the French government the Saint Malo process was something of a surprising opportunity. As the least transatlantic of any of the EU governments, and the keenest to see NATO scrapped at the end of the Cold War, the French government was surprised to be approached by British officials seeking to advance an EU-based security solution (Howarth

The Petersberg Tasks

The Petersberg Declaration announced the readiness of member governments to make available a wide range of conventional military forces for European-led military tasks. The tasks defined by the Declaration include:

- A contribution to the collective defence in accordance with Article 5 of the Washington (NATO) Treaty. (Note: Article 5 says 'that an armed attack against one or more of them in Europe or North America shall be considered an attack against them all'. Consequently they agree that, 'if such an armed attack occurs, each of them, in exercise of the right of individual or collective self-defence recognized by Article 51 of the Charter of the United Nations, will assist the Party or Parties so attacked by taking forthwith, individually and in concert with the other Parties, such action as it deems necessary, including the use of armed force, to restore and maintain the security of the North Atlantic area').

- Humanitarian and rescue tasks;

- Peace-keeping tasks;

- Tasks of combat forces in crisis management, including peacemaking.

The Petersberg tasks have been incorporated in Article 17 of the Treaty on European Union.

2000). Getting the French government on board with plans for Europeanizing security was seen as crucial by the British, as the agreement at Saint Malo had to bring together both ends of the security spectrum—the proactive (French) and highly reactive (British). Officials from both sides concluded that any agreement on security and defence policy would result, in the medium or long term, in a split between the British position, which saw NATO as the security institution of choice in the EU, and the French view that the EU should become a more capable independent security actor.

The Saint Malo meeting and the texts it produced were the high-water mark of Anglo-French cooperation. The agreements struck in December 1998 also demonstrated other facets of European policy making. The influence of the 'Big Three', the UK, France, and Germany, over large initiatives was certainly in evidence in this case. The German government was seen as America's closest European ally in the late 1990s and also had a post-war allegiance to NATO as it was on the front line of a potential clash between NATO and the Warsaw Pact countries. Convinced that ESDP did not aim to undermine the transatlantic alliance, the German government was happy to lend its support to the initiative. Agreement among these governments ensured that the policy would be successful.

After Saint Malo

Through several European Council meetings in Cologne (1999), Helsinki (1999), and Sintra (2000), the ESDP proposals were amended and adapted. Of particular note was the inclusion of what would become 'the Petersberg tasks' (see Box 15.5) and a 'Headline Goal' for the EU—to be able to deploy 60,000 troops, in 60 days, sustainable for up to a year (Rutten 2002). Proposals such as these were transformed into a 'capabilities catalogue', a pool of personnel, expertise, and military equipment pledged by member governments that could be used in EU-sponsored military actions. In connecting capabilities explicitly to the Saint Malo process, its British and French government sponsors aimed to make ESDP more than just an EU paper policy; indeed this was a prerequisite for their involvement.

The ESDP is composed of three elements: military crisis management, civilian crisis management, and conflict prevention. In June 1999, the Cologne European Council placed crisis management and the capabilities required to deliver it at the heart of renewed efforts to strengthen the CFSP. Subsequent European Councils refocused efforts on the military assets available to the EU to conduct autonomous operations—including policing and peace enforcement (see Box 15.6).

ESDP: the military and civilian dimensions

The military side of ESDP was introduced at Helsinki (1999) and developed at the Nice (2001) European Council. Helsinki resulted in the so-called 'headline goal', whilst Nice provided the institutional structures that support the policy, namely the Political and Security Committee (PSC), which is assisted by a politico-military working group, a committee for civilian aspects of crisis management, as well as the Military Committee (EUMC) and the Military Staff (EUMS).

The Feira (1999) and Gothenburg (2001) Councils developed the civilian element of ESDP, which aimed to fill the 'soft' security gaps left by the international community. The Nice Council provided four institutional arrangements to fill these gaps, including a civil-military relations committee, to ensure that interventions run smoothly. The civilian dimension comprises:

- Police Cooperation: creating a capability to deploy 5,000 police officers, including 1,000 within 30 days, for tasks ranging from training local police officers to assisting military forces in restoring order.

- Rule of Law: an ambition to provide up to 200 judges, prosecutors, and other legal experts to areas in crisis.

- Civilian Administration: providing officials to assist in the basic tasks of government administration like establishing education, infrastructure, and elections.

- Civil Protection: the ability to assist in humanitarian assistance at short notice—the EU to be capable, within three to seven hours, of providing two to three assessment teams as well as intervention teams consisting of up to 2,000 people.

- The European Defence Agency (EDA), established in 2004 to identify gaps in the EU's military capability and then to suggest programmes and assist in conducting efforts to fill these gaps.

British and French government negotiators anticipated that the policy would be fully functioning by 2003. However, the member states have been unable to meet the relatively modest targets within the 'capabilities catalogue'. This has been in part due to internal pressures to spend money on more electorally attractive areas such as health and education, whilst foreign and security budgets have been consumed by defence equipment inflation, the conflicts in Afghanistan and Iraq, and a shifting priority in favour of homeland security as a consequence of the terrorist threat to mainland Europe.

The emphasis on Petersberg-style military tasks reinforces the EU's self-constructed soft security identity, and acts as a barrier to military operations like the US/UK invasion of Iraq (2003) or engagement in high-end military posturing, such as the deployment of a US anti-ballistic missile system in Poland (2008). The inclusion of the Petersberg tasks in ESDP supports the view that ESDP is a product of the EU's inability to deal with peacekeeping and peace-enforcement operations like those presented by the Yugoslavian civil war and a realization that the threats to the EU come from non-state military actors in the medium to long term (Smith 2001).

Civil wars and the consequences of failing states, similar to those of the 1990s in the Balkans, demand the sorts of responses the Petersberg tasks aim to deliver: humanitarian and rescue tasks; peacekeeping tasks; peacemaking; and crisis management. To give the EU a chance of tackling these scenarios effectively it was necessary to ensure that the EU had access to NATO assets. The negotiations to secure this access were one of the most important tasks at the periphery of the Nice European Council meeting. The so-called 'Berlin-plus' arrangements were a key marker of whether the ESDP might function as an independent policy area, avoiding duplication with the institutions and assets of NATO and the UN. In this matter the NATO member Turkey (of course, not yet a member of the EU) proved to be a considerable stumbling block to securing EU rights to these assets, with the Turkish government keen to tie access to NATO equipment to their efforts to join the EU. Turkish opposition was removed through intensive diplomacy by NATO and the British and American governments in December 2000.

The Nice Treaty

The negotiations for ESDP were largely conducted outside the formal EU negotiating frameworks so as to avoid the input of Commission officials and MEPs, and were bi-laterally agreed between governments before the final signatures at the Nice European Council. The Cologne, Helsinki, and Sintra Councils had provided the opportunities between Saint Malo in December 1998 and the Nice Treaty negotiations in December 2000 to conclude much of the detail of ESDP before it was codified at Nice. As such, the final negotiations at Nice were concluded quickly.

The Nice Treaty empowered the Commission to ensure that the EU's actions are consistent and designed to meet the objectives laid out by national governments. The Nice Treaty also secured further institutional reform. The Treaty entrenched a move towards supranationalism in the form of Article 24, which allowed the Council to use qualified majority voting (QMV) for decisions relating to internal matters—that is, institutional design or the adoption of Joint Actions. QMV was also to be used where the Council appointed a Special Representative. Moreover, the Treaty replaced the Political Committee with the Political and Security Committee (PSC). The High Representative could chair the PSC instead of a representative from the Presidency, once again suggesting further drift away from the member states to Brussels. Still further evidence of this drift can be found in the role of the so-called CFSP 'ambassadors' who had previously travelled from capital to capital, but who after Nice were to be based in Brussels in semi-permanent session. Despite these changes, the 'Brusselsization' of foreign and security policy is taking place at an incredibly slow pace, with the majority of foreign and security activity in the Union controlled, as ever, by national governments. The stillborn Constitutional Treaty (2005) sought to bring ESDP and CFSP closer to Brussels within a policy named 'Common Security and Defence Policy' and maintained the Maastricht wording of CFSP. The Treaty demanded that all member governments improve their military capabilities to meet the demands of the capabilities catalogue and the Union's international commitments (Article I-41). The EU's commitment to the formation of a common European defence was reaffirmed, although the right of individual governments to veto this and retain independent defence policies remained. Unfortunately for those who drafted these provisions, the Constitutional Treaty fell as a complete document, with its rejection by Dutch and French voters in the summer of 2005.

KEY POINTS

- The end of the Cold War opened the way for new rounds of enlargement.

- NATO's role in European security was initially in doubt but the organization managed to recast its role during the 1990s.

- The Maastricht Treaty established a Common Foreign and Security Policy, which was largely intergovernmental in character. The outcome of the first tests of the CFSP was far from impressive.

- The Amsterdam Treaty revisions sought to rectify some of the institutional problems, but failed to address the question of a European defence policy.

- The British and French governments' agreement in Saint Malo in December 1998 created an overwhelming momentum towards a common European Security and Defence Policy. The negotiations resulted in the production of a capabilities catalogue, which placed an expectation on member states to provide capabilities. As of late 2008 they had yet to provide all of these capabilities.

The Lisbon Treaty and the institutional framework

The subsequent attempts to revive the Constitutional Treaty's security and defence provisions were encapsulated in the Lisbon Treaty (2007). The Lisbon Treaty aimed to move the EU further into security issues, particularly those relating to countering terrorism. The Treaty makes a provision for a common defence response if any EU member is subject to a terrorist attack or natural disaster. It also incorporates changes to the institutional framework (see Boxs 15.7 and 15.8).

Significantly, a High Representative of the Union's Common Foreign and Security Policy (Mr/Ms CFSP') is created by the Treaty (Article 18), and this individual will serve as a Vice-President of the Union, reflecting the seriousness with which external relations are now taken. Similarly, the Commission and the High Representative can submit joint proposals on external action—thus bringing together the economic and military sectors (Article 22-2). The 'Brusselsization' of CFSP is further deepened by the creation of the European External Action Service (Article 27), which acts as the diplomatic corps of the EU, and which is made up of seconded staff from the member states, the Commission, and the General Secretariat of the Council. This is an important move which centralizes foreign policy activity within Brussels, something that is supported by the Enhanced Cooperation Provisions. The latter allow a group of nine states to agree to deepen their cooperation on foreign and defence policy within a European framework, but without having to get the agreement of the remaining member states. The European Parliament continues as the junior partner when it comes to foreign and security policy, with MEPs' views only being solicited twice a year.

Articles 77 and 78 of the Treaty link up internal and external security via policies on border checks and asylum and immigration. This has happened bi- or multilaterally across member states who have been affected by terrorism and mass migration, but it is now subject to some level of European cooperation. This cooperation also applies to the policy on organized crime and counter-terrorism spheres, where member governments are expected to liaise closely on policing issues, operationally, and in the realm of information sharing (Article 87).

The Treaty makes it clear that the member governments should make military assets available for common EU activities, but also that member states should actively support the work of the European Defence Agency (EDA), whose purpose it is to identify operational requirements and then stimulate measures and programmes to fill the gaps. The establishment of the EDA looks like a centralizing initiative, but in fact it strengthens the hand of those governments that have strong defence industries. In effect the EDA provides a shorter route into an expanding European defence market for defence-related businesses and, because of the peculiarities of the trade, a boost to the influence of those governments who sponsor successful manufacturers. The EDA constitutes, therefore, a very Milwardian rescue of the nation state, and whilst in theory seems to address the shortfalls in the capabilities catalogue, is actually premised on a different logic, that of the so-called 'Lisbon Agenda'—the idea of a European economy supported by innovative technologies that trickle down into mainstream manufacturing.

The most important institutions within CFSP and ESDP are the foreign and defence ministries of the member states. Within these institutions policy initiatives are formulated and agreements struck on whether to accept Common Positions and Joint Actions. Neither the Commission nor the High Representative has demonstrated an ability to act in the same way as a domestic ministry. For example, there have been doubts about the quality of internal security in the Commission, with leaked information potentially endangering the safety of officials in the field, something that is particularly sensitive in counter-terrorism operations (Dassu and Missoroli 2002).

The institutions (I)

The European Council: This body is composed of the Heads of Government and the Commission President, who meet at least once every six months to set priorities and discuss the large issues dominating the policy agenda, including CFSP. The European Council lays down the guidelines for CFSP and adopts Common Strategies.

The EU Council (Council of Ministers): The EU Foreign Ministers and the Foreign Policy Commissioner meet at least monthly under the banner of the General Affairs Council. This body makes decisions on external relations issues, including CFSP. Their decisions can lead to Joint Actions and Common Positions, whose implementation is mainly the responsibility of the country holding the EU's Presidency and that of the High Representative, following the ratification of the Lisbon Treaty.

The Presidency: The country holding the six-monthly Council Presidency plays an important role within CFSP, as it sets the agenda for the political decision-making process. It provides the background administration for all meetings and is responsible for trying to resolve disagreements and difficulties on all policy issues. This is particularly important in relation to CFSP as decisions are made unanimously, although the provision for Enhanced Cooperation does change this dynamic slightly. The Presidency is assisted in its work by the Council Secretariat and, since the Amsterdam Treaty, by the Secretary-General/High Representative for CFSP.

Commission: The strengthening of the Council with regard to CFSP has implications for the role of the Commission. The Commission is an important part of the Union, not only because it has such a large role in concluding agreements and managing aid and trade initiatives, but also as it has diplomatic offices (representations) in virtually every country in the world. This is something the Commission jealously guards. It is in many respects the public face of the EU abroad. A Declaration added to the Amsterdam Treaty outlined how the Commission proposed to reorganize its Directorates-General to bring external relations under the remit of a Vice-President, rather than under the control of four Commissioners. However, the former Commission President, Romano Prodi (1999–2004) did not observe the Declaration and appointed four external relations commissioners with functional rather than geographic responsibilities (see High Representative).

The High Representative of the Union for Foreign Affairs and Security Policy: Acts as a Vice-President of the Commission, and presides over the Foreign Affairs Council. The High Representative ensures the consistency of the EU's external actions, along with the Council and the Commission. The High Representative has the right to submit joint proposals with the Commission in other areas of external action. The High Representative is assisted by the European External Action Service.

The European External Action Service: Works with the diplomatic services of member states and comprises officials from relevant departments of the General Secretariat of the Council and Commission as well as seconded officials from national governments.

The European Parliament: The Parliament has no formal CFSP role but is kept informed and consulted on CFSP issues and on the general direction of the policy. MEPs have been very keen to engage in foreign policy issues—they were particularly active through debates and declarations during the Yugoslavian civil war and Afghan and Iraqi campaigns, continually pushing their case for an enhanced parliamentary role in external relations.

The Policy Planning and Early Warning Unit: The Early Warning Unit was established within the Council Secretariat and has a responsibility for monitoring and assessing international developments, as well as analysing emerging threats and crises. The Early Warning Unit's analytical role is important insofar as it provides the member states with the information they require to formulate a common foreign policy.

COREPER: The Committee of Permanent Representatives (COREPER) is composed of member states' ambassadors to the EU and the Commission Deputy Secretary-General who meet at least once a week to prepare Council meetings and decisions, including those related to the General Affairs Council and CFSP. Anecdotal evidence from senior officials shows that COREPER plays a crucial role in organizing the work of CFSP and smoothing over policy disagreements.

The Political and Security Committee (PSC, or COPS): The PSC is central to CFSP and ESDP. It organizes the EU's response to any crisis. It is composed of national representatives. The PSC prepares recommendations on how CFSP (and ESDP) should develop, and also deals with the routine elements of these policies. In the event of a crisis, the PSC is the body that analyses the options open to members and manages the EU's approach to the crisis, but without preventing countervailing decisions being made by other EU institutions.

European Correspondents: A group of 'correspondents' in all EU member states and within the Commission coordinate the day-to-day business of the CFSP and prepare the PSC meetings. The correspondents are also responsible for ensuring that CFSP business is included on the agendas of the General Affairs Council and European Councils.

Relex Counsellors: This group analyses the institutional, legal, and financial aspects of proposals made under the CFSP umbrella. The Counsellors prepare COREPER's work on Joint Actions and try to ensure consistency across the three EU pillars.

CFSP Working Groups: These groups are staffed by experts from EU member states and the Commission, and meet along geographical (that is, regional) and functional lines to examine policy documents and options for the consideration of the various CFSP institutional bodies.

BOX 15.8

The institutions (II)

Within the Council four new committees have been established since 2001 to help the smooth implementation of CFSP.

The European Union Military Committee (EUMC): This committee is formed by Chiefs of Defence Staff, although in practice they are deputized by other military representatives. The EUMC provides the PSC with military advice and recommendations on military issues. The committee has a directorial role over the EU's military activities, including the EU Military Staff. The Chairman of the EUMC is present at Council meetings where defence-related decisions are taken.

The European Union Military Staff (EUMS): The EUMS sits within the Council structure and gives military-related advice and support to ESDP-related operations.

The EUMS provides analysis about emerging threats and conducts some strategic planning. Part of its role is to identify, as an extension of the capabilities catalogue, the forces of member states that can assist in EU-led military activities and the implementation of EUMC policies.

The Politico-Military Group: This group of civil servant researchers and external experts (including academics) functions to explore the politico-military aspects of all CFSP proposals.

The Committee for Civilian Aspects of Crisis Management: This committee gives advice on the political aspects and consequences of non-military crisis management and conflict prevention. Much of its work to date has focused on the role and capabilities of EU policing and strengthening the rule of law in crisis areas.

The global war on terror

The global war on terror (GWOT), as former US President George W. Bush described his quest to eradicate people, groups, and governments whom his administration designated as presenting a threat to liberty and the 'Western way of life', has presented the EU with a new set of security and justice issues. Because of the number of active plots across Europe by Jihadist terrorists, the GWOT is likely to remain one of the largest foreign and security challenges for the EU in the medium to long term. It raises issues that cut across foreign and security policy as well as impinging on the justice and home affairs sphere (see Chapter 19).

GWOT has generated new domestic and external agendas. The domestic agenda has centred on immigration, policing, and intelligence, whilst the external agenda has focused on the expeditionary warfare efforts of the USA and its allies in Afghanistan and Iraq. Since 2003, attention has turned to the extraterritoriality of efforts to identify, contain, and roll back jihadist groups, including state-sponsored kidnapping (extraordinary rendition) and the outsourcing of torture to states in the Middle East and the Maghreb (special measures) which has publicly appalled European governments, even though they had previously given private support to these programmes. The inauguration of President Obama in January 2009 has seen a notable change in the rhetoric away from the extraordinary measures of the Bush era. The policy outputs generated as a result of GWOT have caused lengthy and divisive political debates in the EU and amongst the Union's member governments. Questions of how to cooperate effectively on intelligence and counter-terrorism operations, along with more philosophical debates about human rights, sovereignty, and military interventions have had serious implications for internal political harmony within the EU, with mistrust and rankling over security policy spilling over into ostensibly unconnected issues like agricultural reform and the EU budget.

The invasion of Iraq in 2003, the subsequent removal of Saddam Hussein from power, and the conduct of the counter-insurgency campaign caused a significant strain in relations among the EU member states and also between the EU and the USA. Whilst the 2001 war in Afghanistan had international approval, the 2003 Iraq campaign was deeply divisive and legally problematic, and seemed to be based on the personal enmity felt by the US Administration towards Saddam Hussein. The divisions within Europe over the Iraq war were most starkly seen in the strong opposition to it from the French and German governments, the former for good intelligence-led reasons and the latter for clear electoral reasons (Peterson 2004). The anti-war stance of Belgium, France, and Germany brought them into public disagreement with the USA, and in particular with the then Secretary of State for Defence, Donald Rumsfeld, who described them as 'old' Europe (with overtones of defeatism), whilst implying that the UK and the EU candidate states in eastern and central Europe were clearly 'new' Europe.

The effects of this diplomatic schism were seen almost immediately. The French and British governments, who had worked very closely together on EU security and defence matters between 1998 and 2000, immediately saw a dramatic deterioration in diplomatic relations. President Chirac is even said to have ordered his diplomatic staff not to assist UK diplomats in the further development of ESDP. More recent tensions between the USA and the UK on the one hand and, broadly speaking, the rest of Europe on the other relate to the issue of burden sharing in Iraq and, especially, Afghanistan. The British and American governments feel a particular sense of grievance towards Germany, whose armed forces are tucked away in a relatively quiet part of Afghanistan and who are operating under their own onerous risk-averse rules of engagement; the issue of Iraq is receding as all the Western powers seek to withdraw.

In terms of its homeland security, the EU went to first principles and wrote a European Security Strategy in 2003 that was widely seen as a reply to the National Security Strategy of the United States, written the year before. The Strategy identifies key threats to the EU as terrorism, the proliferation of weapons of mass destruction, regional conflict, failed states, and organized crime, all of which fit into the general thrust of ESDP and its formulation between 1998 and 2000. To complement the focus on terrorism and organized crime, the Commission tabled a proposal that there should be a compulsory sharing of intelligence between national intelligence agencies, but this was strongly rejected by all EU governments. This wholesale rejection came for the very simple reason that all European member states jealously guard their secret intelligence, and intelligence liaison between agencies is conducted on a bilateral basis.

In 2005, the Commission made a proposal that mobile phone and internet data should be stored to help with counter-terrorism efforts. The British and French governments have introduced their own measures along these lines with the Interception Modernization Programme (2008), which would allow the British government to store all UK internet activity for future intelligence use; and the French EDVIGE and CRISTINA programmes (2007–8), which allow the French police and domestic intelligence agency (DST) to store details on the opinions, social circle, and even sexual preferences of anyone over 13 who may be considered, or might become, a person of note within society; this includes teachers, nurses, and accountants within the French government's very wide definition. In sum, the case of intelligence cooperation is inform-ative. This is an area that will remain solely the preserve of member states, so whilst the EU puts forward policies on common arrest procedures, recent precedents indicate that they will be superseded by national governments putting in place their own arrangements.

The terrorist threat to Europe and the policy responses to it have seen some deepening of European integration. These have been pragmatic responses to various plots. Closer police cooperation has brought a greater number of ordinary security competences under European scrutiny and this has produced a greater day-to-day understanding between the police and justice officials of the different member states. Thus European integration in this area has deepened outside the treaty-making conferences and often outside EU frameworks altogether.

KEY POINTS

- The GWOT has focused EU security efforts on 'homeland security' and, in terms of the political debate, on the efficacy of military interventions in the Middle East, and on human rights issues.

- This refocusing of security has seen a large pan-European investment in technology-led measures, such as electronic intelligence (emails, phone calls, global positioning technology) and broader surveillance and control measures.

- These issues have had a mixed effect on the internal harmony and political cohesion of the member states, and the transatlantic alliance, which have occasionally spilled over into unrelated policy spheres.

Conclusion

From the European Community's inception more than 50 years ago, defence, foreign, and security policy has been a controversial and contested policy area. Policies made by the EU, as a large economic trading bloc and 'civilian superpower', have wide-ranging impacts on its global partners, but this economic influence was not transferred across to the foreign, security, and defence sphere. Institutionally and procedurally the main areas of disagreement between the EU institutions and the member states have been the desire of the supranational institu-tions to centralize foreign and security policy and reduce the number of areas where decisions have to be made by unanimity. Whilst member governments have been resolute in their desire to maintain unanimity and therefore a veto over all issues that relate to their security and defence. These controls have been slightly relaxed with the introduction of the Enhanced Cooperation mechanism.

Since 1991 there has been a constant demand for collective EU action in foreign and security policy from governments and groups within member states and from the Parliament and Commission. A common criticism of the EU is that it has not been able to generate sufficient capabilities to meet these demands and has therefore been an ineffective foreign policy actor. The key successes of European policy have been the formulation of Joint Actions and Common Positions, which have helped create international agreement on issues like landmines policy. These policies have been successful because of the cohesion of member governments on the selected issues and because the financing is already in place. Neither Joint Actions nor Common Positions have produced radical or ambitious policies. They have been subject to the tell-tale EU trait of lowest common denominator policy making.

Since 1998 the EU's foreign and security policy agenda has been dominated by the ESDP, while fighting against an emerging reality: without the capabilities gap being addressed, European policy will remain piecemeal and ineffective. However, the foundation of the European Defence Agency and the European External Action Service demonstrates a commitment to bridging military and diplomatic capabilities and fostering cooperation and common positions across the Union.

Relaxing the grip of member governments over these policies may take several decades more, and may never happen at all. For the militarily capable states the power and influence their capability affords them is invaluable, whilst for less capable states the financial investment required to improve their capabilities is just too much for them to contemplate. So the 'soft power' functions seem here to stay whilst a common, actionable vision of European defence remains to be reconciled with a paucity of overall European ambition.

In sum, EU foreign, security, and defence policies have been a mixed bag of successes and failures. The notable successes have come institutionally with the provisions of the failed Constitutional Treaty being enshrined in the Lisbon Treaty. The High Representative, the European External Action Service and the European Defence Agency are all positive institutional developments aimed at stabilizing and developing the EU's foreign and defence policies. The development of bilateral relationships and coordination across police forces and intelligence agencies has been positive in as much as an informal Europeanization is developing in these areas, whilst these developments also herald a determination on the part of national governments to retain control of these competences. Positively, the Europe-wide schism over Iraq seems to have dissipated, but new tensions have emerged over member states' military commitments in Iraq and particularly Afghanistan, and in how to deal with resurgent Russia (in terms of both its military and energy profiles). Greater levels of cooperation between member states will come with greater exposure to collective foreign policy responses and through a shared foreign policy vision, which itself can only come through greater levels of dialogue.

? QUESTIONS

1. To what extent do CFSP/ESDP cover 'soft-security' functions and NATO 'hard-security' issues?

2. Has a 'Europeanized' foreign and security policy strengthened the position of the member states in international affairs?

3. Has the Lisbon Treaty removed the main hindrances to a fully functional common foreign and security policy?

4. What do CSFP and ESDP tell us about the EU as a political entity?

5. Is the EU destined to remain a 'soft security' actor?

6. To what extent do the 'Big Three' (France, Germany, and the United Kingdom) dominate CFSP / ESDP?

7. Would it be desirable for the European Commission and European Parliament to have greater powers over CFSP/ESDP?

8. Does a resurgent Russia mean that the EU should revise its security stance away from homeland security?

 ## GUIDE TO FURTHER READING

■ Howarth, J. Security and Defence Policy in the European Union (Basingstoke: Palgrave, 2007). A comprehensive survey of the history and politics of the ESDP, and the transformation of the EU as an international actor.

■ Kagan, R. *Paradise and Power: America and Europe in the New World Order* (New York: Atlantic Books, 2004). This book has generated a great deal of academic commentary about the nature of the existing transatlantic alliance and the prospects for the future alliance. Key to understanding how US/EU military efforts coexist.

■ Kagan, R. *The Return of History and the End of Dreams* (New York: Atlantic Books, 2008). Suggests the real clash of civilizations is between democracies and non-democracies.

■ Jones, S. *The Rise of European Security Cooperation* (Cambridge: Cambridge University Press, 2007). Provides a compelling yet counter-intuitive account of the EU's strategic relevance in the international system.

■ van der Pijl, K. *Global Rivalries: from the Cold War to Iraq* (London: Pluto Press, 2006). This comprehensive work includes a radical critique of the formation of the European Union and what drives its external relations policy.

■ Smith, M. E. *Europe's Foreign and Security Policy: the Institutionalisation of Cooperation* (Cambridge: Cambridge University Press, 2008). A theoretically informed exploration of the politics of foreign policy cooperation.

 ## WEBLINKS

● http://europa.eu.int/comm/external_relations/   EU external relations website.

● http://www.nato.int   The North Atlantic Treaty Organization's website.

● http://www.cer.org.uk/   The Centre for European Reform based in London publishes useful briefing papers, often on CFSP/ESDP-related issues.

● http://www.epc.eu   The European Policy Centre has a distinct stream of output which focuses on defence and security issues.

● http://www.ceps.be   One of the larger Brussels-based think tanks, which has a research section on EU neighbourhood, foreign and security policies.

 Visit the Online Resource Centre that accompanies this book for lots of interesting additional material. http://www.oxfordtextbooks.co.uk/orc/Cini_Borragan3e/

16 The Single Market

MICHELLE EGAN

Chapter Contents

- Introduction
- Market integration in historical perspective
- From harmonization to mutual recognition
- The free trade umpire: the European Court of Justice and judicial activism
- Market making: the politics of neo-liberalism
- The 1992 Programme: a blueprint for action
- Correcting the market: the politics of regulated capitalism
- Modernizing the Single Market
- Globalization and the Single Market
- Theorizing the Single Market
- Conclusion

Reader's Guide

This chapter charts the evolution of the single market project, from its original conception in the 1950s to its contemporary evolution. The chapter begins with the Treaty of Rome, and focuses first on the association between a single market and the harmonization of national laws at European level. It explores the role of the European Court of Justice in promoting market access; the balance between different economic ideals; and the different regulatory strategies used to foster market integration. The chapter highlights the importance of globalization in encouraging greater competitiveness and modernization in the single market as the European Union seeks to shape global norms and standards. The chapter concludes by examining how traditional International Relations theories of European integration as well as more recent theories of regulation and governance have explained the advent of the single market.

Introduction

The single market is a defining component of the European integration process. Charting market integration from its inception in the 1950s, the chapter establishes a clear difference between market-oriented policies aimed at removing barriers to trade and the integration of national markets; and market-interventionist mechanisms aimed at ensuring the implementation and effectiveness of new legislation while promoting competitiveness and easing burdens on business. The legal dimension of the single market project is analysed in relation to the European Court of Justice (ECJ) and its role in umpiring the economic relationship between public intervention and the market, and the political relationship between the EU and the member states. While initially an intra-European exercise in economic integration, the single market has an important external dimension. Thus the chapter outlines the impact of globalisation on the single market and the EU's leading role in international trade negotiations and liberalization. Notwithstanding the importance of economic imperatives, market integration, and particularly the single market, is also the product of politics. A final reflection on traditional International Relations theories of European integration and on more recent theories of regulation and governance provides an insight into explanations of the dynamics of market integration.

Market integration in historical perspective

In the space of one year, from the Messina Conference in June 1955 to the Venice Conference in May 1956, the idea of economic unification among six West European states had taken root. After months of lengthy discussion, what became known as the Spaak Report, after its principal author, generated the idea of an entirely new kind of inter-state economic relationship as the basis for treaty negotiations (Bertrand 1956: 569). This Report provided a blueprint for a single market in Western Europe, with three main elements: (a) the establishment of normal standards of competition through the elimination of protective barriers; (b) the curtailing of state intervention and monopolistic conditions; and (c) measures to prevent distortions of competition, including the possible harmonization of legislation at the European level. The economic intent of such proposals dovetailed with the federalist agenda (Laurent 1970). Yet turning the single market idea into a political reality has been extremely contentious and protracted.

Based on the Spaak Report, the Treaty of Rome (1957) aimed for a common market by coordinating economic activities, ensuring stability and economic development, and raising living standards. At the core of the proposed European common market was the creation of a customs union (see Box 16.1). This meant that member states would not only abolish all their customs duties on mutual trade, but also apply a uniform tariff on trade with non-EC countries. The other measures proposed to promote internal trade liberalization, including free movement of labour, services, and capital, and a limited number of sectoral policies (agriculture, transport, and competition), were to be regulated and managed at the European level.

The transformation of the Community into a common market was to take place over a period of 12 to 15 years. It began with efforts to address traditional tariffs, starting with the elimination of customs duties and quantitative restrictions in 1958, and by introducing a common external tariff in

1968. Internal tariff reductions were also frequently extended to third countries to limit the discriminatory effects of the customs union, which was politically important in the formative period of the EC (Egan 2001: 41).

Membership of the European Community meant more than simply a customs union, however. The treaty established the 'four freedoms'—the free movement of goods, services, capital, and labour, as central features of the single market. However, the requirements for each freedom varied according to the political exigencies at the time the Treaty was drafted. The removal of trade barriers for *goods* focused on the removal of tariffs and quantitative restrictions, and then on the removal of non-tariff barriers. This meant dismantling quotas, subsidies, and voluntary export restraints, and measures such as national product regulations and standards, public purchasing, and licensing practices which sometimes reflected legitimate public policy concerns but were often a thinly disguised form of protectionism designed to suppress foreign competition (Egan 2001: 42). For the free movement of *capital*, the goal was freedom of investment to enable capital to go where it would be most productive. Yet vivid memories of currency speculation in the interwar period meant that liberalization was subject to particular conditions or 'safeguard clauses', frequently used during recessions. With regard to free movement of *services*, it meant the freedom of establishment for

industrial and commercial activity, that is, the right to set up in business anywhere in the Community. However, the treaty provisions on services contained virtually no detail on what should be liberalized (Pelkmans 1997). For *labour*, the provisions for free movement meant the abolition of restrictions on labour mobility.

National governments were receptive to early efforts to eliminate trade barriers and create a customs union because they were able to use social policies to compensate for the increased competition stemming from market integration. Favourable starting conditions for the European trade liberalization effort were thus due to the fact that it occurred against the backdrop of the mixed economy and welfare state, which were central components of the post-war settlement (Tsoukalis 1997). Yet even with these national policies, it was still felt politically necessary to provide some sort of financial aid at the European level to ease the effects of competition through basic investment in underdeveloped regions, suppression of large-scale unemployment, and the coordination of economic policies (see Spaak 1956; Bertrand 1956).

But while the Community experienced substantial economic growth and increased trade among member states, the transition to a common market did not remove all obstacles to the expansion of trade. The prevalence of domestic barriers to trade and the pervasive role of nation states as regulators of economic activity across all four freedoms signaled the enormity of the task (Tsoukalis 1997: 78).

A major characteristic of European economies has been their historical and national variation in areas such as industrial relations, social welfare, and financial systems (Zysman 1994; Berger and Dore 1996; Rhodes and van Apeldoorn 1998). There are systematic differences in how national economies are organized, and member states have chosen ways of regulating production, investment, and exchange that constitute different varieties of capitalism (Hall and Soskice 2001: 15). Thus efforts to create a single market in Europe have sought to unify disparate interests and market ideologies, and the process of market integration has often been deeply contested.

KEY CONCEPTS AND TERMS 16.2

Characteristics of capitalism

Neo-liberalism

- Market liberalization: removes restrictions to trade; provides regulatory climate attractive to business; laissez-faire approach.

- Regulatory competition among member states: competition among different national regulatory policies rather than harmonization.

- Rejection of greater regulatory power for institutions at EU level; insulation of market from political interference; retention of political authority at the national level.

- Supporters include conservative political parties, multinationals and industry associations and financial institutions.

Regulated capitalism

- Market intervention: government intervention in market.

- Social market economy and social solidarity: emphasis on welfare state and distributive politics.

- Increased capacity to regulate at European level; mobilize particular social groups; reform institutions to generate greater use of qualified majority voting; enhance legislative legitimacy.

- Supporters include Jacques Delors, Social Democrat and Christian Democrat parties.

Source: adapted from Hooghe and Marks (1997).

The clash between laissez faire and interventionist ideologies began in the earliest years of the European Community. The implied commitment to free market economy, stressing the virtues of competition and greater efficiencies through specialization and economies of scale, was balanced by a widespread acceptance of dirigisme and intervention by state agencies and nationalized monopolies. This tension was initially framed as a distinction between 'regulated capitalism' and 'neo-liberalism' (Hooghe and Marks 1997; see Box 16.2). Different and sometimes competing strategies contributed to the fragmentation of the European market, preventing new firms from entering the market and taking advantage of new commercial opportunities. How then did the Community tackle such deep-seated differences in rules, standards, and practices as it sought to create a single European market?

KEY POINTS

- The objective of creating a single European market can be traced to the Spaak Report of 1956 and the Treaty of Rome in 1957.

- The aim of the Treaty was to liberalize trade by dismantling barriers to trade among the six EEC members.

- Distinctive forms of capitalism persist given strong institutionally embedded practices and norms.

From harmonization to mutual recognition

In order to tackle those domestic regulations that thwarted the creation of a common or single market, the European Community promoted a policy of harmonization (or standardization) that was to provide a lightning rod for criticisms of the integration process.

Public opposition mounted over efforts to regulate what many felt were long-standing national

The Single Market programme

The single market programme involved the removal of three kinds of trade barriers: physical barriers to trade; technical barriers to trade; fiscal barriers to trade.

- *Physical barriers:* the removal of internal barriers and frontiers for goods and people. The simplification of border controls (including the creation of a single administrative document for border entry).

- *Technical barriers:* coordinating product standards, testing, and certification (under the so-called 'new approach'); liberalization of public procurement; free movement of capital (by reducing capital exchange controls); free movement of services (covering financial services, such as banking and insurance, to operate under home country control); liberalization of the transport sector (rail, road, and air; rights of cabotage; the liberalization of markets and removal of monopolies, state subsidies, and quotas or market-sharing arrangements); free movement of labour and the mutual recognition of professional qualifications (including non-discrimination in employment); Europeanization of company law, intellectual property, and company taxation (including the freedom of establishment for enterprises; the agreement of a European Company Statute; new rules of trade marks, copyright, and legal protection).

- *Fiscal barriers:* the harmonization of divergent tax regimes. Harmonization of value-added or sales tax; the agreement of standard rates and special exemptions from sales tax; other indirect taxes with the aim of reducing restrictions on cross-border sales.

customs, traditions, and practices (Dashwood 1983; see Box 16.3). Although the Commission drew attention to the benefits of harmonization in creating a large 'barrier-free' single market, this was met with criticisms from member states about the years of fruitless arguments over harmonizing noise limits on lawnmowers, the composition of bread and beer, and tractor rear-view mirrors. However, the reasons for such limited results stem from a number of factors. First, the decision rule of unanimity on single market issues made it extremely difficult to get agreement amongst member states, and allowed individual governments to exercise their veto on specific legislative proposals. Second, harmonization was a complex process, and efforts were hampered by rapid changes in production and technology that often made agreements obsolete by the time they were adopted. The relative lack of political interest in the process of harmonization was understandable, as there was little to be gained by explaining these issues to the wider public (Puchala 1971).

However, the single market took off with the introduction of a new mode of governance, when the principle of mutual recognition was introduced.

Mutual recognition allows member states to recognize regulations as equivalent (Schmidt 2007). As member states do not unconditionally accept such mutual equivalence of rules, they reserve the right to enforce their own regulations due to 'general interest' considerations. Mutual recognition and harmonization reduce the barriers created by national regulations but provide the necessary level playing field. Without this the absence of regulations for product and process standards might lead to a 'race to the bottom' in social and environment standards, if states sought to reduce their domestic measures to attract foreign direct investment and gain significant competitive advantage through social dumping.

KEY POINTS

- Harmonization was the main *dirigiste* strategy used to integrate national markets in the 1960s and 1970s, but it achieved limited results.

- Mutual recognition provided a new mechanism for regulatory coordination and the possibility of mutual equivalence of member state rules.

The free trade umpire: the European Court of Justice and judicial activism

The problems associated with addressing trade restrictions through harmonization did not go unnoticed by the European Court of Justice, which has often used its judicial power for the purposes of fostering an integrated economy (see Chapter 11). Indeed, a large measure of the credit for creating a single market belongs to the judicial activism of the ECJ. Confronted by restrictions on their ability to operate across national borders, firms began to seek redress through the Community legal system. The Court was asked to determine whether the restrictions on imports imposed by member states were legitimate under the Treaty.

Examples of member states' restrictions included Italy's prohibition on the sale of pasta not made with durum wheat, Germany's 'beer purity' regulations prohibiting the sale of any product as 'beer' that was not brewed with specific ingredients, and Belgian regulations that required margarine to be sold only in cube-shaped containers to prevent confusion with butter, which was sold in round-shaped containers. As many of its decisions illustrate, the Court had the task of reconciling the demands of market integration with the pursuit of legitimate regulatory objectives and policy goals advanced by member states.

Several landmark cases limited the scope and applicability of national legislation. One of the most important in this regard came in the *Dassonville* case in 1974. Dassonville imported whisky into Belgium purchased from a French supplier. They were prosecuted by Belgian authorities for violating national customs rules that prohibited importation from a third country without the correct documentation. Dassonville argued that the whisky had entered the French market legally, that it must therefore be allowed to circulate freely, and that restrictions on imports within the EC were illegal. In a sweeping judgment, the Court argued that 'all trading rules that hinder trade, whether directly or indirectly, actually or potentially, were inadmissible'.

National measures that negatively impact trade were therefore prohibited (Stone Sweet and Caporaso 1998: 118). This was softened by the recognition that reasonable regulations made by member states for legitimate public interests such as health, safety, and environment policies were acceptable if there were no European rules in place. The judgment was predicated on the belief that the European Commission should adopt harmonized standards to allow free movement across markets, while at the same time giving the ECJ the opportunity to monitor member states' behaviour and scrutinize permissible exceptions.

In what is probably its best known case, *Cassis de Dijon*, the Court, in 1979, ruled on a German ban on the sale of a French blackcurrant liqueur because it did not conform to German standards in terms of alcoholic content (see Egan 2001: 95). The Court rejected German arguments that Cassis, with its lower alcoholic content, posed health risks, but noted that the protection of the consumer could be aided by the labelling of alcoholic content. Most importantly, it clearly defined what national measures were deemed permissible. The most cited part of the ruling suggested that 'there was no valid reason why products produced and marketed in one member state could not be introduced into another member state'.

The notion of equivalence of national regulations, which this ruling introduced, opened up the possibility that harmonization would not always be necessary for the construction of a single market. This was the crucial step in launching a new regulatory strategy, mutual recognition, which would make for an easier circulation of trade and commerce in the Community. Mutual recognition implies that it is only in areas that are not mutually equivalent that member states can invoke national restrictions, practices, and traditions and restrict free trade in the Community.

In fact, the Court argued that derogations from (or exceptions to) the free trade rule for the purposes of public health, fair competition, and consumer protection were possible, but that they had to be based upon reasonable grounds. Governments, whether national, local, or subnational, must demonstrate that any measure restricting trade was not simply disguised protectionism. Anxious to safeguard the Community-wide market, the Court has continued to determine on a case-by-case basis whether specific laws are valid under the Treaty. However, faced with a growing number of cases, the Court, in the *Keck* case (1993), reduced the scope of judicial scrutiny where cases applied to all traders operating in specific national territory, under certain conditions. Thus the Court would not examine issues such as Sunday trading, mandatory closing hours, or other issues that had a limited effect on cross-border trade and that reflected national moral, social, and cultural norms.

Yet despite lagging behind other areas, case law relating to free movement of services and rights of establishment is now at the centre of a wave of recent legal developments, as the country of origin principle is the starting point in assessing restrictions to free movement. In the seminal cases of *Viking* (2007), *Laval* and *Ruffert*, the importance of freedom of establishment and services is prioritized over social and collective labour rights in economic integration. Judicial activism has thus allowed companies the right to choose the least restrictive regulatory environment to allow for more home country control rules.

The constitutive role of law is crucial in understanding the consolidation of markets in Europe. Market integration involves a substantive legal project that shapes public and private policies. The European Court of Justice has placed state and local laws under its purview, and also determined the economic relationship between public intervention and the market, and the political relationship between member states and the Union. European case law opened up opportunities by reducing much of the cost of innovation and entrepreneurship by shifting the focus towards creating the context for open markets and competition.

KEY POINTS

- Legal rulings by the ECJ in cases such as *Dassonville* and *Cassis de Dijon* have played a key role in addressing non-tariff barriers to trade.

- Mutual recognition is a key concept in trade liberalization, promoting mutual reciprocity of standards rather than harmonization.

Market making: the politics of neo-liberalism

Throughout the 1970s and early 1980s, member states' efforts to maintain import restrictions and discriminatory trade practices thwarted efforts to create a single market. Growing recognition of a competitiveness gap vis-à-vis the United States and Japan, on the one hand, and newly industrializing countries, on the other, led to strenuous efforts to maintain overall levels of market activity and provide conditions for viable markets (Pelkmans and Winters 1988: 6). While past economic policies had succeeded in promoting national economic growth, the tools of national politics could no longer cope with changes in the international economy. Neo-corporatist class compromises and consensual incomes policies, which underpinned Keynesian economic policy, were under immense pressure as government capacity to manage the economy failed. As trade deficits soared, attention focused on the strengthening of European strategies in areas such as research and development as a way to improve the environment in which companies operate.

Assessments were so bleak that, on the twenty-fifth anniversary of the Treaty of Rome, *The Economist* put a tombstone on its cover to proclaim the EC dead and buried. These assessments contributed to a growing consensus among business and political leaders that a collective strategy was needed to stop an 'escalating trade war' (*Financial Times*, 25 July 1980). Through the European Round Table (ERT), heads of European companies put forward numerous proposals to improve European competitiveness. Their influence on the European agenda was accomplished largely through a campaign of proactive lobbying, ambitious proposals, and visible political engagement (*Financial Times*, 20 March 2001). This was complemented by efforts of the American Chamber of Commerce (AmCham) and BusinessEurope, which noted problems of industry standards, border formalities, and export licences, identifying France and Italy as the worst offenders. Responding to this groundswell, the European Commission responded with numerous studies and resolution, and forwarded a list of the most problematic barriers existing in the member states (*Financial Times*, 23 September 1980; *The Economist*, 22 October 1983).

Governments, well aware that their efforts to create national champions, protect labour markets, and maintain public spending were not stemming rising trade imbalances and deficits, sought new solutions. Efforts to contain import competition and stabilize industries had failed. Disenchantment with Keynesian tax-and-spend policies led to a shift towards market liberalization. This did not mean a common consensus around neo-liberalism, however, since different conceptions of the operation of the market economy and the agenda for European integration continued.

While the British government advocated a genuine common market in goods and services, and promoted a radically neo-liberal agenda, the French government argued for the creation of a common industrial space in which trade barriers could be reduced internally, provided that external trade protection would compensate for increased internal competition (Pearce and Sutton 1983). Major steps taken at the European Council meeting in Fontainebleau in 1984 broke the immobility that had stifled progress. Key was an agreement on long-running disputes over Britain's contribution to the Community budget and the pending Iberian enlargement. The meeting also established the Dooge Committee to focus on the reform of the institutional and decision-making structure of the Community.

Further agreement at the 1985 Intergovernmental Conference in Milan to 'study the institutional conditions under which the internal market could be achieved within a time limit' proved critical for the market integration process. This built on several earlier developments including the Spinelli Report, which focused on the need to link national regulations and institutional reform, and the parliamentary draft Treaty on European Union on institutional reform, which included increased parliamentary powers and greater use of qualified majority voting in the Council. At the subsequent intergovernmental conference, the proposed treaty reforms were brought together to become the Single European Act (SEA) (see Chapter 3).

Historically significant as the first substantial treaty reform, the SEA endorsed the single market and altered the decision-making rules for single market measures (with exceptions such as taxation and rights of workers) from unanimity to qualified majority voting (QMV). This linked institutional reforms to substantive goals, and made it more difficult for recalcitrant member states simply to veto legislative action, as had been the case under harmonization. The SEA also strengthened the powers of the European Parliament with respect to single market measures by allowing for the rejection or amendment of proposals under the cooperation procedure.

KEY POINTS

- The tools of domestic policy no longer seemed able to solve the problems of international competitiveness for member states.

- Business engaged in extensive lobbying for single market and supported measures to improve European competitiveness.

The 1992 Programme: a blueprint for action

By early 1985 the stage was set for an ambitious initiative. The newly appointed Commission President, Jacques Delors, and Internal Market Commissioner Lord Cockfield, a British former Secretary of State for Industry, put together a package of proposals that aimed to achieve the completion of the single market by 1992. The 300 proposals—subsequently modified and amended to become 283 proposals—became a Commission White Paper entitled 'Completing the Internal Market'. The final product became known as the '1992 Programme'.

The White Paper contained a comprehensive assessment of the remaining obstacles to trade, grouped together in three major categories: physical, technical, and fiscal barriers. Lord Cockfield used this very simple and deceptive categorization to introduce a series of measures across goods, services, capital, and labour markets to improve market access, prevent distortions to competition and restrictive business practices, and coordinate policies to prevent market failure. The European Commission bolstered support by commissioning a series of economic evaluations on the 'costs of non-Europe' (the Cecchini Report (1988)). Although overly optimistic, the estimated trade and welfare gains from removing barriers to trade were compelling. Not only would there be lower trade costs and greater economies of scale, as firms exploited increased opportunities, but it was expected that there would also be greater production efficiency achieved through market enlargement, intensified competition, and industrial restructuring.

At the core of the single market project was the concept of mutual recognition, the consequence of which would be increased competition not only among firms within the EU, but also among different national regulatory systems (see Sun and Pelkmans 1995). Governments sponsoring regulations that restricted market access would be under pressure since firms from other EC member states would not be required to abide by them, putting their own local firms at a disadvantage. The European Commission sought to apply this innovative strategy to the service sector as well. The concept of 'home country control' was to allow banks, insurance companies, and dealers in securities to offer the same services elsewhere in the Community that they offered at home. A single licence would operate, so that these sectors would be licensed, regulated, and supervised for the most part by their home country.

A policy framework for action on the legislative proposals contained in the White Paper was also required. Building on the legal decisions outlining the doctrine of mutual recognition as a broad free trade principle, and reference to standards as a more flexible regulatory strategy, the Commission drafted a proposal on harmonization and standards in 1985 (Pelkmans 1987). This 'new approach', reflected a critical effort to address barriers to trade by sharing regulatory functions between the public and private sectors. Where possible, there was to be mutual recognition of regulations and standards, and Community-level regulation was to be restricted to essential health and safety requirements. The necessary standards to meet them would be set by the European standards bodies, CEN, CENELEC, and the European Telecommunications Standards Institute (ETSI) (Egan 2001). Such private sector governance allowed states to foster coordination without the agreement costs associated with harmonization, by delegating regulatory authority to private institutions.

The White Paper gained widespread political support by providing a target date for the completion of the single market, and constituted a radical break with Europe's interventionist tradition, emphasizing the merits of economic liberalism. Tapping into these sentiments, the White Paper included a diversity of measures across the four freedoms, such as the abolition of frontier controls, mutual recognition of goods and services, rights of establishment for professional workers, and abolition of capital-exchange controls. While the bulk of the measures outlined in the White Paper focused on market access or negative integration measures, such as removing technical barriers to trade, dismantling quotas, and removing licensing restrictions for cross-border banking and insurance services, they were complemented by a series of market-correcting or positive integration measures such as health and safety standards, rules for trademarks and deposit insurance, and solvency ratios for banks and insurance (see Box 16.4).

While most attention focused on the political deadline of 1992, continued obstacles to cross-border movements were indications of the complexities involved. The resistance to tax harmonization was predictable, since the issue of distortions created by differential tax regimes has been problematic since the early days of the common market. The White Paper also conspicuously avoided a number of issues including a strong social dimension, as well as other politically sensitive areas such as textiles, clothing, and taxation of savings and investment income, despite the evident distortions and restrictions in these areas.

Completion of the single market meant tackling politically difficult dossiers and ensuring that the legislation was put into effect in all member states; otherwise the confidence of consumers and producers in realizing economic benefits would be undermined. Nationally important sectors such as utilities (gas and postal services, for example) were given special exemptions in the single market on the basis of social and economic arguments that 'universal services' must be provided, resulting in natural monopolies and limited competition. With rapid liberalization and technological changes, the traditional economic rationale for such *dirigiste* policies was being undermined. Pressure to open up telecommunications, electricity, and gas markets resulted in the Commission forcing liberalization of these basic services through its competition powers. The competition policy pursued by the European Commission has reinforced a liberalizing bias to the single market—as the specific features of restrictive practices, monopolies, rules governing state aid to industry, and merger policy have all played a substantial role in reducing market distortions.

Given the transformation of European economies over the past two decades, the traditional means of market integration through the removal of trade barriers and sector harmonization appears outdated

CASE STUDY 16.4

The frayed edges of the Single Market: the case of services

The services directive is seen as a critical means to generate growth in the European economy by allowing both free movement of services and rights of establishment. With services as the main driver of growth and jobs, liberalization is expected to deliver tangible benefits. Hampered by numerous barriers, the so-called 'Bolkestein Directive', which aimed to do for services trade what the '1992' agenda did for internal market activity in goods, sparked fierce criticism and protest across Europe. Although a key ambition of the directive was to extend the well understood EU principle of 'mutual recognition' to the service sector, it stoked fears of a flood of cheap labour from new member states under the 'country of origin principle'. Under this principle a firm would be able to operate in a foreign country according to the rules and regulations of its home country, leading to concerns that an influx of cheap labour from Central and Eastern Europe would undercut working conditions, wage levels, and welfare benefits in Western Europe, leading to 'social dumping'. 'Polish plumbers'—emblematic job snatchers—came to symbolize concerns about the effects of liberalization among the old member states. European fears that services liberalization reflected the primacy of market liberalization over social protection made this one of the most disputed pieces of European legislation in recent years (Nicolaïdis and Schmidt 2007; Polanyi 1957).

in the context of changes in technology and innovation, the growth of tradable services, and changes in production. In the post-1945 period, the basic European model was one of growth promotion through lowering barriers to trade and increasing competition (Hamilton and Quinlan 2005: 255). While closer economic cooperation has challenged the sovereign capacity of states in terms of their capacity for autonomous action within their own borders, further integration has run into resistance as the irreversible pressures of market liberalization and economic globalization have challenged the European social model. Although high unemployment, low economic growth, and the resulting sense of insecurity in many European states have fuelled pressure for economic reform, there has been strong resistance as states have sought to protect certain strategic sectors from the competitive effects of market integration. Although Europe has experienced a remarkable expansion of free markets and trade going beyond eliminating tariffs and non-tariff barriers to regulate and harmonize a range of policies in many sectors, it has also triggered a response as

anxieties are stoked and reaction intensifies towards the costs of further integration. Often forgotten is that the internal market agenda is unfinished. A large amount of work remains to be done in the area of financial services, patents, customs, company law, and taxation. Yet in spite of legal and political efforts to address archaic rules in the service sector, the freedom of services and rights of establishment through the concept of home country control sparked a considerable outcry (see Box 16.4). Despite deeper market integration, domestic consumption and investment patterns and labour markets still reveal a distinctive 'home bias' (Delgado 2006).

> **KEY POINTS**
>
> - The White Paper on the single market created a package of measures to liberalize trade that became the 1992 Programme.
>
> - The single market project is still a work in progress, with continued efforts to remove barriers to trade and promote market access.

Correcting the market: the politics of regulated capitalism

The renewed emphasis on market integration through the '1992 Programme' also brought pressures for ancillary policies along social democratic lines (Scharpf 1999). Dealing with the pressures from increased competition led to policy proposals reflecting the ideological cleavages that had always underpinned the Community project. Fearful that excessive competition would increase social conflict, proponents of a regulated capitalism approach (see Box 16.2) proposed a variety of inclusive mechanisms to generate broad-based support for the single market. These included structural policy for poorer regions to promote economic and social cohesion, consumer and environmental protection, and rural development (see Chapter 18). Fiscal

transfers spread the burden of adjustment and assisted the adversely affected countries.

Labour representatives also sought to address the impact of market integration through the creation of an ongoing social dialogue (see Chapter 17). These initiatives were narrower than the traditional social market philosophy and distinct from dirigiste policies of state ownership and control, but they complemented efforts to shift regulation to the European level. The effort to promote a European social dimension also acknowledged that the domestic political pressures on national welfare states meant that they could no longer compensate for the effects of integration as they had done in the past (Scharpf 1999).

The goal of regulating markets, redistributing resources, and shaping partnership among public and private actors led advocates of regulated capitalism to propose provisions for transport and communications infrastructure, information networks, workforce skills, and research and development (Hooghe and Marks 1997). The progressive expansion of activities at the European level brought into focus two long-standing opposing views about the economic role of governments.

Some have argued that the single market has progressively increased the level of statism or interventionism in Europe (Messerlin 2001; Schmidt 2007). The economic consensus in favour of market forces and neo-liberalism under the single market programme in the 1980s have been offset by increased intervention or regulated capitalism in labour markets (minimum wage and working time), and new provisions for culture (broadcast quotas), industry (shipbuilding, textiles, and clothing),

and technology (new energy resources, biotechnology, and broadband networks) in the 1990s. Yet the forms of 'embedded liberalism' have to some degree been overshadowed by growing emphasis on competitiveness in the 1990s, in terms of increased market competition and market discipline through the Lisbon process, a collective strategy across a range of policies in which the single market is a central element to deliver the goals of growth, jobs, innovation, and competition, and drive European recovery.

KEY POINTS

- Proponents of the regulated capitalism approach have proposed a number of policies to generate more widespread support for the EU.
- This has included structural policies, the introduction of social dialogue, and transport policy.

Modernizing the Single Market

As Europe faces the challenges of making the single market deliver to its full potential, greater attention has been given to its governance and management (Radaelli 1998; European Report July 20, 2005; Chatham House 2003). In some instances, poor preparation and lack of commitment by national administrations have accounted for some of these problems. In other cases badly drafted rules were also to blame (Radaelli 1998). To tackle such problems, all of the European institutions have sought to promote regulatory reform and enhance the governance of the market. However, the push for administrative and organizational reform has been motivated by business requests for easing regulatory burdens as a prerequisite for the achievement of a Europe-wide single market (Molitor 1995; Mandelkern Group, 2001; European Commission 1992a). This has led to specific initiatives, including SLIM (Simpler Legislation for a Single Market) in 1996, the Action plan for the

Single Market (1997), and a scoreboard to generate peer pressure to improve compliance (European Report 28 November 1997). Yet there remain problems of infringement of European law, and the difficult challenge of ensuring actual compliance with single market obligations in both new and old member states (Falkner et al 2004). While the Commission has actively pursued infringement proceedings (under Article 226 of the Treaty), whereby they formally notify member states of their legal obligations, they have also created SOLVIT, as a means to find a solution to concerns about single market problems through informal cooperation. Yet the slow pace of standardization, as well as misunderstandings with the application of mutual recognition in practice continues (Nicolaidis and Schmidt, 2007).

Seeking to modernize elements of the single market in response to changes in business strategy and market structure, greater attention has been given to more flexible market instruments. But despite recent reform efforts, it is clear that businesses still believe they face serious obstacles that prevent them from realizing the full benefits of the single market. In economic terms, the single market has promoted trade liberalization, industrial restructuring, and consolidation in numerous industrial sectors. In political terms, integration triggers a reaction from inefficient producers or unions worried about the impact of increased competition. Such market liberalization presents opportunities for mobilization and provides a new context in which opposition can be expressed (Imig and Tarrow 2001). Yet the single market has also enabled the European Union to exercise its authority in multilateral trade negotiations and use market access as an instrument of 'soft power' to promote economic and political reform in Central and Eastern Europe and the Balkans through stabilization and association agreements to eventual membership and accession.

Even though the single market is now well entrenched, its feasibility and effectiveness are dependent on two conditions. First, it requires well defined legal and judicial mechanisms to enforce the rights and obligations of a single market to ensure enforcement and compliance. A second factor in generating political support and legitimacy for economic integration is the pursuit of an acceptable distribution of tangible benefits. In this respect, the relationship between economic rights and social rights needs to be considered since viable and sustainable integration is likely to be more successful if economic growth is fairly distributed.

KEY POINTS

- The operation of the single market is under tremendous political scrutiny to ensure correct implementation and compliance, which requires management and oversight by European institutions.

- Emphasis has been given to designing better regulatory policies to ease burdens on business and promote competitiveness.

Globalization and the Single Market

Globalization has been the source of much discussion in Europe. Some argue that Europeanization contributes to globalization, as the increased flow of goods, services, capital, and people across Europe increases economic opportunities and market openness. Others argue that globalization is a threat to the European social model, and the direct impact on national economies requires coordinated action to manage the tensions and challenges created by increased global competition. While much attention within Europe focused on the need to manage the consequences of industrial decline, foster greater productivity, and ease transaction costs within Europe, such debates about managing economic liberalization have now been transferred to the global level.

As the largest single trading area, the EU has a leading role to play in the context of international trade negotiations and liberalization. Across a broad range of sectors, Europe is increasingly shaping global markets through the transfer of its regulatory rules and standards. The European Union as an international economic regime has sought to play a leading role by promoting key concepts of its regulatory approach in areas such as competition policy, financial regulations, environmental management standards, and food safety. The European Union now seeks to strategically promote its regulatory standards better to take advantage of globalization. Yet European integration takes place in a situation of global sourcing of goods and services, increased tradability of goods and services, and changing patterns of trade and investment. While many studies of globalization have suggested that we are moving towards greater levels of economic integration, they have paid much less attention to other parts of the world. Economic integration is proceeding, but political integration is either not desired or so limited that many debates about territoriality, sovereignty, and governance have not yet been addressed.

Theorizing the Single Market

While market integration in Europe is the most institutionalized form of regional cooperation, there are different theoretical approaches from a variety of disciplinary perspectives that can explain the causes, content, and consequences of the single market (see Pelkmans et al 2008). While many of these studies fall squarely within the major theoretical debates in the field of European integration studies, particularly international relations (see Chapters 5–7), there has been a proliferation of perspectives and approaches to understanding market governance, not just within European borders but beyond those borders.

No matter how diverse the field becomes, the dominant paradigms are still important. Intergovernmentalists (see Chapter 6) claim that the institutional dynamics that underpin the single market project were the result of a convergence of policy preferences in the early 1980s (Moravcsik 1991). Parties that advocated neo-liberal market reforms came to power in a number of states such as the UK, Denmark, and Belgium. Coupled with decisive reversal in France away from Keynesian fiscal policy in 1983, the resulting Single European Act represented a familiar pattern of bargaining and negotiation between the UK, Germany, and France, to reach a common solution.

For intergovernmentalism, national interests and policies are thus expected to constrain integrationist impulses, as state resources, power, and bargaining are the driving factors of economic integration. Garrett (1992) adds to this, arguing that in important areas of legal activity, the Court was constrained by member states' governments. According to Garrett, the Court anticipates reactions from member states, and serves their interests (especially the most powerful member states) in rendering its judgments. By comparison, the neo-functionalist account stresses the importance of supranational actors in shaping the single market agenda. Sandholtz and Zysman (1989) point to the Commission as an innovative policy entrepreneur in shaping the European agenda, supported by business interests seeking to reap the benefits of an enlarged market. Burley and Mattli (1993) add to the neo-functionalist argument by claiming that Court rulings have resulted in interactions between national and European courts, creating a distinctive legal regime that shapes rules and procedures governing markets. When political attempts to create a common market stalled, the Court advanced its supranational authority over national courts, expanding its jurisdictional authority in order to make a pivotal contribution to the promotion of free trade (see Egan 2001; Shapiro 1992). Cameron (1992) seeks to blend these different theoretical perspectives by arguing that the 1992 initiative was the result of the complex interaction of different actors and institutions, simultaneously accelerating economic integration and supranational institution building, while also representing intergovernmental bargaining among states. By contrast, Van Apeldoorn argues that market outcomes are the result of struggles between contending transnational forces, and that economic integration reflects the economic interests of transnational capital strengthened by the deepening globalization processes, and the rise of neo-liberal market ideology within European political economy (Van Apeldoorn 1992). Jabko, on the other hand, focuses on the role of ideas in framing the single market project, drawing on constructivist premises that the market can be strategically used as a political strategy to appeal to various constituencies at different times (Jabko 2006).

More recently, the single market process has been examined through the lens of comparative policy analysis. Empirical studies have shown that European policies are a patchwork of different policy styles, instruments, and institutional arrangements (Héritier 1996). Majone described such changes in governance resulting from the failure of public ownership modes of control and the ensuing turn to privatization policies as generating an increasing transfer of authority to the EU level to deal with market failures and ensure credible commitments to a European single market (Majone 1996). His argument that the EU as a political system specializes in regulation is based on the notion that regulation is the central instrument of governance at the EU level, since with limited fiscal resources at its control, the EU has sought to expand its influence through the supply of regulations where the costs are borne by the firms and states responsible for complying with them. Thus the single market is an effort to reduce transaction costs and resolve problems of heterogeneity through collective action and coordination. Majone (1995) argues that in order to achieve such goals, the European Union requires non-majoritarian institutions such as independent banks, regulatory agencies, and courts to foster collective regulatory outcomes, as they are better suited than traditional political interests, such as parties, legislatures, and interest groups, to achieve the necessary independence and credibility to govern the market.

Focusing on issues of governance, other scholars have stressed the impact of the single market on regions, sectors, and classes by looking at the relationship between economic development and democratic conditions, seeking to demonstrate that the

single market may not be entirely benign in its consequences (Scharpf 1999; Hirst and Thompson 1996; Amin and Tomaney 1995). While political economists have illustrated how the activism of the European polity has increased market competition in sectors hitherto shielded from the discipline of the market (Scharpf 1999), there has been growing attention in comparative politics to the role of public opinion and party politics in intensifying conflict around European policies. Few subjects have generated more debate than the effects of economic integration and globalization on the policy autonomy of governments. Opponents argue that the increasing constraints on national policy choices, especially the pressures on the welfare states and government-owned monopolies, have in fact, contributed to the growing opposition among the populace towards further European integration. As Hooghe and Marks have recently argued, as important as economic imperatives are, market integration is also the product of politics, most notably but not exclusively, tensions and conflicts about sovereignty, identity, and governance in a multi-level polity. There is a strong relationship between economic and political developments, as the single market and its ancillary policies require political support and legitimacy on the one hand, and institutional capabilities and effectiveness on the other. Market integration has revealed that there are disparate ideas about how to stabilize and regulate markets, conflict and bargaining over institutional power and authority, and growing economic insecurity among domestic publics about the effects of a broader breakdown of economic barriers on national identity, culture, and values.

KEY POINTS

- Two main approaches, intergovernmentalism and neo-functionalism, have been used to account for the resurgence of European integration in the mid 1980s.

- Subsequent research in comparative politics and policy studies has focused on the implications of market governance.

Conclusion

Although the single market is at the heart of European integration, considerably less attention has been given to its role and impact in recent years as scholars have focused on new policy areas and new modes of governance. Yet the single market continues to play a fundamental role both internally and externally in shaping economic governance, through serving as a powerful mechanism to promote European norms and standards both multilaterally and bilaterally in a host of issues areas, promoting market access, removing cross-border barriers, and fostering regulatory coordination. Ranging across a number of policy areas, European efforts to remove obstacles and distortions in goods, services, capital, and labour have transformed the European economic landscape. Equally significant, the single market allows the European Union to confront the dynamics of increased competition, and to respond to the changing global environment by fostering collective coordinated action on a range of regulatory issues to shape global rules and norms. In many areas, the single market has enabled the European Union to exercise global leverage and export its regulatory rules and standards in a host of issue areas, both in multinational arenas as well as through bilateral enlargement negotiations and the pressures of conditionality.

Yet European integration has, from the signing of the Treaty of Rome, been deeply contested, as distinctive forms of capitalism persist, given strong institutionally embedded practices and norms. The process was successful in the early period due to rapid economic growth which masked the contradiction inherent between trade liberalization and the mixed economy and welfare state (Pelkmans 1984). However, there are increased concerns about the asymmetries between polity and market, with the legal emphasis on economic provisions of the treaty seeming to come at the expense of the protection of social rights.

There are concerns that rhetorical support for the single market is being undermined by a surge of national protectionism. As the ECJ strikes down economic barriers to trade, promoting market liberalization and economic access, it has also created extensive case law that bolsters equity, economic development, and social welfare (Caporaso and Tarrow 2007). Yet as European integration has become more politicized, and attention has focused on the public opposition to European integration, the implicit premise of economic integration as a positive outcome has faded as increased economic divergence within an enlarged EU has made the impact of market integration more salient in domestic politics.

Stumbling blocks remain to the completion of the single market. Domestic pressures against further liberalization, coupled with opt-outs, derogations, and transition periods, have undermined the uniformity of the single market. Supplementing the traditional legal approaches with soft law mechanisms generated concerns among lawyers about the credibility of market integration. The lack of effective competition and market fragmentation in retail trades, energy, telecommunications, and financial services hamper innovation, create barriers to market entry, and create inefficiencies. As attention shifts from the politics of bargaining and negotiating to the politics of rule enforcement and compliance, the single market has been marginalized in part due to the distractions created by recent constitutional failures. Yet the single market is a work in progress. Market integration has to balance functional, distributional, and territorial pressures. As a result, theorizing about the single market is diverse and cuts across globalization, political economy, comparative politics, policy studies, and international relations.

QUESTIONS

1.   What are the main barriers to trade in the EU?

2.   What type of policy instruments has the EU used to integrate national markets?

3.   How successful has the EU been in establishing a single market free of restrictions to trade and commerce?

4.   What were the driving forces behind the 'relaunch' of the single market project in 1980s?

5.   How have different theories and approaches been used to explain the single market programme?

6.   What role has the ECJ played in addressing barriers to trade?

7.   What accounts for the shift towards modernizing the single market?

8.   Is market integration a shield or conduit for the forces of globalization?

 GUIDE TO FURTHER R\EADING

■ Armstrong, K. and Bulmer, S. *The Governance of the Single European Market* (Manchester: Manchester University Press, 1997). This book examines the single market project from its origins to the mid 1990s, examining the dynamics of the processes involved from both a political and legal perspective.

■ Egan, M. *Constructing a European Market. Standards, Regulation and Governance* (Oxford: Oxford University Press, 2001). This volume draws on literature from several disciplines to develop a comprehensive account of the regulatory strategies and institutional arrangements adopted by the European Union in promoting the single market in goods.

■ Grin G. *Battle of the Single European Market: Achievements and Economic Thought 1985 – 2000* (London; Kegan Paul, 2003). This book focuses on the political, economic, and intellectual debates that have accompanied the history of the Single European Market (SEM), from its inception to 2000.

■ Jabko, N. *Playing the Market: A Political Strategy for Uniting Europe*, 1985 – 2005 (Cornell: Cornell University Press 2006). In this book Jabko traces the political strategy that underlay the move from the Single Market of 1986 through the official creation of the European Union in 1992 to the coming of the euro in 1999.

■ Pelkmans, J., Hanf, D., and Chang, M. *The EU Internal Market in Comparative Perspective*, Economic, Political and Legal Analyses, Volume 8 (Berlin: Peter Lang Publishers, 2008), This book addresses the EU's 'hard core', the internal market, by undertaking a tri-disciplinary analysis of the internal market.

 WEBLINKS

● http://ec.europa.eu/internal_market/score/index_en.htm   The Single Market Scoreboard provides implementation statistics across the EU.

● www.newapproach.org   This explains the new regulatory strategy of standardization.

● http://www.accenture.com/NR/rdonlyres/FAD399B3-1856-4356-95C9-7C9D4CA5B060/0/unfinished_ business.pdf   *Unfinished Business: Making Europe's Single Market a Reality*. A survey about business concerns in the single market.

● http://ec.europa.eu/citizens_agenda/docs/sec_2007_1519_en.pdf   Analysis of the external dimension of the Single Market.

 Visit the Online Resource Centre that accompanies this book for lots of interesting additional material. http://www.oxfordtextbooks.co.uk/orc/Cini_Borragan3e/

17

The EU's Social Dimension

GERDA FALKNER

Chapter Contents

- Introduction
- The EEC and its member states
- The Treaty reforms from Maastricht to the Lisbon Treaty
- The development and scope of European social policy
- The European Social Fund
- New developments: the Open Method of Coordination
- Social partnership at European level
- Conclusion

Reader's Guide

This chapter looks at the way in which European social policy has evolved since the late 1950s. It begins by reflecting on the intergovernmental character of the policy in the early days, and on how the gradual introduction of qualified majority voting (QMV) and the widening scope of the policy allowed the European institutions and European-level interest groups much more of a say in the European social dimension. The chapter also looks at the work of the European Social Fund. Focusing on newer developments, later sections chart the arrival of the Open Method of Coordination, a non-regulatory approach to European policy making in this field, and the growing importance of social partnership: that is, the involvement of interest groups representing employers and labour in making European-level social policy. The chapter concludes by arguing that social regulation will become even more difficult now that the EU incorporates a greater number of the Central and East European (CEE) states at the same time as having to fight the financial and economic crisis.

Introduction

What is social policy? In a famous definition, T. H. Marshall (1975) talked of the use of political power to supersede, supplement or modify operations of the economic system in order to achieve results which it would not achieve on its own. Such a wide definition would include, for example, redistributive EU actions, which provide funding through the EU's structural funds (that is, the social, agricultural, cohesion, and regional funds) (see Chapter 18). This would go far beyond what is usually understood as European social policy and would introduce too vast an array of topics to be covered in this brief chapter. It seems, therefore, more useful to apply a pragmatic understanding of social policy. This involves actions which fall under the so-called 'social dimension of European integration': that is, any acts carried out under the social policy chapter of the European Community (EC) Treaty; policies targeted at facilitating the freedom of movement of workers in the social realm; and last, but not least, action to harmonize the quite diverse social or labour law standards of the member states, whatever the relevant Treaty base may be. It should be added that most writers on EC social policy have chosen a similar approach to this.

This chapter will first outline the division of social policy competences between the European Union and its member states; the interpretation of these Treaty provisions in the day-to-day policy process over time; and the latest formal reforms at Amsterdam and Nice, with an outlook on the Lisbon Treaty. It will then analyse the incremental development of EC/EU social regulation and activities, including the European Social Fund and the so-called Open Method of Coordination. Since patterns of decision making are quite distinctive in the social, as opposed to other, fields of EU politics, this chapter will also outline how the EU-level interest groups participate therein (see also Chapter 12). The conclusion not only summarizes the results of the chapter, but also discusses the performance of European integration within its 'social dimension'.

The EEC and its member states

According to the Treaty of Rome (1957), social policy competences were to remain a largely national affair. It did not provide for the Europeanization of social policies, as too many delegations had opposed this in the negotiations leading up to the Treaty. Some governments (especially the German) pleaded for a neo-liberal, free market approach to social affairs, even in the realm of labour and social security; others opted for a limited process of harmonization. The French delegation, notably, argued that its comparatively high social charges and its constitutional principle of equal pay for men and women might constitute a competitive disadvantage within the newly formed European market, while Italy feared that the opening up of Community borders might prove costly for the southern part of the country, which was already economically disadvantaged. In the end a compromise was found, but this did not include explicit European Economic Community (EEC) competences for active social policy harmonization at the European level. The dominant philosophy of the 1957 Treaty was that improvements in welfare would be provided by the economic growth that arose as a consequence of the liberalization of the European market, and not from the regulatory and distributive form of public policy (see Barnard 2000; Leibfried and Pierson 1995).

Nevertheless, the Treaty contained a small number of concessions for the more interventionist delegations. These were the provisions on equal pay for both sexes (Article 119); the maintenance of 'existing equivalence between paid holiday schemes' (Article 120); and the establishment of a European Social Fund (Articles 123–128). Equal pay and the Social Fund increased in their importance as the European integration process progressed. There was to be no follow up, however, on the equivalence of paid holiday schemes.

While other provisions of the Treaty's Title III on social policy included some solemn social policy declarations, they failed to empower the EEC to act. 'Underwriting this arrangement was the relative feasibility of nation state strategies for economic development in the first decades after World War II. The common market, as it was constructed, was designed to aid and abet such national strategies, not transcend them' (Ross 1995: 360). Yet in other areas of activity the Commission was empowered to present legislative proposals to the Council. These proposals would ultimately become binding law. For social policy, however, the Commission was only permitted to act by undertaking relevant studies, delivering opinions, and arranging consultations both on problems arising at national level and on those of concern to international organizations. In legal terms, then, Article 118 reflected a confirmation of national (as opposed to European) responsibility for social policy.

Paradoxically, the sole explicit Community competence for social policy regulation under the original EEC Treaty was not in the part of the Treaty that dealt explicitly with social policy. It belonged, rather, to Part II, on the Foundations of the Community, which contained provisions on the free movement of goods, labour, services, and capital. Articles 48 to 51 thus provided for the establishment of the freedom of movement for workers as part of the Treaty's market-making activities. This implied the abolition of all discrimination based on the nationality of workers in the member states in the areas of employment, remuneration, and other conditions of work and employment (Article 48). In order to 'adopt such measures in the field of social security as are necessary to provide freedom of movement for workers' (Article 51), the Council was mandated

to establish Community-wide rights to benefits and a way of calculating the amount of those benefits for migrant workers and their dependants.

Yet although there were almost no explicit social policy competences in the Treaty of Rome, an extensive interpretation of the Treaty basis provided, in practice, some room for manoeuvre. This was possible because, where necessary or useful for market integration, intervention in the social policy field was *implicitly* allowed through the so-called 'subsidiary competence' provisions. In other words, laws in the member states which 'directly affect the establishment or functioning of the common market' could be approximated by unanimous Council decision on the basis of a Commission proposal (Article 100). Moreover, if action by the Community should prove necessary to attain (in the course of the operation of the common market) one of the objectives of the Community, and if the Treaty had not provided the necessary powers, the Council was mandated to take the appropriate measures, acting unanimously on a proposal from the Commission and after consulting the European Parliament (Article 235).

From the 1970s onwards, these provisions provided a loophole for social policy harmonization. However, the unanimous Council vote necessary for this to happen constituted a high threshold for joint action. Each government could veto social measures and as a result the EC found itself in what Scharpf (1988) has called a joint-decision trap (see Chapter 6).

In 1987, the Single European Act (SEA) came into force as the first major Community Treaty revision (see Chapters 3 and 16). As in the 1950s, an economic enterprise was at the heart of this fresh impetus in favour of European integration. But parallel to the member states' commitment to a Single Market Programme, the Europeanization of social policy remained controversial. In various policy areas touched by market liberalization, notably environmental and research policy, Community competence was formally extended (see Articles 130r–t and 130f–q; see Chapter 22). But this was not so for social policy, as the delegations representing the national governments seemed unwilling to give the Community a broader role in this field.

However, one important exception was made. Article118a on minimum harmonization concerning health and safety of workers provided an escape route out of the unanimity requirement. For the first time in European social policy, it allowed directives to be agreed on the basis of a qualified majority of the Council members (see Chapter 13). The standards adopted following this article were minimum regulations only. Nevertheless, under this provision reluctant member states could be forced to align their social legislation with the (large) majority of member states, even against their will. It should be stressed that agreement on this article was only possible because occupational health and safety issues were closely connected to the single market.

Governments did not expect this 'technical' matter to facilitate social policy integration in the significant way that it would in the decade to follow. An extensive use of this provision was possible mainly because the wording and the definition of key terms in Article 118a were somewhat vague:

> ❝❝ Member States shall pay particular attention to encouraging improvements, especially in the working environment, as regards the health and safety of workers, and shall set as their objective the harmonization of conditions in this area, while maintaining the improvements made. In order to help achieve the objective laid down in the first paragraph, the Council, acting by a qualified majority on a proposal from the Commission ... shall adopt, by means of directives, minimum requirements for gradual implementation ... ❞❞

This formulation made it easy to play what has since been called the 'treaty base game' (Rhodes 1995). It allowed governments to adopt not only measures improving the working environment (for example, a directive on the maximum concentration of airborne pollutants), but also measures that ensured the health and safety of workers by improving working conditions in a more general sense (for example, limiting working time). It was clear that the reason why this treaty basis was frequently chosen was the fact that only this article allowed for majority voting at the time.

KEY POINTS

- The 1957 EEC Treaty meant that social policy remained largely a national affair. The coordination of social security systems for migrant workers was an exception to this rule in the legislative field.

- The SEA introduced qualified majority voting to a limited area of social policy. Governments did not realize its implications at the time.

The Treaty reforms from Maastricht to the Lisbon Treaty

The 1991 Intergovernmental Conference (IGC) preceding the Maastricht Treaty negotiated the next reform of the social policy provisions. However, under the requirement of unanimous approval by all (then) 12 member states, the social provisions could not be significantly altered because of the strong opposition from the UK government. At the end of extremely difficult negotiations that threatened all other compromises achieved within the IGC, the UK was granted an opt-out from the social policy measures agreed by the rest of the member states. In the *Protocol on Social Policy* annexed to the EC Treaty, all members except the UK were authorized to use the institutions, procedures, and mechanisms of the Treaty for the purpose of implementing their 'Agreement on Social Policy' (sometimes called the Social Chapter).

Because of the UK opt-out (or the 'opt-in' of the other member states), the European Union after Maastricht (from November 1993) had two different legal bases for the adoption of social policy measures. The EC Treaty's social provisions remained valid for all member states. As introduced in the 1986 Single European Act, it allowed for minimum harmonization as well as for QMV in the area of worker health and safety provisions only. By contrast, the innovative social policy provisions of the Social Agreement, applicable to all but the UK, comprised what had been perceived during the IGC as an amendment to the social provisions of the Treaty. These constituted an extension of Community competence into a wide range of social policy issues, including working conditions; the information and consultation of workers; equality between men and women with regard to labour market opportunities and treatment at work (as opposed to only equal pay before); and the integration of persons excluded from the labour market (Article 2.1, Social Agreement). Some issues were, however, explicitly excluded from the scope of minimum harmonization under the Maastricht social policy provisions: namely, pay; the right of association; the right to strike; and the right to impose lock-outs (Article 2.6.).

Additionally, qualified majority voting was extended to many more issue areas than before, including the information and consultation of workers. Unanimous decisions remained, however, for social security matters and the social protection of workers; the protection of those whose employment contract is terminated; representation and collective defence of interests of workers and employers, including co-determination; conditions of employment for third country nationals, that is non-EU nationals, legally residing in Community territory; and financial contributions for promotion of employment and job creation (see Article 3 Social Agreement).

In contrast to the Maastricht negotiations, in the 1996–7 Intergovernmental Conference preceding the Amsterdam Treaty, social policy reform was not a major issue. Because of the fierce resistance to

social policy reforms by the UK's Conservative government (in office until May 1997), the IGC decided to postpone discussion of the topic until the very end of the negotiation period, awaiting the result of the 1997 general election. Under the new Labour government, which came into office at this point, the UK's opt-out from the Social Agreement came to an end. Another significant innovation in the Amsterdam Treaty was the new employment policy chapter (now in Articles 125–130). While excluding any harmonization of domestic laws, it provides for the coordination of national employment policies on the basis of annual guidelines and national follow-up reports. Furthermore, a new Article 13 on Community action against discrimination was inserted. On this legal basis, a couple of important new directives on fighting discrimination based on grounds of sex, race, ethnic origin, belief, disability, age, and sexual orientation have been adopted in recent years.

The Nice Treaty of 2001 was not particularly innovative in terms of social policy matters. In some fields, the Council is now allowed to decide unanimously upon the use of the codecision procedure (see Chapter 13). This applies to worker protection where employment contracts have been terminated; to the representation and collective defence of collective interests; and the interests of third country nationals (see Article 137.2). Furthermore, 'measures' (not legislation) to improve transnational cooperation can now be adopted on all social issues, not just those concerning social exclusion and equal opportunities, as was the case after Amsterdam.

Under the Lisbon Treaty, social security provisions for migrant workers are the only new issue that would fall within QMV in the Council, to the great disappointment of the European Trade Union Confederation (ETUC). Furthermore, the 2000 Charter of Fundamental Rights of the Union would formally come under the Treaty framework and hence finally acquire a higher legal status (see Box 17.1). At the same time, new safeguard procedures could in the future strengthen member state control over their social security systems. Finally, a horizontal 'social clause' would be introduced

KEY CONCEPTS AND TERMS 17.1

The Charter of Fundamental Rights

The Charter of Fundamental Rights of the European Union is the first single document that brings together all of the rights previously found in a variety of legislative instruments, such as national laws and international conventions. At the request of the European Parliament, the Cologne European Council (June 1999) decided to have the rights of European citizens codified, since the 'protection of fundamental rights is a founding principle of the Union and an indispensable prerequisite for her legitimacy'. The Charter was drawn up by a Convention consisting of the representatives of the heads of state or government of the member states, one representative of the President of the European Commission, MEPs and members of national parliaments. The Charter was formally adopted in Nice in December 2000. The Lisbon Treaty gives the Charter binding effect, conferring on it the same legal value as the treaties. Poland and the UK negotiated an opt-out.

The Charter contains a preamble and 54 Articles, grouped in seven chapters. The preamble to the Charter states that the Union is founded on the indivisible universal values of human dignity, freedom, equality, and solidarity, and on the principles of democracy and the rule of law. The preamble specifies that the EU contributes to the preservation and development of these common values 'while respecting the diversity of the cultures and traditions of the peoples of Europe as well as the national identities of the Member States'. The rights enshrined in the Charter are enumerated in six chapters on 'Dignity', 'Freedoms', 'Equality', 'Solidarity', 'Citizens' Rights', and 'Justice' and a final seventh chapter on general provisions.

Chapter I on Dignity declares the inviolability of human dignity, the right to life, the prohibition of torture and inhuman or degrading treatment or punishment, and the prohibition of slavery and forced labour.

Chapter II includes a list of rights and freedoms such as the right to liberty and security, to respect for private and family life and to protection of personal data, the right to marry and found a family, freedom of thought, conscience and religion, of expression and information, of assembly and of association, freedom of the arts and sciences, the right to education, freedom to choose an occupation, and

the right to engage in work, freedom to conduct a business, the right to property, the right to asylum, and the right to protection in the event of removal, expulsion, or extradition.

Chapter III on Equality refers to equality before the law, non-discrimination, respect for cultural, religious, and linguistic diversity, equality between men and women, the rights of children and the elderly, and integration of persons with disabilities.

Chapter IV on Solidarity refers to workers' right to information and consultation within the undertaking, the right of collective bargaining and action, the right of access to placement services, protection in the event of unjustified dismissal, fair and just working conditions, prohibition of child labour, and protection of young people at work, family and professional life, social security and social assistance, health care, access to services of general economic interest, environmental protection, consumer protection.

Chapter V enumerates the rights of European citizens in the framework of the EU, including the right to vote and stand as a candidate at elections to the EP, the right to vote and stand as a candidate at municipal elections, the right to good administration, the right of access to documents, the ombudsman, the right to petition, freedom of movement and residence, diplomatic and consular protection.

Chapter VI on Justice establishes the right to an effective remedy and a fair trial, the presumption of innocence and the right of defence, principles of legality and proportionality of criminal offences and penalties, the right not to be tried or punished twice in criminal proceedings for the same criminal offence.

The final provisions stipulate that 'the provisions of this Charter are addressed to the institutions and bodies of the Union with due regard to the principle of subsidiarity and to the Member States only when they are implementing Union law'. They are to apply these provisions 'in accordance with their respective powers'.

Source: European Navigator, www.ena.lu and SCADPlus, Charter of Fundamental Rights, http://europa.eu/scadplus/leg/en/lvb/l33501.htm.

whose practical significance is very unclear. This means that, in the future, any EU policy must take into account 'requirements linked to the promotion of a high level of employment, the guarantee of adequate social protection, the fight against social exclusion, and a high level of education, training and protection of human health' (Article 9). At least potentially, any new legislative draft might in the future need a 'social impact assessment'.

The development and scope of European social policy

There are a number of important sub-fields of social legislation, the most important of which are labour law; health and safety at the workplace; and anti-discrimination policy. The following sections outline when and how they were developed. During the early years of European integration, social policy consisted almost exclusively of efforts to secure the free movement of workers and in that sense was rather non-controversial. In a number of EC regulations, national social security systems were coordinated with a view to improving the status of internationally mobile workers and their families.

During the late 1960s, however, the political climate gradually became more favourable to a wider range of European social policy measures. At their 1972 Paris summit, the Community heads of state and government declared that economic expansion should not be an end in itself but should lead to improvements in more general living and working conditions. With relevant Community action in mind, they agreed a catalogue of social policy measures that were to be elaborated by the Commission. In the resulting social action programme (that is, a list of intended legislative initiatives, covering a number of years) of 1974, the Council expressed its intention to adopt a series of social policy measures within two years.

That the Council stated that Community social policy should furthermore be conducted under Article 235, which goes beyond purely economic considerations, was a major development. This was confirmation that governments perceived social policy intervention as an integral part of European integration. As a consequence, the Treaty's subsidiary competence provisions were increasingly interpreted in a regulation-friendly manner in day-to-day policy making. Originally, only issues that directly restricted the single market had qualified for harmonization (or 'approximation') under Article 100. During the 1970s, a shift occurred. Henceforth, regulation was considered legitimate if it facilitated the practice of the free movement of production factors, that is, goods, services, labour, or capital. Several of the legislative measures proposed in the 1974 Social Action Programme were adopted by the Council in the years thereafter, and further such Programmes followed the first one.

Figure 17.1 shows the growth in social policy legislation from 1970 onwards. By 2009, approximately 80 binding norms (regulations and directives), approximately 90 amendments and geographical extensions (to the former East Germany, to new member states, and to the UK after Amsterdam) of such norms, and approximately 120 non-binding policy outputs were in existence. Taken together, the two variants of binding rules by far outstrip the non-binding norms. Their slow but rather steady growth has not been stopped by the emergence of the 'softer' modes of governance, as will be explained below.

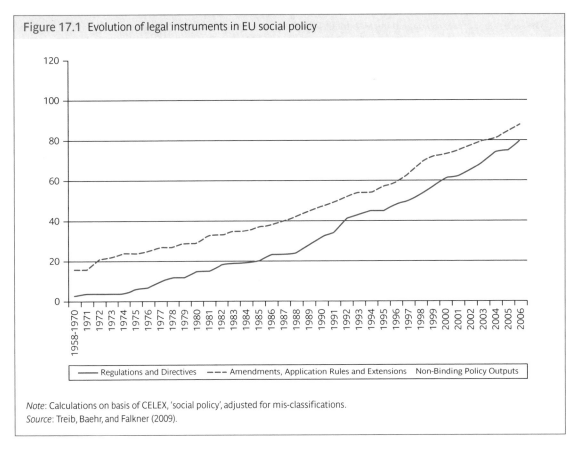

Figure 17.1 Evolution of legal instruments in EU social policy

Note: Calculations on basis of CELEX, 'social policy', adjusted for mis-classifications.
Source: Treib, Baehr, and Falkner (2009).

There are three main fields of EU social regulation: health and safety, other working conditions, and equality at the workplace and beyond. With regard to *equality*, the European Court of Justice (ECJ) had become a major actor ever since it provided a broad interpretation of Article 119 on domestic measures to ensure equal pay for both sexes, opening the way for action on the basis of the subsidiary competence provisions (as outlined above). Matters such as equal pay for work of equal value, the equal treatment of men and women regarding working conditions and social security, and even the issue of burden of proof in discrimination law suits were finally regulated at EU level (Hoskyns 1996; Mazey 1998). Since the Treaty of Amsterdam (new Article 13), a more general equality policy has been developed, targeting discrimination based on sex, racial or ethnic origin, religion or belief, disability, age, or sexual orientation.

In the field of *working conditions*, a number of directives were adopted during the late 1970s, for example on the protection of workers in cases of collective redundancy; the transfer of undertakings; and employer insolvency. Many more directives followed during the 1990s and thereafter, including those on worker information; on conditions of work contract; on the equal treatment of atypical (such as shift, temporary agency, or part-time) workers; and on parental leave.

With regard to *health and safety at work*, the Regulation was based on a number of specific action programmes. Directives include the protection of workers exposed to emissions (or pollutants) and responsible for heavy loads, as well as protection against risks of chemical, physical, and biological agents at work (such as lead or asbestos). Figure 17.2 indicates the number of directives in these three sub-fields.

KEY POINTS

- The development of EC social legislation has increased since the late 1950s, with the 1990s being the most active decade.

- In addition to the issue of free movement of workers and equal treatment in national social security systems, the main areas of regulative European social policy are working conditions; anti-discrimination policy; and health and safety in the workplace.

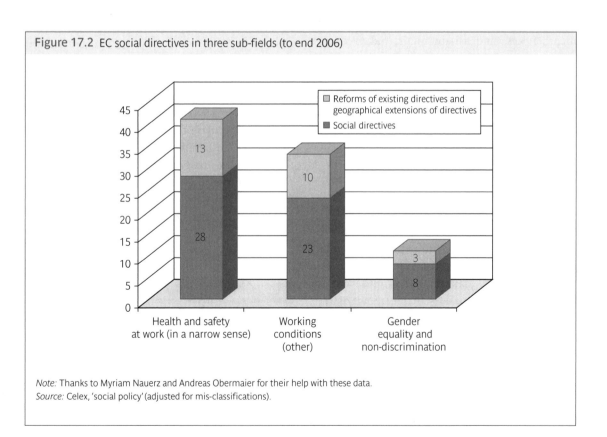

Figure 17.2 EC social directives in three sub-fields (to end 2006)

Note: Thanks to Myriam Nauerz and Andreas Obermaier for their help with these data.
Source: Celex, 'social policy' (adjusted for mis-classifications).

The European Social Fund

European Community policy is largely regulatory, and this is particularly the case in the social field. However, as this and the following section will outline, the relative importance of regulation has declined in recent years, as both funding opportunities and 'soft' forms of governance have increased. In the case of funding, the Treaty of Rome provided for a 'European Social Fund' (ESF). Its goal was to simplify the employment of workers, to increase their geographical and occupational mobility within the Community, and to facilitate their adaptation to change, particularly through vocational training and retraining. Initially, the ESF reimbursed member states for some of the costs involved in introducing and implementing such measures. The Fund did not have any controlling capacity, however, as the transfer of money to the member states' employment services was quasi-automatic. And, in contrast to its original objective of rectifying specifically Italian problems after the opening up of market borders, it tended to be the best funded and best organized domestic labour market administrations who received most of the money (Germany, for example). It was this anomaly in the system that prompted the first major reform of the ESF in 1971. This involved an agreement on the definition of target groups, and the co-funding of only those domestic projects considered appropriate from a Community perspective. After a number of further reforms, the ESF now co-finances projects for young people seeking employment, for the long-term unemployed, for disadvantaged groups, and for promoting gender equality in the labour market. The aim is to improve people's 'employability' through strategic long-term programmes (particularly in regions lagging behind), to upgrade and modernize workforce skills and to foster entrepreneurial initiative.

In addition to the Social Fund, other EU Funds also seek to combat regional and social disparities (see Chapter 18). These are the European Regional Development Fund, the European Agricultural Guidance and Guarantee Fund (Guidance Section) (see Chapter 21), and the Financial Instrument for Fisheries Guidance. Additionally, the Cohesion Fund finances environmental projects and trans-European infrastructure networks in member states whose gross domestic product (GDP) is less than 90 per cent of the EU average. Finally, the European Adjustment Fund for Globalization aims to help workers made redundant as a result of changing global trade patterns to find another job as quickly as possible. It became operational in 2007 with €500 million a year at its disposal, but at least during the initial period fewer applications than expected were submitted by the member states' authorities.

In sum, the EU's social dimension is less regulatory than is often assumed. For 2006, the financial perspective heading on 'structural operations' claimed 31.6 per cent of the of EU's general budget (CEC 2006: 50). Finally, the steering effect of the EU's labour market policy is much stronger than the ESF figures indicate. The latter display only the EU's part of the overall project budgets. The impact of the EU's criteria for project selection is greater than this, since national authorities also apply them, with the prospect of European co-funding in mind (in order to get national contributions back from Brussels). Moreover, the relative importance of EU funding has increased at a time of national spending cuts.

> ## KEY POINTS
>
> - The Treaty of Rome established a European Social Fund. Its aims are narrower than its name suggests as they concern only labour market policy and mostly target specific regions.
>
> - The ESF co-funds projects and programmes in the member states. It has had, since 1971, its own priorities for funding, with a certain steering effect on national policies, as national governments want a share of the EU budget to flow back into their country.

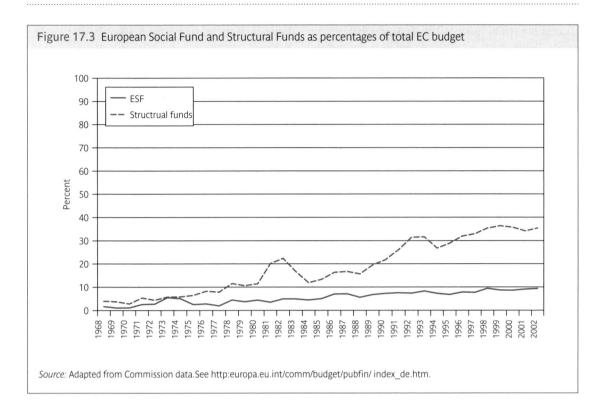

Figure 17.3 European Social Fund and Structural Funds as percentages of total EC budget

Source: Adapted from Commission data.See http:europa.eu.int/comm/budget/pubfin/ index_de.htm.

New developments: the Open Method of Coordination

If the legislative or regulatory track of EU social policy seems to have comparatively less importance by now, this is not due to any significant slowdown in legislative proposals, but because of a new (often called a 'softer') style of intervention known as the Open Method of Coordination (see de la Porte and Pochet 2002; Chapter 13). Thus the EU has a novel role as a motor and, at the same time, as a constraint on national, social, and structural reform (see Goetschy 2002).

The main features of the Open Method of Coordination were developed (initially without Treaty basis) in the field of employment policy, as a follow up to the Essen European Council of 1994. The Amsterdam Treaty's employment chapter later formalized it. Every year since, the EU has adopted employment policy guidelines. Their specification and implementation is left, however, to the national level so that the domestic situation and party political preferences can be taken into consideration. All the same, member states must present regular reports on how they have dealt with the guidelines, and why they have chosen particular strategies in their 'National Action Plans'. They have to defend their decisions at the European level in regular debates on the national employment policy, so that peer pressure comes into play and has, at least potentially, a harmonizing effect on social policies in Europe.

The open method of coordination has recently been extended to new fields, including pension reform, social inclusion, and education. To date, its success is hard to judge, as the lack of reliable data on its practical effects in the member states is only slowly being filled (but see Zeitlin and Pochet 2005; Kröger 2008, 2009). In any case, the net effect of this strategy may have been overstated in the early years of its existence, and it will always be difficult to measure since there is no counter-factual basis of comparison at the researcher's disposal (de la Porte and Pochet 2004). It is plausible to expect that the joint policy learning (Sabatier and Jenkins-Smith 1993) and mutual adaptation (DiMaggio and Powell 1991) that result from this approach will have some beneficial effects, and that EU-level obligations, however loosely defined, will help governments to justify reforms domestically that they might otherwise not have dared to enforce for fear of electoral losses. Where national governments are not ready for policy change, however, the National Action Plans may do no more than either restate pre-existing domestic policies or perform a symbolic function (Scharpf 2002). In such cases the EU is helpless, since EU-level harmonization by means of more formal regulation (new laws) is explicitly ruled out under the open method.

KEY POINTS

- The Open Method of Coordination is a new EU-level approach that has been developed as an alternative to regulation.

- It is based on European guidelines, national action plans, national reports using common indicators, and uses EU-level evaluations that feed into new policy guidelines.

- The practical effects of the Open Method have not yet been evaluated in a sufficiently systematic way up to the present date, and recent studies draw rather pessimistic conclusions.

Social partnership at European level

Contemporary Community social policy making is characterized by a style that some call 'Euro-corporatism' (Gorges 1996). This involves intense cooperation between public and private actors in the EU's social dimension. Corporatism is a way of making policy that includes not only public actors, but also interest groups as decisive co-actors (Streeck and Schmitter 1991; see also Chapter 12). There is general agreement that EU social policy since Maastricht has been characterized by the entanglement of governmental negotiations in the Council and collective bargaining between the major economic interest group federations. As a consequence, the rather particular, closed, and stable policy network in EU social policy may be defined as a 'corporatist policy community' (Falkner 1998).

The legislative procedure in EU social policy now works as follows: when the Commission consults on any planned social policy measure, European-level employer and labour groups may inform the Commission of their wish to initiate negotiations on the matter under discussion in order to reach a collective agreement. This process brings standard EC decision making (see Chapter 13) to a standstill for nine months. If a collective agreement is signed, it can, at the joint request of the signatories, be incorporated in a Council decision on the basis of a prior Commission proposal.

Since 1992, bargaining on social policy issues has therefore been pursued in two quite distinctive arenas, though the two are nevertheless interdependent. The traditional pattern of social policy making is dominated by the Council and its working groups (see Chapter 9), although the adoption of a directive demands a Commission proposal and action by the European Parliament (EP), depending on the specific procedure at stake. The interests represented by politicians and bureaucrats involved are predominantly territorial (in the Council) and party political (in the EP). In this 'intergovernmental arena' for

EU social policy, negotiations proceed according to the detailed rules about decision taking that are specified in the EC Treaty. These are complemented by informal rules that have resulted from decades of EC negotiation practice.

A second, quite different, arena now surrounds negotiations between management and labour. Here procedures are not prescribed in the Treaties, which only contain provisions about 'interface situations' where the intergovernmental procedure and collective bargaining meet, notably specifying the rules on bringing to a standstill standard decision processes, or initiating Council negotiations on implementation. Since the Treaty did not even specify who 'labour and management' should be, this was decided informally. Moreover, the Commission and the Council did not designate the European interest groups as responsible for carrying out the collective negotiations, even if in practice they approved the special status of the Union of Industrial and Employers' Confederations of Europe (UNICE, since 2007 renamed BusinessEurope), the European Centre of Enterprises with Public Participation (CEEP) and the European Trade Union Confederation (ETUC) as the responsible cross-sectoral social partners. These three groups, who wanted and received the leading role in 'negotiated legislation' (Dølvik 1997) on European social policy had already participated in a 'social dialogue' with the Commission since the mid 1980s. When parental leave, the first issue to be discussed under the Social Agreement, was under consideration, the Commission stopped the standard legislative processes on the request of these groups and considered it appropriate to implement the agreement that resulted in a binding directive. Smaller interest groups, excluded from this process, complained about this, but the legal action taken by the Union of Small and Medium Sized Enterprises (UEAPME) was rejected by the ECJ. Thereafter, both BusinessEurope and ETUC have concluded cooperation agreements with smaller groups on the European social dialogue, while ultimately keeping their negotiation prerogatives intact.

Yet it is important to underline the point that the social partner negotiations on social policy issues are by no means entirely independent of the intergovernmental arena. There is intense contact and a large degree of interdependence amongst all relevant actors in social policy at the EU level, that is amongst the Council, the social partners, the Commission, and, to a lesser extent, the EP. To date, three legally binding, cross-sectoral collective agreements on labour law issues have been signed (see Table 17.1) and were implemented in directives (Falkner 2000a): on parental leave (December 1995); on part-time work (June 1997); and on fixed-term work (March 1999).

A number of other negotiations failed to reach agreement, for example on the issue of temporary agency work; or were not initiated, such as on fighting sexual harassment and on information and consultation of employees in national enterprises. Recently, further agreements were concluded or are being negotiated that the social partners (above all, industry) want to be non-binding and/or implemented in accordance with the procedures and practices specific to individual countries, rather than by a directive.

This can be interpreted as a move away from social partner agreements on effective minimum standards that are applicable throughout the EU. At the sectoral level, however, there are a couple of more recent agreements with subsequent binding directives, for example, on working time in various industries.

> **KEY POINTS**
>
> - Since Maastricht, EU social policy has involved a 'corporatist policy community'.
>
> - The organized interests of labour and industry are free to collectively agree social standards that are later made binding in Council directives.
>
> - On the cross-sectoral level, they have done so in three cases, but have failed or have settled for less binding recommendations in others.

Table 17.1 EU-level social partner agreements (cross-sectoral)

year	Agreements Implemented By Council Decision; Monitored By The Commission	Autonomous Agreements; Implemented By The Procedures and Practices Specific To Management and Labour And The Member States; Implementation And Monitoring By the Social Partners
2007		Harassment and violence at work
2004		Work-related stress
2002		Telework
1999	Fixed-term work	
1997	Part-time work	
1995	Parental leave	

Source: Author's compilation on basis of various EU sources.

Conclusion

The preceding sections have indicated that European social policy has been considerably extended and differentiated over time. Treaty bases have been revised several times to extend the range of competences. The ESF has increased its resources, and has had a practical impact on national employment promotion projects. The number of social directives has also increased over time, with the 1990s being the most active decade so far. It should also be mentioned that the ECJ has been influential on a number of social policy issues and, at times, has significantly increased the practical impact of EU social law. The equal treatment of women in the workplace and the protection of worker interests when enterprises change hands are two important examples (Leibfried and Pierson 2000). Most recently, however, controversial cases like Viking and Laval (whose consequences will only be visible in the years to come) have touched the borderlines between the market freedoms and basic social rights such as union action (see Chapter 11).

When judging social policy developments at the EU level, at least four different evaluation criteria seem worth considering (Falkner 2000b). First, the closing of a number of gaps in labour law, introduced or widened by the Single Market Programme, was a major task for EU social policy (Barnard 2000: 62). According to this indicator, the EU performed much better than most experts expected during the early 1990s and all important gaps are now closed. Second, a somewhat more far-reaching criterion for judging EU social law is the differential between Commission proposals and Council legislation. There was a huge gap during the late 1980s and early 1990s, which has been almost completely filled. Even some of the most controversial projects, on sexual harassment in the workplace and on employee consultation in the European Company Statute, have been adopted.

A third indicator of the scope of the EU's social dimension is action taken to prevent reductions in national social standards, potentially induced by the increased competitive pressures of the single market and the Economic and Monetary Union (sometimes called social dumping). One possibility to prevent this from happening would have been to agree on fluctuation margins, which would have stopped any individual country from gaining competitive advantages through lowering social standards. However, such proposals were thought realistic in only a small number of member states, notably Belgium, France, and Germany (Busch 1988; Dispersyn et al 1990). At the level of the Social Affairs Council there was little support. Finally, a fourth evaluation criterion might be the rather small extent to which the EU has forged a truly supranational social order.

In any case, a full evaluation of the success of existing European social law is restricted by the lack of knowledge about its practical effects in the member states. One comparative study of 90 cases of domestic adaptation performance across a range of EU social directives (see Falkner, Treib, Hartlapp and Leiber 2005) has revealed that there are major implementation failures and that, to date, the European Commission has not been able to perform its control function adequately. While all countries are occasional non-compliers, some usually take their EU-related duties seriously. Others frequently privilege their domestic political concerns over the requirements of EU law. A further group of countries neglects these EU obligations almost as a matter of course. Extending this kind of analysis to new member states from Central and Eastern Europe shows that EU standards all too often remain a 'dead letter' (Falkner et al 2008).

Finally, the enlargement of the European Union makes the adoption of joint regulation more difficult, as social policies and preferences differ even more widely in the enlarged EU than they did before. At the same time, common social standards will be of even more importance in the current context of increased competitive pressures in the enlarged market plus a financial and economic crisis.

QUESTIONS

1. Why did the evolution of a 'social dimension' lag behind the market integration aspects of European integration?

2. Why is the treaty base so important for EC social law?

3. What are the main areas of EU social law?

4. To what extent is EU social policy a regulatory policy?

5. How does the European Social Fund influence national policy?

6. What is the Open Method of Coordination and what are its merits in the field of social policy?

7. To what extent is EU social policy corporatist?

8. Which criteria are best used for evaluating the development of the EU's social dimension?

GUIDE TO FURTHER READING

- De Búrca, G., De Witte, B., and Ogertschnig, L. (eds) *Social Rights in Europe* (Oxford: Oxford University Press, 2005). An excellent and recent collection of essays on EU social policy.

- Falkner, G., Treib, O., Hartlapp, M., and Leiber, S. *Complying with Europe. EU Minimum Harmonization and Soft Law in the Member States,* (Cambridge: Cambridge University Press, 2005). This book examines the implementation of six social directives (on, for example, working time, parental leave, part-time work) in 15 member states.

■ Falkner, G., Treib, O., and Holzleithner, E. (with Causse, E., Furtlehner, P., Schulze M., and Wiedermann, C.) *Compliance in the Enlarged European Union: Living Rights or Dead Letters?* (Aldershot: Ashgate, 2008). This book studies the implementation of three EU social and anti-discrimination directives in Central and Eastern European countries.

■ Kröger,s. (ed.) 'What We Have Learnt: Advances, Pitfalls and Remaining Questions of OMC Research' (European Integration Online Papers (EIOP): Special Issue 1(13), 2009). An excellent account of current debates on the Open Method of Coordination.

■ Shaw, J. (ed.) *Social Law and Policy in an Evolving European Union*. (Oxford/Portland: Hart, 2000). An excellent collection of essays on EU social policy.

■ Zeitlin, J. and Pochet, P. (with Lars Magnusson) (eds) *The Open Method of Coordination in Action: The European Employment and Social Inclusion Strategies* (Brussels: PIE-Peter Lang, 2005). This edited book offers insights from various fields of the Open Method.

WEBLINKS

● http://ec.europa.eu/social/ The home page of the European Commission's Directorate-General for Employment and Social Affairs provides up-to-date information on all fields of European social law and policy.

● http://ec.europa.eu/employment_social/social_dialogue/index_en.htm The European Commission's Social Dialogue website.

● http://www.eiro.eurofound.ie/ The 'European industrial relations observatory online' is an excellent source of information on all social dialogue issues, be they at national or EU level.

● http://europeangovernance.livingreviews.org/ The 'Living Reviews in European Governance'(LREG) are an innovative e-journal, publishing solicited state-of-the-art articles in the field of European governance research that will always be kept up to date by their authors.

● http://eiop.or.at/erpa/ The European Research Papers Archive (ERPA) is a common access point for currently nine high-quality online working paper series in the field of European integration research (including, for example, that of the European University Institute). Hundreds of articles can be searched and the full text read for free. 'Social policy' is one the key areas covered.

 Visit the Online Resource Centre that accompanies this book for lots of interesting additional material. http://www.oxfordtextbooks.co.uk/orc/Cini_Borragan3e/

18

Regional Europe

MARCO BRUNAZZO

Chapter Contents

- Introduction
- The origins and development of EU regional policy
- The 2007 reform and beyond
- Regional participation in EU policy making
- Channels for regional representation in Brussels
- Conclusion

Reader's Guide

This chapter examines the effect that European integration has had on regions. It does so by focusing on two aspects. Firstly it addresses the development of the EU regional or cohesion policy, with a focus on the main policy objectives, instruments, and actors involved. Secondly, the chapter outlines the participation of Europe's regions in European governance, both at the European Union (EU) level and within the member states. Thus the chapter describes the main institutional channels for regional representation within the EU, such as the Committee of the Regions (CoR) and the presence of certain regions in the EU Council, as well as the channels created by the regions themselves such as Brussels-based regional offices and interregional associations.

Introduction

The need to address regional disparities across member states has been one of the main challenges facing the European Union (EU) since the early years of integration. While the Treaty of Rome addressed this issue, it was the Single European Act (SEA) that set in motion the development of coordinated Community and national measures to meet the objective of economic and social cohesion. The Maastricht Treaty brought about further changes to regional policy by creating a new Cohesion Fund, which was designed to reduce regional disparities even further, and the Committee of the Regions (CoR), set up to represent regional authorities at the EU level. The Treaty also incorporated the principle of subsidiarity as a way of ensuring that decisions would henceforth be taken as closely as possible to the citizen (see Box 18.1).

Later policy reforms continued the trend initiated in the 1980s, reinforcing the effect of European integration in shaping the relationship between regions, national governments, and EU institutions by granting subnational authorities an increasingly influential role in regional development. As this chapter will show, the transfer of further policy competences to the EU level and the creation of institutionalized channels that involve regional and local authorities have led to a growing presence of the European regions in Brussels. At the same time the impact of Europeanization (see Chapter 25) has fostered a process of devolution in several member states and has contributed to the strengthening of the role of regions in national arenas. This process has affected all member states despite differences in territorial organization and the diverse meaning of the term 'region' in different national contexts (Loughlin 2004 and Box 18.2).

This chapter is organized around three main sections. In the first section, European regional policy is described together with the main stages of policy development and its rationale. In the second section, the chapter focuses on the 2007–13 reform that was a response to the EU's eastward enlargement and which incorporated Lisbon Agenda targets into the policy. The third section outlines the channels for regional participation in European Union policy making, both in Brussels and within the member states, with special attention to the Committee of the Regions, the presence of regions in the EU Council, and the role of regional offices and interregional associations.

 KEY CONCEPTS AND TERMS 18.1

The principle of subsidiarity

The principle of subsidiarity regulates the exercise of powers in the European Union. It is based on the idea that decisions must be taken as closely as possible to the citizen. Subsidiarity was introduced into the Maastricht Treaty as the result of pressure from regions such as the German Länder which saw in the principle a guarantee of their regional autonomy. For member states such as the UK, the principle would potentially limit the Union's ability to intervene and thus further encroach on national sovereignty.

According to Article 5 EC:

The Community shall act within the limits of the powers conferred upon it by this Treaty and of the objectives assigned to it thereto.

In the areas which do not fall within its exclusive jurisdiction, the Community shall take action, in accordance with the principle of subsidiarity, only if and insofar as the objectives of the proposed action cannot be sufficiently achieved by the Member States and can therefore, by reason of the scale or effects of the proposed action, be better achieved by the Community.

Any action by the Community shall not go beyond what is necessary to achieve the objectives of this Treaty.

The principle of subsidiarity was further elaborated in a Protocol on the application of the principle, attached to the Treaty of Amsterdam. For the first time the Lisbon Treaty gives national parliaments direct powers to enforce the principle of subsidiarity. The Treaty sets out how national parliaments can decide whether EU legislation complies with the principle of subsidiarity.

KEY CONCEPTS AND TERMS 18.2

Region

A 'region' refers to the institutional level immediately below the level of the state. A region can be either a political institution, with a directly elected assembly and a more or less powerful regional government, as in Germany or Italy, or an administrative institution, with no legislative powers, fiscal autonomy, or representation at national level, such as in certain Central and Eastern European (CEE) member states. A region can also be conceived of as a functional space whose institutions are directly involved in territorial development planning and implementation, or as a cultural space, characterized by the presence of ethic or linguistic movements, as it is the case of the Basque Country, Catalonia, Wales, or Flanders.

The origins and development of EU regional policy

This section considers the aims and evolution of EU regional policy.

Origins and development

The principal aim of EU regional policy is that of reducing regional economic and social disparities across European states and regions. Territories within the EU have varying levels of wealth, unemployment, and capital income. The wealthiest of the EU's regions are generally located within the geographical line that links London to Milan and then follows the Rhine River. The poorest regions are mainly situated in the periphery of the EU, particularly in Central and Eastern Europe (CEE), Southern Italy, Southern Spain, Portugal, and the northern regions of Sweden and Finland. Attempts to reduce disparities across the Union and thus avoid any negative effect on the development of the common market have been in place throughout the history of European integration.

Even in the Rome Treaty the six founding member states declared that they were 'anxious to strengthen the unity of their economies and to ensure their harmonious development by reducing the differences existing between the various regions and the backwardness of the less favoured regions' and fostering in so doing 'a harmonious and balanced development of economic activities' throughout the Community (Article 2 EC). The Rome Treaty established three instruments that addressed issues of regional imbalance: namely (1) the European Social Fund (ESF), which was set up to sustain and improve mobility in the European labour market through education and requalification initiatives for workers in areas experiencing industrial decline; (2) the European Investment Bank (EIB), which was established to fund projects in the less developed areas; and (3) the Guidance section of the European Agricultural Guidance and Guarantee Fund (EAGGF), which provided support for underdeveloped rural areas (see Chapter 21).

However, it took several years for the Community to implement coordinated decisions aimed at achieving this goal. The reason for this was that while there was a common commitment to remedy regional disparities, the then member states agreed that *national* measures rather than *Community* intervention were best suited to bridge regional differences. Moreover, there was broad consensus that once the common market was created, it would provide the development conditions that would ultimately increase the wealth of the least developed regions. However, these predictions were overly optimistic, not least because the accession of Denmark, the UK, and Ireland in 1973 exacerbated regional disparities. As Gilbert notes:

> OECD figures for 1970 show clearly how Britain has slipped behind the Six in economic terms. British Gross National Product (GNP), which in 1950 had been two-thirds as large as the collective product of the Six, was now less than one-quarter. GNP per head, which had been almost exactly double that of the Six in 1950 ... had declined to three-quarters of the average of the Six.

(Gilbert 2003: 123).

Even so, the UK became a net contributor to the Community budget upon accession and the British government, facing a domestic public opinion sceptical about the benefits of European integration, requested partial economic compensation (Bache 1998: 37). The Community responded by creating the European Regional Development Fund (ERDF) in 1975. The main objective of the ERDF was to promote industry and infrastructures and thus address the problem of unequal development across regions. However, the ERDF achieved only modest results for three main reasons: because it was considered a compensation measure for net contributors to the Community budget rather than an instrument for regional development; because its budget (around 5 per cent of the Community budget in the early years) was too limited to reduce regional disparities significantly; and because the Council of Ministers was in charge of defining the budget on the basis of national quotas, without targeting regions that were lagging behind in terms of development (Bourne 2007: 294–5).

The accession of Spain and Portugal in 1986 doubled the number of European citizens living in regions with a per capita GDP lower than 50 per cent of the Community average. This situation was regarded as a problem by some member states, especially in light of the greater economic integration envisaged by the Single European Act. Thus Greece, Italy, and France, with levels of production comparable to those of the applicant countries, threatened to veto the enlargement to Spain and Portugal if the European Community (EC) failed to protect their agricultural production. To address these concerns, the Commission created the Integrated Mediterranean Programmes (IMPs), a seven-year budgetary commitment to regional economic development in Greece, Italy, and Southern France. The IMPs incorporated the main provisions that would later, in 1988, become the core of EU cohesion policy, such as the leading role of the Commission and the active involvement of regional actors (Leonardi 1995; Hooghe 1996b; Heinelt 1996). In 1986 the SEA established regional policy as a Community competence and social and economic cohesion as a Community goal. Article 130a (now Article 158 EC) established, for the first time, a link between cohesion and the reduction of regional disparities, by stating that 'in order to promote its overall harmonious development, the Community shall develop and pursue its actions leading to the strengthening of its economic and social cohesion. In particular the Community shall aim at reducing disparities between the various regions and the backwardness of the least-favoured regions'. The SEA outlined a number of measures to remove the structural conditions of underdevelopment across European regions through the coordination of the economic policies of the member states (where the Commission is in charge of controlling and giving incentives). It set in place a broader and more operational definition of Community regional policy extending beyond the sectoral logic of most interventions to date; and instructed the Commission to reform the objectives and implementation of the three Structural Funds, namely the ERDF (which was given a treaty base), the ESF, and the guidance section of the European Guidance and Guarantee Fund (EAGGF) (see Box 18.3).

The 1988 reform

A fully fledged cohesion policy was not created until 1988, when the Brussels European Council of that year agreed policy reforms proposed by the European Commission. This reform, known as the Delors-1 package, was aimed at improving the efficiency of

KEY CONCEPTS AND TERMS 18.3

The Structural Funds

The *European Regional Development Fund* (ERDF) finances infrastructure, job-creating investments, local development projects and aid for small firms.

The *European Social Fund* (ESF) promotes the return of the unemployed and disadvantaged groups to the workforce, mainly by financing training and systems of recruitment.

The *'Guidance' section of the European Agricultural Guidance and Guarantee Fund* finances rural development measures and aid for farmers, mainly in regions lagging in development.

The Cohesion Fund was set up in 1993 to provide assistance to the poorest EU member states (those with a GNP per capita below 90 per cent of the EU average), allowing them to finance major projects in the field of environment and transport.

regional policy. It also provided an important increase in regional funding, by doubling the Structural Funds commitments, which by 1992 would amount to 25 per cent of the total EC budget.

The concept of cohesion had two dimensions: the economic dimension concerned with the reduction of economic regional imbalances; and the political dimension, which pointed to a greater involvement of subnational institutions in Community policy making (Hooghe 1996a: 6–7). The new policy was based on the idea that a reduction in territorial disparity was possible only if subnational institutions, and specifically regions, were involved in decision-making and implementation processes, as they were the targets of Community interventions. This new 'integrated approach' aimed to create a common regional policy based on pluriannual programmes. The latter were focused on specific objectives and were managed in close cooperation by the Commission, the national governments, and subnational institutions. Allocations would be based on five principles: programming, concentration, additionality, partnership, and evaluation (see Box. 18.4).

It was clear to the European Commission, which had been charged with drafting the new policy, that not all regional institutions had the means to achieve these goals. For that reason, the Commission promised that it would promote all possible initiatives 'to align agents before the race starts' (Bailey and De Propris 2002: 409). At the same time, however, it also became clear to the Commission that involving regional actors in decision making would help strengthen its own position in this specific policy area as a broker of agreements between the actors involved (Ansell et al 1997; Hooghe 1996a). It is not surprising then that the Commission became an important advocate of regional policy reform.

The 1993 reform

The 1993 reform was framed by the need to address member states' concerns about the operation of the funds (particularly in view of the substantial financial commitment agreed in 1988), the consequences of the coming into force of the Maastricht Treaty, and the likely enlargement to include Finland, Sweden, and Austria (which would take place in 1995). The Maastricht Treaty set the scene for the construction of the Economic and Monetary Union and confirmed the centrality of cohesion policy as a means of reducing socio-economic disparities among the European regions whilst easing the structural constraints that might otherwise impact upon the adoption of the single currency. It also introduced a new generous financial instrument, the Cohesion Fund, to assist those *member states* (not regions) with a GDP lower than 90 per cent of the EU average. This was also intended to help states meet the EMU convergence criteria. This decision followed a threat by Spain, Portugal, Greece, and Ireland to veto the Treaty unless a financial instrument was established to help less developed countries facing serious difficulties in fulfilling the single market criteria. The new Treaty confirmed the basic provisions of the 1988 reform as well as new measures to increase transparency, simplify fund allocation procedures, and specify the role of national governments, subnational institutions, and the European Commission in light of the

KEY CONCEPTS AND TERMS 18.4

The five functioning principles of EU cohesion policy

Programming: Structural Funds will be deployed within programmes: that is to say, the funds will be allocated within a multi-annual framework, based on socio-economic analysis, and on a clear strategy with priorities and objectives. Since 1988, these programmes are prepared by the regions and/or member states and submitted for screening and negotiation to the European Commission, which subsequently adopts them.

Concentration: The largest proportion of EU funds is to be allocated in regions affected by specific problems, for example regions whose development is lagging behind. Five priority objectives have framed the distribution of funding. Only three of these objectives have had an explicit regional dimension:

- Objective 1: aimed at regions with a GDP per capita below 75 per cent of the EU average.

- Objective 2: aimed at converting regions seriously affected by industrial decline and where the unemployment level is above the EU average.

- Obective 5a: funded by the EAGGF (see Box 18.3) and targeting the adjustment of agricultural structures.

Additionality: Co-financing of the programmes by all the actors involved, in particular the EU and the national governments.

Partnership: Refers to the close consultations that take place between the Commission, the member state concerned, and the competent authorities designated by the latter at national, regional, or local level, with each party acting as a partner in pursuit of a common goal.

Evaluation: Documents and activities connected to the funds are evaluated in order to improve their quality, efficiency, and the coherence of their intervention.

---

subsidiarity principle. The TEU also created the Committee of the Regions (CoR), a new consultative institution representing regions and local authorities, which was to report on issues of Structural Fund allocation and implementation (see below).

New territorial challenges in view of the Union's enlargement to include Finland, Sweden, and Austria led to the EU having to address the issue of the least populated areas of Europe—in Scandinavia—for the first time. Hence a new Objective 6 for developing sparsely populated Nordic regions was introduced at this time, while part of Austria gained Objective 1 status (see Box 18.4 on the Objectives).

The 1999 reform

The 1999 reform was also framed by the EU's commitment to support the accession of the Central and Eastern European countries, and the introduction of EMU. As with previous reforms, enlargement prompted changes to regional policy, allowing for the accommodation of new members whose levels

of wealth were considerably lower than those of the EU15 (see Table 18.1). Agenda 2000 outlined the EU's reform plan for addressing the challenge of such a large-scale enlargement. It incorporated proposals to reform regional policy which would enable it to strike a balance between the needs of existing member states and the accession of new members. Crucially it did not foresee increasing spending on the Structural Funds but rather focused on the stabilization of total expenditures. The Commission proposed further concentration in terms of fund allocation and another simplification of procedures. In line with this latter recommendation, the number of objectives was to be reduced to three (thus reducing the coverage of the Structural Funds) and eligibility rules were to be tightened, with a new efficiency principle being added to the existing five principles (referred to above). A greater role was to be delegated to domestic actors in the implementation and monitoring of programmes, thus reducing the Commission's sphere of action and conferring on national and subnational governments a greater room for manoeuvre (Hooghe 2002; Sutcliffe 2000).

Table 18.1 The link between enlargement and reform of the Structural Funds Policy

Enlargement	Reform
1973: Britain, Denmark, and Ireland's accession.	1975: European Fund of Regional Development.
1981: Greece's accession.	1985: Integrated Mediterranean Programmes.
1986: Spain and Portugal's accession.	1988: First Reform of Cohesion Policy.
1995: Austria, Finland, and Sweden's accession.	1993: Second reform of Cohesion Policy; the Cohesion Fund.
1998: Negotiations with CEE countries start.	1999: Third reform of Cohesion Policy.
2004 and 2007: 12 new CEE countries join the EU.	2007: Fourth reform of Cohesion Policy.

KEY POINTS

- Addressing regional disparities has been a long-term challenge of the EU.

- The Treaty of Rome outlined the principles that favoured the creation of a coordinated regional policy.

- The evolution of the regional policy has been characterized by tensions between the need to develop European coordination and the interests of member governments.

- Five principles defined cohesion policy: additionality, partnership, concentration, programming, and evaluation. Efficiency was later added to this list.

The 2007 reform and beyond

The 2007 reform of the cohesion policy is best explained as a process of adaptation to the EU's eastern enlargement and the goals of the Lisbon Agenda, and as an attempt to simplify and decentralize the policy. The reform suffered from the long bargaining process between the Commission and national governments that took place over the adoption of a new 'Financial Perspective' for 2007–13. This negotiation determined how much the EU would allocate to structural and cohesion funding over this period. The Council finally allocated €308 billion (0.37 per cent of the Gross National Income of the EU27) to cohesion policy, 10 per cent less than the initial Commission proposal asked for.

As of 2007 three new (or revised) objectives have defined cohesion policy: convergence; regional competitiveness and employment; and European territorial cooperation. The convergence objective points to the fact that cohesion policy must involve the promotion of economic growth in the regions whose development is far lower than the EU average. This is based on the Commission's Objective 1 experience (see Box 18.4) and the lessons learnt from the operation of the Cohesion Fund. In addition to the Objective 1 criteria, however, this new principle also highlights innovation and knowledge-based society, adaptability to social changes, environmental quality, and administrative efficiency. The convergence objective is supported by the ERDF, the ESF, and the Cohesion Fund.

The aim of the second objective, regional competitiveness and employment, is to strengthen the attractiveness of regions to direct investment and to help to improve employment rates. It brings together the

Table 18.2 Indicative financial allocations for 2007–13 Cohesion Policy (€ million, 2004 prices)

	Convergence objective			Regional Competitiveness and Employment objective		European Territorial Cooperation objective	Total
	Cohesion Funds	Convergence	Statistical Phasing out	Phasing in	Regional Competitiveness and Employment		
Austria			177		1,027	257	1,461
Belgium			638		1,425	194	2,258
Bulgaria	2,283	4,391				179	6,853
Cyprus	213			399		28	640
Czech Republic	8,819	17,064			419	389	26,692
Denmark					510	103	613
Ireland				458	293	151	901
Estonia	1,152	2,252				52	3,456
Finland				545	1,051	120	1,716
France		3,191			10,257	872	14,319
Germany		11,864	4,215		9,409	851	26,340
Greece	3,697	9,420	6,458	635		210	20,420
Hungary	8,642	14,248		2,031		386	25,307
Italy		21,211	430	972	5,353	846	28,812
Latvia	1,540	2,991				90	4,620
Lithuania	2,305	4,470				109	6,885
Luxembourg					50	15	65
Malta	284	556				15	855
Netherlands					1,660	247	1,907
Poland	22,176	44,377				731	67,284
Portugal	3,060	17,133	280	448	490	99	21,511
Romania	6,552	12,661				455	19,668
Slovakia	3,899	7,013			449	227	11,588
Slovenia	1,412	2,689				104	4,205
Spain	3,543	21,054	1,583	4,955	3,522	559	35,217
Sweden					1,626	265	1,891
United Kingdom		2,738	174	965	6,014	722	10,613
Interregional/ Network Cooperation						445	445
Technical Assistance							868
Total	69,578	199,322	13,955	11,409	43,556	8,723	347,410

Note: The figures having been rounded off, the total might not correspond.

Source: http://ec.europa.eu/regional_policy/sources/docgener/informat/pdf/nsrf_cover_en.pdf.

objectives established for the previous Objective 2 (economic and socially backwards regions) and Objective 3 (concerning training systems and employment policies). For 2007–13, development programmes in this category should anticipate and promote economic change through innovation, knowledge-based society, entrepreneurship, protection of environment, and the improvement of regional accessibility. Moreover, by investing in human resources, they should help the workforce adapt to new economic conditions. These programmes grant transitional support to regions previously covered by Objective 1, but whose GDP exceeds 75 per cent of the EU average. A total of 168 regions and 314 million people are covered by this Objective, and the phased-in support concerns regions in 19 member states.

Finally, the Objective for European territorial cooperation supports cross-border cooperation through joint initiatives by local and regional authorities, whilst at the same time fostering interregional cooperation and an exchange of experience. A total of 37.5 per cent of the EU population (that is to say, 181.7 million people) live in border regions, and the Commission has identified 113 transnational cooperation areas. Three programmes have been established to support this Objective: Interact, which encourages organizations involved in cooperative programme management; Urbact, which is a thematic city network; and ESPON (an observation network for spatial planning.

As Table 18.2 demonstrates, 81.5 per cent of all financial allocations are devoted to the convergence objective; 16 per cent supports the regional competitiveness and employment objective; and 2.5 per cent is allocated to the European territorial cooperation objective. In absolute terms, the member states who have benefited most from this assistance are Poland, Spain, Italy, Czech Republic, Germany, and Hungary. The reform further confirmed the principles of intervention defined for the 2000–6 period (programming, additionality, evaluation, partnership, and concentration), but also adopted a number of changes by widening the scope of the partnership principle to include civil society organizations. Moreover, a new proportionality principle was

defined in order to relate the member states' obligations to the total amount of expenditure on an operational programme. Finally, the new cohesion policy is now strictly linked to other EU policies such as the Common Agricultural Policy (CAP) and the Common Fisheries Policy. And cooperation with non-EU countries is no longer part of cohesion policy (as was the case during the previous accession process), as two new initiatives, the European Neighbourhood and Partnership Instrument (ENPI) and the Instrument for Pre-Accession Assistance (IPA) provide funds to that end. The reform did not substantially change the role of the Structural Funds, but three new instruments were introduced to help regions and member states manage their funds.

With regard to the Structural Funds, the ERDF is devoted to the promotion of public and private investment helping to reduce regional disparities across Europe. It supports programmes on regional development, economic change, enhanced competitiveness, and territorial cooperation. Its main priorities are infrastructure investment, especially in regions where development is lagging behind, but also research, innovation, environmental protection, and risk prevention.

The ESF is implemented according to the European Employment Strategy and addresses four main areas: increasing adaptability of workers and enterprises; enhancing access to employment and participation in the labour market; strengthening social inclusion by fighting discrimination and facilitating access to the labour market for disadvantaged people; and promoting partnership for reform in the fields of employment and inclusion.

Finally, the Cohesion Fund is focused on interventions related to the environment and trans-European transport networks in the member states with a GNI of less than 90 per cent of the Community average (mainly the new member states, Greece and Portugal, and, on a transitional basis, Spain). Finally, the three new instruments to help member states and regions to manage funds more effectively and to make good use of the financial resources given by the EIB and by other financial institutions are:

- JASPER (Joint Assistance in Supporting Projects in European Regions), which aims to support cooperation between the European Commission, the EIB, and the ERDF in order to pool expertise and to assist member states and regions in the preparation of major projects.

- JEREMIE (Joint European Resources for Micro and Medium Enterprises) which is promoted by the Commission, the EIB, and the European Investment Fund in order to increase accessibility to EU funds for micro, small, and medium-size enterprises.

- JESSICA (Joint European Support for Sustainable Investment in City Areas), which coordinates the efforts of the Commission, the EIB, and the Council of Europe's Development Bank in the field of sustainable investment in urban areas.

While it is too early to evaluate the impact of this new round of reform, it is, in the context of an enlarged EU, possible to identify some tension between the Lisbon Agenda goals and increased territorial diversity. Key factors informing any final assessment will be the ability of new member states to absorb funds and whether the new reform has really managed to simplify procedures.

KEY POINTS

- The 2007 reform responds to the challenges of EU enlargement and the need to meet the Lisbon Strategy goals.

- After the 2006 reform, cohesion policy had three new objectives: convergence; regional competitiveness and employment; and European territorial cooperation.

- The principles of intervention—namely, programming, additionality, evaluation, partnership, and concentration—have been confirmed and a new proportionality principle has been added to these principles.

- It is too early to evaluate the impact of this latest stage of reform.

Regional participation in EU policy making

The development of cohesion policy has been an essential factor in the mobilization of regions in Brussels. The role assigned to regions in programming and implementing Community programmes has provided them with new competences and has fostered the Europeanization of state systems, although there remains substantial national variation. Within the EU's institutional structure, the European Commission has traditionally been supportive of regional mobilization at the EU level for a number of reasons. First, by being closer to the citizens, regions may be able to bridge the gap between the EU and its citizens and thus help address the democratic deficit. Second, regions can help to communicate better the benefits of EU membership to citizens. Finally, by introducing new actors into the policy-making process, thereby pushing for new intergovernmental alliances and more complex bargaining and agreements, the Commission can counterbalance the influence of the member states (Keating 1998: 172–7). For example, in the 2001 White Paper, the Commission recognized the need to 'organize a systematic dialogue with European and national associations of regional and local government, while respecting national constitutional and administrative arrangements … The principal responsibility for involving the regional and local level in EU policy remains and should remain with national administrations' (European Commission 2001: 12 and 13). This reflects the tension between the Commission's aim to involve regions to a greater degree and the national governments, who in a formal sense remain autonomous when deciding how their states are organized and—where member states are centralized—how their regions participate in European-level activities.

In their turn, and particularly since the mid 1980s, regions have developed a sort of 'foreign policy' towards the EU that displays distinctive features with regard to the framing of issues and their objectives, and makes it different from the kind of diplomacy pursued by national governments (Keating 1998). On issue framing, the region's economic agenda at the EU level is very specific, as it focuses on trying to attract more investment (especially Community funds) and broadening markets via agreements with other regions. Regions with strong territorial identities, nationalistic claims and difficult relations with their central governments seek to internationalize their position so as to find consensus and support for their aspirations of independence or greater autonomy. Regions lacking a strong identity can boost their international profile in this way.

With regard to their objectives, the goals pursued by regions tend to be more specific and focused than those of governments, as they do not really have competences in traditionally defined foreign policy (such as the power to declare war). Similarly, on global economic issues, regions' goals tend to be much more short term than those of the member states. And a region's international agenda is more permeable to specific territorial interests. Business associations, for instance, may push regional governments towards specific alliances or encourage them to follow a particular objective, while at the national level interests are more diverse and dispersed. Finally, institutional factors affect the regions' external outlook more than for the member states. For example, regions with a greater autonomy vis-à-vis the centre (as in the case of federal states) are better placed to construct and promote their interest than weaker ones.

> **KEY POINTS**
>
> - The roles assigned to regions in programming and implementing Community programmes have provided them with new competences.
>
> - The Commission recognizes the need for dialogue with European and national associations of regional and local government, while respecting national constitutional and administrative arrangements.
>
> - Regions have developed a sort of 'foreign policy' towards the EU, which differs from member state diplomacy.

Channels for regional representation in Brussels

European regions have at their disposal several channels of access to EU policy making. These channels differ in relation to their source of legitimacy, as the regions' right to participate in EU policy making may derive from EU legislation or from the application of national law. Access to EU governance is also affected by whether access to EU institutions is direct or occurs through the member states. It is possible to distinguish between direct channels where regions have direct contact with EU institutions, as in the case of the Committee of the Regions, for example; and indirect channels where the national government plays a mediating role across regions and Community institutions (see Table 18.3).

Even though these channels are available to all regions of the EU, the situation still varies from state to state. This variation is more evident in the case of mediated access legitimated by the national government (Table 18.3, cell D), where there are specific legal variations depending on national tradition and operational variations, dependent on how the relationship between state and region is regulated. In the case of direct access with European legitimacy

Table 18.3 Channels for access of regions to the EU

		(Main) Source of legitimacy	
		European	National
Access	Direct	(A) Committee of the Regions	(B) Regional offices, inter-regional associations or networks
	Mediated	(C) EU Council	(D) Consultation of regions by representatives of national governments in Brussels

(Table 18. 3, cell A) national differences as well as the composition of delegates sent to the Committee of the Regions varies from one member state to another; in the case of direct access with national legitimacy (Table 18.3, cell B) the variation is based on the different legal status of regional offices based in Brussels. Mediated access with European legitimacy (Table 18.3, cell C) is relevant mainly to federal systems where one may even find regional politicians with competences allowing them to represent the national government in the EU Council.

The main institutional channel for regional participation in EU policy making is the Committee of the Regions. The CoR is an advisory body that brings together representatives of local and regional authorities. Created in 1994 by the Maastricht Treaty, its main tasks are to give local and regional authorities a voice in EU governance and to help bring the EU closer to its citizens by involving the levels of government located nearest to them. The Treaties require that the Commission and the Council seek the CoR's advice whenever new legislative proposals, which have regional and/or local implications, are initiated. This is particularly the case in relation to economic and social cohesion, trans-European networks in the field of transport, energy and telecommunications, public health, education and youth, culture, employment, social policy, environment, and vocational training. Since it is an advisory body, the CoR's opinion can, however, be ignored by other institutions.

The CoR has 344 members (approximately reflecting each member state's population). Members are appointed for four years by the EU Council. They are selected according to national provisions, but, as Article 263 of the Treaty of Nice establishes, they 'should be required to be elected members of a regional or local authority or be politically accountable to an assembly by direct universal suffrage'. Federal states select most of their representatives from the regional level. Thus the Austrian delegation has 12 members, nine of whom represent the Länder. By contrast, smaller or more centralized states nominate members from cities or municipalities. For instance, the Estonian delegation includes four members from the Association of Estonian Cities as well as three from the Association of Rural Municipalities. In member states with a limited degree of devolution, there is usually a balance between regional, provincial, and municipal representatives. For instance, the French delegation is composed of 12 regional delegates, six representatives of the *départements* and six delegates from the municipalities.

Overall, the CoR represents a broad range and variety of interests. This is often considered an obstacle to the smooth and effective operation of the institution (Christiansen 1996; Christiansen and Linter 2005). In this context, the process of enlargement, which has substantially increased the CoR's membership, making the diversity of interests even broader, inevitably increases the expectation of a growing degree of conflict within the Committee. However, to date, there is little evidence of this having occurred (Brunazzo and Domorenok 2008).

The participation of regions in meetings of the EU Council was introduced in the Maastricht Treaty

(Article 203). It establishes that each state has a seat in the Council for a 'representative at ministerial level'. This means that a minister of a regional government may substitute for a minister of the national government in these meetings. This was a proposal that the German government advanced and strongly defended following a request from the German Länder. The latter feared that in the post-Maastricht period, the Community institutions and the Federal Government would reduce their powers. Even if this norm of ministerial substitution is mainly applied in the case of federal states such as Germany, Austria, and Belgium, it has also been used on occasions by Spain and the UK. However, it should be noted that when acting within the Council, regional representatives are expected to represent the national rather than their own regional interest.

Regional offices are an additional channel of regional participation in EU policy making. There are more than 250 of them, with their number having increased steadily as the EU's competences have grown. They are organized in representations that are directly responsible to the regions and are an integral part of the regional governance structures. The regional offices vary in terms of number of staff, appointment mechanism, function, and scope. The tasks they perform include lobbying community institutions, gathering useful information for the regional actors they represent, promoting visibility of the region at the European level, the informal exchange of information with other regions, and the organization of visits to Brussels (Marks et al 1996: 186–9). However, it is very difficult to assess how effective the regional offices are.

Since the 1970s, European regions and localities have cooperated in creating multiple associations and networks. There are two main types of cooperation agreement: those with a representative task and those with a functional task. The first group comprises cooperation agreements aimed either at promoting or defending broad regional interests. Examples include the Assembly of European Regions (AER), the Council of European Municipality and Regions (CEMR), the Congress of Local and Regional Authorities (CLRA), or Eurocities. Associations with a functional role include those representing territories with similar geographical features such as the Conference of Periphery Maritime Regions (CPMR). Other functional associations represent the richest territories of the EU. This is the case for the Four Motors for Europe, comprising Lombardy, Catalonia, Rhône-Alpes, and Baden-Württemberg, whose activities mainly involve an exchange of experience and knowledge on topics of common interest, the implementation of common projects, and lobbying at the EU level.

An essential part of the involvement of regions in European governance is their participation in national decision-making processes where these involve EU policies. In federal states, the national government has to consult regions on any decision on EU matters that might impinge on their competence. In Germany, Article 23 of the Basic Law (the so-called 'Europe Article'), the Act on Cooperation between the Federation and the Länder in European Union Affairs, and the Federation-Länder Agreement of 29 October 1993 establish the right of the Länder to participate in EU affairs. They participate through the Bundesrat, whose statements are binding for the federal government, particularly where EU proposals affect the Länder's legislative power. Forms of dialogue between national and subnational institutions have also been created in more centralized countries. In Italy, the State–Regions Conference (Conferenza Stato–Regioni) meets twice a year in order to define an Italian position on EU matters involving regional interests. In France, regions participate through the French integrated bureaucracy, by linking local and national policy makers (Keating and Hooghe 2006: 274–5).

KEY POINTS

- Regions can access EU policy making through both institutionalized and ad hoc channels at the national and EU levels.

- The Committee of the Regions, regional representations, and regional associations and networks are the main channels of regional presence in Brussels.

- Dialogue between national governments and regions are becoming the norm across the EU.

Conclusion

Territorial disparities are a major challenge facing the EU. Back in 1957 a common belief was that the market would foster positive effects on the economies of the member states, which would in turn solve the backwardness of certain regions. But the reality proved to be much more complex. The need to develop coordinated action to address this common problem explains the willingness of the member states to pool sovereignties at the EU level and to accept the substantial financial burden demanded of the promotion of economic and social cohesion. Similarly the need for coordinated action explains the leading role of the Commission in this policy field, while the importance of drawing on expertise from the bottom up explains the increasing role afforded to regions and localities in European governance. However, this process begs the question: what does the involvement of Europe's regions in European governance tell us about the EU? As Le Galès and Lequesne (1998: 263–7) point out, regional presence is not a synonym for regional influence, and this fact of life makes it very difficult to establish the actual impact of regional actors on EU governance. But their mere presence reveals itself as yet another example of the EU as a system of multi-level governance, where complex formal and informal processes intermingle, bringing in a range of actors at different institutional levels and to various degrees. In other words, the EU is not only a 'matter of states'; yet neither is there a 'Europe *of* the regions', since regions have not replaced national governments and their role often remains peripheral (as the case of the CoR shows). Therefore it may be more appropriate to define the EU as a 'Europe with the regions' or, given the differing impact of Europeanization (see Chapter 25), as a 'Europe with (certain) regions'.

? QUESTIONS

1. Why does the EU need a regional policy?

2. Why have subsequent enlargements been important for the development of EU regional policy?

3. What is the economic justification for cohesion policy reforms?

4. What does the term 'cohesion' mean?

5. What is the role of the Commission in regional policy?

6. What makes regional diplomacy different from that of national governments?

7. What are the main channels of regional access to EU policy making?

8. Is the EU becoming a 'Europe of the Regions'?

GUIDE TO FURTHER READING

- Aldecoa, F. and Keating, M. (eds) *Paradiplomacy in action: the foreign relations of subnational governments* (London: Routledge, 1999). This volume provides a good overview of the growing subnational involvement in foreign affairs.

■ Bache, I. *The Politics of European Union Regional Policy: multi-level governance or flexible gatekeeping*? (Sheffield: Sheffield Academic Press, 1999). This book provides a review of the key developments in the politics of EU regional policy to 1988.

■ Bache, I. and Fliders, M. *Multi-level Governance*, (Oxford, University Press, 2005). This collection discusses the key concept of multi-level governance.

■ Hooghe, L. and Marks, G. *Multi-level Governance and European Integration* (Lanham, Rowman & Littlefield, 2001). The book explains the emergence of multi-level governance and how it shapes conflict in national and European political arenas.

■ Leonardi, R. *Cohesion Policy in the European Union: The Building of Europe* (London, Palgrave Macmillan, 2005). This volume assesses the implementation of the EU's cohesion policy in Eastern and Southern Europe before 2004 enlargement.

 WEBLINKS

● http://ec.europa.eu/regional_policy/   This is the website covering the European Union's regional policy. It contains information about reports, programmes, in-depth analysis, and official documents.

● http://cor.europa.eu/   The Committee of the Regions website offers up-to-date information on CoR activities, official documents, and declarations.

● http://www.aer.eu/   The Assembly of European Regions (established 1985) is the largest independent network of regions in Europe. The website contains information about AER activities, publications, member regions.

● http://epp.eurostat.ec.europa.eu/pls/portal/url/page/PGP_DS_REGION/PGE_DS_REGION_1   The Eurostat regional statistics site covers the principal aspects of economic and social life in the European Union, including demography, economic accounts, and labour market data.

 Visit the Online Resource Centre that accompanies this book for lots of interesting additional material. http://www.oxfordtextbooks.co.uk/orc/Cini_Borragan3e/

19 Justice and Home Affairs

EMEK M. UÇARER

Reader's Guide

This chapter looks at one of the most recent European policies, Justice and Home Affairs (JHA). JHA comprises policy areas such as immigration and asylum, and police and judicial cooperation, some elements of which are found in the EU's third pillar (see Chapter 3). The chapter focuses first on the early years of cooperation in this policy area, and includes an introduction to the Schengen Agreement. It then reviews the procedural steps taken first by the Maastricht Treaty (1993) and then at Amsterdam (1999) and subsequent institutional developments culminating in the Lisbon Treaty. The second half of the chapter concentrates on policy output, again looking at steps taken at Maastricht and Amsterdam, but also in the landmark Tampere European Council meeting and the Hague Programme. It argues that although steps have already been taken to Europeanize JHA policy, this field continues to be characterized by intergovernmentalism. Moreover, given the inherent tensions in the policy, numerous challenges remain to be resolved.

Introduction

Justice and Home Affairs cooperation has undergone a remarkable ascent from humble beginnings to a fully fledged and vibrant EU policy. JHA is one of the newest additions to the EU mandate. It seeks to engage the EU in the fields of immigration and asylum policy, police and judicial cooperation. Because of the sensitive nature of the issues involved, cooperation has been slow and difficult. However, it has resulted in a body of policies that apply across the EU's internal and external borders, and which have locked previously inward-looking national authorities into a multilateral process. This involved significant political compromise,

which has led to the introduction of a complicated mix of communitarized and intergovernmental institutional procedures peculiar to this field. The EU is now developing a complex immigration and asylum regime, and is also making some progress on police and judicial cooperation. Particularly after the conclusion of the Amsterdam Treaty, the EU's capacity to reach collective and binding decisions in the JHA field has improved considerably, creating momentum towards further cooperation and increasing concerns about the creation of a 'Fortress Europe' into which access is increasingly restricted.

Preludes to cooperation

If in the late 1960s government ministers responsible for home affairs and justice had been told that they would soon need to consult with fellow European ministers while formulating policies on immigration, asylum, judicial, and police matters, they would no doubt have found this a very unlikely and undesirable prospect. Yet, during the 1980s and 1990s, issues falling within the mandate of interior and justice ministries have increasingly become of collective EU concern, provoking efforts to deal with them at the European, rather than exclusively at the national, level. Beginning in the mid 1970s and gathering momentum in the 1980s, immigration, asylum, police, and judicial cooperation increasingly appeared on the collective political agenda. This led to the creation of new, overlapping forums within which these issues could be discussed (see Box 19.1).

There were two broad sets of catalysts that drove this development. The first was the consequences of increased cross-border movements into and across Europe. After the Second World War, Western Europe became an area of immigration. Cross-border movements increased, straining border

patrols and causing delays at points of entry. With this rise came growing concerns about transnational crime, which could proliferate because of weak border controls and a lack of effective communication among European national law enforcement agencies. The second catalyst was the revitalization of the European integration agenda after the signing of the Single European Act (SEA) in 1986 (see Chapter 3). The removal of internal EU border controls had been written into the 1957 Treaty of Rome, even though this had not been fully realized by the early 1980s. With this goal back on the agenda, attention turned to the need to create external Community borders and to develop common and coherent rules on access. Early efforts targeted three groups: the citizens of the EC/EU whose freedom of movement within the Community was to be secured; long-term EU residents of third countries, that is non-EU citizens who had relocated to the EU and who held residence and work permits; and third-country nationals (TCNs), including labour migrants and refugees seeking to enter the collective territory of the EC/EU. Early efforts to cooperate were launched not by the EU but by the Council of Europe (CoE),

---

CASE STUDY 19.1

Catalysts for early cooperation in Justice and Home Affairs matters

Linked to immigration:

- Increase in cross-border movements between West European countries.

- Increase in labour and family unification migration into West European countries.

- Increase in applications for asylum.

- Concerns about cross-border organized crime.

Linked to the European integration project:

- Undesirable impacts of delays at borders on economic activities.

- Desire to complete the creation of the Single Market by gradually removing controls at the Union's internal borders.

- Recognition of the necessity to develop common measures to apply to the external borders before doing away with controls at the internal border.

---

whose membership comprised both East and West European countries. Judicial matters were raised often at CoE meetings. But while the CoE's work was path breaking, the drawbacks of its processes, including slow and modest lowest common denominator policy output, were also clear.

With the shortcomings of the CoE in mind, member states set up the 'Trevi Group' in 1975 as an informal assembly to deal with cross-border terrorism through closer cooperation among EC law enforcement authorities. Trevi was really a loose network rather than an institution, and the meetings concluded in non-binding consultations on organized international crime, including drug and arms trafficking. Subsequently, several other groups were established, including the Judicial Cooperation Group, the Customs Mutual Assistance Group, and the Ad Hoc Groups on Immigration and Organised Crime. These groups

spanned the four policy clusters that were gradually becoming Europeanized, namely immigration policy, asylum policy, police cooperation, and judicial cooperation.

KEY POINTS

- Cooperation in JHA was not foreseen in the Treaty of Rome.

- The Council of Europe (a non-EC institution) was the main forum for the discussion of JHA issues, but it worked slowly and its output was meagre.

- The Trevi Group was set up in 1975 as a loose network within which terrorism might be discussed at European level. It led to the setting up of similar groups in related areas.

The Schengen experiment

Perhaps the most ambitious project of these early years was what became known as Schengen. In 1985, a number of EC member states decided to do away with border controls. This was formalized in the 1985 Schengen Agreement and later the 1990

Schengen Implementation Convention. Belgium, the Netherlands, Luxembourg, Germany, France, and Italy thus created a new system that would connect their police forces and customs authorities. They also created the Schengen Information System

(SIS), an innovative, shared database that stored important information (such as criminal records and asylum applications), and which was accessible by national law enforcement authorities. Schengen's primary objective was to develop policies for the Community's external borders and which would eventually remove the EC's internal borders. This was an ambitious goal and the United Kingdom, Ireland, and Denmark remained extremely sceptical. Despite the fact that the Schengen compromise involved only some member states, Schengen became a model for the EC (and later the Union) as a whole.

Within the Schengen framework, significant progress was made in each of the four emergent areas of cooperation. With respect to asylum, Schengen instituted a new system for assigning responsibility to review asylum claims to one state in order to stop multiple asylum applications and reduce the administrative costs of processing duplicate asylum claims. Schengen also provided the groundwork for an EU-wide visa policy through a common list of countries whose citizens would need an entry visa. Uniform Schengen visas were intro-

duced for the Schengen territory. There was a more modest start in judicial cooperation, with easing extradition procedures between member states. Finally, Schengen involved cooperation on law enforcement, particularly involving drug trafficking. However, since most of this work fell outside the framework of the EC decision-making structure, it was conducted away from the scrutiny of the general public and their elected representatives (see Box 19.2).

KEY POINTS

- The 1985 Schengen Agreement was a commitment by a subset of EC member states to remove controls at their internal borders.

- Steps were taken by the Schengen members to agree on common rules on their external borders, for example with regard to visa policy.

- For those countries involved, Schengen allowed national civil servants in these fields to become accustomed to European-level cooperation.

 KEY CONCEPTS AND TERMS 19.2

What is Schengen?

Named after the small Luxembourg border town where a subset of the member states of the then EC resolved to lift border controls, the Schengen system is considered a path-breaking initiative to provide for ease of travel between member states. In 1985, France, Germany, and the Benelux countries signed the first Schengen Agreement and were later joined by nine other EU members, bringing the total number of participating states to 15. The Schengen accords sought to remove controls on persons, including TCNs, at their internal borders while allowing member states to reintroduce them only under limited circumstances. Member states agreed to develop common entry policies for their collective territory, issue common entry visas to entrants, designate a responsible state for reviewing asylum claims, and jointly combat transnational crime. They also created a novel

database—the Schengen Information System, or SIS—to exchange information between the member states on certain categories of individuals and property. As the original SIS was designed to interlink at most 18 countries, a new version, SIS II, is being developed in 2009, made necessary by the enlarged EU. The current 25 Schengen countries are Austria, Belgium, Czech Republic, Denmark, Estonia, Finland, France, Germany, Greece, Hungary, Iceland, Italy, Latvia, Lithuania, Luxembourg, Malta, Netherlands, Norway, Poland, Portugal, Slovakia, Slovenia, Spain, Sweden, and Switzerland. Three of these countries (Norway, Switzerland, and Iceland) are not members of the EU. Two European Union countries (the UK and Ireland) are not part of the Schengen system, though they have recently chosen to opt-in on an issue-by-issue basis. Bulgaria, Cyprus, Liechtenstein, and Romania have opted-in but implementation is still pending.

Maastricht and the 'third pillar'

The early 1990s represented an intensification of these efforts and a shift in the locus of decision making towards the European institutions. With the coming into force of the Treaty on European Union (TEU) in 1993, JHA was brought under the auspices of the EU, forming the third pillar of the Union. The TEU identified the following areas of 'common interest': asylum policy rules applicable to the crossing of the Union's external borders; immigration policy and the handling of TCNs; combating drug addiction and drug trafficking; tackling international fraud; judicial cooperation in civil and criminal matters; customs cooperation; police cooperation to combat and prevent terrorism; and police cooperation in tackling international organized crime. The Treaty also created a new institutional home for the groups that had been set up in earlier decades, and created a decision-making framework. However, this new JHA pillar was the product of an awkward inter-state compromise. In the run-up to Maastricht, while a majority of member states supported bringing JHA matters into the Union, they remained divided over how this should be done. Some argued that JHA should be handled within the first pillar, as a supranational policy. Others were uncomfortable with handing control over to the European institutions in such a sensitive field and preferred to keep JHA as a largely intergovernmental dialogue.

Title VI of the Maastricht Treaty reflected the institutional consequences of this political compromise. With the third pillar, the Treaty established an intergovernmental negotiating sphere that marginalized the Community institutions, particularly the European Commission, within the JHA decision-making process. This third pillar set-up diverged significantly from standard decision making in the EC (see Chapter 13). The key decision-taking body became the JHA Council. The European Commission's usual function as the initiator of European legislation (see Chapter 8) was diminished by its shared right of initiative in JHA (Uçarer

2001). The role of the European Parliament did not extend beyond consultation, a situation that led to accusations that JHA exemplified the Union's democratic deficit (see Chapter 23). The European Court of Justice, the body that might have enhanced the accountability and judicial oversight of policy, was excluded from jurisdiction in JHA matters (see Chapter 11).

Although bringing JHA into the EU was an important step, critics of the third pillar abounded. Two sets of interrelated criticisms were advanced. Critics lamented the lack of policy progress in the post-Maastricht period. Indeed, what little was accomplished after 1993 seemed to relate to policies that had already been in progress before Maastricht. The problem was that the post-Maastricht institutional arrangements were ill equipped to handle the projected or indeed the existing workload falling under JHA. The decision-making framework was cumbersome, with the often non-binding policy instruments necessitating long-drawn-out (and potentially inconclusive) negotiations. All decisions in the third pillar had to be reached unanimously and this led to deadlock. And when unanimity was reached, the result was often a lowest common denominator compromise that pleased few. Negotiations continued to be secretive and the EP remained marginalized. This was particularly problematic at a time when the Union was trying hard to improve its image vis-à-vis its citizens.

> **KEY POINTS**
>
> - The Maastricht Treaty, which came into effect in 1993, created a 'third pillar' for JHA.
>
> - The institutional framework put in place was intergovernmental and cumbersome and was subject to much criticism in the mid 1990s.

Fixing the third pillar: from Amsterdam to Lisbon

In the run-up to the 1999 Amsterdam Treaty, proposals for reforming JHA included enhanced roles for the Commission, EP, and ECJ; the elimination of the unanimity rule; and the incorporation of the Schengen system into the EU. As with Maastricht, there was a fierce political debate over these issues.

The challenge was to make the Union 'more relevant to its citizens and more responsive to their concerns', by creating 'an area of freedom, security and justice (AFSJ)' (Council of the European Union 1996). Within such an area, barriers to the free movement of people across borders would be minimized without jeopardizing the safety, security, and human rights of EU citizens. The compromise reached at Amsterdam led to three important changes. First, parts of the Maastricht third pillar were transferred to the first pillar, or 'communitarized'. Second, the institutional framework for issues that remained within the third pillar was streamlined. And third, the Schengen framework was incorporated into the Union's *acquis*.

New first pillar issues under Amsterdam

The insertion of Title IV into the Treaty was the most significant development at Amsterdam with respect to JHA matters. This brought a number of third pillar issues into the first pillar. These provisions, captured in Articles 61–4 of the Amsterdam Treaty, called for the Council to adopt policies (within five years of the entry into force of the Treaty, by 1 May 2004) to ensure the free movement of persons within the EU, whilst concurrently implementing security measures with respect to immigration, asylum, and external border controls. Article 67 specified new decision-making rules. For the first five years after the entry into force of the Amsterdam Treaty, a transition period

was foreseen, during which time unanimity was required in the JHA Council following consultations with the EP. The Council would act on a proposal from the Commission or a member state, the latter retaining their shared right of initiative. In other words, the Maastricht decision rules were to remain in place. After five years, however, the Commission would gain an exclusive right of initiative. And while the EP's access to the decision-making procedure would still be limited to consultation in most cases, an automatic shift to the codecision procedure, which would give the EP much more of a say, was foreseen in the area of uniform visa rules and the procedures for issuing visas. The ECJ would receive a mandate for the first time, allowing it to interpret Title IV and to undertake preliminary rulings in policy areas falling within the first pillar, in response to requests by national courts (see Chapter 11). Despite these improvements, however, the new Amsterdam architecture turned out to be a formidable maze created through masterful 'legal engineering' for political ends and opaque for even seasoned experts (European Parliament 1997).

The left-over third pillar: cooperation in criminal matters

The Amsterdam reforms left criminal matters in the third pillar. The amended Title VI included combating crime, terrorism, trafficking in persons and offences against children, illicit drugs and arms trafficking, corruption, and fraud. The Treaty envisaged closer cooperation between police forces, customs and judicial authorities, and with Europol (see below), seeking an approximation of the criminal justice systems of the member states as necessary.

While the new Title VI essentially retained the intergovernmental framework created at Maastricht, the Commission obtained a shared right of initiative for the first time, an improvement over its pre-Amsterdam position. The EP gained the right to be consulted, but that was all. The Treaty constrained the ECJ in a similar fashion in that it recognized the jurisdiction of the Court to issue preliminary rulings (see Chapter 11) on the instruments adopted under Title VI, but importantly it made this dependent on the assent of the member states. While the Commission, Parliament, and Court were to continue to struggle to play an active role in the third pillar, the Council retained its dominant decision-making function, and unanimity remained the decision rule used in third pillar legislation.

Absorbing Schengen

After much debate, Schengen was incorporated into the EU by means of a protocol appended to the Amsterdam Treaty. The Protocol provided for the closer cooperation of the Schengen 13 (that is, the EU 15 minus Ireland and the United Kingdom) within the EU framework. With this development, cooperation on JHA matters became even more complicated, involving various overlapping groupings. There were those EU members that agreed to be bound by the Amsterdam changes (the EU 12): Denmark chose to opt out, and the United Kingdom and Ireland would remain outside unless they chose to opt in. Moreover, there were actually 15 signatories to the Schengen agreement (the Schengen 15), of which 13 were EU members and two were not (Iceland and Norway). The two members of the EU that remained outside the Schengen system, the United Kingdom and Ireland, decided to take part in some elements of Schengen, including police and judicial cooperation. Of the 12 countries that subsequently joined the EU in 2004 and 2007, nine joined the Schengen area fully in 2007. Another non-EU country, Switzerland, partially joined Schengen in December 2008. This makes for quite a complex system: of the current 25 members, 22 are EU members and three (Iceland, Norway, and Switzerland) are not. Three current EU members (Bulgaria, Romania, and Cyprus) and one non-EU country (Liechtenstein) are in line to join. Two current EU members (United Kingdom and Ireland) remain outside the Schengen area and three European non-EU microstates (Monaco, San Marino, and Holy See) are de facto Schengen members because they maintain open borders with their neighbours. In essence, the incorporation of Schengen into the acquis communautaire did not result in desired simplification, but rather maintained, if not amplified, the convoluted system that emerged in the early 1990s. Not surprisingly, some now regard JHA as the ultimate example of a multi-speed or à la carte Europe.

The Treaty of Nice made few substantial changes to the institutional developments highlighted above. Perhaps the biggest change was the extension of a shared right of initiative for the Commission in the otherwise intergovernmental left-over third pillar.

'Normalizing' JHA: the Constitutional Treaty and the Lisbon Treaty

The Convention on the Future of Europe and the 2003–4 IGC, culminating in the October 2004 signing of the Constitutional Treaty (CT), marked the next stage in JHA reform. Leading up to this, a far-reaching overhaul of the JHA field was recommended by the Convention's working party on JHA, which proposed the 'normalization' of JHA by abolishing the pillar structure. Greater use of qualified majority voting (QMV) was proposed to overcome problems in decision making, although unanimity would still need to be retained for judicial and police cooperation in criminal matters. The final text of the CT reflected many of these proposals and eliminated the pillar structure. It retained the shared right of initiative for the Commission and the member states in judicial cooperation in criminal matters but foresaw proposals coming from coalitions composed of at least 25 per cent of the membership of the Union. While the Convention proposed an extension of the use of QMV in judicial cooperation, it qualified this with an additional mechanism through which a member state in significant opposition to the Council could suspend negotiations. These were all efforts to streamline the decision-making process whilst preserving a diminished capacity for member states to block decisions. The CT further provided for a role for national parliaments to monitor the implementation of JHA policies and for a judicial review of compliance by the ECJ. Finally, the Constitution retained the British and Irish opt-ins, and the Danish opt-out.

However, the CT was stalled when it was rejected in referendums in France and the Netherlands. The JHA provisions were later given a new life in the Lisbon Treaty, signed on 13 December 2007. The Lisbon Treaty contains all of the major innovations pertaining to JHA that were present in the Constitutional Treaty and underscores the salience of AFSJ by placing it ahead of EMU and the CFSP in the Union's fundamental objectives. The Lisbon Treaty also incorporates the Prüm Convention (sometimes referred to as Schengen III; see Box 19.3) into the *acquis communautaire*. The Lisbon Treaty also foresees jurisdiction for ECJ to enforce all JHA decisions apart from provisions adopted under the post-Amsterdam Third Pillar. This is subject to limited jurisdiction for a transitional period of five years, after which jurisdiction is to extend to all prior legislation. The EP will operate with codecision authority in almost all cases. However, the Lisbon Treaty's transformative provisions were also brought about by compromises. Opt-outs and opt-ins remain for Denmark, the United Kingdom, and Ireland. The Treaty also provided for 'enhanced cooperation' among pioneer groups of at least nine member states in the current third pillar (see Table 19.1). These concessions are criticized as moving further towards a multi-speed Europe. Nonetheless, if ratified by the current 27 members, the Lisbon Treaty would represent the most significant reform of JHA poised to rectify vexing institutional problems that were created by Maastricht.

KEY POINTS

- The Amsterdam Treaty sought to address the shortcomings of the third pillar by bringing immigration and asylum as well as judicial and police cooperation in civil matters into the first pillar.

- The third pillar, cooperation in criminal matters (police and judicial cooperation), remained intergovernmental.

- Schengen was incorporated into the Treaty, but this did not result in simplification given the overlapping memberships involved in this Agreement.

- The Nice Treaty added few changes to the Amsterdam set-up and extended a right of shared initiative to the Commission in the third pillar.

- The Lisbon Treaty is the most significant reform of JHA to date. It makes important strides in normalizing this policy domain in the aftermath of the failed CT. However, the Treaty cannot be implemented until all member states ratify it.

Policy output: baby steps to bold agendas

There have been several spurts of policy since the beginnings of JHA cooperation, building on the early pre-Maastricht efforts but gathering momentum after Maastricht and Amsterdam. More recently, in addition to making progress on the four main dossiers (immigration, asylum, police cooperation, and judicial cooperation), the EU has acknowledged the importance of the external dimension of JHA, and has embarked on attempts to export its emergent policies beyond the Union.

Table 19.1 Justice and Home Affairs Co operation: from Trevi to Lisbon

	Pre-Maastricht JHA	Post-Maastricht third pillar Title VI TEU Article K	Post-Amsterdam first pillar (Communitarized areas of former third pillar) Immigration, Asylum, Police and Judicial Cooperation in Civil Matters Title IV TEC, Articles 61–69		Post-Amsterdam third pillar (non-communitarized areas of former third pillar) Police and judicial cooperation in criminal matters Title VI TEU Articles 29–42	Lisbon Treaty (not yet ratified) Title IV TEC, Articles 61–69 Consolidated pillars
			1999–2004	Post–2004		
European Parliament	No role	Limited role, restricted to consultation	Consultation	Codecision	Consultation	Codecision
European Court of Justice	No jurisdiction	No jurisdiction	Referral for an obligatory first ruling for national last-instance courts		Preliminary rulings on the validity and interpretation of framework decisions and decisions, on the interpretation of conventions established under Title VI and on the validity and interpretation of the measures implementing them.	Will acquire jurisdiction to enforce all JHA decisions—provisions adopted under the post-Amsterdam third pillar subject to limited jurisdiction for a transitional period of five years. Jurisdiction to extend to all prior legislation thereafter.
Council	No direct role	Dominant actor	Dominant actor but Commission and EP increasingly empowered	Shared power position in decision making	Dominant actor	Shared power position in decision making 'Enhanced cooperation' possible

Commission	Consultative Occasional observer status at intergovernmental meetings	Shared right of initiative for the Commission and member states except judicial and police cooperation matters in which there is no right of initiative	Shared right of initiative (member states have encouraged the Commission to assume an exclusive right for asylum issues)	Exclusive right of initiative	Shared right of initiative (previously not possible)	Exclusive right of initiative except in police and judicial cooperation where the Commission shares its right of initiative with a coalition of at least 25% of EU membership
Decision-making mechanisms	Intergovernmental negotiations Non-binding decisions in the form of resolutions Binding decisions in the form of treaties	Unanimity rule on all issues	Council acts unanimously on proposals from Commission and member states *for the first five years* UK, Ireland, and Denmark not bound unless they choose to opt-in	Council will act unanimously on proposals from the Commission A move towards QMV (except legal migration) UK and Ireland retain opt-in, Denmark retains opt-out	Council acts unanimously on proposals from Commission and member states	QMV for most decisions Denmark has opt-out on judicial cooperation Opt-ins continue for UK and Ireland

Note: This covers asylum policy, the crossing of the external borders of the EU, immigration policy and the handling of third country nationals, combating drug addiction and trafficking, tackling international fraud, judicial cooperation in civil and criminal matters, customs cooperation, and police cooperation to combat and prevent terrorism and organized international crime.

Source: adapted and expanded from Uçarer (2001a).

Post-Maastricht developments in policy

After Maastricht, member states first focused on rules to apply to TCNs entering the Union territory. The Council formulated common rules in this area for employment and education, and recommended common rules for the expulsion of TCNs. It also recommended a common format for 'bilateral readmission agreements' (which would allow for the return of TCNs) between member states and third countries. In 1997, an extradition convention was concluded among the EU member states. Agreement was also reached on the format of a uniform visa as well as on a list of countries whose nationals required a visa to enter EU territory. These agreements, which were relatively unambitious, sought to develop comparable procedural steps for the entry, sojourn, and expulsion of TCNs.

Asylum policies were disappointing for some. The most notable development was the conclusion of the 1990 Dublin Convention, an instrument of binding regional international law, which designated one member state as responsible for the handling of an asylum claim. The politically significant London Resolutions introduced the concepts of safe countries of origin and transit into the EU, rejecting applications lodged by the nationals of countries deemed safe or by those who had passed through safe countries en route to EU territory. Refugee rights activists frowned upon these policies as excessively restrictive, and warned that such rules could potentially weaken refugee protection.

During this period, work began on the EURODAC fingerprinting system, which would allow member states to keep track of asylum seekers, as well as on the negotiation of a common framework for the reception of individuals seeking temporary protection status in Union territory. The Maastricht Treaty also took earlier efforts to cooperate in customs, public safety, and cross-border matters further by embarking on the ambitious agenda to create a European Police Office (Europol), a project that was initiated by Germany in 1991 to enhance police cooperation and information exchange in combat-

ing terrorism and the illicit trafficking of drugs and human beings. Based in The Hague, Europol became operational in October 1998. Ministers of the member states also signed an agreement in 1993 to create a European Drugs Unit (EDU) to assist in criminal investigations. Through the EDU, the Union sought to enlist the help of countries considered to be suppliers contributing to the drugs problem, particularly in the Caribbean and in Latin America.

Amsterdam and Tampere

Following the entry into force of the Amsterdam Treaty, progress in JHA cooperation accelerated substantially, aided by the Tampere European Council dedicated exclusively to JHA. The goal of this summit, which was convened in Tampere (Finland) in October 1999, was to take stock of developments to date, evaluate the impact of Amsterdam, and discuss the future direction of JHA cooperation. Policy steps were outlined towards creating an Area of Freedom, Security, and Justice. Included in the 'Tampere milestones' were a reiterated commitment to a common market complete with freedom of movement; the development of common rules for the fair treatment of TCNs, including guidelines for dealing with racism and xenophobia, the convergence of judicial systems, and the fostering of transparency and democratic control. Among the more far-reaching goals were better controls on and management of migration and the deterrence of trafficking in human beings.

On matters of immigration and asylum, Tampere advocated a 'comprehensive approach', closely linked to the combating of poverty and the removal of the political and economic conditions that compel individuals to leave their homes (Van Selm 2002). At Tampere, it was argued that JHA policies should be linked closely to tools of foreign policy, including development cooperation, and economic relations, rather than imagining JHA solely as 'domestic' EU policy. This called for intensified cooperation between countries of origin and transit to address the causes of flight, empowering neighbouring countries to offer adequate protection to those in flight, and speeding up the removal of illegal immigrants from Union territory.

EU member states committed themselves to creating a Common European Asylum System (CEAS), including common standards for reviewing claims and caring for asylum applicants, and comparable rules for refugee recognition. The Commission was designated as the coordinator of policy proposals dealing with asylum. With this new charge, the Commission soon introduced numerous proposals relating to asylum, including policies on reception conditions for refugees, a common set of minimum standards for the review of asylum claims, as well as common family reunification schemes for refugees. The Union also approved the creation of the European Refugee Fund, designed to aid EU recipient states during massive refugee influxes, such as those experienced during the fallout from Bosnia and Kosovo. By this point, the Dublin Convention had taken effect, and the EURODAC fingerprinting system was now functioning. The creation of the CEAS was in progress.

In matters of judicial and police cooperation, still third pillar issues, the creation of a European Judicial Area (EJA) occupied a prominent place at Tampere. The proposed EJA would ensure the mutual recognition of judicial decisions and cross-border information exchange for prosecutions, as well as minimum standards for civil procedural law. With respect to criminal matters, the Council was required to expedite the ratification of the EU Conventions on extradition.

Tampere also created 'Eurojust'. Composed of national prosecutors, magistrates, and police officers, Eurojust would aid national prosecuting authorities in their criminal investigations of organized crime. A European Police College (CEPOL), which would also admit officers from the candidate countries, and a European Police Chiefs Task Force were also planned. Priorities were established for the approximation of judicial and police practices in the member states, with particular regard to money laundering, corruption, euro counterfeiting, drug trafficking, trafficking in human beings, the exploitation of women, the sexual exploitation of children,

and high-tech and environmental crime. Europol was designated as the lead agency in these efforts. Importantly, Tampere also established benchmarks and set deadlines for the accomplishment of its goals, which enlivened the policy process. In December 2000, the draft EU Charter of Fundamental Rights was completed, and there was progress in the mutual recognition of judicial decisions. The Commission developed a framework decision, under the new Title VI, on combating terrorism, and this was adopted on 13 June 2002.

Nonetheless, debate on the numerous items on the agenda after Tampere proved to be protracted. Blame for the delays was variously attributed. While the member states (operating through the Council) blamed the Commission, critics noted that the Council was in no particular hurry to press forward with the adoption of these measures. There was some progress in 2002 on immigration and asylum, through the adoption of a comprehensive plan to combat illegal immigration and to regulate the management of external borders. The Commission tabled new and revised initiatives relating to asylum procedures, on reception conditions for asylum seekers, on the definition and status of refugees, and on a first pillar instrument to replace the Dublin Convention. Still, the Presidency Conclusions issued at the end of the June 2002 Seville European Council called emphatically for a 'speeding up' of work, suggesting continued frustration with the progress made since Tampere.

The Hague Programme

In June 2004, the Commission published an assessment of the Tampere Programme, characterizing the previous five years as a time of progress hampered by the drawbacks of the decision-making rules (European Commission 2004). The next phase in JHA cooperation, the Commission argued, would involve creating an integrated border management system and visa policy, complete with a Visa Information System (VIS) database to store biometric data of visa applicants, a common policy on the management of migration flows to meet economic and demographic needs, and the creation of the EJA. The Hague Programme that was subsequently adopted at the November 2004 Brussels European Council reiterated the call for the abolition of internal border controls soon after the projected launch of SIS II (see Box 19.3). To compensate for the abolition of internal border controls, a recurring theme since the 1970s, the European Council called for the strengthening of external borders to be set forth through the Hague Programme. Of note in the Programme was the affirmation of the move to QMV (except for measures involving legal migration where unanimity continues to apply) and codecision. The Hague Programme called for the implementation of a common asylum system by the year 2010 and the

gradual expansion of the European Refugee Fund to €150 million per year by 2008. The Hague Programme endorsed the Council Secretariat's SitCen, the situation centre which would provide strategic analyses of terrorist threats, and called for the creation of a European External Borders Agency, with the possible creation of a European System of Border Guards. It invited greater coordination on the integration of existing migrants. As for the external dimension of JHA cooperation, the Hague Programme stressed partnership with countries of origin and/or transit and the conclusion of further readmission agreements as necessary (see below). The Hague Programme arguably gave policy making a push, resulting in the adoption of hundreds of texts in 2007 alone.

KEY POINTS

- Since Maastricht, significant policy progress has been made in the fields of immigration, asylum, police, and judicial cooperation, even though policy output has fallen short of initial expectations.

- Policy making focused on developing common rules for travel within and entry into the Union, harmonizing policies offering protection to asylum seekers and refu-

gees, creating better information exchange and cooperation between law enforcement officials, and developing mutual recognition of judicial decisions within the EU.

- The Hague Programme gave policy making a push by calling for the implementation of a common asylum system, and stressed partnership with countries of origin and/or transit.

Extending JHA cooperation outwards

During the initial phases of JHA cooperation, the immediate goal was to lift barriers to the free movement of persons within the EU. As the 1990s progressed, the planned enlargements projected the collective territory outwards, making it necessary to discuss JHA matters with the Union's *future* borders in mind. Member states began, early on, to involve certain third countries in some of their initiatives, attempting to solidify EU border controls by recruiting other countries to tighten their own border controls (Lavenex and Uçarer 2002). This involved entering into collective agreements with countries of

origin and transit. These attempts to recruit neighbouring countries to adopt close variations of the EU's emergent border management regime were particularly pronounced in Central and Eastern Europe (CEE), the Maghreb, and the Mediterranean basin, because of the proximity of these areas to the EU.

EU policies began to radiate out to neighbouring countries, particularly those applying for membership. Schengen countries collectively signed agreements with Poland, Hungary, and the Czech Republic, in which the latter agreed to readmit individuals returned from EU territory. Most CEE countries were declared safe countries of origin and transit, compelling them to accept asylum seekers who had travelled through their territory to get to the EU. At the 1993 Copenhagen European Council, future membership was made conditional upon the rapid incorporation of the EU's JHA *acquis* which, after Amsterdam, also included the Schengen *acquis*. The accession partnerships included an aid component, some of which was tied to the improvement of border controls. The EU assumed an advisory role for policy making in CEE countries, with the aim of helping them develop policies in line with those of the EU (Grabbe 2000). Applicant countries began adopting the EU's JHA policies even if that meant implementing, often at the risk of souring relations, restrictive policies vis-à-vis countries whose citizens previously enjoyed, for example, visa-free access into their own territories. The 2004 and 2007 enlargements included the majority of these accession countries. Turkey and Croatia, which commenced accession negotiations on 3 October 2005, are required to make similar changes in preparation for membership (see Chapter 26).

JHA's external dimension extends further than would-be member countries, however. The EU expects similar adjustments of countries that are not part of the enlargement process. These expectations are situated in the broader setting of the Union's external relations (see Chapters 14 and 15), and, more specifically, have become part of its aid and trade policies. Thus North African, Mediterranean, and African, Caribbean, and Pacific countries are steered towards adopting some of the EU's deflective immigration and asylum policies to ease migratory pressures into the Union by including sending and transit countries in the screening process. To these ends, by 2009 the EU had concluded readmission agreements with Albania, Bosnia and Herzegovina, the Former Yugoslav Republic of Macedonia, Hong Kong, Macao, Montenegro, Moldova, Russia, Serbia, Sri Lanka, and the Ukraine. The Commission has been authorized to negotiate similar agreements with Algeria, China, Morocco, Pakistan, Russia, and Turkey. The Hague Programme further charged the EU to develop EU Regional Protection Programmes in partnership with the third countries concerned. It further asked for a new European Neighbourhood and Partnership Instrument to create a strategic framework for furthering cooperation and dialogue on asylum and migration with neighbouring countries and for initiating new measures. One of the newest initiatives in this vein is the development of the EU Returns Directive (dubbed the Expulsion Directive by its critics), which seeks to lay down common procedures for returning illegally resident individuals to third countries. Developments in October 2005 in the Spanish enclaves of Ceuta and Melilla, where hundreds of sub-Saharan Africans attempted to jump razor-wire fences to gain access to Spanish territory, and were subsequently expelled to Morocco, intensified calls to cooperate with third countries to secure Europe's borders.

The external dimension of JHA is firmly rooted in the effort to develop compensatory measures, as the EU seeks to manage its collective borders. Yet the EU's efforts to extend its strict border controls outwards, by assisting (and in some cases demanding) the adoption of stricter border control measures elsewhere, involves an irony. While the EU attempts to liberalize the freedom of movement within its territory, it does so by applying potentially illiberal policies at its borders and by advocating such policies in its relations with third countries (Uçarer 2001; and see Box 19.3).

KEY POINTS

- JHA cooperation has developed a significant external dimension, particularly vis-à-vis the EU's neighbours.

- The enlargement of the Union not only pushes its borders (and therefore the Area of Freedom, Security, and Justice) eastward, but also commits applicant countries to adopt JHA rules before their accession.

- JHA policy output also has an impact on countries that are not part of the enlargement process.

Fighting terrorism in the European Union

JHA cooperation owes its genesis partly to the efforts of the Trevi Group, whose main goal was to establish cross-border cooperation in the fight against organized crime and terrorism. These matters were subsequently incorporated into the Union under Title VI of the Maastricht Treaty and revised by the Amsterdam Treaty. EU member states authorized the creation of Europol to facilitate the apprehension and prosecution of transborder criminals and established jointly accessible databases to enhance police cooperation. Noting that terrorism 'constitutes one of the most serious threats to democracy, to the free exercise of human rights and to economic and social development', the Commission began work in late 1999 to develop an instrument that would outline the Union's position on terrorism. The instrument was to address not only terrorist acts directed against member states and the Union itself, but also international terrorism.

Following the 11 September 2001 attacks, JHA ministers were called to an Extraordinary EU Council on JHA, held on 21 September 2001. During this and following meetings, EU politicians expressed solidarity with the USA and confirmed their support for the military operations launched in Afghanistan. The events in the USA gave impetus to the EU's efforts to move speedily towards adopting anti-terrorist policies that were already in preparation. Terrorism was defined as 'offences intentionally committed by an individual or a group against one or more countries, their institutions or people, with the aim of intimidating them and seriously altering or destroying the political, economic, or social structures of a country' (European Commission 2001b). In October 2001, the Council expressed its intention to 'fast-track' the Framework Decisions on Terrorism and the European Arrest Warrant, and committed the Union to adopting a common definition of terrorist offences, a common decision on the freezing of assets with links to suspected terrorists, and establishing the European Arrest Warrant, which was designed to replace the protracted extradition procedures between EU member states with an automatic transfer of suspected persons from one EU country to another. The Council urged better coordination between Europol, Eurojust, intelligence units, police corps, and judicial authorities, and announced work on a list of terrorist organizations, which was adopted in 2001 and later updated. The Framework Decision called for increased vigilance for possible biological and chemical attacks, even though such attacks had never previously occurred in the EU. Finally, linking the fight against terrorism to effective border controls, the Council insisted on the intensification of efforts to combat falsified and forged travel documents and visas (European Council 2001). The Framework Decision on combating terrorism and the Framework Decision for the European Arrest Warrant (which included a list of 32 Euro-crimes) were adopted in June 2002.

The attention to anti-terrorism intensified yet further after the 11 March 2004 attacks in Madrid. While no stranger to terrorist attacks from separatist Basque militants, Spain's trauma sharpened the attention to terrorism, which quickly became the primary preoccupation of the JHA field. The EU and its member states subsequently negotiated a number of cross-border initiatives to enhance their collective capabilities to combat terrorism. Among these was the Prüm Convention, signed by Germany, Spain, France, Luxembourg, Netherlands, Austria, and Belgium on 27 May 2005, which enables signatories to exchange DNA, fingerprint, and vehicle registration data to combat terrorism. The possibility that violent acts could be perpetrated by ill-integrated migrants—highlighted by the widely publicized murder of a prominent Dutch film director allegedly at the hands of a Muslim who held dual Dutch and Moroccan citizenship—rekindled the integration debate. Fears about 'home-grown' terrorism hit another high with the 7 July 2005 London bombings, prompting swift condemnation from JHA ministers at an extraordinary ministerial meeting on 13 July 2005.

The Union is working on improving its information exchange infrastructure to help with its anti-terrorism efforts. Along with a second generation Schengen Information System (SIS II), a new EU Visa Information System (VIS) is in preparation. Envisioned with interactive capabilities, these databases will collect and compare information on persons, also targeting anti-terrorism work. SIS II will include additional information to be entered on 'violent troublemakers' (including football hooligans but potentially also political protesters) and suspected terrorists, and would also store biometric information (digital pictures and fingerprints). In turn, the VIS will collect and store data from all visa applications in all member states, including biometric data in the form of digital photos and all ten fingerprints, something that is criticized for potentially falling foul of data protection measures. SIS II and VIS are expected to become operational in 2009.

While the attention directed towards anti-terrorist measures is warranted, the EU's efforts in this field have already attracted criticism from civil liberties and migrants' rights advocates (Statewatch 2001). Activists caution against a possible backlash against migrants of Arab descent and argue against closing the EU's outer doors even more tightly. As in post-9/11 USA, European anti-trafficking measures have attracted sharp criticism from civil libertarians in Europe. The challenge in Europe is similar to that in the USA: developing policy instruments that meet security needs while protecting the civil liberties of individuals residing in the EU territory. The events of 11 September, 11 March, and 7 July seem to have brought JHA cooperation full circle to its Trevi origins. It is certain that this dossier will remain very lively, if controversial, in the future.

Conclusion

JHA cooperation has come a long way since its obscure beginnings in the 1970s. It currently occupies a prominent and permanent position in EU governance. The European Commission now has a more active role in JHA, facilitated by the creation within it of a new JHA Directorate-General. The status of the EP and the ECJ has also improved since Amsterdam and they remain hopeful about the prospects for further institutional gains in the future. Matters discussed within the JHA framework continue to strain the sovereign sensibilities of the EU's member states, and the policy remains intrinsically intergovernmental. However, few believe that the Union can achieve its common market goals without making significant progress in JHA. As the events of 11 September 2001 in the USA and the attacks in Madrid and London clearly demonstrate, the tackling of transborder issues so typical of the JHA dossier demands coordination and cooperation beyond the state. JHA is a young field compared to the other more established competences of the EU. Its birth pangs, as well as the continuing difficulties it faces, are comparable to the state of affairs in, say, environmental policy some decades ago. But the EU must contend with a number of important, and sometimes conflicting, challenges specific to JHA cooperation. In order to lift internal border controls on people moving within the EU, the Union must articulate and implement policies to manage its *external* borders. These policies should foster the freedom of movement of EU citizens and TCNs within the Union. They should also spell out common rules on the entry of TCNs. To demonstrate its commitment to basic human rights and democratic principles, the EU must protect TCNs against arbitrary actions, uphold their civil liberties, and deter acts of violence against them. To maintain the rule of law, the Union must press forward with judicial and police cooperation, while ensuring the privacy and civil liberties of those living in the EU. To live up to its international obligations, the EU must keep its policies in line with its pre-existing treaty obligations, particularly in the field of refugee protection. To protect its legitimacy and improve its public image, the EU must take pains to address issues of transparency and democratic deficit. And finally, it must undertake these endeavours without raising the spectre of an impenetrable 'Fortress Europe', which some argue already exists. The challenges facing the policy remain substantial.

QUESTIONS

1. What are the catalysts that have led to the Europeanization of JHA policy?

2. Fostering cooperation in JHA matters has not been a straightforward process. What have been the impediments to effective cooperation in this field?

3. The issues dealt with in JHA can also be addressed through unilateral decisions by individual countries, or by bilateral agreements concluded with interested parties. Why, then, is there such an effort to develop multilateral and collective responses in this field?

4. What are some of the lingering shortcomings of post-Amsterdam JHA cooperation?

5. What is meant by 'normalizing' JHA and how does the Lisbon Treaty contribute to such 'normalization'?

6. What are the negative consequences of closer cooperation in JHA matters?

7. How is the EU extending the impact of its JHA policies beyond its borders?

8 To what extent was the European Council meeting held at Tampere a watershed in the evolution of JHA policy?

 GUIDE TO FURTHER READING

■ Baldaccini, A., Guild, E., and Toner, H. (eds) *Whose Freedom, Security and Justice? EU Immigration and Asylum Law and Policy* (London: Hart, 2007). Provides a current survey of most issues pertaining to immigration and asylum.

■ Bieber, R. and Monar, J. (eds) *Justice and Home Affairs in the European Union: The Development of the Third Pillar* (Brussels: European Interuniversity Press, 1995). Covers the third pillar after Maastricht, focusing on the institutional framework and on early policy developments, particularly in the fields of immigration and asylum.

■ Geddes, A. *Immigration and European Integration: Towards Fortress Europe?* (Manchester: Manchester University Press, 2000). One of the first single-authored studies of the EU's immigration regime. Very accessible and well informed.

■ Lavenex, S. and Uçarer, E. (eds) *Migration and the Externalities of European Integration* (Lanham, MD: Lexington Books, 2002). An edited volume that focuses on the external dimension of EU migration policies.

■ Monar, J. 'The Dynamics of Justice and Home Affairs: Laboratories, Driving Factors and Costs', *Journal of Common Market Studies*. vol. 39, no. 4 (2001): 747–64. A useful article that seeks to explain the rapid development of JHA policy, by looking at early 'laboratories' (such as the Trevi Group) and at driving factors (such as challenges to internal security). It also points to the costs of this rapid evolution, in terms of the democratic deficit and other problems with the policy.

■ Peers, S. 'Key Legislative Developments on Migration in the European Issues' (European Journal of Migration Law: Various Issues). These legislative updates capture the policy output as well as providing insightful discussions of the decision making process.

 WEBLINKS

The EU's websites are the best source of information on JHA matters. To foster transparency in this field, the Commission, Council, and Parliament have all created websites that highlight policy initiatives, namely:

● http://ec.europa.eu/justice_home/index_en.htm   European Commission.

- http://www.consilium.europa.eu/cms3_fo/showPage.asp?id=249&lang=en   Council of Ministers.

- http://www.europarl.europa.eu/committees/libe_home_en.htm   European Parliament.

Similarly, the main agencies in JHA have their own websites, which are an excellent source of current developments:

- http://www.europol.europa.eu/   Europol.

- http://www.cepol.net   European Policy College (European Police Cooperation).

- http://www.eurojust.europa.eu/   Eurojust.

OTHER WEBSITES:

- www.statewatch.org   The Statewatch website provides a more critical approach to the JHA role of the EU than you will find on the EU websites.

- www.migpolgroup.com   The Migration Policy Group website, including the monthly *Migration News Sheet*.

 Visit the Online Resource Centre that accompanies this book for lots of interesting additional material. http://www.oxfordtextbooks.co.uk/orc/Cini_Borragan3e/

20 Economic and Monetary Union

AMY VERDUN

Reader's Guide

This chapter provides an introduction to Economic and Monetary Union (EMU). It describes the key components of EMU and what happens when countries join. EMU was the result of decades of collaboration and learning, which have been subdivided here into three periods: 1969–91, taking us from the European Council's first agreement to set up EMU to Maastricht, when the European Council included EMU in the Treaty on European Union; 1992–2002, from when plans for EMU were being developed to the irrevocable fixing of exchange rates; and 2002 onwards, once EMU had been established and banknotes and coins were circulating in member states. Next the chapter reviews various theoretical explanations, both economic and political, accounting for why EMU was created, and looking at some criticisms of EMU. Finally the chapter discusses how EMU has coped with the pressures of financial market and economic turmoil and what we may expect of it in the years to come.

Introduction

The introduction of euro banknotes and coins on 1 January 2002 was a major happening. The euro became legal tender in 12 European Union (EU) member states counting more than 300 million people. All EU member states except Denmark, Sweden, and the United Kingdom (UK) participated. It signalled the start of a new era in the history of the European Union not least because from this point on the majority of EU citizens were, on a daily basis, in contact with a concrete symbol of European integration. Let us look behind the big eye-catching event of 1 January 2002, however, to examine the path that led to the euro.

Economic and Monetary Union (EMU) has been an integral part of European integration since the early 1970s, though those early plans were derailed. Once back on track in the late 1980s and 1990s,

supporters of the idea of monetary union wanted to make sure that the process was done properly. Member states agreed that there should be economic and monetary convergence prior to starting EMU. But at the same time, some member states (for example, the UK) did not want to join EMU because they disliked the idea of giving up their own currency in favour of a European single currency. Today there are still those who are highly sceptical about EMU even if the financial market crisis that began in 2008, and the accompanying currency turmoil, made adopting the euro a more attractive policy objective to those still outside the euro area. Even countries that are not members of the EU, such as Iceland, have become attracted to the idea of becoming an EU member, in part because of the prospect of joining the euro.

What is EMU?

Having a common currency is not unique to the EU; the Roman empire had a single currency. Belgium, France, Italy, Switzerland, and others were part of a Latin Monetary Union (LMU) from 1865 to 1927. They minted francs that were of equal value across their union. In 1872 the Danes, Norwegians, and Swedes launched a single currency, the Scandinavian krona, used until the outbreak of World War I in 1914. Although the nineteenth-century European monetary unions were significant, the scale and scope of EMU in the EU is further reaching, as these earlier unions only harmonized coinage and did not introduce a single monetary policy or a central bank. Thus EMU is without doubt the most spectacular and ambitious monetary union of all time.

The component parts of EMU

EMU, as we know it in the EU, refers to a union in which participating countries have agreed to a single monetary policy, a single monetary authority, a single currency and coordinated macroeconomic policies. Let us clarify these features.

First, what is monetary policy? Central banks conduct monetary policy, in some cases in collaboration with the government, that is, with the ministry of finance and sometimes also with the economics ministry. Monetary policy aims at influencing the money supply and credit conditions. Central banks set a key interest rate. In EMU, monetary policy is no longer formulated at the national level but decided upon at the European level by a single monetary authority: the European Central Bank (ECB).

In December 1991, at the Maastricht summit, the European Council agreed to create a European System of Central Banks (ESCB). This consists of the European Central Bank (ECB) and the already existing national central banks, which in EMU are just 'branches' of the new ECB. The ECB Governing

Council is responsible for formulation of the monetary policy for the 'eurozone' or 'euro area'. The ECB is responsible for the new single currency, sets a key short-term interest rate, and monitors the money supply. To facilitate coordination of economic and financial policies, an informal group has been set up. The so-called 'eurogroup' consists of the ministers of finance, and sometimes economics, who get together to coordinate policies. The group typically meets before the meeting of the Economic and Financial Affairs Council (ECOFIN).

Strictly speaking, EMU could have been introduced without having a single currency. There were two alternatives. Participating countries could have kept their national currencies and fixed their exchange rates irrevocably; or they could have introduced a common currency in parallel to the existing national currencies—something the British government suggested in 1990 (the 'hard ecu proposal') but which did not receive support. While a parallel currency is introduced *alongside* existing national currencies, a single currency *replaces* them. The member states' leaders opted for a single currency as it would reduce the transactions costs that banks charge when currencies are exchanged. It was also politically more attractive as it would signal a full commitment to EMU.

Finally, in order to have a successful mix between fiscal and monetary policies, EMU envisages the coordination of economic policies (Article 99 TEC). To secure the euro as a low-inflation currency there are rules on public debts and budgetary deficits. Article 104 TEC states that member states must avoid budget deficits in excess of a reference value (set in a protocol annexed to the Treaty at 3 per cent of Gross Domestic Product (GDP)), and general government debt should be at or below a reference value (60 per cent of GDP). Furthermore, monetary financing of the debts and deficits would not be permitted: countries could no longer use the printing press to create money to service their debt (some governments had done this in the past, thereby reducing their public debts but at the expense of increased inflation). This so-called 'no bail-out clause' was put in place to reduce

the likelihood of the ECB having to bail out member states should they be unable to pay their debts (Article 103 TEC). Prior to EMU, a member state that ran high budget deficits with inflationary consequences would have been 'punished' by the market as they would have needed to set higher short-term interest rates as a consequence.

If one looks at the acronym, EMU, one sees a union with two components: 'economic' and 'monetary'. This term is a little awkward. In fact, many commentators in daily newspapers erroneously, but not surprisingly, refer to the acronym EMU as 'European' Monetary Union. Indeed, the most prominent feature of EMU is the 'monetary' component. The term *'Economic and Monetary Union'* can be traced back to the discussions in the late 1960s and early 1970s. The policy makers at the time were not sure how best to create EMU. To have fixed exchange rates—and ultimately a single currency—required some coordination of economic policies. Some countries—Belgium, Luxembourg, and France—thought that by fixing the exchange rate the necessary cooperation of the adjacent economic policies would naturally start to occur (the 'Monetarists'). Two other countries—West Germany and the Netherlands—held the opposite position. In their view, economic policies needed to be coordinated *before* fixing exchange rates or introducing a single currency (the 'Economists'). This debate is referred to as the debate between the 'Monetarists and the Economists'. (Note that the term 'Monetarists', used in this context, does not have the same meaning as the term 'Monetarists' referring to the followers of the ideas of Milton Friedman.)

The question of how to reach EMU had already been discussed in some detail by economic thinkers of the 1960s such as Bela Balassa and Jan Tinbergen. According to these and others, economic integration can be subdivided into a number of stages (see also Chapter 16). Originally it was thought that these stages would be consecutive and that they would follow each other at a regular pace. More recently this sequential order has been called into doubt: there is no clarity as to whether they should follow each other, or what the expected timing would be. Yet even though the framework may not be helpful as a predictive tool, it is still a useful analytical device.

The least far-reaching form of integration is a Free Trade Area (FTA). In an FTA, participating members remove barriers to trade amongst themselves but maintain the right to levy tariffs on third countries. The next stage of integration is a Customs Union (CU). In addition to the free trade amongst members, a CU has common external tariffs on goods and services from third countries. A Common Market (CM)—since 1985 renamed Single Market (SM)—is characterized by free movement of goods, services, labour, and capital among the participating states, and common rules, tariffs, and so on vis-à-vis third countries. An Economic Union implies not only a CM/SM but also a high degree of coordination of the most important areas of economic policy, market regulation, as well as monetary policies and income redistribution policies. A Monetary Union contains a CM/SM but also further integration in the area of currency cooperation. However, this is not always the case: the Scandinavian Monetary Union did not contain a Customs Union. A monetary union either has irrevocably fixed exchange rates and full convertibility of currencies, or a common or single currency circulating within the monetary union. It also requires integration of budgetary and monetary policies. An Economic and Monetary Union (EMU) combines the features of the economic union and the monetary union. This combination is what European leaders had in mind when they discussed EMU in 1969 and again in 1988. A Full Economic Union (FEU) implies the complete unification of the economies of the participating member states and common policies for most economic matters. A Full Political Union (FPU) is the term used when, in addition to the FEU, political governance and policy making have moved to the supranational level. Effectively political unification occurs when the final stage of integration has taken place and a new confederation or federation has been created.

The eventual institutional design of EMU in the 1980s and 1990s was an asymmetrical one (Verdun 1996; 2000). It featured a relatively well developed monetary union, but a much less developed economic union. In the sphere of monetary policy a complete transfer of policy making to a new European supranational institution was envisaged, whereas in the area of economic policy making, decisions remained to be made by the national governments. One observes here the difference between positive and negative integration. Positive integration refers to the creation of common rules, norms, and policies. Negative integration is all about taking away obstacles, eliminating rules and procedures that are an obstruction to integration. Regarding EMU, we find that in the area of monetary policy a new institution and a common policy are created. By contrast, in the area of economic union one observes mainly negative integration: the completion of the single market (that is, removing barriers to trade), and the acceptance of only numerical ceilings on budgetary policies, which involves only the coordination of national policies. Neither a common institution nor a common policy was created in this area of policy making. As we shall see in the next section, the reason this asymmetry existed was that in the area of monetary policy a convergence of policy making had already occurred, whereas in the area of economic policy there was still a great deal of divergence.

KEY POINTS

- There have been other European monetary unions, such as the Latin Monetary Union and the Scandinavian Monetary Union.

- EMU consists of a single monetary policy, a single monetary authority, a single currency, and coordinated macroeconomic policies.

- The 'Monetarists' and the 'Economists' differed in opinion as to how best to create EMU.

- There are various stages of integration: from a free trade area to a full political union. The stages are an analytical device.

From The Hague to Maastricht (1969–91)

At the 1969 summit in The Hague, the heads of state and government decided to explore a path to EMU. A group of experts, headed by Pierre Werner, Prime Minister and Finance Minister of Luxembourg, drafted the blueprint. The 1970 Werner Plan proposed three stages to reach EMU by 1980. On the institutional side it recommended setting up two supranational bodies: a Community System for the Central Banks and a Centre of Decision for Economic Policy. The former would pursue monetary policies whereas the latter would coordinate macroeconomic policies (including some tax policies). Most of the recommendations of the Werner Plan were adopted, but EMU did not take off in subsequent years.

There are two reasons why the creation of EMU stalled in the 1970s. First, there were substantial differences among the member states about how to get to EMU. Second, the international economic and monetary situation rapidly changed in the early 1970s, making for a totally different climate for cooperation. The so-called Bretton Woods Agreement, which had facilitated stable exchange rates in Western Europe since 1945, ended in August 1971. West European countries responded by setting up their own exchange rate mechanism, the so-called 'snake', which functioned with moderate success throughout the 1970s, and in which not all member states participated, though several non-EEC members were involved.

Developments leading to the relaunch of EMU in the late 1980s

In 1979 the European Monetary System (EMS), was set up in which all EC member states were to participate. Not all were immediately part of its most important feature, the Exchange Rate Mechanism (ERM)—a system of fixed but adjustable exchange rates. The UK was not part of the ERM during the 1980s but its currency was part of the European Currency Unit (ECU)—the unit of account at the heart of the EMS. In 1991 the British pound did join the ERM, but it was forced to leave on 16 September 1992 ('Black Wednesday') following a period of intense selling of sterling in the financial markets, which the British government was unable to bring to a halt. Italy participated in the ERM from the outset but was initially given more leeway. The rules stipulated that most currencies could not fluctuate more than ± 2.25 per cent from an agreed parity, whereas the bandwidth for those who needed more leeway (for example, Italy) was set at ± 6 per cent from the parity. If a currency threatened to move outside the agreed band, central banks would intervene by buying or selling currencies in order to keep the currency from leaving the band. If an imbalance were persistent, the so-called EC Monetary Committee (MC), an informal advisory body created by the Treaty of Rome to discuss monetary policy and exchange rate matters, would decide whether or not to adjust the parities. In 1999 the MC was renamed the Economic and Financial Committee.

The ERM needed some time to become successful. The first four years (1979–83) were learning years with numerous exchange rates fluctuations and parity adjustments. The participating currencies became more stable in the interim period (1983–7), and thereafter until summer 1992 the ERM witnessed no realignments. By this time, it had become an important 'symbol' of successful European integration. In the 1980s, the German currency, the Deutschmark (D-mark), became the 'anchor currency'. Because it had been

CHRONOLOGY 20.1

Three stages to Economic and Monetary Union

First stage	1 July 1990 to 31 December 1993	• Free movement of capital among member states. • Closer coordination of economic policies. • Closer cooperation among central banks.
Second stage	1 January 1994 to 31 December 1998	• Convergence of the economic and monetary policies of the member states (to ensure stability of prices and sound public finances).
Third stage	From 1 January 1999	• Establishment of the European Central Bank. • Fixing of exchange rates. • Introduction of the single currency.

a strong currency, monetary authorities in ERM countries took German monetary policies as their point of reference, following the decisions of the German central bank (the Bundesbank) quite closely.

A few other developments in the 1980s helped relaunch the EMU process. The 1986 Single European Act (SEA) facilitated the completion of the single market and mentioned the need to relaunch EMU. The 1988 Hanover European Council mandated Commission President Jacques Delors to head a committee composed of the 12 central bank presidents, and one other EC Commissioner and a few experts to draft a blueprint for EMU. Like the earlier Werner Report, the Delors Report (issued in April 1989) proposed a road to EMU in three stages (see Box 20.1). It also envisaged the creation of a European System of Central Banks. In contrast to the Werner Report, it did not find it necessary to set up a similar supranational institution in the economic sphere. But it had the same objectives: full freedom of goods, services, capital, and labour, and, if possible and if the political will was there, the introduction of a single currency. On the basis of the Delors Report the June 1989 Madrid European Council adopted the EMU blueprint, with the first stage of EMU (the liberalization of capital markets) starting on 1 July 1990. An Intergovernmental Conference (IGC) opened in Rome in October 1990 and closed in Maastricht in

1991 to discuss the next stages (see Chapter 3). Strictly speaking, there were two IGCs, one on EMU and another on political union. One of the decisions taken during the IGC negotiations was that countries would have to meet certain criteria, dubbed 'convergence criteria', in order to be allowed to join EMU.

The convergence criteria (see Box 20.2) referred to good performance in the area of inflation rates, interest rates, and exchange rates. Moreover, it was agreed that participating countries should not have excessive budgetary deficits or public debts. Finally, the national central bank needed to be made politically independent, and national monetary authorities could no longer use the printing press to reduce public debts and budgetary deficits (monetary financing). It is important to note that right from the outset there were 'escape clauses' built into the wording of the Maastricht Treaty. It was generally thought the criteria would be applied generously with regard to the debt criterion as it was believed that some countries, such as Belgium and Italy, would never be able to meet the reference value in less than a decade. As for the budgetary criteria, however, these *had* to be met.

It has been speculated that the creation of EMU was assisted by the fall of the Berlin Wall in 1989 and the end of Communist regimes in Central and Eastern Europe in 1990. The observant reader will

---

BOX 20.2

The Maastricht convergence criteria

- Budget deficits should be no more than 3 per cent of Gross Domestic Product (GDP).

- Accumulated public debt should be no more than 60 per cent of GDP.

- Exchange rates should have participated without devaluation or severe tensions in the exchange rate mechanism (ERM-2) for at least the previous two years.

- Inflation should not be more than 1.5 percentage points above the rate of the three best-performing member states.

- Long-term interest rates should be not more than 2 percentage points above the rate of the three best-performing member states.

Source: European Union: consolidated versions of the Treaty on European Union and the Treaty establishing the European Community, article 121 and protocol 21.

---

have noted, however, that the Delors Report had already been completed by April 1989, and therefore preceded these turbulent political developments. Nevertheless, the political determination of the German Chancellor, Helmut Kohl, to secure EMU was connected to his eagerness to move ahead quickly with German Unification. The IGCs were completed in December 1991 and the European Council in Maastricht agreed to revise the Treaty of Rome and accept a new Treaty on European Union. It was signed on 7 February 1992, and came into force on 1 November 1993 after the national parliaments of all 12 member states ratified it (see ratification).

KEY POINTS

- In the 1970s EMU stalled because of differences among member states and due to changing international circumstances

- The EMS and the SEA contributed to the relaunch of EMU in the late 1980s.

- The Delors Report offered a blueprint for EMU.

- The Treaty changes necessary for acceptance and implementation of EMU were negotiated in an Intergovernmental Conference, which was completed in Maastricht in 1991.

- Member states need to meet the 'convergence criteria' to join EMU.

From treaty to reality (1992 – 2002)

The period from 1992 to 2002 posed numerous challenges for EMU, most notably over the ratification of the Maastricht Treaty, the issue of what would happen post-EMU, and the 'real' criteria for membership of the Monetary Union.

Ratification problems and the 'real' convergence criteria

The ratification process of the Maastricht Treaty turned out to be very tricky. Only months after the Treaty was signed, on 2 June 1992, Danish citizens voted against the Treaty in a referendum. A razor-thin majority rejected the Treaty (50.7 per cent against; 49.3 per cent in favour). In a reaction to the Danish referendum, the French President François Mitterrand also decided to hold a referendum in France on 20 September 1992. Against the background of major speculation in the financial markets, which had resulted in the British pound and the Italian lira leaving the Exchange Rate Mechanism days before the referendum, the French referendum resulted in a very slim majority in favour of the Treaty (51.05 per cent in favour; 48.95 per cent against). The result surprised most observers as the French had been overall supporters of European integration. This period cast a shadow over the run-up to EMU. The period from late 1992 through early 1994 was characterized as one of continued exchange rate turbulence, placing the ERM under further pressure. In August 1993 the ERM exchange rate bands were widened from ± 2.25 per cent to ± 15 per cent. After the introduction of the euro, a new system, the ERM II, was set up to succeed the previous ERM. It maintained the ± 15 per cent bands.

In May 1998, the European Council decided that 11 countries would participate in EMU from 1 January 1999—the day when exchange rates would be irrevocably fixed between the participating member states. However, Denmark, Sweden, and the UK did not want to join, whereas Greece was judged ready in June 2000 and joined the euro area as the twelfth member on 1 January 2001.

When eight Central and Eastern European countries and two very small Mediterranean countries joined the EU on 1 May 2004, the accession treaty stipulated that these countries would eventually join EMU. However, they had to wait at least two years and fulfil the convergence criteria before they could adopt the euro. In 2007 Slovenia became the first new member state to join EMU. Two of the Baltic states, Estonia and Lithuania, were also very keen, though in May 2006 the assessment of the European Commission concluded that Lithuania met all the convergence criteria except that of inflation. The assessment caused a public outcry as the Commission had adopted a very strict interpretation of the criterion. However, the two Baltic states decided subsequently to delay joining the euro area. In 2008 Cyprus and Malta joined, and in 2009 Slovakia became the sixteenth member of the euro area.

Managing EMU: the Stability and Growth Pact (SGP)

In the mid 1990s the German Finance Minister, Theo Waigel, proposed rules for countries once in EMU. The Stability and Growth Pact (SGP) was put in place to ensure that no single member state, once it had become a member of EMU, could free ride,

for example by incurring high debts and deficits. Under the SGP, member states that violate the rules to keep their public debt and budgetary deficit low can be penalized and may have to pay a fine. Understandably, the SGP was not without its critics. The rules can be seen as artificial. Furthermore, imposing a fine on a member state is politically undesirable—especially where that member state is in financial difficulties. Indeed, the SGP was designed primarily to work as a deterrent. It is ironic then that Germany subsequently in 2003 became one of the countries to experience problems meeting the rules and objectives of the SGP.

The SGP involves multilateral budgetary surveillance (a 'preventive arm') as well as specifying a deficit limit, the excessive deficit procedure (EDP) (a 'corrective arm') (see Box 20.3). When—on the basis of a Commission recommendation—the Council decides that an excessive deficit indeed exists, the member state concerned is obliged to reduce its deficit below the Treaty's reference value of 3 per cent of GDP; otherwise financial sanctions can be levied against the member state in question.

In 2002, France, Germany, and Portugal were each at different times given an 'early warning' that they were in breach of the Pact. Portugal made the necessary corrections and hence the EDP was abrogated in 2004. But France and Germany failed to make the necessary adjustments to reduce their budgetary deficits. By November 2003 both were heading for the next step in the excessive deficit procedure (Article 104(9) TEC), and thus were coming closer to the financial sanctions set out in the SGP. Neither country was keen to move to the next step, and thus sought to get support from other member states to avoid that situation. At a meeting of the Council of Economic and Financial Affairs Ministers (ECOFIN) on 25 November 2003, a proposal by the Commission to move France and Germany closer to the sanctions was defeated. The result was that the SGP was interrupted for the cases of France and Germany. Other member states, notably Austria, Finland, the Netherlands, and Spain, were outraged at the situation. Their judgement was that France and Germany had been exempted from the process because they were large enough to rally other

---

BOX 20.3

The Stability and Growth Pact

The *Stability and Growth Pact aims* to ensure that member states continue their budgetary discipline efforts after the introduction of the euro.

Dates	Decisions
The Stability and Growth Pact was a European Council resolution (adopted at Amsterdam on 17 June 1997) and two Council Regulations of 7 July 1997. The Council Regulations were revised on 27 June 2005.	• The surveillance of budgetary positions and coordination of economic policies. • Implementation of the excessive deficit procedure.
Annually since 1999	• Member states have undertaken to pursue the objective of a balanced or nearly balanced budget and to present the Council and the Commission with a stability programme. • Member states not taking part in the third stage of EMU are also required to submit a convergence programme. • Opening and closing (where appropriate) of an excessive deficit procedure for EU member states.
The Stability and Growth Pact enables the Council to penalize any participating member state that fails to take appropriate measures to end an excessive deficit. Initially, the penalty would take the form of a non-interest-bearing deposit with the Community, but it could be converted into a fine if the excessive deficit is not corrected within two years. The legal text of the SGP consists of (1) Resolution of the European Council on the Stability and Growth Pact, OJ	1997, C 236/1; (2) Council Regulation No. 1466/97 of 7 July 1997 on the strengthening of the surveillance of budgetary positions and the surveillance and coordination of economic policies, OJ 1997, L 209/1 as amended by Council Regulation 1055/105 of 27 June 2005; and (3) Council Regulation No. 1467/97 on speeding up and clarifying the implementation of the excessive deficit procedure, OJ L 209/6 as amended by Council Regulation 1056/2005

Source: http://ec.europa.eu/economy_finance/sg_pact_fiscal_policy.

---

member states around their cause. The four were particularly upset because they were convinced that if a smaller member state had faced the same situation, it would not have been able to obtain the same support. The crisis atmosphere that resulted from the 25 November 2003 Council decision prompted the European Commission to ask the European Court of Justice (ECJ) whether this Council decision was legal. In July 2004 the ECJ ruled that the November 2003 Council decision was in fact *illegal* as the Council had adopted its own text outside the context of the Treaty. But the ECJ did confirm that the Council has the right not to follow the recom-

mendations of the Commission. The result of all these developments was that the Commission felt that the SGP needed to be adjusted. By the spring of 2005 the SGP was revised so as to include more flexibility over the circumstances under which member states may temporarily run deficits in excess of the 3 per cent reference value; and small adjustments were made to the time schedule.

The preventive arm of the SGP has been strengthened by a more differentiated medium-term orientation of the rules. The new provisions ensure that due attention is given to the fundamentals of fiscal sustainability when setting budgetary objectives. In future, the medium-term budgetary objective of a country will be based on its debt ratio and potential growth. In practice, this will mean that countries with a combination of low debt and high potential growth will be able to run a small deficit over the medium term, whereas a balanced budget or a surplus will be required for countries with a combination of high debt and low potential growth. The preventive arm of the SGP is strengthened because member states have committed to consolidate further their public finances when they face favourable economic conditions, and have accepted that the Commission will be giving them 'policy advice' if this consolidation fails to occur. The new agreement is also more sensitive to the effects of efforts made by member states to make structural reforms. The SGP's corrective arm has also been adjusted by allowing more room for economic judgements and leaving open the possibility that the one-year deadline for the correction of an excessive deficit could be increased to two years.

The first test of the new SGP came in the second half of 2008 when the global financial crisis upset markets and challenged the survival of the banking sector. Member state governments in the EU responded by guaranteeing the savings of consumers, buying out banks, and offering other stimulus packages. The rescue packages were so large that public finances were affected by them. The rules of the Pact still applied, however, even if, because of the economic crisis, these countries were allowed to overshoot the reference value for the duration of the downturn.

KEY POINTS

- The aftermath of the signing of the Maastricht Treaty posed challenges to creating EMU: Treaty ratification difficulties; the ERM crisis; difficulties meeting the convergence criteria.

- Some member states have had difficulties avoiding excessive deficits.

- SGP implementation difficulties led to a crisis and subsequently to its revision.

Explaining EMU

The following section considers two ways in which EMU can be explained—first, from an economics perspective; and second from a political one.

An economics perspective

In the field of economics, there are two schools of thought that offer analytical tools to determine whether or not it made sense for the EU to create an EMU. The first argues that countries should create an economic and monetary union only if they constitute a so-called optimum currency area (OCA). Countries should adopt a single currency only when they are sufficiently integrated economically; when they have mechanisms in place that can deal with transfer payments if one part of the currency union is affected by an economic downturn and the other part is not; and when they no longer need the exchange rate instrument to make those adjustments.

Most analysts claim that the EU is not an OCA, though a few think that a small number of its members come close to it. OCA theory states that if countries do not form an OCA they should not give up their exchange rate instrument, but use it to make adjustments as the economic situation dictates. These analysts argue that the EU should not have moved to EMU. Others who have observed that some countries of the EU do indeed constitute an OCA are less critical of this situation. They see the current group of countries as being well integrated. Furthermore, they use a broader definition of an OCA, claiming that original OCA theory is too rigid and pointing out that, following the original definition, no federation (including Canada, Germany, or the United States) would constitute an OCA! Other developments that have influenced recent thinking about the role of exchange rates are the effects of financial markets on exchange rate policies—particularly on smaller open economies. Foreign exchange markets can create their own disturbances that can be irrational. This effect is worse for smaller open economies than for larger established countries. However, the original OCA theorists did not take the destabilizing effects of exchange rate freedom into consideration.

The second school of thought that reflects on whether or not it makes sense to create an EMU focuses on central bank credibility. It argues that over the past two decades the EU has witnessed long periods of collaboration in central banking. Central banks can only be effective if financial markets have confidence in their policies. In the case of the ERM, participating countries had to keep their exchange rates stable. To do this they focused on the monetary policy of the strongest currency, the German D-Mark. Hence individual central banks followed the policies of the leader (the Bundesbank), and in practice had no opportunity to pursue alternative policies. The most credible way to secure monetary policy is to commit firmly to it in a Treaty. That is in fact what happened with Maastricht. A regime was set up that envisaged full central bank independence and gave the ECB a clear single mandate to maintain price stability.

A political science perspective

Political science has drawn on European integration theories (see Chapters 5–7) to explain EMU. It is noteworthy that scholars from opposing schools of thought have argued that EMU can be explained using different theoretical approaches. For reasons of simplicity we shall focus on the two best known opposing schools in order to capture a larger set of arguments.

A neo-functionalist explanation (see Chapter 5) claims that EMU can be best explained as the result of spillover and incremental policy making. The success of the ERM and the completion of the single market necessitated further collaboration in the area of monetary integration. EMU was needed to maximize the benefits of these developments. Furthermore, significant monetary policy convergence had occurred,

arising out of the collaboration within the framework of the ERM and the tracking of German policies by other member states. Hence EMU could be seen as a natural step forward. Moreover, it is argued that supranational actors were instrumental in creating EMU—which is another characteristic of the neo-functionalist explanation of European integration. Not only were the Commission President and the services of the Commission (in particular the Directorate-General for Economic and Financial Affairs) involved, but also various EC committees, such as the Monetary Committee—and they each proved influential.

An intergovernmentalist explanation (see Chapter 7) argues that EMU can best be understood by examining the interests and bargaining behaviour of the largest member states. This approach sees the European Council meetings as crucial for decisions such as the creation of EMU. By examining the interests of the largest member states, one is able to see why EMU happened. France was in favour of EMU as a way of containing German hegemony. Germany, in turn, was able to secure a monetary policy regime that was sufficiently close to its domestic regime. Some argue that the reason that Germany was in favour of EMU in the early 1990s was that it signalled its full commitment to European integration, in the period following German Unification. The UK was not so much in favour of EMU, but was aware that it was likely to happen. Thus the UK wanted to be involved in agenda setting, in shaping the process, and ensuring EMU would not create a more federal political union at the same time. It has also been argued that EMU served the economic interests of the business communities within these countries, which subsequently led governments to be more supportive of the project.

KEY POINTS

- Economists often use OCA theory to assess EMU.
- Political scientists use theories of European integration to explain EMU.

Criticisms of EMU

EMU is not without its critics, however. Criticisms may involve distinctive national perspectives, but can also rest on institutional grounds.

Countries opposing EMU

The Danes and Swedes are very proud of their political, social, and economic achievements, and many of them doubt that joining EMU will benefit their respective countries. Their populations have been relatively sceptical about the EU, and many see EMU as yet another example of unnecessary or undesirable European integration. In both countries a referendum was held (in Denmark in 2000; in Sweden in 2003) and in both cases the majority of those who voted were against joining EMU. Denmark has an opt-out agreed at Maastricht, and thus can choose to stay outside the euro area; although the Swedish government does not have an opt-out, it pursues policies that guarantee that it does not qualify for EMU.

The UK reflects an even more Eurosceptic population. A large segment of the UK population has had doubts about aspects of European integration ever since the UK first joined the EC in 1973. British citizens, the media, and the Conservative Party seem deeply suspicious about policy making in the rest of Europe and fear they will have to make too many changes if they follow the lead of other European states. Another argument often heard is that citizens are unconvinced that there is a real need to create a single currency. The benefits of the euro have been calculated to be around one per cent of GDP.

The main benefits of EMU are the elimination of transactions costs—costs related to the exchange of money. Other benefits are a strong monetary policy, the fact that a single currency further strengthens the single or 'internal' market, and the dynamic effects that come about as a result of clarity about prices once they are all denominated in the same currency. Yet these benefits are not guaranteed. It is likely, for example, that the single monetary policy may not benefit each member country equally.

EU citizens have generally been supportive of the euro and EMU. Eurobarometer data has suggested that the populations of some countries are outright enthusiastic about EMU (Ireland, Slovenia, Luxembourg, Belgium, Netherlands, with more than 80 per cent in favour, and Finland and France with three-quarters or more in favour). Others still are strongly in favour (such as Romania, Germany, Spain, Austria, and Hungary where a two-thirds majority supports EMU). Other countries have been more subdued (as in the case of Italy, Malta, Slovakia, Portugal, Bulgaria, Estonia, the Czech Republic, Denmark, and Greece, where only a bare majority supports the single currency). The countries where the popular support for the euro is below 50 per cent are Poland (49 per cent); Latvia and Lithuania (48 per cent); Sweden (48 per cent); Cyprus (46 per cent); Sweden (45 per cent); and UK (24 per cent). Figure 20.1 illustrates aggregate support by EU citizens for the euro from 1999 to 2005 (European Commission 2005b).

A recent public poll of attitudes held among inhabitants of the nine new member states not yet part of the euro area shows a majority thinking that the adoption of the euro will have either very positive or rather positive consequences for their countries, while 37 per cent of citizens expect rather negative or very negative consequences at a national level (Commission 2008b: 5).

Criticism of EMU's institutional design

EMU has also been criticized for its poor institutional design. Critics argue that the extreme independence of the ECB may lead to problems of legitimacy and accountability. The argument is developed in three steps. First, the ECB is more independent than any other central bank in the world. Its independence and its primary mandate (to secure price stability—in effect, low inflation) are firmly anchored in the Treaty on European

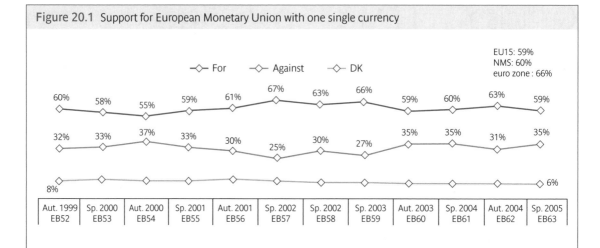

Figure 20.1 Support for European Monetary Union with one single currency

From a socio-demographic point of view, the main supporters of the euro are:

- Men;
- Citizens aged under 55;
- Citizens having a higher level of education;
- Citizens who place themselves on the left of the political spectrum;
- 'Leaders of opinion';
- Citizens who are well informed about the European Union.

Source: European Commission (2005b), Eurobarometer 63, Spring, p. 164.

Union. The Treaty also stipulates that no one is allowed to give instructions to the ECB, nor should it take instruction from anyone. Second, it is close to impossible to change the ECB mandate. A change to the ECB statute demands a treaty change, which requires the unanimity of the heads of state and government of all EU member states as well as ratification by all EU national parliaments (and in some countries referendums too). Third, there are very few checks and balances in place to ensure that policies are pursued that the member states want— except for the one clear one, namely to secure price stability (low inflation). Even on that issue there is not much control: the ECB President gives quarterly reports to the European Parliament (EP), but the EP cannot give instructions to the ECB; and the ECB President speaks to the media after the Governing Council has taken decisions (but no minutes of Governing Council meetings are published). Thus one has to trust that the ECB will pursue policies in accordance with its mandate and that the policy outcome will benefit the EU as a whole. Fourth, no

supranational institution can pursue flanking policies that may correct imbalances occurring as a result of the policies pursued by the ECB. Let us clarify this fourth issue a little further.

Compared to mature federations, the institutional design of EMU is incomplete: there is a strong ECB that decides monetary policies for the entire euro area; yet, there is no equivalent supranational economic institution that sets economic policies for that same area. Budgetary and fiscal policies remain in the hands of national governments. Although countries such as France argued strongly in favour of creating such an 'economic government' (*gouvernement économique*), the choice was made not to go down that route.

What are the advantages and disadvantages of having a European 'economic government'? The advantages would be that policies could then be pursued to correct imbalances throughout EMU that result from a strict monetary policy (one that focuses on combating inflation). However, an economic government would only make sense if a majority of the citizens of the euro area felt comfortable with it. If it did not have that support, then a decision by such a body would be deemed illegitimate. The current situation in Europe is that most citizens feel most comfortable with their national government taking on the role of taxing and spending.

The global financial crisis

In the latter half of 2008 a major financial crisis hit the global economy. The crisis was caused by a series of problems, many of them originating in the USA, culminating in the collapse of the investment bank Lehman Brothers on 15 September 2008. It did not take long for the financial crisis to blow across to the EU. It took the shape of falling stock exchanges, a drying up of credit, and many banks being at risk of collapse. National governments responded by guaranteeing deposits, nationalizing or partially nationalizing banks, and by putting together rescue packages. In early 2009 economic growth statistics showed that the global financial crisis had had major impact on the real economy, with many countries experiencing a sharp drop in growth. In the EU almost all countries were showing negative growth or were in recession (defined as two successive quarters of negative growth).

The global financial crisis put a lot of pressure on the EU and in particular on the institutional design of EMU. As was discussed above, the Stability and Growth Pact requires that budgetary deficits stay below 3 per cent of GDP, even though the SGP contains provisions that allow countries to exceed the limit temporarily in exceptional circumstances. The Commission was quick to decide that these circumstances were indeed exceptional according to that definition. However, member states now running large deficits will remain closely monitored and, once the economic tide turns, the SGP framework will require them to get their public finances in order sooner rather than later. As for the other challenges: as discussed above, the EU lacks an economic government—a supranational body that can make a swift decision on economic policies at such a time of crisis. Instead, in the current context, concerted action can be achieved only by bringing together the various national governments and the EU institutions. To date these voices have been seeking to collaborate, but at various times during the 2008 crisis, uncoordinated national decisions dominated the scene. It will be interesting to watch whether the EU institutional structure and the political behaviour of EU member state governments will support or undermine the EMU edifice, given the challenges of the financial crisis and the subsequent economic downturn.

Conclusion

While euro banknotes and coins were introduced overnight, it has taken more than 30 years to create EMU. It was a long and slow process that ultimately led to the creation of a single monetary policy, the ECB, and rules on budgetary policies and public debts. Behind the fanfare and festivities of the introduction of the new currency lay a lengthy and gradual process of learning about economic and monetary cooperation. Not only was it necessary for countries to have met the convergence criteria, but it was also crucial that member states maintain stable exchange rates, and that they agree on common goals for EMU.

We have seen that there were economic and political motivations underlying the plan to move to EMU. Although one can make a case for a purely economic rationale for monetary union, its ultimate creation cannot be understood without an appreciation of its political dimension. EMU is a new stage in European integration. It signals the capability of EU member states to take firm action together. It also places the EU more clearly on the international map. Yet a number of issues remain unresolved. In discussing the asymmetrical EMU the chapter has indicated how fragile the balance is between 'economic' and 'monetary' union. It is not unthinkable that in the future further integration might be needed in the area of 'economic union' or that steps will have to be taken towards further political unification, if only to redistribute more evenly the costs and benefits of EMU. At the same time, we have seen that European integration is a gradual process which if pushed ahead too quickly lacks legitimacy.

What will the future of the EU be with EMU in place? The continuing presence of the euro may well give the EU a stronger position in world politics, if only because it might offer an alternative to the US dollar (but see Chapter 14 on this point). As such, the euro contributes to the symbolism of European integration. It offers a concrete token representing the rapid and far-reaching process of integration taking place in the EU.

The regional use of the euro has increased quite rapidly from being legal tender in 11 member states in 1999 to 16 member states in 2009. Furthermore, it is not unthinkable that some of the EU member states, such as Denmark and Sweden, may want to join the euro area in the not-so-distant future, as will a number of Central and East European countries, thereby adding more to the euro's credibility and strength. Yet not all monetary unions in the past have lasted. EMU will survive only if it continues to be supported by the citizens and by national and European politicians. Leaders will have to keep listening to the needs of their citizens. If they do so satisfactorily, the euro may well continue to have a very promising future.

? QUESTIONS

1. Why was the term 'economic' and 'monetary' union used? What, in this regard, is an 'asymmetrical EMU'?

2. What was the argument between the 'Monetarists' and the 'Economists'?

3. What are the various stages of economic integration from a Free Trade Area to Full Political Unification, and what does each stage entail? Do all stages have to be passed in sequence?

4. What are the convergence criteria, and why were they invented?

5. Why has the Stability and Growth Pact been difficult to implement? (Think, for instance, about what the impact of the financial crisis has been.)

6. There are two opposing political science theories explaining why EMU happened. What are they? Do you agree that they are opposing theories or are they complementary?

7. What are the main criticisms of EMU?

8. Discuss how the creation of EMU was both an economic and politically driven process.

GUIDE TO FURTHER READING

■ Dyson, K. and Featherstone, K. *The Road to Maastricht: Negotiating Economic and Monetary Union* (Oxford: Oxford University Press, 1999). A very influential political science volume, which looks at the steps leading to the agreement on EMU at Maastricht, and which is based on hundreds of interviews with key informants.

■ Hosli, M. O. *The Euro: A Concise Introduction to European Monetary Integration* (Boulder, CO: Lynne Rienner, 2005). A wonderful short introduction to EMU written in language accessible to the non-specialist.

■ Tsoukalis, L. *The Politics and Economics of European Monetary Integration* (London: George Allen and Unwin, 1977). A seminal book on the history of EMU.

■ Verdun, A. *European Responses to Globalization and Financial Market Integration: Perceptions of Economic and Monetary Union in Britain, France and Germany* (Basingstoke: Palgrave-Macmillan, 2000). A volume on EMU, based on original research, examining perceptions of EMU from the perspective of the member states and considering how actors use EMU to serve or frustrate their interests.

■ Verdun, A. (ed.) *The Euro: European Integration Theory and Economic and Monetary Union* (Lanham, MD: Rowman and Littlefield, 2002). This book focuses on EMU as part of a wider process of European integration. It examines various theoretical approaches that assist us in better understanding the process that led to the introduction of the euro.

 WEBLINKS

● http://www.ecb.int/   The official website of the European Central Bank. The ECB website features exchange rates, speeches by the ECB president, monetary reports, and useful statistics.

● http://ec.europa.eu/economy_finance/the_euro/   The website of the European Commission that deals with EMU and the euro.

● http://www.consilium.europa.eu/   The website of the Council of the EU: click on 'Economic and Financial Affairs'.

● www.euobserver.com   An online source of Eu news and debates

● www.ft.com   The website of the *Financial Times*

● www.economist.com   Each of these websites is full of useful media sources that will allow you to follow current events on relevant matters.

● http://ec.europa.eu/public_opinion/standard_en.htm   This Eurobarometer website offers information about public opinion in the EV.

 Visit the Online Resource Centre that accompanies this book for lots of interesting additional material. http://www.oxfordtextbooks.co.uk/orc/Cini_Borragan3e/

21 The Common Agricultural Policy

EVE FOUILLEUX

Chapter Contents

- Introduction
- The early days of the CAP and the issue of CAP reform
- A dramatic shift in 1992
- An ongoing reform process
- Conclusion: the CAP at a crossroads

Reader's Guide

This chapter examines one of the first European policies, the Common Agricultural Policy (CAP). It does so by focusing on the policy's objectives, instruments, actors, and debates. It looks at the way in which the CAP has evolved since the 1960s, and attempts to explain this evolution by asking and answering a number of important questions. Why has the CAP been so problematic for European policy makers? Why has it proven so resistant to change? Given the constraints identified, how has reform come about? This chapter also looks at some of the challenges facing agricultural policy, as new debates take place among citizens on the social, cultural, and environmental roles performed by agriculture.

Introduction

The Common Agricultural Policy (CAP) has long been of symbolic importance to the European integration process, and has been subject to calls for reform ever since the 1960s. This chapter focuses on this reform process as a way of exploring not only the character of the 'old' CAP, but the form that this controversial policy might take in the future. It begins with a brief introduction to the principles underpinning the CAP, and then provides an explanation of why it has taken (or is taking) so long to reform this policy. The CAP reform of 1992 is the focus of the following section, after which attention turns to the subsequent reforms of 1999, 2003, and 2008. The successive reforms have provoked new thinking in the agricultural policy domain, involving the integration of environmental and social concerns into the policy, rural development, and the introduction of the concept of multifunctionality. Throughout the chapter, emphasis is placed on the role of the international context in providing incentives for reform, and on the national context which, more often than not, acts as a constraint.

The early days of the CAP and the issue of CAP reform

This section presents the main principles and instruments of the CAP and an overview of the CAP's brake mechanisms at national and European levels.

The early days of the policy

The objectives of the CAP, which came into force from 1962, were laid down in the Treaty of Rome in 1957 (Article 39) and subsequently at the Stresa Conference in July 1958. Three general principles underpinned the policy: market unity; Community preference; and financial solidarity. The initial move in establishing a European agricultural market (applying the so-called market unity principle) was the setting up of Common Market Organizations (CMOs) for all agricultural products, and most notably for wheat, barley, rye, corn, rice, sugar, dairy products, bovine meat, pork, lamb, wine, and some fruits and vegetables. The idea was to allow free trade internally within the Community, but also to erect barriers to the outside world, to protect the income of European farmers.

The CMOs usually operated on the basis of three complementary policy tools: a guaranteed price, a public intervention system, and some variable levies at the Community's border. First, the notion of a guaranteed price is crucial to understanding how the CAP operated. The idea was that the specificities of the farming sector (dependence on climatic conditions and vulnerability to natural disasters) and the consequent structural instabilities of agricultural markets made some public intervention necessary to guarantee decent living conditions for farmers. This is why, instead of allowing the market to determine price levels, the prices farmers received for their produce were institutional prices: that is, they were fixed centrally by Community civil servants and politicians. Such a system had the objective of both supporting farmers' incomes and boosting agricultural production; the more farmers produced, the more money they earned. Indeed, with the food shortages of the post-1945 period and the security concerns of the Cold War in mind, the aim of self-sufficiency in foodstuffs was presented as one of the major objectives of the policy. In practice, the level of guaranteed prices was initially set on the basis of a political compromise between France and Germany. In the early 1960s the Germans had a very inefficient cereal sector but numerous politically powerful farmers, and asked for a high level of support for cereals. Although the French were more efficient and had a lower national price for cereals, they did not mind setting guaranteed prices higher under the CAP, as long as they did not have to pay for them. It is for this reason that Germany has ended up as the primary contributor to the CAP since 1962, while France has always been among the main financial beneficiaries.

Second, if the price began to fall due, for example, to an excessive internal supply, which would have had the effect of depressing farmers' incomes, intervention agencies would step in when the price reached a certain level (the intervention price) to buy up the surplus and store it until the market was balanced again, thus keeping prices high. This was clearly an extremely interventionist system.

Third, if the price fixed inside the EC was to be high enough to support farmers' incomes, it was imperative to prevent cheap imports from flooding the common market. Therefore, to achieve the second CAP principle, Community preference, a system of variable levies was set up for each product. Produce could generally only enter the common market if it was priced at or above the internal price; if not, the importer had to pay a tariff equalling the difference to the European budget. Moreover, a system of 'reimbursements' (refunds), similar to export subsidies, was also put in place, enabling European producers to sell their products on the world market at world prices without losing income. These subsidies covered the difference in cost between the world and the higher European prices.

Finally, so as to promote the CAP's third principle, that of financial solidarity, a common fund was set up on the basis of Regulation 25 of 1962 (amended subsequently by Regulation 728/70), to cover the financing of the CAP. This fund is known as the European Agricultural Guidance and Guarantee Fund (EAGGF). EAGGF comprised two parts: guidance and guarantee. While the guarantee section covered costs involved with the market system, such as the costs of intervention and export refunds, the much smaller guidance section was responsible for funding structural policies. The EAGGF originally represented almost the entire general budget of the European Community. However, the proportion of the budget spent on agriculture and rural development has decreased substantially since the early 1980s, falling from 65.1 per cent of the total EC budget in 1986 to 53.8 per cent in 2000, and 41 per cent in 2008.

Reforming the CAP?

Initially this policy was very successful in that it very quickly met its initial objectives of increasing productivity and of achieving European self-sufficiency. However, by the 1970s, overproduction had become a political issue, with the first surpluses having appeared in the form of the famous 'butter mountains' and 'wine lakes' of this period. These problems of overproduction, caused when the supply of agricultural produce outstrips demand, increased throughout the 1980s. And with an ever increasing volume of products surplus to internal requirements being paid for at the guaranteed price, being stored at high cost, and finally being exported out of the Community, with support from the agricultural budget to compensate for lower prices on the world market, the CAP was becoming ever more costly to operate. It is far from surprising, therefore, that the CAP was frequently denounced during this time for being too expensive and for taking up too many EC resources, thereby preventing the development of other potentially important political priorities. As a consequence, agricultural policy began to be a major concern for European policy makers, and the issue of CAP reform appeared on the European political agenda.

The policy has proven very resistant to change, however. Some reforms took place from the late 1970s to the end of the 1980s, but these are generally understood to be marginal and incremental. The economic policy tools that were used during this first period of reform were mainly oriented towards controlling the supply of produce by imposing quantitative restrictions on production

CASE STUDY 21.1

Quotas or price cuts? Two options for CAP reform

From an economic point of view, with the CAP guaranteeing high prices to farmers, there were two ways of dealing with the overproduction of foodstuffs, that is, when the supply of food exceeds demand. The first option was to impose production quotas: this would serve to limit the supply of food by imposing limits on the quantities produced, without touching the guaranteed price. This was the solution chosen by European policy makers during the 1980s. This can be seen as a compromise, allowing EC policy makers to cope temporarily with the CAP budget explosion whilst placating, for electoral purposes, their agricultural constituencies by keeping the guaranteed price intact.

However, since the 1970s, most agricultural economists have opposed production quotas because they tend to freeze production capacity, limiting the competitive advantage of individual producers, and constructing entry barriers for the sector. The second option available, which has been implemented by CAP reforms since 1992, is to cut institutional prices in order to restore the role of market forces in adjusting supply and demand. As prices fall, farmers have less of an incentive to produce more food. Most economists promote the price decrease solution because it gives regulatory powers back to the market. From a social perspective, it also allows farmers' revenues to be supported by the state via direct payments, but decouples those payments from the act of production. For economists, direct payments also have the advantage that they can be more precisely targeted at certain categories of farmers or in rewarding specific practices (those that are environmentally friendly, for example). They also allow for greater transparency.

(See Box 21.1). These took the form of 'guaranteed ceilings' for crops in 1981, milk quotas in 1984, and a regime imposing maximum guaranteed quantities (MGQ) for cereals in 1987–8, generalized to other commodities in 1988–9. Despite these changes, the principle of guaranteed prices for agricultural products remained the core element of the CAP.

This incrementalism can be explained by institutional factors rooted in the workings of CAP decision making. Beyond the formal rules of the process (see Box 21.2), decision taking in this policy area is based on what might be termed an 'inflationist bargaining dynamic'. As the CAP is a redistributive policy, each member state's minister of agriculture is under pressure to bring home the maximum they can get from that part of the EU budget dedicated to agriculture. As a consequence of the number of member states involved in the negotiations (all of them trying to increase their CAP budgetary return), the range of products involved, and the rules that have long governed the CAP, there is an inbuilt inflationary tendency. A typical example of this is in the annual 'price package' review, where each

minister in the Council would agree to price increases in their neighbour's favoured products in order to get the increases that they themselves want. As a consequence, decisions that would lead to a reduction in agricultural costs, or that would change the redistributive effects of the policy, are more than likely to be rejected by the Agricultural Council. This makes it very difficult for a body such as the Commission to propose reforms that cut costs. The CAP is also an excellent example of what happens when there is no real link between the EU institutions and the EU's citizens. In such circumstances it is easy for governments to use the European Commission as a scapegoat for decisions that they really do not want to take. The Commission is restricted in what it can do when this happens, and often ends up taking the blame for a policy it would like to see reformed.

In addition to these European brake mechanisms, the incrementalism of CAP reform can also be explained by national political pressures, which are exported to the EC level through the agriculture ministers of each member state in the Agricultural Council. Due to their ability to mobilize support in

CASE STUDY 21.2

The formal CAP decision-making process

The main actors in the CAP decision-making process are the European Commission, responsible for drafting legislation, and the Agricultural Council that takes decisions. The European Parliament (EP), which in many policy areas now shares decision-making responsibility with the Council, has only a very limited role in agricultural policy, amounting to consultation. The only way for the EP to have any influence on the CAP, through its crucial role in the EU's budgetary decision-making mechanisms, is thus in a very indirect manner. However, this situation could change if the Lisbon Treaty is ratified, with the EP being given codecision powers.

CAP decision making usually begins with a proposal from the Commission that may be made either on the basis of a broadly defined request from the European Council (the heads of government or state), or on a voluntary basis by the Commission. Once formulated, the Commission's proposal is then submitted to the EP for consultation and the Agricultural Council for decision. It is also transmitted to the Committee of Agricultural Organisations (COPA), the

main interest group representing European farmers, and to other institutions as appropriate, such as the Committee of the Regions, representing regional interest, for consultation. The Agricultural Council may reject the Commission's proposal or ask for modifications. Alternatively it may begin to negotiate on the basis of what the Commission has proposed, resulting ultimately in a decision.

The Agricultural Council meets monthly, more frequently than most of the EU Councils. One of these meetings was usually set aside to discuss what was called the 'price package' for the following year, at which the member states decided on such issues as the level of guaranteed prices for each product and the amount of quota by country.

Within the Agricultural Council, the unanimity rule has been in place until very recently, albeit only on an informal basis, as a consequence of the 'empty chair crisis' in the late 1960s (see Chapter 2), because the formal rule is in fact qualified majority voting. This has meant that each member has had the right to veto any decision. Decision rules such as this have had important consequences for the CAP, especially with regard to the pace of reform.

---

many European countries, farmers' organizations are able to exert pressure on governments to support their line on the CAP. Political influence of this kind was particularly intense in France and Germany in the 1970s and 1980s. In both countries, farmers were important in electoral terms, as public opinion, influenced by a deep-rooted affinity for rural life, viewed farmers' interests favourably. In the French case, close links were established from the late 1950s between the government and the main farmers' representative organizations, the FNSEA (Fédération Nationale des Syndicats d'Exploitants Agricoles) and the CNJA (Centre National des Jeunes Agriculteurs). Thanks to their capacity for collective action, these organizations were able to impose their views on both right-wing governments (their traditional allies) and successive socialist ones after 1981. Although the left-supporting farmers did manage to get organized during the 1980s, with the establishment of the Confédération Paysanne in 1987, which had a rather different position, they

were still too weak to challenge the power of the right-leaning FNSEA. Consequently, over the course of the 1980s, the French position on the CAP remained very close to that of the FNSEA.

Farmers' opposition to CAP reform is usually explained by simply referring to their will to protect their economic interests. However, there is an additional factor to be taken into account. The conservatism of farmers' associations has much to do with deep-rooted symbolic issues linked to the identity of the farming community. In the French case, for example, the FNSEA has vehemently refused to replace the guaranteed price system with direct payments, even if the latter were calculated to provide a higher income for farmers than the former. Such a position can be explained by certain ethical and professional values that have been inherited by CNJA and FNSEA leaders, arising out of their early experiences in the 1950s with the Young Christian Movement, the JAC (Jeunesse Agricole Chrétienne). Farmers were considered to be individual entrepreneurs, actively working the land and selling the products they had grown in order to earn their living. It is for this reason that they could not tolerate the idea of living and supporting their families on the back of direct income payments, which were viewed either as salaries or, even worse, as a form of social security/welfare payment.

But a second explanation relates directly to the nature of the CAP itself. In upholding the idea that all farmers should get the same rewards, guaranteed prices symbolically feed the myth of farmer unity. This is something of a paradox, as in practice the CAP provides very different levels of support across the EU, across farmers and across products. For example, the bigger you are as a farmer, the more financial support you get. In fact, guaranteed prices have always been used as a political tool by farming elites and, as such, can even be viewed as fundamental to the FNSEA's monopoly in representing French farmers. Thus, by mobilizing support to defend and promote the level of agricultural prices, particularly when the 'price package' event was taking place in Brussels, they were able to consolidate their own dominant position within the farming community.

KEY POINTS

- The CAP was based on three fundamental principles: market unity; Community preference; and financial solidarity.

- The original CAP comprised the institutional guaranteed price, a system of variable levies at borders, and public intervention (storage).

- The CAP began to pose problems in the 1970s: agricultural surpluses soon began to accumulate, and the cost of the CAP increased dramatically, but an inflationary bias in decision-making prevented reform.

- Farmers' reluctance to change is not only rooted in economic interests. Identity and symbolic dimensions matter too.

A dramatic shift in 1992

Despite these brake mechanisms, a first radical reform took place in 1992, which cast aside the original rationale for the CAP. To examine this 'U-turn', we must consider international factors beyond the EU.

Increasing external pressures on the CAP in the 1980s

World agricultural markets in the early 1980s were affected by massive instabilities. In 1982, member countries invited the OECD Secretariat-General to undertake a review of agricultural policies to analyse their effects on international trade, so as to seek recommendations that would lead to balanced reductions in agricultural protection, to better integrate agriculture into the multilateral trading system—in other words, to liberalize agriculture.

The officials in charge asked a number of academics, mainly agricultural economists, for advice. These economists provided them with both theoretical and technical tools to construct an economic model that enabled estimates to be made of the impact of domestic policies on world prices and trade. These studies were initially used to classify the distorting effects of national policies, and later to rank policies, demonstrating which of them were in most serious need of reform. This process engendered a learning process within the international agricultural policy community, and induced a profound change in the way agricultural policy issues were defined. Most notably, it was concluded that to be less distorting, instruments used within an agricultural policy had to be 'decoupled' from agricultural production, so that they would have no direct impact on the type and quantity of commodity produced by the farmer. This conclusion spoke directly to the CAP's price support system.

The process transformed the ideas and beliefs dominating the agricultural policy community towards more 'liberal' approaches, and led to concrete decisions—ultimately to the end of the so-called 'agricultural exception' in international trade negotiations. In 1986, the GATT (the General Agreement on Tariffs and Trade) 'Uruguay Round' opened. For the first time the negotiations included agriculture. As is often the case in GATT Rounds, the main players were the United States and their allies, the Cairns Group, a group of 14 net exporters of agricultural produce, notably Argentina, Australia, New Zealand, Uruguay, and Thailand. This group was on the offensive from the start, arguing strongly for a radical liberalization of international agricultural markets. The USA denounced the CAP as a system that allowed European farmers to eschew competition with the rest of the world, thereby generating trade distortions for producers in third (or non-EU) countries. They called for an end to all trade-distorting domestic subsidies and tariff barriers on agricultural products. The EU, with traditionally more protectionist countries like Norway and Japan, found itself on the defensive.

At the Heysel Ministerial Conference in December 1990, the US and EU positions were still at odds, leading to a stalemate in the negotiations, and threatening the entire process. To put additional pressure on the Europeans, the Americans and their allies took the decision not to negotiate on any other aspect of the Round until the agricultural issue was resolved.

A radical shift in policy: the MacSharry reform

The 1990 GATT crisis provided a window of opportunity for European reformers. A radical CAP reform was seen as the only solution. At this point, the Commission decided to launch a project that it had been preparing secretly for some months. Using its right of initiative, the Commission delivered its radical CAP reform proposal to the Agricultural Council in February 1991. The spirit of the reform was in line with international requirements, in that it would partly replace the system of agricultural price support with a system of direct support to farmers. In broad terms, the proposal revolved around a dramatic decrease in guaranteed prices for oilseeds, cereals, and beef. As this implied a serious loss of income for the farmers, the price cuts were to be compensated by individual direct payments.

The political decision to implement such a radical shift in policy instruments, agreed by the Council in May 1992, was taken initially by Helmut Kohl and François Mitterrand, the then leaders of Germany and France. Both were very keen to conclude the Uruguay Round. Germany had important interests in the non-agricultural part of the negotiations, and the German industrial policy community put intense pressure on the German government to resolve the impasse. In France, the pressures came from the biggest cereal growers, who had a direct interest in the reform. Thanks to the agreed price decreases, they would be able to gain the upper hand in the European animal food market over US cereal substitutes, which had been sold in the EC at world prices (that is, with a zero border tariff) since 1967. Their pressure was kept secret, however, given the fact that the cereal growers were officially part of the FNSEA, which was vehemently opposed to any price decrease for the reasons mentioned before. Another important lobby was the aeronautical industry, so the outcome of what came to be known as the Blair House Agreement, concluding the Uruguay Round in 1993, was really as much about 'Airbus' as about agriculture.

However, although the political decision to reform the CAP was taken by the heads of government or state, negotiations on precisely how the reform would be implemented took place in the Agricultural Council over a period of 18 months. As a result of the sectoral brake mechanisms described before, the Commission's original proposal was largely rewritten. The price levels of crops (cereals and oilseeds) were reduced by 30 per cent and there was a 15 per cent decrease in the price of beef. In addition, the Commission had proposed a sliding scale of compensation for price decreases, for both equity and budgetary reasons. The biggest producers, it was felt, were strong enough to deal with competition in world markets and were therefore not compensated at all for the reduction in the level of prices. Small producers, on the other hand, who would not be able to cope with market pressures without public support, were to be fully compensated, in part on social grounds. Medium-sized farms would be only partially compensated. This proposal was rejected by the Council, largely due to UK and French opposition, driven by large arable farmers. Direct payments to farmers were finally calculated on the basis of the area of land cultivated and according to historical estimates of yields on the farm and/or in the region over a reference period (an average of the previous three years). This meant that the redistributive effect of the policy among farmers remained exactly as it was in the old CAP. Other so-called 'flanking measures' were also adopted in the reform package proposal, though these remained very marginal from a budgetary point of view. They dealt mainly with agri-environmental issues, early retirement, and forestry.

In sum, the outcome of the 1992 reform was not quite as innovative as it might have been, but the deal that was finally concluded on 21 May 1992 was still regarded in many quarters as historic (see *Financial Times*, 22 May 1992: 1–3).

> **KEY POINTS**
>
> - An agricultural learning process at the international level led to a profound shift in knowledge, beliefs, and ideas about agricultural policy towards more 'liberal' views.
>
> - The inclusion of agriculture in the Uruguay Round of the GATT in 1986 placed an important political constraint on European governments, which led to the reform of the CAP.
>
> - The European Commission used this window of opportunity to advance its own proposals and the CAP was subject to a radical shift in 1992, with a reform based on a decrease of the guaranteed price levels replaced by direct individual payments to farmers ('decoupling').

An ongoing reform process

The MacSharry reform marked the point of departure of a deeper CAP reform process, with three further steps in 1999, 2003, and 2008. In many respects these were similar to the earlier reform, including budget-related concerns and pressures; inter-linked international trade bargains and interests; free riding strategies by specialized farmers' organizations; and brake mechanisms in the Agricultural Council.

Agenda 2000 and the 1999 Berlin Compromise

A further CAP reform was agreed in March 1999 at the Berlin European Council, and was incorporated into the Commission's Agenda 2000 plans. It was prepared and issued in the broader context of the Eastern enlargement of the EU (see Box 21.3). On the basis of this document, ten new regulations were adopted, which were expected to come into force from 2000. The Berlin Agreement continued the reform initiated in 1992 for various products, with price reductions in the form of progressive decreases for cereals and dairy products (15 per cent by 2006) and beef (20 per cent), partially compensated for by direct income payments to the farmers affected. As a response to calls for the decentralization of the policy, some of these direct payments took the form of 'national envelopes' (de facto national allocations) paid to the member states from the EC budget, and which each state could distribute to its farmers to target specific national and/or regional priorities.

CASE STUDY 21.3

Eastern enlargement and the CAP

A first crucial issue regarding EU enlargement and agriculture was the extent to which the CAP would be applied to the ten member states that joined in 2004, and whether CAP instruments would have to be adapted. This raised the question of the economic consequences of applying CAP to the new members in respect of the general structure of farming. Moreover, the question of how the CAP would be financed in future was also of major concern.

The European Commission presented its strategy for dealing with these questions at the beginning of 2002. Its proposal involved offering direct payments to farmers and introducing production quotas for new member countries after they joined. To ease transitional problems in rural areas, and to encourage the restructuring of agricultural sectors, the Commission also proposed complementing its financial support with an enhanced rural development policy. Given that the immediate introduction of 100 per cent direct payments would have frozen existing structures and hampered modernization (and bankrupted the EU), the Commission favoured a gradual introduction over a transition period of ten years, covering 25 per cent in 2004, 30 per cent in 2005, and 35 per cent in 2006, ultimately reaching 100 per cent in 2013.

For existing member states, the northern Europeans had argued that the proposal was too costly, and that there should be no direct aid to the Central and East Europeans in the first few years after accession. The Dutch government pointed out that no direct aid for new members was assumed in the Agenda 2000 agreement of 1997. The Swedes argued that direct aid for the new member states would actually discourage much-needed agricultural restructuring. Germany was more concerned about predictions that its net contribution to

the agricultural budget would grow after enlargement and, as a result, that its budgetary returns would decrease. France, always concerned to keep its own budgetary returns on CAP as high as possible, also expressed concern about the cost of the Commission's strategy, but firmly opposed the suggestion by some members that a more profound reform of the CAP needed to take place before enlargement.

For their part, most of the candidate countries reacted by saying that the Commission's proposal did not offer them enough, and that they needed 100 per cent of direct aid paid from Year One, not just for sectoral, but also for political, reasons, in order to convince their publics to agree to EU membership in the first place.

At the Brussels European Council on 25 October 2002, the EU heads of government and state finally adopted the main lines of the Commission's proposal on CAP and enlargement. In order to address some national concerns (from Germany in particular), they placed their decision in a framework of financial stability from 2007 to 2013. More specifically, this meant that total annual expenditure on CAP direct payments and market-related expenditure for a Union of 25 members would not exceed the corresponding combined ceilings for 2006.

One important aspect of the 'CAP and EU enlargement' debate was the concern that Eastern countries would not have the capacity to implement CAP legislation and control expenditures. Bulgaria and Romania were at the core of especially important debates in this respect in the years before their accession in 2007. In addition to more general concerns in terms of judiciary systems and high-level corruption, agricultural funds control and food safety (animal disease control, BSE regulations in particular) were seen as major areas of concern.

In addition to these subsidiarity/decentralization attempts, the 1999 reform was remarkable in that it placed a renewed emphasis on the environment and on sustainability, which also illustrates the increasing participation in and influence of environmental activist groups on CAP debates (See Box 21.4). Three possible avenues were proposed to the member states in this regard: (i) direct payments explicitly dedicated to agri-environmental issues (the old 'agri-environment measures' of the MacSharry reform); (ii) direct payments conditional upon the observance of generally applicable environmental requirements; or (iii) direct payment attached to specific environmental conditions. However, these options, as well as one that allowed the setting of maximum levels on direct aid received by farmers, were to be implemented on a voluntary basis by the member states. Owing to national difficulties and conservative pressures, these optional measures were very rarely implemented.

Environment as an increasingly important issue in the CAP debate

The environment and, more broadly, issues of sustainable development, have progressively found their way into the agricultural policy debate since the 1980s. The negative effects of modern farming were initially denounced by environmental groups. Problems identified included soil erosion in areas of intensive crop production, pollution by pesticides, water pollution caused by nitrate fertilizers in areas of intensive livestock production, and homogenization of the rural landscape. Until the 1990s, however, due to the opacity of the guaranteed price mechanism, it was not easy to explain to the public how the CAP affected the environment in rural areas by prompting farmers to intensify their practices and thereby exacerbating environmental degradation. With CAP support becoming gradually more transparent in 1992, 1999, and 2003, the situation became clearer and environmentalists could enter the agricultural policy debate more directly. Environmental organizations, like WWF, Friends of the Earth, and BirdLife have thus developed an increasing expertise and discursive capacity on agriculture, and they now actively contribute to the CAP debate.

They argue that farmers should at the very least comply with a minimum set of environmental requirements. They also call for a direct link to be set between the amount of subsidy provided to a farmer, and the environmental performance of their farm and/or the quantity of environmental public goods they actually deliver. As BirdLife International puts it: 'We need to spend EU tax-payers' money more sensibly—let's support those farmers who maintain a healthy, thriving rural environment, and let's stop distributing unjustified and environmentally harmful subsidies' (BirdLife 2008a).

The new active participation of environmentalist groups in the CAP debate does not, however, ensure that their views are taken into account in the final decisions. The 2008 reform, for example, has been denounced as highly disappointing by environmental organizations. According to a Bird Life representative in Brussels after the Agriculture Council's final compromise was made public, it 'completely fails to address the new environmental challenges of the 21st Century ... The patient is still ill and won't get any better with the prescribed treatment' (BirdLife 2008b).

The Agenda 2000 reform also endorsed an important innovation in policy discourse, by making use of the term 'multifunctionality'. This signals that agriculture is not just about production but also incorporates 'non-production' aspects of farming, that is, its social, cultural, territorial, and environmental dimensions. With this concept, however, European policy makers were not only seeking new ways to legitimize the CAP within the EU. They also had the forthcoming World Trade Organization (WTO) Round in mind. When the Uruguay Round was concluded in 1994, the Agreement on Agriculture (AoA) defined three 'boxes' used to distinguish between support for policy programmes that directly stimulated production and consequently distorted trade, and those that were considered to have no direct effect on production and trade. Domestic measures with a direct effect on production were placed in the 'amber box': they had to be cut. Measures considered to be 'decoupled from production', with no linkage between the amount of

payment and the production process, agricultural prices, or factors of production, were placed in the 'green box' and could be freely used. Payments linked to programmes aiming at limiting production went in the 'blue box' and did not need to be reduced as long as certain conditions were met. In the AoA, the post-1992 CAP compensatory payments were classified in the blue box; but in view of the forthcoming international trade negotiations, the strategy decided by the Agricultural Council in October 1999 involved 'securing' CAP payments in the blue box, by arguing that the CAP could not be challenged because it pursued multifunctionality, meaning non-production as well as production goals.

As a conclusion, we can say that although rural development was newly presented as the 'second pillar' of the CAP (note: this has nothing to do with the three pillars of the EU) and as such intended to enhance the 'multifunctionality' of European agriculture in line with a subsidiarity-based approach,

Agenda 2000 was in fact only one small step in this direction, with only a small percentage of total CAP expenditure allocated to it (see Figure 21.1 and Table 21.1).

The 'Mid-term Review' of June 2003

After a new WTO Round was opened in 2001, the European Commission also issued a new CAP reform plan in July of the following year. This plan envisaged a substantial reshaping of the policy (European Commission 2002b) by introducing further reforms for crops and meat and by extending changes to new commodities like milk. The official argument was that public expenditure for farming had to be better justified, that it had to do more to ensure high-quality food and animal welfare, the preservation of the environment, landscapes, and cultural heritage, as well as social welfare and equity. In reality, however, this plan was largely driven by the new WTO negotiations, where the fate of the

blue box became more and more uncertain, making it clear that the EU could only secure CAP payments to European farmers by transferring them to the green box, meaning their further 'decoupling' from production.

While initially supported by the UK, Germany, and other 'northern' governments, the new CAP reform proposal faced very strong French opposition. The French government refused to reduce its support for its larger cereal growers and wanted reform postponed until 2006. The Agricultural Council finally reached a compromise in June 2003. The 2003 'Mid-term Review' (MTR) of the CAP (so called because it was foreseen in the 1999 Berlin Agreement as a simple reviewing exercise) is considered by some commentators as a second revolution in CAP reform (after the 1992 reform).

The June 2003 reform further decreased the intervention price of cereals and introduced changes for durum wheat, rice, dried fodder, protein crops, and nuts, along the same lines as the 1992 and 1999 reforms. It also introduced a new element, the Single Farm Payment (SFP), a unique

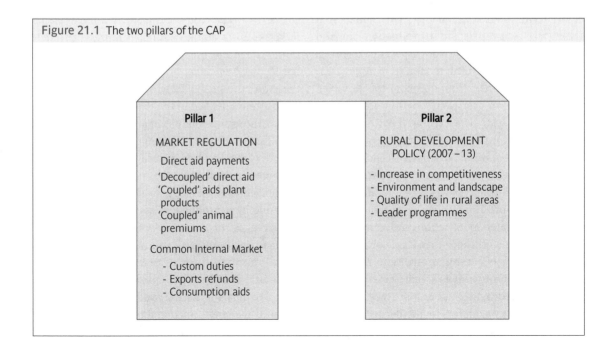

Figure 21.1 The two pillars of the CAP

Pillar 1

MARKET REGULATION

Direct aid payments
'Decoupled' direct aid
'Coupled' aids plant products
'Coupled' animal premiums

Common Internal Market

- Custom duties
- Exports refunds
- Consumption aids

Pillar 2

RURAL DEVELOPMENT POLICY (2007–13)

- Increase in competitiveness
- Environment and landscape
- Quality of life in rural areas
- Leader programmes

Table 21.1 Agricultural expenses 2004 to 2008

		2004	2005	2006	2007 (appropriations)	2008 (appropriations)
PILLAR I	Interventions in agricultural markets (%)	18	16	15	9	8
	Direct aids (%)	63	64	64	71	70
PILLAR II	Rural development (%)	18	19	20	19	22
Other (%)		1	1	1	1	1
Total (%)		100	100	100	100	100
Total (€ millions)		47,467.4	52,698.2	53,538.5	52,015.5	52,457.8

Source: Eur-Lex—General Budget of the EU for years 2006 to 2009—Title 05.

CAP direct payment aimed at achieving a complete decoupling of support and production. Under this system, even a farmer who decides to grow nothing is eligible to receive this payment, as long as they comply with environmental, food safety, animal welfare, and occupational safety standards (see Table 21.5).

Implementation of the reform began in the member states in 2005 or 2006. The SFPs are calculated

---

 CASE STUDY 21.5

Alternative ways of farming

Without public support and in opposition to 'conventional' models of agriculture, 'alternative' farmers have been proving that it is possible to farm differently. Organic farming is the best known example, but there are others, all based on a rejection of the conventional productivist model of agriculture, which is based on the trilogy of intensification-enlarging-investment. In contrast to this conventional model, alternative farmers have proved that farming can simultaneously be friendlier to the environment, offer better working conditions and quality of life for the farmer, and provide a similar or even better income. This sort of farming used to be denounced as old-fashioned and out of line with modernity and technical progress; but thanks to an opening of the agricultural debate to incorporate environmental and sustainability issues (notably under consumer pressure), alternative farming is gaining much more attention at both national and EU levels.

At the EU level, some steps have been taken to support alternative modes of farming since the 1990s. For example, in 1991 the Agricultural Council voted to harmonize production norms for organic vegetal products that have been operational since 1993. Alternative farming is also considered under the CAP's agri-environmental measures, with member states now authorized to support alternative models of agriculture under the EU's co-financing procedures. However, it seems that policy makers do not yet consider these models as real alternatives to the productivist agricultural model. Support for alternative farmers remains very small.

In order to reverse this situation, alternative farmers have become politically active, even though they have relatively scarce resources compared to conventional farming organizations. The *International Federation of Organic Agricultural Movements* regularly publishes position papers on CAP, as they did during the 2008 Health Check debate (see www.ifoam.org). Alternative farmers also build alliances with environmental groups (see Box 21.4). In Paris in 2008, the CIVAM federation, a network of French alternative farmers, organized an important conference with the WWF in the frame of the CAP Health Check debate and made a number of common claims.

Table 21.2 Distribution of total direct aids per tranche for select EU member states, financial year 2006

		United Kingdom	France	Denmark	Portugal	Ireland	Czech Republic	Poland
Total direct aids (€1000)		3,523,571	7,615,739	924,064	538,365	1,202,657	255,950	807,018
Number of beneficiaries		195,080	426,690	70,600	239,580	129,490	20,210	1,464,970
Average amount per beneficiary (€)		60,000	20,000	13,090	2,250	9,290	12,660	1,820
Farmers paid less than €5,000	share of total beneficiaries	49%	34%	36%	92.5%	46%	55%	80%
	share of total amount	3%	3%	6%	29%	11%	8%	99%
Farmers paid between €5,000 and €200,000	share of total beneficiaries	50%	66%	64%	7.5%	54%	44%	19%
	share of total amount	87%	96%	91%	66%	89%	74%	1%
Farmers paid more than €200,000	share of total beneficiaries	1%	1%	Less than 0.1%	Less than 0.1%	Less than 0.1%	1%	1%
	share of total amount	10%	1%	3%	5%	Less than 0.1%	18%	Less than 0.01%

Source: European Commission, http://ec.europa.eu/agriculture/fin/directaid/2006/annex1_en.pdf (raw data), with calculations by the author.

on a historical basis, based on the total payments received for all products in previous years (average payment for the years 2000, 2001, and 2002). In order to redress the imbalances between big and small farmers, individual SFPs are calculated regionally in almost all the member states other than France and the UK where, after pressure from large-scale cereal growers and landowners, the payment was made on an individual basis (see Table 21.2).

The 2008 'Health Check'

Since 2003, further reforms have been decided on the MTR 'decoupling' model for various isolated products like olive oil, cotton, and tobacco in 2003 and 2004, sugar in December 2005, fruits and vegetables in 2007, and wine in 2008. Regarding the global policy, a so-called 'health check' took place in 2007–8. With the WTO Doha Round talks more or less on hold in this period, the 2008 'Health Check' reform was driven mainly by internal rather than external concerns, and the general debate that took place was primarily concerned with budgets and efficiency (see Box 21.6).

A first Green Paper was issued by the Commission in November 2007. This denied any intention to engage in a deep CAP reform at this stage, but proposed some 'adaptations' for the period 2009–13 along three key principles: making farmers respond to market signals; ensuring they receive the 'right' kind of support (in terms of quantity and compliance criteria); and meeting four 'new challenges': climate change, water management, renewable energy, and biodiversity. A formal proposal

---

BOX 21.6

About budgets and transparency: where does the money go?

A first very general feature of the CAP debate set countries like the UK, Sweden, and Denmark against countries like France and Spain. The former ask why such a large amount of EU funds (40.8 per cent of the EU budget in 2007) should go to agriculture instead of other sectors like research (with only 3.5 per cent of the EU budget in 2007), given that farmers represent such a small part of the population (see ECORYS 2008). The latter argue that this is simply because the CAP is the only fully Europeanized policy and that aggregated figures at national and EU levels show a very different picture, with research and development benefiting from 0.677 per cent of the European GNP against only 0.55 per cent for agriculture (Bertoncini 2007). Behind these arguments for and against lies a crucial debate among member states, which has always existed in the CAP: the issue of 'budget return', that is, the benefits of a given country thanks to the CAP, less the contribution of this country to the CAP via the EU budget. This issue, which recalls Margaret Thatcher's famous 'I want my money back' stance in 1984, is present in all bargaining processes in the Agriculture Council, and is responsible for its inflationist spending tendency.

For years, citizens have been left out of these debates. Due to the opacity of the old guaranteed price system, the discussion was very much a technical one and was confined to the elite level. Under the reformed CAP and the direct payment system, CAP support became more understandable and the debate became public. As a consequence, more and more actors have been asking for a greater transparency about

'where' and 'to whom' the money goes. Although data on individual payments were initially kept secret, from 2004 onwards lists of the main beneficiaries of the CAP were progressively published in the member states. And it came as a surprise when citizens discovered that huge CAP payments were allocated to the late British Queen Mother, to Prince Rainier of Monaco, to big companies and food industries, and to members of governments (including an Agriculture EU Commissioner, Mariann Fisher Boel)! In France there was a scandal when it was revealed (see *La Tribune*, 3 November 2005: 2–3) that the first beneficiary on the list for 2004 was allocated more than €850,000 to produce rice in the south of France; and the second, almost the same for 1,500 hectares of irrigated maize in south-west France (one of the less environmentally friendly crops in this area!). More recently, in October 2007, the Council agreed to the full disclosure of all recipients of financial support under the Common Agricultural Policy and decided that data would have to be made publicly available in all member states as of the end of 2008 for the second pillar and at the start of 2009 for the first pillar (see Table 21.2).

In sum, with the distribution of CAP support suddenly becoming more visible, the question of social justice has been raised. As did the environmental issue (see Box 21.4), this shift in the debate had important consequences in the farming community. It created tensions within traditional farmers' unions, notably between the different kinds of producers—for example, intensive crop growers versus extensive cattle growers. It also allowed left-wing farmers' unions to gain additional support.

---

followed in May 2008 and launched a bargaining process in the Council. The final agreement, the aforementioned 'Health Check' was approved in November 2008. This abolished milk quotas—to be phased out progressively to 2015—cancelled compulsory set-aside, reformed some remaining intervention instruments, and further decoupled CAP support by shifting all kinds of support to the SFP (except for suckler cows, goats, and sheep, for which a certain level of coupling is still allowed). It also increased modulation, that is, the shifting of funds

from the first to the second CAP pillar (see Figure 21.1). However, with only 10 per cent shifted to the second pillar, and an additional 4 per cent for payments above €300,000, the final Council agreement strongly departed from the Commission's initial proposal on this point (see Box 21.7).

The European agricultural community is now awaiting 2013 when the policy will be reformed again, probably in a rather more substantial manner, given that a general review of the European budget will take place at the same time.

The long road towards rural development

Since the early years of the CAP, the European Commission has tried to introduce a socio-economic dimension into the policy. The very first attempt of this kind was made by the Dutch Agricultural Commissioner, Sicco Mansholt, in the late 1960s. He proposed a radical revision of CAP's market measures, together with an active *structural agricultural policy* at the European level, in order to help the restructuring of the sector. Strongly rejected by the Council, the proposal gave birth to a very timid structural policy in 1972, providing funds for such things as new technologies and equipment. Differing from other CAP measures, these structural measures were co-financed by member states through fixed, multi-annual budgetary 'envelopes'. Despite an increase in allocations since the mid 1980s, only an extremely small part of the European agricultural budget has ever been devoted to structural measures, most of the budget being spent on market- (production-) related expenditures.

In the following decades, structural measures were replaced by efforts to create a *rural development policy* in the frame of the CAP, with social, forestry, and agri-environment measures supplementing structural goals. The European Commission has made various attempts to promote rural development as a parallel approach to agricultural policy since the beginning of the 1990s. Its Directorate-General for Agriculture was renamed 'Agriculture and Rural Development', and it published numerous documents promoting its 'sustainable rural development' strategy. An important event organized in this perspective was 'the European Conference on Rural Development' (Cork, Ireland, 7–9 November 1996), initially planned as a way of building an ambitious 'integrated' approach to the countryside within the CAP. The Cork Declaration invited European policy makers to switch their public support from financing market measures to assisting rural development and agri-environmental programmes. But the member states remained reluctant to adopt such an approach, and the conference was seen as a failure.

Some progress was made in pursuing this agenda in 1999, with structural measures converted into the 'second pillar' of the CAP alongside agri-environmental measures. However, this new 'pillar' remained marginal from a budgetary point of view. Subsequently, some commentators expected the eastern enlargement to provide an opportunity to reinforce rural development measures in the CAP, but this did not really happen (see Box 21.3). The 'modulation' measure, decided in 2003, was the first really concrete measure. A new regulatory framework for rural development was also adopted in September 2005 (Council Regulation No. 1698/2005), with three different themes: 'improving the competitiveness of the agricultural and forestry sector'; 'improving the environment and the countryside'; and 'improving the quality of life in rural areas and encouraging diversification of the rural economy'. By 2007, all member states had to define their rural development programme(s) for the period 2007–13 by spreading funds between the three themes, with some additional support available for so-called 'LEADER initiatives', that is, highly individual projects designed and implemented by local partnership to solve local problems. Ninety-four rural development programmes were approved for the 2007–13 period.

The 2008 Health Check was initially planned to continue this trend. In its initial proposal, the Commission had asked for a basic modulation rate of 13 per cent by 2013, rising to 23 per cent on individual payments over €100,000, 38 per cent above €200,000 and 58 per cent above €300,000. Owing to (among others) German pressure in the Council—since reunification, Germany has some very big farms—the final agreement includes a much lower modulation scheme, with a basic rate of 10 per cent in 2013, and only an additional 4 per cent for individual payments above €300,000. The revenues from this modulation policy are to be used by the member states to finance 'new challenges' (global warming, water, renewable energy, biodiversity) and a 'soft landing' in the dairy sector as milk quotas get dismantled.

In sum, a major issue regarding EU rural development policy remains the persistent weakness of the second pillar, which is allocated only 19 per cent of the CAP budget, as against 81 per cent allocated to the first pillar (in 2007). Furthermore, EU rural development policy is often criticized as being too 'farming'-oriented. While agriculture is no longer the sole engine for rural development, it still consumes almost all available funds, with rural development actors outside the farming sector only benefiting from very scarce resources. In order to address this issue better, some commentators argue for a shift in rural development from the CAP to EU regional policy, a proposal strongly resisted by the agricultural policy community, who argue that 'the money must stay green' as a means of guaranteeing that it is 'really spent on the countryside, and not on large centres of population that call themselves rural' (see Figure 21.1 and Table 21.1).

KEY POINTS

- A new CAP reform was agreed in December 1999, in light of forthcoming enlargements. This introduced the concept of multifunctionality and the concept of the two pillars of the CAP.

- The policy was further reformed in June 2003 to avoid a clash within the WTO. This reform introduced the Single Farm Payment system, which can be seen as a second 'revolution' in the policy after the 1992 reform.

- A 'Health Check' of the CAP was made in November 2008, which notably abolished the milk quota system.

- Despite a number of proposals encouraging greater social justice and a more environmentally friendly policy, change is still resisted by certain members of the Council who continue to support large payments to big farmers.

Conclusion: the CAP at a crossroads

Originally intended to make Western Europe self-sufficient in food, the CAP was equipped with 'productivist' instruments that led to an overproduction of agricultural produce and serious budgetary problems for the EC. In the 1980s, the first reforms introduced supply control measures, such as quotas. At the beginning of the 1990s, due to international developments, new policy beliefs inspired the 'decoupling' of farm support from production. This provoked a radical reform of the CAP in 1992, which shifted policy instruments from market or price support to direct income support. This decreased centrally planned prices, compensating for these cuts through direct payments to farmers. This new path has continued in subsequent CAP reforms, with further 'decoupling' for an increasing number of products, and attention paid to the environmental and social dimension of the CAP.

The evolution of the CAP since the 1980s is an excellent illustration of the complexity of the links that exist between national, European, and international political arenas. Intersectoral deals that are not easily understood at national level become even more complicated when various governments, coalitions of interests, and European and international institutions enter the game. Caught in the crossfire between national interest and international bargains, the EU's political system is complex, intricate, and competitive. The only way to deconstruct this complexity is by examining the actors involved in the policy process and the nature of the political exchanges that take place amongst them.

The CAP also provides a good example of how a reform can feed back into discussions about the very purpose of the policy. The shift from an opaque set of instruments (the guaranteed price mechanism) to a more transparent system of direct payment proved to have very direct impacts on the actors engaged in the process and the balance of power across member states, as well as on the substantive content of debates on the kind of agricultural policy Europe ought to have (see Boxes 21.4 and 21.6).

QUESTIONS

1. Why did the CAP originally seek to maintain high prices for agricultural produce?

2. What were the negative consequences of the CAP's price support mechanism?

3. How did European policy makers try to deal with the problems of overproduction and increasing budgetary costs in the 1980s?

4. Why did the 1992 reform take place?

5. What do the 1992, 1999, 2003, and 2008 CAP reforms have in common?

6. To what extent does the current round of international trade negotiations pose a threat to the CAP?

7. What is multifunctionality? What implications does it have for agricultural policy?

8. Which new issues entered the agricultural policy debate from the late 1990s on, and why?

 GUIDE TO FURTHER READING

■ Garzon, I. *Reforming the Common Agricultural Policy: History of a Paradigm Change* (Basingstoke: Palgrave Macmillan, 2007). The book provides a comparison of the 1992, 1999, and 2003 CAP reforms, and argues that policy feedbacks of each reform led to a change in policy paradigm.

■ Greer, A. Agricultural policy in Europe (Manchester: Manchester University Press, 2005). This book provides a unique comparative analysis and shows that despite the CAP, substantial agricultural policy variations exist across the EU.

■ Jones, A. and Clark, J. *The Modalities of European Union Governance: New Institutionalist Explanations of Agri-environmental Policy* (Oxford: Oxford University Press, 2001). An excellent study of the relationship between agricultural and environmental policy in the EU, exploring in the process many of the intricacies of the CAP.

■ Moyer, W. and Josling, T. *Agricultural Policy Reform. Politics and Process in the EU and US in the 90s* (London: Ashgate, 2002). This book provides a detailed, accurate, and well informed presentation of agricultural policy reforms in the 1990s in the USA, EU, and GATT/WTO.

■ Shucksmith, M., Thomson, K., and Roberts, D. (eds) *CAP and the Regions. The Territorial Impact of Common Agricultural Policy* (Wallingford: CABI Publishing, 2005). Through detailed statistical analysis and case studies, this book assesses the regional impact of the EU's CAP and Rural Development Policy, asking how far these policies are compatible with more general objectives of territorial cohesion across the enlarged European Union.

 WEBLINKS

● http://commonagpolicy.blogspot.com/ Professor Wyn Grant's excellent blog on the CAP, regularly updated and with lots of useful information.

● http://europa.eu.int/comm/commission_barroso/fischer-boel/index_en.htm Mariann Fischer Boel's web page, with lots of information on ongoing work on CAP reforms.

- http://europa.eu.int/comm/agriculture/index_en.htm   The home page of the European Commission's Directorate-General for agriculture.

- http://farmsubsidy.org   An online database, with detailed data on who gets what from the CAP (on a country basis).

- http://caphealthcheck.eu/   This blog brings together contributions of researchers, activists, and analysts who share a reformist approach to the CAP.

 Visit the Online Resource Centre that accompanies this book for lots of interesting additional material. http://www.oxfordtextbooks.co.uk/orc/Cini_Borragan3e/

22 Environmental Policy

DAVID BENSON AND ANDREW JORDAN

Chapter Contents

- Introduction
- The development of environmental policy: different perspectives
- Linking different perspectives: the underlying dynamics of environmental policy
- Future challenges
- Conclusion

Reader's Guide

The EU is, at root, an economically oriented organization dedicated to the liberalization of trade. Nonetheless, it has developed an extensive array of policies and institutions dedicated to protecting and preserving the environment. Through this process, environmental concerns have shifted from being a marginal aspect of the European integration process to one that routinely grabs newspaper headlines and, unlike many other policy areas in which the EU is active, receives strong political support from its citizens. Moreover, these policies have shown themselves to be remarkably resilient to economic and deregulatory pressures. This chapter documents and explores the reasons behind this relatively rapid and remarkably enduring transformation, explores the main dynamics of policy making in the environmental sector from different perspectives, and identifies a number of future challenges.

Introduction

At its founding in 1957, the EU had no environmental policy, no environmental bureaucracy, and no environmental laws. In fact, the word 'environment' was not even mentioned in the Treaty of Rome. The EEC was primarily an intergovernmental agreement between six like-minded states to boost economic prosperity and repair political relations in war-torn Europe. Over 50 years later, EU environmental policy is 'broad in scope, extensive in detail and stringent in effect' (Weale et al 2000: 1). It now conforms to a set of guiding principles, has its own terminology (see Box 22.1), is the focus of significant activity amongst a dedicated network of environmental actors, is underpinned by a binding framework of environmental laws, and has an explicit basis in the founding treaties. In short, it has successfully evolved from a set of 'incidental measures' (Hildebrand 2005: 16) to a mature system of multi-level environmental governance. Virtually all environmental policy in Europe is now made in, or in close association with, the EU. It is therefore 'impossible to understand the environmental policy of any of the … Member States without understanding [EU] environmental policy' (Haigh 1992: xi) as the two are now inextricably intertwined.

What is especially striking about this process of transformation is how quickly the EU assumed control over policy powers 'that in a federal state would have been ceded to the centre only grudgingly, if at all' (Sbragia 1993: 337). Moreover, as a sector, environmental policy has consistently shown itself to be remarkably resilient to deregulatory pressures and/or declining public demands for ever higher standards. This chapter documents the reasons behind this rapid and remarkably enduring transformation (see Box 22.2), identifies the main dynamics of policy making from a range of different perspectives and explores a number of future challenges.

 KEY CONCEPTS AND TERMS 22.1

Sustainable development

The policy principle that states human development should address the needs of present generations without comprising the ability of future generations to meet their needs.

New environmental policy instruments (NEPIs)

Non-legislative alternatives to environmental regulation, that is, self-enforced management standards, voluntary agreements between governments and polluters, and market-based instruments such as taxes and tradable permits.

Emissions trading

A market-based instrument that offers polluters economic incentives to reduce their emissions. It works by creating a market in which tradable allowances are bought and sold.

Environmental Impact Assessment (EIA)

A systematic assessment procedure conducted on proposed developments in order to predict their impacts on the environment.

Kyoto Protocol

A 1997 protocol to the 1992 United Nations Framework Convention on Climate Change (UNFCCC), which commits signatory countries and the EU to achieve specified greenhouse gas emissions reduction by 2008–12.

Ecological modernization

A political philosophy that maintains environmental protection can be reconciled with, and indeed help to generate, economic growth and technological innovation.

CHRONOLOGY 22.2

The evolution of EU environmental policy

1972 Heads of state meeting in Paris request the Commission to prepare a common statement of environmental policy.

1973 The Commission adopts the First Environmental Action Programme.

1981 Reorganization of the Commission leads to the creation of a dedicated Directorate-General for the environment.

1987 The Single European Act provides a more secure legal basis.

1993 The Maastricht Treaty enters into force and extends QMV to almost all areas of environmental policy.

1993 Publication of the Fifth Environmental Action Programme: explores the systematic pursuit of sustainable development.

1997 The Treaty of Amsterdam: makes the promotion of sustainable development and environmental policy integration central objectives of the EU.

2002 A Sixth and more binding Environmental Action Programme is adopted.

2008 The EU adopts a comprehensive climate and energy package committing member states inter alia to a 20 per cent reduction in greenhouse gas emissions by 2020 and a sharp increase in the use of renewable energy sources.

The development of environmental policy: different perspectives

There are several different ways to comprehend the evolution of EU environmental policy. One is to explore the content of the six environmental action programmes (EAPs) drafted by the European Commission since 1973. A second is to examine the main policy outputs, namely Directives, Regulations and Decisions. A third is to scrutinize the periodic amendments to the founding treaties, starting with the Single European Act (SEA) and concluding with the (as yet unratified) Lisbon Treaty. Finally, the dynamic interplay between the main actors at the international, EU, and national levels can be examined. The remainder of this section is structured around these four perspectives.

The environmental action programmes

Six EAPs have been adopted by the Commission since the early 1970s. Initially, these were essentially 'wish lists' of new legislation, but have gradually become more comprehensive and programmatic in nature. The first (1973–6), identified a number of pressing priorities, namely pollution and other threats to human health. Just as importantly, it also established several key principles (see Box 22.3) which were subsequently enshrined in the founding treaties (see below). They were not particularly novel (many derived from national and/or OECD best practice), but they represented an innovative attempt to apply them together in a new (that is, supranational) setting.

The second (1977–81), followed the same approach as the first, but emphasized the importance of monitoring and collecting information to inform decision making, through procedures such as environmental impact assessment (EIA). Importantly, it also underlined the Commission's desire to become more heavily involved in international-level policy-making activities (see below). By

BOX 22.3

Key principles of EU environmental policy

Environmental management

Prevention: preventing problems is cheaper and fairer than paying to remedy them afterwards.

Action at source: using the best available technology to minimize polluting emissions.

Integrated pollution control: ensuring that, for example, attempts to remedy water pollution are not transformed into air or land pollution problems.

Specification of environmental standards

Resource conservation: environmental protection as a goal in its own right.

High level of protection: aiming for the highest level of protection possible.

Precaution: acting to protect the environment even when cause – effect relationships are not fully understood.

Allocation of authority

Appropriate level of action: acting at the 'right' level.

Subsidiarity: only acting at EU level when problems cannot be tackled at national level.

Policy integration

Polluter pays: the polluter (rather than society as a whole) should pay to address problems.

Environmental policy integration: integrating an environmental dimension into the development of new sectoral policies such as agriculture and transport.

Source: Weale et al (2000: 62 – 3); Knill and Liefferink (2007: 28).

contrast, the third (1982–6) and fourth (1987–92) were more programmatic in nature, setting out an overall strategy for protecting the environment before problems occurred. In contrast to the first programme, they were significantly more ambitious, identifying many more priority areas (Weale et al 2000: 59). They also underscored the benefits of prevention by fitting the best available abatement technology to factories and vehicles.

The fifth (1993–2000) and sixth (2002–12) accelerated this shift to a more strategic approach to planning. The fifth introduced the notion of sustainable development, explored new ways to enhance policy implementation through non-legislative instruments (known as new environmental policy instruments, or 'NEPIs'), and identified new ways to embed greater environmental policy integration (EPI) (see Box 22.3). The sixth developed this approach still further by initiating seven thematic strategies. Crucially, the sixth—and current—programme has greater legislative force, having been coadopted by the Parliament and the Council.

Key items of policy

Looking at the content of all six, a steady trend is visible away from a rather ad hoc, reactive approach driven by the Commission, to a more strategic framework, co-developed by multiple stakeholders. A similar picture emerges from a cursory inspection of the number of legal measures adopted annually (see Figure 22.1). In the 1960s and 1970s, the output of legislation was relatively slow, but then it rocketed in the 1980s and 1990s, tailing off again in the 2000s. By the late 1990s, more effort was being devoted to consolidating, streamlining and reforming the environmental *acquis communautaire* via more framework-type legislation. Key measures here have included the framework directives on air quality (1996), water (2000), and chemicals (2006).

However, if we look at the changing purpose of all these measures, a slightly different pattern emerges. Thus the first few environmental directives addressed areas such as cars and chemicals: in other words, traded products. In the 1980s and particularly the 1990s, the EU began to diversify into new

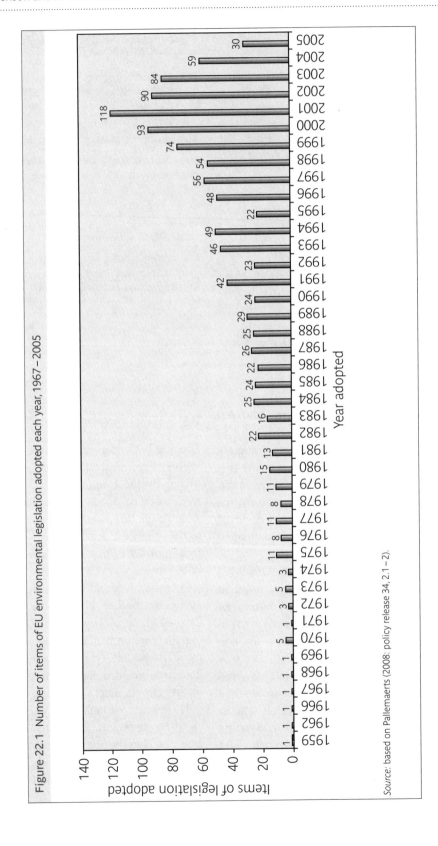

Figure 22.1 Number of items of EU environmental legislation adopted each year, 1967 – 2005

Source: based on Pallemaerts (2008: policy release 34, 2.1 – 2).

areas including access to environmental information, genetically modified organisms, and even zoos, a trend that exemplified the rising political demand for environmental protection 'for its own sake'. The overall pattern of policies therefore resembles more an inconsistent 'patchwork' (Héritier 2002a) than a comprehensive and carefully designed framework. It also nicely illustrates the fact that the EU is a 'regulatory state' (Majone 1996) in the environmental sphere; non-legislative instruments (i.e. NEPIs) are still conspicuous by their absence at EU level.

The evolution of the treaties

Another way to comprehend the development of EU environmental policy is to analyse the environmental provisions of the EU's founding treaties. At one level, the legal codification of the environmental *acquis communautaire* has followed the same gradual but ever increasing pattern noted above. Thus the original Treaty of Rome contained no reference at all to environmental matters. New environmental measures consequently had to rely either on Article 100 (now Article 94), relating to the internal market, or on Article 235 (now Article 308), which allowed the EU to move into new policy areas to accomplish its goals. The former proved to be legally more secure and hence politically less contested than the latter, hence the tendency (noted above) for early measures to target traded products.

In one sense, the Single European Act did establish a more secure legal basis, with qualified majority voting (QMV) for issues with a single market dimension. This undoubtedly allowed the EU to enter new, and less 'obvious', areas such as access to environmental information, the conservation of wildlife habitats, and the performance of wastewater treatment facilities—all somewhat removed from the development of an internal market. In another sense, it simply codified the status quo: over a hundred items of policy had already been adopted when it was ratified in 1987 (Wurzel 2008: 66). The Maastricht and Amsterdam Treaties drew new policy principles (such as sustainable development,

precaution, and EPI), see Boxes 22.1 and 22.3 into the founding treaties. Crucially, they also extended QMV to almost all areas and greatly increased the European Parliament's powers. By the late 1990s, most environmental policy followed one decision-making route (that is, QMV in the Council plus codecision). But immediately prior to this, there were several legislative routes anchored in different treaty bases. This encouraged actors to fight with one another to select the legal base that maximized their bargaining power (Hovden 2002). The fact that the Nice (Jordan and Fairbrass 2005) and Lisbon Treaties (Benson and Jordan 2008) were so lacking in new environmental content rather suggests that the legal underpinnings of environmental policy had essentially been settled by the late 1990s.

Actor dynamics

By now it should be evident that the development of environmental policy has not followed a single pattern. There have been periods of continuity and periods of significant change. Furthermore, some aspects (for example, the action programmes) have evolved in a fairly gradual and systematic manner, whereas others (for example, the types of policies) have emerged in much more unpredictable and opportunistic ways. In order to explore these similarities and differences, one needs to look at the main actors, examine their motivations, and the evolving constraints under which they operate.

More so than any other actor, the Commission deserves the bulk of the credit (or, depending on one's point of view, blame) for developing an environmental policy at the EU level. In the early phases, it worked hard to establish a case for EU involvement. Undaunted by the absence of high-level political support (no Commission President has consistently championed environmental policy, and some have appeared more than willing to sacrifice it for other political objectives), a weak treaty basis, and limited administrative capacities (there was no designated environmental Directorate-General until 1981 and no environment Commissioner until 1989), the Commission soon realized that it would have to be creative to thrive. Even today, its DG Environment is still rather limited in size; it is dwarfed, for example, by its opposite number in the USA, the federal Environmental Protection Agency (Sbragia 1996: 244). The Commission is not, of course, monolithic; debates between the DGs responsible for environment, trade, and industry are often just as intense as those between the Commission and other actors.

Given these limitations, DG Environment very quickly learnt to exploit opportunities and colonize institutional niches as and when they appeared. In many ways, this was the very essence of Monnet's neo-functionalist method of integrating 'by stealth', whereby incremental integration by the EU in key economic sectors creates so-called 'spillover' incentives for political integration in others (Weale 2005) (see also Chapter 5). In the environmental sector, the Monnet Method succeeded brilliantly. But as the political and legal basis of EU policy became more secure, the Commission focused more of its efforts on managing and governing instead of trying to expand into new areas. This has gone hand in hand with a more open, inclusive, and less opportunistic modus operandi.

Until the 1980s, the chief policy-making body was the Council of Ministers (now usually called the EU Council). The first meeting of the Environment Council took place in 1972. The participants—mostly national environment ministers—soon learnt that they could adopt policies in Brussels that were frankly unattainable in their national governments. Pushed hard by a 'troika' of environmental 'leader' states comprising the Netherlands, Denmark, and West Germany, the Council began to adopt more and more ambitious legislation in the 1980s. After 1982, West Germany emerged as a strong advocate of new policies, partly to address domestic political concerns but also to boost its fledgling environmental technology industry (Sbragia 1996: 241). In many ways, its underlying philosophy—that of 'ecological modernization'—now underpins all aspects of EU environmental policy. Advocates of this philosophy argue that high levels of environmental protection are reconcilable with, and can even promote, economic growth (Box 22.1).

Less ambitious or what are sometimes referred to as 'laggard' states (typically from the Mediterranean region but also including Ireland and the UK) were rather slow to catch on to what was happening in Brussels, and ended up adopting some key policies almost 'absent-mindedly' (Weale et al 2000: 359). Sbragia (1996: 237) has argued that the outcome of these actor constellations was a 'push–pull' dynamic: '[t]he internal politics of the ... progressive States 'pushes' the process in Brussels along ... "pulling" most of the Member States towards levels of environmental protection, which, left to their domestic devices, they most probably would not adopt'.

By the 2000s, the once stark division between 'leaders' and 'laggards' had begun to dissolve. New member states had entered the fray (for example, after 2004) and some existing participants (the UK, for example) had changed their preferences and bargaining tactics as a result of their involvement in EU policy making (Jordan 2002). Consequently, new alliances began to open up that criss-crossed the traditional binary divide between richer and poorer states. These were often more strongly associated with how to achieve policy goals (for example, what policy instruments or style of enforcement should be applied?), than whether to pitch standards at a higher or lower level (Sbragia, 2000: 295).

Two other things are important to note about the behaviour of states in the Council. First, given the right contextual conditions, the Presidency of the EU matters a great deal. When a 'leader' state is in charge there tends to be more substantive policy outputs than if a 'laggard' state is at the helm. Second, other than periodically issuing general, high-level affirmations, the European Council has never really taken an active and sustained role in environmental policy making. In some ways, this was to the benefit of environmental policy because it allowed the Monnet Method to flourish below the political radar of most EU leaders (Wurzel 2008: 83-4).

The European Parliament is often described as the greenest of all the EU institutions (Burns 2005), although it did not actually establish its own dedicated environment body—a committee—until somewhat later than the rest, in 1979. At first, it developed its influence indirectly by cultivating informal links with national actors and other EU institutions, whose opinions might otherwise have been neglected. During the 1970s and 1980s, it helped draw attention to new environmental issues such as animal protection and policy implementation, which were subsequently taken up by other actors and fed into formal policy-making processes. With the appearance, first, of the cooperation and then later the codecision-making procedures, its formal influence grew still further. Although it is now arguably far stronger than its opposite numbers at the national level, its green ambitions remain essentially undiminished. That said, its influence remains largely reactive in nature. It also struggles, for example, to hold the Council to account in environmentally important areas (such as agriculture, land use planning, energy, and taxation) where unanimous voting still remains the norm.

The ECJ played a pivotal role in establishing the legal importance (and hence legitimacy) of EU environmental policy via rulings on the direct effect of directives. Although by no means an unqualified supporter of stronger environmental powers, during the 1970s and 1980s it was drawn into adjudicating some of the Treaty games noted above, often resolving them in favour of the Commission. Earlier rulings also supported the Commission's right to participate in international environmental policy making (Sbragia 2005) (see

below). As the legal basis of EU policy became simpler and more secure, the ECJ's focus shifted to resolving disputes over lax policy implementation (see below).

Interest groups constitute the final category of policy actors. Soon after the formal inauguration of EU-level policy making in 1972, national-level environmental pressure groups created (in 1974) an EU federation to coordinate their efforts in Brussels. The European Environment Bureau (EEB) now has over 140 member organizations drawn from 31 countries, including all 27 member states. These range from large and very well established national bodies to much smaller and more local ones. In the 1980s and 1990s, the number of environmental pressure groups lobbying directly in Brussels mushroomed—another good indicator of how far European integration has proceeded in this sector. The EEB in turn belongs to the Green 8, a looser coalition of the eight largest environmental pressure groups. Although all these organizations are manifestly better organized than in the 1970s, they are comprehensively out-resourced by business interests that can hire the very best public relations firms to get their views heard by policy makers in Brussels. Nonetheless, they are drawn to Brussels because they perceive that they can achieve things there that would be unattainable back home. They also lobby the EU in an attempt to influence international-level policy dynamics in issue areas such as climate change, of which more below.

KEY POINTS

- At its inception in 1957, the EU had no environmental policy. Environmental issues were not explicitly mentioned in the Treaty of Rome.

- Over the last 50 years, the EU has developed a broad-ranging environmental *acquis communautaire*.

- Environmental policy development can be understood by examining, inter alia: the six Environmental Action Programmes; key policy outputs; EU treaty amendments; and the interplay between policy actors at multiple levels.

- Several actors are important within this system. Most notably, the Commission has been instrumental in driving policy development, often 'by stealth' (Weale 2005). Other influential actors include the EU Council, the European Parliament, the European Court of Justice, and civil society groups.

Linking different perspectives: the underlying dynamics of environmental policy

Having now introduced the main actors, policies, and legal frameworks, we are better placed to explore the changing dynamics of EU policy making. One reason that these dynamics are changing is that there are many more actors operating at EU level today than in 1972. Another is that the range of issues has expanded from quite localized concerns such as water pollution and habitat protection to highly complex, cross-sectoral concerns such as unsustainable consumption, climate change, and widespread biodiversity loss. Finally, public demands for higher standards have, of course, fluctuated, but have generally cycled in an upward direction. Consequently, at any point in time there will be at least one group of actors in Brussels that is seeking to pioneer higher standards at EU level (Wurzel 2008: 68) or resist the dilution of existing standards.

Although these policy dynamics may have changed, the underlying societal demand for higher environmental standards remains as strong as ever. Consequently, EU policy appears capable of withstanding periodic political demands for environmental policy to be nationalized (as occurred in the 'great subsidiarity debate' of the early 1990s) or for economic issues to be prioritized (for example, in the economic recessions of the early 1990s and late 2000s). In fact, a raft of new EU policies on car emissions, renewable energies, and carbon-capture technology was successfully adopted during the 2008 'credit crunch'. In one sense, this does reaffirm that ecologically modernist ideas have staying power, but are by no means dominant.

In the past, it was possible to explain EU environmental policy in terms of one particular dynamic (for example, regulatory competition) and/or in rather binary terms (leaders v. laggards; EU institutions v. member states; industry v. environment).

But as the sector has matured and become more and more deeply entangled with other sectors, these analytical devices no longer seem sufficient (Lenschow 2005). Moreover, the nature of policy outputs and their differentiated outcomes on the ground seem too complex and contingent (Sbragia 1996: 241) to fit into a single model or framework. In order, therefore, to better understand how policy is made, analysts have started to explore policy developments in particular sub-areas of environment policy using more governance-centred approaches (Lenschow 2006). These studies have revealed the salience of three interacting dynamics: Europeanization; internationalization; and cross-sectoral policy integration.

Europeanization

Europeanization is the process through which EU-level policies affect domestic systems. In the last ten years, analysts have started to investigate the domestic implications of the shift towards more multilevel governance in the environmental sector (see Chapter 25). The picture that is emerging from these studies is one of differential Europeanization. In other words, every state appears to have been affected by EU membership, *even* those so-called leader states that worked the hardest to shape EU policy in the first place. Moreover, they have been changed in different ways: the content of their policies has been more deeply affected than their style (for example, anticipatory or reactive; consensual or adversarial) or administrative structures. And while some aspects of national policy have become more similar, no long-term convergence towards a common 'European' model is apparent (Jordan and Liefferink 2004). For now, national policies and policy systems appear to be far too strongly rooted in national history to respond in precisely the same way to policy demands emerging from Brussels. In other words, growing multi-level environmental governance in the EU has not yet created more uniform environmental governance (Weale et al 2000: 468).

Internationalization

The discussion thus far may have given the impression that EU policy has been mostly unaffected by external drivers. In fact, a far larger proportion of EU policy derives from international-level discussions than is commonly thought. After all, it was the 1972 UN conference in Stockholm that first gave EU actors an impetus to discuss their respective approaches, build new institutions, and, eventually, develop common policies. An internal–external dynamic has therefore been apparent since the very dawn of the EU's involvement.

What does this particular dynamic entail? First and foremost, it involves EU-level actors (chiefly the Commission and the Presidency) working alongside the member states in international-level discussions. However, in practice the point at which member state control ends and EU control begins varies from one issue area to the next. This has engendered highly complex and—it has to be said— rather introspective discussions about who should take the lead in a given issue area and according to what decision-making procedure (Lenschow 2006: 426). In the 1970s and 1980s, the ability of 'laggard' states to prevent the EU from developing a more progressive collective position forced it to trail behind the USA in emerging global issue areas such as stratospheric ozone depletion (Sbragia 2005). In the 1990s, changing internal political and legal conditions allowed the EU to adopt a more progressive position in areas such as global climate change, biodiversity protection and sustainable development (Jordan et al 2010). However, effective international leadership outside the EU partly depends on the presence, amongst other factors, of stronger internal policy coordination and delivery structures

within it (Vogler and Stephan 2007). This takes us to a second dimension: the drive to give the EU an international environmental face has, in turn, boomeranged back and affected internal EU policies via a process which is rather analogous to Europeanization. For example, the EU had to develop a suite of internal policies to control chemicals (such as chlorofluorocarbons) that deplete the ozone layer; a policy area originally formalized and transformed by two important UN agreements brokered in Vienna (1985) and Montreal (1987). In the coming years, international climate change commitments entered into at Kyoto (1997) and Copenhagen (in 2009) will similarly affect established areas of internal EU policy making such as agriculture, transport, and energy.

Integration

Environmental policy integration is a long-standing goal of EU policy (see Boxes 22.2 and 22.3). In recent years it has been linked to the achievement of more sustainable forms of development. In practice, integration means ensuring that economically powerful sectors such as transport, agriculture, and energy build an environmental dimension into their policy design and implementation processes. In the past, DG Environment approached integration from a somewhat weaker and more defensive position, that is, by issuing regulations to compel these sectors to take environmental issues into account. The obvious benefit of this rather segmented approach was that a large amount of ambitious legislation could be adopted relatively quickly. The drawback was that a great deal of it was either watered down in the Council or systematically ignored by cognate sectors at the implementation stage.

In the 1990s, the environmental sector mapped out the move towards a more systematically integrated approach in the Fifth and Sixth Action Programmes, the post-1998 Cardiff Process of integrating environmental considerations into the work of all policy sectors (Jordan and Schout 2006), and the 2001 sustainable development strategy. Moving out of the environmental 'policy ghetto' (Sbragia

1993: 340) was always going to be fraught with difficulty, given the inherently (and perhaps even infinitely) expansive nature of environmental issues. But it seemed to offer the tantalizing prospect that the sectors might eventually bear more of the responsibility for adopting strong *and* implementable environmental policies. At the time, some environmentalists wondered whether this approach might, if pushed to its logical end point, eventually

put environmental policy makers out of their jobs. Other commentators, however, were a lot less worried about this problem. Liberatore (1993: 295), for example, warned of the risks of 'policy dilution'—a situation in which the sectors adopted and implemented new environmental measures but in a greatly 'diluted and piecemeal' form. The next section examines which of these predictions proved to be closest to the mark.

KEY POINTS

- The evolution of EU environmental policy has been characterized by multiple dynamics, including a growth in the number of participating actors, an expansion in issue areas addressed, and increasing public demands for higher environmental quality.

- EU environmental policy now exhibits a number of particular features that do not conform to a single theoretical perspective. More governance-centred approaches have revealed the salience of three interacting dynamics: Europeanization; internationalization; and policy integration.

- Differential Europeanization is apparent: member states have been shaped by the EU in a non-uniform manner.

- The EU has become an active participant in international environmental agreements via a process known as internationalization.

- The Integration of the environment into sectoral policies has become a key EU objective but its implementation remains rather incomplete.

Future challenges

In the 2000s, the interplay between these three dynamics has moved centre stage. They have certainly shaped the EU's response to climate change, which before 2000 comprised little more than an amalgam of national policies, but is now arguably *the* most dynamic and high-profile area not only of environmental policy but of EU integration as a whole (Jordan et al 2010). Thus in a bid to achieve international leadership at the 1997 Kyoto conference of the parties to the UN Convention on climate change ('internationalization'), the EU took on the most far-reaching policy targets of any party (−8 per cent from 1990 levels by 2008–12). Sbragia and Damro (1999: 53) claim that this transformed

the EU from a 'Vienna laggard' to the 'Kyoto leader'. The progressive and proactive stance adopted by the EU resulted from simultaneous pushing by greener member states and the Commission. Ten years on, however, the EU is struggling hard to implement this commitment ('Europeanization') while at the same time busily preparing itself for a new, 'post-Kyoto' agreement ('internationalization'). Given that all sectors of the EU generate greenhouse gas emissions (and hence need to mitigate them) and/or stand to be affected by rising temperatures (cue discussions on adaptive actions), it is apparent that climate change requires unprecedented levels of cross-sectoral policy coordination ('integration'). In spite of these undoubted achievements, a number of hugely important challenges remain to be addressed in the environmental sector, namely improving integration, coping with enlargement, improving policy instrumentation, and strengthening implementation. The remainder of this section looks at how these four are playing out specifically in the area of climate change.

Integration or consolidation?

In the late 1990s, greater integration leading to more sustainable forms of development was the 'big idea' in the environmental sector. Various strategic processes to embed integration were initiated, but many environmentalists feel that the results thus far have been rather disappointing. Integration is, of course, inherently difficult to achieve when political priorities are constantly changing and the sectors are busy delivering their own equally legitimate policies. The institutional and cognitive barriers to better coordination in a complex, multi-level system such as the EU are extremely daunting (Jordan and Schout 2006). It is hardly a surprise to discover that the sectors did not willingly accept responsibility for 'greening' their own activities. On the contrary, they used some of the new integrating systems and structures to 'reverse integrate' economic and social factors into environmental policy making in precisely the manner predicted by Liberatore (1993). However, the worsening economic climate in the 2000s and growing fears that Europe was falling behind emerging economic powers in Asia was what really blunted the Commission's enthusiasm for integration. The Barroso Commission (2005–9) pointedly identified the delivery of the Lisbon Agenda of more 'Jobs and Growth' as its overriding priority. The Cardiff Process of environmental policy integration was disbanded, the production of the thematic strategies envisaged in the Sixth EAP was repeatedly delayed, and the 2001 sustainable development strategy eviscerated of binding targets and secure implementing structures.

In the mid to late 2000s environmental policy went 'back to basics'. For sure, integration remains an objective, but this time it is organized around and implemented through the delivery of climate change policies. The comprehensive new package of climate and energy policies adopted by the EU in late 2008 requires unprecedented degrees of coordination between the environment, transport, agriculture and energy sectors. And the presence of a clear environmental threat (of runaway climate change) and strong international commitments (that is, Kyoto) appear to be more forceful drivers of integration than the far broader (and hence politically weaker) legal commitments to integration and sustainable development contained in the Amsterdam Treaty.

Strengthening implementation

Agreeing upon and adopting integrated environmental policies is one thing, but implementing them is another entirely different challenge. Policy implementation was effectively a 'non-issue' until the Parliament politicized it in the 1980s. Poor implementation is of course an endemic problem in very many EU policy areas. But in contrast to the competition and fisheries sectors, the Commission lacks inspection powers, being reliant on other actors (for example, pressure groups) to bring cases of non-compliance to its attention. Naturally, these groups have a vested interest in presenting failures in the worst possible light, thus making implementation problems appear worse than they really are. The exact size of the implementation 'gap' in the EU remains a matter of academic and policy debate. But the continuing presence of poor implementation—however significant—is undoubtedly a factor in the ongoing failure to arrest declining levels of environmental quality across many parts of Europe (EEA 2007).

What is abundantly clear is that monitoring and enforcement capacities in the environmental policy sector are much weaker than those at national level. Moreover, in spite of continuing pressure from, among others, the European Parliament, member states remain fiercely opposed to strengthening them. Hence implementation remains 'a policy problem without a political solution' (Jordan 2005).

Finally, an implementation perspective also points to a slightly different—and some might say much more cynical—explanation for the remarkably rapid development of EU environmental policy; that is, member states accepted it because they never really had any intention of fully implementing it. In the climate sector, poor implementation has not really been a significant problem until now. On the contrary, emission reduction targets have lagged well behind accepted international scientific advice. Where they have been met, they have been achieved somewhat fortuitously (that is, as the unintended by-product of economic restructuring in the UK and Germany), rather than because of targeted policy interventions. However, as international (and hence EU) targets become more stringent, poor implementation is likely to become far more problematic.

Coping with enlargement

EU environmental policy managed to cope remarkably well with previous enlargements, but the 2004 and 2007 accessions were always expected to pose problems for the policy process in Brussels as well as in the new entrant states. The underlying problem was that their size, number (12 in total), and relatively poor economic performance were unprecedented in the history of the EU. Prior to entry, they were granted financial assistance to upgrade their administrative systems and implementation structures, but it is still too early to determine whether this will prevent them from exacerbating the EU's ongoing implementation problems. What is abundantly clear, however, is that in the area of climate change policy making (as opposed to implementation), they are quite prepared to fight their corner in Brussels if they have to. During the adoption of the climate–energy package in late 2008, Poland led a group of eight Eastern European states that called for their relatively weak 'economic potential' to be taken into account at a time of 'serious financial difficulty' (ENDS Europe Daily 2637). This was the first occasion on which the new entrants had acted as a negotiating bloc in the environmental sector. But some did not join them (in fact, France and Germany were also active in demanding concessions), which adds weight to the argument (outlined above) that binary analytical categories are no longer as useful as they once were. The more immediate practical problem for the Commission, however, was that having done it once and succeeded, these newer members may well be tempted to do it again. In the climate change arena they are in a very powerful position. During the late 1990s and early 2000s the contraction of their domestic economies helped to dampen the growth in emissions across the whole of the EU. But in the remainder of the Kyoto compliance period (2008–12), their emissions are expected to rise steeply (EEA 2008: 8). Looking even further forward, were Turkey to eventually join the EU, it would further complicate the process of allocating (or sharing) emissions reductions targets ('burdens'). Currently it has no Kyoto Protocol target and while its per capita emissions are relatively low at present, they are predicted to rise sharply in the future (EEA 2008: 8).

Enlarging the toolbox

In principle, the available toolbox of environmental policy instruments is relatively full. There has been an active technical debate over the (de)merits of 'new' instruments since the late 1960s (Jordan et al 2005). These include voluntaristic instruments such as informal management standards, voluntary agreements (amongst polluters but also between polluters and the state), and market-based instruments such as environmental taxes and emissions trading. Nonetheless, despite significant learning and borrowing interactions between states, regulation remains the EU's instrument of choice (Jordan et al 2005). Why does such a liberally inclined organization with high environmental ambitions such as the EU find itself relying so heavily on the 'illiberal instrument' of regulation (Weale et al 2000: 458)? The lack of a sound legal base in the treaty for fiscal measures has certainly played a part in retarding the use of environmental taxes, as has resistance from large polluters. Meanwhile, voluntary agreements have been trialled but not extensively employed.

However, in the climate change domain the international and scientific pressure to hold down emissions has encouraged the EU to dip a little deeper into the environmental toolbox, but with rather mixed success. The most prominent example of a voluntary agreement at EU level was supposed to reduce CO_2 emissions from new cars but failed to meet expectations and has now been replaced by a (2010) Regulation. In contrast, the EU has managed to pioneer an entirely new kind of instrument—emissions trading (see Box 22.4)—but it too has experienced serious implementation problems.

BOX 22.4

Emissions trading: a case of policy entrepreneurship?

In the 1990s, the EU tried—unsuccessfully, as it turned out—to adopt an EU-level carbon-energy tax, but was thwarted by a blocking coalition of member states unwilling to cede more power to EU institutions. As a result, climate policy fell into the doldrums and the EU struggled to exert international leadership. However, EU influence over climate policy has grown since the late 1990s, due in large part to the emergence of the Emissions Trading Scheme or ETS. This scheme, based on the trading of greenhouse gas emissions allowances (see Box 22.1), is not a fiscal instrument and therefore did not fall foul of the unanimity requirement in the Council. Spotting a political opportunity to exploit this legal loophole in the treaties and noting that several member states had already adopted their own trading schemes at national level, the Commission proposed an EU-wide emissions trading system. When this proposal was debated, the UK and Germany made it clear that they wanted a voluntary approach, whereas most other member states were willing to accept the Commission's plan for a mandatory scheme (van Asselt 2010). The Commission was nonetheless able to get its proposal accepted by offering concessions to the UK and Germany. An emissions trading Directive was subsequently adopted with amazing speed, quickly becoming the keystone of the EU's new climate – energy package. What does this tale reveal? First, it reveals that the opportunistic and unpredictable nature of EU policy making—a hallmark of the 1970s and 1980s (see above)—has not entirely disappeared (Jordan et al 2010). In other words, integration 'by stealth' (Weale 2005) is still a powerful way of progressing EU environmental policy. Second, it also neatly illustrates that national governments retain strong control over events. Finally, it also emphasizes the fact that the EU is not hermetically sealed from the outside: emissions trading was originally suggested by the US government in the Kyoto Protocol negotiations.

KEY POINTS

- The addition of new competences in the environmental sector has become harder to sustain, primarily due to fears over international competitiveness. However, the climate change and energy agendas offer new scope for building EU environmental policy and promoting environmental policy integration.

- The poor implementation of environmental policies is likely to become an increasingly significant issue.

- Recent enlargement of the EU has presented new problems for environmental policy making, with some accession states in Eastern Europe prioritizing economic development over environmental protection.

- EU policy is also likely to remain heavily reliant on regulation despite repeated rhetorical commitments to employ 'new' instruments.

Conclusion

In some respects it is obvious why the EU had to become heavily involved in environmental policy making. High levels of environmental quality are often held to be somewhat of a luxury. As the EU is made up of some of the world's most affluent states, it is hardly surprising that its economically focused governance system was quickly confronted with the problem of how to ensure that different national environmental standards did not disrupt free trade. Nonetheless, it is remarkable how quickly the EU's role expanded in comparison with similar systems of multi-level governance such as the USA. Where problems span borders or involve a strong trade dimension, the 'value added' of EU involvement seems self-evident. But many issues now governed by the EU do not exhibit these characteristics: zoos, bathing and drinking water quality, waste water treatment, bird habitats, and renewable energy supplies, to name just a few.

Putting to one side all the legal and administrative constraints noted above, the underlying reason for the rapid transformation in EU environmental policy is probably political. That is to say, once the basic idea had been accepted that the environment should be protected 'for its own sake', it was but a relatively short step to the regulation' of these and other apparently 'local' issues (Sbragia 1996: 253). The absence of a fixed constitutional blueprint, relatively weak policy coordination structures, and growing support from environmental pressure groups, allowed (and perhaps even tacitly encouraged) the Commission to behave in an opportunistic and entrepreneurial manner in the environmental 'ghetto'.

To summarize, once a side project, the environment is now a key area of EU competence and a dynamic site of everyday politics. Its focus has shifted over time from remedying problems to 'designing them out' of sectoral policies in accordance with the sustainability and environmental integration principles. But as the focus of environmental policy has become more diffuse, so have the opportunities grown for the sectors to 'reverse integrate' their concerns into environmental policy. Contrary to earlier expectations, environmentalists have had to learn that policy integration is a 'two-way street'.

Nonetheless, the tide of new environmental policy shows no sign of receding. Recent years have admittedly witnessed a shift 'back to basics', centring on the production of new regulations that address climate change and energy security concerns. Noting the political salience of these topics amongst EU citizens (vis-à-vis the rather dry and technocratic nature of the Lisbon Agenda), the Barroso Commission of 2004–9 began to use the environment as a pretext for driving the EU into new policy areas (chiefly energy supply). In terms of its political popularity and institutional permanence, environmental policy undoubtedly represents one of the EU's greatest 'success stories'. However, important challenges remain, not least that of translating active policy making into tangible and enduring improvements in environmental quality 'on the ground'. Environmental policy has come a very long way in a short space of time, but it remains very much a 'work in progress'.

? **QUESTIONS**

1. Why did the EU first become involved in environmental policy making in the late 1960s and what kinds of obstacles stood in its way in the early years?

2. What roles do the Council, the Commission, and the European Parliament play in environmental policy making at EU level and how have these changed over time?

3. In what ways does EU environmental policy interact with and affect national and international policies?

4.   How 'effective' has EU environmental policy been?

5.   What are the environmental provisions of the Lisbon Treaty?

6.   How likely is it that the Lisbon Treaty will radically transform environmental policy making?

7.   How and to what extent has EU policy Europeanized national policy since the late 1960s?

8.   What challenges are EU environmental policy makers likely to face in the future?

GUIDE TO FURTHER READING

■ Jordan, A. (ed.) *Environmental Policy in the European Union*, 2nd edn (London: Earthscan, 2005). A collection of more advanced chapters by leading thinkers in the field, on the actors, institutions, and processes of environmental policy making.

■ Jordan, A. and Liefferink, D. (eds) *Environmental Policy in Europe: The Europeanization of National Environmental Policy* (London: Routledge, 2004). The first and most comprehensive analysis of the Europeanization of national environmental policy in different member states.

■ Jordan, A. et al (eds) *Climate Change Policy in the European Union* (Cambridge: Cambridge University Press, 2010). The first book-length account of policy making in this rapidly evolving and politically salient area.

■ Knill, C. and Liefferink, D. *Environmental Politics in the European Union* (Manchester: Manchester University Press, 2007). A concise analysis of the evolution of EU environmental politics.

■ McCormick, J. *Environmental Policy in the European Union* (Basingstoke: Palgrave, 2001). A comprehensive undergraduate text but now becoming rather dated.

■ Weale, A., Pridham, G., Cini, M., Konstadakopulos, D., Porter, M., and Flynn, B. *Environmental Governance in Europe* (Oxford: Oxford University Press, 2000). A highly detailed empirical analysis of how and why the EU created such a complex and multi-level system of environmental governance.

WEBLINKS

● http://www.eea.europa.eu/   The website of the European Environment Agency contains a wide-ranging database of statistics and reports on the state of the environment across the EU.

● http://ec.europa.eu/environment/index_en.htm   The home page of the European Commission's Directorate-General for Environment.

● http://www.ieep.eu/   The Institute for European Environmental Policy (IEEP) is an independent body undertaking research and consultancy on policy across Europe.

● http://www.endseurope.com/   A private provider of daily news in both print and e-formats.

● http://europa.eu/abc/treaties/index_en.htm   An EU website listing all the major treaty agreements from Rome to Lisbon.

Visit the Online Resource Centre that accompanies this book for lots of interesting additional material. http://www.oxfordtextbooks.co.uk/orc/Cini_Borragan3e/

PART FIVE

Issues and Debates

23 Europe's Contested Democracy

DIMITRIS N. CHRYSSOCHOOU

Chapter Contents

- Introduction
- Making sense of the 'democratic deficit'
- Consociation or republic?
- Democracy and treaty reform
- Conclusion

Reader's Guide

This chapter examines the notion of a democratic deficit in the European Union (EU) and explores its origins, development, and various meanings. It discusses divergent proposals for rectifying the deficit by distinguishing between its institutional and socio-psychological perspectives. While the former focus on issues of power sharing, the latter address the absence of a fully fledged European demos. These complementary perspectives imply different strategies for democratic reform. As yet, there remains no consensus over the future of the EU. The chapter emphasizes this point by asking which form or understanding of democracy best captures the nature of the EU polity, and which is likely to be an appropriate blueprint for the future. It also considers whether treaty reforms, such as the failed Constitutional Treaty (CT) and the Lisbon Treaty, have addressed the democratic deficit.

Introduction

Integration theory, especially during periods of transformation, has yielded new insights into processes of social and political change, both internationally and regionally. This has certainly been the case for Europe's integrative journey. The focus of this chapter is the changing democratic character and path of that journey and the scholarly efforts that have been made to theorize about the kind of democracy currently taking shape within the evolving EU polity.

Much of the scholarly writing on European democracy claims that attempts to 'constitutionalize' the EU have failed to bestow on the system a stronger sense of social legitimacy and common destiny. Instead, signs of civic apathy at the grassroots have appeared following the rejection by the French and Dutch publics of the constitutional project in the referendums of 2005. In the 'reflection period' that followed, the EU reassessed how best to proceed with the changes necessary after enlargement. The end result was yet another classical treaty-amending process, the Lisbon Treaty, which attempted to rescue most of the Constitutional Treaty reforms.

But before proceeding further, let us pose the central question of this chapter: what is the democratic deficit? A general answer is that it refers to a negative side effect of European integration: the growing dissonance between the requirements of modern democratic rule and the actual conditions upon which the governance of the EU is based. To be more specific than that is to pre-empt the discussion below, which stresses the essentially contested nature of the democratic deficit (see Box 23.1).

The chapter begins by explaining what the democratic deficit is. It distinguishes between institutional and socio-psychological perspectives. Whereas the former focus on institutional power sharing and on institutional reform as a solution to the perceived problems of EU-level democracy, the latter are concerned with questions of European civic identity and large-scale demos formation. The chapter then goes on to consider different variants of democratic governance and the extent to which recent treaty reforms have helped to democratize the EU political system. The general assessment is that the EU still remains closer to a *system of democracies* than to a *democratic polity* in its own right. It is perhaps best explained as an 'organized synarchy' (Chryssochoou 2009), a term which refers to political systems in which there is extensive sovereignty sharing.

🔑 KEY CONCEPTS AND TERMS 23.1

Definitions of the democratic deficit

The idea behind the notion of a 'democratic deficit' is that decisions in the EU are in some ways insufficiently representative of, or accountable to, the nations and people of Europe.
(Lord 2001: 165).

It has become a received wisdom that the EU suffers from a 'democratic deficit'. It suffers from deficiencies in representation, representativeness, accountability and support. The problem is not merely that of the establishment of an additional layer of governance, further removed from the peoples of Europe. It is also that this process contributes to the transformation of the Member States, so that each Member State can no longer claim to be the source of its own legitimacy.
(Eriksen and Fossum 2002: 401).

The limited ability of Europeans to influence the work of the major EU institutions is a problem that has become so entrenched as to merit its own label: the democratic deficit.
(McCormick 1999: 147)

The democratic deficit is '... the combination of two phenomena: (a) the transfer of powers from the Member States to the European Community; and (b) the exercise of those powers at the Community level by institutions other than the European Parliament, even though, before the transfer, the national parliaments held power to pass laws in the areas concerned.'
(European Parliament 1988: 10–11, quoted J. Smith 1999: 13).

What is democracy?

Democracy is a method of organizing public life that allows the concerns and interests of citizens to be articulated within government. Democracy's defining properties are its institutional controls, the peaceful resolution of conflicts in society, meaningful legislative representation, as well as civic inclusion and political participation. Important in understanding democracy is the concept of the demos. This is more than simply the people; it also represents the idea of a political community of shared values and identities. One possible model of democracy involves the demos participating in the making of decisions that affect its members (Arblaster 1987: 105).

Democracy may be defined as an institutional arrangement for arriving at publicly binding decisions, with the legitimacy of those decisions resting on competitive elections. This suggests that the institutions of democracy are ends in themselves. But democracy may also be viewed as a means of realizing the common good through the electoral process. Here, institutions are merely means to much deeper ends. Democracy may also be defined in terms of active civic involvement in the affairs of the polity (democracy in input) or by focusing more on policy outcomes (democracy in output) (Scharpf 1999). Whatever the definition, democracy comprises a mixture of an ideal and a procedural arrangement. As such, it involves principles, norms, and values that are shared amongst citizens, and which provide the means through which ideals are embodied in political institutions and through which the demos engages actively to arrive at binding decisions, whilst holding government to account for its actions or lack of action.

Making sense of the 'democratic deficit'

When the integration process began, back in the late 1950s, no one gave much thought to its democratic credentials. In the decades after, the European Community (EC) rested on a 'permissive consensus': namely, the tacit agreement of the member states' citizens. The political legitimacy of the European project came from elsewhere: that is, the peace and prosperity that integration would bring to Western Europe rather than from its aspirations to become a democracy (Newman 2001: 358; see Box 23.2). But since the ratification crisis prompted by the signing of the Maastricht Treaty, this consensus has broken down. In its place new and far more complex discourses have arisen, which offer conflicting solutions to the problem of democratizing the EU.

All this raises new questions for the EU, such as how it might be possible for citizens, who belong to different political systems, who have distinctive cultural experiences and traditions, and who aspire to diverse understandings of what polity is and how it might best be governed, to hold EU decision makers to account. Questions of this kind reflect democratic concerns that have grown as the EU has evolved away from being merely a diplomatic forum for inter-state bargaining towards a fully-fledged political system. While there is some measure of agreement in the literature that the EU political system is *not* democratic, at least when compared to most member states, there is as yet no consensus on how the EU might become democratic. Two quite different yet interrelated understandings of what the democratic deficit is help to expand on this point. The first adopts an institutional approach which highlights the flawed inter-institutional relationships that characterize the EU and the need to enhance its accountability. The second is socio-psychological, and is thereby interested in the development of a European civic identity and the extent to which there is a feeling of community amongst Europeans. The subsections that follow look more closely at these two perspectives.

The democratic deficit: an institutional perspective

The orthodox view of the EU's democratic deficit is that the transfer of legislative powers from national parliaments to the EU institutions has not been matched by an equivalent degree of democratic accountability and legislative input on the part of the European Parliament (EP), the only directly elected institution at EU level. This has been the dominant view of the democratic deficit since the first EP elections of 1979, and one that has become more convincing since the Single European Act extended the scope of EU competences and the use of qualified majority voting (QMV) in the Council. Although the latter has increased decisional *efficiency*, it has exacerbated the already marginal role that national parliaments enjoy within the integration process, as there is no guarantee that national parliamentary scrutiny will matter when member governments are outvoted in the Council.

This orthodox view also brings together a second form of institutional democratic deficit: alongside the 'de-parliamentarization' of national political systems exists the growing influence of the executive (Chryssochoou et al 2003); and the transfer of decision-making authority from the national (or subnational) to the EU level. Implicit in this reading of the democratic deficit is that such a transfer has benefited executive decision makers at the expense of parliamentarians. This weakens the link between the electorate and elected legislators. An obvious solution to the democratic deficit would therefore seem to involve a shifting of control of the integration process away from national governments and the national civil servants who support them and, indeed, from the unelected European institutions. Thus the most familiar argument is that a loss of control by national parliaments must be compensated for by a process of parliamentarization at EU level. In other words, the EP must be given more powers if it is to perform the functions of a 'real' parliament. This would seem to imply a move towards a bicameral system, comprising both direct and popular representation (via the EP) and indirect, territorial representation (via the Council).

Yet the EP, and others supporting the 'parliamentarization' of the EU, recognize that the Parliament's gains have not entirely compensated for losses at national level, and that integration remains very much controlled by national and EU-level executives. Further measures to extend the EP's involvement both in the legislative process and in scrutinizing the executive have been proposed—for example, in the form of an extension of the codecision procedure so that all provisions falling under codecision also operate on the basis of QMV in the Council; or through an increase in the EP's involvement in the appointment of the Commission, possibly by allowing MEPs to choose the President of the Commission from a shortlist put forward by the European Council. But there is also growing support for increasing the involvement of national parliaments in the EU policy process. National MPs or deputies already have an important role to play in scrutinizing EU legislation, though in practice they are often unable to perform that function very effectively. One suggestion is that national parliaments should have a say over whether EU legislation has been made on the basis of the subsidiarity principle. This would allow a judgement to be made as to whether decisions are being taken at the most appropriate level. Such a proposal was in fact incorporated into the Lisbon Treaty.

The political agenda of those who favour a greater role for national parliaments sometimes stretches even further, however, to support a de facto renationalization of EU policies. For the advocates of this approach, arguments about the democratic deficit may mask a more general hostility to the EU project. Alternatively, it may assume that the EU is incapable of substantive democratic reforms and that the only viable solution is for the EU institutions to play less of a role in domestic politics and for the EU to become more state-centric.

Moreover, as integration is said to privilege executives at the expense of directly elected legislatures, the criticism is also that non-elected bodies possess too many powers. In this vein, many in the past have attacked the European Commission for being an archetypal undemocratic institution, in that it is a civil service composed of appointed members who possess substantive policy-making, if not legislative, powers (see Chapter 8). This issue is really about accountability and institutional autonomy: the extent to which the Commission, as an executive body, is accountable to European citizens; or the degree to which it has been able to break free from the control of national governments and parliaments to act independently of them, thereby directly influencing policy and integrative outcomes. While there was clearly an extension of the scrutiny role of the EP over the Commission in the treaty revisions of the 1980s and 1990s, the Commission retains a degree of discretion over how it performs its initiative function in most policy domains. But whether this means it is undemocratic or not is disputed.

It is not only the Commission that is subject to criticism of this kind, however. The European Court of Justice (ECJ) has also been attacked for its teleological pro-integrationist bias. While the Court has an obligation to interpret the Treaties, and has also been instrumental in pushing the boundaries of European law, there is once again little agreement on the extent to which it plays an autonomous role in EU integration and in the EU policy process. While the role played by the Court may be inventive, it is also very much in line with the spirit of the Treaties that it was set up to interpret (see Chapter 11).

Finally, the Council too has been the object of some criticism in that it is the Council rather than the EP that has the final say in crucial legislative matters. An important point here is that the Council is a secretive and arcane body (see Chapter 9) when compared to the other EU institutions.

Underpinning arguments that the non-parliamentary EU institutions need to be more accountable is the view that the EU has traditionally been a technocratic institution, and has valued expertise and effectiveness much more than representation and democracy. Since the early 1990s, the democracy debate within the EU has been extended so that even where it remains institutionally orientated, it has become inextricably linked to issues of public participation in the EU policy process. Thus democratizing the EU is not just about rejigging the Union's institutional balance; neither is it solely reliant on the representative role of parliaments. It is also about bringing the EU closer to ordinary people, ensuring that integration is no longer simply elite driven, distant, or even irrelevant for the vast majority of European citizens. There are various dimensions to these arguments, ranging from that of strengthening the representation of regions and localities in the EU (see Chapter 18) to increasing transparency and simplification (Dinan 2000: 133). In the latter case, democracy is said to be facilitated through greater institutional openness, such as the availability of Council minutes or enhanced public consultation by the Commission in advance of legislative proposals. It is worth noting here that the Lisbon Treaty (moving in the same direction as did the CT) attempts to engage with civil society agents and to acknowledge the importance not only of representative democracy but also of direct democracy (through a novel public initiative process) as a means of tackling some acute legitimacy issues in the EU.

KEY POINTS

- An important perspective on the democratic deficit is the institutional perspective.

- This focuses on the absence of representative and direct democracy within the European Union.

- All institutions can be considered from this perspective, though most emphasis is placed on the role of the European Parliament and—though to a lesser extent—national parliaments in helping to democratize the EU.

The democratic deficit: a socio-psychological perspective

The problem with institutional approaches to the democratic deficit is that they leave the equally important socio-psychological dimension of this phenomenon unexplored. This dimension shifts the emphasis from the question of 'Who governs and how?' to the more demanding question of 'Who is governed?', thereby focusing more on the treatment of the disease than on its symptoms. The starting point for this discussion is that at the heart of the EU's democratic deficit lies the absence of a European demos and, by extension, an absence of 'civic we-ness'—that is, a sense of common identity amongst Europeans (Chryssochoou 2000a).

This perspective on the democratic deficit builds on the wider assumption that democracy, in the form of representative and responsible government, presupposes a popular infrastructure upon which certain basic properties, such as adherence to and acceptance of majority rule, apply in any given political community. A transnational demos can be defined as a composite citizen body, whose members share an active interest in the governance of the larger polity and who can direct their democratic claims to and via the central institutions. Thus it is the demos itself that endows the EU with legitimacy. It follows that the transformation of the EU 'from democracies to democracy' requires the positive feelings of the member publics to be stronger than any divisive issues that may arise as integration proceeds. As Cohen states, 'there can be no larger part unless the larger part and the smaller parts are indeed parts of one whole' (Cohen 1971: 46).

The more the EU relies on democratic credentials, the more important it is for citizens to have feelings of belonging to an inclusive polity. In this context, the emergence of a European civic identity out of the democratic traditions that currently exist in the EU is imperative, not only for the viability of EU democracy but also if the democratic integrity of the constituent populations is to be respected, and for cultural variation and multiple identity-holding to be fostered. For a European demos to exist, its members must recognize their collective existence. Merely being granted citizenship rights, as happened in the Maastricht Treaty, is far from adequate. What matters is how Europeans think about themselves and the way that they view the communities to which they belong.

As the polity of the EU cannot be detached from its constituent identities, transnational demos formation does not imply a melting-pot type of society in which pre-existing (mainly territorial) identities are assimilated into a new supranational identity. Rather, it projects an image of a pluralist polity, within which the civic demos emerges as the unchallenged unit of transnational authority and the ultimate focus of political purpose. 'Many people, one demos', rather than 'many demoi, one people', epitomizes this, implying 'a many turned into one without ceasing to be many'. A European demos can be said to exist when the constituent publics see themselves as part of a democratic whole, and are given the means to mark their impact in EU governance even though they retain their constituent identities. It is thus possible to identify the following as necessary for EU demos formation: the democratic self-consciousness of citizens; adherence to shared democratic values; public awareness of the larger polity; and a desire to shape the democratic future of the plurality of interrelated peoples.

KEY POINTS

- Different models of democratic governance resonate with different aspects of the EU.

- The socio-psychological perspective of the democratic deficit stresses the absence of a European demos.

- This approach seeks to identify what it would take to construct a European civic body as a means of constructing a more democratic European Union.

Consociation or republic?

Resolving the democratic deficit is no easy task, as it would require some form of agreement about the sort of model of democratic governance to which the EU should adhere. Up to now, the EU has evolved incrementally, and despite various reforms, there has been no consensus on its future shape. The Convention on the Future of Europe discussed these issues with a view to agreeing a Constitutional Treaty in 2004 (see Chapter 4). The section that follows aims to develop a greater understanding of the democratic deficit, keeping in mind the uniquely observed nature of the EU political system. Put differently, the EU is not a classical representative majoritarian political system, for it involves different, and often competing, sources of legislative representation; it is not based on the separation of powers between executive and legislative institutions; and its quasi-majoritarian system (qualified majority with potential veto players) does not allow executives to govern as long as they enjoy the confidence of a majority in a directly elected parliament. The EU thus deviates considerably from a conventional parliamentary democracy, as the latter presupposes some form of social unity that allows the minority to identify with the decisions taken by the central institutions. For the moment, QMV still applies to areas of EU action that are not prone to intense conflict among national representatives: that is, in areas where the member state governments want to see collective progress, rather than to hold on to their national prerogatives (Taylor 1996: 85–8). Major reform initiatives take place through formal treaty revision on the basis of unanimity (see Chapter 9). Where majority decisions are at issue, they are often subject to a lowest common denominator approach, with the informal norm of consensus usually overriding the idea of a decision at any cost. No single state is prepared to be outvoted on a regular basis in the Council: 'Majority voting merely cloaked the continuing need to obtain the assent of all states … In a system of sovereign states, it could not be otherwise' (Taylor 1996: 86).

At a general level, the image of the EU as a sui generis system of collective governance involves the merging of distinct politically organized states and diverse publics into some form of (consensually agreed upon) union, without losing either their collective (national) identities or their individual sovereignty. It thus resembles a confederal structure that highlights the treaty-based nature of the union and its essentially state-centric character. In that context, EU democracy is linked to the notion of a democratically organized society of states, rather than a constitutional, state-like polity. Moreover, the EU favours the diffusion of authoritative decision-making power to the segments rather than to a regional centre, with the larger union referring to a 'treaty-constituted body politic, rather than … [a] constituted unity of one *people* or *nation* (Forsyth 1981: 15–16). More importantly, integration 'falls short of a complete fusion or incorporation in which one or all of the members lose their identity as states' (Forsyth 1981: 1). State sovereignty is still the order of the day, although in practice the EU depends on power sharing, which in turn involves the management of certain policies over which there is a form of joint sovereignty. In that regard, the EU provides an alternative to the creation of a new political centre 'beyond the nation state': it becomes an exercise in 'co-governance', incorporating a wide variety of institutional possibilities, whilst resting upon the separate constitutional orders of states. The fact that formal treaty reform requires the unanimous consent of all member governments makes this point even more resonant. Likewise, it is the states themselves, rather than a self-conscious European demos, that bestow the EU with political legitimacy. This projection recognizes that the EU seeks to reconcile the parallel demands for greater union of the whole with adequate guarantees for the autonomy of the parts: 'unity without uniformity'.

As neither federalism nor confederalism captures the essential character of the EU as a 'sympolity' of states and peoples' (Tsatsos 2009)—a composite union that combines different forms of representation and sources of legitimacy—in the absence of a European demos, majoritarian politics would imply serious exclusionary practices harmful to minorities. As a consequence, a consociational understanding of governance might provide a more constructive point of departure for addressing the EU's democratic deficit.

Consociationalism has four main features: a *grand coalition* or 'cartel of elites' (Dahrendorf 1967: 267) where decisions are taken among the elites; *proportionality*, whereby all societal forces are represented within the government, in a way that reflects their size; *segmental autonomy*, with each elite having control over their own particular territory in areas that do not impinge on other elites; and *mutual vetoes* where each segment acts as a potential veto player. From this perspective we might see the EU as a kind of European consociation resting as it does on the politics of accommodation. This is exemplified by the Council's closed meetings, which often result in carefully negotiated package deals; and by the fact that different states are assigned different votes in the Council according to their size and/or population, while all are represented in the central institutions. Moreover, EU states retain their distinctive features as separate constitutional polities and remain responsible for dealing with issues that are exclusive to their jurisdiction, at the same time as being allowed to block decisions of which they strongly disapprove.

The EU thus represents a compound polity whose units are bound in a consensual form of union. Its aim is to further certain common ends without sacrificing collective national identities or resigning individual sovereignty to a higher central authority. Crucial to the workings of the European consociation is the practice of political codetermination— the common management of separate sovereignties through means and objectives that have been agreed in advance. The result is a system of interconnectedness coexisting with high levels of segmental autonomy, allowing for a less rigid understanding of sovereignty than is found in classical federal structures. In brief, national and collective systems of governance are bound together in a symbiotic relationship that accommodates divergent expectations

in joint decisions. As for democracy, in this model it is not an end in itself, but rather an institutional device used to arrive at mutually acceptable compromises among sovereign states. From this rather instrumental view, however, stems the model's greatest deficiency: the lack of horizontal integration among the members' demoi.

In contrast to the consociationalist perspective lies the idea of a 'Republic of Europeans' (Lavdas and Chryssochoou 2007)—a composite union composed of diverse publics along the lines of a *res publica composita*. *Res publica* means that which belongs to the public. It has three primary objectives: justice through the rule of law; the common good through a mixed and balanced constitution; and liberty through active citizenship. Love for a virtue-centred life constitutes the raison d'être of the *res publica*, marking its impact in the search for 'the good polity' (Schwarzmantel 2003). Republican thought applied to the EU case has contributed to a 'normative turn' (Chryssochoou 2000b, 2001, 2002) in EU studies, comprising a paradigm shift 'from policy to polity'. Also drawing on constructivist discourses in international relations theory (Wendt 1999), this has opened the way for novel conceptualizations of the EU as 'an entity of interlocking normative spheres' (Bankowski, Scott and Snyder 1998) and as an ordered political arrangement for diverse communities and arenas for collective action.

Sitting in this republican tradition, Bellamy and Castiglione (2000: 181) capture the complexity of the EU through a theory of democratic liberalism that is founded upon 'a pre-liberal conception of constitutionalism that identified the constitution with the social composition and form of government of the polity'. This amounts to 'a political system that disperses power within civil society … and encourages dialogue between the component parts of the body politic' (Bellamy and Castiglione 2000: 172). The point here is that, '[i]nstead of the constitution being a precondition for politics, political debate becomes the medium through which a polity constitutes itself' (Bellamy and Castiglione 2000: 182). Democratic liberalism brings the members of the polity into an equilibrium with each other, and aims 'to disperse power so as to encourage a process of controlled political conflict and deliberation' (Bellamy and Castiglione 2000:181). This accords with MacCormick's (1997) conceptualization of the EU order as a 'mixed commonwealth', within which the subjects of the constitution represent a mixture of agents that share in the sovereignty of the larger unit. Bellamy and Castiglione (1997: 443) explain: 'The polycentric polity ... is a definite departure from the nation state, mainly because it implies a dissociation of the traditional elements that come with state sovereignty: a unified system of authority and representation controlling all functions of governance over a given territory'. MacCormick's notion of a lawfully constituted European commonwealth of post-sovereign states allows the EU to conduct itself as a 'community of law'. Here, the rule of law emerges as the most fundamental constitutional guarantee of the system, 'as all other [legal] values depend on it, for them to be upheld at all' (Piris 2000: 12). Political authority is neither proportionately nor symmetrically vested in a single decision-making centre. Rather, it is distributed through overlapping arrangements, with the polity being characterized by various degrees of decentralization and sources of loyalty holding.

Republican theory embodies a normative commitment to civic deliberation for the promotion of the public interest and to 'balanced government'. This offers citizens 'undominated' (or quality) choice. But it is not the latter that causes liberty. Instead, liberty is constituted by the legal institutions of the republican state (Pettit 1997: 106–9). Brugger (1999: 7) explains: 'whereas the liberal sees liberty as essentially presocial, the republican sees liberty as constituted by the law which transforms customs and creates citizens'. In short, the rule of law,

opposition to arbitrariness, and the republican constitution are constitutive of civic freedom. 'Balanced government' is therefore forged both negatively, through the prevention of tyranny, and positively, by ensuring a deliberative mode of public engagement, 'within which the different "constituencies" which made up civil society would be encouraged to treat their preferences not simply as givens, but rather as choices which were open to debate and alteration' (Craig 1997: 114). From this perspective, liberty is best preserved within a mixed polity, with no single branch of government being privileged over the others. These issues are of relevance to the distribution of political authority within the EU, as it allows for 'a stable form of political ordering for a society within which there are different interests or constituencies' (Craig 1997: 116).

> **KEY POINTS**
>
> ● Different models of democratic governance highlight different aspects of the EU polity.
>
> ● The absence of a European demos seems to preclude the application of a federal model.
>
> ● Confederal governance finds it difficult to capture the polity aspects of a dynamic, composite union of states and peoples.
>
> ● Consociationalism's inherently elitist nature fails to provide an adequate avenue for democratizing the EU political system.
>
> ● Republican conceptions of the EU project a more participatory and balanced form of collective governance and citizenship.

Democracy and treaty reform

Although the Maastricht Treaty preserved the confederal nature of the EU, it also introduced a number of federal principles such as codecision, subsidiarity, and proportionality. Taylor (1996) argues that after

Maastricht, the EU and the member states became increasingly locked together in a mutually reinforcing relationship that left much to be desired from a democratic standpoint. Yet at the same time the issue of democracy occupied a more prominent position in subsequent treaty negotiations, a reflection of public concern over the EU's democratic deficit. But even though a widespread consensus emerged during the Amsterdam Treaty negotiations that the EU had to find ways of developing closer links with its citizens, ultimately this did not leave much of a mark on the Treaty itself.

Hailed by some as a 'reasonable step', but criticized by others as 'lacking in ambition', the Amsterdam Treaty consolidated state competences by preserving the EU's three-pillar structure (see Chapter 3). As Devuyst put it: '[r]ather than focusing on pre-emptive institutional spillover in preparation for enlargement, the Amsterdam negotiation was characterized by a "maintaining national control trend"' (Devuyst 1998: 615). The crucial question that the Amsterdam process failed to address concerned the institutional structure that would facilitate the future enlargement of the EU. The end result was a lack of agreement on the delicate question of the reweighting of votes in the Council, even if, on the credit side, it increased the role of the EP by extending the scope of codecision and simplifying the conciliation process. But the Amsterdam reform also failed to address more fundamental issues of parliamentary involvement in EU decision making: namely, whether codecision would always be used with QMV, or whether EP involvement in third pillar issues should also cover the financial implications of such policies. The largest deficiency of the Amsterdam process was that it prioritized specific policy issues over broader questions relating to the EU's future. It reflected the member states' preference for a managerial type of reform that would improve the *effectiveness* of policy output rather than its democratic character. Those who had hoped that the new Treaty would forge a new democratic EU polity had no grounds for celebration, as political pragmatism won the day. It is not overstating the case to argue that Amsterdam was characterized by a profound lack of democratic vision over the future of Europe.

Similarly, the Treaty of Nice, signed in 2001, provides a good example of the limits of EU polity building. The 'declaratory' Charter of Fundamental

Rights, signed at Nice but not incorporated into the Treaty, seemed a missed opportunity for EU democracy. The institutionalization of fundamental rights within the EU would most likely strengthen the credibility of national commitments to protect the rights of persons residing within their territory, whilst empowering the ECJ to ensure that principles underpinning the Charter are respected. It would also advance the fight against various forms of discrimination within the EU, contributing to the preservation and further development of shared values, while respecting and protecting the diversity of constituent cultures, traditions, and identities. Three points deserve our attention regarding the Nice process and EU democracy building. First, although the EU sought to create Europe-wide civil society, the development of a shared civic identity among its constituent publics has not yet materialized. Second, the EU is still characterized by its diversity and, moreover, by a lack of agreement on where integration will end. Despite the increase in substantive policy competences, the EU has not become a federation, and remains a consensual form of governance. Third, by acknowledging how important it is that states retain ultimate control over treaty changes, the Nice reforms have revealed the limits of democratization in the EU. In failing to strengthen common citizenship rights and decouple EU legitimacy from policy performance, Nice, like Amsterdam, has been a missed opportunity for EU democracy.

As far as the CT is concerned, its rejection by the French on 29 May 2005 and by the Dutch a few days later threw the EU into a profound political crisis. Many analysts have asserted that the institutional changes proposed would have contributed to a more functional, viable, and balanced form of decision making in an enlarged EU of 27 or more members, coupled by a strengthening of the EU's international role (see Chapter 4). But even if the Treaty had been ratified, the EU would still have rested on an international treaty or, at best, on a quasi-constitutional system of checks and balances designed to organize political authority in a non-state polity.

With regard to the process leading up to the CT (see Chapter 4), the following questions are in order. Did the Convention act as a 'constituent assembly'? Were the deliberations on the new Treaty legitimized by European public opinion? Would the envisaged Treaty have taken the EU further down the road towards a federal system? The answer to all these questions is 'no'. First, the drafting process was characterized by a lack of a genuine European constituent power, as the Convention was composed of appointed delegates, albeit drawn from a wider sociopolitical spectrum than has previously been the case. Second, the outcome agreed by the Convention could be (and was) changed by the IGC that followed it, with the latter retaining the right to a final say over the end product through classical forms of intergovernmental bargaining. Third, the outcome of the IGC failed to produce a Constitution 'proper' that derived its social legitimacy directly from a European demos.

The general assessment then is that state-centrism was the order of the day when it came to bestowing the EU with a system of 'basic law' provisions. Nor could the constitutional project have transformed a constellation of democracies into a democratic polity, as it could only follow the previous path of sovereign-conscious states wishing to bring about a moderate reordering of the treaties. The CT would not therefore have endowed the EU with 'a new basis of sovereignty' able to transcend the sovereignty of its parts. In brief, the EU is about the preservation of those state qualities that allow its members to survive as distinct polities, whilst engaging themselves in a polity-building exercise that transforms their traditional patterns of interaction.

The Brussels European Council in June 2007 opened the way for a Reform Treaty (now called the Lisbon Treaty), which was initially expected to be ratified by 1 January 2009. The Treaty was signed by EU leaders on 13 December 2007 with the aim of 'rescuing' most of the Constitutional Treaty's envisaged reforms, whilst removing its symbolic dimension. It was to be ratified by national parliaments, with the exception of Ireland, which was committed to holding a referendum. This represented the long-awaited response of the EU to a prolonged political crisis, conveniently termed, if not camouflaged, as a 'reflection period'. The Irish rejected the Lisbon Treaty on 12 June 2008, bringing the EU yet again into a state of crisis, but leaving the door open for a second referendum to take place in the second half of 2009 which produced a positive result.

The overall assessment of the Lisbon Treaty (its content is dealt with in Chapter 4) is that it represented a compromise among divergent and, more often than not, conflicting national interests. Too many reservations, opt-outs, references to the retention of states' prerogatives in relation to competences and reform practices, along with a considerable delay of applying the double majority system of the Constitutional Treaty (not before 2017, although from 2014 a new version of the 1994 Ioannina Compromise will take effect), deprived the EU of any possible consolidation of its political identity that might signal a shift in the basis of its legitimation. The Lisbon Treaty was therefore much on a par with the Amsterdam and Nice reform outcomes in that it lacked the democratic vision that might have (re)ignited the public's interest in EU affairs.

KEY POINTS

- The Amsterdam Treaty was little more than a managerial reform that aimed to increase policy effectiveness.

- After Nice, there was still no evidence of the emergence of a European civic identity.

- The rejection of the Constitutional Treaty by the French and Dutch publics threw the EU into a prolonged political crisis.

- The Lisbon Treaty represents a balanced yet moderate reform outcome.

Conclusion

Viewing the EU as an organized synarchy of entwined sovereignties helps us rethink democracy in the EU. The notion of 'synarchy' as presented earlier in this chapter does not invalidate the sovereignties of the member states, however; nor does it threaten the member states' legitimizing role. Rather, it brings to the fore a commonly shared perception that states can act as constituent units with the capacity to coexercise their sovereignties. The image projected is of an organized 'multiplicity of autonomies', not an 'autonomous multiplicity'. Thus presenting the EU as a 'synarchy' does not point to the emergence of a new sovereignty, as would occur had a federal state been created; nor does it sweep away its members' demoi in any imposed form of homogenization. Rather, it rests on the rise of a cooperative culture based on mutually reinforcing perceptions about how collective life might be organized.

The study of the EU exposes new understandings of state sovereignty, which is embodied in the right of the constituent polities to be involved in coexercising common competences whilst claiming an active role in the representation of their interests in the larger system. States are recognized as sovereign, not on the basis of what they can do on their own, but on the basis of their ability to participate in collective systems.

The initial prospects for a smooth ratification of the Lisbon Treaty raised expectations that the fragmented European demos might be endowed with a common civic identity. The treaty reforms of the 1990s and 2000s have failed to produce not only a common democratic vision but even the belief that such a vision is within reach in the foreseeable future. The outcome of the reforms is much more a product of utilitarian calculus led by the dominant national elites. Such an elite-driven EU process would seem to work against the interests of citizens as they seek to become the decisive agents of civic change.

In conclusion, then, the discussion of Europe's contested democracy in this chapter is underpinned by a belief that it is increasingly important for the EU to continue to address issues of democratic governance and to ensure that its decisions are informed by a principled public discourse. Yet, like any other polity that aspires to become a democracy, the EU has to engage itself in a constitutive process based on a new framework of politics capable of addressing both the institutional and the socio-psychological aspects of the democratic deficit. Although the EU is closer to a synarchy of entwined sovereignties, rather than to a *res publica*, the current situation is not an ideal end state, as it is likely to hinder the development of a European demos. And as the EU was founded and is still based on an international treaty, its transition to a participatory form of polity is likely to be neither easy nor linear.

? QUESTIONS

1. What is the 'democratic deficit' and how might one rectify it?
2. Why is democracy important for the making of a European polity?
3. Is a European demos necessary for the promotion of European democracy?
4. Which model of governance is most likely to democratize the EU?
5. What merits and weaknesses does consociational democracy entail for the EU?
6. What are the limits and possibilities for the making of a European res publica?

7. Have the treaties of Amsterdam and Nice enhanced democracy in the EU?

8. Had it been ratified, how would the Constitutional Treaty have strengthened democracy in the EU?

 GUIDE TO FURTHER READING

- Bellamy, R., Castiglione, D., and Shaw, J. (eds) *Making European Citizens: Civic Inclusion in a Transnational Context* (London: Palgrave, 2006). Assesses the limits and possibilities of European civic competence through an examination of the actors and processes involved in the making of a composite yet identifiable European citizenry.

- Chryssochoou, D. N. *Theorizing European Integration*, 2nd edn (London and New York: Routledge, 2009). Aims to sketch out a general image of the whole, as a reflection of a particular kind of European reality captured by the term 'organized synarchy'.

- Fabrini, S. (ed.) *Democracy and Federalism in the European Union and the United States: Exploring Post-National Governance* (London and New York: Routledge, 2005). Yields comparative and post-national insights into the different experiences of federalism and democracy with reference to the evolution of the EU and the US political systems.

- Nanz, P. *Europolis: Constitutional patriotism beyond the nation-state* (Manchester: Manchester University Press, 2006). Advances a normative thesis on the European public sphere through the lens of what the author calls 'situated constitutional patriotism': an idea rooted not in a single European demos, but rather on multiple co-existing demoi.

- Smith, V. A. *Democracy in Europe: The EU and National Polities* (Oxford: Oxford University Press, 2006). Assesses the democratic dialectics in the emerging relationship between the EU as a democratic polity in the making and its democratic subsystems.

 WEBLINKS

- http://www.eui.eu/RSCAS/Research/EUDO/ The European Union Democracy Observatory (EUDO) at the European University in Florence produces a permanent and periodic assessment of democratic practices within the EU

- http://www.reconproject.eu/projectweb/portalproject/RECONWorkingPapers.html The RECON Online Working Paper Series publishes current research on democracy and the democratization of the political order in Europe.

- http://europa.eu.int.comm/public_opinion/Eurobarometer The portal for Eurobarometer, which provides opinion poll data and analysis on European integration issues.

- http://democracy.livingreviews.org/index.php/lrd/index *Living Reviews in Democracy* is an e-journal that publishes the latest research on the topic of democracy, including the EU.

- www.statewatch.org/ A UK-based NGO that campaigns for the protection of civil liberties. It focuses substantially on the EU.

 Visit the Online Resource Centre that accompanies this book for lots of interesting additional material. http://www.oxfordtextbooks.co.uk/orc/Cini_Borragan3e/

24 Public Opinion and the EU

LAUREN M. MCLAREN

Chapter Contents

Reader's Guide

This chapter provides an overview of trends in public opinion toward the European Union. The chapter also discusses the key factors thought to explain differences in mass opinion regarding the EU. These include: rational utilitarianism (opinions stemming from calculations about the costs and benefits of the EU); perceptions of the national government; knowledge of the EU and cognitive mobilization (attentiveness to politics); concerns about the loss of national identity; and distrust of the EU institutions.

Introduction

The European Union began primarily as an elite-driven process. The early days of agreements and negotiations were seen as too complicated for the ordinary citizen, and so most decisions were taken outside the public spotlight. Hence, early observers of public opinion toward the European project remarked on what was perceived as a 'permissive consensus' of public opinion (Lindberg and Scheingold 1971), whereby citizens generally held neutral opinions regarding what their governments were doing in Brussels, giving these governments considerable leeway to pursue policies outside the purview of an attentive public. It was only after the addition of Eurosceptic member states (particularly the UK and Denmark) in the first enlargement (1973) that we finally saw the beginnings of consultation with mass publics on issues related to European integration (see Box 24.1). Even then, such consultation tended to be limited and was focused on referendums. In general, through the mid 1980s, EU member governments and bureaucrats have been interested in limited public involvement in the integration process. The Single European Act seems to have marked a turning point in this regard, as member state governments began selling their varying visions of a renewed European project that would contribute to the further economic development of the member states. It is also at this point that more EU policies began to impinge upon national policy making because of the increased level of economic coordination within the EU.

Nowadays it would be difficult to argue that mass European publics are providing a 'permissive consensus' for EU-level policy making. Referendums in the past decade or so have come very close to putting the brakes on European integration. The 2005 referendums in France and the Netherlands on the Constitutional Treaty and the subsequent rejection

---

 KEY CONCEPTS AND TERMS 24.1

Euroscepticism

The term *Euroscepticism* was first used in 1986 to describe British Prime Minister Margaret Thatcher (*The Times*, 30 June 1986) and later was used in the 26 December 1992 issue of *The Economist* to describe the increasingly negative German public opinion regarding European integration after Germany was ordered to adjust its rules on beer purity to conform with the internal market (Hooghe and Marks 2007). In academic discourse, the term has tended to refer to 'doubt and distrust on the subject of European integration' (Flood 2002: 73). The terms 'hard Euroscepticism' and 'soft Euroscepticism' have been used to describe the varying types and degrees of Euroscepticism:

Hard Euroscepticism is where there is a principled opposition to the EU and European integration. It can therefore be seen in parties who think that their counties should withdraw from membership, or whose policies towards the EU are tantamount to being opposed to the whole project of European integration as it is currently conceived.

Soft Euroscepticism is where there is not a principled objection to European integration or EU membership but where concerns on one (or a number) of policy areas lead to the expression of qualified opposition to the EU, or where there is a sense that 'national interest' is currently at odds with the EU's trajectory (Taggart and Szczerbiak 2002: 7).

Kopecky and Mudde (2002) develop a four-part typology to describe public opinion regarding the EU: 'Eurorejects' are those who oppose the ideal of integration and the reality of the EU; 'Euroenthusisasts' support both the EU and the ideal of ever closer union; 'Europragmatists' do not support integration, but view the EU as useful; and 'Eurosceptics' support the idea of integration but not its realization through the current EU. As Ray (2007) indicates, although this conceptualization has the theoretical appeal of separating out Europe from the actual EU, it is not clear as to whether this distinction appears in political debate. Thus, for the most part experts on the topic tend to imply a range of negative opinions on European integration, including outright opposition to the EU when using the term 'Eurosceptic' (Hooghe and Marks 2007).

of the revised treaty, the Lisbon Treaty, in Ireland in 2008 (see Boxes 24.2 and 24.3), highlight the important role that the mass public plays in the integration project in the modern day. Moreover, it is clear that public opinion plays a role in constraining integration outside referendum settings as well. A key example of this is the constraint that British public opinion placed on then prime minister Tony Blair's

---

 CASE STUDY 24.2

The referendums on the Constitutional Treaty in France and the Netherlands

In 2001, European Union member states established a European Convention for the purpose of drafting a Constitutional Treaty for the EU member states. The creation of a European constitution was to be both symbolically and substantively important, and implied a further move toward supranational governance in the EU. While the majority of EU member states ratified the Constitutional Treaty, in 2005 French and Dutch voters put a brake on the process by voting 'no' in referendums held on 29 May 2005 and 1 June 2005, respectively. Why?

While the French are not overly Eurosceptic, trends in support for the EU indicate that positive feelings about the EU have been in decline since the early 1990s (see McLaren 2006). Thus, in considerable contrast to the Netherlands (see below), the French 'no' vote was perhaps less of a surprise. Indeed, previous experience indicates that even when feelings about the EU are generally positive, votes in EU referendums in France can be very close indeed. This was the case with the vote on the Maastricht Treaty on European Union, in which a bare majority of 51.05 per cent voted to support the Treaty. While there was some discussion of the vote in the 2005 French referendum being a vote on Turkey's eventual membership of the EU, in fact, the 'no' vote in France appears to be related to a few key issues: the French economy and opposition to the government. Several concerns about France's future economic outlook developed during the referendum campaign. Amongst these were general worries about the state of unemployment in France, fears about the relocation of French business and the decline of small business, and anxiety about decline of the French 'social model', along with the failure of the Constitutional Treaty to address the issue of 'social Europe'. These were predominantly concerns amongst the French left. At the same time, the national government—and French President Jacques Chirac in particular—was becoming increasingly unpopular, and for many French voters the referendum turned into a confidence vote on the government of the day. To some extent, the 'no' vote was also partly motivated by nationalistic concerns. Thus, on 29 May 2005, 54.7 per cent voted against the Treaty (with 70 per cent voter turnout).

While referendums in France are relatively common nowadays, they are far less so in the Netherlands. In fact, the Constitutional referendum held on 1 June 2005 was the first such referendum in modern Dutch history. The Dutch are generally amongst the most enthusiastic EU supporters, and so it was widely expected that they would provide resounding support to the referendum, ratifying the Constitutional Treaty. However, with a relatively high turnout of 62 per cent, 61.8 per cent voted against the treaty. While the referendum was to be consultative only, most major parties had pledged to respect the voters' wishes, whatever the outcome.

Given general widespread support of the EU and European integration in the Netherlands, the big question posed about the referendum result is 'Why?!'. One of the key explanations seems to be that Dutch citizens were unclear as to what they were being asked to approve. The referendum campaign got off to a very slow start, and media and politicians struggled to find ways to frame the debate about the referendum. Moreover, in the absence of clear information as to what the Constitution meant for the EU and for the Netherlands, many Dutch citizens relied on the sorts of cues discussed in this chapter—especially opposition to the government. There may have been some EU-related reasons for the 'no' vote as well, however. One of these is connected to the budget contribution of the Netherlands; another is connected to unhappiness with the Dutch government's adoption of the euro, at which time—according to many commentators—the Dutch guilder had been devalued against the euro. It was also perceived that the introduction of the euro had led to an increase in prices. The prospect of Turkish membership of the EU also contributed to the 'no' vote, both because of the threat of cheap labour and because of the perceived threat to Dutch culture. Finally, as the EU has continued to expand, two fears have subsequently developed. One is whether this small (original) member state can continue to wield influence in the new Europe and the other is whether Dutch interests can still be protected within the EU. Ultimately, however, the 'no' vote may have been in great part a result of the disorganization of the 'yes' campaign.

CASE STUDY 24.3

The Irish rejection of the Lisbon Treaty

Since their entry into the EU, the Irish have been amongst the most enthusiastic supporters of the EU. This is likely to be, in great part, due to the large-scale economic development of the country shortly after becoming a full EU member state, with many Irish citizens attributing this development specifically to the EU. Thus Irish votes against EU projects tend to come as fairly major surprises. The most recent of these occurred on 12 June 2008 when the revised Constitutional Treaty, named the Lisbon Treaty, was rejected by 53.4 per cent Irish voters (with a turnout of 53.1 per cent). Unlike the cases of France and the Netherlands in 2005, Ireland was required to hold a referendum on this treaty: in 1987 the Irish Supreme Court established that any significant amendment to the Treaties of the European Union would require an amendment to the Irish Constitution. In turn, all Constitutional amendments must be approved by public vote.

Although Irish enthusiasm for the EU might be expected to guarantee a 'yes' vote, events in previous years provided clues that a 'yes' was far from secure. In 2001, Ireland voted against the Nice Treaty which was primarily stipulating rules regarding voting and the functioning of EU institutions in preparation for the 2004 enlargement. At that time, the rejection mostly revolved around issues of Irish neutrality, prompted by provisions within the Nice Treaty on Common Foreign and Security Policy. The Irish eventually supported a revised treaty that took these concerns into consideration.

Why did the Irish vote 'no' again in 2008? (Note that an Irish referendum on the Constitutional Treaty was scheduled for 2005 but was cancelled following the Dutch and French referendums.) The answer seems to mirror the events in the Netherlands from 2005: namely, the Irish vote appears to be a result of the failure of the 'yes' campaign to inform and mobilize. In the absence of a coordinated 'yes' campaign, the 'no' camp was able to spread fear regarding the impact of the treaty on Irish neutrality, abortion laws, taxation laws, and workers' rights. At least some portion of the negative vote also appears to be connected to dissatisfaction with the government of the day. Ultimately, ordinary citizens were—yet again—able to put the brakes on EU plans regarding institutional reform.

---

promised referendum on joining the eurozone. There are, of course, other factors that are likely to have prevented the holding of such a referendum, such as then Chancellor Gordon Brown's opposition to the idea, but the public's clear opposition to joining the euro at the very least bolstered the Brown camp's position. Thus, importantly, after promising in 1997 to take Britain into the eurozone, Blair left office without even taking the promised public consultation on this issue, in great part because it was fairly clear which way the public would vote.

Ultimately, it is difficult to argue nowadays that the European mass public is irrelevant in European-level decision making. Indeed, the stated purpose of the proposed Constitutional Treaty was to make an anxious public more comfortable with its European institutions. If public opinion is increasingly important in the realm of European politics, the next question to ask is why some people feel hostile toward the EU, others are more positive about it, while others are still fairly neutral. This chapter outlines the leading explanations for differences of opinion regarding the EU. It begins, however, with an overview of general trends in the European public's opinions toward the Union.

General perceptions of the EU

Since the early 1970s, the European Commission has sponsored regular opinion polls that monitor public support for various aspects of the European project (along with a whole host of other topics). The reports—known as Eurobarometer polls—are published by the Commission and are freely available at: http://europa.eu.int/comm/public_opinion/index_en.htm.

Here I will summarize the survey items found in Eurobarometer polls that are generally used in the academic literature to describe the public's perceptions of the European project. These items are:

• Generally speaking, do you think that [OUR COUNTRY'S] membership of the European Union is a good thing, a bad thing, or neither good nor bad?

• Taking everything into consideration, would you say that [OUR COUNTRY] has on balance benefited or not from being a member of the European Union? (benefited, not benefited, don't know)

Trends for the first of these items indicate that in the period leading up to the Maastricht Treaty ratification there was a marked increase in levels of Euro-enthusiasm (McLaren 2006; see also Chapter 3). By 1991, approximately 70 per cent of Europeans (on average across the EU) were claiming that their country's membership of the European Union was a good thing. Also of interest is that by the time of the signing of the Amsterdam Treaty in 1997, enthusiasm had waned and less than 50 per cent of European citizens were claiming that their country's EU membership was a good thing. While some of this trend can be explained by the entry of three relatively Eurosceptic member states in 1995 (Austria, Finland, and Sweden), the same sort of downward trend in enthusiasm can be found in the Original Six (Western Germany, France, Italy, and the Benelux countries) and in the Southern Enlargement countries (Greece, Spain, and Portugal), groups of countries that can usually be counted amongst the most enthusiastic EU supporters.

In terms of country differences, it is generally apparent that citizens in the Original Six tend to be more positive about their country's EU membership than citizens of other member states, although Germany and France were leaning in the Eurosceptic direction toward the late 1990s. Similarly, the Southern Enlargement countries tend to be relatively enthusiastic about EU membership, but not to the same degree as many of the Original Six (particularly the Netherlands, Luxembourg, and Italy). On the other hand, citizens in countries included in the First Enlargement and 1995 Enlargement lean in the Eurosceptic direction, with approximately 30–40 per cent in countries like the UK, Finland, Austria, and Sweden claiming that their country's membership of the EU had been a good thing by the late 1990s. Not surprisingly, Ireland is a clear exception to this pattern, as well as to the general EU pattern: while positive attitudes to the EU were dropping across other member states in the 1990s, the Irish became more and more Euro-enthusiastic between the mid 1990s and late 1990s. This is generally attributed to the economic miracle in Ireland that is thought to have been stimulated by the budgetary outlays coming from the EU.

Another key survey item often investigated is the question of whether one's country has benefited from membership of the EU. Cross-time trends in responses to this item exhibit the same enthusiasm followed by scepticism or ambivalence in the 1990s, but the cross-time changes are not nearly as dramatic (McLaren 2006; see also Chapter 3). From the 1980s through to the present period, the majority of EU citizens have believed that their country has benefited from EU membership. However, there are also clear country differences: citizens of the UK, Finland, Austria, and Sweden are consistently below the EU average for this item, and by the early twenty-first century, Germans are also considerably below average. Amongst the newer member states, Hungary, Bulgaria, and Cyprus currently display the lowest levels of agreement that their country has benefited from EU membership.

Most of the research that has been conducted on public support for the European Union or the European integration project has been based on the EU 12 or EU 15. Recent publications have, however, investigated attitudes to the EU amongst the member states that joined the EU in May 2004 and January 2007. One of the key points to note about public opinion regarding the EU in most of these countries is that it is—perhaps surprisingly—fairly lukewarm (McLaren 2006; see also Chapter 26). The cross-time trends in the Central and East European Candidate Barometers conducted by the European Commission prior to the entry of these countries into the EU indicate that even in the early 1990s the image of the EU in Central and Eastern Europe was not all that positive. Moreover, amongst many of the CEE candidates, citizens became less and less positive toward the EU through the mid 1990s, presumably as a result of the EU's initially hesitant response

to the prospect of a CEE enlargement. It was only after the EU finally opened accession talks with these countries in 1997 that its image received a bolster amongst their mass publics. Moreover, when asked, prior to entry in May 2004, whether their country's membership of the EU would be a good thing, the response was mixed (McLaren 2006; Chapter 26). Rather interestingly, citizens in the candidate countries that were not accepted for entry in 2004—Bulgaria, Romania, and Turkey—were amongst the most positive about their country's EU membership prior to 2007. Levels of enthusiasm remain relatively high in Romania and Turkey but appear to have declined fairly dramatically in Bulgaria, where by 2008 only 48 per cent thought that their country's membership of the EU was a good thing. (This is only 2 percentage points below the EU average, however, so Bulgaria is still not counted as being amongst the Eurosceptic countries.) In general, at the low end of support for the EU nowadays, we find Latvia and Hungary, along with the UK, where only roughly 30 per cent thought that their country's membership of the EU was a good thing by 2008.

The chapter now turns to some of the key explanations provided for individual differences in Euroscepticism (see Box 24.1). Our discussion will be focused upon the main theories and hypotheses raised in scholarly literature to explain varying attitudes to European integration.

KEY POINTS

- Trends in public opinion toward the EU are collected through regular opinion surveys known as Eurobarometer polls.

- Enthusiasm for the European integration project was generally on the rise until 1991.

- Enthusiasm for European integration was considerably reduced by 1997.

- Citizens of Latvia, Hungary, and the UK are currently amongst the most Eurosceptic mass publics, while the Original Six and Southern Enlargement member states, plus the Irish and Romanians, are amongst the most enthusiastic.

- Enthusiasm for the EU declined across the 1990s in every member state except Ireland, and enthusiasm has also declined in most of the 2004 Enlargement member states, as well as Bulgaria.

Political economy and rationality

In the mid 1980s, the discipline of political science was becoming heavily influenced by rational, utilitarian approaches. More specifically, models of political behaviour were being developed around the assumption that individuals rationally pursue their self-interest. This approach has had a considerable impact on the study of attitudes to European

integration. Some of these theories have been *egocentric* in nature—that is, individuals support or oppose the integration project because they have personally benefited (or will benefit) from it or have been harmed (or will be harmed) by it. Other approaches that would fit within this context are more *sociotropic* in nature: citizens of some of the

EU member states are more supportive of the European project because their *countries* have benefited from the European project.

With regard to the egocentric utilitarian theories, the contention is that individuals from certain socio-economic backgrounds are doing far better economically than individuals of other backgrounds as a result of European integration. In particular, the opening up of the Single Market and the introduction of the common currency are thought to benefit top-level business executives the most, as they no longer face trade barriers and exchange rate differences across (most of) the EU. Similarly, individuals with higher levels of education will be more likely than those with little education to feel that their knowledge and skills will serve them well in a wider EU market. Furthermore, those with higher incomes are argued to be more favourable toward European integration because of the freed capital markets and monetary union that make it more possible for such individuals to move capital across the EU to earn better interest rates. On the other hand, those with poor job skills, educations, and incomes are expected to be the most fearful of a common market and monetary integration. As business executives are free to look across the EU-wide market for lower-paid or higher-skilled workers, domestic *manual* workers in particular are likely to feel vulnerable to job loss. Moreover, without any Europe-wide social safety net and with member state governments being pressured by EU-wide agreements and the European Commission to reduce social welfare budgets (or increase taxation to fund these benefits), those at the lowest levels of occupational skill, education, and income are expected to be most hostile to the EU as a whole (Gabel 1998).

These theories are generally supported empirically. For instance, according to Eurobarometer No. 57.1 published in spring 2002, while 70 per cent of professionals and executives claim that their country's membership of the EU has been a good thing, only 48 per cent of manual workers say the same; similarly, only 46 per cent of the unemployed across the EU think that their country's membership of the EU has been a good thing. In addition, while 47 per

cent of those with lower levels of education are happy about their country's membership of the EU, an overwhelming 66 per cent of those at higher levels of education claim that their country's EU membership is good. There are almost identical percentages for income. It must be noted, however, that the lack of positive attitudes to the EU does not necessarily translate into negativity; in general, those who are not thought to do very well from an expanded market lean towards neutral responses more heavily than groups like professionals and executives. Thus, the potential losers in EU integration do not appear to perceive themselves as such and instead tend to be generally neutral about the project. Although it might have been expected that these relationships would be reversed in the newer member states because workers and those with lower education and skills levels would eventually benefit from the free movement of labour within the EU, it appears that even in this group of countries it is the educated professional class that is generally most positive about the EU (McLaren 2006).

In addition to proposing the notion of egocentric utilitarianism, rational approaches have also focused upon the sociotropic costs and benefits that the EU brings. Namely, the EU can provide economic benefits to member states in two realms: trade and budgetary outlays (Eichenberg and Dalton 1993). Analyses indicate that these factors explain attitudes to integration fairly consistently. A country's EU budget balance in particular has a strong impact on the percentage in the country saying that EU membership is a good thing (McLaren 2006, Chapter 3). The evidence indicates that key net contributors to the EU budget—the UK and Germany—contain the smallest percentage of citizens claiming that their country's EU membership is good (at about 30 per cent in the UK and 40 per cent in Germany). On the other hand, citizens in countries that have been the largest beneficiaries of the EU budget—particularly Spain and Ireland—are far more positive about their country's membership of the EU, with approximately 65 per cent in Spain and 75 per cent in Ireland claiming to feel positively about EU membership. Moreover, the trend across member states is fairly linear, in that attitudes to EU membership become more positive in proportion to the amount of money the member state contributes to or receives from the EU budget. The trend for trade benefits is not quite as clear, however (McLaren 2006). Thus, the most powerful of the sociotropic explanations appears to be that related to the budget balance. At the time of writing it is still to be determined whether this relationship will continue to hold in the EU 27, but it is expected that budget outlays will indeed continue to bolster support for the EU in the future.

KEY POINTS

- *Egocentric utilitarianism* explains support for the European Union in terms of the economic costs and benefits of the European project to the individual.

- Those with higher levels of education, better job skills, and higher incomes are argued to be amongst the most supportive of European integration because their skills and incomes put them in a superior competitive position in a free market.

- However, those without such skills are not necessarily hostile to the project, but instead display indifference.

- *Sociotropic utilitarianism* explains support for the EU in terms of the benefits that the EU has brought to the country, specifically budgetary outlays and increased trade.

Attitudes to the national government

The arguments presented above assume that EU citizens are able to consider rationally the impact of economic costs and benefits of EU membership on their own personal lives or on their countries. The approaches discussed in this section and the next make very different arguments about how individuals come to feel the way they do about the EU. Namely, these approaches argue that support for or opposition to integration may have very little to do with perceived economic gains or losses. This is because it is unlikely that most Europeans are able to calculate whether they have indeed benefited or not from European integration. That is, the egocentric utilitarian models in particular demand a great deal of knowledge of both the integration process and the economy, and for the ordinary European to come to any conclusion about whether they are going to be harmed by the process is likely to be extraordinarily difficult. Thus many researchers have argued that because of the complexity of the integration process (and the EU institutions), the EU is often perceived in terms of *national* issues rather than European-level ones. This effect is seen most clearly in the context of referendums (Franklin, Marsh, and McLaren 1994), in that referendums on European issues often turn into a vote on the national government's popularity. For example, the French nearly voted against the Maastricht Treaty in 1992, not because of opposition to the components of that treaty (such as monetary integration) but because of unhappiness with the government of the day (see Box 24.2). Further, it is likely that the French and Dutch votes in the 2005 Constitutional Treaty referendums were also driven to some extent by unhappiness with the government of the day. Moreover, it has been argued that European elections are generally fought on national issues rather than European-level issues (van der Eijk and Franklin 1996).

Even outside the context of referendums and elections, some have argued that general feelings about the EU are also driven in part by feelings about the national government. As argued by Christopher Anderson (1998), survey after survey shows that few Europeans know much about the details of the European project; so they must be formulating their opinions toward it from something other than their own knowledge and experience. Anderson's contention is that such attitudes are in part projections of feelings about the national government: that is, hostility to the national government is projected onto the EU level while positive feelings about one's national government also translate into positive feelings about the EU.

Political psychology: cognitive mobilization and identity

Early studies of attitudes to European integration conceptualized the project in terms of cosmopolitanism and contended that those who were more 'cognitively mobilized', specifically those who think about and discuss political issues, would gravitate toward the new supranational organization. It was also contended that differences in opinion regarding the European Community were likely to stem from familiarity with the project itself: the more people knew about it, the less fearful they would be of it and thus the more supportive they would be. Evidence indicates that those who talk politics with their friends and family—the cognitively mobilized—are indeed more supportive of the European integration project (Inglehart 1970). Moreover, knowledge of the EU appears to have positive implications for public opinion: those who are able to pass a 'knowledge quiz' about the history and institutions of the EU are on the whole more enthusiastic about the project than those who know very little about the EU (see Karp, Banducci, and Bowler 2003).

The quest for rational explanations of individual-level feelings toward the EU discussed above was motivated by the assumption that the European project was mostly economic in nature. Such an assumption is not unreasonable, in that much of the integration that has occurred has indeed been in various sectors of the economy. However, the overriding

goal of such integration has always been political—namely, the prevention of war on the European continent. As the most recent of these large-scale wars (World War II) is often perceived as being motivated in part by nationalist expansion, one of the phenomena to be thwarted was therefore the roots of such expansion. And while the project as a whole has mostly been sold to Europeans as an economic one, particularly through the 1980s and 1990s, some are likely to perceive it not in economic terms but instead in terms of threat to one of their key identities.

The body of work known as social identity theory leads us to the firm conclusion that identities are terribly important for people and that protectiveness of 'in-groups' (social groups an individual belongs to and identifies with) can develop even in the context of seemingly meaningless laboratory experiments and even when individuals expect no material gain for themselves by maintaining such identity (Tajfel 1970). The reasons for such behaviour are still not entirely clear, but the major explanations are that many people use in-group identity and protectiveness to bolster their self-esteem, while others use identity to help them simplify and understand the world (Turner 1985).

European integration may be perceived by Europeans as a potential threat to a basic identity that they have used for either (or both) of these purposes, namely their *national* identities. Table 24.1 explores the degree to which EU citizens do indeed worry that the European project will bring about a loss of national identity. It is apparent from the figures

Table 24.1 Fear that European integration means loss of national identity

	Currently afraid of it (%)	Not currently afraid of it (%)	Don't know (%)	Number asked
Austria	45	50	5	1,020
Belgium	33	67	1	1,024
Bulgaria	34	51	15	1,001
Croatia	49	46	5	1,000
Cyprus (Republic)	50	46	3	502
Czech Rep	30	68	2	1,161
Denmark	37	60	2	1,032
Estonia	38	57	5	1,000
Finland	39	60	2	1,028
France	41	56	3	1,009
Germany	39	59	3	1,021
Greece	44	56	0	1,000
Hungary	26	69	5	1,000
Ireland	49	44	7	1,009
Italy	34	57	9	1,000
Latvia	42	52	6	1,033
Lithuania	42	50	8	1,020
Luxembourg	40	57	4	510
Malta	42	54	4	500
Netherlands	39	59	2	1,041
Poland	28	67	5	1,000
Portugal	43	49	7	1,003
Romania	22	61	17	1,000
Slovakia	40	56	4	1,096
Slovenia	37	60	3	1,034
Spain	25	63	12	1,015
Sweden	26	70	3	1,033
UK	63	32	4	1,320
Total	39	55	6	29,430

Question wording: Some people may have fears about the building of Europe, the European Union. Here is a list of things which some people say they are afraid of. For each one, please tell me if you, personally, are currently afraid of it, or not ... Loss of national identity and culture ...

Source: Eurobarometer No. 65 (spring 2006).

presented here that concern about the loss of national identity as a result of European integration varies widely across the member states. In the UK, for instance, 63 per cent currently claim to be afraid of the loss of national identity arising from European integration; in Cyprus, concern about the impact of the EU on national identity is relatively high, with 50 per cent of Cypriots claiming to be concerned. On the other hand, only 22 per cent of Romanians, 25 per cent of Spaniards, 26 per cent of Hungarians, and 28 per cent of Poles are worried about this possibility.

To what degree do such fears affect general feelings about the EU? Table 24.2 provides the tabulation between fear of loss of national identity and feeling that EU membership has been a good thing. While 34 per cent of those who worry about the loss of their national identity due to European integration claim that EU membership is a good thing, 62 per cent who do not fear the loss of their national identity believe EU membership to be a good thing. As argued by Liesbet Hooghe and Gary Marks (2004), however, what may be important is the *exclusiveness* of national identity. Indeed, the figures in Table 24.2 indicate that many people who are afraid the EU will lead to a loss of their national identity still think their coun-

try's membership of the EU is good. Thus the important distinction may be between those who hold multiple territorial identities and those who identify only with their nationality. In fact, exclusively national identity seems to vary widely across the EU. In the Original Six member states as well as in Spain and Ireland, less than half of those surveyed by Eurobarometer tend to see themselves in exclusively national terms, while clear majorities of the samples in the UK, Lithuania, Hungary, and Estonia claim to identify exclusively as nationals. Table 24.3 also indicates that this factor is important in explaining general feelings about the EU. For instance, only 32 per cent of those who see themselves as British only, Hungarian only, and so on believe EU membership is a good thing, while 62 per cent of those who see themselves as nationals first but also Europeans, and 71 per cent of those who see themselves as European first but also nationals, think EU membership is a good thing. However, both Tables 24.2 and 24.3 also indicate that while some of the exclusively national identifiers and those who fear the loss of national identity are openly hostile to the EU, it is more generally the case that such fears translate into ambivalence toward the EU rather than outright hostility.

Table 24.2 Fear of loss of identity and attitudes to EU membership

	Currently afraid of it (%)	Not currently afraid of it (%)	Don't know (%)
A good thing	34	62	32
A bad thing	24	9	12
Neither good nor bad	38	28	34
Don't know	4	2	21
	10,271	13,676	977

Question wording column variable: Some people may have fears about the building of Europe, the European Union. Here is a list of things which some people say they are afraid of. For each one, please tell me if you, personally, are currently afraid of it, or not? ... Loss of national identity and culture.

Question wording row variable: Generally speaking, do you think that (OUR COUNTRY'S) membership of the European Union is a good thing, a bad thing, or neither good nor bad?

Source: Eurobarometer No. 64.2 (autumn 2005).

Table 24.3 Exclusive national identity and attitudes to EU membership

	(NATIONALITY) only (%)	(NATIONALITY) and European (%)	European and (NATIONALITY) (%)	European only (%)	Don't know (%)
A good thing	32	62	71	66	36
A bad thing	24	8	7	9	17
Neither good nor bad	39	28	20	21	34
DK	5	2	1	3	13
	10,621	11,824	1,465	479	535

Question wording column variable: In the near future, do you see yourself as (NATIONALITY) only, (NATIONALITY) and European, European and (NATIONALITY) , or European only?

Question wording row variable: Generally speaking, do you think that (OUR COUNTRY'S) membership of the European Union is a good thing, a bad thing, or neither good nor bad?

Source: Eurobarometer No. 64.2 (autumn 2005).

KEY POINTS

- People who discuss politics frequently are said to be *cognitively mobilized*. Cognitively mobilized Europeans are amongst the strongest supporters of the European project.

- Those who know more about the EU (either self-professed or in a knowledge quiz) are also generally more enthusiastic.

- *Social identity theory* points to the fundamental importance of identity for humans. European integration is perceived as a threat to one of the key identities of Europeans, their national identities.

- Worry about the loss of national identity varies considerably by country. *Exclusiveness* of identity may be more important than concern about the loss of identity in explaining hostility to the EU.

The perceived poverty of EU institutions

In contrast to the above two approaches, which contend that in the face of little specific knowledge of the EU, citizens are likely to use proxies such as their feelings about the national government of the day or to revert to concerns about the loss of national identities, other recent approaches to the study of public opinion and the EU assume that people are at least familiar with some aspects of the EU; in particular, people may perceive that EU institutions are deficient and become hostile to the project as a whole because of the perceived poor quality of these institutions (Rohrschneider 2002). As illustrated in Table 24.4, levels of trust in the key policy-making institutions of the EU vary considerably across

Table 24.4 Trust in EU institutions, 2002

	European Parliament (%)	European Commission (%)	Number asked
Austria	47	44	1,020
Belgium	65	64	1,024
Bulgaria	57	51	1,001
Croatia	39	37	1,000
Cyprus (Republic)	55	53	502
Czech Rep	58	54	1,161
Denmark	63	53	1,032
Estonia	61	58	1,000
Finland	59	57	1,028
France	52	45	1,009
Germany	47	43	1,021
Greece	59	57	1,000
Hungary	59	56	1,000
Ireland	54	50	1,009
Italy	53	49	1,000
Latvia	41	38	1,033
Lithuania	57	55	1,020
Luxembourg	64	57	510
Malta	64	59	500
Netherlands	58	62	1,041
Poland	52	47	1,000
Portugal	57	53	1,003
Romania	63	55	1,000
Slovakia	70	63	1,096
Slovenia	62	61	1,034
Spain	57	52	1,015
Sweden	57	52	1,033
UK	27	27	1,320
Total	54	50	29,430

Question wording: For each of these, please tell me if you tend to trust it or tend to not trust it? ...... The European Parliament; ... The European Commission.

Source: Eurobarometer No. 70 (autumn 2008).

member states. For instance, only 27 per cent of the UK public trusts the European Parliament and the European Commission. In contrast, in Slovakia, Belgium, and Malta, trust in the EP is generally widespread; trust in the European Commission is also relatively high in these countries. In general across the EU, roughly half of the public trusts each of the key EU institutions. Moreover, empirical analyses consistently point to the conclusion that distrust in these institutions or the perception that the EU institutions are deficient has a substantial effect on general attitudes to the EU.

There are several reasons why some citizens of the EU may be more distrusting of its institutions. One key explanation is that, in some cases, distrust of EU institutions is connected to the functioning of national institutions: when national institutions function poorly—that is, they are corrupt and/or inefficient—citizens look to the EU to provide better governance than is possible with these national institutions. This has been suggested as one of the primary reasons why citizens in most of the Southern European member state countries were traditionally so positive about the EU and its institutions. On the

KEY POINTS

- Many Europeans are opposed to the EU because they do not trust European institutions; in many cases, it is argued that this is because national institutions work relatively well, making a shift to supranational governance unnecessary.

- On the other hand, many EU citizens are said to trust the EU's institutions because their own national institutions function poorly.

- Other explanations for distrust in EU institutions include exclusive national identity and utilitarian cost–benefit analysis regarding the benefits the EU has brought to one's personal life.

- However, an overall majority of EU citizens claims to trust the European institutions, and this helps to produce positive feelings about the EU as a whole, thereby increasing its popular legitimacy.

other hand, when national political institutions function well, citizens do not perceive any need to add a layer of supranational governance. Naturally, this argument will require some consideration in the post-2004 enlargement era.

Also of importance in explaining perceptions of the EU's main institutions are some of the explanations outlined above: exclusive national identity and utilitarian cost–benefit analysis. That is, those who identify exclusively as French, Polish, and so on find it far more difficult to trust the EU institutions than those who identify as French or Polish *and* European. In addition, individuals who claim to have benefited personally from their country's EU membership are also more trusting of the EU's institutions.

Conclusion

The analyses discussed above point to several conclusions. The first is that feelings about the EU seem to range from ambivalence to support. Only very small numbers across the EU are openly hostile to it. However, these proportions do vary by country, and hostility is far greater in countries like the UK, Hungary, and Latvia than in the rest of the EU.

This chapter also outlined the explanations for differences of opinion regarding the EU. First, some of the difference in opinion was argued to be *utilitarian* in nature. There were said to be two components to this utilitarian approach: egocentric and sociotropic. Egocentric utilitarians support the EU because it has brought them economic benefits or is likely to bring them such benefits; others in this category are ambivalent toward the project because they have not received any benefits themselves. Sociotropic utilitarians support or oppose the project because of the budgetary outlays they have received from the EU, which have presumably increased economic development and growth, or because of the large amount that their country contributes to the EU budget.

Second, some of the differences in attitudes to the EU are thought to be related to perceptions of the national government. That is, some individuals project their feelings about their own government onto the EU level: when they feel positively about the national government, the EU gets an extra boost of support, but when they feel negatively about the national government, the EU is punished.

Third, the chapter introduced two political psychology explanations for differences in opinion regarding the EU: cognitive mobilization and identity. With regard to cognitive mobilization, it was argued that higher levels of political discussion (or cognitive mobilization) and greater knowledge of the EU both appear to lead to more positive opinions about the EU. Those who do not talk politics much with friends and family and who do not know much about the EU tend to be far more ambivalent about the European project. In addition, some portion of public opinion toward the EU is argued to be driven by concerns regarding the loss of national identity. More specifically, individuals who identify exclusively in national terms (vis-à-vis Europe) are either more hostile or in some cases more ambivalent to the EU.

Fourth, Euroscepticism (ambivalence and hostility) seems to stem partly from perceived deficiencies in the EU institutions. Thus, it is not only academics who worry about democracy in the EU; ordinary citizens are also concerned about this issue.

Overall, then, we have a fairly good idea as to why some individuals are positive about the EU, some are negative, and many others are simply ambivalent. Still, even when we take all of the above-mentioned factors into account, it is also clear that there is room for improvement in our explanations. Thus, it is highly likely that research in this field will continue to develop further alternative theories in the near future.

QUESTIONS

1. What is Euroscepticism?

2. To what extent is European public opinion still marked by a 'permissive consensus'?

3. What explains votes against EU treaties in countries where citizens are generally positive about the EU, such as France, the Netherlands, and Ireland?

4. To what extent are European citizens utilitarian in their approach to the EU?

5. Why does cognitive mobilization contribute to positive feelings about the EU?

6. What role does identity play in public opinion regarding the EU?

7. Is distrust in EU institutions widespread? What explains distrust in these institutions?

8. What is the relationship between perceptions of national institutions and perceptions of EU institutions?

GUIDE TO FURTHER READING

■ Gabel, M. J. *Interests and Integration: Market Liberalization, Public Opinion, and European Union* (Ann Arbor: University of Michigan Press, 1998). This book provides an analysis of the utilitarian approaches to the study of public opinion and the EU.

■ Hooghe, L. and Marks, G. (eds) 'Sources of Euroscepticism'. Special issue of *Acta Politica*, Volume 42, Numbers 2–3, July 2007.

■ McLaren, L. M. *Identity, Interests and Attitudes to European Integration* (Basingstoke: Palgrave, 2006). This book re-analyses the utilitarian approach and introduces the concepts of group conflict and identity to explain public opinion toward the EU.

■ Niedermayer, O. and Sinnott, R. (eds) *Public Opinion and Internationalized Governance* (Oxford: Oxford University Press, 1995). This edited volume provides chapters by separate authors on multiple topics related to the EU and public opinion.

WEBLINKS

● http://www.gesis.org/en/data_service/eurobarometer/ Eurobarometer data: the German Social Sciences Infrastructure Services is the key European archive for Eurobarometer data. Access to codebooks and data can be gained through this site.

● http://europa.eu.int/comm/public_opinion/index_en.htm Eurobarometer reports: the Public Opinion unit of the European Commission writes regular reports on Eurobarometer and Candidate Barometer Polls. These reports can be found at this web address.

● http://www.europeanelectionstudies.net/ European Election Studies: the European Election Studies group has led the way in studying voting behaviour in European elections since 1979. This website provides information about the group's research activities.

Visit the Online Resource Centre that accompanies this book for lots of interesting additional material. http://www.oxfordtextbooks.co.uk/orc/Cini_Borragan3e/

25

Europeanization

TANJA A. BÖRZEL AND DIANA PANKE

Chapter Contents

- Introduction: what is Europeanization?
- Why does Europeanization matter?
- Explaining top-down Europeanization
- Explaining bottom-up Europeanization
- Towards an integrated perspective on Europeanization?
- Conclusion

Reader's Guide

The first section of the chapter explains what Europeanization means and outlines the main approaches to studying this phenomenon. The second section explains why this concept has become so prominent in research on the European Union (EU) and its member states. In the third section, the chapter reviews the state of the art with particular reference to how the EU affects states (top-down Europeanization). It illustrates the theoretical arguments using empirical examples. Similarly, section four examines how states can influence the Union (bottom-up Europeanization) and provides some theoretical explanations for the empirical patterns observed. The final section of the chapter presents an overview of research that brings bottom-up and top-down Europeanization together and considers the future of Europeanization research.

Introduction: what is Europeanization?

Europeanization has become a prominent concept in the study of the European Union and European Integration (see Box 25.1). While Europeanization generally refers to interactions between the EU and its member states or third countries, there is no consensus on the definition of the term. Broadly, one can distinguish between three different notions of Europeanization: bottom-up Europeanization, top-down Europeanization, and an attempt to bring the two perspectives together.

The bottom-up perspective analyses how member states and other domestic actors shape EU policies, EU politics and the European polity. For bottom-up Europeanization approaches, the phenomenon to be explained is the European Union itself. This research analyses whether and how member states are able to upload their preferences to the EU institutions by, for example. giving the European Parliament (EP) more powers; by extending policy content and scope—as in the case in the liberalization of services; or by focusing on political processes, for example, in increasing the areas where the codecision procedure applies. European integration theories, such as neo-functionalism, liberal intergovernmentalism, and supranationalism, address such uploading efforts by member state governments (see Chapters 5, 6, and 7). They conceptualize the EU as a political arena in which actors from multiple levels of government compete and cooperate over the making of EU policies and the shaping

of the European integration process (Hooghe and Marks 2001).

In the top-down perspective, the phenomena to be explained and the causes are reversed. Here the focus is on how the EU shapes institutions, processes, and political outcomes in both member states and third countries (Andersen and Eliassen 1993; Ladrech 1994). The phenomenon to be explained is whether and how states download EU policies and institutions, which subsequently give rise to domestic change. In other words, how does the EU impact on domestic institutions, policies, or political processes? To what extent, for example, has the shift of policy competences from the domestic to the EU level undermined the powers of national parliaments by reducing their functions to that of merely transposing EU directives into national law? Is the EU responsible for a decline of public services by forcing France or Germany to liberalize telecommunications, postal services, or their energy markets? And to what extent has European integration empowered populist parties, such as the Front National, Die Linke, or Sinn Féin, which seek to mobilize those who feel they have lost out because of the Single European Market?

Top-down Europeanization approaches search for causes at the EU level that explain domestic change. They share the assumption that the EU can (but does not always) cause adaptations of domestic policies, institutions and political processes, if there is a misfit between European and domestic ideas and institutions (see, for example, Héritier 2001; and Börzel et al 2007). The incompatibility of European and domestic norms only facilitates top-down changes if it creates material costs or challenges collectively shared knowledge or beliefs about how to address societal problems. For instance, it raises the question of whether it is more appropriate to protect the environment by preventing pollution (the German approach); or by fighting environmental pollution where it becomes too damaging (the British approach).

KEY CONCEPTS AND TERMS 25.1

Europeanization

Europeanization captures the interactions between the European Union and member states and third countries (including accession and neighbourhood). One strand of Europeanization research analyses how member states shape EU policies, politics, and polity while the other focuses on how the EU triggers domestic change.

Finally, the integrated perspective combines the focus on uploading and downloading by analysing policy cycles or long-term interactions between the European Union and its members (Radaelli 2003; Kohler-Koch and Eising 1999). Member states are not merely passive takers of EU demands for domestic change. They proactively shape European policies, institutions, and processes, which they have to download and to which they later have to adapt. Moreover, the need to adapt domestically to European pressure may also have significant effects at the European level, where member states seek to reduce the misfit between European and domestic arrangements by shaping EU decisions. For example, when Germany succeeded in turning its air pollution regulations into an EU directive, it did not have to introduce any major legal and administrative changes and German industry had little difficulty in complying with EU air pollution standards. The UK, by contrast, was forced to overhaul its entire regulatory structure, and British industry had to buy new abatement technologies for which German companies were the market leaders.

The integrated approach is not a new research avenue, but rather synthesizes the top-down and bottom-up Europeanization approaches. It analyses how member states shape the European Union (uploading); how the EU feeds back into member states (downloading); and how the latter react in changing properties of the EU (uploading) (see Börzel and Risse 2007).

KEY POINTS

- Europeanization has become a key but disputed term in research on European integration.

- Top-down Europeanization seeks to explain how the European Union induces domestic change in member states or third countries.

- Bottom-up Europeanization analyses how member states and other domestic actors shape EU policies, EU politics, and the European polity.

- The integrated approach to Europeanization synthesizes the merits of top-down and bottom-up Europeanization.

Why does Europeanization matter?

A search of any university library catalogue or research database shows that Europeanization is a very active research field. Why is it that Europeanization has attracted so much attention from scholars?

For a start, the EU has become ever more important for the daily lives of its citizens. The EU has gained more and more policy competences, which now range from market creation and trade liberalization policies, and health, environmental, research, and social policies, to cooperation in the fight against crime and to foreign policies. As a consequence, it is very important to explain how the EU has obtained these competences and how its policies have been formulated. Which actors and which coalitions are active in shaping the EU?

Why is it that we observe a general broadening and widening of integration where the member states have been willing to give the EU ever more power on fighting crime and illegal immigration while resisting any significant sovereignty loss with regard to conflict prevention and conflict resolution? Are the big three (the UK, France, and Germany) in a better position to make their interests heard in the EU than Luxembourg, Ireland, Latvia, or Malta?

Likewise, it is very important to examine how the EU affects the domestic structures of its member states. Europe has hit virtually all policy areas. What kind of domestic change (of policies, institutions, or political processes) does the EU trigger? Do Greece, the UK, Poland, Luxembourg, France, or Denmark download EU policies in a similar way or do national and regional differences remain even after Europeanization?

A second reason why research on Europeanization has been thriving is that European integration does not only affect member states but can also have intended or unintended side effects on third countries. The EU is actively seeking to change the domestic structures of its neighbours and other third countries by exporting its own governance model. Examples of what is often referred to as 'external Europeanization' are the EU's enlargement policy with the famous Copenhagen Criteria, which prescribe liberal democracy and market economy for any country that seeks to join the club (see Chapter 26), and the EU's neighbourhood policy that stipulates similar requirements. Both seek to induce third countries to implement the *acquis communautaire*, particularly in the fields of the Single European Market and Justice and Home Affairs. Thus, the EU has not only talked France, Germany, Spain, Greece, and the Central and Eastern European (CEE) countries into granting their citizens general access to environmental information. It has also asked Ukraine, Georgia, Armenia, and Azerbaijan to make data on the environmental impact of planned projects accessible to the public. Conditionality and capacity building provide a major incentive for accession and for neighbourhood countries to adapt to Europe. Finally, Europeanization can have more elusive effects on member states and third countries, effects that are not necessarily intended by the EU. For instance, domestic actors can use the European Union for their own ends, and induce domestic changes in the name of Europe (Lavenex 2001). For example, gay and lesbian groups in Poland have used the EU to push for the rights of sexual minorities in the absence of any specific EU legislation. Almost all political parties in the 27 EU member states have incorporated a European dimension into their manifestos (Bolleyer and Panke 2009). Even the Irish Green Party praised the EU as 'the creation of structure for the development of peace-

ful, mutually beneficial relations between states' when it was still in the Eurosceptic camp fiercely opposing the Niece Treaty (Green Party/*Comhaontas Glas* 2002: 24). Countries that are not current or would-be members of the EU are subject to the indirect influence of the EU too. Norway, for instance, became part of the Schengen Agreement because it forms a passport union with the Scandinavian member states of the EU. Outside Europe, farmers in developing countries in Latin America and Africa have to suffer the consequences of the Common Agricultural Policy that effectively shuts their products out of the single market.

The European Union has penetrated the lives of its citizens in many respects. It not only regulates the quality of their drinking water, the shape of their vegetables, the length of parental leave, or roaming fees for mobile phones; Europeanization has also fundamentally affected core institutions of the member states and accession countries by, for example, disempowering national parliaments (Schmidt 2006). At the same time, the EU is a multi-level system of governance, in which the member states shape the policies made in Brussels. A good illustration of this is the Bolkestein Directive, which seeks to open up certain domestic markets to foreign service providers.

KEY POINTS

- Europeanization has become a key concept in the study of European integration for three main reasons. First, the EU has obtained many policy competences over the course of more than 50 years of integration and affects various aspects of the daily lives of EU citizens. Second, the EU affects third countries, which may or may not want to become members, by pushing for market liberalization, democracy, human rights, and good governance. Third, European integration has had unintended effects on states both within and outside the EU.

Explaining top-down Europeanization

As explained above, top-down Europeanization seeks to explain the conditions and causal mechanisms through which the EU triggers domestic change in its member states and in third countries. It starts from the empirical puzzle that European norms facilitate domestic change but do not provoke the convergence of national polities, politics or policies. It also posits that EU policies and institutions are a constant impetus of domestic change for all states (for example, Cowles et al 2001; Liefferink and Jordan 2004). To solve the puzzle, the literature has drawn on two different strands of neo-institutionalism (see Chapter 7). While they both assume that institutions mediate or filter the domestic impact of Europe, rationalist and constructivist approaches to top-down Europeanization differ in their assumptions about exactly how institutions matter.

Rational choice institutionalism argues that the EU facilitates domestic adaptation by changing opportunity structures for domestic actors. In a first step, a misfit between the EU and domestic norms creates demands for domestic adaptation. In a second step, the downloading of EU policies and institutions by the member states is shaped by cost–benefit calculations of the strategic actors whose interests are at stake. Institutions constrain or enable certain actions by strategic rational actors by rendering some options more costly than others (Scharpf 1997; Tsebelis 1990). From this perspective, Europeanization is largely conceived of as an emerging political opportunity structure which offers some actors additional resources to exert influence, while severely constraining the ability of others to pursue their goals. Domestic change is facilitated where the institutions of the member states empower domestic actors to block change at veto points or to facilitate it through supporting formal institutions (Börzel and Risse 2003: 64). For example, the liberalization of the European transport sector empowered internationally operating

road hauliers and liberal parties in highly regulated member states, such as Germany or the Netherlands, which had been unsuccessfully pushing for privatization and deregulation at home. But while the German reform coalition was able to exploit European policies to overcome domestic opposition to liberalization, Italian trade unions and sectoral associations successfully vetoed any reform attempt (Héritier et al 2001). Likewise, public agencies in the UK supported the appeal of women's organizations in support of the equal pay and equal treatment directives to further gender equality by providing them with legal expertise and funding to take employers to court. In the absence of such formal institutions, French women were not able to overcome domestic resistance by employers and trade unions to implement EU equal pay and equal treatment policies (Caporaso and Jupille 2001).

Other research in the Europeanization literature draws on sociological institutionalism (see Chapter 7). This specifies change mechanisms based on the ideational and normative processes involved in top-down Europeanization. Sociological institutionalism draws on the 'logic of appropriateness' (March and Olsen 1989), which argues that actors are guided by collectively shared understandings of what constitutes proper, socially accepted behaviour. These collective understandings and intersubjective meaning structures strongly influence the way actors define their goals and what they perceive as rational action. Rather than maximizing their egoistic self-interest, actors seek to meet social expectations in a given situation. From this perspective, Europeanization is understood as the emergence of new rules, norms, practices, and structures of meaning to which member states are exposed and which they have to incorporate into their domestic structures. A normative or cognitive misfit between what the British believe or know about protecting the environment best and what EU policies prescribe is a necessary, but not sufficient, condition for domestic change in response to top-down Europeanization. If there is such a misfit, norm entrepreneurs such as epistemic communities or advocacy networks socialize domestic actors into new norms and rules of appropriateness through persuasion and social learning. Domestic actors then redefine their interests and identities accordingly (Börzel and Risse 2003: 66–9). The more active norm entrepreneurs are and the more they succeed in making EU policies resonate with domestic norms and beliefs, the more successful they will be in bringing about domestic change. For example, in the case of the single currency, the coalition of central bankers and national technocrats successfully advocated a monetarist approach that produced dramatic changes in domestic monetary policy, even in countries like Italy and Greece which had to undergo painful adaptation by dramatically cutting state expenditures (Dyson and Featherstone 1999; see also Chapter 20).

Moreover, collective understandings of appropriate behaviour strongly influence the ways in which domestic actors download EU requirements (see Box 25.2). First, a consensus-oriented or cooperative decision-making culture helps to overcome multiple veto points by rendering their use for actors inappropriate. Cooperative federalism prevented the German Länder from vetoing any of the Treaty revisions that deprived them of core decision powers. Obstructing the deepening and widening of European integration would have not been acceptable to the political class (Börzel 2002). Likewise, the litigious German culture encouraged German citizens to appeal to national courts against the deficient application of EU law, while such a culture was absent in France, where litigation is less common (Conant 2002). Second, a consensus-oriented political culture allows for a sharing of adaptational costs, which facilitates the accommodation of pressure for adaptation. Rather than shifting adaptational costs onto a social or political minority, the 'winners' of domestic change compensate the 'losers'. For example, the German government shared its decision powers in European policy making with the Länder to make up for their EU-induced

power losses. Likewise, the consensual corporatist decision-making culture in the Netherlands and Germany facilitated the liberalization of the transport sector by offering compensation to employees as the potential losers of domestic changes (Héritier et al 2001). In short, the stronger informal cooperative institutions are in a member state, the more likely domestic change will be.

While Europeanization has affected the policy, polity, and politics of all member states, the degree of change differs significantly. If we take the example of environmental policy, the EU has promoted change towards a more precautionary problem-solving approach, particularly in the area of air and water pollution control. It also introduced procedural policy instruments such as the 'Access to Environmental Information and the Environmental Impact' Directives. Equally, EU policies have led to tighter standards in virtually all areas of environmental policy. While the EU has affected the policy content of all member states, the environmental latecomers (Spain, Portugal, Greece, Ireland, the UK, and more recently the Central and Eastern European countries that joined the EU in 2004 and 2007) have been much more Europeanized than the environmentally progressive 'leader' states (Denmark, Sweden, Finland, the Netherlands, Germany, and Austria) (see Chapter 22). The Europeanization of administrative structures paints a similar picture, although domestic change has been more modest. In old and new member states, the domestic impact of Europe has fostered the

---

 KEY CONCEPTS AND TERMS 25.2

Explaining downloading and taking

The top-down Europeanization literature uses the concepts 'downloading' and 'taking' as synonyms. Both terms capture the response of member and third states to the European Union. States are good in taking or downloading policies, if they are able to respond swiftly to impetuses for change coming, for example, from the EU in the form of EU law, EU neighbourhood policy, or EU development policy.

centralization of environmental policy-making competences in the hands of central government departments and agencies at the expense of subordinate levels of government. While regional governments in highly decentralized states have to some extent been compensated by codecision rights in the formulation and implementation of EU environmental policies, the main losers of Europeanization are the national and regional parliaments. Regulatory politics, by contrast, have been much less affected by European integration. While the Europeanization of environmental policy making has created new political opportunities, particularly for citizens and environmental groups, it has reinforced existing consensual and adversarial styles rather than changed them. The only exceptions are the three northern countries that joined the EU in 1995. In Austria, Sweden, and to a lesser extent Finland, the need to implement EU environmental policies in a timely fashion has reduced the scope for extensive consultation with affected interests thus undermining the traditionally consensual patterns of interest intermediation. Moreover, the legalistic approach of the Commission in the monitoring of compliance with EU law has constrained the discretion public authorities used to exercise in the implementation of environmental regulations in the UK, Ireland, and France.

External Europeanization also corroborates the differential impact of Europe. Europeanization has had a more similar effect on accession and neighbourhood countries than it has on member states when it comes to the strengthening of core executives and the increase in their autonomy from domestic political and societal pressures. It has also led to the development of a less politicized civil service and to a degree of decentralization and regionalization, at least when compared with the Communist legacy (Schimmelfennig and Sedelmeier 2005). At the same time, however, Europeanization effects on institutions and politics vary considerably. EU political conditionality was successful only in cases of unstable democracy, where it strengthened liberal politics (as in Slovakia or Serbia), while being irrelevant in those countries that already had

strong democratic constituencies (most of the CEE countries) or in autocratically ruled states (in Belarus or Azerbaijan (Schimmelfennig et al 2006). In general, there has been little institutional convergence around a single European model of governance.

In sum, the top-down impact of Europeanization is differential. EU policies and institutions are not downloaded in a uniform manner. Denmark, the UK or Sweden are better takers than France, Italy, or Greece because they have more efficient administrations (Börzel et al 2007). Thus we should not be too surprised that we find hardly any evidence of convergence towards an EU policy or institutional model. Convergence is not synonymous with Europeanization. Member states can undergo significant domestic change without necessarily becoming more similar.

By focusing on 'goodness of fit' and mediating factors, such as veto players, facilitating formal institutions, or norm entrepreneurs, we can therefore account for the differential impact of Europe. These factors increasingly point to complementary rather than competing explanations of Europeanization. As such, students of Europeanization primarily seek to identify scope conditions under which specific factors are more likely to influence the downloading of EU policies and institutions by the member states.

KEY POINTS

- Top-down Europeanization explains how the EU triggers domestic change. A central concept in this regard is 'misfit'. Only if domestic policies, processes, or institutions are not already in line with what is required by the EU, can the latter causally induce domestic change.

- If misfit is present, the impact of the European Union can be explained through different theoretical approaches, namely sociological or rational choice institutionalism.

- A frequent question of top-down Europeanization research is whether the policies, politics, and polity of states converge over time as an effect of membership, or whether states maintain distinct features.

Explaining bottom-up Europeanization

Bottom-up Europeanization research analyses how states upload their domestic preferences to the EU level. These preferences may involve EU policies, such as environmental standards; they may relate to European political processes, such as how far day-to-day decision making should involve the European Parliament; or they can touch on issues of institutional design regarding, for example, whether the European Commission should get additional competences in Justice and Home Affairs matters (see Box 25.3). Bottom-up Europeanization studies can be divided into those which analyse Intergovernmental Conferences (IGCs) (Moravcsik 1993, Lodge 1998) and those that examine the daily decision-making process within the first, second, or third pillar (Bailer 2004; Hug and König 2002; Thomson et al 2006). In order to conceptualize how bottom-up Europeanization works and how states are able to upload their preferences, students of the EU have drawn on rationalist and constructivist approaches. Rationalist approaches assume that actors have fixed and predefined interests and pursue them through recourse to their power resources (often economic strength or votes in the Council) in strategically calculating the costs and benefits of different options. Constructivist approaches assume that actors are open to persuasion and change their flexible interests in the wake of good arguments.

One of the most prominent rationalist decision-making approaches is intergovernmentalism (Hoffmann 1966; Hoffmann 1989) and its newer version, liberal intergovernmentalism (Moravcsik 1998; see also Chapter 6). Intergovernmentalism assumes that states with many votes in the EU Council and high bargaining power are in a better position to shape outcomes in EU negotiations than states with fewer votes. Moreover, powerful states are more likely to influence successfully the content of EU law if the policy at stake is very important for them and if they manage to form winning coalitions through concessions (package deals or side payments) or through threats, such as the disruption of further cooperation, stopping support in other issues, or reducing side payments. Hence the higher the bargaining power of a state and the higher the issue salience for that state, the more likely it is that this state will shape the content of the European policy (successful bottom-up Europeanization).

Quantitative studies of European decision making attribute different causal weight to formal rules, ranging from traditionally power-based studies to more institutionalist approaches. The former assume political and material power as being the crucial explanatory factor governing EU negotiations (Widgren 1994), whereas the latter put more emphasis on formal rules such as decision-making procedures or the share of vote (Tsebelis and Garrett 1997; Tsebelis and Garrett 1996). A recent collaborative research project entitled 'The European Union Decides', investigating eleven different EU decision-making models, showed that 'powerful actors who attach most salience to the issues receive the largest concessions from other negotiators' (Schneider et al 2006: 305; Thompson and Hosli 2006: 21). Hence the share of votes a member state has in the EU Council is an important negotiation resource, but does not determine outcomes. This is due to an informally institutionalized consensus norm, according to which 'powerful and intense actors are conciliates, even when they might be legally ignored'

 KEY CONCEPTS AND TERMS 25.3

Explaining uploading and shaping

The bottom-up Europeanization literature uses two concepts interchangeably in order to describe how states influence policies, politics, or institutions of the European Union. These are 'uploading' and 'shaping'. An EU member state is a successful shaper (or uploader) if it manages to make its preferences heard, so that an EU policy, political process or institution reflects its interests.

(Achen 2006: 297). Moreover, in order to influence policies successfully, states have to create coalitions. There is some evidence of the rationalist account of bottom-up Europeanization, but a considerable amount of empirical variation is left unexplained (Achen 2006: 295; Schneider et al 2006: 303–10; Thomson et al 2006).

Qualitative studies also demonstrate that bargaining and voting power are very important for bottom-up Europeanization, as power influences the opportunities that states have to upload national preferences to the EU level (Richardson 1996; Liefferink and Andersen 1998). For example, a study by Eugénia da Conceição-Heldt (2004) on the Common Fisheries Policy highlights that power, preferences, and preference intensity influence the outcomes of complex, iterated negotiations under conditions of uncertainty (Box 25.4). Another example of the importance of bargaining power in the shadow of votes is the European Working Time Directive. During the two years of COREPER negotiations prior to an agreement, a potential compromise shifted the outcome towards the UK as a strong veto player. A majority of states favoured the Directive. Although member states could have voted according to qualified majority voting, they abstained from proceeding this way but rather sought to bring the UK on board as well. As a result, the UK achieved key concessions before the Directive was passed (Lewis 2003: 115–19). In line with the findings of the 'The European Union Decides' project above, the bargaining power of a big state with high preference intensity mattered in the case of the Working Time Directive. Even though proceeding to vote could have secured support for the Directive against British interests, all large states' interests were accommodated. Therefore it is clear that qualitative studies lend support to major quantitative findings in showing that when it comes to hard bargaining in the shadow of votes, the size of member state matters in shaping its likely influence.

Constructivist supranational approaches assume that the preferences of states and non-state actors are not completely fixed during interactions, but can change in the wake of good arguments (Risse 2000). Actors have an idea of what they want when they start negotiating in the European Union, but can change their preferences if another actor makes a convincing statement, for example, should new scientific insights be made available. According to this approach, policy outcomes and integration dynamics are shaped by processes of arguing among member states, typically involving supranational institutions such as the Commission, or policy experts and epistemic communities (Haas 1970; Sandholtz and Zysman 1989). Good arguments are the ones that resonate well with all interests. If an argument wins the competition of ideas, it influences outcomes. States are more successful in shaping policy outcomes (successful bottom-up Europeanization) the better their arguments resonate with the beliefs and norms of other actors.

While quantitative studies do not (yet) test the power of ideas and good arguments, qualitative studies can trace ideational processes. They demonstrate that the power of argument is highly important in influencing the opportunity a member state has to influence the content of European laws, European institutions, or EU political processes. In the first pillar, fewer than 15 per cent of all Council positions on a Commission proposal are actually decided at the level of the EU Council. COREPER and especially the working groups of the Council are the forums in which the vast majority of political decisions are taken (see Chapter 9). In both lower-level arenas, hard political bargaining, in which states resort to the threat of hierarchical delegation and voting, is rare. The usual way of doing business is based on the exchange of arguments (Joerges and Neyer 1997; Lewis 1998; Elgström and Jönsson 2000). A study of the 1994 Local Elections Directive shows, for example, that high-quality arguments can convince others, even if the point is put forward by a small state with limited bargaining and voting power, such as Belgium. This leads Lewis to conclude that the possibility of persuading others with a convincing argument and the norms of mutual responsiveness works as a great equalizer in COREPER negotiations. As a result, smaller member states who articulate sound arguments and/or clearly explain their positions can often punch above their weight (Lewis 2005b: 951). This case lends support to the constructivist hypothesis on bottom-up Europeanization.

The two theoretical accounts of the shaping of European policies are compatible rather than being mutually exclusive. We know empirically that in EU institutions, actors sometimes engage in bargaining (as expected by the rationalist intergovernmental approach) and sometimes argue (as expected by the constructivist supranational approach). Therefore both explanations of bottom-up Europeanization can account for different parts of social reality (Panke 2006).

KEY POINTS

- Bottom-up Europeanization explains how states can trigger changes in the EU.

- Misfit is a necessary condition for EU-induced changes. If states' preferences are not already in accordance with EU policies, politics, or polity, states can induce European-level changes.

- Different theories focus on different means available to states to make their voices heard, such as economic and voting power or argumentative and moral power.

- Two prominent questions of bottom-up Europeanization research are whether large states, such as Germany, France, the UK, or Poland, are more successful in influencing European policies than smaller states and under which conditions small states can punch above their weight.

KEY CONCEPTS AND TERMS 25.4

Bottom-up Europeanization: the Common Fisheries Policy

The fisheries case is a good illustration of how states make use of their voting power and the threat of a negative vote in order to obtain better deals for themselves. Back in 1976, the European Commission proposed rules on fishing quotas and member states' access to fishing areas. This policy required unanimity among the member states. Everyone agreed to the proposal, with Ireland and the UK opting for higher quotas and limitations of the equal access principle. Ireland and the UK had high bargaining power, because their agreement was required to pass the policy. In the course of several years of bargaining the Irish government accepted the Commission's modified proposal because it

achieved concessions in the form of quota increases. The UK, however, maintained its opposition and was only brought back into the 'boat' later, as the fisheries policy was linked to the UK's budget contribution in a comprehensive package deal. At that point, however, Denmark turned into a veto player because it became dissatisfied with the quota system. Denmark demanded higher and more flexible fishing quotas and created a stalemate by evoking the Luxembourg Compromise. To the threat of continued blockade, the Community responded with higher offers. Only after Denmark received higher quotas as side payments, could the Common Fisheries Policy finally come into existence in 1983.

Source: da Conceição-Heldt (2006).

Towards an integrated perspective on Europeanization?

As explained earlier in the chapter, the integrated perspective seeks to explain both the shaping and taking of EU policies and institutions. Few students of Europeanization have made an attempt to bring

the two approaches together, although some studies consider 'shaping' as the cause of 'taking' or vice versa (Héritier 1996; Van Keulen 1999; Andersen and Liefferink 1997). Member states that have the power and capacity to upload successfully their preferences, and shape EU policies accordingly, have fewer difficulties in taking and downloading them. This explains why Southern European member states are such laggards when it comes to implementing EU environmental policies (Börzel 2003). Portugal and Greece simply lack the policies, the capacities, and the power to shape EU policy making successfully. They face a higher 'misfit', incurring significant implementation costs. Not only do the Southern laggards have to invest more resources to make EU polices work on the ground, but domestic opposition also becomes more likely. Problems in taking EU policies can provide member states with important incentives to engage in (re-)shaping, in order to reduce the 'misfit'. France, for example, which had already deregulated its transport sector when it met the EU demands for liberalization, pushed for re-regulating the impact of liberalization in order to safeguard public interest goals (Héritier et al 2001).

The more successful member states are in shaping EU policies, the fewer problems they are likely to face in taking these policies. For example, if a state with high regulatory standards in the environmental policy field, such as Denmark, manages to upload its environmental policy preferences to the European level, it has to invest fewer resources in implementing EU policies later on, which in turn reduces the risk of Denmark violating EU environmental law (for example, Börzel 2003). But are successful shaping and taking explained by the same factors or do the two stages of the policy process require different explanations? Some factors might be more important to shaping than to taking, or vice versa. They could also have contradictory effects. However, so far only a small number of Europeanization studies have systematically combined and compared the causal influence of different factors in the two stages of the EU policy process.

> **KEY POINTS**
>
> - The bulk of Europeanization research focuses either on top-down or on bottom-up processes.
>
> - Integrated approaches analyse interaction effects between the shaping and the taking of European policies.
>
> - There is limited research that identifies the interaction between unsuccessful uploading of preferences to the EU level and implementation problems at the national level.
>
> - There is great potential for future research that seeks to integrate top-down and bottom-up Europeanization approaches.

Conclusion

The chapter has introduced the concept of Europeanization and has reviewed the research that has been undertaken thus far on this topic. The chapter has focused attention on the theoretical literature around the concepts of top-down and bottom-up Europeanization by identifying their explanatory quality and by contextualizing them in the wider political science literature. The empirical examples have shown how the EU has contributed to changing structures, processes, and behaviour in national arenas, but also under what conditions member states are able to incorporate their preferences into EU policies, politics, and processes. Moreover, the chapter has addressed the external dimension of Europeanization as the EU is able to affect third countries by pushing for socio-economic and political reform. The chapter has also presented a summary of a more integrated understanding of Europeanization that brings together the merits of top-down and bottom-up Europeanization approaches and possible avenues for future research. Ultimately, the chapter allows the reader to conclude that Europeanization is a concept that is here to stay. In other words,

Europeanization research will continue to be an important field of EU research for the foreseeable future. This does not mean that all EU research needs to fall under the rubric of 'Europeanization', but it is clear that it will be an unavoidable point of reference.

QUESTIONS

1. What is Europeanization and what are the differences between bottom-up and top-down Europeanization?

2. Why is Europeanization an important research field?

3. What is 'misfit'?

4. How can we explain why member states respond differently to Europeanization?

5. How can we explain member states' ability to shape EU policies and institutions successfully?

6. Are some states better equipped to shape EU policies than others?

7. What do the terms 'uploading' and 'downloading' mean?

8. Can states be subject to Europeanization without being members of the EU?

GUIDE TO FURTHER READING

■ Cowles, M. G., Caporaso, J. A., and Risse, T. (eds) *Transforming Europe. Europeanization and Domestic Change* (Ithaca: Cornell University Press, 2001). This edited volume gives a good overview of empirical studies on top-down Europeanization in the EU 15.

■ Eilstrup-Sangiovanni, M. *Debates on European Integration* (Basingstoke: Palgrave, 2006). This book brings together and assesses the most influential scholarly contributions that have fashioned the debate on bottom-up Europeanization.

■ Featherstone, K. and Radaelli, C. (eds) *The Politics of Europeanisation* (Oxford: Oxford University Press, 2003). This book gives a comprehensive overview of the various theoretical approaches and dimensions of top-down Europeanization.

■ Menz, G. *The Political Economy of Managed Migration. Nonstate Actors, Europeanization, and the Politics of Designing Migration Policies* (Oxford: Oxford University Press, 2009). This book is one of the few studies that seek to combine bottom-up and top-down approaches to Europeanization.

■ Schimmelfennig, F. and Sedelmeier, U. (eds) *The Europeanization of Central and Eastern Europe* (Ithaca, NY: Cornell University Press, 2005). This book provides an excellent account of top-down Europeanization in accession countries and new member states.

WEBLINKS

- http://ec.europa.eu/community_law/infringements/infringements_annual_report_en.htm This website contains the European Commission's Annual Reports on the application of European law in its member states (top-down Europeanization).

- http://ec.europa.eu/prelex/apcnet.cfm?CL=en The European Union hosts a website on decision making and the preparation of EU policies (PreLex database). This provides insights into bottom-up Europeanization.

- http://europeangovernance.livingreviews.org/About/whoweare_me.html The *Living Reviews in European Governance* is an online peer-reviewed journal. The main focus of the articles is on European integration and European governance, and it reflects the whole spectrum of Europeanization research.

- http://www.qub.ac.uk/schools/SchoolofPoliticsInternationalStudiesandPhilosophy/Research/PaperSeries/EuropeanisationPapers/ The Queens University of Belfast (UK) hosts a working-paper series on Europeanization. The papers reflect the range of up-to-date scholarly work on Europeanization.

 Visit the Online Resource Centre that accompanies this book for lots of interesting additional material. http://www.oxfordtextbooks.co.uk/orc/Cini_Borragan3e/

26 Enlargement

IAN BARNES AND PAMELA BARNES

Chapter Contents

- Introduction
- Why enlargement?
- The accession process
- Conditionality
- The impact of enlargement on the EU
- Twenty-seven and beyond: the prospects for future enlargement
- Conclusion

Readers' Guide

The European Union (EU) had grown from an organization of six member states in 1958 to 27 states by 2007. The process of enlargement has transformed the EU from an essentially Western European entity into a pan-European organization. The analysis presented in this chapter begins by reviewing the process of enlargement, concentrating on the period since the collapse of communism in 1989. The criteria that determine whether candidates can join, the process of joining (the accession process), and the use of conditionality are then assessed in some depth. The impact of enlargement on the European Union is outlined, as well as the prospects for and viability of further enlargement.

Introduction

Prior to 1989, European borders appeared to be fixed. Since then, the membership of the European Union has become a source of constant debate. The EU has grown from six to 27 member states since the 1950s, and has become an attractive model of economic and political development for neighbouring states. Enlargement is the most successful foreign policy tool that the EU has at its disposal in terms of influencing the behaviour of its near abroad. It is an indication of the Union's resilience that there is a queue of states wishing to join, despite the commitments that come with membership (see Box 26.1).

The EU provides an exemplar for states seeking to develop market economies in a politically stable framework. This has not meant that the EU has taken over this role from national governments. The EU remains a union of strong independent and sovereign states that cooperate and collaborate

for their mutual benefit. Few of the new or aspiring members wish to sacrifice their freedom to join a **superstate**, whilst long-term members such as the UK and Denmark have consistently defended their sovereignty against an over-intrusive Union. The EU has spread geographically to the north, south, and east, thus becoming a more heterogeneous entity. Member states are at various stages of political and economic development, but all of them can claim that they have met certain standards in order to qualify for membership, including the requirement that they are liberal democratic market economies; that they respect human rights and the rule of law; and that they are European in a geographical sense. These broad-ranging commitments were articulated in the 1993 Copenhagen Criteria, when enlargement to the east first became a real prospect.

KEY CONCEPTS AND TERMS 26.1

Enlargement

EU enlargement generally means increasing the size of the Union by incorporating additional members. This is a process that can take a number of years, as the candidate states attempt to align their economy and regulatory structures to those agreed to by the existing members. The decision to

apply means that the candidate state has to agree to accept EU values, and pool sovereignty with other members.

Alternate views of enlargement (not discussed here) stress the widening of EU influence beyond the borders of the member states and the deepening of relationships within the organization.

Why enlargement?

Since its creation, the European Union has experienced five phases of enlargement. While this process was on the political agenda when the organization was initially set up, the first enlargement did not take place until 1973. The motive for states joining is largely associated with changing political and economic circumstances. The Southern European states (Greece, Portugal, and Spain) that joined in the

1980s were looking to enhance their economic development and consolidate their democracies after the collapse of fascist regimes. The 1995 enlargement was largely associated with Sweden, Finland, and Austria's attraction to a growing and dynamic Single Market and the commitment that membership would not compromise their neutrality. As for the European Union, its motives for accepting new members have varied over time, but at its root has been the wish to maintain and spread liberal democratic ideals and the market economy principle across the mainland of Europe. This was a particularly important motive following the collapse of communism in Central and Eastern Europe after 1989 (see Box 26.2). Some members have also been keen to see the EU grow bigger and stronger as a consequence of the enlargement process. Consequently, at various times enlargement has been supported by the current members as a means of deepening the EU's political and economic integration.

Following the collapse of communism in 1989, new states emerged as peoples across Europe rediscovered their national identity and escaped from the tyranny of the Soviet Union, as in the case of the Baltic States; or broke away from the Yugoslav Federation, as did Slovenia. The EU was not really prepared for these dramatic events or for the rapid expressions of interest in accession from its newly democratic eastern neighbours. On 22 June 1993, the Copenhagen European Council set out very general terms of membership. These so-called Copenhagen Criteria, as will be explained below, were important because they set an agenda for transition and indicated that the EU was prepared to go much further than it had done in the past to influence the applicant states. The EU had already agreed Association Agreements with Malta and Cyprus, which established a framework for cooperation, dating back to 1971 and 1973 respectively. After the Copenhagen Council, Association Agreements were then signed with all aspiring members from Central and Eastern Europe.

The accession negotiations started on 31 March 1998 with six applicant countries: Hungary, Poland, Estonia, the Czech Republic, Slovenia, and Cyprus. At that stage it appeared that the fifth enlargement would be a drawn-out affair. However, on 13 October 1999, the Commission recommended to the EU Council that negotiations should also begin with Romania, Slovakia, Latvia, Lithuania, Bulgaria, and Malta. All but Bulgaria and Romania achieved membership on 1 May 2004. (These two states achieved membership on 1 January 2007.) The

delayed accession of Bulgaria and Romania reflected their slow progress in meeting the EU's standards for membership. The fifth enlargement reflected the profound changes that had taken place in all the applicant states, spurred on by the prospect of membership. Latvia and Lithuania, which appeared to be left behind because of their slow pace of economic transition, were able to achieve market economy status. The behaviour of Vladimir Meciar's government appeared problematic on political grounds and threatened Slovakian accession.

 CHRONOLOGY 26.2

Past enlargements

1973 The United Kingdom (UK) joined the EC along with Denmark and Ireland. France had rejected the UK's application in 1962, but by the 1970s the UK's strong democratic credentials were regarded as being a major asset. At that time both the Irish and Danish economies were more closely tied to the UK (the first enlargement).

1981 Greece joined the EC, followed later by Portugal and Spain in 1986. In these cases, the need to consolidate emergent democracies after periods of right-wing dictatorship was the primary driving force (the second and third enlargements).

1995 Austria, Finland, and Sweden joined the EU because they were no longer bound by the post-war political settlement. These states were in many ways ideal members as they were relatively affluent and had a tradition of stable democratic government (the fourth enlargement).

2004 Eight Central and Eastern European (CEE) states— the Czech Republic, Hungary, Estonia, Latvia, Lithuania, Poland, Slovakia, and Slovenia—joined the EU, along with two of the Mediterranean states, Malta and Cyprus. The CEE states were the first of the former communist states to join, although the German Democratic Republic had been absorbed into the Federal Republic of Germany as early as October 1990. This enlargement was motivated by the desire to end the historical divisions in Europe (the fifth enlargement).

2007 Bulgaria and Romania joined the EU. The accession of these two states completed the fifth enlargement. Their membership was delayed because of their slowness to match the conditions of membership.

But once this government lost power in 1998, the road to membership was open, and an Association Agreement with the EU was signed in 1999. Cyprus was included in the enlargement process, largely at the insistence of the Greek government, despite the division of the island dating back to the Turkish invasion of 1974 (see Table 26.1).

An analysis of the EU's enlargement process draws upon theoretical perspectives that range across a number of disciplines. In recent times the debate has been rooted in international relations between rationalism and constructivism (Box 26.3). Adopting a rationalist perspective enables an analysis of the self-interest of the actors concerned. The assumption

Table 26.1 The fifth enlargement: some landmark dates

Date	Event
14 April 1987	Turkey applies for membership of the EC.
19 December 1989	The PHARE programme is established to provide financial and technical assistance to the Central and Eastern European (CEE) states.
3 and 16 July 1990	Cyprus and Malta apply for EU membership.
22 June 1993	The Copenhagen European Council establishes the criteria for joining the European Union.
31 March and 5 April 1994	Hungary and Poland apply for EU membership.
1995	Applications for membership are received from Slovakia (21 June); Romania (22 June); Latvia (13 October); Estonia (24 November); Lithuania (8 December); and Bulgaria (14 December).
1996	Applications for membership are received from the Czech Republic (17 January); and Slovenia (10 June).
12–13 December 1997	The Luxembourg European Council commits to launching the enlargement process.
10–11 December 1999	The Helsinki European Council agrees that accession talks will be held with 12 candidate countries. Turkey is considered to be a candidate country 'destined to join the Union'.
13 December 2002	Agreement is reached with ten candidate countries that they may join the EU on 1 May 2004 (Bulgaria and Romania are to join later).
21 February 2003	Croatia applies for EU membership.
16 April 2003	The ten accession treaties are signed in Athens.
22 March 2004	Macedonia applies for EU membership.
1 May 2004	The ten states join the EU.
17 December 2004	The Brussels European Council endorses the closure of negotiations with Bulgaria and Romania. The Council also defines conditions for the opening of accession negotiation with Croatia and Turkey.
25 April 2005	Accession Treaties with Bulgaria and Romania are signed in Luxembourg.
3 October 2005	Croatia and Turkey begin membership negotiations.
16 December 2005	Macedonia given candidate status by the European Council but no date given for the start of negotiations.
3 June 2006	Montenegro separates from Serbia.
1 January 2007	Bulgaria and Romania join the EU.

is that the organization (in this case the EU) is not autonomous and that it possesses a driving sense of purpose. The interests of the constituent parts (in this case the existing member states and the applicant states) and their interaction are also important (Moravcsik and Vachudová 2003; Schimmelfennig and Sedelmeier 2005; and see also Chapter 6, which draws on the same example). Their concerns relate to the financial costs and benefits that arise out of a more effective organizational structure. However, the organization itself can be important if it is a source of legal authority or technical expertise. Member states will try to minimize the extent of any gains by applicant countries if they are perceived to be at their own expense. This explains the restrictions that some member states have placed upon the free movement of workers from candidate countries. Their ability to impose such restrictions is related to the power asymmetries that exist between the existing members and the candidates. The candidate states may be left with a 'take it or leave it' approach, as they are aware that a successful accession depends upon unanimity in the Council. Moreover, by refusing to move the application process forward, it is possible for member states less supportive of enlargement to gain side payments related to internal EU policies from those members who wish the enlargement to proceed. For example, the Cohesion Fund introduced by the Maastricht Treaty, while designed to assist Greece, Ireland, Italy, Spain, and Portugal with specific regional issues, also helped to ensure their support for the 1995 accession of Austria, Sweden, and Finland (see Chapter 18). Whilst side payments and the pursuit of national self-interest are identifiable in the enlargement process, it is also expected that member states will want to protect their collective interest and not enlarge beyond the capacity of the EU to absorb new members.

The problem with the rationalist perspective is that it does not explain why the existing EU member states would want to accept new members at all. The cost of funding the aspirations of the poorer states and the potential of new states to undermine the coherence of the decision-making process would be a rational justification for *not* engaging in the process. However, in the case of the fifth enlargement, access to markets, considerable amounts of foreign direct investment, and access to structural funds were part of the accession package on offer to the CEE states, while the subsidies going to the southern member states were reduced only gradually and at the expense of the EU's budget.

The constructivist interpretation of enlargement, on the other hand, is concerned with the overall sharing of norms and values, in this case between the applicant countries, the existing member states, and the EU itself (Kubicek 2003; Jacoby 2004). From a constructivist perspective, if there is evidence of shared norms and values and an overall sense of common purpose, then states will seek institutional ties with an organization because they are able to identify with its aims and policies. In such circumstances it is possible to explain the decision by the EU15 to enlarge eastward in 2004 and 2007. For the EU and its existing members, enlargement would be little more than a continuation of existing policy,

---

🔑 **KEY CONCEPTS AND TERMS 26.3**

Rationalism and constructivism in explaining EU enlargement

Rationalism

Rationalists tend to assume individualism and materialistic self-interest amongst the actors in the policy process. They seek to put in place rules that maximize their position in negotiations and in the way that rules are articulated;

Constructivism

Constructivists seek to identify shared norms and values as reasons for the decision to enlarge, so they are concerned with the spread of European values, identification with the EU, and the legitimacy of the EU's demands of applicant states.

hence the EU's attempts to clarify its objectives and the increasing use of conditionality.

assuming that the policy environment had not changed. The process was more problematic for applicant states from CEE because they had to engineer a major economic and political reorientation in order to become acceptable as EU members. Similarly, constructivism helps us explain why the prospect of Iceland joining the EU following the financial crisis of 2008–9 was greeted with some enthusiasm amongst the member states, as this small Nordic state was expected to fit perfectly with the norms and values shared by all existing members. On the other hand, the prospect of Turkey's accession to the EU raises a number of issues about identity and shared values. Is the EU an economic bloc or is it a religious one? Is there a danger that the EU will be accused of having double standards if Turkey does not achieve membership? Both interpretations enlighten our understanding of different aspects of enlargement. The constructivist perspective is important in selecting likely candidates, but the actual process of negotiating membership depends upon the rationalist perspective, with each participant in the process evaluating the likely costs and benefits of membership to themselves.

KEY POINTS

- There have been five rounds of enlargement since the 1950s.

- The pace of enlargement depends upon the EU's capacity to absorb new members.

- The EU's model of the market economy and liberal democracy is widely accepted throughout Europe.

- The fifth enlargement of 2004 and 2007 was more complex than those of the past due to the number of states involved and their more limited economic development.

- It is possible to explain enlargement from both the constructivist and rationalist perspectives.

The accession process

At the time of the first enlargement in 1973 the process of accepting new members was relatively unsophisticated and the negotiations went ahead without a detailed structure in place. The processes were governed by Article 237 of the EEC Treaty, which has now been replaced by Article 49 of the TEU. According to this article any European state may apply for membership, providing that it respects the principles of liberty and democracy, and shows respect for human rights and fundamental freedoms (as set out in Article 6(1) TEU). The membership application has to be addressed to the Council. For the application to be successful the Commission has to be consulted and the European Parliament (EP) has to support the application. The unanimous support of the Council is required and the ratification of membership is subject to the constitutional processes in place in the member states (usually a parliamentary vote, and sometimes also a referendum). This makes individual member states an important part of the process.

After 1989 the prospect of the arrival of a large number of potential applicant states resulted in the introduction of measures to bring greater clarity into the formal application process and greater detail about the requirements of membership. It was during the Copenhagen European Council of 1993 that the framework of political and economic conditions was established that would subsequently determine whether the Central and Eastern European states might become member states of the EU. The Copenhagen Criteria require that an applicant country must: have stable institutions guaranteeing democracy, the rule of law, respect for human rights, and the protection of minorities; have a functioning market economy capable of withstanding the competitive pressures of membership; have the ability to take on the obligations of political, economic, and monetary union; adopt the *acquis communautaire* (the body of EU regulation and norms). In 1997 procedures for negotiations with the prospective candidate states were agreed and it is these procedures, together with the Copenhagen Criteria, that continue to form the basis of the formal discussions with prospective member states (see Box 26.4)

Once the application for membership is successful, the process of accession begins. This is a highly technical exercise that has to be completed by each applicant state and which is managed and coordinated for the European Union by the European Commission's Enlargement Directorate-General. The main activity of the Commission is to establish timetables for the body of EU legislation to be both transposed and implemented by the prospective member state. The Commission's annual monitoring of the progress made by the applicant is a crucial

element, as each stage of the process must be completed before the applicant state may move to the next. Following the unanimous approval of an application by member governments, the Commission is invited to begin to prepare an opinion (or *avis*) on the suitability of the applicant, against the conditions set out in Article 49 TEU. A questionnaire is also forwarded from the Commission to the applicant government, requesting information about a range of issues on the preparedness of the state to take on the responsibilities of membership.

The European Commission does not rely solely on the responses received from the national government, however. In the case of Croatia, for example (still negotiating its accession to the EU in 2009), information was also sought from the EU member states, the Council of Europe, the Organization for Security and Cooperation in Europe (OSCE), the United Nations High Commission for Refugees (UNHCR), the International Criminal Tribunal for the Former Yugoslavia (ICTY), the International Monetary Fund (IMF), the World Bank, the European Bank for Reconstruction and Development (EBRD), the European Investment Bank (EIB), and representatives

---

KEY CONCEPTS AND TERMS 26.4

Membership criteria

Article 49 of the Treaty on European Union (TEU) says that any European state can apply to become a member, providing it is prepared to abide by the organization's principles. Article 6 of the TEU says that:

1. The Union is founded on the principles of liberty, democracy, respect for human rights and fundamental freedoms, and the rule of law, principles that are common to the Member States.

2. The Union shall respect fundamental rights, as guaranteed by the European Convention for the Protection of Human Rights and Fundamental Freedoms signed in Rome on 4 November 1950 and as they result from the constitutional traditions common to the Member States, as general principles of Community law.

3. The Union shall respect the national identities of its Member States.

4. The Union shall provide itself with the means necessary to attain its objectives and carry through its policies.

Article 49 then states that an application for membership shall be addressed to the Council, '... which shall act unanimously after consulting the Commission and after receiving the assent of the European Parliament, which shall act by an absolute majority of its component members'.

The application for membership does not have to be accepted; indeed, this is just the first phase of a process to ensure that applicants are suitable. Because unanimity applies, any one member state can veto membership. Because there is no attempt to define what Europe is geographically and the criteria for membership are generally vague, it is up to each successive generation to interpret who should actually qualify.

of international and national non-governmental organizations dealing with issues of minority representation. In addition, progress on the implementation of the Stabilization and Association Agreement (SAA) for Croatia was also reviewed as part of the Commission's opinion. The SAA is part of the 'road map' to membership prepared for each of the applicant states in the Western Balkans, which outlines the concrete measures to be completed in preparation for accession. The SAA is an important initial stage, which is used to establish that there is a sufficient degree of political and economic stability for the opening of negotiations. The proper implementation of the SAA is the best basis on which to gauge the readiness of a state to move from potential to actual candidate status.

Following a favourable opinion and a recommendation from the Commission to the European Council, an applicant state, by unanimous vote, may be considered a candidate for accession to the EU (see Box 26.5). This is only the first stage, however, in what may be a lengthy process. During the accession period, the candidate state has to demonstrate that the political criteria have been met (including full cooperation with the ICTY if relevant), and that significant progress is being made on meeting the economic criteria and the obligations of membership. The monitoring of progress is undertaken by the Commission and regular progress reports are prepared for the EU Council and the European Parliament.

The post-2007 enlargement has become more complicated and diverse as negotiations take place with Turkey, a large country with many unique and specific problems, and also with a number of the smaller states of the Western Balkans. The negotiations are an open-ended process with an outcome that cannot be guaranteed beforehand. The speed of the negotiations depends on progress made by the state on the implementation of EU rules and standards. The introduction of 'safeguard clauses' and the prospect of a suspension of negotiations if insufficient progress is made—as happened to Croatia in early 2009 because of a border dispute—may slow the process further. Despite the involvement of the Commission and the EP, the whole process remains one that is essentially intergovernmental, as individual member states tend to guard their own individual interests rather than thinking in terms of their collective interest.

The confirmation of candidate status for an applicant state is a political acknowledgement that a closer relationship between the EU and the candidate state has been initiated. It also activates a number of supportive measures that are intended to assist the candidate state as it prepares for accession. The main financial instrument for assistance for the period 2007–13 is the Instrument for Pre-Accession Assistance (IPA), which covers the Western Balkans and Turkey (note that in this case it also includes the potential candidates). The actual level of assistance depends upon the progress made towards achieving the EU's goals, as measured by the Commission's evaluations and annual strategy papers. IPA support amounted to €1.4 billion for 2008. About one-third of the money was set aside to enhance governance, promote the rule of law, and develop civil society. In addition, an Infrastructure Projects Facility is in place, which works with the EBRD, the EIB, and the Council of Europe Development Bank (CEB).

 KEY CONCEPTS AND TERMS 26.5

Who are the candidates?

Candidate countries are states that, upon a positive opinion from the Commission, have been declared ready by the European Council to start accession negotiations. In 2009 there were three candidate countries: namely, Croatia, Turkey, and the Former Yugoslav Republic of Macedonia.

Potential candidate countries are states that have been promised the prospect of EU membership as and when they are ready, in other words, as soon as the Commission produces a positive opinion and their candidate status is approved by a unanimous vote in favour in the European Council. In 2009 the potential candidate countries were Albania, Bosnia and Herzegovina, Montenegro, Serbia, Kosovo (the latter under UNSC Resolution 1244/99) and Iceland.

Support for the technical process of accession is provided by the EU in the form of European Partnerships. These are established to identify the short-term and medium-term priorities for each stage of the pre-accession process. In return, the candidate states are required to provide Action Plans to identify how these priorities will be met. The last technical step before the start of negotiations is the adoption in the EU Council by unanimity of a Negotiating Framework. In the case of Turkey, this was proposed by the Commission on 29 June 2005, and was adopted by the Council on 3 October 2005. The Negotiating Framework for Croatia was agreed by the Council on 16 March 2005, but the initiation of negotiations was delayed until outstanding issues with respect to ICTY were resolved. The adoption of the Negotiating Framework marks the formal convening of the Intergovernmental Conference for the conduct of the negotiations. For the European Union the negotiations are conducted by ministers or the members of COREPER. The Presidency of the Council is responsible for setting the negotiating agenda and for providing the Chair for the deliberations. Each applicant state provides a Chief Negotiator and an expert team. The Council Secretariat working with a secretariat from the candidate state provides support for the negotiations. The role of the Commission in all this includes the drafting of the EU's common negotiating position and of benchmarks for the unanimous approval of the existing member states.

Negotiations cover the adoption of the EU's *acquis* broken down into policy areas known as chapters. For the 2004 enlargement 31 chapters were identified, whereas a preliminary list of 35 was identified in 2005 for the negotiations with Turkey. The first stage of the negotiations involves a screening of the chapters. Screening is done in two stages. First the Commission carries out a formal examination of each chapter to enable it to explain the chapter to the relevant authorities in the candidate states, to assess the preparations for the negotiations in each area and to identify preliminary issues (analytical screening). The second stage involves the applicant state explaining its laws to the Commission (detailed or bilateral screening). In the Turkish case, for example, the screening of the chapters relating to the customs union began in 2000. The opening of negotiations in November 2005 meant that chapters were opened, but in December 2006 the formal completion of chapters was suspended because of a lack of progress regarding Turkey's policy on Cyprus. Negotiations were resumed again in March 2007.

Following the screening of the chapters, negotiations can begin, but the process is essentially a 'take it or leave it' one for the candidate states in terms of the substance of the EU legislation. The negotiations are largely about the timing of the transition, such as how long the candidate state has to implement legislation or whether the existing members can hold back certain benefits until a later date, for example, the right to free movement of labour. Transitional measures, that is, additional time to implement legislation, are expected to be limited. The actual issues have varied over time, reflecting the readiness of applicants for membership and the changing global context. Thus, for example, agricultural derogations (exceptions) were particularly important in the 1973 enlargement and in 1995, whilst derogations from the implementation of environmental measures became a central feature of the 2004 and 2007 enlargements.

Once concluded, the results of the negotiations form part of an Accession Treaty. For the accession process to be completed the Treaty must be approved by the European Parliament and ratified by the appropriate procedures of all the existing member states and the acceding state. Many candidate countries have chosen to have a referendum on membership prior to joining. In the case of Norway there has twice been a 'no' result from their referendums (1972 and 1994), resulting in failure to complete EU accession. The 'yes' results in the accession referendums in Slovakia, Hungary, Poland, the Czech Republic, Malta, Latvia, Estonia, Slovenia, and Lithuania ratified these countries' commitment to EU membership.

- Although all institutions of the EU are involved in the approval of membership applications, the process remains one that is based on intergovernmental decision making.

- Accession negotiations are a highly technical exercise, managed for the EU by the Commission and by a team of negotiators from the applicant states.

- The purpose of the negotiations is to determine the readiness of the applicant state for accession to the EU and the EU's capacity to absorb a new member state.

Conditionality

It is normal practice to expect new members of an organization to believe in the purpose of the club and to agree to abide by its rules. The conditions of membership are therefore of importance to both the existing members and the new ones. Enlarging the EU ('Club Europe') operates in much the same way, but the conditions of membership have grown more onerous over time, because the process of deepening integration has made the rules of the game more complex. At the same time, most of the states that fitted best with the EU's ideal-type membership have already become members. Those ideal-type states that have not joined, such as Norway and Switzerland, have made a conscious decision not to belong, but do work very closely with the EU. What is left, to both the south and east of the EU, is a group of states that have found the process of change to be very difficult; Iceland is the only exception.

For the EU, conditionality has become a source of power over states who wish to join the Union (Box 26.6). But it is an effective tool only when a candidate has a strong desire to become a member. Its effectiveness also depends on the degree of clarity about what is required of those who wish to join (Pridham 2007). The present conditionality rules take the membership requirements beyond the rather vague 1993 Copenhagen Criteria and make them more specific in terms of the actions that are required of aspiring members. Through conditionality, the provision of policy models, financial and technical assistance, the twinning of administrative staff, benchmarking, and gatekeeping (Grabbe 2006), the EU induces domestic change in the applicant countries. The process has incentives built into it, such as enhanced funding to implement change and the ultimate prize of membership. There are also sanctions, including delay or even an outright refusal to proceed with accession.

The purpose of setting conditions is to ensure that states are prepared for membership, whilst reassuring existing members that new ones will not undermine the organization. For this reason, it is important for there to be clarity about what is expected, if only to assist domestic politicians to move the reform process along. However, the more prescribed the membership process becomes, the more likely it is that ordinary citizens in the applicant states are distanced from the process. Citizens find themselves having to accept the EU's *acquis* and measures to ensure the process's implementation without much opportunity to debate the process. So, for example, the reforms being pushed through in preparation for Turkey's eventual membership may well go too far for many of

Conditionality

Conditionality is a tool to encourage and persuade candidate states to reform in line with the model laid down by the EU. It implies rewards, in terms of additional funding in the short term and eventual membership in the longer term.

the country's citizens, and could ultimately be rejected by them. For the EU, however, tighter conditions help to overcome the so-called 'enlargement fatigue' provoked by the effort and consequences of expanding the EU further. Countries with significant political and social problems tend to be poorly regarded in the member states because they are perceived by some as a drain on resources, possibly undermining the global image of the Union. A useful example of conditionality at work is the safeguard clauses and sanctions used when the ten new members joined in May 2004. An economic safeguard clause was to apply if markets were disrupted after enlargement. This comes into effect where trade liberalization causes disruption to the economies of the new members or existing members. Measures can be introduced to protect the markets of one of the existing member states for a period of three years after membership. The Commission must agree to any restrictions. Similarly, if a new member state fails to implement legislation related to the internal market or justice and home affairs, the EU can impose sanctions that remove some of the benefits of membership. Any sanctions against new members must be proportional and can result in funding being denied. These sanctions can apply for a period of up to and beyond three years if the shortfalls have not been remedied. The existence of these safeguards means that there is an incentive for new members to move quickly to achieve their specific membership commitments. The record of the 2004 new member states with respect to implementing EU legislation has generally been good, especially with respect to the internal market (see Pridham 2008). The exception to this was the Czech Republic in 2008, which faced an official complaint from the European Commission and the possibility of financial sanctions over its failure to introduce into law a new anti-discrimination directive. More specific conditions were applied to Romania and Bulgaria, which meant that if either of the two states had been manifestly unprepared for membership in January 2007, the Commission could have recommended a delay until January 2008. In July 2008, €500 million of EU funding was withheld from Bulgaria because of its poor use of funds but with the promise that the funding would be restored if the Bulgarian government took corrective action.

KEY POINTS

- Conditionality describes the process of laying down and monitoring the conditions for new states to become members of the EU.

- Conditionality helps to maintain the confidence of existing EU members.

- There is now more detailed monitoring of the conditions of membership.

The impact of enlargement on the EU

The enlargement of any organization will inevitably have an impact upon both the joining party and the organization itself. The degree of the impact will depend upon the scale of the event. For example, when the German Democratic Republic merged with the Federal Republic of Germany in 1990, the impact upon the EU in an organizational sense was minimal. It did, however, cause some stresses in certain policy areas, most notably in progress towards monetary integration, and in increasing demands on the EU's Regional Development Fund. Yet foreseeing the significant impact of the fifth enlargement on an EU initially designed for six members, the Union embarked on efforts to adapt its institutional structure and decision-making mechanisms as early as 1998 (at Amsterdam) and subsequently though revisions made by the Treaties of Nice and Lisbon (see Chapters 3 and 4).

With the fifth enlargement the number of member states almost doubled and the national agendas became more diverse (see Table 26.2). The balance of smaller states relative to the larger ones changed

Table 26.2 The impact of enlargement upon the EU	
Positive	**Challenges**
EU becomes a more important global actor.	EU becomes more diverse in terms of its culture, society, and economy.
Increased size of the internal market.	Institutions may find it more difficult to reach important decisions.
Widening of the eurozone over time.	Competition from cheaper labour in the new member states.
Convergence in living standards over time.	Demands on the structural funds.
Relationships with the new members become more intense.	Greater pressure on the Common Agricultural Policy.

dramatically; thus new alliances have been forged in the EU Council and in the EP. Moreover, there are now many more states with low incomes (see Best, Christiansen, and Settembri 2008; Wallace 2007). Similarly, the fifth enlargement increased the number of officials employed by the EU by about 19 per cent, although the population increased by 26 per cent. Most of the additional officials are linguists, as there are now 23 official languages and 506 official language combinations. This has further consolidated the use of English as the main working language. In addition to the formal institutional changes, the different representative bodies of industry and interest groups also changed to reflect the enlarged membership (Pérez-Solórzano Borragán 2004; Blavoukos and Pagoulatos 2008). Public opinion, on the other hand, is not always willing to accept the impacts of membership. Perhaps this is because the process of negotiating enlargement tends to be kept well away from the people until the final decision is about to be made (see Chapter 24). Indeed, in the case of the then EU 15, the Eurobarometer data reflect a decline in overall support for enlargement since 2000. The 2001 polls, for example, show that only 44 per cent of EU citizens supported enlargement (with opposition being greatest in France, Austria, and Germany). By the spring of 2006, two years after the 2004 enlargement, the support had not increased substan-

tially, with 45 per cent of Europeans in favour and 42 per cent against. In 2007 the figure supporting enlargement had risen marginally to 49 per cent. The outcome of the fifth enlargement, while not provoking a general opposition to future enlargements, has not fostered an overwhelming wave of support across the board. So-called enlargement fatigue appears to characterize the tendency in the EU 27 to associate enlargement with mass migration, and concerns regarding the accession of Turkey.

The economic case also illustrates the ultimate impact of enlargement. The integration of the CEE states into the European economy started very soon after the fall of communism and, as such, had been in process for up to 14 years prior to the 2004 enlargement. Trade was quickly liberalized, in some cases too quickly, in order to meet the demands from the domestic consumers for more western goods. The CEE states' trade became dominated by imports and exports from the EU (albeit with the exception of energy). At the time of the 2004 enlargement, the new members were achieving economic growth rates almost twice that of the EU 15. The better managed economies had growth rates in excess of 6 per cent per year for the first three years of membership. Growth remained mostly positive, even with the onset of recession in 2008, but by 2009 a number of the new members faced a severe

Table 26.3 The size impact of the different waves of enlargement

Date	New members	Additional population %	Added GDP (PPP) %	GDP per capita of new members (% of existing)
1973	Denmark, Ireland, UK	33.4	31.9	95.5
1981	Greece	3.7	1.8	48.4
1986	Portugal, Spain	17.8	11.0	
1995	Austria, Finland, Sweden	6.3	6.5	103.6
2004	Cyprus, Czech Republic, Estonia, Hungary, Latvia, Lithuania, Malta, Poland, Slovakia, Slovenia	19.6	9.1	46.5
2007	Bulgaria, Romania	6.4	2.4	37.5

Source: Eurostat, IMF, OECD.

economic downturn. Yet, even if growth rates in the CEE economies are maintained at an annual rate of 2 per cent above those of the EU 15, it will take between 25 and 60 years for these states to catch up with the EU average GDP.

The trend above is likely to continue if the EU enlarges further to the south-east. Croatia, with an estimated population of 4.41 million people, has an income per head of about 54 per cent of the EU average. The Former Republic of Macedonia (FYROM) has a population of 2.04 million and an income per head of about 30 per cent of the EU average. And Turkey's average income per head is only 44 per cent of the current EU average, with a population of 69.89 million in 2007. The impact of these trends is that they make the existing EU members seem better off in a relative sense, though the downside is that any EU funding related to relative poverty will go to the new members. This has the effect of reducing some of the membership benefits to those states that were considered poor prior to the 2004 enlargement, such as Greece, Spain, and Portugal (see Table 26.3).

KEY POINTS

- The EU has become much more diverse as a result of enlargement.

- Enlargement has had a significant impact on the running of the EU.

- The states that joined in 2004 and 2007 were all poorer than the EU average, and this trend may continue should the EU enlarge further.

Twenty-seven and beyond: the prospects for future enlargement

With the historical duty to help the ten CEE countries to return to Europe completed after the latest enlargement, the EU's concerns now focus on its ability to accept more members and, crucially, on ensuring the security and stability of an enlarged Union bordered by unstable neighbouring countries. Commissioner

Olli Rehn, when responsible for enlargement, made it clear that the enlargement process:

> ❝ ... does not continue at the pace of a high-speed train, but rather that of a local one. Yet, it is important that the process stays on track. It is in the best interest of the entire Europe to promote democratic transformation in the Western Balkans and make Turkey an anchor of stability in one of the most unstable regions in the world. Enlargement is one of the EU's most important security guarantees ❞

(Rehn 2009).

Despite the Union's commitment to enlargement, it is obvious that prospective candidates will be faced with more complex accession negotiations as the *acquis communautaire* grows. The number of EU member states has risen, and candidates now have to meet more complicated and rigorous requirements. Similarly, the EU has been trying to find coordinated solutions to the economic crisis against a background of citizen dissatisfaction with the direction of the integration project and a more critical approach to future enlargements.

As with the previous enlargement, the countries attracted by closer ties with the EU, or even accession, are a heterogeneous group with regard to their economic status, political regime, ethnic composition, and geopolitical location (see Table 26.4). Of the current candidate countries, namely Croatia, FYROM, and Turkey, it is Croatia that—from the perspective of 2009—is most likely to join the Union first. Croatia applied for EU membership in 2003 and its candidacy was confirmed in June 2004. Its accession prospects have regularly been overshadowed by its relationship with the International Criminal Tribunal for the Former Yugoslavia (ICTY). In 2005 concerns were dissipated after the capture of General Ante Gotovina, yet the EP is still worried about evidence of local hostility to the ICTY. While the accession negotiations proceeded well into 2008 and 2009, challenges were posed to the final stages by Croatia's dispute with Slovenia over fishing rights in Piran Bay, its ratification of the Kyoto Protocol to reduce greenhouse gas emissions, and the need for Croatia to reform the judicial system and improve its public administration to make it more transparent.

Table 26.4 The main economic indicators for prospective member states (after 2007)

	Population 2007 (millions)	GDP 2007 (EU 27 = 100)	Unemployment 2006 (%)	Economic growth 2007 (%)	Inflation 2007 (%)
Albania	3.2	24	13.8	6	3.1
Bosnia and Herzegovina	3.8	29	29.0	6.8	1.5
Croatia	4.4	54	9.6	5.6	3.2
FYROM	2.0	30	35.0	4.0	0.9
Serbia	7.4	33	18.3	7.5	7.0
Montenegro	0.68	41	19.3	8.6	3.9
Kosovo	2.1	19	43.6	5.0	2.8
Turkey	69.8	44	10.0	4.5	8.8
EU 27	497.5	100	7.1	2.5	2.1

Source: Eurostat.

The Former Yugoslav Republic of Macedonia applied for EU membership in 2004, gaining candidate status in December 2005, but membership negotiations had not started as of mid 2009. There were several reasons for this. First, there was a long-running dispute between the governments in Athens and Skopje about the name adopted by the former Yugoslav state, as it coincides with that of the northernmost Greek province. (This dispute also prevented FYROM from joining NATO.) Second, the country failed to meet international standards for the conduct of free and fair elections in line with Copenhagen political criteria. Finally, while the country's economy enjoys price stability, its isolation and generally poor business climate have led to stagnation and a recorded unemployment rate of about 35 per cent. Hence membership would place a considerable financial burden on the EU.

Turkey has often been considered a special case in the context of EU enlargement. The country signed an Association Agreement in 1963 that provided for the gradual establishment of a customs union in industrial and agricultural products, freedom of movement and establishment for workers, freedom of movement for services, and the application of the Community's rules on competition. The issue of Turkish accession has been on the table since 1987, when the country applied for membership. At that time, the Commission of the European Communities did not question the eligibility of Turkey for accession but considered its application premature. Candidate status was awarded in 1999 and accession negotiations were started in 2005. However, Turkey's accession is controversial and has been characterized by an absence of overwhelming support by the citizens of the EU because of the country's human rights record, its large population, which would make it one of the largest member states, its sensitive geographical and geo-political situation, its huge agricultural sector, and its predominantly Muslim population. The Commission believes that Turkey has a functioning market economy, but that there are many internal reforms that must take place before the country can achieve membership, most

notably its treatment of minorities and a solution to the Cyprus conflict.

Potential candidate countries, such as Albania, Bosnia and Herzegovina, Montenegro, Serbia, and Kosovo (under UNSC Resolution 1244/99), see in EU membership the prospect of political and economic stability. Indeed, Montenegro and Albania have formally applied for membership. The EU has a commitment to the rule of law and it will be difficult for the region to move forward unless the legacy of the past has been settled. Therefore a condition of EU membership for all the states of the former Yugoslavia is that the atrocities that were committed by all sides during the conflict of the 1990s are resolved either domestically or via the ICTY. The main challenges facing Albania, now that it is broadly stable, are the fight against corruption and organized crime, the establishment of a fair judiciary, and the embedding of democratic practices. Externally, relations with ethnic Albanians in Kosovo and FYROM are likely to remain an issue of concern.

Iceland, with a population of 313,000 people, is a different matter. Until 2008 the micro-state seemed to be managing remarkably well on its own. It had an income per head well above the EU average. Yet the financial crisis that hit the global economy in 2008 had a particularly damaging effect on the Nordic country, with three of its major banks collapsing and the currency losing two-thirds of its value against the euro in the space of a year. As a consequence of the demise of its financial sector, Iceland had to seek significant outside help to stabilize its economy. It had never applied for EU membership before 2009 largely because of the country's reliance on its fish stocks (and its consequential hostility to the EU's Common Fisheries Policy). However, the events of 2008 meant that it began to be regarded as a prospective member, with the adoption of the euro offered as an incentive for membership. The country's involvement in the European Economic Area (EEA) has placed Iceland in a good position to comply with core (internal market) membership requirements very quickly, and Iceland is already a member of the Schengen area.

A reminder of the importance of the EU's relationships with European states to the east of the enlarged Union came in August 2008 with the crisis over the deployment of Russian Federation troops in Georgia. The EU's mechanism for ensuring the maintenance of its shared values with the countries bordering the Union to the east is the European Neighbourhood Policy (ENP). This may be further strengthened with the introduction of the Eastern Partners Initiative, which was launched during the Foreign Ministers Council in May 2008. These initiatives are not necessarily meant to lead to EU membership, even though Georgia, Moldova, and Ukraine could be considered in this light at some point in the future. All have experienced a democratization process and have moved away from the direct political influence of the Russian Federation. However, these states represent a low priority on the enlargement agenda because of the likely impact on the EU's budget, the poor state of their economies, and the need to consolidate political reforms at home before considering accession.

In sum, the pace of any future enlargement of the EU will depend upon the perceptions of the current members as to the capacity of the organization to absorb additional members. That is, the organization must maintain its ability to function. Membership is not ruled out for any suitably qualified European state. The likelihood is that Iceland, the states of the West Balkans, and Turkey will be considered in preference to those further east, largely because of the need to honour existing commitments.

> **KEY POINTS**
>
> - As of 2009, Croatia is likely to become the next new EU member state.
> - Turkey's membership is controversial.
> - The opening of negotiations with FYROM depends primarily on resolution of the controversy with Greece over its name.
> - The potential candidate countries regard EU membership as a way of promoting political and economic stability.
> - The EU's mechanism for ensuring the maintenance of shared values beyond its borders is the European Neighbourhood Policy.
> - The post-2008 financial crisis explains Iceland's application for EU membership.

Conclusion

As this chapter has shown, no enlargement of the EU has been unproblematic, though the process has been successful in most cases. However, the development gap between the existing members and potential candidates has widened as the EU moves forward with its own internal agendas. Those countries most obviously qualified to join have now become members, setting aside states who have either chosen not to join or who have left the process of reform until very late in the day.

Whilst enlargement is a very powerful tool of EU foreign policy, the EU's primary concern will surely be its own internal survival. This ultimately depends upon ensuring that post-enlargement decision making is effective, and that coherent policies can be agreed upon. There is also a need to ensure that the general public are happy with developments. The failure of the referendum on the Constitutional Treaty in 2005 illustrated the problem of leaving negotiations in the hands of political elites. Only 47 per cent of the population of the EU surveyed in March–May 2008 supported the idea of further enlargement, with only 33 per cent of Germans and 31 per cent of French in favour. It was the new members who joined in 2004 and 2007 that were generally most enthusiastic about further enlargement. However, when the survey asked about the desirability of specific states becoming members in the future, over 70 per cent supported Norwegian, Swiss, and Icelandic membership, but only 31 per cent supported Turkish membership (Eurobarometer No. 69, November 2008).

There is a limit to the size of the EU. In theory this is based upon perceptions of where Europe ends and other continents begin. Whilst enlargement does create a dynamic to the European project, it also creates significant stresses within it. With each additional member, a new point of view must be accommodated and the organization becomes more diverse. The federalist aspiration of a highly integrated United States of Europe is unlikely to be realized. Indeed, the problem of a significantly enlarged EU is more likely to be lack of identity and an absence of a sense of purpose. Moreover, if there is further enlargement to the east, there will inevitably be competition with Russia.

The issues that govern the future of enlargement are those relating to the EU itself. Enlargement does create tensions about the allocation of resources, especially as the need to respond to the budgetary demands of the poorer states will mean some states that are only slightly better off will lose out. Agricultural spending, which dominates the EU budget, will remain a prominent issue, as poorer countries seek to gain the same benefits as the richer ones. The migration of workers will also remain a controversial issue if unemployment is unacceptably high within the more affluent EU states. An enlarged EU will also be faced with the prospect of ever more complex ethnic relationships, especially in the border areas. Finally, there is a concern that the EU will become more inward-looking as it tries to cope with enlargement. Issues such as relations with the developing world, with North Africa and the USA, may all—as a consequence—have to take second place, no matter how politically unpalatable that may seem.

KEY POINTS

- The hope of EU membership is a major incentive for reform amongst prospective members.
- There is a large development gap between the EU and some potential members, which makes meeting membership conditions increasingly difficult
- The EU is becoming more diverse.

QUESTIONS

1. Why has the European Union enlarged since 1989?
2. What is meant by the term 'enlargement fatigue'?
3. What role does conditionality play in the enlargement process?
4. Why does the EU continue with the enlargement process?
5. What are the key policy issues facing the EU in the next round of enlargement?
6. How has the enlargement process changed the EU?
7. Why are the accession criteria important?
8. Why is Turkish membership of the EU so controversial?

GUIDE TO FURTHER READING

■ Best, E., Christiansen, T., and Settembri, P. (eds) *The Institutions of the Enlarged European Union: Continuity and Change* (Cheltenham: Edward Elgar, 2008). An excellent volume outlining the impact of the EU's eastward enlargement on the EU's institutions and policy processes.

■ Cremona, M. (ed.) *The Enlargement of the European Union*, (Oxford: Oxford University Press, 2004). An examination of the enlargement process and its impact upon the EU and the candidate states.

■ Grabbe, H. *The EU's Transformative Power: Europeanization through Conditionality in Central and Eastern Europe* (Basingstoke: Palgrave Macmillan, 2006). An excellent account of the impact of the EU's conditionality on the candidate countries during the fifth enlargement.

■ Schimmelfennig, F. and Sedelmeier, U. (eds) *The Politics of European Union Enlargement Theoretical Approaches* (London: Routledge, 2005). The strength of this volume is its application of theoretical issues to enlargement.

■ Sjursen, H. *Questioning EU Enlargement. Europe in Search of Identity* (London: Routledge, 2006) This book addresses the rationale behind enlargement as well as different national perspectives on the process.

 WEBLINKS

● http://ec.europa.eu/enlargement/index_en.htm   The European Commission's enlargement website is a very good starting point for key policy documents, country reports, and the latest developments.

● http://www.one-europe.ac.uk/   The British Economic and Social Research Council's 'One Europe or Several?' programme finished at the end of April 2003. However, this site still contains information on and access to a series of very good quality monographs.

● http://www.euractiv.com/   The Euractive website is constantly being updated and contains dossiers on enlargement themes and on candidate and applicant states.

● http://www.europarl.eu.int/enlargement/default_en.htm   The European Parliament's website has details of the Parliament's role in the enlargement process as well a clear description of its main events

● http://europa.eu.int/comm/economy_finance/publications/enlargementpapers_en.htm   European Economy Enlargement Papers provide information on the economies of the candidate countries and on the economic implications of enlargement.

 Visit the Online Resource Centre that accompanies this book for lots of interesting additional material. http://www.oxfordtextbooks.co.uk/orc/Cini_Borragan3e/

Glossary

Accession: in a general sense, 'increasing by addition', meaning membership or the process of joining (the EU).

Accession Treaty: is an international agreement concluded between the member states of the EU and the acceding country. It defines the accession conditions of the new member states and the subsequent adaptations and adjustments of the EU Treaty.

Accountability: the requirement for representatives to answer to the represented on how they have performed their duties and powers, and for them to act upon criticisms and accept responsibility for failure, incompetence, or deceit.

Acquis (communautaire): the *acquis* is the Community patrimony, the body of common rights and obligations that bind the member states together. It includes the content of the Treaties, legislation, international agreements and other measures.

Advocacy networks: a network of institutional and non-institutional actors that interact together to defend a common cause.

Agenda 2000: an influential action programme adopted by the Commission on 15 July 1987, which set out the reforms needed for the EU to enlarge.

Agenda-setting: the process by which an issue or problem emerges onto the political scene and is framed for subsequent debate.

À la carte: a non-uniform method of integration which would allow member states to select policies as if from a menu.

Amending Treaty: see Reform Treaty.

Amsterdam (Treaty of): signed in October 1997, and in force from 1 May 1999, the Treaty amended certain provisions of the Treaty on European Union and the European Community Treaties.

Altiero Spinelli: an important federalist thinker and politician (1907–86), responsible for the influential Ventotene Manifesto of 1941, and for the European Parliament's Draft Treaty on European Union (1984), which helped to shape the European political agenda of the late 1980s.

'Anoraks': a British English slang term for a 'geek' or a 'nerd', drawn from the coats worn by trainspotters, implying someone who spends a large amount of time collating information on a very specific subject.

Association Agreement: is an agreement between the EU and a third country that creates a framework for cooperation in several policy fields such as trade, socio-economic issues, and security, as well as the creation of joint institutional structures.

Assent: a legislative procedure in which the Council must first obtain the European Parliament's approval before certain important decisions can be taken. It applies to the accession of new members to the European Union.

Asymmetric military threats: usually refers to chemical, biological, or cyber terrorism or the potential for less powerful actors/states to attack effectively those who are ostensibly more powerful.

Authority: the right or capacity (or both) to have proposals, prescriptions, or instructions accepted without recourse to persuasion, bargaining, or force; more simply, the power or right to control, judge or prohibit the actions of others.

Benchmarking: is one of the mechanisms of the open method of coordination (OMC) that allows for the comparison and adjustment of the policies of member states on the basis of common objectives.

Best practice exchange: is one of the OMC mechanisms that encourages member states to pool information, compare themselves to one another, and reassess policies against their relative performance.

Benelux: short for 'Belgium, Netherlands, and Luxembourg'. The term originally related to the 1944 Customs Union between these three countries, and is said to have been coined by the Brussels correspondent of *The Economist* in 1947.

Barriers to trade: protectionist technical and fiscal rules, and more physical constraints that carve up or prevent the creation of the internal market.

Bi-cameral: involving two chambers. Usually refers to parliaments divided into an upper and lower house.

Bipolarity: refers to the understanding of the international system before the end of the Cold War as being structured around the two major superpowers, namely the United States and the Soviet Union.

Blair House agreement: is an agreement on agriculture signed between the United States and the European Community in 1992 dealing mainly with limits on oilseed subsidies in the European Union. It paved the way for the Uruguay Round Agreement.

Bolkestein directive: the directive on services in the internal market, which aims to break down barriers to trade in services across the EU. It has been controversial because while some believe it will boost European competitiveness, critics feel it promotes social dumping.

Bologna process: is a series of reforms aimed to make European Higher Education more compatible and comparable, more competitive and more attractive for Europeans and for students and scholars from other continents. It was agreed in the Bologna Declaration of June 1999 by the ministers responsible for higher education in the member states.

Bretton Woods: is an agreement signed by 44 countries in July 1944 to support an international monetary system of stable exchange rates. Its aim was to make national currencies convertible on current account, to encourage multi-lateral world trade, and to avoid disruptive devaluations and financial crashes.

Budgetary deficits: governmental shortfalls of current revenue over current expenditure.

Bureau-shaping: the bureau-shaping approach to public sector organization and its reform originates in the work of Patrick Dunleavy. The approach contends that public officials have preferences for the type of work they handle and thus they will develop individual and collective strategies to pursue these preferences. Collective bureau-shaping strategies are likely to be pursued to shape organizations by a variety of means.

Cabotage: in road haulage, the transport of loads that have both their origin and their destination in a foreign country.

Cairns Group: is a coalition of 19 agricultural exporting countries bringing together developed and developing countries from Latin America, Africa, and the Asia-Pacific region. It has been an influential voice in the agricultural reform debate since its formation in 1986 and has continued to play a key role in pressing the WTO membership to meet in full the far-reaching mandate set in Doha.

Candidate countries: these are countries whose application to membership of the EU has been accepted by the European Council.

Capabilities catalogue: a document listing the military capabilities necessary to carry out the Petersberg Tasks.

Central banks: these are national banks that provide services for their countries' governments and commercial banking systems. They manage public debt, control the money supply, and regulate the monetary and credit system.

Charles de Gaulle: he was President of France 1959–69. Responsible for keeping the UK out of the EEC in the 1960s, and for the 'empty chair policy' which is said to have slowed down the European integration process after 1966. See 'empty chair policy'.

Charter of Fundamental Rights: is the first formal EU document to combine and declare all the values and fundamental rights (economic and social as well as civil and political) to which EU citizens should be entitled. The text of the Charter does not establish new rights, but assembles existing rights that were previously scattered over a range of international sources. It was drafted through a convention and proclaimed at the 2000 Nice European Council.

Citizen's initiative: is one of the measures incorporated into the Lisbon Treaty to enhance democracy and transparency in the EU. According to the Treaty provision, one million citizens from a number of member states will have the possibility to call on the Commission to bring forward new policy proposals.

Civic identity: refers to the identification of citizens with a particular political structure such as the EU or the political institutions of the nation state.

Civil society: an intermediate realm between the state and the individual or family; or a particular type of political society rooted in principles of citizenship.

Closer cooperation: established by the Amsterdam Treaty, it introduces instruments that allow groups of states who wish to integrate further than provided for in the Treaties to do so. It was renamed 'enhanced cooperation' at Nice.

Codecision (procedure): a complicated three-stage decision-making procedure that involves both the EU Council and the European Parliament in making European legislation, thereby enhancing the role of the Parliament in the legislative process. It was introduced in the Treaty on European Union at Maastricht (Article 251, ex. 189b) and simplified in the subsequent Amsterdam Treaty. Codecision refers to decision making jointly by the Parliament and the Council.

Co-determination: refers to employee participation in company decision-making, through, for example, works councils.

Cognitive mobilization: the capacity to articulate basic implications of a value system and act accordingly.

Cohesion: a principle which favours the reduction of regional and social disparities across the European Union.

Collective bargaining: an agreement negotiated by trade unions and employers or their associations on incomes or on the working conditions of employees.

Collective goods: those who do not pay for a collective good cannot be excluded from sharing or using it (such as 'clean air').

Collegiality: a principle which implies that decisions taken by one are the collective responsibility of all.

Comitology: refers to the network or procedures of committees designed to oversee the agreement of implementing measures taken by the EU's executive bodies.

Common external tariff: a central element of any customs union. A set of common tariffs, agreed by all members, imposed on goods coming into the Union from outside its borders.

Common market: an economic agreement that extends cooperation beyond a customs union, to provide for the free movement of goods, services, capital, and labour.

Common Market Organizations: these are systems operating for individual items of agricultural produce which involves public intervention, a price guaranteed for farmers, and levies at the EU's borders.

Common strategy: overall policy guidelines for EU activities within individual non-member countries.

Communitarization: the shift of policy activity from the intergovernmental pillars to the Community pillar.

Community method: the use of the 'established' process of EC decision-making, which involves a Commission legislative initiative being agreed by the Council, and now usually the European Parliament. It also implies that the European Court of Justice will have jurisdiction over any decision taken.

Community preference: the fact that EU agricultural products are given preference and price advantage over imported products.

Competences: legal capacity to deal with a matter (also competency).

Compound polity: is characterized by federal or regionalized institutional structures with a high diffusion of power through multiple authorities. This is the opposite category to a 'simple polity' characterized by the concentration of power in the executive.

Compulsory spending: the EU's budget expenditure is divided into compulsory and non-compulsory expenditure. In the case of compulsory expenditure, the underlying principle and the amount are legally determined by the treaties, secondary legislation, conventions, international treaties, or private contracts. The Council has the last word in deciding compulsory expenditure (see also non-compulsory expenditure).

Concentric circles: a concept that envisages a Europe structured out of subsets of states which have achieved different levels of integration.

Conciliation (process): the third stage of the codecision procedure, at which point an equal number of representatives of the Parliament and Council get together to try to work out an agreement acceptable to all.

Conciliation committee: the committee that as part of the conciliation process brings together equal numbers of representatives from EP and Council to broker an inter-institutional agreement on outstanding problems with the proposed legislation.

Conditionality: the principle that applicant states must meet certain conditions before they can become members of the European Union.

Confederal: see confederation.

Confederation: a political model which involves a loose grouping of states, characterized by the fact that the centre has fewer powers than the states or regions.

Consensual: type of decision-making which involves the agreement of all, even where this is not formally a requirement.

Consociational(ism): a political model which brings together distinct communities in shared decision-making, whilst protecting the interests of the minority.

Consolidated treaties: these are versions of the treaties that incorporate all the amendments made since the original Treaty of Rome.

Constitutional Treaty: the Treaty sometimes known as the EU Constitution, which was signed on 24 October 2004, but which has not been ratified, not least because of the negative referendums in France and the Netherlands in 2005.

Constitutionalization: the formalization of the rules of the game, which in an EU context might involve a process whereby the Treaties become over time—de jure or just de facto—a Constitution.

'Constitutive' tradition: an understanding of the world which problematizes the relationship between theory and reality, which are deemed to be tied closely one to the other.

Constructive abstention: a provision that allows member states to abstain in the Council on common foreign and security policy decision, without blocking a unanimous agreement.

Constructivism: or 'social constructivism'. A theoretical approach which claims that politics is affected as much by ideas as by power. It argues that the fundamental structures of political life are social rather than material.

Constructivist: see constructivism.

Consultation: the original EC decision-making procedure, which gave the Commission the exclusive right of initiative, the Council the ability to take the decision, but which only allowed the Parliament a consultative role in the legislative process.

Convention (on the Future of Europe): a body set up in 2002 to debate alternative models and visions of the European Union, and to prepare a draft Constitution which could be used as the basis of discussion in the Intergovernmental Conference of 2004.

Convergence criteria: the rules that member states had to meet before they could join Economic and Monetary Union in 1999.

Convertibility: where one currency is freely exchangeable into other currencies.

Cooperation: usually implies government-to-government relations (with little supranational involvement).

Cooperation procedure: a legislative procedure introduced in the Single European Act (Article 252, ex. 198c), which allows the European Parliament a second reading of draft legislation. Since Amsterdam, it is hardly used, as most policies originally falling under cooperation now come under the codecision procedure.

Copenhagen criteria: the criteria which applicant states have to meet in order to join the EU. It was agreed at the Copenhagen European Council meeting in 1993.

Core Europe (or 'hard core'): the idea that a small group of countries able and willing to enter into closer cooperation with one another might 'leave behind' the less enthusiastically integrationist members of the Union.

Co-regulation: is the mechanism whereby a Community legislative act entrusts the attainment of the objectives defined by the legislative authority to parties which are recognized in the field (such as economic operators, the social partners, non-governmental organizations, or associations). It is one of the modes of governance developed in the context of the Lisbon Strategy to simplify and improve regulation in the EU.

COREPER: the Permanent Representatives Committee or 'Coreper' is responsible for preparing the work of the Council of the European Union. It consists of the member states' ambassadors to the European Union (Permanent Representatives) and is chaired by the member state which holds the Council Presidency.

Cosmopolitanism: relating to 'citizenship of the world'.

Council of Europe: a European political organization with 49 members, distinct from the EU, set up in 1949. It has been particularly involved in assisting post-communist states to democratize after 1989.

Credit conditions: the criteria used for the grant of credit by banks.

Critical juncture: is a key concept of historical institutionalism. This literature assumes a dual model of institutional development characterized by relatively long periods of path-dependent institutional stability and reproduction that are punctuated occasionally by brief phases of institutional flux (referred to as critical junctures) during which more dramatic change is possible. Junctures are critical because they place institutional arrangements on paths or trajectories which are then very difficult to alter.

Customs union: an economic association of states based on an agreement to eliminate tariffs and other obstacles to trade, and which also includes a common trade policy vis-à-vis third countries, usually by establishing a common external tariff on goods imported into the union.

Davignon Report: a document issued by EC foreign ministers in 1970, outlining how the Community might develop its own foreign policy, and setting out some initial steps to that end.

Decoupling: refers to divorcing the grant of direct aid to farmers from production in the context of the CAP.

Deepening: a term usually describing an intensification of integration processes and structures.

Delegated legislation: legislation usually made by executive bodies on behalf of legislatures. It often involves the making of administrative rules, and the filling in of gaps in existing legislation.

Delegation: an act which allows a legitimate political institution to hand powers over to a body which then acts on its behalf.

Delors Report: the report drafted by central bankers in 1989, which later formed the basis of the monetary union section of the Treaty on European Union. The Committee that produced the Report was chaired by Jacques Delors, then Commission President.

Democratic deficit: the loss of democracy caused by the transfer of powers to the European institutions and to member state executives arising out of European integration. It implies that representative institutions (parliaments) lose out in this process.

Democratic liberalism: a democratic form of government limited by a constitutionally guaranteed set of individual rights that ensure that a person has significant freedom to choose the shape of their life.

Demography: the scientific study of human population.

Demographic change: variations in the composition and structure of human populations.

Demos: the people of a nation as a political unit; a politically defined public community.

Dependent variable: the object of study; the phenomenon one is trying to explain.

Derogations: temporary exceptions to legislation.

Differentiated integration: see differentiation.

Differentiation: the idea that subsets of member states might engage in European integration projects that do not involve all existing members; contrasts with the notion of the EU as a uniform Community.

Diplomacy: the art and practice of conducting (international) negotiations by accredited persons.

Direct actions: cases brought directly before the European Courts.

Direct implementation: the putting into effect of European legislation by the European institutions (rather than by national governments).

Direct support: in the context of CAP, agricultural subsidies given directly to farmers, decoupled from production.

Directives: legislative instruments that specify the aims to be achieved, but which generally leave the question of how to achieve those ends up to national governments or their agents.

Directly effective: having a quality which allows provisions of Community law to be enforced in national courts, and which imposes obligations on those against whom they are enforced.

Dirigiste: see interventionist.

Dooge Committee: a committee set up after the Fontainebleau European Council in 1984 to discuss the institutional reforms required to complete the internal market and solve the paralysis provoked by the excessive use of unanimity in the Council. It submitted its final report to the European Council in March 1985 which identified a number of priority objectives necessary to deepen integration such as restricting the use of unanimity in the Council, strengthening the legislative role of the EP, and giving more executive power to the Commission. The Dooge Committee conclusions paved the way to the Single European Act.

Dual majority (system of voting): this voting system takes into consideration number of votes and population to achieve a majority. During the negotiation of the Nice Treaty, the member states failed to agree on a dual majority mechanism. However, if the Lisbon Treaty is ratified, it will be based on the principle of the double majority. Decisions by QMV in the EU Council will need the support of 55 per cent of member states representing a minimum of 65 per cent of the EU's population.

Dumping: selling at below cost, often to force competition out of the market.

ECOFIN: the EU Council of Economics and Finance Ministers.

Economic and Monetary Union (or EMU): refers to a form of integration that combines the features of the economic union (which implies the existence of a single market but also a high degree of coordination of the most important areas of economic policy, market regulation, as well as monetary policies and income redistribution policies) and the monetary union which implies further integration in the area of currency cooperation. The process involves three stages and the fulfilment of the so-called convergence criteria by all participating countries. Not all member states have joined EMU.

Economic union: is a form of integration that implies the existence of a single market (and therefore free movement of goods, services, labour, and capital among the participating states and common rules, tariffs, and so on, vis-à-vis third countries) but also a high degree of coordination of the most important areas of economic policy, market regulation, as well as monetary policies and income redistribution policies.

Economists: refers to those supporting one of the possible strategies to achieve economic and monetary union (the other one being monetarist). In the 1960s and 1970s, the economists camp postulated that economic policies needed to be coordinated before fixing exchange rates or introducing a single currency (see also monetarist).

Efficiency: the ratio of output to input of any system.

Eftan: relating to the countries of EFTA, the European Free Trade Association.

Empty Chair Policy: refers to the empty chair crisis that affected the European Community after July 1965 when France boycotted the meetings of the Council in opposition to Commission proposals addressing the financing of the Common Agricultural Policy. France also insisted on a political agreement concerning the role of the Commission and majority voting if it were to participate again. This crisis was resolved thanks to the Luxembourg compromise in January 1966 (see Luxembourg compromise).

Enforcement: the process of ensuring that (Community) rules are implemented. It may involve taking action in the European Courts.

Engrenage: the enmeshing of EU elites, which may arise out of a process of socialization in Brussels.

Enhanced cooperation: see closer cooperation.

Environmental Action Programmes (EAPs): since 1973, the EU's environmental action programmes define the future orientations of EU policy in the environmental field and suggest specific proposals that the Commission intends to put forward over the next years.

Enlargement: the expansion of the European Union to include new member states.

Epistemology: theory of knowledge, which accounts for the way in which knowledge about the world is acquired.

Epistemic communities: are networks of knowledge-based experts or groups with an authoritative claim to policy-relevant knowledge within the domain of their expertise.

ERASMUS: Erasmus is the European Commission's flagship educational programme for Higher Education students, teachers, and institutions. It encourages student and staff mobility for work and study, and promotes trans-national cooperation projects among universities across Europe.

Euro area: that part of the EU which uses the single currency (see eurozone).

Eurobarometer: a Europe-wide public opinion survey of attitudes.

Eurogroup: an informal group comprising those member states of the ECOFIN Council that are members of the single currency.

European Agricultural Guarantee and Guidance Fund (EAGGF): is one of the funds supporting the Common Agricultural Policy. The EAGGF is composed of two sections, the Guidance section and the Guarantee section. Within the framework of European economic and social cohesion policy, the EAGGF supports rural development and the improvement of agricultural structures.

European Arrest Warrant: replaces the lengthier extradition procedures amongst EU member states, simplifying the arrest and return of suspected criminals across the Union. Introduced after 11 September 2001.

European Central Bank (ECB): established in Frankfurt in 1999, the ECB is responsible for the single monetary policy of the 'euro-zone'.

European Coal and Steel Community (ECSC): established by six states in April 1951 by the Treaty of Paris, the ECSC allowed for the pooling of authority over coal and steel industries. As it was based on a 50-year treaty, the ECSC ceased to exist on 23 July 2002.

European Currency Unit (ECU): the unit of account under the European Monetary System, composed of a 'basket of currencies'. Was replaced by the euro.

European Free Trade Association (EFTA): an international organization set up in 1960 to promote free trade amongst its members. Most of its original members have since joined the European Union.

European integration: one of various definitions is the process of political and economic (and possibly also cultural and social) integration of the states of Europe into a unified bloc.

European Investment Bank (EIB): was created by the Treaty of Rome in 1958 as the long-term lending bank of the EU. The EIB's task is to contribute towards the integration, balanced development, and economic and social cohesion of the EU member states.

European Monetary System (EMS): a regulated exchange rate system established in the EC in 1979 after failures to set up an economic and monetary union earlier in the decade. The EMS aimed to promote monetary cooperation and exchange rate stability.

European Political Cooperation (EPC): foreign policy cooperation prior to Maastricht, set up after 1970 and formalized by the Single European Act.

European Social Fund (ESF): was set up in 1957 to sustain and improve mobility in the European labour market through education and requalification initiatives for workers in areas experiencing industrial decline.

European System of Central Banks (ECSB): brings together the national central banks together with the European Central Bank.

European Working Time Directive: the EWTD is set to protect the health and safety of workers in the European Union. It lays down minimum requirements in relation to working hours, rest periods, annual leave, and working arrangements for night workers.

Europeanization: defined in various ways (see Chapter 22). For example, it may refer either to the process of European integration itself, or as a shorthand for the Europeanization of domestic institutions, politics, and identities.

Eurosceptic: someone who is opposed to European integration, or is sceptical about the EU and its aims.

Eurosclerosis: a word used to characterize the period of EC history between 1966 and the early 1980s, when the process of integration appeared to have slowed down, and when the common market objective was not implemented.

Eurozone: the economic area which covers the countries that have so far joined the EU's single currency.

EU citizenship: was introduced by the Maastricht Treaty as a supplement not a substitute to national citizenship. It confers on every European citizen the right to move and reside freely in the Union; the right to vote for and stand as a candidate at municipal and European Parliament elections in whichever member state they may reside; the right to petition to the EP and the European Ombudsman and the right to diplomatic and consular protection. Such rights were further extended at Amsterdam which incorporated an anti-discrimination clause and member states' commitment to raise the quality and free access to education.

Excessive Deficit Procedure: the EMU procedure which has the potential to sanction those member states who fail to control their budget deficits.

Exchange Rate Mechanism (ERM): the main element of the European Monetary system—a mechanism which aimed to create a zone of monetary stability within Western Europe.

Exclusive competences: refer to specific areas where only the EU is able to legislate and adopt legally binding acts. The member states may intervene in the areas concerned only if empowered to do so by the Union or in order to implement Union acts (see also shared competences).

Executive(s): branch of government, responsible for implementing laws taken by parliament; the administration.

Extraordinary rendition: rendition means the handing over or surrender of a fugitive from one state to another, and providing such transfers comply with national and international law, it is an accepted legal process. Rendition becomes extraordinary or unlawful when a suspect is handed over without the permission of a judicial authority or, after the transfer, that person is tortured or held in breach of their human rights.

Federal: see federalism.

Federalist: promoting federal ideas or ideology.

Federalism: an ideological position which suggests that everyone can be satisfied by combining national and regional/territorial interests in a complex web of checks and balances between a central government and a multiplicity of regional governments. In an EU context it tends to imply an ideological approach which advocates the creation of a federal state in Europe.

Federation: a way of organizing a political system which involves the constitutionally-defined sharing of functions between a federal centre and the states. A federation will usually have a bicameral parliament, a constitutional court and a Constitution.

Finalité politique: the EU's final constitutional settlement.

Financial Perspective: the EU's multi-annual spending plan.

Financial solidarity: the sharing of financial burdens across the EU members.

Flexibility: is one of the mechanisms, first introduced in the Amsterdam Treaty, that allows the EU to pursue differentiated integration.

Fouchet Plan: a plan proposed in 1961 and pushed by the French government, which would have led to the creation of a European intergovernmental defence organization, but which was rejected by the EC's member states.

Founding fathers: are the principal architects of European integration following the end of the Second World War. These include Konrad Adenauer, Winston Churchill, Alcide de Gasperi, Walter Hallstein, Jean Monnet, Robert Schuman, Paul Henri Spaak, and Altiero Spinelli.

Framework directive: see directive.

Framing integration: refers to integration which does not involve legally enforceable rules, but which rests on mechanisms such as sharing ideas, benchmarking and 'naming and shaming'.

Franco–German axis: see Paris–Bonn axis.

Free ride: to free ride is to reap the benefits of a collective agreement without having participated in efforts to forge the agreement or to implement it. See also 'collective goods'; a free rider is someone who benefits from collective activity without participating in it.

Free trade area: a group of countries who agree progressively to reduce barriers to trade, such as quotas and tariffs, which are often imposed at borders.

Full Economic Union (FEU): implies the complete unification of the economies of the participating member states and common policies for most economic matters.

Full Political Union (FPU): is the term used when, in addition to full economic union, political governance and policy making have moved to the supranational level. Effectively political unification occurs when the final stage of integration has taken place and a new confederation or federation has been created.

Functional 'spillover': the knock-on effect of integration in one sector, which is said by neo-functionalists to provoke integration in neighbouring sectors.

Game theory: is an interdisciplinary rational approach to the study of human behaviour where 'games' are a metaphor for a wide range of human interactions. It analyses the strategic interaction among a group of rational players (or agents) who behave strategically. A strategy of a player is the predetermined rule by which a player decides their course of action during the game.

Each player tries to maximize their pay-off irrespective of what other players are doing.

General Agreement on Tariffs and Trade (GATT): was first signed in 1947. The agreement was designed to provide an international forum that encouraged free trade between member states by regulating and reducing tariffs on traded goods and by providing a common mechanism for resolving trade disputes. It lasted until the WTO's creation on 1 January 1995 (see WTO).

Geo-political: refers to the relationship between geography, politics, and international relations.

Globalization: a contested concept, which usually refers to the growing economic interdependence of states and non-state actors worldwide. Often associated with increased capital mobility and the spread of neo-liberal ideas. Implies that market authority is enhanced at the cost of formal political authority.

Governance: the intentional regulation of social relationships and the underlying conflicts by reliable and durable means and institutions, instead of the direct use of power and violence.

Governance turn: the shift in interest in EU studies which included the increased application of theories of governance, comparative politics and public policy, as well as the study of the EU as a political system in its own right.

Grand theory: a theory which tries to explain the entirety of a political process, such as European integration.

Gross National Product (GNP): a measure of the country's total economic activity.

Guarantee price: in the context of CAP the (agricultural) price at which member states intervene in the market to buy up produce (also known as the 'intervention price').

Hard ecu proposal: one of the alternatives to introduce a single currency into the EU. This proposal foresaw the introduction of a common currency in parallel to the existing national currencies. This suggestion was not implemented.

Hard law: another way of saying 'the law', emphasizing its enforceability.

Harmonization: the act of setting common European standards from which states are unable to deviate (either upwards or downwards).

Headline goal: initially a political commitment agreed at the Helsinki European Council in 1999 to deploy by 2003 50,000–60,000 troops in 60 days, sustainable for a year (a Rapid Reaction Force) to meet the requirements of the Petersberg Tasks. It has since been superseded by a new headline goal.

Hegemony: power, control, or influence exercised by a leading state over other states.

Heterarchical: related to the definition of the EU as a heterarchy or a system where political authority is not centralized as in the hierarchical order of the state model nor is it decentralized as in an anarchical order. Rather the units of the system pool their sovereignty.

Hobbesian state of nature: Thomas Hobbes's 'war of all against all'; the contention that in a state of nature humans would act badly towards each other.

Ioannina Compromise: the Ioannina Compromise takes its name from an informal meeting of foreign ministers in the Greek city of Ioannina on 29 March 1994. The resulting compromise lays down that if members of the Council representing between 23 votes (the old blocking minority threshold) and 26 votes (the new threshold) express their intention of opposing the taking of a decision by the Council by qualified majority, the Council will do all within its power, within a reasonable space of time, to reach a satisfactory solution that can be adopted by at least 68 votes out of 87. Following the re-weighting of votes in the Council of Ministers, the Treaty of Nice put an end to the Ioannina compromise.

Independent variable: a factor contributing to an explanation of some phenomenon (to a dependent variable).

Individual direct payments: agricultural subsidies paid directly to individual farmers.

Infringement proceedings: the act of initiating a procedure for breach of European law which may result in a court case.

Institutional isomorphism: a term used by diMaggio and Powell (1983) to denote the tendency for institutions within a similar environment to come to resemble each other.

Integration: a general concept, which implies the act of combining parts of a unified whole—a dynamic process of change. European integration is usually associated with the intensely institutionalized form of cooperation found in Western Europe after 1951.

Integration theory: sometimes used generally as a shorthand for all theoretical and conceptual approaches that discuss European integration; otherwise, it refers more specifically to supranational (especially neo-functionalist) theories of European integration.

Interdependence: a condition in which the actions of one state impact upon others.

Interest intermediation: the process of translating interests into policy, through the medium of interest organizations.

Interest rate: the rate of return on savings, or the rate paid on borrowings.

Intergovernmental (cooperation): cooperation that involves sovereign states, and which occurs on a government-to-government basis, without the extensive involvement of supranational actors.

Intergovernmentalism: a theory of European integration which privileges the role of states.

Intergovernmentalist: see intergovernmentalism.

Intergovernmental Conference (IGC): structured negotiations among the EU's member states, which usually lead to a Treaty revision.

Interlocutory: rulings that are interlocutory are made during the course of a court case, rather than at its end.

Interpretivist: the interpretivist tradition developed largely as a criticism of the dominant theory of positivism. Interpretivists argue that the positivist idea of a chain of causation is quite logical in the natural world where a particular stimulus consistently produces a given effect, but does not apply in the social world. People do not merely react to stimuli. Rather, they actively interpret the situations in which they find themselves and act on the basis of these interpretations.

Intervening variables: explain the relationships between independent and dependent variables.

Intervention price: see guarantee price.

Interventionist: interventionism refers to governments involving themselves in the regulation of markets; through government policy, rather than leaving markets to regulate themselves.

Jacques Poos: in 1991 he was one of the negotiators of the Brioni Agreement that ended the ten-day war in Slovenia. He is a strong defender of the centralization of the European Parliament in Brussels, thus doing away with its seat in Strasbourg.

Jean Monnet: one of the founders of the European integration project. The driving force behind the 1950 Schuman Plan which led to the establishment of the European Coal and Steel Community, Monnet became the first head of the ECSC's High Authority. He continued to play an active role in European integration throughout his life, though often behind the scenes.

Jihadist: from the word 'Jihad', meaning holy war, a jihadist refers to any Muslim involved in or supporting war in the name of religion.

Joint-decision trap: the idea promoted by Fritz Scharpf in 1988 that while it might be increasingly difficult in future for further integration to take place, it will also be impossible for states to go back on agreements already made. As such, states were 'trapped' within the European integration process.

Joint Action: coordinated action by member states to commit resources for an agreed (foreign policy) objective.

Judicial review: the right of a court to review a law or other act for constitutionality or its violation of some fundamental principle.

Kaliningrad: a Russian enclave between Poland and Lithuania on the Baltic Sea. The issue of overland access to the city from Russia was particularly contentious in the 1990s.

Keynesian: a position which supports J. M. Keynes's economic theory, and which has as its starting point the assumption that state finances should be used to counteract cyclical economic downturns. The argument implies that governments should focus on issues of employment and economic growth, rather on variables such as inflation.

Konrad Adenauer: first Chancellor of the Federal Republic of German after the end of the Second World War. He held office for 14 years, and was responsible for overseeing the reconstruction of Germany in the 1950s, particularly in the context of European integration, of which he was a key supporter.

Laissez-faire: an economic position which argues that the state (governments) should play only a minimal regulatory role in economic affairs, with decisions left mainly to the market.

League of Nations: an international organization set up in 1922 which had as its rationale the maintenance of peace in Europe.

Legal basis: see Treaty basis.

Legitimacy: the idea that a regime's procedures for making and enforcing laws are acceptable to all its subjects; the right to rule.

Liberal-democratic: a system of representative government which has universal adult suffrage, political equality, majority rule, and a constitutional check on the power of rulers.

Liberal intergovernmentalism: Andrew Moravcsik's update on classical intergovernmentalism (see chapter 6).

Liberalization of capital markets: the removal of exchange controls by states, allowing capital to flow freely across state borders.

Liberalization of services: the removal of barriers to the establishment and provision of services across state borders.

Lisbon Agenda or Lisbon Strategy: the EU's strategy intended to turn the Union into the most competitive and dynamic economy in the world by 2010.

Lisbon Process: see Lisbon Agenda.

Lisbon Treaty: revises the Nice version of the TEU; was signed in 2007 and after a successful second Irish referendum in october 2009 is pending retification.

Lock-outs: a situation where employers lock employees out of their place of work as a consequence of a labour dispute.

Luxembourg Compromise: an intergovernmental agreement arrived at in January 1966 between the member states which solved the 'empty chair' crisis. It states that when vital interests of one or more countries are at stake, members of the Council will endeavour to reach solutions that can be adopted by all while respecting their mutual interests.

Maastricht (Treaty): see Treaty on European Union.

Maastricht Treaty ratification: the process that lead to the approval—in both national parliaments and in some cases in referendums—of the Treaty on European Union, which came into force in 1993.

Macro-economic policies: economic policies which deal with aggregates such as national income and investment in the economy.

Majoritarian: application of majority rule. The principle that the majority should be allowed to rule the minority.

Market citizenship: the concept introduced to the EC in the 1950s whereby citizens of member states became endowed with certain rights as workers within the European Community.

Market integration: the breaking down of barriers to trade amongst the EU's member states, plus any regulation necessary to ensure the smooth running of the single market. It does not involve an explicitly political dimension.

Market-making measures: refers to measures that involve the prohibition of certain types of market behaviour.

Market-shaping measures: refers to measures that lay down an institutional model which shapes market behaviour.

Market unity: the removal of protection across the Union, allowing agricultural produce to move freely across borders.

Middle-range theories: theories that aim to explain only part of a political process and that do not have totalizing ambitions.

Milwardian: related to Alan Milward who in his seminal work, *The European Rescue of the Nation-State* argues that the purpose of the European Community was not to supersede but to reinforce the nation state.

Mixed commonwealth: conceptualization of the 'EU order' within which the subjects of the constitution represent a mixture of agents that share in the sovereignty of the larger unit.

Modulation: the transfer of agricultural subsidies to agri-environmental and other rural development projects.

Modus operandi: Latin expression that means 'method of operating or proceeding'.

Monetarists: refers to those supporting one of the possible strategies to achieve economic and monetary union (the other one being economists). In the 1960s and 1970s, the economists' camp postulated that by fixing the exchange rate the necessary cooperation of the adjacent economic policies would naturally start to occur (see also economist).

Monetary union: is a form of integration that usually contains a single market (and therefore free movement of goods, services, labour, and capital among the participating states and common rules, tariffs, and so on, vis-à-vis third countries) and has further integration in the area of currency cooperation. A monetary union either has irrevocably fixed exchange rates and full convertibility of currencies, or a common or single currency circulating within the monetary union. It also requires integration of budgetary and monetary policies.

Money supply: the stock of liquid assets in an economy that can be freely exchanged for goods and services.

Monnet Method: see 'Community Method'.

Multifunctionality: the notion in agricultural policy that the policy can be used to serve a range of functions, including environmental protection and rural development.

Multilateral budgetary surveillance: against the background of the Stability and Growth Pact, the objective of the multilateral budgetary surveillance is to ensure that national economic policy is broadly consistent with the SGP and thus with the proper functioning of EMU.

Multi-level governance: an approach to the study of EU politics which emphasizes the interaction of the many different actors who influence European policy outcomes.

Multi-speed (Europe): a method of differentiated integration whereby common objectives are pursued by a group of member states, able and willing to advance further than others in the integration process.

Mutual recognition: the principle that an economic product sold in one member state should not be prohibited from sale anywhere in the EU. This was upheld in the famous *Cassis de Dijon* (1979) case brought to the European Court of Justice. Exceptions can be made in cases of public health and safety, however.

National envelopes: in the context of the Common Agricultural Policy, these are de facto national allocations paid to the member states from the EC budget, and which each state can distribute to its farmers to target specific national and or regional priorities.

Negative integration: a form of integration which involves the removal of barriers between the member states.

Neo-corporatist: is a model of policy making which links producer interests to the state, and where interest organizations are incorporated into the system. The neo- prefix was added in the 1970s to distinguish this from corporatism in the past—particularly in the fascist era.

Neo-functionalism: a theory of European integration which views integration as an incremental process, involving the spillover of integration in one sector to others, ultimately leading to some kind of political community.

Neo-functionalist: see neo-functionalism.

Neo-liberalism: an economic school, which advocates the reduction of state influence in the market, the liberalization of the economy, the privatization of state-owned firms, tight control of money supply, and supports a general trend towards deregulation.

Neo-realism: an International Relations theory, associated with the work of Kenneth Waltz, which claims that the international state system is anarchic, and as such that state uncertainty is a given. States will want to maintain their independence, and survival will be their primary objective, but they may all the same engage in European integration if this serves their ends.

Net contributors: those countries that receive less from the EC budget than they contribute.

Net recipients: those countries that receive more from the EC budget than they contribute.

New approach: it refers to a new approach to regulating internal market rules as established in the Commission's White Paper on Completing the Internal Market (1985) in which legislative acts would set out only the main objectives and detailed rules would be adopted through private standardization bodies.

New institutionalism: a conceptual approach to the study of politics which restates the importance of institutional factors in political life. It takes a number of very different forms, from rational institutionalism and historical institutionalism to sociological institutionalism.

Nice Treaty: treaty revision agreed at Nice in December 2000, signed in February 2001, and ratified in 2002. It introduced a number of institutional reforms which paved the way for the enlargement of the Union in 2004 and after.

Non-compulsory spending: the EU's budget expenditure is divided into compulsory and non-compulsory expenditure. In the case of non-compulsory expenditure, the budgetary authority is free to choose the amount to be spent. The European Parliament has the last word in deciding on non-compulsory expenditure.

Non-majoritarian institutions: those governmental entities that possess and exercise specialized public authority, separate from that of other institutions, but are neither directly elected by the people, nor directly managed by elected officials.

Non-tariff barriers: see barriers to trade.

Non-state actors: usually any actor that is not a national government. Often refers to transnational actors, such as interest groups (rather than to international organizations).

Normative: refers to value judgements, 'what ought to be', as opposed to positive statements about 'what is'.

Ontology: relates to the nature of being; an underlying conception of the world; that which is being pre-supposed by a theory.

Open Method of Coordination: is an approach to EU policy making which is an alternative to regulation and which involves more informal means of encouraging compliance than 'hard' legislation.

Optimum Currency Area (OCA): a theoretical notion which implies that monetary union will only work effectively when the states participating are economically very similar.

Organized synarchy: a term which refers to political systems in which there is the idea of extensive sovereignty sharing.

Original Six: the original signatories of the Treaty of Rome, namely, France, Germany, Italy, Belgium, Luxembourg, and the Netherlands.

Paris-Bonn axis: the relationship between France and Germany, which is often said to lie at the heart of the European integration process.

Parity: equality in amount, status or character.

Parsimony: a theory which is parsimonious is a theory which provides an extremely simplified depiction of reality.

Path-dependence: the idea that decisions taken in the past limit the scope of decisions in the present (and future).

Peace dividend: a political term denoting the economic benefit of reducing defence spending.

Permanent representation: is the diplomatic delegation of any member state vis-à-vis the EU in Brussels.

Permissive consensus: the political context which allowed elites in the post-1945 period to engage in European integration, without involving Europe's citizens.

Pillar: one of three parts of the European Union, which since its inception at Maastricht has been divided into pillar 1 (the EC pillar), pillar 2 (foreign and security policy) and pillar 3 (formerly justice and home affairs, now just police and judicial cooperation in criminal matters).

Plan 'D': commissioner Margot Wallstrom's communication strategy, emphasizing democracy, dialogue, and debate.

Pluralist: pluralism is a general approach which implies that organized groups play an important role in the political process.

Policy convergence: the tendency for policies (in different countries) to begin to take on similar forms over time.

Policy network: a set of actors who are linked by relatively stable relationships of a non-hierarchical and interdependent nature. These actors share common interests with regard to a policy and exchange resources to pursue these shared interests acknowledging that cooperation is the best way to achieve common goals.

Policy style: sets of characteristics which describe different ways of making policy (for example, in a particular sector, or across a particular country).

Policy transfer: the replication of policies pursued in one context (country; sector) to others.

Political codetermination: codetermination refers to a complex set of legal and social institutions that shape employee participation in company decision-making through works councils and representation in the supervisory boards of large firms. Political codetermination applies this model to the political process.

Political opportunity structure: describes the various characteristics of a political system which influence elements within it such as social movements, organizational forms and the way in which political actors behave.

Polity: a politically organized society.

Positive integration: a form of integration which involves the construction of policies and/or institutions.

Positive-sum outcomes: outcomes that constitute more than the sum of their parts. It is often talked of in EU terms as an 'upgrading of the common interest'.

Post-national: refers to forms of governance beyond the nation-state.

Power: the ability to control outcomes. The capacity of A to force B to do something in A's interest.

Preliminary rulings: acts of the ECJ, which arise as responses to questions of European law posed in domestic courts.

Presidency: the EU Presidency is held on a six-monthly basis by member states in rotation. The Presidency performs various functions, for example, presenting a programme for the period concerned, and chairing European Council and EU Council meetings.

Price support: the system of agricultural support which involves keeping food prices higher than the market price so as to give farmers a higher and more stable income.

Primus inter pares: Latin expression that means 'first amongst equals'.

Primus super pares: Latin expression that means 'first above anyone else'.

Proportionality: a principle which implies that the means should not exceed the ends; applies to decision-making/the legislative process.

Public debts: the amount of money owed by the state.

Public goods theory: a branch of economics that studies how voters, politicians, and government officials behave from the perspective of economic theory.

Qualified Majority Voting (QMV): system of voting in the EU Council, which attributes a number of votes to each member state (very roughly related to their size). A majority of these votes (currently 71 per cent) is needed for legislation to be agreed in the Council, implying that some states will be outvoted, but will have to apply the legislation all the same.

Rapid Reaction Force: a transnational military force managed by the European Union.

Ratification: formal approval. In the EU context, it implies approval of Treaty revisions by national parliaments and sometimes also by popular referendum.

Ratification crisis (1992): the crisis provoked by the Danish 'no' vote in their 1992 referendum on the Maastricht Treaty.

Rational choice: see rationalist.

Rational utilitarianism: where opinions stem from calculations involving the weighing up of costs and benefits.

Rationalist: theories that are rationalist assume that individuals (or states) are able to make rank orderings of their preferences and to choose the best available preference.

Realism: a rationalist theory of International Relations.

Realist: see Realism.

Rebate: the 'abatement' granted to the UK in 1984 to compensate it for being a net contributor to the Community budget at a time when its economy was weak.

Recession: a temporary depression in economic activity or prosperity.

Redistributive: policy which transfers wealth from one group to another.

References: see Preliminary rulings.

Reference value: a baseline. A measure from which assessment of economic process can be made.

Reflection group: a group established prior to an intergovernmental conference to prepare preliminary papers on relevant issues.

Reflectivist: reflectivist perspectives centre on ontological and epistemological questions not answered to a satisfactory degree by the rationalist, behaviourist, positivist perspectives, such as the nature of knowledge, its objectivity or subjectivity, and the nature of international politics. Reflectivism questions the existence of objective truth and our ability to possibly discover such truths.

Reform Treaty: a Treaty that amends the provisions of existing EU treaties. The difference between a reform treaty (operating within the framework of existing treaties) and a constitution (that would consolidate all the rules governing the EU and give rise to a new set of legal principles) shaped the debates over the ratification of the Lisbon Treaty and member states' justification not to hold referendums.

Regime(s): principles, norms, rules, and decision-making procedures around which actors' expectations occur. An international regime is usually considered to take the form of an international organization. It is a concept associated with neo-realism.

Regulation: the act of making rules or legislation in order to provoke certain policy outcomes.

Regulation: one of the legislative instruments used by the EU. Regulations are directly effective, spelling out not just the aims of legislation, but what must be done and how.

Regulatory competition: a situation where regulators try to offer a regulatory environment to attract business from abroad. This may involve deregulation.

Representation: the principle by which delegates are chosen to act for a particular constituency (group of electors).

Republican: a state or nation in which supreme power rests with voters, and in which the head of state has been elected.

Res public composita: a composite union composed of diverse publics.

Right of association: the democratic right of people to form groups such as trades unions.

Robert Schuman: French foreign minister and one of the 'founding fathers' of the European Coal and Steel Community, through his 'Schuman Plan' of 1950.

Rural development policy: the EU's common rural development policy aims to address the challenges faced by rural areas, and to unlock their potential. Rural development addresses three key areas: improving the competitiveness of the agricultural and forestry sector;

improving the environment and the countryside; and improving the quality of life in rural areas and encouraging diversification of the rural economy.

Schengen: an agreement to create a border-free European Community. It was originally outside the EC, but was incorporated into it at Amsterdam.

Schuman Plan: signed on 9 May 1950, it led to the setting up of the European Coal and Steel Community.

Sectoral integration: a description of or strategy for integration which involves an incremental sector-by-sector approach. See also spillover.

Separation of powers: a condition of democratic political systems where the executive, legislature, and judiciary are separate, and provide checks and balances which serve to prevent abuses of power.

Shared competences: refer to specific areas where the member states and the EU have powers to legislate and adopt legally binding acts. The member states exercise their powers in so far as the Union has not exercised, or has decided to stop exercising, its competence. Most of the EU's competences fall into this category (see also exclusive competences).

Single European Act (SEA): the first of the large-scale Treaty revisions, signed in 1986. It came into force in 1987, and served as a 'vehicle' for the single market programme.

Single Farm Payment (SFP): a unique CAP direct payment aimed at achieving a complete decoupling of support and production. Under this system, even a farmer who decides to grow nothing is eligible to receive this payment, as long as they complie with environmental, food safety, animal welfare, and occupational safety standards.

Single market: the idea of having one unified internal EU market, free of (national) barriers to trade. While the idea was included in the Treaty of Rome, the single market is usually associated with the revitalization of the Community from the mid 1980s.

Single monetary policy: common monetary policy across the euro area (see EMU).

'Snake': a system aimed to stabilize exchange rates within the EC in the 1970s.

Social Chapter: agreed at Maastricht, the Social Chapter establishes minimum social conditions within the EU.

Until Amsterdam, the Chapter was annexed to the Treaty, as the UK Conservative government had decided not to sign up to it.

Social constructivism: see constructivism.

Social dialogue: joint consultation procedure involving social partners at EU level, to discuss and negotiate agreements where relevant.

Social dumping: the undercutting of social standards in order to improve competitiveness.

Social partner(s): refers to labour (the unions) and capital (employers) acting together. The two sides of industry.

Social spillover: a recent neo-functionalist concept which divorces social from political spillover in order to explain the learning and socialization processes that help drive the European integration process.

Sociotropic: relating to voting behaviour which maximizes social welfare (implying solidarity).

Soft law: documents that are not formally or legally binding but which may still produce political effects.

Sovereignty: a condition in which states are not subject to any higher authority; supreme, unrestricted power (of a state).

Spillover: a mechanism identified by neo-functionalist theorists who claimed that sectoral integration in one area would have knock-on effects in others, and would 'spill over', thereby increasing the scope of European integration.

Stability and Growth Pact (SGP): an agreement of the EU member states concerning conduct over their fiscal policy, which aimed to ensure that the constraints on member states prior to the introduction of the single currency would continue after EMU was in place.

State-centrism: a conceptual approach to understanding European integration which gives primacy to the role of state actors within the process.

Statecraft: wisdom in the management of public affairs.

Statehood: the condition of being a state. See stateness.

Stateness: the quality of being a state, that is, a legal territorial entity with a stable population and a government.

Strong currency: a situation arising out of relative levels of exchange rate whereby the value of national money is increased. This has the effect of lowering the price of imports (making imported goods cheaper), but also of increasing the price of exports, making exports less competitive in international markets.

Subsidiarity: the principle that tries to ensure that decisions are taken as close as possible to the citizen.

Superstate: a political term, which implies that the aim of supporters of European integration is to turn the EU into a (national?) state, with connotations of the detachment of elites and the European institutions from ordinary citizens.

Supranational(ism): that which is above the national level. It may refer to institutions, policies, or a particular 'type' of cooperation/integration; or an approach to the study of the EU, which emphasizes the autonomy of the European institutions and the importance of common European policies.

Supranational governance: a theory of European integration proposed by Wayne Sandholtz and Alec Stone Sweet which draws on neo-functionalism, and provides an alternative approach to Moravcsik's liberal intergovernmentalism.

Sustainability: or 'sustainable development'. The ability to meet the needs of the present without compromising the needs of future generations.

Sympolity: is a composite union that combines different forms of representation and sources of legitimacy.

Tampere: city in Finland at which a summit meeting in 1999 agreed to create an 'area of freedom, security and justice' in Europe.

Teleological: in the context of the EU's legal doctrine, teleological arguments are those drawn from the objectives that the norms (Community law) establish either implicitly or explicitly. A typical teleological argument is the reference to the need to achieve a single European market.

Third country nationals: citizens of countries outside the European Union.

Third pillar: that part of the European Union that deals with police and judicial cooperation in criminal matters. From Maastricht to Amsterdam it was labelled Justice and Home Affairs.

Transaction costs: costs related to the exchange of money.

Transfer payments: payments not made in return for any contribution to current output. Usually refers to agricultural subsidies.

Transparency: a term used in the EU to refer to the extent of openness within the EU institutions.

Transposed: see transposition.

Transposition: the translation of European law into domestic law.

Treaty base: the provision of the Treaty which underpins a particular piece of European legislation.

Treaty base game: the act of selecting a treaty base (in a 'grey area') for political ends.

Treaty of Rome: signed in 1957, the Rome Treaty formally established the European Economic Community (EEC) and EURATOM (the European Atomic Energy Community).

Treaty of Nice: see Nice Treaty.

Treaty on the Functioning of the EU (TFEU): this Treaty organizes the functioning of the Union and determines the areas of, delimitation of, and arrangements for exercising its competences (see Lisbon Treaty).

Trevi (Group): a forum for internal security cooperation, which operated from the mid 1970s until 1993.

Troika: refers to (i) the country holding the Presidency together with the previous Presidency and the forthcoming Presidency; or (ii) in CFSP: the Presidency, the High Representative for CFSP, and the Commission.

Unanimity: the principle that all member states must vote in favour for an agreement to be reached. It implies that each member state holds a potential veto.

Utilitarian theories: theories that relate to choosing the greatest good for the greatest number of people.

Variable geometry: an image of the European Union which foresees the breakdown of a unified form of cooperation, and the introduction of a 'pick and choose' approach to further integration.

Variable levies: in the context of the Common Agricultural Policy, variable levies are raised on produce before

it enters the common market so that it is priced at or above the internal price. A system of 'reimbursements' (refunds), enables European producers to sell their products on the world market at world prices without losing income.

Veto players: according to Tsebelis, for policy change to occur, a certain number of individual or collective actors (veto players) have to agree to the proposed change.

Voluntary agreements: agreements resulting from the autonomous social dialogue at EU level are 'voluntary' in that they proceed without the initiative or participation of the Commission and in that their implementation is not subject to legal enforcement (see social dialogue).

Werner Plan: the 1970 Werner Plan drafted the blueprint for economic and monetary union. It proposed three stages to reach EMU by 1980. On the institutional side it recommended setting up two supranational bodies: 'a Community System for the Central Banks' and a 'Centre of Decision for Economic Policy'. The former would pursue monetary policies whereas the latter would coordinate macroeconomic policies (including some tax policies). Most of the recommendations of the Werner Plan were adopted.

Western European Union (WEU): a collaborative defence agreement and extension of the 1948 Treaty of Brussels, signed in 1955. It was designed to allow for the rearmament of West Germany. It was revitalized in the 1980s, and subsequently served as a bridge between NATO and the EU. Its functions have lately been subsumed within the European Union.

Widening: generally refers to the enlargement of the EU, but may also be used to denote the increasing scope of Community or Union competences.

World Trade Organization (WTO): is an international organization that oversees the global trade in goods and services.

Zero-sum game: a game played (by states) in which the victory of one group implies the loss of another.

Zollverein: a customs union between German states in the eighteenth century under Bismarck. The economic basis for German unification.

References

Abromeit, H. (1996), *Democracy in Europe: legitimizing politics in a non-state polity* (Oxford: Berghahn Books).

Achen, C. H. (2006), 'Evaluating political decision-making models' in R. Thomson, F. N. Stokman, C. H. Achen, and T. Koenig (eds) *The European Union decides* (Cambridge: Cambridge University Press): 264–98.

Allen, D. (2002), 'The common foreign and security policy' in J. Gower (ed.) *The European Union Handbook* (London: Fitzroy Dearborn Publishers).

Alter, K. (2001), *Establishing the supremacy of European law* (Oxford: Oxford University Press).

Amato, G. and J. Ziller et al (2007), *The European constitution: cases and materials in EU and member states' law* (Cheltenham: Elgar).

Amin, A. and J. Tomaney (1995), *Behind the myth of European Union: prospects for cohesion* (London: Routledge).

Anderson, C. J. (1998), 'When in doubt, use proxies: attitudes toward domestic politics and support for European integration', *Comparative Political Studies*, 31/5: 569–601.

Andersen, S. S. and K. A. Eliassen (eds) (1993), *Making policy in Europe: the Europeification of national policy-making* (London: Sage).

Andersen, M. S. and D. Liefferink (eds) (1997), *European environmental policy: the pioneers* (Manchester: Manchester University Press).

Anderson, J. J. (1995), 'The state of the (European) Union: from the single market to Maastricht, from singular events to general theories', *World Politics*, Vol. 47, April.

Ansell, C. K., C. A. Parsons, and K.A. Darden (1997), 'Dual networks in European regional development policy', *Journal of Common Market Studies*, 35/3: 347–57.

Arblaster, A. (1987), *Democracy* (Minneapolis: University of Minnesota Press).

Armstrong, K. and S. Bulmer (1998), *The governance of the single European market* (Manchester: Manchester University Press).

Arnull, A. (2006), *The European Union and its Court of Justice* 2nd edn (Oxford: Oxford University Press).

Arnull, A. (2008), 'Me and my shadow: the European Court of Justice and the disintegration of EU Law', *Fordham International Law Journal*, 31, 1174–2007.

Arnull, A. and D. Wincott (eds) (2002), *Accountability and legitimacy in the European Union* (Oxford: Oxford University Press).

Aron, R. and D. Lerner (1957), *France defeats EDC* (London: Thames and Hudson).

Aspinwall, M. and J. Greenwood (1998), 'Conceptualising collective action in the European Union: an introduction' in J. Greenwood and M. Aspinwall (eds) *Collective action in the European Union: interests and the new politics of associability* (London: Routledge).

Aspinwall, M. and G. Schneider (2001), 'Institutional research on the European Union: mapping the field' in M. Aspinwall and G. Schneider (eds) *The rules of integration: institutionalist approaches to the study of Europe* (Manchester: Manchester University Press).

Athanassopoulou, E. (ed.) (2008), *United in diversity? European integration and political cultures* (London: I. B. Tauris).

Axelrod R. (1984), *The evolution of co-operation* (New York: Basic Books).

Bache, I. (1998), *The politics of European Union regional policy: multi-level governance or flexible gatekeeping?* (Sheffield: Sheffield Academic Press).

Baldaccini, A., E. Guild, and H. Toner (eds) (2007), *Whose freedom, security and justice? EU immigration and asylum law and policy* (London: Hart).

Bailer, S. (2004), 'Bargaining success in the European Union', *European Union politics*, 5/1: 99–123.

Bailey, D. and L. De Propris (2002), 'The 1988 reform of the European Structural Funds: entitlement or empowerment?', *Journal of European Public Policy*, 9/3: 408–28.

Balme, R. and D. Chabanet (eds) (2008), *European governance and democracy: power and protest in the EU* (Lanham: Rowman & Littlefield).

Bankowski, Z., A. Scott, and F. Snyder (1998), 'Guest editorial', *European Law Review*, 4/4: 227–40.

Barber, L. (1995), 'The men who run Europe', *Financial Times*, 11–12 March, Section 2: 1–2.

Barnard, C. (2000), 'Regulating competitive federalism in the European Union? The case of EC social policy' in J. Shaw (ed.) *Social law and policy in an evolving European Union* (Oxford: Hart).

Barzanti, S. (1965), *The underdeveloped areas within the common market* (Princeton: Princeton University Press).

Baumgartner, F. and B. Leech (1998), *Basic interests: the importance of groups in politics and political science* (Princeton: Princeton University Press).

Baun, M. J. (1996), *An imperfect union: the Maastricht Treaty and the new politics of European integration* (Boulder, CO: Westview)

Beetham, D. and C. Lord (1996), *Legitimacy in the European Union* (London: Addison Wesley Longman).

Behrens, P. and M. Smyrl (1999), 'A conflict of rationalities: EU regional policy and the single market', *Journal of European Public Policy*, 6/3: 419–35.

Bellamy, A. (2002), *Kosovo and the International Society* (New York: Palgrave).

Bellamy, R. and D. Castiglione (1997), 'Building the union: the nature of sovereignty in the political architecture of Europe', *Law and Philosophy*, 16/4: 421–45.

Bellamy, R. and D. Castiglione (2000), 'Democracy, sovereignty and the construction of the European Union: the republican alternative to liberalism' in Z. Bankowski and A. Scott (eds) *The European Union and its order* (London: Blackwell).

Bellamy, R., D. Castiglione, and J. Shaw (eds) (2006), *Making European citizens: civic inclusion in a transnational context* (London: Palgrave)

Bellamy, R. and A. Warleigh (eds) (2001), *Citizenship and governance in the European Union* (London: Continuum).

Benson, D. and A. Jordan (2008), 'Grand bargain or "incomplete contract": the environmental implications of the EU reform treaty', *European Environmental and Energy Law Review*, 17/5: 280–90.

Benz, A. (1998), 'Politikverflechtung ohne Politikverflechtungsfalle – Koordination und Strukturdynamik im europäischen Mehrebenensystem', *Politische Vierteljahresschrift*, 39/4: 558–89.

Berger, S. and R. Dore (1996), *National diversity and global capitalism* (Cornell: Cornell University Press).

Bergman, T. and T. Raunio (2001), 'Parliaments and policy-making in the European Union', in J. Richardson (ed.) *European Union: power and policy-making* 2nd edn (London: Routledge).

Berkhout, J. and D. Lowery (2008), 'Counting organized interests in the European Union: a comparison of data sources', *Journal of European Public Policy*, 15/4: 489–513.

Bertoncini, Y. (2007), *The EU budget as an instrument to finance collective goods: key points for the debate*, paper presented at the Notre Europe seminar 'The EU budget: what for?', held on 19 April 2007, Brussels, htpp://www.notre-europe.eu.

Bertrand, R. (1956), 'The European common market proposal', *International Organization*, 10/4: 559–74.

Best, E., T. Christiansen, and P. Settembri (eds) (2008), *The Institutions of the Enlarged European Union: Continuity and Change* (Cheltenham: Edward Elgar).

Beyers, J., R. Eising, and W. Maloney (eds) (2008), 'The politics of organised interest in Europe: lessons from EU studies and comparative politics', *West European Politics* 31/6: 1129–46.

Bieber, R., and J. Monar (eds) (1995), *Justice and home affairs in the European Union: the development of the third pillar* (Brussels: European Interuniversity Press).

BirdLife (2008a), 'Europe's farmland birds continue to suffer from agricultural policy', 2 December: http://www.birdlife.org/news/news/2008/12/monitoring.html

BirdLife (2008b), 'CAP Health Check: the environment gets a placebo treatment', 11 November: http://www.birdlife.org/news/extra/europe/health_check.html

Blavoukos, S. and G. Pagoulatos (2008), 'Enlargement waves and interest group participation in the EU policymaking system: establishing a framework of analysis', *West European Politics*, 31, 6, 1147–65.

Blondel, J., R. Sinnott, and P. Svensson (1998), *People and parliament in the European Union: participation, democracy and legitimacy* (Oxford: Clarendon Press).

Bolleyer, N. and D. Panke (forthcoming), 'The Irish Green Party and Europe: An Unhappy Marriage?', *Irish Political Studies*.

Bomberg, E. and Peterson, J. (2000), 'Policy transfer and Europeanization: passing the Heineken test?', Queen's Papers in Europeanization no. 2, Queen's University, Belfast.

Borrás, S. and Greve, B. (2004), 'Concluding remarks: new method or just cheap talk', *Journal of European Public Policy*, 11/2: 329–36.

Borrás, S. and Jacobsson, K. (2004), 'The open method of co-ordination and new governance patterns', *Journal of European Public Policy*, 11/2: 185–208.

Börzel, T. A. (2001), 'Non-compliance in the European Union: pathology or statistical artefact?', *Journal of European Public Policy*, 8/5: 803–24.

Börzel, T. (2002), 'Pace-setting, foot-dragging and fence-sitting: member state responses to Europeanisation', *Journal of Common Market Studies*, 40/2: 193–214.

Börzel, T. A. (2003), *Environmental leaders and laggards in the European Union: why there is (not) a southern problem* (London: Ashgate).

Börzel, T. A. (2005), 'Europeanization: how the European Union interacts with its member states', in S. Bulmer and C. Lequesne (eds) *The member states of the European Union* (Oxford: Oxford University Press): 45–69.

Börzel, T. A. and T. Risse (2000), 'When Europe hits home: Europeanization and domestic change', *European Integration Online Papers*, 27, 29 November.

Börzel, T. A. and T. Risse (2003), 'Conceptualising the domestic impact of Europe' in K. Featherstone and C. M. Radaelli (eds) *The politics of Europeanisation* (Oxford: Oxford University Press).

Börzel, T. A., and T. Risse (2007), 'Europeanization: the domestic impact of EU politics', in K. E. Jorgensen, M. A. Pollack, and B. Rosamond (eds) *Handbook of European Union Politics* (London: Sage): 483–504.

Börzel, T. A., M. Dudziak, T. Hofmann, D. Panke, and C. Sprungk (2007), 'Recalcitrance, inefficiency, and support for European integration: why member states do (not) comply with European law', Harvard University, Center for European Studies Working Paper Series, No. 153.

Börzel, T. A., Y. Pamuk, and A. Stahn (2008), 'The European Union and the promotion of governance in its near abroad: one size fits all?', SFB 700 working paper no.19, SFB-Governance Research Centre, Berlin.

Bourne, A. K. (2007), 'Regional Europe' in M. Cini (ed.) *European Union politics* (Oxford: Oxford University Press): 287–303.

Brugger, B. (1999), *Republican theory in political thought: virtuous or virtual?* (London: Macmillan).

Buiter, W. (2000), 'Optimal currency areas: why does the exchange rate regime matter?', *Scottish Journal of Political Economy*, 47: 213–50.

Bulmer, S. (1983), 'Domestic politics and European Community policy-making'. *Journal of Common Market Studies*, 21/4: 349–63.

Bulmer, S. and W. Wessels (1987), *The Council: decision-making in the European Community* (London: Macmillan).

Burley, A. M. and W. Mattli (1993), 'Europe before the court: a political theory of legal integration', *International Organization*, 47/1: 41–76.

Burns, C. (2005), 'The European Parliament' in A. Jordan (ed.) *Environmental Policy in the European Union* 2nd edn (London: Earthscan): 87–105.

Busch, K. (1988), *The corridor model—a concept for further development of an EU social policy* (Brussels: European Trade Union Institute).

Cameron, D. (1992), 'The 1992 initiative: causes and consequences' in A. Sbragia (ed.), *Europolitics* (Washington DC: Brookings).

Cameron, F. (1999), *The foreign and security policy of the European Union: past, present and future* (Sheffield: Sheffield University Press).

Cameron F. (ed.) (2004) *The future of Europe: integration and enlargement* (London: Routledge).

Caporaso, J. A. (1974), *The structure and function of European integration* (Pacific Palisades, California: Goodyear).

Caporaso, J. A. and J. Wittenbrinck (2006), 'The new modes of governance and political authority in Europe', *Journal of European Public Policy*, 13/4: 471–80.

Caporaso, J. A. and J. Jupille (2001), 'The Europeanization of gender equality policy and domestic structural change' in M. G. Cowles, J. A. Caporaso, and T. Risse (eds) *Transforming Europe: Europeanization and domestic change* (Ithaca: Cornell University Press): 21–43.

Caporaso, J. A. and S. Tarrow (2007), 'Polanyi in Brussels: European institutions and the embedding of markets in society', paper presented for the Cornell University Government Department seminar on comparative and international politics, 30 November.

Carrubba, C. J. (2003), 'The European Court of Justice: democracy, and enlargement', *European Union Politics*, 4/1: 75–100.

Chalmers, D. and A. Tomkins (2007), *European Union public law* (Cambridge: Cambridge University Press).

Cecchini, P. (1988), *1992: The European Challenge* (Aldershot: Gower).

Chatham House (2003), *Unfinished business: making Europe's single market a reality* (London: Chatham House/RIIA).

Checkel, J. T. (1998), 'The constructivist turn in international relations theory', *World Politics*, 50: 324–48.

Checkel, J. T. (2001), 'A constructivist research programme in EU studies', *European Union Politics*, 2/2: 219–49.

Christiansen, T. (1996), 'A maturing bureaucracy: the role of the Commission in the policy process' in J. Richardson (ed) *European Union: Power and Policymaking* (London: Routledge).

Christiansen, T., K. E. Jørgensen, and A. Wiener (1999), 'The social construction of Europe', *Journal of European Public Policy*, 6/4: 528–44.

Christiansen, T., K. E. Jørgensen, and A. Wiener (eds) (2001), *The Social Construction of Europe* (London:Sage).

Christiansen, T. and T. Larsson (eds) (2007), *The role of committees in the policy process of the European Union* (Cheltenham: Edward Elgar).

Christiansen, T. and P. Lintner (2005), 'The Committee of the Regions after 10 years: lessons from the past and challenges for the future', *EIPAScope*, 1, 7–13.

Chryssochoou, D. N. (2000a), *Democracy in the European Union* (London: Taurus).

Chryssochoou, D. N. (2000b), 'Metatheory and the study of the European Union: capturing the narrative turn', *Journal of European Integration*, 22/2: 123–44.

Chryssochoou, D. N. (2001), *Theorizing European integration* (London: Sage).

Chryssochoou, D. N. (2002), 'Europe's republican moment', *Journal of European Integration*, 24/4: 341–57.

Chryssochoou, D. N. (2009), *Theorizing European integration*, 2nd edn (London and New York: Routledge).

Chryssochoou, D. N., M. J. Tsinisizelis, S. Stavridis, and K. Lavdas (2003), *Theory and reform in the European Union* (Manchester: Manchester University Press).

Church, C. H. (1996), *European integration theory in the 1990s*, European dossier series (London: University of North London).

Church, C. and D. Phinnemore (1996), *The Penguin Guide to the European treaties: from Rome to Maastricht, Amsterdam, Nice and beyond* (London: Penguin).

Citi, M. and M. Rhodes (2007), 'New modes of governance in the EU: common objectives versus national preferences', CONNEX *European Governance Papers*, 7/1, http://www.connexnetwork.org/eurogov/pdf/

Clark, A. (1993), *Diaries* (London: Weidenfeld and Nicolson).

Coen, D. (1997), 'The evolution of the large firm as a political actor in the European Union' *Journal of Public Policy*, 4/1: 91–108.

Coen, D. (1998), 'The European business interest and the nation state: large firm lobbying in the European Union and member states' *Journal of European Public Policy*, 18/1: 75–100.

Cohen, B. J. (1971), *The future of sterling as an international currency* (London: Macmillan).

Conant, L. J. (2002), *Justice contained: law and politics in the European Union* (Ithaca: Cornell University Press).

Coombes, D. (1970), *Politics and bureaucracy in the European Community. A portrait of the Commission of the E.E.C.* (London: George Allen & Unwin).

Corbett, R. (1998), *The European Parliament's role in closer EU integration* (London: Macmillan).

Council of the European Union (1996), *The European Union today and tomorrow, adapting the European Union for the benefit of its peoples and preparing it for the future: a general outline for a draft revision of the treaties* (Brussels: EU Council).

Cowles, M. G. (1995), 'Seizing the agenda for the new Europe: the ERT and EC 1992'. *Journal of Common Market Studies*, 33/4: 501–26.

Cowles, M. G. (1997), 'Organizing industrial coalitions: a challenge for the future?' in H. Wallace and A. R. Young (eds) *Participation and policy-making in the European Union* (Oxford: Clarendon Press).

Cowles, M. G. (2001), 'The transatlantic business dialogue and domestic business–government relations' in M. G. Cowles, J. A. Caporaso, and T. Risse (eds), *Transforming Europe. Europeanization and domestic change* (Ithaca, NJ: Cornell University Press).

Cowles, M. G., J. A. Caporaso and T. Risse (eds) (2001), *Transforming Europe. Europeanization and domestic change* (Ithaca, NJ: Cornell University Press).

Craig, P. P. (1992), 'Once upon a time in the West: direct effect and the federalization of EEC law', *Oxford Journal of Legal Studies*, 12/4: 453–79.

Craig, P. P. (1997), 'Democracy and rule-making within the EC: an empirical and normative assessment', *European Law Review*, 3/2: 105–30.

Craig, P. and G. de Búrca (2007), *EU law: text, cases and materials* 4th edn (Oxford: Oxford University Press).

Cram, L. (1994), 'Calling the tune without paying the piper?', *Policy and Politics*, 21/2: 135–46.

Cram, L. (1999), 'The Commission' in L. Cram, D. Dinan and N. Nugent (eds) *Developments in European Union Politics* (Basingstoke: Macmillan).

Cremona M. (ed.) (2004), *The Enlargement of the European Union* (Oxford: Oxford University Press).

Curtin, D. (1993), 'The constitutional structure of the Union: a Europe of bits and pieces', *Common Market Law Review*, 30/1: 17–69.

Curtin, D. and M. Egeberg (2008), 'Tradition and innovation: Europe's accumulated executive order', *West European Politics*, 31/4: 639–61.

da Conceição-Heldt, E. (2004), *The common fisheries policy of the European Union: a study of integrative and distributive bargaining* (London: Routledge).

da Conceição-Heldt, E. (2006), 'Taking actors' preferences and the institutional setting seriously: the EU common fisheries policy', *Journal of Public Policy*, 26/3: 279–99.

Dahrendorf, R. (1967), *Society and democracy in Germany* (London: Weidenfeld and Nicolson).

Dashwood, A. (1983), 'Hastening slowly the Community's path towards harmonisation' in H. Wallace, W. Wallace and C. Webb (eds) *Policy-making in the European Community* 2nd edn (Chichester: John Wiley).

Dassu, M. and A. Missoroli (2002), 'More Europe in foreign and security policy: the institutional dimension of CFSP', *The International Spectator*, 37/2 :79–88.

Davies, A. C. L. (2008), 'One step forward, two steps back? The Viking and Laval cases in the ECJ', *Industrial Law Journal*, 37/2: 126–48.

de Bassompierre, G. (1988), *Changing the guard in Brussels: an insider's view of the EC presidency* (New York: Praeger).

de Búrca, G. (2003), 'The constitutional challenge of new governance in the European Union', *European Law Review*, 28/6: 814–39.

De Búrca, G., B. De Witte, and L. Ogertschnig (eds) (2005), *Social rights in Europe* (Oxford: Oxford University Press),

de Grieco, J. M. (1995), 'The Maastricht Treaty, economic and monetary union and the neo-realist research programme', *Review of International Studies*, 21/1: 21–40.

de Grieco, J. M. (1996), 'State interests and international rule trajectories: a neorealist interpretation of the Maastricht Treaty and European economic and monetary union', *Security Studies*, 5/2: 176–222.

de la Porte, C. and P. Pochet (2002*), Building social Europe through the open method of co-ordination* (Berlin: PIE Peter Lang).

de la Porte, C. and P. Pochet (2004), 'The European employment strategy: existing research and remaining questions', European briefing, *Journal of European Social Policy*, 14/1: 71–8.

Delgardo, J. (2006), 'Single market trails home bias', Bruegel policy brief, no. 2006–05, Brussels, 7 October.

Devuyst, Y. (1998), 'Treaty reform in the European Union: the Amsterdam process', *Journal of European Public Policy*, 5/4: 615–31.

Diebold, W., Jnr (1959), *The Schuman Plan: A Study in Economic Cooperation, 1950-1959* (New York: Praeger).

DiMaggio, P. and W. Powell (1991), 'The iron cage revisited: institutional isomorphism and collective rationality in organizational fields' in P. DiMaggio and W. Powell (eds) *The new institutionalism in organizational analysis* (Chicago: University of Chicago Press).

Dinan, D. (2000), *Encyclopedia of the European Union* (Basingstoke: Macmillan).

Dispersyn, M., P. Vandervorst et al (1990), 'La construction d'un serpent social européen' *Revue Belge de Sécurité Sociale*, 12: 889–979

Dølvik, J. E. (1997), *Redrawing boundaries of solidarity? ETUC, social dialogue and the Europeanization of trade unions in the 1990s,* ARENA report no 5, Oslo.

Dover, R. (2007), 'For Queen and company: the role of intelligence in the UK arms trade' *Political Studies,* 55/4: 683–708

Dowding, K. (2000), 'Institutional research on the European Union: a critical review', *European Union Politics,* 1, 1, 125–44.

Duff, A. (1994), 'Building a parliamentary Europe', *Government and Opposition,* 29/2: 147–65.

Duff, A. (2006), *The Struggle for Europe's constitution* (London: Federal Trust/I.B. Tauris).

Dyson, K. and K. Featherstone (1999), *The road to Maastricht: negotiating economic and monetary union* (Oxford: Oxford University Press).

Dyson, K., and K. H. Goetz (eds) (2004), *Germany, Europe, and the politics of constraint* (Oxford: Oxford University Press).

Eberlein, B. and D. Kerwer (2002), 'Theorising the new modes of European Union governance', *European Integration Online Papers,* 6/5: 1–21.

Eeckhout, P. (2004), *External relations of the European Union: legal and constitutional foundations* (Oxford: Oxford University Press).

ECORYS (2008), 'Progress on EU sustainable development strategy', final report, Brussels.

Egan, M. (2001), *Constructing a European market: standards, regulation and governance* (Oxford: Oxford University Press).

Egeberg, M. (2006a), 'Executive politics as usual: role behaviour and conflict dimensions in the college of European commissioners', *Journal of European Public Policy,* 13/1: 1–15.

Egeberg, M. (ed.) (2006b), *Multilevel Union administration: the transformation of executive politics in Europe* (Basingstoke: Palgrave).

Egeberg, M. and A. Heskestad (2008), 'The denationalisation of the *cabinets* in the European Commission: a research note', ARENA Working Paper No. 25, ARENA Centre for European Studies, University of Oslo.

Egeberg, M., G. F. Schaefer, and J. Trondal (2003), 'The many faces of EU committee governance', *West European Politics,* 26/3: 19–40.

Eichenberg, R. C. and R. J. Dalton, (1993), 'Europeans and the European Community: the dynamics of public support for European integration', *International Organization,* 47/4: 507–34.

Eising, R. (2004), Multi-level governance and business interests in the European Union', *Governance,* 17/2: 211–46.

Eising, R. (2009), *The political economy of state–business relations in Europe: capitalism, interest intermediation, and EU policy-making* (London: Routledge).

Eising, R. (2007), 'The access of business interests to EU institutions: towards elite pluralism?' *Journal of European Public Policy,* 14/3: 384–403.

Elgström, O. and C. Jönsson, (2000), 'Negotiating in the European Union: bargaining or problem-solving?', *Journal of European Public Policy,* 7/5: 684–704.

ENDS (2008), 'EU climate change plans survive summit test', ENDS Europe Daily 2637, 16.10.08 (London: ENDS).

Eriksen, E. O. and J. E. Fossum (eds) (2000), *Democracy in the European Union* (London: Routledge).

Eriksen, E. O and J. E. Fossum (2002), 'Democracy through strong publics in the European Union?', *Journal of Common Market Studies,* 40, 3, 401–24.

Eriksen, E. O., J. E. Fossum, and A. J. Menendez (eds) (2005), *Developing a constitution for Europe* (London: Routledge).

European Commission (1970), 'Report to the Council and the Commission concerning the implementation in stages of economic and monetary union in the Community', *Bulletin of the European Communities,* Supplement 11, no. 19, Brussels.

European Commission (1973), *Report on regional problems in the enlarged Community,* Brussels.

European Commission (1989), *A guide to the reform of the Community's structural funds,* Luxembourg.

European Commission (1992a) *The internal market after 1992: meeting the challenge,* (the Sutherland report), SEC (92) 2044, Brussels, October.

European Commission (1992b), *An open and structured dialogue between the Commission and special interest groups,* SEC (92) 2272 final, Brussels.

European Commission (1997), *Agenda 2000,* COM (97) 2000, 15 July, Brussels

European Commission (1999), *The Commission and non-governmental organisations: building a stronger partnership* Commission discussion paper presented by President Prodi and Vice-President Kinnock, COM (2000) 11 final, 18 January, Brussels.

European Commission (2001a), *European governance: a white paper,* COM (2001) 428 final, Brussels, 25 July.

European Commission (2001b), *Proposal for a Council framework decision on combating terrorism,* COM (2001) 521 final, Brussels.

European Commission (2002a), *Communication from the Commission—towards a reinforced culture of consultation and dialogue—general principles and minimum standards for consultation of interested parties by the Commission,* COM (2002) 704 final, 11.12.2002, Brussels.

European Commission (2002b), *The mid-term review of the Common Agricultural Policy,* COM (2002) 294 final, Brussels.

European Commission (2002c), *A project for the European Union,* COM (2002) 394 final, Brussels

European Commission (2004), *Communication from the Commission and the European Parliament: area of freedom, security and justice. Assessment of the Tampere programme and future orientations,* Brussels.

European Commission (2005a), *Enlargement strategy paper*, COM (2005) 56, Brussels, 9 November.

European Commission (2005b), Eurobarometer 63, spring.

European Commission (2006a), *Green Paper: European Transparency Initiative*, COM (2006) 194 final, Brussels, 3 May.

European Commission (2006b), *General Budget of the European Union for the financial year 2006, The figures*, SEC (2006) 50, Brussels.

European Commission (2008a), *Communication from the Commission—European Transparency Initiative. A framework for relations with interest representatives (Register and Code of Conduct)*, COM (2008) 323 final, 27 May, Brussels.

European Commission (2008b), '*Education & training 2010'*: main policy initiatives and outputs in education and training since the year 2000 (Brussels: Commission of the European Communities).

European Commission (2008c), *Enlargement Strategy and Main Challenges 2008–2009*, COM (2008b) 674 (final), (Brussels: European Commission, 5 November).

European Commission (2008d), *Croatia 2008 Progress Report*, SEC(2008) 2694, Brussels: European Commission, 5 November.

European Commission (2008e), *Turkey 2008 Progress Report*, SEC(2008) 2699, Brussels: European Commission, 5 November.

European Commission (2008f), *Education & Training 2010': Main Policy Initiatives and Outputs in Education and Training Since the Year 2000* (Brussels: Commission of the European Communities): http://ec.europa.eu/education/policies/2010/doc/compendium05_en.pdf

European Council (2000), *Presidency conclusions*, Lisbon European Council, 23 and 24 March 2003, http://ue.eu.int/ueDocs/cms_Data/docs/pressData/en/ec/00100-r1.en0.htm

European Council (2001), *Declaration by the heads of state or government of the European Union and the president of the Commission: follow-up to the September 11 attacks and the fight against terrorism*, SN 4296/2/01 Rev 2, Gent.

European Council (2003), *Council conclusions on reference levels of European average performance in education and training (benchmarks) document*, 891/03 EDUC83, 7 May, http://ec.europa.eu/employment_social_gender_equality/docs/benchmark_council_8981_03.en.pdf

European Council (2004b), 'Treaty establishing a constitution for Europe', *Official Journal of the European Communities*, 47, C310, 16 December.

European Environment Agency (EEA) (2007), *Europe's environment—the fourth assessment* (Copenhagen: EEA).

European Environment Agency (EEA) (2008), *Greenhouse gas emission trends and projections in Europe 2008* (Copenhagen: EEA).

European Parliament (1997), *Note on the European Parliament's priorities for the IGC and the new Amsterdam treaty: report and initial evaluation of the results*, http://www.europarl.eu.int/topics/treaty/report/part1_en.htm

European Parliament (2001), *EP resolution on the Commission white paper on European governance*, A-5-0399/2001.

European Public Affairs Directory (2005), *The comprehensive guide to opinion-formers in the capital of Europe* (Brussels: Landmarks).

European Report (1997), *Single Market: slim achievements and prospects for legislative streamlining*, No. 27, Brussels, 28 November 1997, p. 1.

European Report (2005), *Single Market: member states improve EU Law implementation record*, (Brief Article), Brussels, 20 July 2005.

European Union (1997), 'Treaty on European Union', *Official Journal of the European Communities*, C340: 145–72.

Fabrini, S. (ed.) (2005), *Democracy and federalism in the European Union and the United States: exploring post-national governance* (London: Routledge).

Falkner, G. (1998*), EU social policy in the 1990s: towards a corporatist policy community* (London: Routledge).

Falkner, G. (2000a), 'The Council or the social partners? EC social policy between diplomacy and collective bargaining', *Journal of European Public Policy*, 7/5: 705–24.

Falkner, G. (2000b), 'EG-Sozialpolitik nach Verflechtungsfalle und Entscheidungslücke: Bewertungsmaßstäbe und Entwicklungstrends', *Politische Vierteljahresschrift*, 41/2: 279–301.

Falkner, G., M. Hartlapp, S. Leiber, and O. Treib (2004), 'Non-compliance with EU directives in the member states: opposition through the backdoor?', *West European Politics*, 27/1: 2–73.

Falkner, G., O. Treib, M. Hartlapp, and S. Leiber (2005), *Complying with Europe: EU minimum harmonisation and soft law in the member states* (Cambridge: Cambridge University Press).

Falkner, G., M. Hartlapp, S. Leiber, and O. Treib (2005), 'Die Kooperation der Sozialpartner im Arbeitsrecht: Ein europäischer Weg?', in R. Eising and B. Kohler-Koch (eds) *Interessenpolitik in Europa* (Baden-Baden: Nomos): 341–62.

Falkner, G., O. Treib, and E. Holzleithner (with E. Causse, P. Furtlehner, M. Schulze, and C. Wiedermann) (2008), *Compliance in the enlarged European Union: living rights or dead letters?* (Aldershot: Ashgate).

Farrell, D., S. Hix, M. Johnson, and R. Scully (2006), 'A survey of MEPs in the 2004–09 European Parliament', paper presented to the annual conference of the American Political Science Association, Philadelphia.

Farrell, D. and R. Scully (2007), *Representing Europe's citizens? Electoral institutions and the failure of parliamentary representation* (Oxford: Oxford University Press).

Flood, C. (2002), 'The challenge of Euroscepticism' in J. Gower (ed.) *The European Union Handbook* 2nd edn (London: Fitzroy Dearborn).

Foreign and Commonwealth Office (2005), 'Treaty establishing a constitution for Europe: commentary', Cm 6459, London, 26 January.

Forster, A. (1998), 'Britain and the negotiation of the Maastricht Treaty: a critique of liberal intergovernmentalism', *Journal of Common Market Studies*, 36/2: 347–68.

Forster, A. (2002a), *Euroscepticism in contemporary British politics* (London: Routledge).

Forster, A. (2002b), 'Britain and the negotiation of the Maastricht Treaty: a critique of liberal intergovernmentalism' *Journal of Common Market Studies*, 36/3: 347–68.

Forsyth, M. (1981), *Unions of states: the theory and practice of confederation* (Leicester: Leicester University Press).

Franklin, M. N., M. Marsh, and L. M. McLaren (1994), 'The European question: opposition to unification in the wake of Maastricht', *Journal of Common Market Studies* 32/4: 455–72.

Gabel, M. J. (1998), *Interests and integration: market liberalization, public opinion, and European Union* (Ann Arbor, MI: University of Michigan Press).

Galloway, D. (1999), 'Keynote article: Agenda 2000—packaging the deal', *Journal of Common Market Studies Annual Review*, 37s1: 9–35.

Galloway, D. (2001), *The Treaty of Nice and Beyond* (Sheffield: Sheffield Academic Press).

Garman, J. and L. Hilditch (1998), 'Behind the scenes: an examination of the informal processes at work in conciliation', *Journal of European Public Policy*, 5/2: 271–84.

Garrett, G. (1992), 'International cooperation and institutional choice: the European Community's internal market', *International Organization*, 46/2: 533–60.

Garrett, G. and G. Tsebelis (1996), 'An institutional critique of intergovernmentalism', *International Organization*, 50, 269–99.

Garzon I., (2007), *Reforming the common agricultural policy: history of a paradigm change* (Basingstoke: Palgrave).

Geddes, A. (2000), *Immigration and European integration: towards fortress Europe?* (Manchester: Manchester University Press).

Geddes, A. (2003), *The politics of migration and immigration in Europe* (London: Sage).

George. S. and I. Bache (2001), *Politics in the European Union* (Oxford: Oxford University Press).

Gilbert, M.F. (2003), *Surpassing realism: the politics of European integration since 1945* (Lanham: Rowman and Littlefield).

Goetschy, J. (2002), 'The European employment strategy, multi-level governance and policy coordination: past, present and future' in J. Zeitlin and D. Trubek (eds) *Governing work and welfare in a new economy: European and American experiments* (Oxford: Oxford University Press).

Gomez, R. and J. Peterson (2001), 'No one is in control: The EU's impossibly busy foreign ministers', *European Foreign Affairs Review*, 6/1: 53–74.

Gorges, M. J. (1996), *Euro-corporatism? Interest intermediation in the European Community* (London: University Press of America).

Grabbe, H. (2000), 'How does the EU measure when the CEECs are ready to join?' in C. Jenkins (ed.) *The Unification of Europe? An Analysis of EU Enlargement* (London: Centre for European Reform).

Grabbe, H. (2004), 'How the EU should help its neighbours', Policy Brief, Centre for European Reform, London.

Grabbe, H. (2006) *The EU's Transformative Power: Europeanization through Conditionality in Central and Eastern Europe* (Basingstoke: Palgrave Macmillan).

Grande, E. (1994), *Vom Nationalstaat zur europaischen Politikverflechtung. Expansion und Transformation moderner Staatlichkeit—undersucht am Beispiel der Forschungs—und Technologiepolitik* Habilitationschift, Universität Konstanz.

Green Party / *Comhaontas Glas* (2002) *Electoral Manifesto*: http://www.michaelpidgeon.com/manifestos/party/gp/Green%20Party%20GE%202002.pdf

Greenwood, J. (2007), *Interest representation in the European Union* (Basingstoke: Palgrave).

Green, A. (2005) Agricultural policy in Europe (manchesters: manchester university press).

Grin G. (2003), *Battle of the single European market: achievements and aconomic thought 1985–2000* (London: Kegan Paul).

Gros-Verheyde, N. (2007) 'Treaty of Lisbon: here is what changes', *Europolitique*, 3407, 7 November, www.europainfo.at/dokumente/Europolitics_3407_special_treaty

Grote, J. R. and A. Lang (2003), 'Europeanization and organizational change in national trade associations: an organizational ecology perspective' in K. Featherstone and C. M. Radaelli (eds) *The politics of Europeanization* (Oxford: Oxford University Press).

Grote, J. R., V. and Schneider (2006), 'Organizations and networks in a globalizing economy: British and German chemical interest associations', in W. Streeck, J.R. Grote, V. Schneider, and J. Visser (eds), *Governing Interests: Business Associations Facing Internationalization* (London: Routledge).

Guay, T. R. (1996), 'Integration and Europe's defence industry: A "reactive spillover" approach', *Political Studies Journal*, 24/3: 404–16.

Haas, E. B. (1958), *The uniting of Europe: political, social and economic forces, 1950–1957* (Stanford: Stanford University Press).

Haas, E. B. (1961), 'International integration. The European and the universal process', *International Organization*, 15/3: 366–92.

Haas, E. B. (1970), 'The study of regional integration: reflections on the joy and anguish of pretheorizing', *International Organization*, 24/4: 607–46.

Haas, E. B. (1971), 'The study of regional integration: reflections on the joy and anguish of pretheorizing', in L. N. Lindberg and A. Scheingold (eds) *Regional integration theories and research* (Harvard: Harvard University Press).

Haas, E. B. (1975), *The obsolescence of regional integration theory*, research studies 25, (Berkeley, Cal: Institute of International Studies)

Haas, E. B. (1976), 'Turbulent fields and the theory of regional integration', *International Organization*, 30/2: 173–212.

Haas, E. B. (2001), 'Does constructivism subsume neo-functionalism?' in T. Christiansen, K. E. Jørgensen and A. Wiener (eds) *The social construction of Europe* (London, Sage).

Haas, E. B. (2004), 'Introduction: institutionalism or constructivism?' in *The Uniting of Europe: political, social and economic forces, 1950-1957* 3rd edn (Notre Dame, IN: University of Notre Dame Press).

Haas, E. B. and P. C. Schmitter (1964), 'Economic and differential patterns of political integration: projections about unity in Latin America', *International Organization*, 18/3: 705–38.

Haigh, N. (ed.) (1992), *Manual of environmental policy* (London: Longman).

Hall, P. (1986), *Governing the economy: The politics of state intervention in Britain and France* (Cambridge: Polity Press)

Hall, P. and D. Soskice (2001), *Varieties of capitalism* (Oxford: Oxford University Press).

Hall, P. A. and R.C. R. Taylor (1996), 'Political Science and the three institutionalisms', *Political Studies* XLIV, 936–57.

Hamilton, D. and J. Quinlan (eds) (2005), *Deep integration: how transatlantic markets are leading to globalization* (Brussels: Centre for Transatlantic Relations/Centre for European Policy Studies).

Hartley, T. (2007), *The foundations of European Community law* 2nd edn (Oxford: Oxford University Press).

Harvey, B. (1993), 'Lobbying in Europe: the experience of voluntary organizations' in S. Mazey and J. R. Richardson (eds) *Lobbying in the European Community* (Oxford: Oxford University Press).

Haverland, M. (2000), 'National adaptation to European integration: the importance of institutional veto points', *Journal of Public Policy*, 20/1: 83–103.

Hayes-Renshaw, F. and H. Wallace (1997), *The Council of Ministers* (New York: St. Martin's Press).

Helfferich, B. F. and Kolb (2001), 'Multilevel action coordination in European contentious politics: the case of the European women's lobby' in D. Imig and S. Tarrow (eds), *Contentious Europeans. Protest and Politics in an Emerging Polity* (Lanham: Rowman & Littlefield Publishers).

Heinelt, H. (1996), 'Multilevel governance in the European Union and the structural funds', in H. Heinelt and R. Smith, *Policy Networks and European Structural Funds* (Aldershot: Avebury): 9–25.

Heinelt, H. (1998), 'Zivilgesellschaftliche Perspektiven einer demokratischen Transformation der Europäischen Union', *Zeitschift für Internationale Beziehungen*, 5/1: 79–107.

Heritier, A. (1996), 'The accommodation of diversity in European policy-making and its outcomes: regulatory policy as patchwork', *Journal of European Public Policy*, 3/2: 149–67.

Héritier, A. (2001), 'Differential Europe: national administrative responses to Community policy', in M. G. Cowles, J. A. Caporaso, and T. Risse (eds) *Transforming Europe: Europeanization and domestic change* (Ithaca, NY: Cornell University Press): 44–59.

Héritier, A. (2002a), 'New modes of governance in Europe: policy making without legislating?' in A. Heritier (ed.) *Common Goods: Reinventing European and International Governance* (Boulder, CO: Rowman and Littlefield): 185–206.

Héritier, A. (2002b), 'The accommodation of diversity in European policy-making and its outcomes' in A. Jordan (ed.) *Environmental Policy in the European Union*, (London: Earthscan): 180–97.

Héritier, A., D. Kerwer, C. Knill, D. Lehmkuhl, M. Teutsch, and A.-C. Douillet (2001), *Differential Europe: the European Union impact on national policymaking* (Lanham, MD: Rowman and Littlefield).

Héritier, A., C. Knill, and S. Mingers (1996), *Ringing the changes in Europe: regulatory competition and the redefinition of the state: Britain, France, Germany* (Berlin, New York: De Gruyter).

Hey, C. and U. Brendle (1994), *Unweltverbände und EG: Strategien, politische Kulturen und Organisationformen* (Opladen: Westdeutscher Verlag).

Hildebrand, P. M. (2005), 'The European Community's environmental policy, 1957 to 1992' in A. Jordan (ed.) *Environmental Policy in the European Union* 2nd edn (London: Earthscan): 19–41.

Hill C. and M. Smith (eds) (2005), *International relations and the European Union* (Oxford: Oxford University Press).

Hingel, A. J. (2001), 'Education policies and European governance—contribution to the interservice groups on European governance', *European Journal for Education Law and Policy*, 5, 1–2, 7–16.

Hirst, P. and G. Thompson (1996), *Globalization in question: the international economy and the possibilities of governance* (Cambridge: Polity Press).

Hix, S. (1994), 'The study of the European Union: the challenge to comparative politics', *West European Politics*, 17/1: 1–30.

Hix, S. (1999), *The political system of the European Union* (Basingstoke: Macmillan).

Hix, S. (2002), 'Parliamentary behaviour with two principals: preferences, parties and voting in the European Parliament', *American Journal of Political Science*, 46/3: 688–98.

Hix, S. (2005), *The political system of the European Union* (Basingstoke: Palgrave).

Hix, S. and R. Scully (eds) (2003), *The European Parliament at fifty: special issue of the Journal of Common Market Studies*, 41/2.

Hix, S., A. Noury, and G. Roland (2006), *Democracy in the European Parliament* (Cambridge: Cambridge University Press).

Hoffmann, S. (1966), 'Obstinate or obsolete? The fate of the nation-state and the case of western Europe', *Daedalus*, 95/3: 862–915.

Hoffmann, S. (1989), 'The European Community and 1992', *Foreign Affairs*, 68/4: 27–47.

Hoffmann, S. (1995), 'Introduction' in S. Hoffmann (ed.) *The European Sisyphus: essays on Europe 1964–94* (Oxford: Westview).

Hogan, M. J. (1987), *The Marshall Plan, Britain and the Reconstruction of Western Europe, 1947–1952* (Cambridge: Cambridge University Press).

Holland, M. (2002), *The European Union and the third world* (Basingstoke: Palgrave).

Hooghe, L. (ed.) (1996a) *Cohesion policy and European integration: building multi-level governance* (Oxford: Oxford University Press).

Hooghe, L. (1996b), 'Introduction: reconciling EU-wide policy and national diversity', in L. Hooghe, *Cohesion policy and European integration: building multi-level governance* (Oxford: Oxford University Press): 1–24.

Hooghe, L. (2001), *The European Commission and the integration of Europe: images of governance* (Cambridge: Cambridge University Press).

Hooghe, L. (2002), 'The mobilisation of territorial interests and multilevel governance', in R. Balme, D. Chabanet, and V. Wright (eds) *L'action collective en Europe* (Paris: Presses de Sciences Po): 347–74.

Hooghe, L. and G. Marks (1997), 'The making of a polity: the struggle over European integration', *European integration online Papers* (EIoP), 1/4, http://eiop.or.at/eiop/texte/1997-004a.htm.

Hooghe, L. and G. Marks (2001), *Multi-level governance and European integration* (Boulder, CO: Rowman and Littlefield).

Hooghe, L. and G. Marks (2004), 'Does identity or economic rationality drive public opinion on European integration?', *PS*, 37/3: 415–20

Hooghe, L. and G. Marks (2006), 'The neo-functionalists were (almost) right: politicization and European integration' in C. Crouch and W. Streeck *The diversity of democracy: corporatism, social order and political conflict* (Cheltenham: Edward Elgar): 205–21.

Hooghe, L. and G. Marks (eds) (2007), 'Sources of euroscepticism', special issue of *Acta Politica*, 42/2–3: 119–27.

Horspool, M. and M. Humphreys (2008), *European Union law* (Oxford: Oxford University Press).

Hoskyns, C. (1996), *Integrating gender* (London: Verso).

Hoskyns, C. and M. Newman (eds) (2000), *Democratizing the European Union* (Manchester: Manchester University Press).

Hosli, M. O. (2005), *The euro: a concise introduction to European monetary integration* (Boulder: Lynne Rienner).

Hovden, E. (2002), 'The legal basis of European Union policy: the case of environmental policy', *Environment and Planning C*, 20/4: 535–53.

Howarth, J. (2000), 'Britain, NATO, CESDP: fixed strategies, changing tactics', *European Foreign Affairs Review*, 16/3: 1–2.

Howarth, J. (2007), *Security and defence policy in the European Union* (Palgrave: Basingstoke).

Hudson, J. and S. Lowe (2004), *Understanding the policy process* (Bristol: Policy Press)

Hug, S. and T. König (2002), 'In view of ratification: governmental preferences and domestic constraints at the Amsterdam intergovernmental conference', *International Organization*, 56/2: 447–76.

Hurrell, A. and A. Menon (1996), 'Politics like any other? Comparative Politics, International Relations and the Study of the EC', *West European Politics*, 19, 2, 386–402.

Imig, D. and S. Tarrow (eds) (2001), *Contentious Europeans: protest and politics in an emerging polity* (Lanham: Rowman and Littlefield).

Inglehart, R. (1970), 'Cognitive mobilization and European identity', *Comparative Politics*, 3/1: 45–70.

Jabko N. (2006), *Playing the market: a political strategy for uniting Europe, 1985–2005* (Ithaca, NJ: Cornell University Press).

Jachtenfuchs, M. (1997), 'Conceptualizing European governance' in K. E. Jørgensen (ed.) *Reflective Approaches to European Governance* (Basingstoke: Macmillan).

Jachtenfuchs, M. (2001), 'The Governance Approach to European Integration', *Journal of Common Market Studies*, 39, 2.

Jacobs, F., R. Corbett, and M. Shackleton (2005), *The European Parliament* 5th edn (London: John Harper).

Jacoby, W. (2004), *The Enlargement of the EU and NATO: Ordering from the Menu in Central Europe* (Cambridge: Cambridge University Press).

Jensen, C. S. (2000), 'Neofunctionalist theories and the development of European social and labour market policy', *Journal of Common Market Studies*, 38/1: 71–92.

Joerges, C. and J. Neyer (1997), 'From intergovernmental bargaining to deliberative political processes: the constitutionalisation of comitology', *European Law Journal*, 3/3: 273–99.

Joergensen, K. E., M. Pollack, and B. Rosamond (eds) (2007), *Sage Handbook of European Union politics* (London: Sage).

Jones, A. and J. Clarke (2001), *The modalities of European Union governance: new institutionalist explanations of agri-environmental policy* (Oxford: Oxford University Press).

Jones, S. (2007), *The rise of European security cooperation* (Cambridge University Press: Cambridge).

Jordan, A. (2002), *The Europeanization of British Environmental Policy* (Basingstoke: Palgrave).

Jordan, A. (2005), 'The implementation of EU environmental policy' in A. Jordan (ed.) *Environmental policy in the European Union*, 2nd edn (London: Earthscan): 1–15.

Jordan, A. and J. Fairbrass (2005), 'European Union environmental policy after the Nice summit' in A. Jordan (ed.) *Environmental policy in the European Union* 2nd edn (London: Earthscan): 42–6.

Jordan, A. and D. Liefferink (eds) (2004), *Environmental policy on Europe: the Europeanization of national environmental policy* (London: Routledge).

Jordan, A. and A. Schout (2006), *The coordination of the European Union* (Oxford: Oxford University Press).

Jordan, A., R. Wurzel, A. Zito, and L. Brückner (2005), 'European governance and the transfer of "new" environmental policy instruments in the EU', in A. Jordan (ed.) *Environmental policy in the European Union* 2nd edn (London: Earthscan): 317–35.

Jordan, A. J., D. Huitema, H. van Asselt, T. Rayner, and F. Berkhout (eds) (2009), *Climate change policy in the European Union* (Cambridge: Cambridge University Press).

Kagan, R. (2004), *Paradise and power: America and Europe in the new world order* (London: Atlantic Books).

Kallas, S. (2005), *The need for a European transparency initiative*, SPEECH/05/130, the European Foundation for Management, Nottingham Business School, Nottingham, 3 March.

Kassim, H. (1994), 'Policy networks, networks and the European Union: a sceptical view', *West European Politics*, 17, 4, 15–27.

Karp J. A., S. A. Banducci, and S. Bowler (2003), 'To know it is to love it? Satisfaction with democracy in the European Union', *Comparative Political Studies*, 36/3: 271–92.

Katzenstein, P. J. (1996), *The Culture of National Security: Norms and Identity in World Politics* (Boulder: Westview Press).

Katzenstein, P. J. (ed.) (1997), *Tamed power: Germany in Europe* (Ithaca: Cornell University Press).

Katzenstein, P., R. O. Keohane, and S. Krasner (1998), The sovereignty of global society', *World Politics*, 51, 1–35.

Keane, R. (2004), 'The Solana process in Serbia and Montenegro: coherence in EU foreign policy', *International Peacekeeping*, 11/3: 491–507

Keating, M. (1998), *The new regionalism in Western Europe: territorial restructuring and political change* (Cheltenham: Edward Elgar).

Keating, M. and L. Hooghe (2006), 'Bypassing the nation state? Regions and the EU Policy Process' in J. Richardson (ed) *European Union: Power and Policymaking* (London: Routledge).

Keohane, R. O. (1988), 'International institutions: two approaches', *International Studies Quarterly*, 32/4: 379–96.

Keohane, R. O. (1989), *International institutions and state power: essays in international relations theory* (Boulder, CO: Westview).

Keohane, R. O. and S. Hoffmann (eds) (1991), *The new European Community: decision making and institutional change* (Boulder, CO: Westview).

Keohane, R. O. and J. Nye (1975), 'International interdependence and integration', in F. Greenstein and N. Polsby (eds) *Handbook of political science* (Andover, MA: Addison-Wesley).

Keohane, R. O. and J. Nye (1976), *Power and interdependence: world politics in transition* (Boston:, MA: Little, Brown)

Kerwer, D. and M. Teutsch (2001), 'Elusive Europeanisation: liberalising road haulage in the European Union', *Journal of European Public Policy*, 8/1: 124–43.

Knill, C. (2001), *The Europeanisation of national administrations: patterns of institutional change and persistence* (Cambridge: Cambridge University Press).

Knill, C. and D. Liefferink (2007), *Environmental politics in the European Union* (Manchester: Manchester University Press).

Kohler-Koch, B. (1997), 'Organized interests in the EC and the European Parliament', *European integration online papers*, 1/9, http://eiop.or.at/eiop/_texte/1997-009.htm.

Kohler-Koch, B. (1999), 'The evolution and transformation of European governance' in B. Kohler-Koch and R. Eising (eds) *The transformation of governance in the European Union* (London: Routledge).

Kohler-Koch, B. and R. Eising (eds) (1999), *The transformation of governance in the European Union* (London: Routledge).

Kopecky, P. and C. Mudde (2002), 'Two sides of Euroscepticism: party positions on European integration in East Central Europe', *European Union Politics* 3, 3, 297–326.

Kreppel, A. (2002), *The European Parliament and the supranational party system: a study in institutional development* (Cambridge: Cambridge University Press).

Kröger, S. (2008), 'The open method of coordination: nine years later and so little wiser'. Paper presented at the workshop 'The OMC within the Lisbon Strategy: empirical assessments and theoretical implications'. Institute for European Integration Research, 28–29 November, Vienna.

Kröger, S. (2009), 'The open method of coordination: part of the problem or part of the solution?' Paper presented at the workshop on 'Nouveaux' modes de gouvernance et action publique européenne of the Section d'études européennes de l'AFSP, PACTE/IEP de Grenoble, 23 January, Grenoble.

Kröger, S. (ed.) (2009) 'What We Have Learnt: Advances, Pitfalls and Remaining Questions of OMC Research', *European integration online papers*, 1/13, Special Issue, http://www.eiop.or.at

Kubicek, P. J. (2003), 'International norms, the European Union, and democratization: Tentative theory and evidence' in P. J. Kubicek (ed) *The European Union and Democratization* (London: Routledge) pp. 1–29.

Kurpas, S., C. Grøn and P. M. Kaczynski (2008), 'The European Commission after Enlargement: Does more Add up to less?', CEPS Special Report (Brussels: Centre for European Policy Studies).

Ladrech, R. (1994), 'Europeanization of domestic politics and institutions: the case of France', *Journal of Common Market Studies*, 32/1: 69–88.

Laffan, B. and C. Shaw (2006), 'Classifying and mapping OMC in different policy areas' report for NEWGOV, 02/D09, www.eu-newgov.org/database/DELIV/D02D09_Classifying_and_Mapping_OMC.pdf

Lasswell, H. (1950), *Politics: Who gets what, when and how* (New York: Smith).

Laurent, P. H. (1970), 'Paul-Henri Spaak and the diplomatic origins of the common market, 1955–56', *Political Science Quarterly*, 85/3: 373–96.

Lavdas, K. A. (2000), *Mixed government and fragmentation in the European polity: a republican interpretation*, UWE papers in politics, 6 February.

Lavdas, K. A. and D. Chryssochoou (2007), 'A republic of Europeans: civic unity in polycultural diversity in L. Bekermans et al (eds) *Intercultural dialogue and citizenship* (Venice: Marsello).

Lavenex, S. (2001), 'The Europeanization of refugee policy: normative challenges and institutional legacies', *Journal of Common Market Studies*, 39/5: 825–850.

Lavenex, S. and W. Wallace (2005), 'Justice and home affairs: towards a "European public order"', in H. Wallace, W. Wallace and M. Pollack (eds) *Policy-making in the European Union* 5th edn (Oxford: Oxford University Press).

Lavenex, S. and E. M. Uçarer (eds) (2002), *Migration and the externalities of European integration* (Lanham, MD: Lexington Books).

Le Galès, P. and C. Lequesne (1998), *Regions in Europe* (London: Routledge).

Lehmkuhl, D. (2000), *The importance of small differences: the impact of European integration on road haulage associations in Germany and the Netherlands* (Amsterdam: Thela Thesis).

Leinen J. and I. Méndez de Vigo (2001), 'Report on the Laeken European Council and the future of the Union', European Parliament, A5-0368/2001, Brussels, 23 October.

Lenschow, A. (2005), 'Environmental policy', in H. Wallace, W. Wallace and M. Pollack (eds) *Policy-making in the European Union* 5th edn (Oxford: Oxford University Press): 305–72.

Lenschow, A. (2006), 'Environmental policy in the EU', in K. E. Jorgensen, M. A. Pollack, and B. J. Rosamond (eds) *Handbook of European Union politics* (London: Sage): 413–31.

Leonardi, R. (1995), *Convergence, cohesion, and integration in the European Union* (London: Macmillan).

Lewis, J. (1998), 'Is the 'hard bargaining' image of the Council misleading? The committee of permanent representatives and the local elections directive', *Journal of Common Market Studies*, 36/4: 479–504.

Lewis, J. (2003), 'Institutional environments and everyday EU decision making: rationalist or constructivist?' *Comparative Political Studies*, 36/1: 97–124.

Lewis, J. (2005a) 'Is the Council becoming an upper house?' in C. Parsons and N. Jabko (eds) *With US or against US? The state of the European Union*, volume 7 (Oxford: Oxford University Press).

Lewis, J. (2005b), 'The janus face of Brussels: socialization and everyday decision making in the European Union', *International Organization*, 59/4: 937–71.

Liberatore, A. (1993), 'Problems of transnational policy making: environmental policy in the EC', *European Journal of Political Research*, 19/2–3: 281–305.

Liebfried, S. and P. Pierson (eds) (1995), 'Semisovereign welfare states: social policy in a multi-tiered Europe' in S. Liebfried and P. Pierson (eds), *European Social Policy: Between Fragmentation and Integration* (Washington: Brookings Institution).

Liebfried, S. and P. Pierson (2000), 'Social policy: left to court and markets?' in H. Wallace and W. Wallace (eds) *Policy-making in the European Union* 4th edn (Oxford: Oxford University Press).

Liefferink, D., and M. S. Andersen (1998), 'Strategies of the 'green' member states in EU environmental policy-making', *Journal of European Public Policy*, 5/2: 254–70.

Liefferink, D., and A. Jordan (2004), 'Measuring Europeanization of policy convergence: national baseline conditions', in A. Jordan and D. Liefferink (eds) *Environmental policy in Europe: the Europeanization of national environmental policy* (London: Routledge): 32–46.

Lindberg, L. N. (1963), *The political dynamics of European economic integration* (Stanford: Stanford University Press).

Lindberg, L. N. (1971), 'Political integration as a multidimensional phenomenon requiring multivariate measurement' in L. N. Lindberg and S. A. Scheingold (eds) *Regional integration: theory and research* (Harvard: Harvard University Press).

Lindberg, L. N. and S. A. Scheingold (1970), *Europe's would-be polity: patterns of change in the European Community* (New Jersey: Prentice-Hall).

Lindberg, L. N. and S. A. Scheingold (eds) (1971), *Regional integration: theory and research* (Harvard: Harvard University Press).

Lodge, J. E. (1998), 'Intergovernmental conferences and European integration: negotiating the Amsterdam Treaty', *International Negotiation. A Journal of Theory and Practice*, 3/3: 345–62.

Lodge, M. (2006), 'The Europeanization of governance: top down, bottom up or both?' in G. F. Schuppert (ed.) *The Europeanisation of governance* (Baden-Baden: Nomos): 60–76.

Lord, C. (1998), *Democracy in the European Union* (Sheffield: Sheffield Academic Press).

Lord, C. (2001), 'Assessing democracy in a contested polity', *Journal of Common Market Studies* 39, 4 641–61.

Loughlin, J. (2004), *Subnational Democracy in the European Union: Challenges and Opportunities* (Oxford: Oxford University Press).

Lynch, P. N., N. W. Neuwahl, and N. Rees (eds) (2000), *Reforming the European Union from Maastricht to Amsterdam* (London: Longman).

MacCormick, N. (1997), 'Democracy, subsidiarity and citizenship in the "European commonwealth"', *Law and Philosophy*, 16/4: 331–56.

Mahoney, C. (2008), *Brussels versus the Beltway: advocacy in the United States and the European Union* (Washington DC: Georgetown University Press).

Majone, G. (1994), 'The rise of the regulatory state in Europe', *West European Politics*, 17/3: 77–101.

Majone G. (1995), 'The development of social regulation in the European Community: policy externalities, transaction costs, motivational factors', EUI Working Paper, Florence.

Majone, G. (1996), *Regulating Europe* (London: Routledge).

Majone, G. (2005), *Dilemmas of European Integration: the Ambiguities and the Pitfalls of Integration by Stealth* (Oxford: Oxford University Press).

Mandelkern Group (2001), Final Report, Brussels, 13 November.

March, J. G., and J. P. Olsen (1989), *Rediscovering institutions: the organizational basics of politics* (New York: Free Press).

March, J. G., and J. P. Olsen (1998), 'The institutional dynamics of international political orders', *International Organization*, 52/4: 943–69.

Marks, G. (1992), 'Structural policy in the European Community' in A. Sbragia (ed.) *Europolitics: institutions and policy-making in the 'new' European Community*, (Washington DC: Brookings Institute).

Marks, G., and Hooghe, L. (2001), *Multi-level governance and European integration* (Lanham: Rowman & Littlefield).

Marks, G., and McAdam, D. (1999), 'On the relationship of political opportunities to the forms of collective action: the case of the European Union', in D. Della Porta, H. Kriesi, and D. Rucht (eds), *Social movements in a globalizing world* (Basingstoke: Macmillan): 97–111.

Marks, G., F. Nielsen, J. Salk and L. Ray (1996), 'Competencies, cracks, and conflicts: regional mobilization in the European Union', *Comparative Political Studies*, 29/2: 164–93.

Marshall, T. H. (1975), *Social policy* (London: Hutchinson).

Mattli, W. (2005), 'Ernst Haas's evolving thinking on comparative regional integration: of virtues and infelicities', *Journal of European Public Policy*, 12/2: 327–47.

Mazey, S. (1998), 'The European Union and women's rights: from the Europeanisation of national agendas to the nationalisation of a European agenda?', in D. Hine and H. Kassim (eds) *Beyond the market: the EU and national social policy* (London: Routledge).

Mazey, S. and J. R. Richardson (2002), 'Pluralisme ouvert ou restreint? Les groupes d'interêt dans l'Union européenne', in R. Balme, D. Chabernet, and V. Wright (eds) *L'action collective en Europe/Collective Action in Europe* (Paris: Presses de Science Po): 123–61.

McAleavy, P. (1993), 'The politics of the European regional development policy: additionality in the Scottish coalfields', *Regional Politics and Policy*, 3/2: 88–107.

McCormick, J. (1999), *Understanding the European Union* (Basingstoke: Macmillan).

McCormick, J. (2002), *Understanding the European Union* 2nd edn (Basingstoke: Palgrave).

McGowan, L. (2007), 'Theorising European integration: revisiting neofunctionalism and testing its suitability explaining the development of EC competition policy', *European Integration online Papers* (EIoP), 11/3: 1–17.

McGuire, S. and M. Smith (2008), *The European Union and the United States: competition and convergence in the global arena* (Basingstoke: Palgrave).

McLaren, L. N. (2006), *Identity, interests and attitudes to European integration* (Basingstoke: Palgrave).

Mearsheimer J. J. (1990), 'Back to the future: instability in Europe after the Cold War', *International Security*, 15/1: 5–56.

Messerlin, P. (2001), *Measuring the costs of protection in Europe* (Washington: IIE).

Metcalfe, L. (1996), 'Building capacities for integration: the future role of the Commission', *Eipascope*, no. 2: 2–8.

Milward, A. S. (1999), *The European Rescue of the Nation State* (London: Routledge).

Mitrany, D. (1943), *A working peace system: an argument for the functional development of international organization* (London: Royal Institute of International Affairs).

Molitor, B. et al (1995), *Report of the group of independent experts on legislation and administrative simplification*, COM (95) 288, Brussels, 21 May.

Monar, J. (2001), 'The dynamics of justice and home affairs: laboratories, driving factors and costs', *Journal of Common Market Studies*, 39/4: 747–64.

Monar, J. and W. Wessels (eds) (2001), *The European Union after the Treaty of Amsterdam* (London: Continuum).

Moravcsik, A. (1991), 'Negotiating the single European act: national interests and conventional statecraft in the European Community', *International Organization*, 45/1: 19–56.

Moravcsik, A. (1993), 'Preferences and power in the European Community: a liberal intergovernmentalist approach', *Journal of Common Market Studies*, 34/4: 473–524.

Moravcsik, A. (1997), 'Taking preferences seriously: a liberal theory of international politics', *International Organization*, 51/4: 513–53.

Moravcsik, A. (1998), *The choice for Europe: social purpose and state power from Messina to Maastricht* (London: UCL Press).

Moravcsik, A. (2001), 'A constructivist research programme for EU studies', *European Union Politics* 2/2: 219–49

Moravcsik, A. (2005), 'The European constitutional compromise and the neofunctionalist legacy', *Journal of European Public Policy*, 12/2: 349–86.

Moravcsik A. and M. A. Vachudová (2003), 'National interests, state power and EU enlargement', *East European Politics and Societies*, 17, 1, 42–57.

Morgenthau, H. (1985), *Politics among nations: the struggle for power and peace* 6th edn (New York: Knopf).

Moyer, W. and T. Josling, *Agricultural policy reform: policies and process in the EU and US in the '90s* (London: Ashgate).

Nanz, P. (2006), *Europolis: constitutional patriotism beyond the nation-state* (Manchester: Manchester University Press).

Naurin, D. and H. Wallace (eds) (2008), *Unveiling the Council of the European Union: games governments play in Brussels* (London: Palgrave).

Niemann, A. (2006), *Explaining decisions in the European Union* (Cambridge: Cambridge University Press).

Neunreither, K. (2000), 'Political representation in the European Union: a common whole, various wholes, or just a hole?' in K. Neunreither and A. Weiner (eds) *European integration after Amsterdam: institutional dynamics and prospects for democracy* (Oxford: Oxford University Press).

Newman, M. (1996), *Democracy, sovereignty and the European Union* (London: Hurst).

Newman, M. (2001), 'Democracy and accountability in the EU' in J. Richardson (ed.) *European Union: power and policy making* (London: Routledge).

Newman, A. L. (2008), 'Building transnational civil liberties: transgovernmental entrepreneurs and the European data privacy directive', *International Organization*, 62/1: 103–30

Nicolson F. and R. East (1987), *From Six to Twelve: The Enlargement of the European Communities* (Harlow: Longman).

Nicolaïdis, K. and S. Schmidt (2007), 'Mutual recognition on trial: The long road to services liberalization', *Journal of European Public Policy*, 14(5): 717–34.

Niedermayer, O. and R. Sinnott (1995), 'Democratic legitimacy and the European Parliament' in O. Niedermayer and R. Sinnott (eds) *Public opinion and institutionalized governance: beliefs in government*, vol. 2 (Oxford: Oxford University Press).

Noël, E. (1967), 'The committee of permanent representatives', *Journal of Common Market Studies*, 5/3: 219–51.

Nugent, N. (1999), *The government and politics of the European Union* 4th edn (Basingstoke: Macmillan).

Nutall, S. (1992), *European Political Co-operation* (Oxford: Oxford University Press).

Nye, J. S. (1971), 'Comparing common markets: a revised neo-functionalist model', in L. N. Lindberg and S. A. Scheingold (eds) *Regional integration: theory and research* (Harvard: Harvard University Press).

Obermaier, A. J. (2008), 'The national judiciary: sword of European Court of Justice rulings: the example of the Kohll/Decker jurisprudence', *European Law Journal*, 14/6: 735–52.

Obradovic, D. (2005), 'Civil society and the social dialogue in European governance' NEWGOV (Integrated projects on new modes of governance), working paper series, http://www.eu-newgov.org/public/EUROGOV.asp

O'Brennan, J. (2006), *The eastern enlargement of the European Union* (London: Routledge).

Olsen, J. P. (1996), 'Europeanization and nation-state dynamics', in S. Gustavsson and L. Lewin (eds), *The future of the nation-state* (London: Routledge): 245–85.

Olsen, J. P. (2002), 'The many faces of Europeanisation', *Journal of Common Market Studies*, 40/5: 921–52.

O'Neill, M. (1996), *The politics of European integration. a reader* (London: Routledge).

Padoa-Schioppa, T., M. Emerson, M. King, J. C. Milleron, J. H.P. Paelinck, L. D. Papademos, A. Pastor, and F. W. Scharpf (1987), *Efficiency, stability, equity* (Oxford: Oxford University Press).

Pallemaerts, M. (ed.) (2008), *Manual of European Environmental Policy: The EU & Britain* (Leeds: Maney Publishing).

Panke, D. (2006), 'More arguing than bargaining? The institutional designs of the European convention and intergovernmental conferences compared', *Journal of European Integration*, 28/4: 357–79.

Pearce, J. and J. Sutton (1983), *Protection and industrial policy in Europe* (London: Routledge).

Peers, S. 'Legislative Updates', *European Journal of Migration and Law*—various issues.

Pelkmans, J. (1984), *Market Integration in the European Community—Studies in Industrial Organization v. 5* (Kluwer Academic Publishers)

Pelkmans, J. (1987), 'The new approach to technical harmonisation and standardization', *Journal of Common Market Studies*, 25: 249–69.

Pelkmans, J. (1997), *European integration, methods and economic analysis* (London: Longman).

Pelkmans, J. and A. Winters (1988), *Europe's domestic market* (London: Royal Institute of International Affairs).

Pelkmans, J., D. Hanf, and M. Chang (2008), *The EU internal market in comparative perspective, economic, political and legal analyses*, vol. 8 (Berlin: Peter Lang Publishers).

Pentland, C. (1973), *International theory and European integration* (New York: Free Press).

Pérez-Solórzano Borragán, N. (2004) 'EU accession and interest politics in Central and Eastern Europe', *Perspectives on European Politics and Society*, 5, 2, 243–72,

Peterson, J. (2004), 'Keynote article: Europe, America, Iraq: worst ever, ever worsening?', *Journal of Common Market Studies*, 42s1: 9–26.

Peterson, J. (1995), 'Decision Making in the European Union: towards a framework for analysis', *Journal of European Public Policy*, 2/1: 69–93.

Peterson, J. and E. Bomberg (1999), *Decision-making in the European Union* (Basingstoke: Macmillan).

Pettit, P. (1997), *Republicanism: a theory of freedom and government* (Oxford: Oxford University Press).

Philip, A. and M. Porter (1997), 'Business alliances, network construction and agenda definition: recent development in lobbying activities in Brussels and Strasbourg', paper presented at the fifth biennial conference of the European Union Studies Association (EUSA), 29 May to 1 June.

Pierson, P. (1998), 'The path to European integration: a historical institutionalist analysis', in W. Sandholtz and A. Stone Sweet (eds) *European integration and supranational governance* (Oxford: Oxford University Press).

Piris, J.-C. (2000), 'Does the European Union have a constitution? Does it need one?' Harvard Jean Monnet Working Paper, No. 5/00, Harvard Law School.

Poidevin, R. and D. Spierenberg (1994), *History of the High Authority of the European Coal and Steel Community* (London: Weidenfeld and Nicolson).

Pollack, M. A. (1997a), 'Delegation, agency and agenda-setting in the European Community', *International Organization*, 51/1: 99–134.

Pollack, M. A. (1997b), 'Representing diffuse interests in the European Union', *Journal of European Public Policy*, 4/4: 572–90.

Pollack, M. A. (2002), *The engines of integration: delegation, agencies and agenda-setting in the EU* (Oxford: Oxford University Press).

Polanyi, K. (1957), *The Great Transformation* (Boston: Beacon Press).

Pridham, G. F. M. (2007) 'Change and continuity in the European Union's political conditionality: aims, approach, and priorities', *Democratization*, 14, 3, 446–71.

Pridham, G. F. M. (2008) 'The EU's political conditionality and post-accession tendencies: comparisons from Slovakia and Latvia', *Journal of Common Market Studies*, 46, 2, 365–87.

Puchala, D. (1971), *International politics today* (New York: Dodd Mead).

Putnam, R. (1988), 'Diplomacy and domestic politics: the logic of two-level games', *International Organization*, 42/3: 427–60.

Radaelli, C. M. (1998), *Governing European regulation: the challenge ahead*, RSC policy paper no. 98/3, European University Institute, Florence.

Radaelli, C. M. (2003), 'The Europeanization of public policy' in K. Featherstone and C. M. Radaelli (eds) *The politics of Europeanization* (Oxford: Oxford University Press).

Radaelli, C. M. (2003), 'The open method of coordination: a new governance architecture for the European Union?' SIEPS Report 2003/1, Swedish Institute for European Policy Studies, Stockholm.

Rasmussen H. (2007), 'Present and future European judicial problems after enlargement and the post-2005 ideological revolt', *Common Market Law Review*, 44/6: 1661–87.

Ray, L. (2007), 'Mainstream Euroskepticism: trend or oxymoron?', *Acta Politica*, 42, 153–72.

Rehn, O. (2009) *The Rationale of Enlargement*, available at http://ec.europa.eu/commission_barroso/rehn/work/index_en.htm

Rhodes, M. (1995), 'A regulatory conundrum: industrial relations and the "social dimension"' in S. Leibfried and P. Pierson (eds), *Fragmented social policy: the European Union's social dimension in comparative perspective* (Washington DC: Brookings Institution).

Rhodes, M. and B. van Apeldoorn (1998), 'Capital unbound? The transformation of European corporate governance', *Journal of European Public Policy*, 5/3: 407–28.

Richardson, J. (2001), 'Policy-making in the EU: interests, ideas and garbage can of primaeval soup' in J. Richardson (ed.), *European Union. Power and Policy-making* (London: Routledge).

Risse-Kappen, T. (1996), 'Exploring the nature of the beast: international relations theory and comparative policy analysis meet the European Union', *Journal of Common Market Studies*, 34/1: 54–81.

Risse, T. (2000), '"Let's argue!" Communicative action in international relations', *International Organization*, 54/1: 1–39.

Risse, T. (2004), 'Social constructivism' in A. Wiener and T. Diez (eds), *European integration theory* (Oxford: Oxford University Press).

Risse, T. (2005), 'Nationalism, European identity and the puzzles of European integration', *Journal of European Public Policy*, 12/2: 291–309.

Risse, T., M. G. Cowles, and J. A. Caporaso (2001), 'Europeanization and domestic change: introduction', in M. G. Cowles, J. A. Caporaso, and T. Risse (eds) *Transforming Europe: Europeanization and domestic change* (Ithaca: Cornell University Press): 1–20.

Rittberger, B. (2005), *Building Europe's parliament: democratic representation beyond the nation state* (Oxford: Oxford University Press).

Rohrschneider, R. (2002), 'The democracy deficit and mass support for an EU-wide government', *American Journal of Political Science*, 46/2: 463–75.

Rosamond, B. (2000), *Theories of European integration* (Basingstoke: Palgrave).

Rosamond, B. (2005), 'The uniting of Europe and the foundations of EU studies: revisiting the neofunctionalism of Ernst B. Haas', *Journal of European Public Policy*, 12/2: 237–54.

Rosenau, J. N. and M. Durfee (1995), *Thinking theory thoroughly: coherent approaches in an incoherent world* (Boulder, CO: Westview).

Ross, G. (1995), 'Assessing the Delors era and social policy', in S. Leibfried and P. Pierson (eds), *European social policy: between fragmentation and integration* (Washington DC: Brookings Institution).

Ruggie, J. G. (1998), *Constructing the World Polity: essays on international institutionalisation* (London: Routledge).

Ruggie, J. G., P. J. Katzenstein, R. O. Keohane, and P. C. Schmitter (2005), 'Transformation in world politics: the intellectual contribution of Ernst B. Haas', *Annual Review of Political Science*, 8: 271–96.

Rutten, M. (2002), 'From Saint-Malo to Nice: European defence—core documents', Institute for Security Studies, Paris.

Sabatier, P. A. and H. C. Jenkins-Smith (eds) (1993), *Policy change and learning: an advocacy coalition approach* (Boulder, CO: Westview).

Sandholtz, W. (1998), 'The emergence of a supranational telecommunications regime' in W. Sandholtz and A. Stone Sweet (eds) *European integration and supranational governance* (Oxford: Oxford University Press).

Sandholtz, W. and J. Zysman (1989), '1992: recasting the European bargain', *World Politics*, 42: 95–128.

Sbragia, A. M. (1993), 'EC environmental policy' in A. W. Cafruny and G. G. Rosenthal (eds) *The state of the European Community* (Boulder, CO: Lynne Rienner): 337–52.

Sbragia, A. M. (1996), 'Environmental policy: the "push–pull" of policy-making', in H. Wallace and W. Wallace (eds) *Policy-making in the European Union* 3rd edn (Oxford: Oxford University Press).

Sbragia, A. M. (2000), 'Environmental Policy', in H. Wallace and W. Wallace (eds) *Policy-making in the European Union* 4th edn (Oxford: Oxford University Press): 293–316.

Sbragia, A. M. (2005), 'Institution building from below and above: the European Community in global environmental politics' in A. Jordan (ed.) *Environmental policy in the European Union* 2nd edn (London: Earthscan): 201–24.

Sbragia, A. M. and C. Damro (1999), 'The changing role of the European Union in international environmental politics', *Environment and Planning C*, 17/1: 53–68

Scharpf, F. W. (1988), 'The joint-decision trap: lessons from German federalism and European integration', *Public Administration*, 66/3: 239–78.

Scharpf, F. W. (1997), *Games real actors play: actor-centered institutionalism in policy research* (Boulder: Westview).

Scharpf, F. W. (1999), *Governing in Europe* (Oxford University Press).

Scharpf, F. W. (2002), 'The European social model: coping with the challenges of diversity', *Journal of Common Market Studies*, 40/4: 645–70.

Schimmelfennig, F. (2004), 'Liberal Intergovernmentalism' in A. Wiener and T. Diez (eds) *European integration theory* (Oxford: Oxford University Press).

Schimmelfennig, F., S. Engert and H. Knobel (2006), *International socialization in Europe: European organizations, political conditionality and democratic change* (Basingstoke: Palgrave).

Schimmelfennig, F. and U. Sedelmeier (2005), *The Europeanization of Central and Eastern Europe* (Ithaca, NY: Cornell University Press).

Schmidt, V. A. (2006), *Democracy in Europe: the EU and national polities* (Oxford: Oxford University Press).

Schmidt, S. K. (2007), 'Mutual recognition as a new mode of governance', *Journal of European Public Policy*, 14/5: 667–81.

Schmidt, S. K. and C. Nicolaïdis (2007), 'Mutual recognition on "trial": the long road to services liberalization', *Journal of European Public Policy*, 15/4: 717–34.

Schmitter, P. (1969), 'Three neofunctional hypotheses about international integration', *International Organization*, 23/1: 161–6.

Schmitter, P. C. (2000), *How to democratize the European Union ... and why bother?* (Lanham: Rowman and Littlefield).

Schmitter, P. C. (2005), 'Ernst B. Haas and the legacy of neofunctionalism', *Journal of European Public Policy*, 12/2: 255–72.

Schneider, G., B. Steunenberg, and M. Widgren (2006), 'Evidence with insight: what models contribute to EU research' in R. Thomson, F. N. Stokman, C. H. Achen, and T.

Koenig (eds) *The European Union decides* (Cambridge: Cambridge University Press): 299–316.

Scott, J. and D. M. Trubek (2002), 'Mind the gap: law and new approaches to governance in the European Union', *European Law Journal*, 8/1: 1–18.

Schwarzmantel, J. (2003), *Citizenship and identity: towards a new republic* (London: Routledge).

Scully, R. (2000), 'Democracy, legitimacy and the European Parliament' in M. G. Cowles and M. Smith (eds), *The state of the European Union Vol. 5* (Oxford: Oxford University Press).

Scully, R. (2005), *Becoming Europeans? Attitudes, behaviour and socialisation in the European Parliament* (Oxford: Oxford University Press).

Shackleton, M. (2006), 'The European Parliament' in J. Peterson and M. Shackleton (eds) *The institutions of the European Union* 2nd edn (Oxford: Oxford University Press): 104–24.

Shapiro, M. (1992), 'The European Court of Justice' in A. M. Sbragia (ed.) *Europolitics* (Washington DC: the Brookings Institution).

Shaw, J. (ed.) (2000), *Social law and policy in an evolving European Union* (Oxford: Hart).

Shucksmith M., K. Thomson and D. Roberts (eds) (2005), 'CAP and the regions: the territorial impact of common agricultural policy (Wallingford: CABI Publishing).

Simonian, H. (1985), *The Privileged Partnership: Franco-German Relations in the European Community, 1969-84* (Oxford: Clarendon).

Smismans, S. (2003), 'European civil society: shaped by discourses and institutional interests', *European Law Journal*, 9/4: 482–504.

Smismans, S. (2004), *Law, legitimacy, and European governance: functional participation in social regulation* (Oxford: Oxford University Press).

Smismans, S. (2006a), 'New modes of governance and the participatory myth', *European governance papers*, 6/1: 1–23.

Smismans, S. (ed.) (2006b), *Civil society and legitimate European governance* (Cheltenham: Edward Elgar).

Smith, J. (1999), *Europe's elected Parliament* (Sheffield: Sheffield Academic Press).

Smith, M. (2001), 'The common foreign and security policy' in S. Bromley (ed.) *Governing the European Union* (London: Sage).

Smith, M. E. (2008), *Europe's foreign and security policy: the institutionalisation of cooperation* (Cambridge University Press: Cambridge).

Smith, S. (2001), 'Reflectivist and constructivist approaches to international theory', in J. Baylis and S. Smith (eds) *The Globalization of world politics: an introduction to international relations* 2nd edn (Oxford: Oxford University Press).

Smith, V. A. (2006), *Democracy in Europe: The EU and national polities* (Oxford: Oxford University Press).

Spaak, P.-H. (1956), *The Brussels Report on the General Common Market* (the Spaak Report), Brussels, June.

Statewatch (2001), 'The "conclusions" of the special justice and home affairs council on 20 September 2001 and their implications for civil liberties: http://www.statewatch.org/observatory2.htm.

Stone Sweet, A. (2004), *The judicial construction of Europe* (Oxford: Oxford University Press).

Stone Sweet, A. and T. L. Brunell (1998), 'Constructing a supranational constitution: dispute resolution and governance in the European Community', *American Political Science Review*, 92/1: 63–81.

Stone Sweet, A. and J. Caporaso (1998), 'From free trade to supranational polity: the European Court and integration' in W. Sandholtz and A. Stone Sweet (eds), *European integration and supranational governance* (Oxford: Oxford University Press).

Stone Sweet, A. and W. Sandholtz (1998), 'Integration, supranational governance, and the institutionalization of the European polity' in W. Sandholtz and A. Stone Sweet (eds) *European integration and supranational governance* (Oxford: Oxford University Press).

Streeck, W. and P. C. Schmitter (1991), 'From national corporatism to transnational pluralism: organized interests in the single European market', *Politics and Society*, 19/2: 133–65.

Sun, J. M. and J. Pelkmans (1995), 'Regulatory competition in the single market', *Journal of Common Market Studies*, 33/1: 67–89.

Sutcliffe, J. B. (2000), 'The 1999 reform of the structural regulations: multi-level governance or renationalization?', *Journal of European Public Policy*, 7/2: 290–309.

Sutton, M. (2007), 'The IGC 2007: the European Union comes of age?', *European Public Law*, 14/1: 55–68.

Suvarierol, S. (2008), 'Beyond the myth of nationality: analysing networks within the European Commission', *West European Politics*, 31/4: 701–24.

Taggart, P. and A. Szczerbiak (2002), 'Europeanization, Euroscepticism and party systems: party-based Euroscepticism in the candidate states of Central and Eastern Europe', *Perspectives on European Politics and Society*, 3. 1, 23–41.

Tajfel, H. (1970), 'Experiments in intergroup discrimination', *Scientific American*, 223/2: 96–102.

Tallberg, J. (2006), *Leadership and negotiation in the European Union* (Cambridge: Cambridge University Press).

Taylor, P. (1975), 'The politics of the European Communities: the confederal phase', *World Politics*, 27/3: 335–60.

Taylor, P. (1990), 'Regionalism and functionalism reconsidered' in P. Taylor and A. J. R. Groom (eds), *Frameworks for international cooperation* (London: Pinter).

Taylor, P. (1993), *International organization in the modern world—the regional and the global process* (New York: Pinter).

Taylor, P. (1996), *The European Union in the 1990s* (Oxford: Oxford University Press).

Thompson, R., and M. O. Hosli (2006), 'Explaining legislative decision-making in the European Union', in R. Thomson,

F. N. Stokman, C. H. Achen and T. Koenig (eds) *The European Union decides* (Cambridge: Cambridge University Press): 1–24.

Toal, G. (2005), 'Being geopolitical' *Political Geography*, 24/3: 365–72.

Tranholm-Mikkelsen, J. (1991), 'Neo-functionalism: obstinate or obsolete? A reappraisal in the light of the new dynamism of the EC', *Millennium: Journal of International Studies*, 20/1: 1–22.

Treib, O., H. Bähr, and G. Falkne (2009), 'Social policy and environmental policy: comparing modes of governance' in U. Diedrichs and W. Wessels (eds) *The Dynamics of Change in EU Governance: Policy-making and System Evolution.* (Cheltenham: Edward Elgar)

Trondal, J., C. van der Berg, and S. Suvarierol (2008), 'The compound machinery of government: the case of seconded officials in the European Commission', *Governance*, 21/2: 253–74.

Truman, D. B. (1951), *The Governmental Process. Political Interests and Public Opinion* (New York: Alfred A. Knopf. Reprint by the Institute of Governmental Studies, University of California, Berkeley 1993).

Tsatsos, D. T. (2009), *The European sympolity: new directions in democratic thinking* (Brussels: Bruylant)

Tsebelis, G. (1990), *Nested games: rational choice in comparative politics* (Berkeley: University of California Press).

Tsebelis G. (1994), 'The power of the European Parliament as conditional agenda-setter', *American Political Science Review*, 88, 128–42.

Tsebelis, G., and G. Garrett (1996), 'Agenda setting power, power indices and decision making in the European Union', *International Review of Law and Economics*, 16/3: 345–61.

Tsebelis, G. and G. Garrett (1997), 'Agenda setting, vetoes and the European Union's co-decision procedure', *Journal of Legislative Studies*, 3/3: 74–92.

Tsoukalis, L. (1977), *The politics and economics of European monetary integration* (London: George Allen and Unwin).

Tsoukalis, L. (1997), *The new European economy revisited* (Oxford: Oxford University Press).

Turner, J. C. (1985), 'Social categorization and the self-concept: a social cognitive theory of group behavior' in E. J. Lawler (ed.) *Advances in Group Processes*, 2: 77–122.

Uçarer, E. M. (2001), 'Managing asylum and European integration: expanding spheres of exclusion?', *International Studies Perspectives*, 2/3: 291–307.

van Apeldoorn, B. (1992), *Transnational Capitalism and the Struggle over European Integration* (London and New York: Routledge).

van Asselt, H. (2010), 'Emissions trading: the enthusiastic adoption of an alien instrument?', in A. Jordan et al (eds) *Climate Change Policy in the European Union* (Cambridge: Cambridge University Press).

van der Eijk, C. and M. Franklin (eds) (1996), *Choosing Europe? the European electorate and national politics in the face of Union*, (Ann Arbor, MI: University of Michigan Press).

van der Pijl, K. (2006), *Global rivalries: from the Cold War to Iraq* (Pluto Press: London).

van Hüllen, V. and A. Stahn (2009), 'Comparing EU and US democracy promotion in the Mediterranean and the Newly Independent States' in A. Magen, M. McFaul and T. Risse (eds) *Democracy promotion in the US and the EU compared* (Basingstoke: Palgrave).

van Keulen, M. (1999), *Going Europe or going Dutch: how the Dutch government shapes European policy* (Amsterdam: Amsterdam University Press).

van Selm, J. (2002), 'Immigration and asylum or foreign policy: the EU's approach to migrants and their countries of origin' in E. M. Uçarer (ed.) *Migration and the externalities of European integration* (Lanham, MD: Lexington Books).

Vandenbroucke, F. (2002), 'Sustainable social justice and open coordination in Europe', in G. Esping-Andersen and D. Gallie (eds) *Why we need a new welfare state* (Oxford: Oxford University Press).

Verdun, A. (1996) 'An "asymmetrical" economic and monetary union in the EU: perceptions of monetary authorities and social partners,' *Journal of European Integration*, 20/1: 59–81.

Verdun, A. (2000), *European responses to globalization and financial market integration: perceptions of economic and monetary union in Belgium, France and Germany* (Basingstoke: Palgrave).

Verdun, A. (2002), *The euro: European integration theory and economic and monetary union* (Lanham, MD: Rowman and Littlefield).

Vogler, J. and H. Stephan (2007), 'The EU in global environmental governance', *International Environmental Agreements*, 7/4: 389–413.

Wæver, O. (2004), 'Discursive approaches' in T. Diez and A. Wiener (eds) *European Integration Theory* (Oxford: Oxford University Press).

Wallace, H. (1971), 'The impact of the European Communities on national policy-making', *Government and Opposition*, 6/4: 520–38.

Wallace, H. (2000), 'The institutional setting: five variations on a theme', in H. Wallace and W. Wallace (eds), *Policy-making in the European Union* 4th edn (Oxford: Oxford University Press): 3–37.

Wallace, H. (2002), 'The Council: an institutional chameleon', *Governance*, 15/3: 325–44.

Wallace, H. (2005), 'An institutional anatomy and five policy modes' in H. Wallace, W. Wallace, and M.A. Pollack (eds) *Policy-making in the European Union* 5th edn (Oxford: Oxford University Press)

Wallace, H. (2007), *Adapting to Enlargement of the European Union: Institutional Practice since May 2004* (Brussels: TEPSA)

Wallace, H. and F. Hayes-Renshaw (1995), 'Executive power in the European Union: the functions and limits of the Council of Ministers', *Journal of European Public Policy*, 2/4: 559–82.

Wallace, W. (1982), 'European as a confederation: the Community and the nation-state', *Journal of Common Market Studies*, 21/1: 57–68.

Waltz, K. (1979), *Theory of international politics* (New York: McGraw Hill).

Warleigh, A. (2000), 'The hustle: citizenship practice, NGOs and policy coalitions in the European Union—the cases of auto oil, drinking water and unit pricing', *Journal of European Public Policy*, 7/2: 229–43.

Warleigh, A. (2001), 'Europeanizing civil society: NGOs as agents of political socialization', *Journal of Common Market Studies*, 39/4: 619–39.

Warleigh, A. (2003), *Democracy in the European Union: theory, practice and reform* (London: Sage).

Warleigh, A. (2006), 'Conceptual combinations: multilevel governance and policy networks' in M. Cini and A. Bourne (eds) *Palgrave Advances in European Union Studies* (Basingstoke: Palgrave).

Weale, A. (2005), 'European environmental policy by stealth' in A. Jordan (ed.) *Environmental policy in the European Union* 2nd edn (London: Earthscan): 336–54.

Weale, A., G. Pridham, M. Cini, D. Konstadakopulos, M. Porter, and B. Flynn (2000), *Environmental governance in Europe* (Oxford: Oxford University Press).

Wendt, A. (1999), *Social theory of international politics* (Cambridge: Cambridge University Press).

Wessels, W. (1997), 'Ever closer fusion? A dynamic macro-political view on integration processes', *Journal of Common Market Studies*, 35/2: 267–99.

Wessels, W. and D. Rometsch (1996), 'Conclusion: European Union and national institutions' in D. Rometsch and W. Wessels (eds) *The European Union and member states: towards institutional fusion?* (Manchester: Manchester University Press).

Westlake, M. and D. Galloway (2004), *The Council of the European Union* 3rd edn (London: Cartermill).

Widgren, M. (1994), 'Voting power in the EC decision making and consequences of the different enlargements', *European Economic Review*, 38/4: 1153–70.

Wiener, A. (2006), 'Constructivism and sociological institutionalism' in M. Cini and A. K. Bourne (eds) *Palgrave Advances in European Union Studies* (Basingstoke: Palgrave).

Wincott, D. (1994), 'Human rights, democratization and the role of the Court of Justice', *Democratization*, 1/2: 251–71.

Wincott, D. (1995), 'Institutional interaction and European integration: towards an everyday critique of liberal intergovernmentalism', *Journal of Common Market Studies* 33/4: 597–609.

Wishlade, F. (1996), 'EU cohesion policy: facts, figures and issues' in L. Hooghe *Cohesion policy and European integration: building multi-level governance* (Oxford: Oxford University Press).

Wonka, A. (2008), 'Decision-making dynamics in the European Commission: partisan, national or sectoral?', *Journal of European Public Policy*, 15/8: 1145–63.

Wurzel, R. (2008), 'Environmental policy' in J. Hayward (ed.) *Leaderless Europe* (Oxford: Oxford University Press).

Young, A. R. (1997), 'Consumption without representation? Consumers in the single market' in H. Wallace and A. R. Young (eds) *Participation and policy-making in the European Union* (Oxford: Clarendon Press).

Young, A. (2002), *Extending European cooperation: the European Union and the 'new' international trade agenda* (Manchester: Manchester University Press).

Zeitlin, J. and P. Pochet, with L. Magnusson (eds) (2005), *The open method of co-ordination in action: the European employment and social inclusion strategies* (Brussels: PIE Peter Lang).

Zysman, J. (1994), 'How institutions create historically-rooted trajectories of growth', *Industrial and Corporate Change*, 3/1: 243–83.

Index